T0331986

ESCAPING PATERNALISM

The burgeoning field of behavioral economics has produced a new set of justifications for paternalism. This book challenges behavioral paternalism on multiple levels, from the abstract and conceptual to the pragmatic and applied. Behavioral paternalism relies on a needlessly restrictive definition of rational behavior. It neglects nonstandard preferences, experimentation, and self-discovery. It relies on behavioral research that is often incomplete and unreliable. It demands a level of knowledge from policymakers that they cannot reasonably obtain. It assumes a political process largely immune to the effects of ignorance, irrationality, and the influence of special interests and moralists. Overall, behavioral paternalism underestimates the capacity of people to solve their own problems, while overestimating the ability of experts and policymakers to design beneficial interventions. The authors argue instead for a more inclusive theory of rationality in policymaking.

MARIO J. RIZZO is a professor of Economics, Director of the Foundations of the Market Economy Program, and Co-Director of the Classical Liberal Institute at New York University. He is the co-author of *Austrian Economics Re-Examined: The Economics of Time and Ignorance*. He has published in such journals as the *Journal of Legal Studies*, the *Columbia Law Review* and the *UCLA Law Review*.

GLEN WHITMAN is a professor of Economics at California State University, Northridge. He is the co-editor of *Economics of the Undead: Zombies, Vampires, and the Dismal Science*. He has published in such journals as the *UCLA Law Review*, the *Journal of Legal Studies*, and the *Journal of Economic Behavior and Organization*.

CAMBRIDGE STUDIES IN ECONOMICS, CHOICE, AND SOCIETY

Founding Editors

Timur Kuran, *Duke University*
Peter J. Boettke, *George Mason University*

This interdisciplinary series promotes original theoretical and empirical research as well as integrative syntheses involving links between individual choice, institutions, and social outcomes. Contributions are welcome from across the social sciences, particularly in the areas where economic analysis is joined with other disciplines such as comparative political economy, new institutional economics, and behavioral economics.

Books in the Series:

BENJAMIN POWELL *Out of Poverty: Sweatshops in the Global Economy*
MORRIS B. HOFFMAN *The Punisher's Brain: The Evolution of Judge and Jury*
PETER T. LEESON: *Anarchy Unbound: Why Self-Governance Works Better Than You Think*
TERRY L. ANDERSON and GARY D. LIBECAP *Environmental Markets: A Property Rights Approach*
CASS R. SUNSTEIN *The Ethics of Influence: Government in the Age of Behavioral Science*
JARED RUBIN *Rulers, Religion, and Riches: Why the West Got Rich and the Middle East Did Not*
JEAN-PHILIPPE PLATTEAU *Islam Instrumentalized: Religion and Politics in Historical Perspective*
TAIZU ZHANG *The Laws and Economics of Confucianism: Kinship and Property in Preindustrial China and England*
ROGER KOPPL *Expert Failure*
MICHAEL C. MUNGER *Tomorrow 3.0: Transaction Costs and the Sharing Economy*
CAROLYN M. WARNER, RAMAZAN KILINÇ, CHRISTOPHER W. HALE and ADAM B. COHEN *Generating Generosity in Catholicism and Islam: Beliefs, Institutions, and Public Goods Provision*
PAUL DRAGOS ALICIA *Public Entrepreneurship, Citizenship, and Self-Governance*
RANDALL G. HOLCOMBE *Political Capitalism: How Political Influence Is Made and Maintained*
NOEL D. JOHNSON *Persecution and Toleration: The Long Road to Religious Freedom*
VERNON L. SMITH and BART J. WILSON *Humanomics: Moral Sentiments and the Wealth of Nations for the Twenty-First Century*
ANDREAS THIEL, WILLIAM A. BLOMQUIST and DUSTIN E. GARRICK *Governing Complexity: Analyzing and Applying Polycentricity*
MARIO J. RIZZO and GLEN WHITMAN *Escaping Paternalism: Rationality, Behavioral Economics, and Public Policy*

Escaping Paternalism

Rationality, Behavioral Economics,
and Public Policy

MARIO J. RIZZO

New York University

GLEN WHITMAN

California State University, Northridge

CAMBRIDGE
UNIVERSITY PRESS

CAMBRIDGE
UNIVERSITY PRESS

University Printing House, Cambridge CB2 8BS, United Kingdom

One Liberty Plaza, 20th Floor, New York, NY 10006, USA

477 Williamstown Road, Port Melbourne, VIC 3207, Australia

314–321, 3rd Floor, Plot 3, Splendor Forum, Jasola District Centre,
New Delhi – 110025, India

79 Anson Road, #06–04/06, Singapore 079906

Cambridge University Press is part of the University of Cambridge.

It furthers the University's mission by disseminating knowledge in the pursuit of
education, learning, and research at the highest international levels of excellence.

www.cambridge.org
Information on this title: www.cambridge.org/9781107016941
DOI: 10.1017/9781139061810

© Mario J. Rizzo and Glen Whitman 2020

First published 2020

A catalogue record for this publication is available from the British Library.

ISBN 978-1-107-01694-1 Hardback
ISBN 978-1-108-76000-3 Paperback

Contents

Figures

Tables

Preface

This book is the product of many years of thinking about economic rationality, its critique by behavioral researchers, and the impact of both on public policy, especially paternalistic public policy. Much has been written about whether real people are "rational" and the kinds of errors they may be subject to. Unfortunately, economists, and perhaps other social scientists as well, have been boxed into an excessively narrow and technical concept of rationality. This has left its imprint on the influential heuristics-and-biases literature, which claims people are not fully rational relative to that standard.

It worries us that much of the core behavioral literature is often presented as essentially settled, and many alleged biases have now attained the status of truisms. One of our tasks in this book is to show that the evidence is far weaker than has been often assumed. Similarly, the behavioral policy goal of moving people in the direction of their "true preferences" – that is, their well-considered preferences purged of all cognitive and behavioral contaminants – is often a mirage. The behavioral policy discussion frequently suffers from significant empirical difficulties and conceptual confusions.

Furthermore, the political economy of behavioral policy is fraught not only with the usual public-choice problems, but with an amplification of them due to the peculiar moralistic character of paternalist legislation. To the extent that ordinary people are afflicted by cognitive biases, we must confront the likelihood that policymakers suffer from them as well. Finally, the supposedly gentle and moderate character of behavioral policy initiatives is not a sustainable state of affairs, as we hope a reasonable analysis of their dynamic consequences will show.

We are indebted to many people, including the following: Nathan Berg, Simon Bilo, Peter Boettke, Donald Boudreaux, William Butos, Bryan

Caplan, Young Back Choi, Malte Dold, Pablo Duarte, Richard Epstein, Pierre Garello, Gerd Gigerenzer, David Harper, Daniel Hausman, Clare Hill, Andreas Hoffmann, Sanford Ikeda, Jonathan Klick, Roger Koppl, Jason Kuznicki, Peter Leeson, Craig McKenzie, Maria Pia Paganelli, Shruti Rajagopalan, Vernon Smith, Ilya Somin, Richard Wagner, Will Wilkinson, and Todd Zywicki. We are indebted to Cass Sunstein and Richard Thaler, whose provocative work has induced us to devote so much time and effort to this topic. We also owe a special thanks to Harry David, whose expert editing made this a much better book. Finally, we wish to thank our respective partners, Daniel Chiarilli and Brynn Malone, for their unfailing patience and support.

We should also acknowledge our debt to our previous work and publishers. Some sections of Chapter 3 are based on Whitman and Rizzo, "The problematic welfare standards of behavioral paternalism," *Review of Philosophy and Psychology*, 6 (2015). Chapter 7 is adapted from Rizzo and Whitman, "The knowledge problem of new paternalism," *Brigham Young University Law Review* (2009). Portions of Chapter 8 and much of Chapter 9 appeared previously in Rizzo and Whitman, "Little Brother is watching you: New paternalism on the slippery slopes," *Arizona Law Review*, 51 (2009).

Introduction

Puppets and Puppet Masters

How many misfortunes have happened to me. But I deserved them, for I am an obstinate, passionate puppet. I am always bent upon having my own way, without listening to those who wish me well, and who have a thousand times more sense than I have! But from this time forth I am determined to change and to become orderly and obedient. For at last I have seen that disobedient boys come to no good and gain nothing.

—Carlo Collodi, *Pinocchio*

One of the nice things about puppets is that it's your own hand in there. You can make it do anything you want it to.

—Jim Henson, *It's Not Easy Being Green*

Carlo Collodi's *Pinocchio*, first published in 1881, tells the tragicomic story of an impulsive young puppet who obstinately refuses to behave as a puppet should. A normal puppet, of course, cannot misbehave. It performs only such actions as the puppeteer commands and its design permits. But Pinocchio is different. He has a will of his own, which he exercises constantly and to his great misfortune, in ways that never appear in the more familiar Disney version. In fact, Collodi's original story, later changed by popular demand, concluded with the disobedient puppet's execution by hanging (Rich 2011). The moral of the story? Bad behavior leads to terrible punishment – and to avoid it, you need to follow the rules like a good puppet.

At its heart, Pinocchio is a paternalistic tale, albeit with a brand of paternalism so harsh that readers of the 1880s demanded a change. Modern readers would be even less sympathetic to the hanging of a child, even a truly criminal one. Yet we find something compelling in the metaphor of a puppet – the good kind that does what it's supposed to – as a model of behavior for real human beings. What makes Pinocchio a bad puppet is his failure to behave as the puppet masters say he should. And what makes some of us bad humans is our failure to behave as others think we should.

But who are the puppet masters in this scenario, and what gives them the authority to decide what is proper behavior? That question will arise repeatedly in this book, in various forms, as we critically evaluate a new form of paternalism that has taken the academic and policy worlds by storm. Unlike earlier forms of paternalism, this new brand of paternalism promises to employ gentler means while respecting people's chosen ends. But like those earlier forms, it seeks to make people conform better to an idealized model of behavior, and in so doing it treats humans as puppets to some degree. Not surprisingly, we use the words *puppet masters* and *puppets* as metaphors for paternalists and the real people whose behavior they wish to improve. But we also intend them as metaphors for economists and the abstract models they use to understand the world. Many difficulties that arise in the former relationship, we will argue, trace back to difficulties in the latter.

THE RISE OF THE NEW PATERNALISM

Several years ago, one of us (Whitman) went on a diet. Although he used a variety of strategies to control his calorie intake, one proved particularly effective: placing snack foods in a high cabinet. The new placement of food slightly increased the cost of snacking; he had to reach a little higher. But more importantly, it made him acutely aware – every time he reached to get a snack – that he was breaking his resolution. Of course, this didn't completely prevent him from snacking, but it did help him cut back.

This strategy didn't work for all foods. For pretzels and cookies, the high cabinet was good enough. But ice cream, which could only be stored in the freezer, he banned from the house altogether. Any ice cream in the freezer would have been consumed in short order.

Strategies such as these are hardly novel. People who want to lose weight have adopted all manner of devices for changing their behavior, including banning temptations from the household, eating desserts only on holidays and weekends, joining weight-loss clubs, making weight-loss pacts with friends, and so on. Smokers trying to quit have been known to flush their remaining cigarettes down the toilet, avoid locations where they will be tempted to smoke, and make themselves put money in a jar every time they have a cigarette.

Such behaviors are commonplace. Yet they are surprisingly difficult to reconcile with traditional economic theory. Why? Because they seem to conflict with conventional notions of *rationality* employed in economics. Simply put, why would you deliberately take action – maybe even incur costs – to *reduce* your options? After all, you could just ignore the options you don't prefer. Don't want to eat the potato chips? Then don't eat the potato chips! Don't want to smoke? Then don't smoke! In theory, a rational person will simply select the best option from those available; there is no reason to take the undesired options off the table unless it's costly to keep them there.[1]

The burgeoning field of behavioral economics attempts to make choices such as these understandable. It does so by arguing that people have biases and cognitive limitations that cause them to deviate substantially from an ideal standard of perfect rationality – a standard that has been dominant in economic theory for generations. Behavioral economists have endeavored to take off the blinders, allowing economists to better grasp how real human beings make choices. A number of books, including Daniel Kahneman's *Thinking, Fast and Slow*, Dan Ariely's *Predictably Irrational*, and Charles Duhigg's *The Power of Habit*, have brought these insights to the general public. To the extent that behavioral economics has exposed the genuine failings of the old rational-choice models, it has been a boon to the economics profession.

But there has been a downside. The conclusions of behavioral economics have also been used to craft a new justification for paternalistic policies – that is, policies designed to influence, manipulate, or coerce individuals for their own good, as distinct from the good of others. Rational-choice models imply that, by and large, people act consistently with their own preferences and values. By challenging that claim, behavioral economics has opened the door to the possibility that some government interventions might actually make us better off, even by our own lights. A number of economists and policy analysts have walked through that door, championing a wide range of government policies to "fix" the errors and biases in human decision-making. Leading works in this literature include Cass Sunstein and Richard Thaler's *Nudge*, David Halpern's *Inside the Nudge Unit*, and Sarah Conly's *Against Autonomy*, as well as numerous academic articles aimed at intellectual elites rather than the general public.

---

[1] In fairness, not all economists failed to consider these issues. For example, in *The Reason of Rules*, Buchanan and Brennan (1985, 76–83) discuss temptation and self-constraining behavior in a rational-choice framework. Their analysis makes no use of behavioral economics. It hadn't been developed yet. Analytically their discussion rests on an extension of the work of Becker (1965) and Schelling (1978).

We call the use of behavioral economics to justify paternalistic interventions "behavioral paternalism" – or, when we wish to distinguish it from the older variety of paternalism, "the new paternalism." The purpose of this book is to show why behavioral paternalism is mistaken.

Our response to behavioral paternalism will have several prongs, which we will outline shortly. But for now, let's return to the examples with which we started: high shelves, flushed cigarettes, and so on. Behavioral economists sometimes point to behaviors such as these as evidence of real-world irrationality. Yet, oddly, these examples all demonstrate both the problem *and* the solution. Yes, people have weaknesses and bad habits that may thwart their goals. But they also respond by adopting deliberate strategies to control them, and it is perfectly rational to do so. Apparently, rationality is not such a simple matter; it seems to have levels.

A number of questions naturally arise: How do we know whether people who adopt self-control strategies such as these have done too little, too much, or just enough? What is the *right amount* of self-control? Whose preferences or values should we use to judge? What are the individual's *true* preferences about present enjoyment versus future health and wealth – and how would we know?

These questions, as we shall see, are only the tip of the iceberg. The relevant objections to behavioral paternalism range from the deeply philosophical to the thoroughly pragmatic. We contend that behavioral paternalists have hardly begun to respond to most of these objections, much less overcome them.

THE OLD VERSUS THE NEW PATERNALISM

As far back as memory reaches, there have been those who would tell others how to live. So, what makes this new variety of paternalism "special"?

For most of history, paternalists have drawn their support from religious or moral notions of goodness. They have claimed special knowledge, from God or some other source, about how people ought to live. The overtly religious character of temperance movements in the nineteenth and early twentieth centuries exemplifies this kind of "old" paternalism. Given their moral convictions, the old paternalists did not usually appeal to the preferences and desires of those whose behavior they wished to regulate. The very desire for alcohol – or drugs, or deviant sex – was condemned directly.

Old paternalism is still with us, but its strength has waned. In the modern era, especially in liberal democracies, greater respect for personal choice and individual preference has dampened support for old-style paternalism – notwithstanding some obvious exceptions, most notably the prohibition of recreational drugs.

Popular resistance to paternalism took root in the economics profession as well. The traditional economic case against paternalism derived from two key assumptions. First, there was the notion of *subjective preference*: the idea that preferences are individualized, and there is no objective standard by which we can say those preferences are right or wrong. Technically, the assumption of subjective preferences is strictly descriptive; it is a claim about what motivates people to take action. If we want to understand the choices that real people make, we must consider their internal values and desires, rather than some external set of values and desires they may or may not share. But for many economists, subjectivism has a normative side as well; it reflects a level of respect for the fact that we don't all value the same things in the same degree. We differ in our values, and that's okay.

Second, there was the notion of *preference revelation*: the idea that people act consistently with their subjective preferences, whatever they might be.[2] Consequently, people's true preferences are revealed by their actual choices. Whatever someone chooses, it must be the option they like best, all things considered, of the options available; otherwise, they would choose something else. A corollary of preference revelation is deep skepticism about *cheap talk* – that is, preferences expressed in words but not in actions, such as when someone professes a desire to quit smoking while continuing to smoke. A verbal statement of preference might reveal what the speaker wants others to *hear*, but it does not necessarily reveal what she really wants to *do*.

Together, subjectivism and preference revelation imply that each individual does the best he can do, according to his own standards, given his circumstances and constraints. That doesn't mean he couldn't do better under other circumstances, because various features of the world can get in the way.[3] *But taking as given the totality of an individual's circumstances,* including the choices of other people, he could not be doing any better.

---

[2] In this chapter we use the term "preference revelation" instead of the more familiar "revealed preference" to distinguish an appreciative or informal interpretation of the formal theory of revealed preference. Here we mean simply the idea that actions demonstrate a person's preferences, without the methodological and behaviorist baggage that accompanied the formal theory of revealed preference. In Chapter 3 and its appendix we discuss the formal theory.

[3] For instance, there may be externality or public good problems. In these circumstances, even if individuals are fully rational in the traditional sense of that term, they may fail to maximize their collective welfare. These issues are beyond the scope of this book. Our focus is on individual welfare losses that may be attributable to failures of rationality.

Of course, mainstream economists have long conceded the possibility of errors. However, in the traditional view, if people make mistakes, they presumably balance each other out. A person might overestimate or underestimate their hunger when ordering food, for example, but those errors are assumed to be equally likely, so that on average they make choices that match their subjective preferences. Thus, subjectivism-plus-preference-revelation leaves little room for paternalist policies (again, policies designed to alter an individual's choices for his own good, not the good of others). Far from making people better off, such policies would just prevent people from making the choices that maximize their own well-being as they perceive it.

Behavioral economists, like most economists, still accept subjectivism. However, they have rejected the notion of accurate preference revelation. Experimental evidence suggests that individuals may *systematically* deviate from the behavior that would best satisfy their own preferences. The list of alleged deviations from strict rationality includes – but is not limited to – status quo bias, optimism bias, susceptibility to framing effects, poor processing of information, and lack of willpower or self-control. To the extent that these phenomena cause people to make errors, paternalist policies can in principle help them to do better – not by some exogenous standard, but by their own standards.

This is the defining feature of new paternalism that distinguishes it from the old: *the new paternalists claim to help people better achieve their own preferences, not someone else's.*

Philosopher Sarah Conly, for example, explicitly condemns paternalism based on anything other than people's own goals:

I argue, though, that the only reasonable form of paternalism is one that helps people act according to their own values, rather than imposing foreign values upon them. I will argue that objective views about welfare – that regardless of what we ourselves want, some ways of living are better than others – are implausible in general, and that using them as a guide for governance is both implausible and impractical. *Rather, paternalist regulations are designed to help us reach our own goals.*

(Conly 2013, 11–12, emphasis added)

Cass Sunstein and Richard Thaler, coming from an economic perspective, support policies that will make people better off "in terms of their own welfare." That welfare is best advanced by the choices people would make "if they had complete information, unlimited cognitive abilities, and no lack of willpower" (Sunstein and Thaler 2003, 1162). In other words, Sunstein and Thaler define the correctness of choices in terms of what people would choose for themselves – if only they were not afflicted with cognitive biases.

Similarly, Colin Camerer and coauthors advocate policies that will help individuals "make better decisions and come closer to behaving in their own best interest" (Camerer et al. 2003, 1218). Acting in their own best interest means acting as they would if they were fully rational, and rationality is defined as maximizing the satisfaction of well-defined preferences that accurately reflect true benefits and opportunity costs. In conditions of risk, rational individuals also have well-formed beliefs about the world, contingent on various events occurring, and will update their probability assessments on the basis of Bayes' rule (Camerer et al. 2003, 1214–1215).

These authors' concern with people's "own goals," "own welfare," and "own best interests" reflects their continued acceptance of subjectivism, despite their rejection of preference revelation. The essential problem, as behavioral paternalists see it, is that cognitive and behavioral biases prevent people from doing what's best by their very own standards. Behavioral paternalist policies aim to fix that.

A SAMPLING FROM THE BEHAVIORAL PATERNALIST AGENDA

This line of reasoning could in principle justify a dazzling array of policies – and indeed, the behavioral paternalist policy agenda seems to be growing rapidly. Rather than attempt a comprehensive list, we will offer seven illustrative proposals: sin taxes, default enrollment in savings plans, cooling-off periods for consumer purchases, risk narratives, graphic images, employee-friendly terms in labor contracts, and outright bans. With each proposal, we also introduce the alleged biases that behavioral paternalists have used to justify them.

Sin Taxes

Some analysts, notably Cremer et al. (2012), O'Donoghue and Rabin (2003, 2006), and Gruber and Köszegi (2001), propose to impose sin taxes – for example, a tax on fattening foods – to induce better personal consumption choices.

The behavioral justification for sin taxes is that individuals are afflicted by present bias or insufficient willpower. Simply put, individuals place too much weight on the present relative to the future (O'Donoghue and Rabin 2015; Frederick et al. 2003, 65). This creates a bias toward getting benefits now and incurring costs later: people spend too much and save too little, eat too much and exercise too little, procrastinate, become addicted to drugs, and so on.

We will have much more to say about present bias and willpower in later chapters. For now, we will observe that in traditional economic theory, there is nothing per se irrational about placing more weight on the present than the future. What traditional theory does require, however, is that people be *consistent* about how much they discount the future relative to the present. Behavioral research, however, indicates that real people are not so consistent.[4] They appear to place additional weight on the present simply because it is the present, and as a result, their choices sometimes display *time inconsistency*: they make decisions about future trade-offs, and then reverse those decisions later. For instance, if offered a choice between $850 in ten years and $1,000 in eleven, a typical person might choose the larger sum. Yet when a decade has passed, she might reverse her earlier choice and take the smaller sum immediately. This sort of inconsistency is taken by behavioral economists as evidence of irrationality or bounded rationality.

Intuitively, people's inconsistent behavior reflects their vulnerability to temptation when temptation is near. With regard to eating, for example, an overweight person might promise to start a diet tomorrow, but then reverse that decision once tomorrow has become today. In the present, the desire to eat dessert is too strong to resist. A properly calibrated sin tax on fattening foods, behavioral paternalists argue, would make the overeater fully account for the future costs of her present choices.

Present bias has been invoked to advance other paternalist policies as well. Specifically, it has played a role in Oren Bar-Gill's case for greater regulation of credit cards. The idea is that present bias causes naïve consumers to underestimate their future tendency to borrow, thereby making them respond positively to low annual fees and other short-term inducements offered by credit card companies while paying insufficient attention to interest rates and penalties. To mitigate this supposed problem, policymakers might "categorically prohibit the use of excessive late and over-limit fees, negative amortization rates, and even some types of teaser rates in unsolicited offers" (Bar-Gill 2004, 1378). Regulators might also restrict the ability of firms to offer benefits programs, such as frequent-flyer miles and travel rewards, with their credit cards (p. 1421). The same argument could even justify the revival of usury laws, including interest

---

[4] See Cohen et al. (2016) and Frederick et al. (2003) for reviews of the relevant literature on experiments of this nature.

rate ceilings on credit cards, although Bar-Gill himself is reluctant to go that far (pp. 1422–1423).

Default Enrollment in Savings Plans

Some behavioral paternalists, most notably Thaler and Sunstein, have advocated automatic enrollment of new employees in savings plans from which they could voluntarily opt out (as opposed to the more common practice of not enrolling employees until they opt in). It is unclear in most of the literature whether this is solely a recommendation for employers, or if the behavioral paternalists would also have the government require employers to implement automatic enrollment as is currently done in the United Kingdom. Sunstein and Thaler say the law "might require employers to provide automatic enrollment and allow employees to opt out," but they do not *explicitly* advocate this policy (Sunstein and Thaler 2003, 1176). Camerer and coauthors strongly imply that mandatory savings default rules may be necessary because firms lack sufficient incentive to offer optimal defaults (2003, 1251–1252).

One behavioral argument in favor of default enrollment is the same as that used for sin taxes: individuals are afflicted by present bias. In this case, the cognitive costs of deciding whether to enroll in an employer-sponsored retirement program – and, if so, what vehicle to use for savings – are overweighted relative to the expected benefits. This causes individuals to procrastinate, delay enrollment, and thus save too little (O'Donoghue and Rabin 1998).

Other times behavioral paternalists base their case for default enrollment on inertia or status quo bias: the psychological tendency of people to stick with current arrangements whatever they might be.[5] Sunstein and Thaler say that employees often simply fail to enroll under an opt-in system, even though they would choose to enroll if they took the time to think carefully (2003, 1172–1173). Default enrollment would, they argue, place employees in a new status quo that is more likely to match their considered preferences.[6]

---

[5] For a detailed discussion see Samuelson and Zeckhauser (1988) and Dean et al. (2017).

[6] Status quo bias and present bias are not always clearly distinguished in the case for default savings enrollment. For instance, Sunstein and Thaler state that "[e]ven a trivial action, such as filling in some form and returning it, can leave room for failures due to memory lapses, sloth, and procrastination" (Sunstein and Thaler 2003, 1181). Although they do not specifically invoke the notion of hyperbolic discounting, that is the leading explanation among behavioral economists for present bias and procrastination in areas such as dieting and saving.

Cooling-Off Periods

There are two types of cooling-off period. One kind creates a mandatory waiting period before a purchase or other decision can be made; the other creates a mandatory period following a purchase or other decision during which it can be reversed by one of the parties (Camerer et al. 2003, 1240). For example, a cooling-off period for marriage requires a certain number of days to pass between acquiring a marriage license and actually getting married, whereas a cooling-off period for new cars gives a car buyer the right to return the car within a few days of the sale without penalty.[7]

Behavioral paternalists argue for cooling-off periods based on evidence that people make different decisions depending on whether they are in a "hot" or "cool" state – a tendency that has been dubbed the *hot–cold empathy gap* (Loewenstein 2000). As Sunstein and Thaler put it, "The essential rationale [for cooling-off periods] is that under the heat of the moment, consumers might make ill-considered or improvident decisions" (Sunstein and Thaler 2003, 1188). Camerer and coauthors point to evidence that people make choices when they are in a biologically "hot" state (such as anger, fear, excitement, or sexual arousal) that they would not make if they were in a "cool state" (calm, reflective, and sober). Often these choices are costly or even irreversible. A cooling-off period would either force someone to delay making a final decision until he is in a cooler mental state, or allow him to reverse his decision once he is in a cooler state.

A related idea, based on similar reasoning, is the proposal to require people to acquire a license to smoke. In the version explored by Le Grand and New (2015, 157–158), an individual would acquire a license at the beginning of the year to purchase a certain number of cigarettes per week or per month during that year. This is similar to a cooling-off period inasmuch as it prevents making spur-of-the-moment decisions, instead requiring individuals to plan for future smoking. Anyone who wants to smoke has to go through a deliberate process and then determine his cigarette consumption far in advance. This deliberate decision is presumably made in a cool state rather than in the heat of nicotine craving.

---

[7] Without an *ex post* penalty, that is. The initial purchase price might be higher to account for costs associated with having a cooling-off period.

Risk Narratives

How should consumers be informed of the potential risks posed by dangerous products and activities? One possibility is to provide them with oral or written warnings, perhaps accompanied by statistical summaries of the likelihood of various harms. Another possibility, suggested by Christine Jolls and Cass Sunstein (2006, 212–215), is to expose consumers to real-life accounts about people who have suffered harm from the product or activity in question. Jolls and Sunstein propose that such narratives could be required by law. We refer to this policy as "risk narratives."

The behavioral justification for this policy is that people often display *optimism bias*, which causes them to underestimate their *personal* likelihood of suffering adverse consequences (Viscusi and Magat 1987; Jolls 1998). For example, many people underestimate their odds of getting into an automobile accident (Jolls and Sunstein 2006, 205). Because of optimism bias, people are too likely to expose themselves to risks. Jolls and Sunstein propose to correct optimism bias by exploiting a different bias: the *availability heuristic* (Tversky and Kahneman 1973, 1974), meaning the tendency of people to judge the likelihood of an event based on "an assessment of how easily examples of the event can be called to mind" (Jolls and Sunstein 2006, 204). For instance, someone who has just seen a news report about an airplane crash might overestimate the likelihood of such an accident. Risk narratives harness the availability heuristic to counter optimism bias, since exposing people to vivid stories about specific harms to specific people should induce them to consider that kind of harm more likely.

Graphic Images

In some cases it may be thought that simple statements of risk, or even risk narratives, might not be enough – that they might be ignored or dismissed and therefore not have the desired effect. A desire to make sure consumers take risks seriously might justify somewhat different policies. The Centers for Disease Control and Prevention have included in their national anti-tobacco campaign not only personal stories from smokers suffering from smoking-related diseases – i.e., risk narratives – but also graphic images of individuals (or their internal organs) in bad medical condition (Emery et al. 2014). Many nations and territories now require "pictorial warnings" to be placed directly on packs of cigarettes (Canadian Cancer Society 2016).

From a behavioral perspective, one rationale for graphic images is the same as for risk narratives: to exploit availability bias to offset possible optimism bias (Sunstein 2014, 45, 64). But a somewhat different behavioral rationale has also been offered: to affect the *salience* of certain messages in the consumer's mind (Veer and Rank 2012). Salience means the tendency for some features of a situation to be more noticeable or prominent than others. Someone eyeing a pack of cigarettes may be fully aware of the possible health consequences, yet they may not be sufficiently vivid or present in her mind to alter her choice. Graphic images constitute attempts to increase the salience of certain facts or risks in the viewer's mind. Unlike standard warning labels, which could be purely informative, these methods are more intensely visceral. They can be described as attempts to induce "psychological distress" (Gass and Seiter 2015, 348) or to trigger "a heightened awareness of one's own mortality or mortality salience" (Veer and Rank 2012, 226) in the service of smoking cessation.

Salience has also been invoked to bolster other paternalistic interventions, particularly in the area of consumer finance. Earlier, we discussed how present bias has been used to justify regulation of credit card offers. Recall that credit card companies can supposedly attract present-biased customers with credit card offers featuring attractive upfront characteristics (such as annual fees) and unattractive delayed characteristics (such as interest rates and penalties). But even if consumers are present-biased, why don't they foresee the impact of that bias? Shouldn't likely borrowers pay *more* attention to interest rates and penalties? The reply is that upfront characteristics of credit offers will be more salient to consumers than delayed ones, meaning they pay too much attention to the former and not enough to the latter (Bar-Gill 2012, 95; 2014, 473–474). Aside from the previously discussed interventions, salience-based concerns suggest the possibility of enhanced disclosure requirements. Such requirements would go beyond simple disclosure of relevant facts by requiring "typical usage" information, thereby boosting the salience of product characteristics that the consumer might otherwise neglect. Salience has been blamed for distortions of various nonfinancial consumer choices as well (Bordalo et al. 2013).

Employee-Friendly Terms in Labor Contracts

Sunstein and Thaler (2003) suggest that labor law could be modified to assume, by default, various terms in labor contracts for the benefit of employees. For instance, they suggest making "for cause" rather than "at will" the default termination rule (p. 1175); lengthening the presumed amount of paid vacation time (p. 1176); and presuming protection against age discrimination unless the employee negotiates not to have such protection (p. 1177). To be clear, Sunstein and Thaler do not explicitly endorse these policies, but they strongly suggest that such policies would qualify as "libertarian paternalism," their preferred variety of behavioral paternalism.

In addition to suggesting new default terms that are fully waivable, Sunstein and Thaler suggest other policies (including some existing policies) that are only partially waivable. For instance, as an example of existing policies that "embody libertarian paternalism," they offer the provision of the Model Employment Termination Act that replaces "at will" with "for cause" termination. This right can be waived by agreement, but only if the employer agrees to make a severance payment equal to one month's salary in the event of a not-for-cause termination (2003, 1186–1187). Note that employees cannot waive "for cause" termination for any smaller compensation. As another example, Sunstein and Thaler mention a provision of the Fair Labor Standards Act that says that employees cannot be required to work more than forty hours per week (2003, 1178). This provision may be waived in return for time-and-a-half pay, but not for any lower rate of pay (including the regular rate) that employer and employee might agree upon.

The behavioral justification for changing default rules – and sometimes making them costly to change – begins with the observation that people are vulnerable to *framing effects*. This means their choices are sensitive to seemingly irrelevant aspects of how the choice situation is described. Altering defaults may also be justified by the closely related *endowment effect*, which refers to people's tendency to demand more money to give something up (their willingness to accept or WTA) than they would have paid to acquire that same thing (their willingness to pay or WTP).[8] This behavior is not consistent with standard economic rationality, which would hold the default should not matter and therefore WTP and WTA should be equal, at least if switching costs are low and the value of the item is small relative to the chooser's wealth. Therefore, the endowment effect raises a red flag that perhaps something is "wrong" with decision-making

---

[8] For instance, students "endowed" with a university mug demanded more to part with the mug than they would have paid to buy it; see Jolls and Sunstein (2006, 205). Given the mug's low value relative to the students' wealth, the two situations are effectively identical: they are being asked to choose between a mug and money. Regardless of whether they were given the mug to begin with, both mug and money were options. Yet the students' choices differed.

in these cases. By shifting default rules of contract, policymakers can potentially harness the WTA–WTP gap to induce ostensibly better outcomes. Employees might demand more compensation to eliminate a "for cause" clause than they would sacrifice to insert it, or they might demand more compensation to give up additional vacation time than they would sacrifice to acquire it. The idea, then, is to structure defaults in labor contracts to increase the likelihood of employees getting favorable terms.

Outright Bans

In some cases, behavioral paternalists have argued for banning certain options altogether. We saw a hint of this in the previous discussion of default rules. When the default rule can only be waived in specified ways – as in the case of the forty-hour work week, which can be waived for time-and-half pay but nothing less – some options are taken off the table completely. A cooling-off period can also be characterized as a kind of ban, inasmuch as it rules out concluding a *final sale* before the required time has passed.

Some of the leading behavioral paternalists, notably Sunstein and Thaler, have shied away from outright bans. Their "libertarian paternalist" framework is largely premised on encouraging better choices rather than mandating them. However, the intellectual framework behind libertarian paternalism is broad enough to include bans. Sunstein and Thaler characterize libertarian paternalism as lying on a continuum, with costless opting-out at one end and very costly opting-out at the other (2003, 1185–1186). If it's not obvious that outright bans lie at one pole of this continuum, Sunstein and Thaler drive home the point with the example of mandatory helmet laws: "Almost all of the time, even the non-libertarian paternalist will allow choosers, at some cost, to reject the proposed course of action. Those who are required to wear motorcycle helmets can decide to risk the relevant penalty, and to pay it if need be" (2003, 1189–1190).

Although Sunstein and Thaler stop short of *explicitly* advocating bans, other behavioral paternalists do not. Sarah Conly offers a short list of things that should be banned (or required, which means banning the alternative): "We should, for instance, ban cigarettes; ban trans-fats; require restaurants to reduce portion sizes to less elephantine dimensions; increase required savings, and control how much debt individuals can run up" (2013, 1).

The behavioral justification for outright bans typically involves a combination of the biases discussed earlier, and sometimes other biases we haven't mentioned. For instance, Conly (citing Robert Goodin) says,

[T]he choice to smoke typically involves the cognitive biases of "wishful thinking" – when we believe something is safe only because we are in fact already engaged in doing it; "anchoring" – falsely assuming that since smoking has not perceptibly hurt us in this one instance, it never will; and "time-discounting" – disproportionately discounting future pains when trading them off against present pleasures.

(Conly 2013, 169)

But why a ban, instead of some weaker measure? The idea is that in some cases, the biases will simply be too strong to resist, and therefore weaker measures will not suffice to overcome them. Some people may never be able to resist the temptation of present pleasures with high future costs; others may be able to resist, but only with great effort. A ban removes the temptation altogether. Similarly, some people may have an optimism bias so strong that it resists any attempt at presenting the true risk or cost associated with certain activities. Only a ban will suffice.

It is worth observing that, while behavioral paternalism has often been associated with left-wing views, it is not limited to the left. In fact, Camerer and coauthors' (2003) paper on the subject was titled "Regulation for Conservatives." The motivation to limit consumption of "sin" goods such as alcohol and drugs has often come from the political right, and behavioral arguments could bolster that case. Many conservatives might share the left's desire to see people save more for retirement. It is not hard to imagine behavioral paternalist arguments, based on the existence of present bias or hot–cold empathy gaps, for traditionally conservative policy goals such as discouraging sexual promiscuity and encouraging marriage. Thus, we do not see ourselves as taking sides in a partisan debate. We have deep concerns about behavioral paternalist arguments regardless of who offers them.

A GAUNTLET OF CHALLENGES

From the behavioral paternalist point of view, all of the cognitive phenomena previously discussed – hyperbolic discounting, status quo bias, optimism bias, the hot–cold empathy gap, vulnerability to framing – and many others as well – constitute *errors in decision-making*.[9] The use of the term "bias" in many of the labels reflects this perspective. (For simplicity, we will also use the term "bias," though we are not convinced it is always accurate.)

---

[9] For the rather large list of cognitive biases that have been identified, see the Wikipedia entry "List of Cognitive Biases" (List of Cognitive Biases n.d.).

As behavioral paternalists see it, they are simply advocating policies that will help correct mistakes, thereby leading to better choices.

In principle, if people make mistakes, then correcting those mistakes should make them better off. So what's wrong with behavioral paternalism?

Our case will consist of a series of challenges – in effect, hurdles that behavioral paternalist proposals must clear in order to be justified as a matter of policy. We will begin with the most abstract and conceptual, then proceed to more pragmatic and applied challenges.

In Chapters 2 and 3 we address the concept of rationality. The behavioral paternalist case hinges crucially on the idea that people deviate systematically from rational choice. Their policies are intended to push people toward more rational behavior. In other words, despite having rejected rationality as a model of how people *do* behave, the behavioral paternalists still accept rationality as a model of how people *ought* to behave.

But what does it mean to be rational? The answer is far from simple. More than one definition of rationality is possible. In mainstream economics, rationality has become associated with a set of highly restrictive assumptions – not just about how people seek to achieve their preferences, but about the structure of the preferences themselves. Specifically, to qualify as rational, preferences must satisfy the technical assumptions of *completeness* and *transitivity*, as well as certain corollaries of them. These restrictive assumptions were adopted not because they were especially plausible – from either a descriptive or normative perspective – but because they were analytically convenient. They made it easier to engage in mathematical modeling. Nevertheless, behavioral economists have swallowed those assumptions whole for prescriptive purposes. For all the radicalism of their critique of mainstream economics, in this respect, behavioral economists *have not been radical enough*.

We refer to the traditional economic definition of rationality, adopted by mainstream and behavioral economists alike, as "puppet rationality." It is a brand of rationality well suited for building models of how the world works. Models are not unlike stage plays, and puppets are the players. The puppets are always well behaved. They play the roles they were designed to play. They follow the rules. They have no motive force of their own. Real human beings, however, are not puppets. Their preferences and behavior may deviate from what is expected of agents in a model. But such deviation does not provide sufficient warrant for deeming them irrational.

We do not, however, claim that everyone is always fully rational. We are happy to concede that they are not. But it is one thing to say people make mistakes; it is another to clearly and definitively identify which actions are, in fact, mistakes. In the rush to characterize certain "anomalies of choice" as violations of rationality, behavioral paternalists have been insufficiently subjectivist. Despite their stated desire to justify policy on the basis of people's own values and preferences, behavioral paternalists have unintentionally applied an external set of values – specifically, those captured by the too-restrictive neoclassical definition of rationality. Furthermore, an important part of rationality is experimenting with different choices, discovering one's preferences over time, learning from one's mistakes, structuring one's environment, adopting strategies for self-control, and working with groups of other decision-makers. These behaviors do not fit nicely into the straitjacket of "puppet" rationality, but they are perfectly sensible behaviors for real people. In sum, we argue for an *inclusive concept of rationality*.

In Chapter 4 we delve further into the research on heuristics and biases, particularly in reference to supposed biases of preference. In many, perhaps most, of these the evidence for their existence is far from unambiguous. In some cases there is reason to doubt their existence altogether. Furthermore, to the extent they do exist, their designation as "biases" often seems quite arbitrary because a good case can be made for their reasonableness or inclusive rationality. And when biases do not in practice cause people to incur unwanted costs, doubts about their rationality seem misplaced.

When rationality is stripped of unnecessary and artificially confining restrictions or assumptions, many (though not all) of the behavioral paternalists' best arguments dissolve. Many alleged violations of rationality, on which they base their case for correction, are in fact violations of analytical assumptions that are not welfare-relevant. In short, much "irrational" behavior may be nothing of the sort.

Neoclassical economists have also packed into their notion of rationality some restrictive ideas about how people process information – or, at least, how they should. Specifically, rational people must strictly adhere to the rules of classical logic and probability, they must have well-formed prior beliefs about the likelihood of events, and they must update those beliefs according to Bayes' rule. In Chapter 5 we question whether these rules constitute the uniquely rational way to process information and form beliefs. We argue that other modes of information-processing and belief-formation may be superior in many real-world contexts. We also argue that beliefs perform important functions other than truth-tracking. They can increase the quality of the agent's performance and can have direct utility-enhancing effects. Furthermore, many of the classic cognitive "fallacies" of logic and probability can be shown, in appropriate contexts, to be either reasonable responses to questions as perceived by the agent or pragmatically effective mechanisms of perception and calculation in real-world environments.

In Chapter 6 we examine some general deficiencies in the research underlying the policy recommendations of behavioral paternalism. Much of the evidence for "failures of rationality" derives from experimental settings that are effectively context-free. Such experiments may identify "raw" or unmodified propensities in human behavior in the laboratory. But they do not tell us how strong those propensities are "in the wild," where people make real decisions. Furthermore, in the real world, such findings are highly contextual and do not reach the level of generality required as a basis for policymaking. In particular, the quantitative magnitudes of such psychological propensities do not necessarily generalize to all situations in the real world, including those relevant to policy.

We also argue that people are often (though not always) aware of their cognitive biases, and sometimes they act to counteract or control them. People "self-debias" in myriad and idiosyncratic ways, including through small-group decision-making. Some of these methods are more effective than others, and some may be entirely ineffective. But to the extent they are effective, they reduce the *operative* level of bias in real choices and thereby weaken the case for government involvement.

In Chapter 7 we present the knowledge problem of paternalism. To implement behavioral paternalist policies that successfully bring individuals closer to satisfying their own subjective preferences, policymakers must possess a high level of knowledge about the actual content of those preferences – knowledge that they do not, and often cannot, possess.

By rejecting preference revelation, paternalists have stumbled into an epistemological dilemma. If actions do not reveal preferences, then what does? Experiments only yield data on people's actions, not the content of their minds. Surveys only produce data on what people say they want, not necessarily what they do want. So in order to discern "true" preferences, behavioral paternalists are forced to observe a complex set of (sometimes contradictory) actions, and then determine that *some* actions are more revelatory than others. Often, there is no basis at all for that determination.

Even if behavioral paternalists could discern people's true preferences, that's not enough. To craft effective policies, they must also know the extent of people's biases, how much people have self-debiased, how their biases interact with and offset each other, and how policies may induce compensatory behaviors and substitution effects. And to make the whole problem harder, policymakers must have extensive knowledge of the heterogeneity of all these factors in the population of decision-makers. Without such knowledge, behavioral paternalists cannot reasonably hope that their policies will achieve their stated goal of improving the satisfaction of subjective preferences.

In Chapter 8 we address the political economy, or public choice, problem of paternalism. Public choice is the field of economics that studies the incentives of policymakers – including voters, politicians, bureaucrats, and judges – and how those incentives lead to the construction of actual policies. A consistent prediction of the public choice literature is that policymakers will often fail to deliver policies that are truly in the public interest. Instead, policies will often reflect the influence of special interests, including groups both within the government and outside of it.

We argue that behavioral paternalist policies are in no way immune from the usual public choice pressures, and in some ways they may be especially vulnerable. Some pressure groups will have a financial interest in paternalist legislation – for instance, firms that market products that compete with those subject to sin taxes. Other pressure groups may be traditional "old-school" paternalists who want to reward some lifestyles and punish others for moral, religious, or ideological reasons. As a result, we predict that behavioral paternalists could find themselves in a classic "Bootleggers and Baptists" coalition (to use Bruce Yandle's evocative phrase), in which they unwittingly aid the efforts of people who don't share their goal of better satisfying people's true preferences.

To make matters worse, there is little reason to believe that legislators and bureaucrats will engage in the kind of careful, modest, data-driven policymaking that behavioral paternalists envision. Lacking sufficient knowledge of people's "true" preferences (for reasons discussed in Chapter 7), but nevertheless charged with creating policy, policymakers will inevitably find some other basis on which to do so. Even when they are not manipulated by pressure groups, policymakers are likely to rely on simple rules of thumb and unjustified assumptions. They presumably share the behavioral and cognitive biases that paternalists have attributed to private decision-makers, but they lack the effective incentives that the latter have to correct to their own failings. Consequently, we argue that policymakers will tend to promote some combination of their own preferences, socially approved preferences, or special-interest preferences – none of which are synonymous with the real preferences of people targeted by paternalist laws.

In Chapter 9 we discuss the slippery-slope problem of paternalism – that is, the possibility that seemingly small or moderate paternalist interventions will increase the likelihood of more intrusive (and less justified) interventions in the future.

Many authors have claimed that slippery-slope arguments are fundamentally fallacious, but that claim is mistaken. A recent literature, to which we have contributed, has illuminated the various processes or mechanisms by which slippery slopes do in fact occur, as well as the circumstances under which slippage is most likely.[10] Applying the insights of this literature to behavioral paternalist policies suggests that these policies are particularly susceptible to expansion. This is true even if policymakers are rational. Furthermore, we argue that the risk of slippery slopes is especially great if policymakers share the same behavioral and cognitive biases that behavioral economists have attributed to regular people.

Although we believe the slippery-slope argument is valid (otherwise we would not present it), we have noticed a tendency for the slippery-slope argument to eclipse other arguments in the public debate. Some behavioral paternalists seem to believe that the slippery slope is the *only* argument against their position. We therefore wish to emphasize that dealing with the threat of slopes is only one hurdle among many that behavioral paternalism must clear.

Finally, in Chapter 10 we bring together all of the arguments we have made, consider possible defenses of the paternalist paradigm against our critique, and recommend better ways to approach policymaking. The key conclusion is that we need to reject the paternalism-generating framework and adopt a paternalism-resisting framework instead.

We don't expect that every reader will find all of our challenges to paternalism equally compelling. Some may find our conceptual objections persuasive, others may see the knowledge problem as definitive, etc. But our hope is that, taking the gauntlet of challenges *as a whole*, readers will recognize just how tenuous the entire new-paternalist enterprise is. Behavioral paternalism's proponents often present it as just common sense – a set of smart, simple, straightforward corrections that will make us all better off. *All we're trying to do is correct some mistakes; who could be opposed to that?* But the reality is far more difficult, complicated, and even dangerous.

---

[10] Walton (1992); Ikeda (1997); Volokh (2003); Rizzo and Whitman (2003); Lode (1999); Schauer (1985).

CAVEATS AND CLARIFICATIONS

Before proceeding to our gauntlet of challenges to behavioral paternalism, we wish to make a few caveats and clarifications to stave off potential confusions.

Arguments versus Policies

Although we have been talking about "paternalist policies," this is slightly inaccurate. Any given policy may have multiple justifications, some of which may be paternalistic and others not. It would therefore be more accurate to speak of "paternalistic arguments," as well as "policies supported wholly or in part by paternalistic arguments." But for brevity, we will often speak simply of paternalist policies.

The distinction matters because classically paternalist policies are sometimes bolstered with nonpaternalist arguments. For example, the leading purpose of mandatory helmet laws is to save the lives of motorcycle riders, but they are often supported on grounds of limiting emergency-room expenditures as well. The latter argument is not strictly paternalistic; it is about protecting the interests of others (the taxpayers who subsidize emergency rooms) rather than the riders themselves. Similarly, cigarette taxes and (hypothetical) fat taxes have been defended as a means of reducing, or at least reimbursing, Medicaid and Medicare expenditures caused by smoking-related and obesity-related illnesses. Edgar Browning (1999) has coined the term "fiscal externality" to refer to this kind of argument. To take another example, restrictions on public smoking might be justified for the good of the smokers themselves *and* for the good of bystanders who could be exposed to secondhand smoke.

In this book, we will focus on strictly paternalist justifications for policy – and specifically, *behavioral* paternalist justifications. Other kinds of argument are simply beyond the scope of this work. However, given how often the fiscal externality argument is used to support the case for otherwise paternalist policies, we will offer our objections to that position in a section of Chapter 10.

Conversely, some seemingly nonpaternalist policies might nevertheless receive support from paternalist arguments. For instance, new corporate average fuel economy (CAFE) standards are typically justified by the need to limit emissions into the environment – a nonpaternalist goal. However, regulators now also include the benefits of lower fuel costs to the car owners themselves (Viscusi and Gayer 2015, 984). To the extent that consumers care about lower fuel costs, that factor should already affect their buying decisions – and thus the incentives of automakers. So the appeal to the lower fuel costs arguably involves an implicit paternalist claim that consumers irrationally ignore those benefits for some reason.

To take another example, consider the abortion debate. The leading argument for restricting abortion relates to the supposed interests of the fetus, which abortion opponents regard as a person with a right to life. Whatever its merits or demerits, this is *not* a paternalist argument. However, abortion opponents sometimes bolster their position by arguing that women who have abortions experience regret and other adverse psychological consequences after the fact.[11] To the extent that abortion opponents rely on this kind of argument – in essence saying that women should be prevented from having abortions for their *own* good as well as the fetus's – their case takes on a paternalistic aspect. (This is also another good example of how paternalistic arguments can come from the right as well as the left.)

Our objections to paternalism, therefore, apply also to paternalist arguments in favor of otherwise nonpaternalist policies – without necessarily committing us to opposing those policies entirely. We may or may not agree with their nonpaternalist justifications.

Behavioral Arguments for Nonpaternalist Policies

Not every policy application of behavioral economics involves paternalism. Instead, policymakers may use behavioral insights to achieve nonpaternalistic goals. For instance, a government might change the default rule for organ donation from "opt in" (you must state in advance that you wish to donate organs in the event of your death) to "opt out" (you must state in advance that you do *not* wish to donate organs). Behavioral research indicates that the latter rule tends to induce more organ donation. Although the success of this policy hinges on behavioral economics, its goal is entirely nonpaternalistic: to save the lives of other people.

Policies such as these are not our primary target in this book. However, *some* of our challenges to behavioral paternalist policies – particularly those that question their efficacy – may also apply to nonpaternalist policies supported by behavioral research. For instance, in Chapters 6 and 7 we discuss how some paternalistic interventions can backfire because

---

[11] See, for instance, Iowa Right to Life's page on "Post Abortion Syndrome": www.iowartl .org/get-the-facts/abortion/post-abortion-syndrome/

the cognitive bias in question is not well understood, or because its interaction with other biases is uncertain. This kind of objection might apply to behaviorally justified nonpaternalist interventions as well. However, we will leave it to the reader to discern which of our arguments have this broader applicability.

Freedom and Autonomy

Many opponents of paternalism make a straightforward appeal to freedom or autonomy. John Stuart Mill is one prominent example, although he makes many other arguments as well. Some behavioral paternalists have responded by explicitly questioning the value of freedom and autonomy; most notably, Conly titled her defense of paternalism *Against Autonomy*. Other behavioral paternalists, such as Sunstein and Thaler, concede – even emphasize – the value of freedom and autonomy, but they weigh these values in a cost–benefit analysis versus the beneficial consequences of paternalism.

We admit to finding the argument from freedom and autonomy persuasive. But we have little to add in support of it. As economists, we think our comparative advantage lies in presenting the *conceptual* and *consequentialist* case against behavioral paternalism. Inasmuch as the case for behavioral paternalism rests on its supposedly beneficial consequences, our response in most respects constitutes an immanent critique. However, to the extent that the case for new paternalism, either in a cost–benefit calculation or in some other way, depends upon the claim that autonomy is infringed only slightly, we do have something to add. In Chapter 9 we discuss the tendencies within the paternalist framework to expand its reach to ever greater violations of autonomy. To the extent that the case for behavioral paternalism rests on its minimal intrusiveness, we contend that it fails on its own terms. Thus, even in this context, our position remains an immanent critique.

PEOPLE, NOT PUPPETS

Frank Oz once said of his longtime collaborator Jim Henson, "Jim had a lot of respect for puppetry, but not much for the puppet as a physical object. It was a means to an end. If he was giving a live demonstration, he didn't care if people saw him put his hand in the puppet, and he didn't try to sustain the illusion once the performance was over" (Finch 1993). We believe it's time for economists, and the policymakers they advise, to set down their puppets. The puppets used in economic models have their valid purposes, and often they perform them well. But it is a profound mistake to confuse the puppets with reality. Real human beings do not display puppet rationality, yet they display a wide range of behaviors that we can reasonably call "rational." When we confuse puppet rationality with real rationality, we run the risk of treating real people as puppets – and turning self-appointed experts into puppet masters.

2

What Is Rationality?

Properly construed, rationality is as wide-ranging and complex as the domain of intelligence at large.

—Nicholas Rescher, *Rationality*

A map is not the territory it represents, but, if correct, has a similar structure to the territory, which accounts for its usefulness.

—Alfred Korzybski, *Science and Sanity*

Are human beings rational? It is a question often posed by philosophers, economists, and others. It is also a question central to the behavioral paternalist project of rescuing people from their own irrationality. But it is not easily answered, because the word "rational" has many meanings.

Rationality can simply mean purposefulness, that is, trying to use the best means available to satisfy your goals or preferences given your beliefs about the world. It can mean taking an abstract approach to solving problems, applying universal systems of thought and inference, and following scientific methods. It can mean avoiding errors of logic and reasoning. It can mean revising one's beliefs in accordance with Bayes' Rule. It can mean having preferences that conform to certain axioms – transitivity, completeness, and so forth – which together guarantee the preferences are internally consistent and have a certain structure. In neoclassical economic theory, it has historically meant *all of the above*. Interestingly, while behavioral economists have cast doubt on this kind of rationality as a description of how people *do* behave, they follow the neoclassical economists in saying it describes how people *should* behave. We call this kind of rationality *neoclassical rationality*. But we also call it *puppet rationality*, as it describes agents who always conform to a specified model of behavior; they do only what they are programmed to do.

Another possibility is that rationality means successfully adapting to some task environment – that is, acting on the basis of beliefs, habits, and heuristics that function well in a specific environment to attain the agent's goals. Todd and Gigerenzer call this form of rationality *ecological rationality* (Todd et al. 2012). This is distinct from the more abstract notion of rationality described previously and used by most economists, which purports to have universal validity irrespective of the individual's situation.

In this book, we will defend what we call *inclusive rationality*. Inclusive rationality means purposeful behavior based on subjective preferences and beliefs, in the presence of both environmental and cognitive constraints. This notion of rationality preserves the core notion of purposefulness, and in that sense it should seem familiar. But unlike other notions of rationality – many of which were invented for modeling purposes but have since taken on a life of their own – inclusive rationality does not dictate the normative structure of preferences and beliefs a priori. Instead, it allows a wide range of possibilities in terms of how real people select their goals, form and revise their beliefs, structure their decisions, and conceptualize the world. Their preferences and beliefs may be inchoate, incomplete, inconsistent, mutable, and dependent on context. Inclusive rationality can thus encompass choices and strategies that would not make sense under more restrictive notions of rationality. To be specific, real people may do all of the following and still qualify as inclusively rational:

- Experience internal conflict that has not yet been (and may never be) resolved;
- Have preferences that change over time;
- Have preferences that are indeterminate or incomplete – i.e., that do not specify attitudes over all possible decisions at all possible times and states of the world;
- Have preferences that are in the process of being created or discovered;
- Have preferences that depend on context, including both the options available and the way in which decisions are framed;
- Hold beliefs that serve purposes other than truth-tracking, such as providing motivation or intrinsic satisfaction;
- Make inferences based not on the strict rules of classical logic, but on contextual and linguistic cues they have learned from human interaction;
- Indulge "biased" modes of decision-making when the costs are low and rein them in when the costs are high;

- Economize on scarce mental resources by refusing to impose perfect consistency on their preferences and beliefs;
- Structure their environments, possibly in ways that constrain their own choices;
- Adopt personal rules and resolutions that create internal incentive systems;
- Enlist the help of friends, family, and other groups to assist in attaining goals;
- Rely on institutions, social customs, and market structures to assist in attaining goals;
- Employ heuristics that minimize cognitive effort and/or informational input.

From our perspective, rationality does not demand a universal structure that works for all people in all places and times. Rationality is practical or pragmatic in nature. As such, its tools may be both contextual (i.e., specific to an environment) and idiosyncratic (i.e., specific to an individual). In the real world, agents can and do employ a variety of decision-making tools, which can be quite effective while nevertheless deviating from the strictures of neoclassical rationality. (In taking this position, we draw heavily on Todd and Gigerenzer's notion of ecological rationality, but we do not limit ourselves to it.) Furthermore, rationality does not depend solely on cognitive abilities, let alone conscious cognitive abilities. Reason is cunning. Reason is adaptive. We can find it where we least expect it. Human beings are far more rational in the relevant sense than a reading of the behavioral economics literature would lead us to expect.

That does not, of course, mean that human beings are never irrational. They may indeed exhibit behaviors that are not well adapted to their environments. They may have failures of agency, in the sense that they sometimes fail to act upon their genuine preferences. Following the behavioral economists, we will refer to these true failures of rationality as "biases." But finding clear evidence of such failures is another matter. It is easy to show that real people deviate from the predictions of economic models built on the assumptions of neoclassical rationality. That is not the same as showing they have acted irrationally in the broader, more inclusive sense that is most relevant to the agents themselves. As Vernon Smith puts it, "My point is simple: when experimental results are contrary to standard concepts of rationality, assume not just that people are irrational, but that you may not have the right model of rational behavior. *Listen to what your subjects may be trying to tell you*" (2005, 149, emphasis in original). To take just one example, it can be difficult to determine whether someone has acted contrary to their own preferences versus simply having preferences that fail to conform to the model's requirements. They may have preferences over things that the modeler doesn't think they should. They may have mutable preferences . . . or no relevant preferences at all.

As we shall see in subsequent chapters, many claims of bias suffer from a dogmatic adherence to axioms about the structure of preferences that can be violated in perfectly reasonable ways. For example, people can have intransitive preferences and still function perfectly well in the world. Furthermore, many alleged biases rest on flimsy evidence – studies based on the same inadequate designs employed over and over again.

Our conception of rationality is fundamentally liberal. While this doesn't necessarily mean liberal in the political or ideological sense, it does mean being tolerant of deviations from specialized and restrictive notions of sensible behavior. Those who are keen to evaluate behavior sharply and to separate the world neatly into rational and irrational decisions will find much of what we say frustrating. They may be irked by our efforts to find the reasonable or understandable aspect of behavior they wish to fix or improve. In social science, as in many areas of life, it is best to understand from the perspective of the agents themselves before engaging in criticism.

EXPLICIT AND IMPLICIT COMPONENTS OF PURPOSEFUL BEHAVIOR

Much of economics builds upon the pre-theoretical "folk psychology" insight that human beings engage in purposeful behavior. They have purposes and beliefs that both motivate and rationalize their decisions. This is where we start as social scientists. It is how we make sense of much of what people do in everyday life, including the activities of scientists. The interactions of daily life presuppose a common mental structure based on purposeful behavior. Other people may have different beliefs and purposes than we do, but normally we can – perhaps with significant effort – understand the meaning of their actions. In the social sciences, the interpretation of much behavior as purposeful has been very successful in understanding social phenomena.

Behavior can be *consciously* purposeful; that is, the individual explicitly knows what she wants and uses what she considers the best means to get it. While this is a useful ideal type, it is easy to see that purely and thoroughly conscious choice is an illusion. The individual's background beliefs about the world are not always conscious. The means by which an individual infers conclusions from what she already knows may be intuitive. Thus behavior may be *unconsciously* purposeful. It may go even further along the continuum of unconsciousness to a reconfiguration of the entire choice-problem. For example, individuals may tacitly downgrade how much they value immediate goals in order to enhance their attainment of longer-run goals. Strong temptations may paradoxically and unconsciously trigger strong self-control (Geyskens et al. 2008). The distinction between consciously and unconsciously purposeful behavior is important because, among other things, unconscious behavior seems to require fewer cognitive resources.

RULES AS A TOOL OF RATIONALITY

Human beings exercise purpose not just in a narrow, action-by-action sense, but also through rule-following and rule-conforming behavior. Especially in a world of true uncertainty, following rules is often the best way to attain the satisfaction of goals. For our purposes, a rule might be thought of as a generalized "if–then" imperative: if an event or cue of a certain kind occurs, then the individual will (or should) perform a certain action or infer a certain thing about the world. Rules and heuristics may be applied consciously (rule-following behavior) or implicitly without conscious awareness (rule-conforming behavior). The rules may be taught or acquired through trial-and-error experience.

Many examples of explicit, conscious rules can be found among those that govern driving: stopping at stop lights, yielding to pedestrians in a crosswalk, and so forth. Many examples of implicit, unconscious rules come from language; speakers typically follow their native language's rules of grammar and syntax without conscious thought. Whether the rules are explicit or implicit, following or conforming to them is pragmatically rational in that doing so typically helps the individual achieve his goals (such as reaching his destination or communicating successfully with others).

Rules can also be adopted to channel one's own behavior. A person can resolve to exercise more to compensate for overeating. She can choose to eat cake only on weekends. She can always store junk food in an inconvenient place. Rationality does not imply that individuals must allow themselves to be subject to every momentary passion. Rational behavior includes the *self-imposition* of constraints.

Heuristics, sometimes called rules of thumb, can make it easier to learn about the world and make better choices. Examples include the *recognition heuristic* and *Take the Best* (TTB), both of which provide a means of choosing between two alternatives according to some criterion, such as guessing which of two named cities has the higher population.[1] As it turns out, the recognition heuristic and TTB actually work better in certain environments than more data-hungry methods such as multiple-regression analysis, and they also enable the individual to economize on cognitive effort.[2]

Often rules can enhance the attainment of ends, and people follow or conform to them for that reason. However, there are some cases where individuals follow rules consciously without much awareness of the rules' functions. Moral rules can be of this character. Some of these rules may have individual or social functions that are identifiable by analysts and in that sense are still instrumentally rational. But others may be atavistic or provide purely intrinsic satisfaction. In these cases, their instrumental rationality is attenuated and it may be best to look at these rules as either ends in themselves (if the individual has internalized them as important) or as exogenous constraints on the attainment of other ends (if the individual conforms to them primarily to avoid social sanctions).

BOUNDED RATIONALITY AND THE LIMITS OF MODELS

It is common now in economics to refer to agents who have limits upon their reasoning capacities as "boundedly rational." For the most part, the term is used synonymously with "irrationality," albeit with a less judgmental edge. Nevertheless, on a policy level, it tends to generate similar prescriptions – typically paternalistic ones.[3]

What would it mean to have unbounded rationality? Any particular instantiation of rationality is bounded relative to another. Suppose, for instance, we choose the reasoning capacity of the smartest person on earth

---

[1] The recognition heuristic simply means choosing a recognizable option over an unrecognized one. Take the Best (TTB) involves searching sequentially through a sequence of cues that might predict the correct answer, such as whether a city is the capital, whether a city has a soccer team, and so on, with the cues ordered roughly in terms of their predictive accuracy. See Gigerenzer (2015, 107–139).

[2] TTB will work better than linear regression when the following conditions hold: (1) the cue validities and weights have the ranking as in the regression model and (2) the weight of each cue is not exceeded by the sum of the weights of the subsequent cues. This is called a "noncompensatory environment." See Marewski et al. (2010, 112).

[3] Jolls and Sunstein (2006), for example.

as the relevant standard; then anyone else's reasoning will certainly fall short. This smartest person will see the rest of us as "boundedly rational."

In the more typical case, the appropriate standards are chosen by a model-builder. For example, expected utility theory is often presented as a model of perfect or unbounded rationality. But even this framework is bounded because it cannot accommodate uncertainty that is not reducible to risk. It presupposes the consequences of all alternatives are known, at least in probabilistic terms, and it tolerates no ambiguity in the assignment of utility to an outcome. The model's agents can only think and act within confines specifically constructed for them. They do what their creators program them to do and no more.[4] We can certainly imagine a broader and more inclusive model that permits true uncertainty and so on, although that model might be mathematically intractable or cumbersome. This is the nature of *all* models of behavior that exhibit agent rationality. Modeled rationality is always incomplete and bounded relative to what it could be in another model. Recognizing this fact does not automatically open the door to normative criticism. There will *always* be some standpoint from which agents are deficient. The key issue is whether that standpoint is important and relevant *to the agents themselves*.

When behavioral economists invoke bounded rationality, they are in essence claiming that the bounds of the traditional models are not appropriate for explaining real people's choices. For example, Daniel Kahneman (2011, 278–288) argues that prospect theory is an alternative to expected utility theory that better explains actual behavior. Agents in prospect theory do not seek to maximize their expected level of wealth; instead, they are concerned with asymmetrically valued gains and losses relative to a reference point such as the status quo. Normatively, this and other alternative assumptions are considered "failures of rationality" (2011, 286), but it is not clear why. It is true that, in the long run, agents who are more affected by the desire to avoid losses than by the desire to obtain gains do not maximize wealth. Kahneman says these agents thus have valuations that "are unreasonably short-sighted" (2011, 286). Strictly speaking, they are not short-sighted because they are still attentive to long-run gains and losses and do not suffer from present bias. The "problem" is simply that the long-run outcome generated by such valuations is not consistent with the neoclassical model, which remains the

---

[4] When agents *appear* to be omniscient it is simply because they are modeled to know everything the model-builder, as model-builder, knows. The bounds of the creature are the same as the bounds of its creator.

standard of rationality. It is not at all clear why, if prospect-theory agents attach utility to gains and losses rather than levels of wealth, they should be considered bounded in their rationality. To put the point another way, why shouldn't *expected utility agents* be considered limited or bounded because they are *not* sensitive to gains and losses (except to the extent that they affect absolute levels of wealth)? The attitude Kahneman takes on this issue shows just how much his view of normative rationality is a slave to the particular standard framework that, ironically, Kahneman may have done more than anyone else to falsify as a positive model of human behavior.

It is perhaps surprising that Kahneman does not frame his critique of expected utility theory in terms of its exceedingly high knowledge and computational requirements. But other criticisms of the standard neoclassical models have been made along these lines. We think that many of them are powerful – yet the wrong lessons have been drawn. The heuristics and biases literature has promoted the view, shared by most economists, that the full use of all of the available information is always better than ignoring some pieces of information. In this view, it is only the limited cognitive capacity of the human mind that prevents the use of the most sophisticated and most efficacious methods of inference and choice. On the contrary, sometimes more information and more computation are worse, even if the cognitive costs are zero. The aforementioned recognition and TTB heuristics are examples of methods that can, under the right circumstances, perform better at real-world prediction tasks. These heuristics, among others, can use less information and produce better decisions – a topic we will discuss in greater depth in Chapter 5.

THE FUNCTIONAL VALUE OF BIASES AND ERRORS

A closely related problem is that heuristic-driven biases are often examined in isolation from the functions they serve in a more integrated picture of the human mind. Consider the matter of perfect recall. One individual who had a near-perfect memory had so many details in his head that he was unable to generalize or to even recognize the same face from moment to moment as it underwent slight changes (Gigerenzer 2008, 75–76). The ability to make abstractions is rooted in the ability to suppress details. Furthermore, forgetting has a role in emptying the mind of information that, because it is not frequent or recent in the person's environment, is unlikely to be needed for the pursuit of current or future goals (Marewski et al. 2010, 115). It has also been found that intermediate rates of forgetting increase the efficacy of the recognition heuristic as out-of-date information is cleared away (Schooler and Hertwig 2005). Thus there can be too little forgetting.

The issue of cognitive limitations has also been confused by a failure to recognize the opportunity costs of "executive functions" such as focus, self-control, and vigilant monitoring (Kurzban et al. 2013). The cognitive resources that underlie such functions tend to be finite but also flexible so that they can be used in multiple alternative tasks. Accordingly, there is an allocation problem. It has been suggested, with considerable evidence (Kurzban et al. 2013), that the subjective feeling of effort and fatigue that accompanies these executive functions reflects the opportunity cost of applying the same or similar cognitive mechanisms elsewhere. For example, if a young lawyer's resolve to give up smoking begins to weaken under the pressure of studying for the bar exam, we cannot consider this a simple failure of willpower or self-control. It may be that the fatigue from applying self-control to resist smoking is signaling that, at least for a time, self-control and focus resources are more urgently needed for studying. The "failure" is thus efficient.

Sometimes, however, paternalists argue that nudges or other policies employing external pressure can substitute for scarce self-control resources. If a policy intervention – such as a high sin tax or gruesome images on the cigarette pack – enabled the lawyer to attain her goal of not smoking without having to exert self-control, then she would not have to choose between concentrating on the bar exam or controlling her urge to smoke; she could do both. However, we cannot assume that paternalistic interventions will simply augment self-control or reduce the need for it. A tax doesn't reduce the lawyer's craving for a cigarette; it just activates her interest in saving money. The cravings are still there. So, she redirects her existing self-control resources toward the paternalist's goal – and away from other goals. The lawyer may focus more on not smoking and less on studying. There is an opportunity cost.

Furthermore, even if paternalistic interventions did somehow expand an agent's self-control, the improvement could be short-lived. In the long run, the substitution of external pressure for self-control resources may result in an overall reduction of self-control. This can be seen from studies showing that the exercise of self-control in one area can increase the amount of self-control resources available in entirely unrelated areas over time (Gailliot et al. 2007).[5] The diminished capacity for self-control in the long run

---

[5] For a further discussion of this issue see Rizzo and Whitman (2009b, 957–960). The "long run" in the study by Gailliot et al. (2007) is as little as two weeks.

(relative to what it would have been) constitutes another form of opportunity cost.

Another issue is whether errors can play a functional role in the learning process. It is not hard to find examples of individuals making poor predictions, especially in laboratory settings, and often such prediction errors will be attributed to some kind of bias. What this approach neglects is that repeated divergence of outcomes from predictions – particularly about rewards and punishments – can motivate the learning processes that lead to more accurate predictions over time (Schultz and Dickinson 2000). To the extent this is so, policies that aim to prevent errors may have the unintended effect of short-circuiting cognitive processes of self-correction. We will expand on the relationship between errors and learning in Chapter 6.

The overall lesson here is that useful concepts of rationality must respect human cognitive limits. It is tempting to say that, if cognitive control of a behavior can be improved by some policy, the original behavior was irrational or boundedly rational. But this can be misleading. If the improvement cannot be made at a justifiable cost, then it is idle to call the behavior irrational.[6] What is the opportunity cost of improving the cognitive quality of some decision? Without an answer to that question, we cannot conclude that the low quality of the decision demands correction. As we saw previously, the opportunity cost will equal the forgone benefit of self-control, focus, or other cognitive effort that was diverted from another activity or lost entirely because of the policy. Since this can occur in an entirely unrelated area, it will not necessarily be easy for policymakers to determine the cost.

In any case, certain conclusions should be evident. First, individuals should not be held to a standard of rationality that is infeasible or cannot be attained in a cost-justified manner. Second, policymakers should be alert to the unseen opportunity costs of interventions designed to correct poor decision-making. Third, the individual's goals may differ from what an outsider thinks they should be, which makes the meaning of "improvement" less than obvious. Finally, the cognitive processing abilities of individuals may not be the major problem; all they may need is better information. I may have the best cognitive processing abilities in the world, but if I do not have the train timetable, I may not get to my destination.

---

[6] This is analogous to the discussion of whether states of affairs should be considered "inefficient" if there is no feasible policy that could improve them at justifiable cost. See Demsetz (1969).

The value of information was, of course, well established long before behavioral economics. We will expand on all of these arguments in later chapters.

POSITIVE, NORMATIVE, AND PRESCRIPTIVE

Economists and other social scientists often rely on the distinction between positive and normative statements, as well as the related distinction between descriptive and prescriptive statements. As we will lean heavily on these distinctions in future chapters, it's worth defining them explicitly.

By *positive* or *descriptive* statements, we mean statements of fact or potential fact. Positive models and theories attempt to explain, describe, or predict how people do behave or could behave. By *normative* statements, we mean statements that make a judgment of value: good or bad, right or wrong, better or worse, should or should not. Some normative statements are narrow, in that they only apply within a particular model – for example, a firm should set price in a particular way in order to maximize profits. But more often, normative statements are meant to have broader application, as they purport to state how people should behave in the real world, not merely within a model. We will sometimes use the term *prescriptive* to refer to such broader normative judgments.

The core of instrumental rationality – purposeful behavior – has been developed into many specific forms and applied to a variety of human behavior. The models constructed on the basis of this core help to make human behavior intelligible in positive terms. Given assumptions about beliefs and preferences, such models enhance our ability to make predictions about what individuals or groups of individuals will do. By specifying much more narrowly the nature or structure of preferences, the content of beliefs, and the rules for rational thinking, analysts can make relatively precise predictions about human behavior. Whether these predictions are corroborated or falsified will depend on the appropriateness of the particular model in realistic environments.

In most cases, standard neoclassical economists have assumed that rational actors are just like them, or at least how they imagine themselves to be. They think like economists. They use the same models. They are expected utility maximizers, perfect logicians, and Bayesian updaters.[7] Cognitive differences between actors and analysts are minimized, if they

---

[7] Gigerenzer and Marewski (2015) criticize the mechanical application of Bayes' rule in much of the "heuristics and biases" literature.

exist at all. Therefore, it is natural that tests of the rationality of individuals have proceeded along the lines of testing whether they behave like economists (or as economists would ideally behave). They are usually tests of the individual's ability to use decision-making and cognitive techniques that are the subjects of academic training. Stated in this way, it does seem very strange, but its strangeness has largely been suppressed by the familiarity and frequency of the practice. Most economists are so wedded to the idea that rationality can only mean adherence to the tools of standard theory that they cannot break out of the box of their own creation. If people don't behave as the model predicts, something must be wrong with them! Consequently, there has been a tendency to conflate the normative and the positive: "we are testing to see if people *do* behave as they *should* behave."

However, neoclassical rationality only specifies how individuals "should" behave *if* they are to behave according to the dictates of the standard model. In principle, that is all there is to it. There is no necessary implication that real-world individuals *should* behave as rational-choice models predict in the actual environments in which they find themselves. Standard rationality norms are not *ipso facto* prescriptive norms for successful behavior. We discuss this in much greater depth in the chapters that follow, but here we offer a preview.

When real people take tests designed to test neoclassical rationality norms, they do not leave their inclusive and contextually shaped rationality at the testing room door. Instead, they may behave as they do in the real world. For example:

- They may assume, in accordance with ordinary conversational norms, that experimenters provide only information that is relevant to solving the problem – i.e., no irrelevant or "tricky" information. They do not immediately assume the experimenters are trying to fool them.
- They may resist the distinction between the validity of a syllogistic inference (e.g., "People with red hair are Martians, John has red hair, therefore John is a Martian") and the truth of a conclusion itself (John is *not* a Martian). Normally, in everyday life, it is the truth that is more important.
- They may not assume that prior probabilities about something – such as the likelihood that someone has a disease – must be equal to the "base rates" from the population provided to them. Instead, their priors may be affected by their evaluation of the significance of the base rates to a particular problem in front of them – say, whether a

specific person who chose to visit the doctor and chose to take a test has the disease. Treating priors in this way is fully consistent with the subjectivist Bayesian view that prior probabilities are subjective – a fact frequently ignored in the rush to deem subjects "irrational."

- They may not agree with model-builders on the informational equivalence of different descriptions of a situation. Instead, they may infer implicit information or advice from how a problem is presented. For example, they may perceive an important difference between a stated probability of success equal to 0.7 and a stated probability of failure equal to 0.3. Perhaps the former conveys greater optimism, despite the formal mathematical equivalence of the two statements. Conversational norms and expectations do not always align with logic and probability theory. The former can be adaptive in the real world while the latter is adaptive on experimental tests. Which is more important?
- They may attach satisfaction or utility to things other than what the analysts expect. For instance, they may value an object more because it is theirs already. Or they may care about feelings of gain and loss experienced during the experiment, not just how much money they have when they leave the laboratory. Or they may gain satisfaction purely from having a particular belief, irrespective of its truth ("My wife is beautiful and my children are gifted").

This is only a partial list, and we will expand on these examples in later chapters. Here, our point is that we must distinguish the intellectual tools and skills needed by agents in an artificial model from the tools needed by real people pursuing their own ends in the real world. There is no automatic overlap. The "should" of standard economic theory is internally generated. Rational agents in many models are *defined* to have certain characteristics irrespective of whether these characteristics pass the test of enhancing adaptability in the wild.

Because our notion of inclusive rationality is very broad, we might be accused of offering a theory that cannot be falsified. We should therefore clarify that we do believe positive claims should, in principle, be falsifiable. But some claims are more easily tested than others, and there is no guarantee that the most easily tested claims are also normatively relevant. Behavioral economists have set about testing the specific claims of neoclassical rationality, and in some cases those claims have been found wanting (i.e., they have been falsified). We have no problem with this process. The testing of specific and sometimes narrow claims about human behavior can be highly useful in elucidating how real people behave. The error creeps in when the analyst assumes, implicitly or explicitly, that the falsification of any particular claim automatically has normative import.

In general, more restrictive positive claims are easier to test and potentially to falsify. For scientific purposes, then, more restrictive claims are often useful. But if the claims in question lack normative status, then although their falsification may tell us *more* about the world, it does not tell us that anything is *wrong* with the world. To make valid normative conclusions, we may need to consider less restrictive positive claims – which can be more difficult to test.

Standard models based on a narrow conception of rationality *do* sometimes pass falsification tests and may be the best explanation we have in many areas. In other contexts, they do not perform as well. The important question for us is: what is the significance of the *failure* of narrow rationality to predict or explain behavior in specific cases?

From a strictly positive perspective, failure simply suggests that a new approach may be needed to explain the phenomenon. As theories of behavior, standard rationality models are attempts to understand the world. When the world says "no," the scientist must go back to the drawing board. The failure of individuals to act as the scientist predicts is, in principle, no different from electrons not behaving as predicted by the Bohr model of the atom. However, economists often label people "irrational" or "boundedly rational" without sufficiently emphasizing that this simply means that the individuals are not behaving according to one narrow stipulation of rational behavior. In other words, economists are saying, in a roundabout fashion, that their theory of the phenomenon is wrong.

To carry the claim further and say that the *individuals* are "wrong" is a leap that cannot be made without additional argument. In a framework of inclusive rationality, the ultimate standard by which individuals' behavior is evaluated is the degree of successful attainment of goals in the actual environment in which they find themselves. The simple fact that individuals do not behave in accordance with standard theories is not evidence of failure in this broader normative sense. It is certainly not evidence in favor of fixing their behavior. The norms of standard neoclassical rationality are not prescriptions for better behavior. Behavioral economists have unfortunately accepted the *prescriptive* relevance of the received theory even as they have rejected its *predictive* accuracy in a wide range of behavior. In this book we are mainly concerned with the normative and prescriptive aspects of rationality. Therefore our disagreement is with both standard and behavioral economics, given that both are wedded to the same prescriptive view of rationality.

3

Rationality for Puppets*

The fundamental fact . . . is that we lay down rules, a technique, for a game, and then when we follow the rules, things do not work out as we had assumed. That we are therefore as it were entangled in our rules.

—Ludwig Wittgenstein, *Philosophical Investigations*

A foolish consistency is the hobgoblin of little minds, adored by little statesmen and philosophers and divines.

—Ralph Waldo Emerson, *Self-Reliance*

Do I contradict myself?
Very well then I contradict myself,
(I am large, I contain multitudes.)
—Walt Whitman, *Song of Myself*

The case for behavioral paternalism is fundamentally *normative* in character; it prescribes or recommends policies to make people better off. As such, its justification cannot rest on positive (i.e., factual) research alone. It is ultimately necessary to consider the normative assumptions on which it is based. Yet any normative analysis must at least begin with a clear statement of the evaluative standard. Therefore we ask: what welfare criteria justify the use of insights from behavioral economics to support paternalistic policies? As presented by its leading proponents, behavioral paternalism aims to make people better off *according to their own (true) preferences*. In appealing to individual preferences, it appears to rely on the same normative standards as neoclassical welfare economics, which may be loosely characterized as a form of preference-based utilitarianism. Although utilitarianism has (of course) been subjected to many

---

* Some sections of this chapter first appeared, with some differences, in Whitman and Rizzo (2015).

philosophical criticisms, it might seem that behavioral paternalism raises no *additional* concerns beyond those raised by standard welfare economics.

But in fact, behavioral paternalism raises deep concerns that do not arise in traditional welfare economics. In the traditional approach, agents are simply assumed – as a matter of fact – to meet the definition of rationality used in that approach. Thus, no questions arise regarding how to judge the welfare of agents who do not satisfy that definition. Behavioral economics challenges the *positive* validity of neoclassical rationality in describing human behavior. Nevertheless, behavioral paternalism maintains neoclassical rationality as a *normative* standard to which agents *ought* to conform. Thus, it is crucial for us to examine closely what neoclassical rationality really means.

In sharp contrast to the highly contextual concept of rationality introduced in Chapter 2, today's dominant economic paradigm relies on a concept of rationality that is formal, axiomatic, and context-independent. It is a creature of at least two philosophical movements: the classical behaviorism of the early to mid-twentieth century, which eschewed all but observable entities; and the mathematical philosophy of Bourbakism,[1] which sought the development of axiomatic systems independent of content. These influences combined with the particular concerns of economists to produce a mental construct of the "rational agent" that has little to do with the depth and breadth of human reason – and still less to do with how we as human beings ought to behave.

Our primary interest here is the normative aspects of the standard view rather than its descriptive realism. Whether people *do or do not* behave as axiomatic agents does not necessarily affect the claim that they *ought* to behave that way. The neoclassical position says that people are by and large rational, while the behavioral position argues that they are not, at least much of the time and in important contexts. In the standard approach, there are no decision-making failures to remedy. Agents rigorously adhere to the rules of neoclassical rationality. In the behavioral approach, agents violate the rules. But both approaches affirm that agents *ought* to follow the rules.

We have been calling the rationality of axiomatic theory "neoclassical rationality," but it could aptly be called "rationality for puppets." Agents

---

[1] "Bourbakism" refers to the philosophy of mathematics of a group of French mathematicians who wrote under the nom de plume of Nicolas Bourbaki, a fictional person. They wished to ground mathematics on a formal and self-contained axiomatic system.

equipped with this kind of rationality do not have minds of their own. They are mental constructs, that is, hypothetical or idealized agents who have been endowed by economists with certain primitive characteristics of preference and choice. These agents are puppets because they evaluate or choose exactly as they have been programmed to do by their handlers (Machlup 1974; Schutz 1962).[2]

As with all scientific constructs, the puppets have been created for specific purposes.[3] It is important not to lose sight of these. When economists adopted axiomatic rationality, their purposes were: (1) to give preference theory a solid logical foundation, (2) to make precise the necessary and sufficient conditions that must be placed on preferences or choices to build a utility function, and (3) to use that function as part of theories with predictive or explanatory value.[4] This was not fundamentally a normative project. However, the normative value of axiomatic rationality has come to be stressed as its predictive and explanatory value has suffered setbacks (Hands 2015). The separation of this idealization of rationality from its original purposes has created the impression of a free-floating or all-purpose formalization of practical rationality.

This chapter is devoted to examining the axiomatic definition of rationality of preference and choice under conditions of certainty. We will focus

---

[2] "Yet these models of actors are not human beings living within their biographical situation in the social world of everyday life. Strictly speaking, they do not have any biography or any history, and the situation into which they are placed is not a situation defined by them but defined by their creator, the social scientist. He has created these puppets or homunculi to manipulate them for his purpose. A merely specious consciousness is imputed to them by the scientist which is constructed in such a way that its presupposed stock of knowledge at hand (including the ascribed set of invariant motives) would make actions originating therefrom subjectively understandable, provided that these actions were performed by real actors within the social world. But the puppet and his artificial consciousness is not subjected to the ontological conditions of human beings. The homunculus was not born, he does not grow up, and he will not die. He has no hopes and no fears: he does not know anxiety as the chief motive of all his deeds. He is not free in the sense that his acting could transgress the limits his creator, the social scientist, has predetermined. He cannot, therefore, have other conflicts of interests and motives than those the social scientist has imputed to him. He cannot err, if to err is not his typical destiny. He cannot choose, except among the alternatives the social scientist has put before him as standing to his choice" (Schutz 1962, 41).

[3] "A choice of axioms is not a purely objective task. It is usually expected to achieve some definite aim – some specific theorem or theorems are to be derivable from the axiom – and to this extent the problem is exact and objective" (von Neumann and Morgenstern 1944, 25).

[4] Usually these theories are directed toward explaining market or aggregate behavior and not individual behavior per se (Machlup 1974). Therefore, the empirical adequacy of the axioms is not tested directly.

on philosophical or "in principle" objections to neoclassical rationality as a normative standard. In Chapter 4, we will delve more deeply into behavioral research that casts doubt on the interpretation of so-called anomalies of choice as necessarily irrational. And in Chapter 5, we will extend our analysis to the rationality of beliefs and choice under uncertainty.

THE AXIOMS OF PREFERENCE RATIONALITY

Are we correct to claim that behavioral paternalism has adopted neoclassical rationality as a welfare standard? After all, behavioral economics is often presented as a refutation of rational choice. This is particularly true in the behavioral paternalist literature. Camerer et al. (2003), for instance, offer this summary:

The standard approach in economics assumes "full rationality." While disagreement exists as to what exactly full rationality encompasses, most economists would agree on the following components: First, people have well-defined preferences (or goals) and make decisions to maximize those preferences. Second, those preferences accurately reflect (to the best of the person's knowledge) the true costs and benefits of the available options. Third, in situations that involve uncertainty, people have well-formed beliefs about how uncertainty will resolve itself, and when new information becomes available, they update their beliefs using Bayes's law – the presumed ability to update probabilistic assessments in light of new information.

Behavioral economics challenges all of these assumptions and attempts to replace them with more realistic approaches based on scientific findings from other social sciences.

(pp. 1214–1215, italics added, footnotes omitted)

Similarly, Sunstein and Thaler (2003) say:

The false assumption is that almost all people, almost all of the time, make choices that are in their best interest or at the very least are better, by their own lights, than the choices that would be made by third parties. This claim is either tautological, and therefore uninteresting, or testable. *We claim that it is testable and false, indeed obviously false.*

(p. 1163)

Yet when they advocate policies designed to improve or correct behavior, what they mean is encouraging behavior that conforms more closely to the neoclassical ideal that they believe is factually false. We will justify this claim later, but first we should be more specific about the requirements of neoclassical rationality.

We focus in this chapter on the first of the neoclassical rationality criteria listed by Camerer and coauthors: having well-defined preferences.

"Well-defined" is economics jargon for preferences that satisfy two axioms: *completeness* and *transitivity*.[5] Both axioms are stated in terms of a binary preference relation R, meaning "is ranked at least as highly as," or in the usual jargon, "is weakly preferred to."

> *Completeness*: For *any* two objects (x, y) in the set of alternatives (X) we must have xRy or yRx or both. This means that the agent ranks x at least as highly as y, or ranks y at least as highly as x, or is indifferent between the two if both xRy and yRx are the case. In the case where xRy but not yRx, we say x is strictly preferred to y. Simply put, the agent is supposed to have an unambiguous preference between any two alternatives.
>
> *Transitivity*: For *all* x, y, z in the set of alternatives, if xRy and yRz, then xRz. In words, if x is at least as highly ranked as y, and y is at least as highly ranked as z, then x is at least as highly ranked as z. Any strict preference in the premises also flows to the conclusion; for instance, if x is strictly preferred to y, and y is at least weakly preferred to z, then x is strictly preferred to z.

Although transitivity is sometimes considered a principle of the "logic of preference" (von Wright 1963), it does not have the same status as a principle of classical logic. We will discuss some illustrations shortly.

These axioms have two corollaries, which are worth stating explicitly because they figure so prominently in the behavioral literature:

> *Independence of Irrelevant Alternatives* (IIA): If xRy when z is available, then xRy when z is not available, and vice versa. That is, an agent's preference between two options x and y should not be affected by the presence or absence of a third option z. IIA is directly implied by completeness, provided that completeness is defined independently of the choice set (as it is here).[6]
>
> *Framing Invariance*: If xRy for any description of the choice situation, then xRy for all equivalent descriptions of the choice situation. In other words, preference relations are entirely unaffected by the manner in which the alternatives are described.

---

[5] "The hypothesis of rationality is embodied in two basic assumptions about the preference relation . . . : *completeness* and *transitivity*" (Mas-Colell et al. 1995, 6).

[6] See, for instance, Gintis (2016). Gintis's definition of completeness has the preference relation defined with respect to specific choice sets, so that x might be preferred to y for one choice set and y to x for another. Then he introduces IIA as a third axiom, and notes: "Because of the third property [IIA], we need not specify the choice set and can simply write [that x is preferred to y]" (2016, 92, bracketed changes made for consistency of notation).

Both completeness and transitivity impose a kind of consistency on preferences. Furthermore, a violation of completeness that takes the form of contradictory preferences technically violates transitivity as well:[7] if x is strictly preferred to y, and y is strictly preferred to x, then transitivity would imply x is strictly preferred to itself, which is ruled out by the definition of strict preference.[8] As a result, the axioms are not always clearly distinguished in the literature, nor are they always mentioned by name. Instead, preferences that satisfy both axioms (and their corollaries) are typically said to be "well-defined" or "well-behaved," while preferences that reveal any form of inconsistency are said to be "not well-defined" or "not well-behaved."

The axioms, and consequently the deductions from them, are independent of their economic interpretation. For example, the alternative objects of preference may be physical commodities at one location, at different locations, at one point in time, at different times, in particular states of the world, and so forth. An abstract system enables us to adapt our analysis in these ways while preserving the same essential structure. However, the axiomatic framework must define the alternatives *objectively and independently* of each other. There are many difficult issues compressed into the words "objectively and independently," as we shall see.

We now turn to the proposition that ties rational preference to rational choice. It is usually called an "axiom" (Green 1971, 24), but not always:

> *Rational Choice*: If x is *chosen* from a set of alternative options, then for all x_i in that set, xRx_i. That is, if the agent chooses an option, it must be at least as good as any other available option.

As in the previous axioms, the preference relation is stated in terms of weak preference. This is important because it shows that the axiom does

---

[7] Contradictory preferences violate completeness for the following reason. For any x and y, completeness requires the agent to have xRy or yRx or both. By definition, xRy & $\sim(yRx)$ $\rightarrow xPy$ (strict preference), yRx & $\sim(xRy)$ $\rightarrow yPx$ (strict preference in the other direction), and xRy & yRx $\rightarrow xIy$ (indifference). Therefore, completeness requires that an agent have one and only one of the following: xPy, yPx, or xIy.

[8] Or by reflexivity, which is sometimes regarded as a separate axiom. But usually, reflexivity is taken to be implied by the definitions of indifference and strict preference in terms of weak preference: if A is weakly preferred to B and vice versa, then A ~ B; if A is weakly preferred to B but not vice versa, then A is strictly preferred to B. By these definitions, it's simply impossible to have A strictly preferred to A.

not make a definitive statement about indifference. If, for example, the agent chooses x_1 but is indifferent between x_1 and x_2 in the set of alternatives, the axiom does not tell us that x_1 is necessarily always chosen. We would not be surprised if x_2 had been chosen. A choice of either option is consistent with the axiom. If there is strict preference, then the agent will choose the option that is strictly preferred.

In short, the axiom says that the rational preference relation, defined in terms of completeness and transitivity, governs choice behavior. A potentially restrictive implication of the rational-choice axiom is that it prima facie excludes the idea of weakness of will. The agent cannot simultaneously know what is better for herself (all things considered) and yet choose the worse altcınative. There can be no sense that the agent "really" prefers to choose x_2 but instead chooses x_1.

The epistemic status of the rational-choice axiom is crucially important. Some economists treat it virtually as a definition: "chosen" and "R" mean the same thing. This idea goes back to the economics profession's early infatuation with classical behaviorism – about which, more later. Other economists see rational choice as an axiomatic statement about how people behave: in accordance with their preferences. And the behavioral economists see it as a falsifiable hypothesis about how people behave: they *might* act in accord with their preferences.

All of the axioms and corollaries can be summarized in a single word: *consistency*. Completeness and transitivity require that preferences be internally consistent. Framing invariance and independence of irrelevant alternatives require that preferences be consistent across equivalent descriptions and across differing menus. Rational choice requires that choices be consistent with preferences.

Earlier, we noted that it can be difficult to distinguish completeness violations from transitivity violations. It can also be difficult to distinguish violations of either axiom from violations of rational choice. For instance, if the agent chooses x over y but also y over x – perhaps because of a difference of framing – this could be characterized as a violation of completeness: the agent has both xRy and yRx.[9] Alternatively, it could be characterized as a violation of rational choice: the agent really has xRy and not yRx, but one framing of the problem induces the agent to act against his preferences and choose y anyway.

---

[9] We set aside the possibility of indifference; suppose that in both cases, the agent is willing to pay a small amount for the first option, thereby demonstrating strict preference.

NEOCLASSICAL RATIONALITY AS THE BEHAVIORAL WELFARE STANDARD

Have behavioral paternalists actually embraced neoclassical rationality as a welfare standard, as we claim? Although they have not always been explicit about this, we believe the answer is yes. The evidence comes from both their analytical approach and their rhetorical stance.

Virtually all behavioral paternalist policy recommendations start from the failure of real-world agents to satisfy the standard rationality requirements. A short list will suffice. We have already introduced each of the following anomalies, as well as the paternalist interventions they have been used to justify, in Chapter 1.

Hyperbolic and Quasi-hyperbolic Discounting: Empirical evidence indicates that many people may be hyperbolic or quasi-hyperbolic discounters. This means that an agent will prefer (x) a larger reward at time $t + 1$ to (y) a smaller reward at time t, and yet prefer y to x when nothing has changed except the passage of time – that is, t and $t +1$ have both come closer to the present (Frederick et al. 2002). This can be characterized as a violation of either completeness, transitivity,[10] or both, and it has been used to justify imposing sin taxes, among other policies. (Alternatively, hyperbolic discounting may be characterized not as a violation of transitivity or completeness, but as a violation of *stationarity*, a lesser-known axiom that requires preferences not to change over time [Manzini and Mariotti 2009, 243–246]. Like the better-known axioms, stationarity imposes a form of consistency on preferences – one that is even harder to justify on normative grounds. For now, we will stick with the interpretation of hyperbolic preferences as a transitivity or completeness violation.)

Hot–Cold Empathy Gaps: Agents are more inclined to make certain choices such as impulse purchases when in a "hot" state (such as fear, excitement, or sexual arousal) than when in a "cold" state (calm and sober). Thus, the agent prefers A to B when choosing in a hot state, and B to A when choosing in a cold state (Loewenstein 2000). This appears to be a violation of completeness and/or transitivity, and it

---

[10] See note 7 for a proof of why completeness rules out contradictory preferences of the form xPy and yPx. But suppose the agent has xPy and yPx anyway. If xPy and yPx, then transitivity would require xPx, i.e., x is preferred to itself. That's either a violation of transitivity or a violation of the lesser-known axiom of reflexivity.

has been used to justify imposing cooling-off periods on various transactions.

Framing Effects: Given a choice situation described in two different but logically equivalent ways, the agent's choice may differ depending on the description. For instance, a patient is more likely to opt for surgery described as having a 90 percent survival rate than surgery described as having a 10 percent death rate (Redelmeier et al. 1993). Since framing results in having both x preferred to y and y preferred to x for what the analyst regards as the same choice situation, framing effects are regarded as violations of completeness or transitivity – and, of course, framing invariance. Framing effects can be difficult to separate from the next two choice anomalies – endowment effects and status quo bias – and have been used to justify some of the same policies (Sunstein and Thaler 2003, 1179–1182).

Endowment Effects: Willingness to pay (WTP) is what an agent will pay for an item when he doesn't already own it. Willingness to accept (WTA) is what an agent will accept to sell an item when he does already own it. When WTA exceeds WTP, as has been shown to occur in experimental results (Kahneman et al. 1991), then we can choose a price P in between WTP and WTA and use it to generate a violation of completeness. E.g., if WTP = \$4 and WTA = \$6, let P = \$5. Then the individual will prefer the item over \$5 when he already owns the item, but he will prefer \$5 to the item when he does not already own the item. Technically, these two situations aren't precisely the same, because ownership of the item increases the agent's wealth. But because wealth effects are negligible – that is, the value of the item is very small relative to the agent's base wealth – the observed behavior is tantamount to a violation of completeness or transitivity (or both). This phenomenon has been used to support changing default rules of labor contracts by (for instance) assuming two weeks of paid vacation, for-cause rather than at-will termination, and other allegedly labor-friendly terms.

Status Quo Bias: People more often choose an option over an alternative when it is perceived as the default or the status quo – i.e., when they would have to opt out of it rather than opting in (Kahneman et al. 1991). Because what is perceived as the status quo can be affected by how the situation is described, status quo bias sometimes overlaps with framing effects. Although arguably the choice situations for opting in and opting out aren't identical – because any act of opting out involves some effort – behavioral paternalists have nevertheless treated status quo bias as evidence of an inconsistency because "the cost of turning in a form is trivial" (Sunstein and Thaler 2003, 1171). If this is true, then status quo bias constitutes a violation of completeness, transitivity, or both. This is used to justify some of the same policies as the endowment effect, as well as automatic enrollment in savings plans (p. 1172).

We will have much more to say about these choice anomalies and the evidence supporting them in the chapters to come. But we take them as given for now, because the question at hand is this: *assuming that the behavioral paternalists are right* in characterizing these behaviors as demonstrating inconsistencies of choice, what does that imply about their welfare criteria?

Let us clarify the analytical move the behavioral paternalists are making. In keeping with the notion of subjectivism, they have not tried to characterize any preference *in isolation* as necessarily irrational. There is nothing per se irrational about eating unhealthy foods, splurging on the present rather than saving more for the future, buying an expensive car in a moment of excitement, or demanding a high price to part with a recently acquired treasure. Leading behavioral paternalists admit this.[11] How, then, can behavioral paternalists be confident that people are making inferior choices? Their argument relies crucially on demonstrating *inconsistencies* of choice and preference, including those described previously, and using them as a jumping-off point for recommending policies to "fix" bad behavior.

The leading behavioral paternalists, particularly Sunstein and Thaler, have not *explicitly* adopted transitivity and completeness as welfare norms. Thaler has said, "A demonstration that human choices often violate the axioms of rationality does not necessarily imply any criticism of the axioms of rational choice as a normative idea" (Thaler 1991, 138). But that was in 1991, many years before "libertarian paternalism," so it is possible that his

---

[11] See, for instance, Sunstein and Thaler (2003, 1168): "Of course, rational people care about the taste of food, not simply about health, and we do not claim that everyone who is overweight is necessarily failing to act rationally"; Sunstein (2014, 75): "I am interested in defending paternalists who respect choosers' own views about their ends, and who seek to increase the likelihood that their decisions will promote those ends"; Sunstein (2014, 96): "With respect to diet, savings, exercise, romance, credit cards, mortgages, cell phones, health care, computers, and much more, different people have divergent tastes and situations, and they balance the relevant values in different ways"; Sunstein (2014, 108): "There is no claim that life must be dry, chocolate-free, and long."

view has evolved.[12] In any case, approval of neoclassical rationality norms is implicit in the form of Sunstein and Thaler's argument, and is also evident in the work of other behavioral paternalists.

First, Sunstein and Thaler repeatedly say that welfare must be judged according to people's own preferences – "as judged by themselves" or "by their own lights" (e.g., Sunstein and Thaler 2003, 1163, 1170). Thus, they eschew an objective notion of welfare that is independent of what people really want; as in the neoclassical approach, their notion of welfare is subjectivist.

Second, behavioral economists question "the rationality of many judgments and decisions that individuals make" (Sunstein and Thaler 2003, 1168) in order to argue that people are making "inferior decisions" (p. 1162). As evidence for these claims, they point to behaviors that deviate from the neoclassical model, including inconsistencies. If it were not for these deviations, their argument for paternalism could not even get off the ground, as there would be nothing to fix. Decision-making failure is demonstrated by departures from the neoclassical model.

Third, they advocate policies designed to help people come closer to full rationality. This is stated most clearly by Sunstein: "Some forms of paternalism move people in the directions that they would go if they were fully rational. Paternalism, whether hard or soft, creates 'as if' rationality. Indeed, that is a central point of good choice architecture" (2014, 154). If inconsistencies are evidence of the problem, then improvements presumably must involve choices that display fewer such inconsistencies. Ideal choice behavior would conform to some set of subjective preferences that satisfy the neoclassical axioms, including completeness and transitivity.

It is conceivable that Sunstein and Thaler do not fully embrace the neoclassical definition of rationality, but instead have some different – perhaps looser – notion of rationality in mind. But if so, they have not stated it clearly. Furthermore, whatever notion of rationality they have in mind, it must involve some kind of consistency requirement; otherwise, the inconsistencies they point to as evidence of irrationality and inferior decision-making would be irrelevant.

---

[12] The view that behavioral models are positive while neoclassical models are normative was common in the early days of behavioral economics. Floris Heukelom observes, "Contrary to [Herbert] Simon, [Daniel] Kahneman and [Amos] Tversky argued that there was nothing wrong with economists' theory of expected utility maximization. It was only that this was the normative theory, and not an accurate description of actually observed human behavior" (2014, 127).

Other behavioral paternalists have also relied on neoclassical rationality as a normative benchmark. Camerer and coauthors replicate Sunstein and Thaler's approach almost exactly. After citing inconsistencies of choice (among other things) as violations of rationality, they conclude: "It is such errors – apparent violations of rationality – that can justify the need for paternalistic policies to help people make better decisions and come closer to behaving in their own interest" (Camerer et al. 2003, 1218).

Bernheim and Rangel (2007) have been more explicit than other behavioral paternalists in their use of neoclassical rationality as a welfare norm:

> A natural analytic strategy involves endowing the individual with *well-behaved lifetime preferences*, while simultaneously specifying a decision process (or decision criterion) that does not necessarily involve selecting the maximal element in the preference ordering. To conduct positive analysis, one employs a model of the decision process (or criterion). *To conduct normative analysis, one uses a model of lifetime preferences.*
>
> (Bernheim and Rangel 2007, 16, emphasis added)

The key phrase here is "well-behaved lifetime preferences." Again, "well-behaved" is economics jargon for satisfying completeness and transitivity. To be more specific, Bernheim and Rangel (2007, 10) list the following assumptions of the neoclassical approach that they adopt for normative analysis: agents (1) have "coherent, well-behaved preferences," (2) defined over "the set of lifetime state-contingent consumption paths," (3) that are "constant across time and states of nature," (4) with "no mistakes," in the sense that the agent "always selects the most preferred alternative for the feasible set." Violations of these are viewed as "anomalies."

The centerpiece of Bernheim and Rangel's approach is the following analytical strategy, which we derive from their article:

1. *Assume* that agents have well-behaved "true preferences" and that they are attempting to maximize the satisfaction of these.
2. Observe actual choices and identify violations of the standard preference-choice criteria or axioms.
3. Identify decision-making aberrations that manifest themselves as the violations of the standard axioms and are thus responsible for the inability of agents to maximize the satisfaction of true preferences.
4. Uncover the agent's true preferences by using choice and non-choice data (e.g., choices in related areas and answers to surveys).
5. Conceptualize what the agent's true preferences must be, consistent with the standard normative (axiomatic) structure.

6. Compare these with actual choices to determine the normative–descriptive gap.
7. Craft policy to attempt to move agents toward the satisfaction of the true preferences constructed in 5.

The dependency of this strategy on the standard neoclassical welfare norms is clear. Biases or anomalies are defined in terms of violations of these standards; they are signs that something has gone wrong. Preferences expressed in nonstandard ways cannot be "true preferences" because true preferences would conform to the standard norms. There is an inner neoclassical agent struggling to overcome the "randomly encountered conditions that trigger systematic mistakes" (Bernheim and Rangel 2007, 16). Thus Bernheim and Rangel are saying more than the vague platitude that people should be helped to attain what they really want. What people really want is *assumed* to have a particular neoclassical structure.[13] (We should also note that Bernheim's perspective on paternalism has evolved somewhat since his work with Rangel; we address Bernheim's revised view in Chapter 7.)

Beshears et al. (2008) have expressed a similar view. The actual choices of agents are "jointly determined by both normative preferences and other factors such as analytic errors, myopic impulses, inattention, passivity, and misinformation" (p. 1787). These observed choices deviate from normative status because of the influence of various behavioral shocks. True preferences are implicitly assumed to have standard neoclassical form. For example, one of the "red flags" of distorted or biased preferences is the existence of two intertemporal rates of discount – a short-term rate and a long-term rate (p. 1788). For these authors, it is not conceivable that both rates can represent true preferences because they are said to be "dynamically inconsistent." Standard neoclassical economics assumes a single intertemporal rate of discount.[14] Thus, in this view, normative time discounting must also employ a single rate.

---

[13] Why do Bernheim and Rangel assume or create this structure? First, the structure is what economists know. It allows the behavioral welfare economists to fill in the blanks with identified true preferences but retain the basic axiomatic form. With that, such constructs as behavioral utility functions or demand curves might be derived. Economists can then play a very similar game as they have become used to. Second, Bernheim and Rangel assume that the standard axiomatic requirements are prescriptively attractive (with the appropriate content substitutions). We believe that the convenience of the first reason drives their welfare economics. At this point, it might be useful to reflect on the axiom of the analytical philosophers: you can't derive an "ought" from an "is" – especially when the "is" is an assumption or analytical convention.

[14] Whether one of the observed rates is the true rate of intertemporal preference is a separate question to be discussed later in this chapter.

In this regard, note that two pairs of authors who have advocated sin taxes on behavioral grounds, Gruber and Köszegi (2001) and O'Donoghue and Rabin (2003, 2006), adopt as their normative standard an intertemporal utility function with exponential rather than hyperbolic or quasi-hyperbolic time-discounting. Note that exponential utility functions satisfy the neoclassical axioms (including stationarity) and thus produce no inconsistencies of choice, whereas hyperbolic or quasi-hyperbolic ones do. To impose exponential time-discounting is to impose internal consistency of intertemporal preferences.

Even where Beshears et al. (2008) deal with intermediate preferences and knowledge biases, the normative reference point is the decisions that would be made in a frictionless, neoclassical world of perfect knowledge and well-behaved preferences. When that framework fails to exist, decision-makers fail to choose according to their true preferences. Outside of the standard framework, there is room for biases to take hold. But inside that framework there would be no decision-making biases because the model is constructed not to have any. Biases are understood as deviations from the standard model; the standard model is the prescriptive norm.

Finally, we should note that we are not the first to characterize behavioral paternalists as having adopted neoclassical rationality as a welfare norm. After documenting the increasing willingness of economists to make policy prescriptions based on behavioral research, Berg and Gigerenzer observe: "This evolution in boldness about looking for prescriptive implications of behavioral economics does not, unfortunately, imply increased boldness about modifying the neoclassical axiomatic formulations of rationality as the unquestioned gold standard for how humans ought to behave" (2010, 147).

The behavioral paternalist case rests, then, on the *normative* strength of the neoclassical rationality axioms that are violated by decision-making anomalies – or, perhaps, on some looser criteria that nevertheless impose a similar requirement of consistency.

THE ORIGIN OF NEOCLASSICAL RATIONALITY IN ECONOMIC THEORY

We now turn to the history of the neoclassical rationality axioms. This history is relevant because it helps us to understand why they were accepted in the past, and hence why they are still accepted – for the most part uncritically – by economists today. One might assume, given the decades-long pedigree of these axioms in economic theory, that they had already been fully justified. But it turns out that these axioms lacked a prescriptive justification from the start. They originally entered economic analysis primarily as positive statements in the form of assumptions, devoid of prescriptive content. They were introduced to provide a logical foundation for microeconomic theory – particularly the existence of utility functions and demand curves.

To the best of our knowledge, the first influential definition of rationality in strictly axiomatic terms comes from Von Neumann and Morgenstern (1944), specifically in the context of developing a theory of choice under uncertainty (or, more accurately, risk). They posited four axioms – including completeness and transitivity – that were sufficient to justify the assumption of numerical utility values for rational decision-makers. They did not posit these axioms as a *unique* definition of rationality, nor did they imbue them with normative significance.[15]

The axiomatic approach was then applied outside the theory of choice under uncertainty by Kenneth Arrow, in his work on social welfare order-ings and his famed Impossibility Theorem (Arrow 2012 [1951]). That work had an undeniable normative component, as the Impossibility Theorem shows the impossibility of simultaneously satisfying several normative goals for deriving a social welfare ordering from individual preference orderings. But the "rationality" requirements of completeness (which Arrow called "connectedness") and transitivity did not appear among the normative goals (which Arrow called "conditions"). Rather, they appeared among the book's initial *assumptions*, without which the analysis could not proceed: "Throughout this analysis it will be assumed that individuals are rational, by which is meant that the ordering relations R_i satisfy Axioms I [completeness] and II [transitivity]" (p. 19). Completeness and transitivity ensured that Arrow could speak unambiguously of an individual's "ordering" of alternatives for the rest of the book.

The usefulness of Arrow's approach elsewhere in microeconomic theory soon became clear. Debreu (1954) proved the existence of a continuous utility function on the assumptions of completeness, transitivity, and the additional axiom of continuity.[16] Arrow and Debreu (1954, 169) put that

---

[15] As Leonard Savage (1954, 97) said later, "One idea now held by me that I think von Neumann and Morgenstern do not explicitly support, and so far as I know they might not wish to have attributed to them, is the normative interpretation of the theory."

[16] A few years earlier, Houthakker (1950) had proven that the weak axiom of revealed preference (WARP) and the strong axiom of revealed preference (SARP) were jointly necessary and sufficient for the existence of a utility function. In the revealed preference

proof to immediate use when they assumed the existence of continuous utility functions for all consumers en route to proving the existence of equilibrium in a competitive economy. Neither of these works used the word "rational" to describe the axioms. Later, Uzawa (1956) and Arrow (1959) merged the axiomatic approach with the revealed preference approach, and in these papers the word "rational" was reintroduced – as a description of various conditions that a choice function (that is, a function that maps sets of alternatives into choices) might satisfy. None of these papers offered any defense of completeness or transitivity as a normative standard.

Arrow's and Uzawa's merger of axiomatic rationality with revealed preference represented the confluence of two separate trends in economics in the early twentieth century. Axiomatic rationality arose from the influence of Bourbakism. The mathematicians who subscribed to this philosophy valued the rigor of mathematic structures above intuition, and abstraction over application. Their influence spread to economics primarily through the influence of Debreu (Weintraub 2002, 101–154), who attempted to build up the essential corpus of economic theory from abstract mathematical axioms and structures that were decidedly not chosen for intuitive content. It should not be surprising to find that axioms lacking in intuitive content also lack normative appeal.

Revealed preference, in its original form, was born from the popularity of behaviorism in early twentieth-century social science. Despite the similar name, behaviorism has no important connection to modern behavioral economics. Behaviorism tried to eschew all reference to the internal mental states of agents, instead limiting itself to descriptions of behavior (in contrast to modern behavioral economics, which attempts to understand behavior as resulting from mental processes). As revealed preference theory was originally conceived, "preferences" were simply descriptions of actual choices, without reference to mental states. This serves to underline that, in the context where rationality acquired its modern axiomatic definition, prescriptive concerns were strictly background; the focus was on objective description or on the development of a useful analytical construct.

Later, some economists began to use the term "revealed preference" to mean what it sounds like: that underlying mental preferences are revealed through choices. We refer to this *appreciative* notion of revealed preference

approach, WARP and SARP perform roles analogous to completeness and transitivity in the axiomatic tradition. For a fuller explanation, see the Appendix to this chapter.

as "preference revelation." In the Appendix to this chapter, we address the question of whether strict adherence to revealed preference in its original form offers any salvation for the normative status of neoclassical axioms. But the short answer is no, for the simple reason that the behaviorist approach says nothing about mental states – and hence nothing about welfare from the perspective of the agents themselves.

To summarize, the neoclassical rationality axioms were originally adopted by the economics profession for their descriptive usefulness, not their normative value. Consequently, if we wish to find their normative justification, we will need to find it elsewhere.

RATIONAL VIOLATIONS OF "RATIONAL PREFERENCE"

The purpose of this section is to demonstrate that there are many possible violations of neoclassical preference axioms that, from an inclusive perspective, are quite reasonable and hence *inclusively rational*. Our concern is not whether these axioms have ever been violated nor whether economic theorists could construct a nonstandard utility function without some of these axioms. Those are concerns of positive economics; we are concerned with the normative issue. Is there something inadequate, from an appropriately inclusive rationality perspective, about people who do not have complete, transitive, framing-invariant, IIA preferences? In general, we argue there is not.

Perhaps surprisingly, the completeness axiom was long ago declared to be of doubtful plausibility. In 1944, von Neumann and Morgenstern (1953, 630) said, "it is very dubious, whether the idealization of reality which treats this [completeness] postulate as a valid one, is appropriate or even convenient." Robert Aumann (1962, 446) made clear that his doubts were not limited to the descriptive accuracy of the axiom: "we find it hard to accept even from a normative viewpoint."[17] We may fairly ask: What is rational about always having preferences over objects in hypothetical situations that may be quite unfamiliar or complex?

Transitivity, too, faced early criticism. Lionel Robbins (1935, 92) tied the normative status of transitivity to the costs of achieving it: "The time and attention which such exact requirements require are better spent in other ways." Ludwig von Mises (1949, 102) considered the assumption of a transitive scale of values simply a "constructed tool of thought" and that

---

[17] Von Neumann and Morgenstern and Aumann are talking about preferences over lotteries. Nevertheless, the point is valid for all complex or novel alternatives.

it is "impermissible" to use it as a "yardstick for the appraisal of real actions."[18]

Modern texts still offer completeness and transitivity as axioms that guarantee a "total preorder" of alternatives and that, along with the assumption of continuity, guarantee the existence of a continuous utility function. But the definitions are often accompanied with qualifications; Mas-Colell et al. (1995) is illustrative:

> The strength of the completeness assumption should not be underestimated. Introspection quickly reveals how hard it is to evaluate alternatives that are far from the realm of common experience. It takes work and serious reflection to find out one's own preferences. The completeness axiom says that this task has taken place: our decision makers make only meditated choices.
>
> (p. 6)

> Like completeness, the transitivity assumption can be hard to satisfy when evaluating alternatives far from common experience. As compared to the completeness property, however, it is also more fundamental in the sense that substantial portions of economic theory would not survive if economic agents could not be assumed to have transitive preferences.
>
> (p. 7)

Note that the argument in the last sentence is strictly a "necessity" defense: transitivity *needs to be* true in order for (descriptive) economic theory to work. It is not a claim that transitivity makes sense as a prescription.

In essence, the axioms require an individual to have *pre-rationalized* his attitudes about the universe of all possibilities before making any actual choices in the world. This is closely akin to the "equilibrium always" assumption that characterizes so many neoclassical models. All relevant forces are presumed to have fully worked themselves out so that no further adjustment is necessary. The observed situation thus constitutes a point of rest and balance – like a pendulum that has finally settled into an unmoving vertical position.[19]

In practice, "equilibrium always" may be true enough to be useful for some descriptive purposes. But normatively, there is no reason to insist that, in order to be considered rational, every agent should have *already* arrived at fully consistent preferences – no more than an entrepreneur should have *already* created and implemented a full business plan,

---

[18] These views echo even earlier ones by Böhm-Bawerk (1959 [1889], 202) and Wicksteed (1910, 29–36).

[19] Robbins (1935, 92) analogizes the existence of transitive preferences to the attainment of "perfect equilibrium" or the elimination of "internal arbitrage" opportunities.

purchased all inputs, and commenced production. These are processes that play out in real time. An inclusive rationality, grounded in reasonability and responsiveness to costs and benefits, would not impose such an arbitrary requirement. Let us consider some of the reasons why the preferences of an agent who is rational in this sense might not be fully rationalized in advance.

Preference Discovery

People may not yet know their own preferences. The process of making choices is thus one of gradually learning one's preferences. Implicit here is the notion that a person has a true, underlying set of preferences waiting to be uncovered. The person may make choices that deviate from those as-yet-unknown preferences, including choices that contradict each other. But such "mistakes" are perfectly reasonable for a person engaged in exploration. Just as an entrepreneur may experiment with different business concepts to discover as-yet-unrealized profit opportunities (see Hayek 1948), individuals may experiment with different choices and combinations of choices to discover which best satisfy their underlying preferences.

Rationality does not imply that human beings have their minds fully made up on the first day about the relative desirability of *all* alternatives in *all* states of the world at *all* points in time. To assert this is an artificial construct of modeling. Whatever the usefulness of the construct in explaining or predicting aggregate behavior, we can see no plausible argument for declaring individuals "irrational" who may be simply undecided. They are in a process of self-discovery. They do not need fixing.

Learning about one's preferences becomes especially relevant when we consider the difference between *intrinsic* goods and *intermediate* goods (Binmore 2009, 6). The former are valued directly, while the latter are valued for their capacity to produce something else. Although the axiomatic framework makes most sense when applied to intrinsic goods, in practice it is often applied to intermediate goods as well. The reason is that intrinsic goods tend to be more abstract and less visible; the most intrinsic goods of all are security, comfort, personal connection, and so on. Intermediate goods, on the other hand, are more concrete. Most goods and services that we think of as such – the everyday items we buy in grocery and hardware stores, for instance – have only instrumental value. We buy them because we hope they will help us attain our more fundamental ends. Now, it is one thing to know your own mind well enough to have preferences across all intrinsic goods. It is quite another to have preferences across all of the goods, including intermediate goods, that are presented for your consideration. Then you would have to know the complex technical relationships between intermediate goods and the final-valued goods as well as technical trade-offs among inputs. This is clearly omniscience rather than rationality. Real people, therefore, have to experiment with intermediate goods to find out how well, and in what combinations, they deliver intrinsic goods.

Preference Formation

The notion of preference discovery requires preferences that preexist the act of choice. There is another possibility: that preferences are formed during the process of choice. As James Buchanan puts it, "I am here advancing the more radical notion that *not even* individuals have well-defined and well-articulated objectives that exist independently of choices themselves" (1979, 111). Choice-making is a creative process in which the individual changes along with the constraints she faces and the choices she makes. Buchanan again: "Individuals do not act so as to maximize utilities described in *independently existing functions.* They confront genuine choices, and the sequence of decisions taken may be conceptualized, *ex post* (after the choices), in terms of 'as if' functions that are maximized. But these 'as if' functions are, themselves, generated in the choosing process, not separately from such process" (1982).

The leading behavioral paternalists have lent support to this position. Sunstein and Thaler (2003, 1161) state, "in many domains, people lack clear, stable, or well-ordered preferences. What they choose is strongly influenced by details of context . . . These contextual influences render the very meaning of the term 'preferences' unclear." Indeed, the authors say that people may have "ill-formed" or "ill-defined" preferences, or lack "well-defined" or "well-formed" preferences, at least fourteen times throughout the article (pp. 1159, 1161, 1164, 1165, 1174, 1177, 1178, 1179, 1181, 1182, 1201).

How does embracing an ongoing process of preference formation affect the behavioral paternalists' normative project? To be blunt, it robs them of the Archimedean point that they would use to judge outcomes. If preferences do not exist independently of the act of choice, then there is no preference set against which to judge the individual's choices as deficient.

Economizing on Cognitive and Noncognitive Effort

Whether preferences are formed in the process of choice or merely waiting to be discovered, another argument explains why we should not expect an equilibrium to emerge in which preferences are fully consistent. As suggested by Mas-Colell and coauthors (1995), the process of considering (possibly hypothetical) pairs of options, settling on preferences over them, and making sure that all such preferences are mutually consistent (through all possible chains of binary comparisons) is costly. Even if carried out strictly in the mind, the process involves time and cognitive effort. If carried out in real life and real time, as in Buchanan's perspective, it involves noncognitive resources as well. The expected marginal benefit of discovering and/or forming these preferences presumably declines as the compared options get further from one's likely future experience. Therefore, a rational person (in the inclusive sense) who compares costs and benefits will not, and *should* not, have complete and transitive preferences.

Preference Rotation

Finally, let us consider an argument for why inconsistent preferences could be desirable in principle, and thus would not necessarily settle into a consistent pattern *even given unlimited time and cognitive resources.* Inconsistent preferences may provide a means of forcing an agent to serve multiple partly conflicting values rather than consistently neglecting some values in favor of others. Here, we draw an analogy to an argument Buchanan has made about Condorcet's Paradox in voting theory. Condorcet's Paradox demonstrates that majority voting can yield an intransitive social ranking of policies – policy A is chosen over B, policy B is chosen over C, and policy C is chosen over A – because different majorities can prevail in each pairwise vote. Usually, this kind of voting cycle is regarded as problematic for social choice, but Buchanan (1954, 118–121) argues that it can be desirable because it can help avert a tyranny of the majority. Without such cycling, a single policy may dominate forever over its alternatives; but with cycling, each winning policy has a chance of being overturned and replaced. As Buchanan puts it, majoritarian voting "serves to insure that competing alternatives may be experimentally and provisionally adopted, tested, and replaced by new compromise alternatives approved by a majority group of ever changing composition" (p. 119).

This possibility is part of what makes majoritarian decision-making acceptable even to those temporarily in the minority.

Now, this argument may or may not be persuasive in the social context. But consider its application in the individual context. If someone has intransitive preferences, it seems plausible that the competing preferences involved correspond to different values that she holds to some degree. (In our list of illustrative examples to follow, we include a specific example of an intrapersonal preference cycle that works in this way.) A perfectly consistent preference ordering could result in making essentially the same choices again and again, particularly if her preferences remain fixed over time as well. The result could be some of her values getting short shrift. Intransitivity, on the other hand, will tend to push the individual to cycle amongst options that serve her values to different degrees, sometimes favoring one, sometimes favoring another. The cycling could facilitate a process of exploration and discovery, as described earlier, in which case the agent may eventually settle into a consistent preference ordering. But it's also possible that the cycling itself might constitute an equilibrium of sorts, inasmuch as it creates a balance over time among competing values. If so, the inconsistency serves a purpose.

Illustrative Examples

With these general considerations in mind, let us consider a series of examples. These examples are designed to illustrate the reasonableness of incompleteness, intransitivity, or both. In some of these examples, the agent's less-than-well-defined preferences could be characterized as happening because the agent is in a state of disequilibrium – i.e., still forming or discovering their preferences. But in other examples, we could imagine these ill-defined preferences persisting even when the agent has had plenty of time for deep thought and consideration.

1. Let us begin with a silly, but instructive, game. It is called "Would You Rather?" The object is to present another player with two unfamiliar options and to ask which she prefers, such as, "Would you rather eat a bowl of crickets or push a needle through your hand?" The person is supposed to say which she prefers and give the reason. Obviously, the repulsiveness of the options is an important factor in the entertainment value of the game. However, it could easily be extended to include presumably positive but still unfamiliar options: "Would you rather have ten more IQ points or perfect hair for the rest of your life?" Of course this

question might not be as entertaining as the first. The game does demonstrate, however, the difficulties that people have stating their preferences among unfamiliar objects.

The game's requirement that the individual make and justify the (hypothetical) choice is also interesting. The rationale given will often be one that amuses the other players and yet has an air of truth surrounding it. It takes time and creativity to come up with a not-always-truthful answer. Nevertheless, the game is limited in two respects for our purposes. First, the player does not in fact get her choice. Not much is at stake. Second, the rules of the game force an answer where, in reality, the person may not have one. This phenomenon might manifest itself in an uncooperative player responding, "I quit. I have no preference and I will not be forced into a choice." End of game for her. And yet this response might be the truly rational one in real-world cases where the choice is supposed to be actual. Suppose you're in a store that has two shirts you like, but you can only afford one, and you cannot decide which you prefer. Consequently, you may just leave the store and spend the money on something else (or return when your indecision has resolved). Even if some external factor (such as a gun to your head) forces you to choose, your choice may not reflect a true preference for one option over the other, but simply a preference for either one over the bullet.

2. Suppose that a close friend reveals, in confidence, that he has been cheating on his wife. Should you inform the wife or not? To whom do you have the greater obligation, the friend or the friend's wife? To some people the answer will be obvious, but surely it's understandable that someone might wrestle with the question. An individual may be conflicted in the application of his moral values, which are not always explicitly known and traded off beforehand. Alternatively, he may believe that certain values ought not to be traded off against each other at all. Which should dominate? In cases where the individual is genuinely undecided between two options, he might sometimes choose one alternative and sometimes the other without changing his underlying, but indecisive, standard(s) of evaluation. This is vacillation and inconstancy. But it is not properly inconsistency because the individual has not adopted a rule of decision. There is nothing to be *inconsistent* with. His preferences are simply incomplete.

The broader point is that sometimes two distinct objects of choice are very close in terms of the individual's standard of evaluation. Indeed, an individual may be unable to say which of the two is definitively better than the other. Behaviorally, it may be difficult to distinguish this from simple indifference. But indecisiveness is not indifference. Moral dilemmas, as in the example above, can be seen as cases of indecisiveness.

3. When preferences are formed by reference to multiple criteria, the individual may have no "rational" basis for a single binary judgment. Consider Nicolas, who is trying to decide among three women to pursue. (Assume, optimistically, that all three women might be interested in Nicolas.) He has three criteria in mind: looks, personality, and intelligence. He weights each of these equally. Suppose there are three women: Adele (a), Betty (b), and Claire (c). Their characteristics are ranked as follows:

Looks: aPb, bPc.
Personality: bPc, cPa.
Intelligence: cPa, aPb.

This can be seen as an intrapersonal version of the Condorcet Voting Paradox. It is as if Nicolas has three voters in his head, each of whom cares exclusively about one characteristic. When he is with Adele he prefers Claire. When he is with Claire he prefers Betty. When he is with Betty he prefers Adele, and so forth. In this state of irresolution, he will continue to vacillate. In this example, a violation of transitivity results in cyclical preferences.[20]

Now, is Nicolas irrational to have such preferences? Some might argue that he errs by failing to consider the relative intensity of his desires (how much more attractive is Adele than Betty, etc.) and then compare them with each other. If he did so, surely he would arrive at a transitive ranking. But this amounts to saying that Nicolas ought to have a different means of evaluating his romantic options – i.e., that he *ought* to attach utility values to differences along each dimension of attraction (looks, personality, intelligence) and that he *ought* to be able to compare utility differences across those dimensions. If he fails to think in this way, then he is deemed irrational. We see no reason to make that assumption.

Nicolas could fairly be criticized if his indecision leads to bad consequences. If he continues to dither, he might lose his opportunity with all three women! This, however, is a pragmatic argument for making a

---

[20] If Nicolas were to be asked which of the *three* he preferred, suppose he would answer Adele. There is no a priori reason that the answer given in ternary evaluation should be consistent with the answer given in a series of binary evaluations (Anand 1995). The case in the text would illustrate "benign" cyclical preferences (Rabinowicz 2000, 131).

choice – not a principled argument for why Nicolas should not have these preferences to begin with. Faced with the possibility of ending up single, Nicolas might find a way to resolve his indecision – without necessarily resolving the fundamental indeterminacy of his preferences. He might, for instance, choose randomly or ask a friend to choose for him. These would be *pragmatically* rational ways to make a decision without having transitive preferences.

Furthermore, if we recast the example so the options correspond to types of women, rather than specific individuals, then the cyclic character of Nicolas's preference could motivate him to experiment with different choices in his romantic life – "shopping around," as the old song puts it. Doing so could help him to figure out what he really values in a partner. We might hope that, eventually, he would settle into fully consistent preferences rather than shopping forever. But we could surely find other, nonromantic aspects of life where a more permanent cycle could be sustained because long-term commitments are not expected. Cyclic preferences can thus facilitate rotation and balance among underlying values.

For a less frivolous example, recall the distinction we made earlier between intrinsic and intermediate goods. Economists often imagine agents having preferences over physical objects such as apples, cars, houses, and so forth. This is convenient for illustrative purposes. But it is really not the objects themselves that produce satisfaction. Their *characteristics* have a better claim to either being or delivering intrinsic goods. If we think of consumers as directly valuing characteristics and only indirectly physical goods, then a given physical good is likely to exhibit more than one characteristic over which people have preferences. From this point of view, the idea of multiple criteria of evaluation seems quite natural and widely applicable. Take apples, pears, and figs. They can be evaluated by sweetness or tartness, bulk (fiber), juiciness, and pleasant color. An individual can have definite preferences across these characteristics that nevertheless produce an inconclusive ranking of the three fruits. The detailed argument is essentially the same as in the romantic choices example. Thus it is not hard to imagine a rational decision-maker who might not have a decisive rank ordering of fruits.

If this example is unpersuasive because the reader believes people *should* have a single scale for comparison of options, consider the next example:

4. Casey is a football fan. In binary competitions, it turns out that Team A is better than Team B, Team B is better than Team C, but Team C is better than Team A. "Betterness" here is ability to beat the paired team.

This will depend on the comparative strengths and weaknesses of each team against its competition.[21] Now suppose Casey prefers the team likely to win. That is the basis of her comparative evaluation. So she will prefer A to B, B to C, and C to A. The preference relation is intransitive, but Casey is not irrational in any meaningful sense.[22] She prefers what she likes according to the criterion relevant to her: winning. This example shows that it's possible for an agent to have intransitive preferences *even when the agent has a single scale of value.*

5. Thus far we have assumed that either preferences are precise and complete or, if they are incomplete, those preferences that do exist are precisely defined. But now we consider a case of *vague* preferences. Suppose Jane likes men with "a lot" of hair on their heads. She prefers them to men with "a little" hair. Now Dick comes along. He definitely has a lot of hair. On the other hand, Yule has only a little hair on his head. Jane definitely prefers Dick to Yule. Poor Dick, however, is taking a medicine that is reducing the hair on his head by one hair each day. We now put Jane to the test. Each day she is asked whether she prefers Dick on the current day to Dick as he was the day before. We assume her basic tastes are unchanged. The tests reveal that on day one she preferred Dick to Yule, and then she was indifferent among the various incarnations of Dick for many, many days until the nth day. On day $n + 1$ she prefers Yule to Dick. The chain of indifference thus ends with the reversal of her preference. This is a violation of the transitivity of preferences.[23]

To make sense of this from an inclusive conception of rationality, we need to distinguish between a failure of perception and a lack of preference. It is no doubt true that most people cannot distinguish between 100,000 hairs and 99,999 hairs. But the problem at issue here does not depend on the imperceptibility of a one-hair difference. We are not referring to a cognitive limitation.[24] We could imagine Jane to perceive the difference in hair without that fact making any difference to her preference (Aldred 2007, 382–384). For instance, we could equip Jane with a reliable hair-counting device that provides an exact count of Dick's hair

---

[21] To be precise, different properties will dominate in each pairwise comparison such as speed in one or accuracy in throwing the ball in another.

[22] We postpone money pump issues until we deal with choices in a later section.

[23] More specifically, the chain violates the transitivity of indifference and consequently the transitivity of weak preference.

[24] Contrast the example in Mas-Colell et al. (1995, 7), which does depend on imperceptible differences.

on each day; nevertheless, she remains indifferent between the different versions of Dick for many days, even after seeing the day's hair count. The crux of the intransitivity is that her preferences are based on a vague predicate: "a lot" of hair (or not). And we should add that this is not simply a vagueness of language; the phrase "a lot" stands in for Jane's general appreciation for an imprecisely defined but relatively large quantity of hair.

Are vague preferences or vague predicates irrational? Some philosophers, such as Gottlieb Frege and Bertrand Russell (Read 1995, 176–177), have argued that vagueness produces incoherence and should be eliminated from scientific and logical discourse. Without taking a position on the nature of proper scientific discourse (there is disagreement about whether Frege and Russell were correct in this regard), it seems unreasonable to demand that economic agents think without recourse to vague predicates. Ordinary life is filled with observations of this kind: smart, handsome, pretty, hairy, bald, hungry, hard, and so forth. The boundaries between these terms and their negations are not sharp.[25] Given this, agents should not be faulted for having preferences that are defined over these predicates.

6. Are manners irrational? They may be from a puppet rationality perspective. Consider a dinner party of at least moderately polite people (Sen 1997, 753). You are a guest and you are going to be offered some fruit. Before being offered anything, you check your complete preferences. You prefer a large apple to an orange, and you prefer an orange to a small apple. But now your host appears with one large apple and one small apple – and no orange. You once again check your binary preferences. You think: I cannot take the *large* apple. That would be impolite as it would leave only the small one for the other guest. So you prefer the small apple. Manners are preserved, but you are "irrational" since transitivity would imply that you prefer the large apple. And that is not all. You have also violated independence of irrelevant alternatives because you are affected by the menu. This example demonstrates the importance of context to decision-making – yet the neoclassical framework is context-free. (We will discuss later whether it's possible to modify the example to avoid this problem in a manner that is consistent with neoclassical rationality.)

---

[25] Of course, with respect to any vague predicate we could stipulate a precise meaning. For example, hairy or "a lot of hair" could be defined at 10,000 hairs or more. But hairy is an *observational* predicate, not a measured one (Read 1995, 179). Agents do not count the hairs, even if it were feasible. Agents have preferences over objects *as they see them*.

7. Consider the following illustration from John Broome (1999, 70). Maurice has the following binary preferences. As between going mountaineering in the Alps (*M*) and touring Rome (*R*), he prefers to tour Rome. When he compares staying at home (*H*) and touring Rome, he prefers to stay at home. So far, so good. But now when he is comparing staying at home with mountaineering, he prefers mountaineering. *RPM, HPR*, but *MPH*. Transitivity, however, would require *HPM*. What's going on? When asked to explain himself, Maurice answers that if he were to prefer to stay home, it would show cowardice about going up into the Alps. But then we ask: why did it not show cowardice to prefer touring Rome to mountaineering in the Alps? He answers that such a choice is really pitting culture against mountaineering and it is fine to prefer culture. And what about his preference for staying home over touring in Rome? Maurice says that it is fine to put relaxing at home above the cultural education of touring Rome. Obviously, Maurice has an issue with cowardice. Is this irrational?

We might try to convince Maurice to think carefully about his issues with cowardice. However, unless economists are going to become psychotherapists, Maurice's reasoning will have to suffice as a rational, that is, a coherent, noncontradictory, and plausible basis for preferences. Of course, Maurice may engage in self-reflection and critically evaluate the meaning he attaches to the preference between staying home and mountaineering. But what might cause him to be self-critical is the *nature of the reason* he has for preferring mountaineering to staying at home. He could also reflect on the *reasons* he has for preferring to stay at home to touring in Rome, or any other aspect of his preference system. At the end of this self-reflection, Maurice might amend his preferences – or he might decide his original reasons were good enough. There is no necessary connection between the intransitivity of a preference system and the agent's desire to re-examine his reasons. The reasons do all the work for rationality. Transitivity is irrelevant. This example shows that perfectly coherent psychological reasons can generate an intransitivity of preferences.

8. Consider a story based on an example from Amartya Sen (1997). A well-mannered and rather conservative woman, Lady Trevelyan, has the following initial preferences: she would prefer to have tea with her long-lost cousin Timothy to not having tea with him. Then Timothy gives her an additional option: to have tea *and* some LSD with him. But with that option on the table, Lady Trevelyan decides she would rather not have even a simple tea with him. Thus while a simple tea is chosen over no tea when the third option is not available, this choice is reversed when all three

options are available. Thus, Lady Trevelyan appears to violate completeness and independence of irrelevant alternatives.

Now, it is not hard to resolve the apparent contradiction. The new option itself (tea plus LSD) tells Lady Trevelyan something about her cousin – that he is the kind of person who would consume illicit drugs. Thus, the menu conveys information. So, a defender of neoclassical rationality could argue that the two choice situations are not really the same because they involve different information. Yet the information does not arrive exogenously or prior to the decision; it comes to Lady Trevelyan *via the menu itself*. Preferences and beliefs cannot easily be distinguished in a case such as this. We can only conclude that Lady Trevelyan's preferences "really" satisfy the neoclassical axioms by digging into the deeper reasons behind her preferences. Only then can we realize that the menu allows her to infer information that interacts with her conservative attitudes so as to reverse her initial ranking of options.

From the foregoing examples, we can glean some general lessons about transitivity. The case for transitivity of preferences hinges on the acceptance of an *analogy* of preference ordering to measurement – specifically as ordering along a real-number line. Therefore the transitivity of preference is the result of a choice to think of preferences in a certain way (Anand 1995, 60–61). It is not part of the meaning of preference itself. We may argue about whether the analogy produces a useful approach to describing or predicting choices, but surely it is difficult to argue that agents *must* evaluate their alternatives in a way that conforms to the measurement analogy. Some methods of evaluation will conform and others will not. The plausibility of the preference-measurement analogy is dependent on the basis of preference formation – the grounds on which people make evaluations. Thus it is not context-free. As we have seen from the examples, particularly #6 (fruit choices at a dinner party) and #7 (Maurice's vacation options), people can have plausible methods of evaluation that turn on situational context.

WHAT ABOUT THE MONEY PUMP?

One common argument in favor of transitivity as a rationality requirement is the money pump. The argument is as follows. Suppose Frances has intransitive preferences: aPb, bPc, and cPa. We assume that they do not change over the relevant period of time. If Frances starts at c, a smart bookmaker can now offer her b in exchange for c plus a very small payment ε that does not alter her strict preference for b. If she accepts, the smart bookmaker continues with a similar offer: a in exchange for b plus another ε. If that is accepted, then he offers c in exchange for a plus another ε. Voilà! Frances has been pumped for 3ε and she is back where she started.

The story seems to provide a pragmatic argument for the "irrationality" or self-defeating character of cyclic preferences. Such preferences will impose costs on those who act in accordance with them and thus make them worse off by their own lights. In principle, this is a good approach to the question of whether behavior is rational or not. And yet it does not succeed in making the case that intransitive preferences are irrational.

First, the money pump is not an argument for why it would be irrational to have intransitive preferences in one's head – only for why *acting upon them* might be problematic in practice. That means we need to focus on the real-world circumstances in which someone's intransitive preferences might actually be exploited. Without hyper-aware and omnipresent bookmakers ready to take advantage of any given intransitivity – such as Nicolas's preferences about women, or the dinner guest's preferences about fruit, or Maurice's preferences about vacation time – the problem may not arise at all. Indeed, it is difficult to imagine how the money pump would even be implemented in cases such as these. The money pump is a purely hypothetical dilemma.

Second, even in a world of omniscient bookmakers, the money pump would not occur with intransitive agents who are equally omniscient. If both the bookmaker and the target had equal knowledge of the target's intransitive preferences, and equal ability to predict the future, then the process would simply never get under way. It would be as if the bookmaker offered to take all of the target's money in exchange for nothing. In commonsense terms, if the target knows where this is going, why start? (Nozick 1993, 140n).[26] And even if the target were insufficiently aware to say "no" from the beginning, it seems the process could only go on for so long before the target sees what is happening and puts a stop to it (by reassessing her preferences or simply refusing to act upon them). For the process to continue indefinitely, the situation would require both a high degree of awareness and cleverness on the part of the bookmaker and a complete lack of awareness on the part of the target.

---

[26] If common sense is not enough, we could follow through the argument from backward induction. The agent *knows* that at the last node in the process she will go from a to c. This is rational at that stage. At the penultimate stage she will see that the exchange of b for a is really an exchange of b for c, which she strictly disprefers. The same argument could be made for the first stage. Thus, it never gets off the ground if the agent has perfect foresight, makes no errors, and acts in accordance with her preferences at each stage (Aldred 2003, 63).

Third, let us introduce transactions costs. It takes time and effort to carry out transactions such as those in the money pump. For the money pump to work effectively, the bookmaker must be willing to carry out the process for numerous cycles. If the target knows that her intransitive preferences cannot be effectively exploited because the transactions costs of exploitation exceed the potential gains to the bookmaker, then she can indulge her intransitive preferences without anxiety or cost.[27]

What, then, is the significance of the money pump? It is a pragmatic objection masquerading as a theoretical one. It gives us no reason to reject intransitive preferences per se, only a reason to think they could be exploitable in practice. Yet we are not aware of any examples of real-world money pumps. In a literature search of 107 articles on the subject, Arkes et al. (2016, 23) did not find a single instance of a person being money-pumped. Supposing, however, that any real-world money pumps do exist, they might indicate a problem for pragmatic rationality in those specific situations. Then again, provided these pumps do not instantaneously empty the bank accounts of the people involved, they might simply show that some people are willing to pay the price for their intransitive preferences (perhaps buying time before finally resolving them). In that respect, intransitive preferences are no different from many run-of-the-mill preferences. After all, most of us willingly exchange money for food, and then consume food for energy, and then expend energy for money, year after year after year!

DESCRIPTION AND REDESCRIPTION

The axioms of transitivity and completeness can always be rescued by an appropriate redescription of the alternatives facing an individual. This can be illustrated best using example #7. Maurice's preferences over vacation options are intransitive. But now let us redefine the alternatives in their menu context. We can say that Maurice prefers touring Rome *when the alternative is mountaineering*. This is not the same as preferring Rome

---

[27] There are a number of ways that transactions costs might assert themselves. In particular, money-pumpers must know the specific pattern of intransitive preferences the agent has and transform this pattern into tradable opportunities. Consider, for example, the cases of the large apple and manners, Jane's preferences about hairy men, and Nicolas's indecision and intransitive preferences regarding Adele, Betty, and Claire. Who is to do the pumping? How is the bookmaker supposed to find out about these patterns? The money pump arguments gain from their usual abstraction and lose credibility when we attempt to think of realistic scenarios.

simpliciter or from all possible menus. We can make such adjustments to all of the binary preferences, and rewrite Maurice's preference system like so: H_rPR_h, R_mPM_r, M_hPH_m, where the subscripts represent the alternative considered. The intransitivity has now been dissolved under the power of redescription, because preferring M when the alternative is staying at home is not the same as preferring M when the alternative is going to Rome.[28] The menu is now part of the alternative's description.[29] An obvious question now arises: what is the rationale for this redescription? The obvious answer is the reasons that Maurice gave when we interrogated him. But if we can redefine the alternatives in this case, what is to stop us from redescribing the alternatives in *every* apparent case of intransitivity?

At this point, we should note that standard theory has no general answer to the question of how the alternatives should be described. This is quite startling when you think about it, given that intransitivities can be created or dissolved by virtue of description. Which intransitivities we "allow" by means of redescription, and which intransitivities we "prohibit" by refusing to redescribe, turns on the analyst's opinion as to the plausibility or acceptability of the reasons given. Once we allow redescription, transitivity does none of the work.

As a general matter, economists of both the neoclassical and behavioral stripe tend to resist redescription. Completeness and transitivity are nearly always defined over menu-independent options, which is why both framing invariance and independence of irrelevant alternatives follow as corollaries of the main axioms. Allowing redescription whenever we encounter seemingly justifiable violations of the axioms reeks of ad

---

[28] Broome (1999) redescribes the options in this way but then asks what transitivity implies at this level of description. Following out the chain of preferences H_rPR_h, R_mPM_r, M_hPH_m, and with his assumptions that R_hIR_m and M_rIM_h, transitivity implies that H_rPH_m. This means that if Maurice's higher-level preference system is to be transitive, he *must* prefer to be faced with the alternatives of staying at home or touring Rome to the alternatives of staying at home or mountaineering. If he can give "good reasons" for this then the meta-transitivity is justified and, derivatively, the original *in*transitivity will be considered by the economist as "rational." Why the reader must go through all of this is unclear. If the rationality of a higher-order preference relation depends on Maurice's reasons, then the rationality of his lower-order intransitive preference relation can be assessed by whether Maurice has given good reasons for that preference. Broome's analysis seems like a last-ditch attempt to save the transitivity axiom by shifting its applicability to a different level.

[29] Anand (1993, 103–105) uses a similar method to illustrate how redescription can cause intransitivity to vanish. He also shows how redescription can cause transitivity to vanish. He has a "translation theorem" that says, "All intransitive behaviours can be redescribed in such a way that transitivity is not violated, and all transitive behaviours can be redescribed in such a way that transitivity is violated" (p. 103).

Table 3.1 *The Allais paradox*

Decision 1				Decision 2			
Option A		Option B		Option C		Option D	
Outcome	Chance	Outcome	Chance	Outcome	Chance	Outcome	Chance
$1 million	100%	$1 million	89%	$0	89%	$0	90%
		$0	1%	$1 million	11%	$5 million	10%
		$5 million	10%				

hoc-ism. Yet, as we have seen, there exist plausible violations that can reasonably be resolved via redescription.

Amos Tversky (1975) showed that the consistency of choices in certain decision problems depends on the interpretation (i.e., description) of the objects of choice. In one of the examples he discusses, the agent will appear inconsistent if we assume the objects of choice are purely monetary pay-offs. However, if regret is also involved when a monetary payoff occurs, then the agent's choices may not seem so inconsistent. For this example, we must briefly venture into the theory of choice under uncertainty. The famed Allais Paradox involves two decisions over risky options, summarized in Table 3.1.

For Decision 1, most people would choose A over B. For Decision 2, most people would choose D over C. But it turns out that Decision 1 and Decision 2 are equivalent once we ignore identical aspects of the options. In Decision 1, observing that both A and B involve at least an 89 percent chance of $1 million, we can focus on the remaining 11 percent chance of $1 million (in A) versus the 1 percent chance of nothing and 10 percent chance of $5 million (in B). In Decision 2, observing that both C and D involve at least an 89 percent chance of getting nothing, we can focus on the remaining 11 percent chance of $1 million (in C) versus the remaining 1 percent chance of nothing and 10 percent chance of $5 million (in D). With these adjustments, A is equivalent to C while B is equivalent to D – which makes choosing both A and D, as many people would, inconsistent.

But must this inconsistency be regarded as irrational? Using our redescription strategy, we could call the $0 in Option B "$0 when the other option was $1 million for sure," and the $0 in Option D "$0 when the other option would probably have also yielded $0." Now that $0 is not the same across situations, the agent will not be seen, in effect, as rejecting a risky option in one case and accepting the very same risky option in the other. Thus, the axioms of rationality cannot be applied without an interpretation. *But the interpretation is not part of puppet rationality.* In Tversky's words, "The axioms of utility theory can be regarded as maxims of rational choice only in conjunction with an intended interpretation, and the criteria for the selection of an interpretation are not part of utility theory" (Tversky 1975, 172).

To understand the profound difficulty of this problem for both standard and behavioral economists, we must analyze more closely how we have gotten to framing invariance. In the standard approach, the ultimate objects of choice are imagined to be simply objects to which *one can point* in the world. They are supposed to be independent of their description. And yet how can this be? The perfume industry creates not only scents but scents with a certain image portrayal. Thus, when people buy a perfume, they also buy the aura or image that the manufacturer and others associate with the scent. *This* is the product, and so too with many other goods. Human beings do not *simply* choose objects with a certain molecular structure or chemical composition ignoring all else, nor should they.

Framing invariance can be looked at in at least two ways, which are importantly different in their implications. Compare the statement of Burkett (2006, 140):

Neoclassical economists assume that all informationally equivalent descriptions of alternatives elicit identical choices.

With that of Tversky and Kahneman (1986, S253):

An essential condition for a theory of choice that claims normative status is the principle of invariance: Different representations of the same choice problem should yield the same preference. That is, the preference between options should be independent of their description.

The important differences are: (1) Burkett adds the characteristic of being "informationally equivalent" while Tversky and Kahneman (T-K) simply talk of "descriptions" or "representations" of the "same" problem; and (2) Burkett is making a positive or descriptive statement, with no necessary normative implication, while T-K are making a normative claim.

Set aside for the moment the issue of informational equivalence and the related idea of logical equivalence. What can T-K possibly mean by the "same choice problem" irrespective of its description? This is not clear. It could mean that the agent has, at some deep level, determined what he desires and has identified the feasible options that will produce what he desires, and yet gets "confused" by a particular description of these options in an experimental situation. After all, he simply wants apples and should not care how they are described. Presumably, if they are alternatively described as objects with a certain physical shape or chemical composition or by how they are digested, and so forth, it should not matter to the individual's preferences. In other words, the decision situation simply involves a certain physical object to which we can point. The various possible descriptions are extensionally equivalent; they point to the same object. The agent's deep preferences are assumed to be defined over these elementary objects. Invariance to equivalent descriptions could also mean invariance to the descriptions that *T-K consider* equivalent. This is probably the operational meaning of equivalence here. But in either case, the assumption is fundamentally at variance with the long-established idea in economics that the relevant characteristics of a good are those the *agent* deems relevant.[30]

Suppose an individual is contemplating a heart transplant operation in order to save her life. She wonders if this is her only prospect of survival and just how good that prospect is. We take it for granted that the individual desires to survive, but not necessarily at all costs. Obviously, the medical opinions of the doctors are crucial to the individual's beliefs. Clearly, there may be disagreements about this among qualified professionals. Yet the individual must determine which opinions are most convincing.[31]

We assume that the individual has settled upon what she accepts as the objective facts of her surgery and survival prospects. But how should these facts be seen? The patient still has to decide whether the operation is worth it *overall*. To make this determination the individual herself may want to be exposed to the immediate facts of the operation itself as one set of elements in her decision process:

To begin with, the facts in question would have to be represented in a particular medium, and there is more than one medium available. I can state the facts, I can

---

[30] "The standard characterization of framing effects refers ... to 'equivalent descriptions of a decision problem' but what does it mean for a pair of descriptions to be 'equivalent'? And what *must* it mean for a pair of descriptions to be equivalent if equivalent descriptions leading to different decisions is to raise normative eyebrows? That is, just what is the *invariance* in 'descriptive invariance'? To our knowledge, these elementary questions have not been satisfactorily addressed in the literature on framing effects and description invariance" (Sher and McKenzie 2006, 468).

[31] Even a single doctor's opinions rarely will be univocal and of the form: "If you don't get the operation now you have only *n* months to live; if you get the operation you will live *n* +*m* months." There are ambiguities and uncertainties that the individual must somehow resolve.

picture them, I can diagram or map them, and their motivational impact may well depend on their medium of representation. Surely mental pictures of open-heart surgery would affect me differently from a mental flow chart or narration. Furthermore, each medium of representation affords me considerable latitude in style and perspective. For instance, I can describe the operation in medical jargon, using words like "incision," "suture," "clot," and "hemorrhage"; or I can describe it in layman's terms with words like "slice," "sew," "gob," and "gush." If I choose instead to picture the operation, I can picture platelets and leucocytes rushing to the scene of damaged tissue; or a seething chest cavity laid bare by steel instruments; or an operating table surrounded by machines and gowned figures; or perhaps even a quiet Midwest town in which there stands a gleaming hospital, whose operating theater is bustling with activity one dark winter morning.

(Velleman 1988, 365–366)

Similar presentational or framing matters will arise in the statement of all of the other aspects of the transplant, including prognoses. T-K would say that the agent *should* ignore the mode of presentation. Under any description, the heart operation is a heart operation. "Look, we can point to the same 'object' in either case," they would say. But the facts must be presented, and they must be apprehended by the patient. They do not magically appear in her brain. There is no rigorous meaning to "options independent of their description."[32] Options are only perceived as such through their descriptions.

Furthermore, in the absence of a correct preference or choice in this decision problem (economics alone cannot tell us whether the individual should prefer or choose the transplant), the only normative issue is the possible inconstancy of the agent's decision across frames. The frames themselves are neither correct nor incorrect; so while the agent's preference might display puppet irrationality, the economist cannot point to the "rational preference." Thus the main implication of framing susceptibility for behavioral economics is the "choice arbitrariness" (Cartwright 2011, 34–39) of agents. As we shall see later in this chapter, the policy relevance of such putative choice arbitrariness is to undermine the significance of the agent's free decisions without providing a clear case for a better alternative.

Returning now to Burkett's statement of framing invariance, we see that his statement does not necessarily carry any normative implications. It refers to the idea that standard economics has traditionally assumed that descriptions such as those given previously do not matter or do not

---

[32] How could we *say* what the options are independently of their description? If we cannot *say* it then we probably cannot *think* it.

supersede the decisions based on "objective" data alone. But, in fact, there is evidence to the contrary. This may create problems in trying to predict what people will choose, but that is a purely positive concern. The framing effect has no normative implications.

THE NON SEQUITUR OF RESOLVING
PREFERENCE INCONSISTENCIES

To demonstrate the existence of irrationality, behavioral economists often point to inconsistencies of choice that imply inconsistent preferences. Then they propose policies designed to correct these inconsistencies – that is, to induce behavior that conforms to a consistent preference ordering.

In the preceding sections of this chapter, we have argued that inconsistent preferences do *not* necessarily mean the individual is irrational in any normatively significant sense. Preferences that violate the axioms of completeness and transitivity (and the corollaries of framing invariance and independence of irrelevant alternatives) can be perfectly reasonable for a variety of reasons. We hope to have persuaded the reader of this point. But now, let us suppose for argument's sake that such inconsistencies do, in fact, constitute irrationality. Does it follow that policies that successfully move people toward more consistent preferences make them better off?

The simple answer is no. The existence of an inconsistency does not provide any grounds for a third party, such as a behavioral economist or policymaker, to resolve it by choosing which among the inconsistent preferences should be followed consistently. If an agent shows evidence of having both Preference Set X and Preference Set Y, there is no analytical basis for designating X or Y as the "true" underlying preference set of the agent. Maybe it's both; maybe it's neither. To choose one over the other is simply a non sequitur. If Sunstein and Thaler are correct in their oft-repeated claim that agents may simply lack well-defined preferences, then the analyst lacks "true" preferences by which to judge choices. There's no there there, so to speak.

In Chapter 7, we will discuss the knowledge problems associated with behavioral paternalism. We will argue, among other things, that paternalist planners have no means of determining which of the conflicting preferences reflect the agent's *true* preferences. But here, we focus on a deeper philosophical challenge: that the agent may not even *have* true preferences (i.e., *underlying* preferences, not enacted in choice, that satisfy the neoclassical axioms). Even an omniscient planner cannot have knowledge of what does not exist.

To be more specific, consider some of the specific inconsistencies of choice:

Hyberbolic or Quasi-hyperbolic Discounting: For an agent who seemingly has two rates of time preference, there are at least two possible ways to induce an individual with this kind of discounting to behave consistently: (1) make her follow her *more* patient rate of time preference consistently, or (2) make her follow her *less* patient rate of time preference consistently. Or we could (3) make her consistently follow some intermediate rate. Behavioral paternalists have, with little justification, chosen (1).

Hot–Cold Empathy Gaps: For agents who choose differently depending on their mental state, there are at least two ways to "correct" the chooser's inconsistency: (1) make him always behave as he would when in a hot state, or (2) make him always behave as he would in a cool state. Behavioral paternalists have, with little justification, chosen (1).

Framing Effects: Take the case of paid vacation time, which we assume the agent tends to prefer when it's presented as the default, but not to prefer when it's not the default. (If it seems obvious that paid vacation is better, keep in mind that wages and other forms of compensation can and probably do adjust to compensate. So the question here is whether the agent is willing to *buy* or *sell* the vacation time.) Again, there are at least two possible fixes: (1) consistently favor the paid vacation or (2) consistently favor the lack of paid vacation. Behavioral paternalists have, with little justification, chosen (1).

In the first two cases, the selected preference seems to be the socially preferred one; after all, "everyone knows" that saving more, avoiding unhealthy foods, and resisting impulse purchases is responsible behavior. In the third case, the selected preference seems to derive from a progressive ideology that says employers ought to treat their employees better. But none of these preferences is derived from the individual himself – except in a trivial sense that could equally well justify the opposite policies. By picking and choosing among preference sets, the behavioral paternalists effectively abandon their stated welfare standard of the individual's own preferences – which, to reiterate, may not even exist – in favor of an *external* set of preferences.

Even our phrasing of the examples above may be somewhat misleading, as it might suggest the possibility that the paternalists have chosen preference set (1) when they *should* have chosen preference set (2) or (3). The key issue is that it requires an unjustified leap of logic to choose *any* of these answers, or indeed to assume that there *is* an answer.

Some defenses have been offered for favoring some preferences over others in cases of conflict, but we find these defenses weak:

> *Verbal Statements and Survey Responses*: When asked, people may say they would rather behave differently or have different preferences. For instance, smokers may say they would rather not smoke, and overweight people may say they would like to eat less. It is indeed *possible* that these statements reveal "true" preferences. However, the incentives for speech differ from the incentives for other kinds of action. Behavioral research has cast doubt on many economic principles previously taken as given, but the principle that *talk is cheap* remains intact. Speakers who say one thing while doing another may simply be expressing what they regard as socially approved attitudes – a phenomenon known as *social desirability bias* (King and Bruner 2000; Grimm 2010). Or their statements may simply reflect "experienced opportunity cost," i.e., the dissatisfaction that always results from options the agent has forgone.
>
> *Regret*: A person may feel, and express, feelings of regret about the choices they have made: "I wish I had not done that." Although regrets are real, they do not necessarily reflect all costs and benefits associated with an action. Especially for intertemporal choices, such as getting inebriated last night and having a hangover today, the regret is typically experienced while the cost is being experienced in the present and the benefit is already in the past. That does not mean the costs outweighed the benefits *at the moment of choice* – only that the *remaining* costs outweigh the *remaining* benefits. In addition, it's worth noting that regret can also be felt about the kinds of choices that behavioral paternalists favor. When approaching death, people often express regret at not having lived a more spontaneous and present-oriented life (Ware 2012). If regret may be experienced regardless of the action taken, then it offers little guidance to the paternalist about which preferences are "true." As with verbal statements, regret can simply reflect the experience of opportunity cost.
>
> Furthermore, as discussed in the context of the Allais Paradox, regret can explain why seemingly *identical* decision situations are not, in fact, identical. Regret means that an agent's future satisfaction may be affected by the other options that were on the menu. Behavioral paternalists cannot simultaneously *reject* regret as the source of a reasonable violation of framing invariance or independence of

irrelevant alternatives, yet *embrace* regret when trying to glean some-one's "true" preferences.

Self-Constraint and Commitment Devices: People will often use various devices and strategies to try to keep their vices under control: planning automatic deductions for savings, avoiding locations where they will be tempted to smoke or drink, etc. These activities do provide further evidence of conflicting preferences, and we will discuss them more in future chapters. They do not, however, show which preferences are superior. Commitment devices reveal one set of preferences at work – but other choices show other preferences at work. Furthermore, the outside observer has no means of knowing whether the *right amount* of self-constraint has been performed. The level of self-constraint the person has already chosen might represent a delicate balance between their conflicting preferences. Or there may not be any correct balance to be found, inasmuch as the individual's true (fully consistent) preferences could be a chimera.

Planned versus Unplanned Choices: Behavioral paternalists often favor the preferences of a "planning self" over the spontaneous or "acting self." The idea is that the planning self is more likely to take all costs and benefits into account and render a considered decision. But the planning self does not necessarily represent a disinterested party; rather, the planning self may represent only the longer-term and more self-denying parts of one's personality (Cowen 1991). This becomes most apparent in the case of extreme behaviors such as anorexia, where the planning self dominates an acting self that might wish to indulge more often.

INTERPRETING BEHAVIORAL INCONSISTENCY

When real people display seemingly inconsistent behavior – that is, choices that appear to contradict each other – what can economists infer? What assumption are the subjects violating? Consider that most neoclassical models of choice typically make all of the following assumptions:

- The agent's preferences are well-defined; that is, they satisfy completeness and transitivity (and their corollaries).
- The agent has preferences that remain the same over time.
- The agent acts consistently with her preferences. We have dubbed this assumption "Rational Choice."

In principle, these assumptions are distinct. In practice, it is very difficult to distinguish violations of one from violations of the others. Thus far, we've focused on the first interpretation: that the agent's preferences violate one or more of the preference axioms (completeness, transitivity, or one of their corollaries). We have argued that such violations do not tell us anything of normative significance. But now we must consider the others.

The second interpretation is that the agent's preferences have simply changed over time. In other words, if someone chose A over B on Monday but B over A on Tuesday, that could be the result of consistent (complete and transitive) preferences on Monday, and a *different* set of consistent (complete and transitive) preferences on Tuesday.

In general, economists resist preference change as an explanatory strategy because it feels ad hoc. Virtually any change in behavior can be rationalized as resulting from changing preferences, but economists usually wish to show the reasons why behavior may change *even if tastes do not* – for example, because of changing relative prices. To resort to saying preferences have changed seems like cheating. These are valid concerns from a positive perspective. But from a normative perspective, they hold little weight. There is no reason a person's preferences *should* remain fixed. Rational people may change their minds – and we have not encountered anyone arguing otherwise. Behavioral paternalists have not emphasized this interpretation, but it's possible they should. At least some observed behavioral inconsistencies could be traced to changing preferences.[33]

The third interpretation is that the agent has internally consistent preferences that do not change over time, but for some reason does not act upon them. In other words, the agent violates what we have called the Rational Choice assumption. Some behavioral paternalists have emphasized this interpretation. The usual form of the argument is that agents suffer momentary *errors or breakdowns in decision-making processes*. From this perspective, "true preferences" simply *must* have a standard well-defined structure. Anything that interferes with the implementation of these true preferences constitutes a distortion or malfunction in the relevant psychological decision-making processes. This position is explicitly stated by Bernheim and Rangel, who explain, "We assume that people attempt to optimize given their true preferences, but randomly encounter conditions that trigger systematic mistakes" (2007, 16). In essence, the advocates of this approach treat the preference axioms as hard constraints.

---

[33] Many of the alleged inconsistencies of choice are inferred from a differences-between-groups approach, meaning there is no opportunity for preferences to have changed over time.

To defend these axioms, they place all "blame" for choice inconsistencies on process errors.[34]

The implicit metaphysical assumption, nowhere explicitly defended, is that each person has a neoclassical agent deep inside that is struggling to surface. Decision-making processes are thus deemed to be malfunctioning insofar as they fail to produce choices consistent with the standard preference structure. In other words, malfunction is not independently defined; it is whatever does not make standard choice theory descriptively accurate. This approach thus *assumes away* the possibility of individuals who simply do not have preferences that satisfy the neoclassical axioms of transitivity and completeness.

Behavioral economists who (implicitly or explicitly) blame inconsistencies of choice on process errors, rather than deeper inconsistencies of preferences, typically point to alleged errors in how people form and revise their beliefs, how they apply rules of logic and probability, and how they treat information in general. We will address these claims directly in Chapter 5. For now, what's important is to see how the neoclassical preference axioms are used to justify the process-error position. If we assume that the agent's true preferences *must* satisfy completeness and transitivity – and also that true preferences are stable over time – then process error is the only remaining explanation for a behavioral inconsistency. The agent *must* be making a mistake! But if you assume, as we do, that real people may have incomplete and intransitive preferences, or even no relevant preferences at all, then behavioral inconsistencies do not necessarily imply mistakes.

CONCLUSIONS

Behavioral paternalists rest their case on evidence that normal people violate basic tenets of rationality. But what do they mean by rationality? It turns out behavioral economists use the same definition of rationality as their neoclassical counterparts. Neoclassical or "puppet" rationality rests on two axioms – completeness and transitivity – that together impose a form of consistency on the structure of people's preferences. Other characteristics of neoclassical rationality, such as framing invariance and independence of irrelevant alternatives, derive from these more basic axioms. Although behavioral paternalists have rejected neoclassical rationality as a

---

[34] Another possible explanation of violations of the Rational Choice assumption is "deficient willpower." See Rizzo (2016).

positive description of human behavior, they have nevertheless maintained it as a normative standard.

In this chapter, we have argued that this was a mistake. The axiomatic definition of rationality was developed primarily, if not entirely, for positive (i.e., descriptive or explanatory) analysis. The axioms justified the use of utility functions, an important step along the path to proving propositions such as the existence of a competitive market equilibrium. They made economic models mathematically tractable, and they facilitated the generation of testable hypotheses. In short, they enabled the creation of simple, functional, and often quite useful puppets to populate economic models, thereby satisfying the needs of the model-builders.

But however useful the neoclassical axioms may have been for positive purposes, they never had a strong normative justification. They may be violated in many reasonable ways. Normal people may be found in the process of discovering their preferences, or even the process of creating them. They may decide, consciously or otherwise, that the costs of completely rationalizing their preferences exceed the benefits of doing so, and so they allow their preferences to remain inconsistent. A variety of examples show that people's preferences may be incomplete or intransitive for understandable reasons that do not obviously demand correction. Our inclusive notion of rationality allows for all of these deviations from the neoclassical structure. The simplistic axioms of puppet rationality cannot capture the breadth and variety of how real human beings evaluate options and make choices.

Many of the problems discussed in this chapter are not new, but presenting them together here demonstrates that the normative case for puppet rationality is extraordinarily weak, at least outside of special cases. The neoclassical axioms of preference may have descriptive or explanatory value – or, given the work of behavioral economists, they may not. But to call them "rationality requirements" is normatively arbitrary. If we gave them another name – say, "structural assumptions" – they would still perform the function for which they were created without deceiving economists or the public into thinking that nonconforming behavior or preferences need to be "fixed."

APPENDIX TO CHAPTER 3: Revealed Preference

The term "revealed preference" appears relatively often in the behavioral literature, though it is not always clearly defined. Sometimes it seems to mean mental states – relative evaluations – that have been revealed through actions. Other times it seems to simply mean actual choices, which may or may not correspond to people's "true" evaluations. It's worth asking whether a return to the *original* notion of revealed preference offers any hope of giving behavioral paternalism a coherent normative foundation. To answer, we need to dig more deeply into the revealed preference approach.

The "revealed preference" approach arose from the behaviorist philosophy of science that became popular in the early twentieth century. As such, it represented the implementation of a philosophical project: to rid economics of unobservable constructs such as preferences (in the sense of mental evaluations). For one alternative to be "revealed preferred" to another was simply a way of saying that one was *chosen* over another. In contrast to the *preference-primitive* axiomatic system discussed in Chapter 2, revealed preference aimed to be a *choice-primitive* system.

We should note that the name "revealed preference" is a double misnomer. The "preferences" involved are not at all what normal people mean by that word; they are not attitudes, but choices. And if we are unwilling to make reference to invisible mental states, then there is nothing to be "revealed." Choices are simply observed, period. The misleading label has contributed, we believe, to an *appreciative* notion of revealed preference that is both common in the profession and more in keeping with normal English usage: that people have preferences in their heads, and these preferences are revealed (perhaps imperfectly) through choices. We have dubbed the appreciative notion of revealed preference "preference revelation." But here, we focus on the original notion of revealed preference.

The revealed preference approach works through the application of a set of restrictions that impose a certain degree of consistency on choice. Many economists think of the consistency requirements as a form of rationality requirement. But since the economic agents do not have minds in the behaviorist approach – or at least we are not allowed to refer to them – it must be rationality from the point of view of the economist, who presumably does have a mind.

The restrictions classically imposed are two: (1) the weak axiom of revealed preference (WARP) and (2) the strong axiom of revealed preference (SARP). These provide the structure that the economist must be able to impose on the agent's behavior in order to deem it rational. And yet this structure cannot stand alone as a set of normative criteria, as we shall see.

Paul Samuelson (1938) proposed that economists could dispense with mental preferences and still derive several important properties of demand curves that previously were derived by means of utility theory. By placing a weak consistency requirement (WARP) on the observed choices, the economist could derive the single-valuedness of the demand function, the homogeneity of degree zero of demand functions, and the Slutsky equation without recourse to unobservable entities (Wong 2006, 54).[35]

Weak Axiom of Revealed Preference: If for some set of available options (a budget set) with distinct bundles x and y the agent chooses x, then for any other budget set with x and y the agent must never choose y over x. Therefore, for example, if from the set $\{x,y\}$ the agent chooses x over y, we *cannot* observe y chosen over x from the set $\{x,y,z\}$.[36]

WARP bears a resemblance to the axiom of completeness, in that it requires a single ordering of any two options x and y. But the resemblance is misleading, because despite its name, WARP says nothing about *preferences* (in the sense of mental evaluations), only about *choices*. Choices, of course, can only be observed in real time. Unlike completeness, which at least in principle requires only consistency of evaluations at a moment in time, WARP demands consistency of choices over time.

As with completeness, WARP also implies "menu independence" – though again with respect to choices, not mental evaluations. If an alternative is chosen over another in a set of two alternatives, this will never be

---

[35] In other words, for a given price-budget the individual will choose the same bundle, a proportional change in all prices and income leaves quantities demanded unchanged, and demand changes can be decomposed into an income effect and a substitution effect.

[36] Technically, the agent can choose y if he also chooses x. This would mean that *in a long series of cases* in which he confronts the same choice problem the choice set would be $\{x, y\}$ – sometimes x and sometimes y (Mas-Colell et al. 1995, 10). In this interpretation one would not know whether WARP is violated until the series is completed.

reversed in a larger set that includes the rejected alternative. This is sometimes called "expansion consistency." Similarly, if an alternative is chosen over another from a larger set, the choice will never be reversed in a smaller set that contains the rejected alternative. This is sometimes called "contraction consistency." Thus, the agent is consistent or constant in his choice of x over y regardless of menu "manipulation" or changes.[37]

To show the compatibility of the choice-primitive axiomatic system with the preference-primitive axiomatic system, and thereby with "rationality," a new axiom had to be introduced (Houthakker 1950). A recursive closure of WARP was developed to accomplish this:

Strong Axiom of Revealed Preference: For every sequence of distinct bundles $x^0, x^1, \ldots x^n$, where x^0 is chosen over x^1, and x^1 is chosen over x^2, ... and x^{n-1} is chosen over x^n, it is not the case that x^n is chosen over x^0.

SARP is a special case of WARP where "consistency" is extended over choices that are both directly and indirectly preferred to others. It does not matter how long the chain of indirect preference relations is. Just as WARP bears a resemblance to completeness, SARP bears a resemblance to transitivity. But the same caveat is required: it is not a statement about preferences-as-mental-states, but about choices. And like WARP, SARP also requires consistency over time, not just at a moment in time.

We need to stop for a moment here and ask the question: "What do WARP and SARP have to do with rationality – even puppet rationality?" It is clear that while WARP and SARP are consistency requirements, they guarantee neither completeness nor transitivity of a hypothetical underlying preference relation (Mas-Colell et al. 1995). Even if they accurately described choices – which they do not – they would say nothing about mental states, even if we were willing to refer to such things. Nevertheless, those who are interested in whether behavior is rational in the neoclassical sense will find violations of WARP or SARP to be a quick way to test for neoclassical rationality. A preference relation that satisfies both completeness and transitivity – as well as being fixed over time – necessarily implies WARP and SARP. Therefore, if WARP and SARP are not satisfied then the preference relation is not neoclassically rational (or not static, if the WARP/SARP violations happen over time).

However, this result is not as useful as it might seem. The reason extends deeply into the program of treating choice as the primitive in an axiomatic system. "Choice" in the sense of revealed preference *appears* to be a

---

[37] WARP implies menu independence and menu independence implies WARP (Isaac 1998, 22).

phenomenon that is definable without reference to mental states. This is completely false. For example, a choice is not an apple or even the movement of an apple into the hands of an individual.[38] It is an action – an intentional physical movement with a specific meaning directed to a purpose.

Once we appreciate the constitutive role of meaning and intention in choice, we can see that the "consistency" of revealed preference is simply an unchanged or constant physical event. Physical movements or pure behaviors cannot be inconsistent with each other, although they can be different.[39] Therefore, to see an inconsistency we must first have *inter preted* behavior. The same physical movement under different circumstances can have a different meaning, and different physical movements under different circumstances can have the same meaning (Hayek 1955). This criticism goes to the heart of the idea that we can have an axiomatic structure of rationality independent of content. We cannot.

RECOVERY OF THE UTILITY FUNCTION FROM REVEALED PREFERENCES

Economists working in the revealed preference tradition sometimes talk about "recovery" of the utility function from (actual or hypothetical) observations of choice. When choices do satisfy WARP and SARP, it is possible to find a utility function (or functions) that would generate those choices.[40] What does this mean, and does it have any normative implications?

The term "recovery" is highly misleading. It *seems* to mean that the utility function was there in the background all along but that we had simply turned our attention temporarily to choice observations.[41] This is false. The utility function is being *constructed* on the basis of actual and

---

[38] Schumpeter (2010, 31–34) thought of exchange as the simple movement of a physical object (commodity) from one location to another where the "locations" are different individuals.

[39] Sen (1993, 449) says something quite similar, but the argument is very confusing because he accepts the use of the terms "action" and "choice" to mean an *uninterpreted* physical movement even as he is trying to show that employing the terms in that way is highly problematic. This accounts for Sen's claim that we must refer to factors "external" to choice to understand ideas such as choice-consistency. At the same time, we would say that one cannot understand "choice" by reference to physical movements or physical objects only. It is necessary to understand *all* of the constituents of choice, including meaning and intention. These are not external to choice but internal to it.

[40] A somewhat more general set of utility functions can be found if the "Generalized axiom of revealed preference" (essentially a long-chain transitivity requirement) is satisfied.

[41] What it really means is that historically economists used to concern themselves with utility functions and then, under the influence of classical behaviorism, switched to revealed preference – but now are recovering that historical concern.

hypothetical observations of choice. It merely summarizes the data in the revealed preference relation (Jehle and Reny 2011, 13). It is a mathematical representation of revealed preferences. As such, it bears the marks of its behavioristic origins: no mental states, just observations of "choices." Therefore, the utility function so constructed says nothing about the mental causes of choices. The function simply describes what a pattern of consistent (from the point of view of the economist) choices would look like even if they were produced by a machine.[42] The reexpression of revealed preference in terms of a utility function is solely for the purpose of greater mathematical tractability in constructing hypotheses. Consequently, the inference of a utility function from revealed preference data does nothing to buttress the normative plausibility of WARP and SARP.

RATIONAL VIOLATIONS OF "REVEALED PREFERENCE"

Let us return to the example of Lady Trevelyan. This example showed a seeming violation of completeness: both preferring tea to nothing (when those are the only options) but also nothing to tea (when LSD is an option). If Lady Trevelyan's choices exhibited a similar inconsistency – say, making plans with Timothy before he offered LSD, and canceling them afterward – we would have a violation of WARP as well. The violation of completeness was resolved by reference to the agent's beliefs and how the menu affected them. As we suggested earlier, that solution is not entirely satisfactory. But even this limited solution is unavailable in the revealed preference approach, inasmuch as that approach abstracts from the beliefs or knowledge of the agent (Hausman 2000). Trying to evaluate the rationality of choices independently of the knowledge of the agent is futile. Practical rationality is concerned with whether the reasons for actions are sufficient, good, coherent, and so forth. Reasons and knowledge go together.

This has not been lost on the defenders of revealed preference. The typical response has been to modify it to include factors such as the subjective perception by the agents of the available alternatives as well as their knowledge of the context in which the choices take place (Gul and Pesendorfer 2008, 22–23; Rubinstein and Salant 2008, 117).

---

[42] Ken Binmore (2009, 19) puts this point succinctly: "In revealed-preference theory, it isn't true that Pandora [the agent] chooses *b* rather than *a* *because* the utility of *b* exceeds the utility of *a*. This is the Causal Utility Fallacy. It isn't even true that Pandora chooses *b* rather than *a* because she prefers *b* to *a*. On the contrary, it is because Pandora chooses *b* rather than *a* that we say that Pandora prefers *b* to *a*, and assign *b* a larger utility."

The problems with this solution are many. First, it sows conceptual confusion because many economists still adhere to the historically correct meaning of revealed preference that eschews subjective states (Varian 2010, 118–125; Kreps 2013, 67–78; Mas-Colell et al. 1995, 5–28).[43] Second, when viewed from the perspective of saving the WARP criterion, the defensive stratagem makes little sense. In the Lady Trevelyan case, we could redescribe the option of having tea when she doesn't know about Timothy's fondness for LSD as different from having tea when she does know about it. This alteration in the feasible options she faces renders the WARP criterion not satisfied, but inapplicable. Thus WARP is saved by refusing to confront it with a possible violation. But the problem does not rest with a single example. How would we treat such putative violations of WARP more generally?

According to this updated version of revealed preference, in order to test WARP we must hold constant the knowledge of the agent. More precisely, all factors that make the set of feasible options either smaller or larger between the compared cases must be held constant. Effectively this means that cases of violation are transformed into cases of inapplicability. Normally, economists would not tolerate this stratagem unless, in some way, it yielded compensating analytical benefits. Whatever these benefits might be in a purely positive or descriptive sense (for example, building a utility function), they are not helpful from a normative perspective. WARP itself does no normative work for us. It simply requires mental contortions to evade its straitjacket. The rationality of choice will depend, for example, on whether it makes sense in terms of her own conservative values for Lady Trevelyan to avoid tea at all with Timothy now that she knows what he is really like. WARP does not help decide this.

What the Lady Trevelyan example does for WARP, the Maurice example does for SARP. If we observed Maurice choosing Rome over the Alps, the Alps over home, and home over Rome, that would violate SARP. In the preference-primitive system, we could at least attempt to "rescue" the axioms by delving into Maurice's personal psychology to discover his concerns about cowardice. But revealed preference, by eschewing reference to mental states, forecloses that option. All we can see from Maurice's behavior is a violation of an axiom, which tells us nothing about the

---

[43] We object, on the basis of preserving clarity of thought, to the admixture of mental and subjective concepts with the "principle of revealed preference" as in Rubinstein and Salant (2008, 116–124). Gul and Pesendorfer (2008, 1–39) make the same doctrinal error but they are less systematic about it.

rationality or reasonability of his doing so. Redescription of the options could resolve the seeming inconsistency in an ad hoc way, but SARP cannot tell us whether such a redescription would be rationally justified.

Ultimately, revealed preference – in its pure form – cannot rescue neoclassical rationality. Indeed, it makes the problems of neoclassical rationality even more intractable. Completeness and transitivity are already difficult to justify on a normative level, given the many reasonable violations thereof. WARP and SARP magnify the difficulty by ruling out the use of mental states to explain away apparent violations. Like completeness and transitivity, WARP and SARP's original purpose was strictly positive. They had no normative content to begin with, and they cannot be imbued with it without venturing far outside the revealed preference paradigm.

SARP AND THE MONEY PUMP

But can SARP be justified on grounds that a violation of it could lead to a money pump? The idea here is that whatever else we may think of SARP violations, they could be problematic from a practical perspective: a SARP violator can be drained of all her money!

We have discussed money pumps before, and some of our objections there apply here as well. But in the revealed preference context, the money pump argument is even more problematic. To see why, we must depart from the insistence of the pure revealed preference approach on not referring to mental states. As we have seen, without mental states, we simply can't engage in normative analysis at all. So let us assume that a SARP violator has some genuine underlying desires or interests that could be harmed by a money pump. But here is the problem: even if an agent's revealed preferences (i.e., choices) are intransitive, this does not mean that her evaluative preferences are intransitive. This is so for at least two reasons.

First, a WARP violation (choice intransitivity) can be generated by a change in an agent's underlying evaluative preferences during the period under consideration. Clearly, there can be no *normative* prohibition against preferences changing. If they have changed, then although the bookmaker makes money, the agent's welfare is not reduced. Each transaction makes her better off according to her then-current preferences.[44]

---

[44] We abstract from what normative meaning welfare could have in the revealed preference world of "mindless" agents.

Furthermore, a choice intransitivity generated by changes in evaluative preferences does not imply that money-pumping is possible. Suppose the agent exchanges *a* for *b* and then *b* for *c*, and then her evaluative preferences change so that she is *now* willing to exchange *c* for *a*. It does not follow that she will now exchange *a* for *b* again. Her initial evaluative preferences ranked *c* over *b* over *a*, but her new evaluative preferences might be exactly the opposite (or any other ranking that places *a* over *c* without putting *b* over *a*).

Second, a choice intransitivity can be generated by incomparability of options. Isaac Levi (2002, S237–S238) has explored an interesting example of this case. Suppose George has before him three options about spending his week's wages:

1. 70 percent of the week's salary for meeting the needs of his family and 30 percent for savings;
2. 50 percent for the family and spending 50 percent on cigarettes, whiskey, and wild women;
3. 35 percent for the family, 30 percent for cigarettes, whiskey, and wild women, and 35 percent for savings.

Unfortunately, George is conflicted. "Good George" would prefer *a* to *b* to *c*. But then there is "bad George" who would prefer *b* to *c* to *a*. Think of George as consulting the two Georges in his head. Luckily, they can agree on one thing: *b* is preferred to *c*. All things considered, George will strictly prefer *b* to *c* and when that option comes up he will be decisive. What about his preferences between *a* and *b* and then between *a* and *c*? Since each George in his head gets only one vote, there is disagreement. As long as this persists, the binary options are incomparable. Nevertheless, he "must" make a decision: time's awastin'. He could simply choose randomly in a pairwise choice. Suppose he does not. Instead he thinks that he could decide on the basis of a secondary consideration – the amount of savings. He has been hearing a lot of talk from mutual fund companies that Americans don't save enough. Therefore, as between *a* and *b*, he acts as a savings maximizer. He chooses *a* because in that option he saves 30 percent. Similarly, in a pairwise choice between *a* and *c* he chooses *c* because in that option he saves 35 percent. His *revealed* preferences are now like so: *aPb*, *bPc*, and *cPa*. They appear as intransitive strict preferences. And yet they are not, except for the first pairwise comparison, all-things-considered preferences. They are the consequence of being forced to choose when George has not yet resolved his internal conflict.

Now, can George be money-pumped? For the same reasons presented in our earlier discussion, it seems unlikely. But suppose he can be pumped because, say, he is substantially less alert or intelligent than the bookmaker (and transaction costs are small enough to make the pump worthwhile). Does this mean he is "irrational"? Put aside the possibility that being less intelligent than a bookmaker makes one irrational. Is it objectively irrational to incur a cost in order to gain more time to resolve internal conflicts?[45] In the meantime, George is satisfying a secondary objective. That must count for something, too. Vulnerability to "exploitation" by a money pump does not, in itself, reveal irrationality. The reason for intransitivity is important. It is not irrational to incur costs for more time to make up one's mind.

SOME CONCLUSIONS ABOUT REVEALED PREFERENCE

We have taken an extended detour through revealed preference, and it's worth asking why. Most behavioral paternalists do not follow a pure revealed preference approach. Like most modern economists, they readily refer to people's mental states to explain their actions.

However, consideration of the problems with revealed preference shines a spotlight on problems of the behavioral paradigm. Behavioral economists rely on various forms of data, often experimental data, to show violations of rationality axioms such as transitivity and completeness. But what they are in fact finding, at least in many cases, are violations of WARP and SARP. That is, they find *choices* that exhibit some kind of inconsistency. In order to draw any normative conclusions, they, like revealed preference analysts, must reach outside the axiomatic framework and surmise the underlying reasons for the inconsistencies. In some cases, the choice inconsistencies might simply result from changing preferences. We have yet to hear any argument for why changing one's preferences is necessarily irrational. In other cases, the choice inconsistency might trace back to genuine violations of the neoclassical preference axioms (completeness and transitivity). But such violations may occur for a variety of reasons that cannot be dismissed as irrational from an inclusive perspective.

---

[45] We say "objectively irrational" because, by assumption, George did not know in advance that he would be subject to this "tax" on his indecision. If he had known, he could have avoided it.

4

Preference Biases

I hate and I love. Why do I do this, perhaps you ask?
I do not know, but I feel it happening and I am tortured.
—Catullus, *Carmina LXXXV*

Wisdum don't konsist in knowing more that iz new, but in knowing less that
iz false.
—Josh Billings, *Everybody's Friend*

The cognitive biases used by behavioral paternalists to justify policy often possess an appealing simplicity, even as they represent a challenge to received models of human behavior. Hyperbolic discounting? That just means that we are *impatient*; we like to experience rewards sooner and costs later. The endowment effect? That's a fancy way of saying we value something more simply *because we already have it*. Empathy gaps? That simply means we're *affected by our emotions* when we make decisions. We have all had experiences to match these descriptions. And we may even have associated those experiences with personal failure, which makes the next step in the argument – claiming that these phenomena demand correction – easier to swallow.

But what do we really know about cognitive biases? Do we know what functions they might serve in human decision-making? In Chapter 3, we largely took the cognitive biases as given, while questioning their implications for human rationality. Now that we have dispensed with the notion that mere inconsistency (a common implication of these biases) is per se irrational, we can look at the cognitive biases with fresh eyes. In this chapter, we will dive more deeply into the logic and empirical research on those cognitive biases most often used to justify paternalist policies. In many cases, we will see that the evidence for a bias is flawed or incomplete. In other cases, the evidence has been misinterpreted. In every case, we find that the phenomenon is not nearly as simple as commonly presented, especially by those who would use it to justify paternalist intervention.

In Chapter 3, we highlighted the non sequitur of resolving preference inconsistencies: if an agent seems to be driven by two conflicting sets of preferences, there is no strictly logical basis for privileging one preference set over the other. In this chapter, we will go a step further: we will show that the preferences deemed better or more "true" by paternalists are often just as questionable on behavioral grounds, if not more so.

INTERTEMPORAL TRADE-OFFS AND TIME-DISCOUNTING INCONSISTENCIES

The standard neoclassical model of time discounting is exponential. This means that an outcome at time t is evaluated now ($t = 0$) as $\delta^t u(x)$, where δ is a constant discount factor and $u(x)$ is an undated utility function defined on outcomes.

This formulation implies several things. The first is that the discount factor itself is stationary; it does not change as the individual evaluates sequences of outcomes in the more distant future. Second, the comparative evaluation of a smaller reward sooner and a larger reward later is not reversed for a given interval between the two outcomes depending on the time at which it is evaluated. So, for example, if today an individual prefers an immediate one dollar to two dollars tomorrow, he cannot simultaneously prefer two dollars in a year and a day to one dollar in a year. If this were to be the case, then as the future became the present, the individual would "reverse" his preference so that once again one dollar now would be preferred to two dollars tomorrow. Third, intertemporal preferences are transitive and thus cyclical preferences are ruled out.

These three characteristics constitute consistent intertemporal preferences, according to behavioral and standard economists alike. Unfortunately for the *descriptive* aspect of the exponential discounting model, there is abundant empirical evidence of violations of these consistency properties. Nevertheless, the model is treated by behavioral economists as a *prescriptive* norm – or, at least, that its failure to hold is a red flag for the presence of some undesirable behavior.

Stationarity is not an obvious prescriptive norm. It is certainly convenient, but why the individual should not be "allowed" to treat trade-offs in the farther future differently from more immediate trade-offs is a puzzle. Strictly speaking, the individual is not even being inconsistent in doing so. It is quite usual in economics to treat the same goods available at different dates as different economic goods. Similarly, with respect to the second characteristic above, there is no real reversal when time elapses and so one dollar available in a year becomes a dollar available now, and two dollars available in a year and a day becomes two dollars available tomorrow. Why not? Because the dollar amounts are *no longer the same objects* after the passage of time. They are closer in time to the decision-maker. Intransitivity in this case, as in many others, may be the benign outcome of applying a perfectly consistent rule or heuristic in comparative evaluations across time (McNamara et al. 2014; Gigerenzer 2000, 194–195). And, as we have argued previously in this book, the pragmatic rationality of violations of standard norms can only be assessed relative to the consequences. Evidence that nonstandard agents who violate exponential discounting norms will face the frustration of their goals has not been provided.[1] The usual claim is that nonexponential discounting *causes* people to save less for the future, which could be deemed a pragmatically bad outcome – but as we shall see, this link has not in fact been established.

Under the usual behavioral interpretations, any conflict in discount rates must be adjudicated. Only one can be the "true" intertemporal preference. The statement that there can only be one true preference is based simply on the *assumption* that it must be so. That the standard model has a single discount rate is not a reason in itself to claim prescriptive significance. This model was created for analytical convenience and because it exhibited pleasing properties from a mathematical perspective. This is not equivalent to a powerful and general normative argument for a unique rate of discount.

In the now common quasi-hyperbolic discounting model, there are *two* rates of discount: an immediate rate that applies when the present time period is involved, and a long-term rate that applies across all other periods. In keeping with the behavioral acceptance of the neoclassical norm of one discount rate, the immediate rate – today versus tomorrow in our previous example – is seen as contaminated or distorted by a present bias. The overall model of quasi-hyperbolic discounting "now functions as a default option for analyzing the *misbehavior* of economic agents" (Prelec 2004, 511, emphasis added). The misbehavior or bias is usually attributed to psychological weakness: temptation, visceral attraction, myopia, impulsiveness, hot-state decision-making, and other similar terms with bad everyday connotations. These interpretations imply a need to explain the immediate

---

[1] See the section "Do Nonstandard Intertemporal Decision-Makers Suffer?"

rate while not taking seriously the need to explain the long-term rate.[2] More comprehensive interpretive efforts make clear that neither rate is free of "behavioral" influences. As we shall see, choices between dated rewards in the farther future are affected by the agent's inability adequately to distinguish the relevant attributes or utility levels associated with future options.

Furthermore, behavioral economists have used quasi-hyperbolic discounting primarily because of its analytical tractability (Ainslie 2001, 210 n29, 214 n21; Angeletos et al. 2001, 50), but there is evidence that actual behavior more closely resembles *true* (not quasi-) hyperbolic discounting (Bleichrodt et al. 2016). Under true hyperbolic discounting, discount rates decline continuously as a function of how far an option is from the present. This means that adjudicating between conflicting discount rates actually involves adjudicating among *many* discount rates, all of which might be construed as "suspect."

Time: Objective and Subjective

At the most fundamental level, the difficulties in choosing a prescriptive rate of discount become apparent if we focus on the general nature of time discounting. There is laboratory research questioning the applicability of a simple linear model to trade-offs in time (Zauberman et al. 2009).[3] People do not necessarily perceive time in the way that the calendar or the number-line portrays it. When asked, "How long do you consider the duration between today and a day some distance in the future," with the interval ranging from three months to thirty-six months, people answer in a nonlinear fashion. For example, while the time horizon from three months to one year grows 300 percent by calendar measure, it grows only 35 percent in subjective duration. Similarly, a calendar lengthening from three months to three years grows 1,100 percent in calendar time but only 89 percent in subjective duration.[4] This psychological

---

[2] Notice how the rate-out-of-step (immediate rate) *is modeled* as a mathematical transformation of the long-term or exponential discounting rate. The model is used to suggest a fundamentally neoclassical man who is shocked by some distortive influence every time he seeks to make a short-term intertemporal choice but who is left undisturbed when he makes choices for the farther future. This, however, is an artifact of a certain fitting of the data. Recently, even one of the main supporters of the hyperbolic discounting model, David Laibson, has admitted that simple heuristics fit the data better than any form of delay discounting. See Ericson et al. (2015). In any event, no prescriptive inferences can be drawn from a descriptive model.

[3] See also Buss and Rüschendorf (2010).

[4] To measure subjective time in most of these experiments, the authors had subjects mark durations (such as three months, one year, and three years) on a 180 mm line, with endpoints labeled "very short" and "very long." If subjective time were equivalent to

compression of time has dramatic implications for discount rates. For example, consider observed discount rates of 100 percent for one year and 45 percent for three years. This difference is indicative of hyperbolic discounting in calendar time. However, when adjusted for psychological duration, the longer-term rate of discount rises, causing the difference in rates of discounting to disappear.[5] There appears to be a constant discount rate across psychological time horizons.[6]

Looking at this from a slightly different perspective, if we imagine a constant discount rate being applied to segments of time defined psychologically, then the observed calendar discount rate within some initial period will be larger than within later calendar periods of the same length. As the agent looks farther into the future, the passage of calendar time is psychologically increasingly compressed. Delays will appear to be shorter. He will have to be paid less for waiting a given amount of calendar time. Thus a lower and lower discount rate will be applied to the successive calendar periods. The *observed* discount rate will continue to fall even as the *psychological* discount rate is constant.

Figures 4.1 and 4.2 illustrate the phenomenon of time compression and its consequences for discounting based on one of the experiments conducted by Zauberman et al. (2009).[7] Figure 4.1 shows the relationship between objective and subjective time. Objective or calendar time is shown by a 45-degree line (a month is a month, a year is a year, etc.). The line for subjective time is much flatter, indicating that from a psychological perspective, longer durations are increasingly compressed. Figure 4.2 shows what happens when discount rates are calculated using subjective time

---

objective time, then (for instance) the ratio of the twelve-month distance to the three-month distance would be exactly four. Deviation from objective ratios thus provides a measure of subjective time. In one set of experiments the authors normalize the subjective time estimate on the basis of three calendar months. Thus, in effect, the comparisons mean that one year *feels* only 35 percent longer than three months *feels*, and so forth. There is no independent measure of just *how* expected durations feel.

[5] Intuitively, the adjustment takes place by keeping the calendar discount rate constant but compressing the amount of time elapsed in accordance with the experimental data. For example, suppose an elapsed time of three calendar years is the equivalent of only 1.3 years in subjective duration. Then when a relatively large amount of calendar-time discounting takes place within a compressed psychological time, the "annual" rate in psychological time becomes considerably larger.

[6] Since there is normalization on three months, the constant psychological discount rate is approximately 320 percent. See Figure 4.2.

[7] "Time compression" is our term for this phenomenon. Kim and Zauberman (2009) refer to it as either "time contraction" or "non-linear perception of time." We find our term more intuitive.

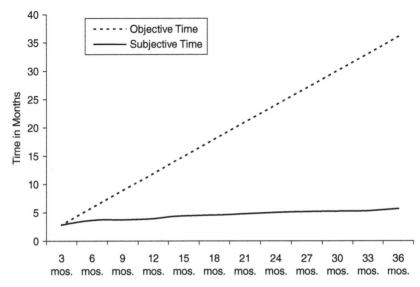

Figure 4.1 Objective and subjective time
Source: Zauberman et al. (2009)

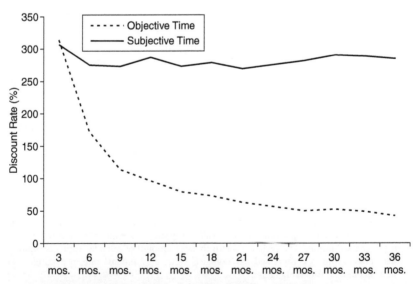

Figure 4.2 Discount rate calculated with objective and subjective time
Source: Zauberman et al. (2009)

rather than objective time. Discount rates calculated based on objective time decrease with duration, as predicted by hyperbolic discounting. But discount rates calculated based on subjective time are relatively constant.

Is this psychological perspective on time a cognitive bias or error? Let us examine the two possibilities. If, on the one hand, nonlinear time perception is construed *not* as an error but as an allowable human trait, then the characterization of short-run higher rates of discount as biased must be reassessed. Whether the agent is applying one rate of discount or more than one will have to be measured relative to psychological time. If we do so, it seems that most of the inconstancy of rates disappears, at least in the experiments discussed. In the real world, the observed inconsistency of discount rates may be attributable, at least in part, to the manner in which people perceive the passage of time.[8] The normative case for correction of present bias disappears.

On the other hand, if nonlinear perception of time is construed as an error, then what sort of error is it? Kim and Zauberman (2009) attribute most of the hyperbolic discounting effect of time compression to *diminishing time sensitivity*, meaning that each additional unit of time (as measured from the present) is perceived as psychologically smaller than the previous one.[9] The analogy with distance perception is helpful: the

---

[8] All time reckoning is relative to something else. In the calendar case it is relative to the rotation of the earth around its axis or the movement of the earth around the sun. *The subjective perception of time is relative to the concerns of the agent.* From an efficiency perspective, it may not be worthwhile to distinguish between particular time periods in the more distant future because the difference in the present value of what is to be gained between these periods may not be significant (Andriani and Sonderegger 2014, 4).

[9] Kim and Zauberman (2009) attribute the nonlinear perception of time (which we have called time compression) to two phenomena: *diminishing time sensitivity* and *overall time contraction*. The latter is a linear (i.e., multiplicative) effect, which affects all time periods equally. An agent whose time perception is characterized by overall time contraction but *not* by diminishing time sensitivity would exhibit exponential discounting, which is time consistent. Although behavioral paternalists have usually treated exponential discounting as rational, if overall time contraction is regarded as a "bias" then it would challenge the rationality of some exponential discounting; someone could have a consistent but too-impatient rate of discount. When an agent's time perception is characterized by *both* overall time contraction and diminishing time sensitivity, overall time contraction has the effect of amplifying the effect of time sensitivity: it makes the agent's behavior "more hyperbolic" than it would be otherwise. Kim and Zauberman (2009, 96) estimate the average (regression-estimated) relationship between calendar time (t) and perceived time (T) as $T = 1.05t^{0.72}$, where 1.05 corresponds to overall time contraction and 0.72 corresponds to diminishing marginal time sensitivity. They find that both parameters significantly affect the "degree of hyperbola" (p. 98). However, for the regression-estimated values, it is clear that overall time compression is relatively slight (on average) and that marginal time sensitivity causes most of the deviation from linear time perception.

farther away something is, the smaller it looks. Now, if this is the source of supposed bias, then it is far from obvious that it's the perception of the present that is distorted. On the contrary, it's distant time periods that are most affected by diminishing sensitivity, while those close to the present are perceived most accurately. In that case, contrary to the usual conclusion that short-run discount rates are too high, we would conclude that long-run discount rates are *too low*. Alternatively, we could assert that diminishing time sensitivity implicates all time periods; the present looks too large and the future looks too small. In that case, we would say the perception of some intermediate time period (and the associated discount rate) is the "correct" one. Either way, the simple characterization of short-run discount rates as the only distorted ones must be discarded.

Preference Reversal

The logical relationship between preference reversal and nonconstant discounting is complex. Hyperbolic discounting has been offered as the leading explanation or "rationalization" of intertemporal preference reversal, that is, the reversal of choices from larger-later (LL) to smaller-sooner (SS) as the delay to the set of options shrinks. This preference reversal is the directly observed phenomenon, rather than hyperbolic discounting itself.[10]

Typically, preference reversals have been observed in experiments where subjects are asked to choose between SS and LL rewards separated by a constant interval but with different delays to the earliest payment (front-end delays). Thus an individual may be asked to choose when each reward is relatively far from the present, and also when the same two rewards are each closer to the present (usually with the SS reward to be received immediately). No appreciable amount of time actually passes between when the subject makes these two choices.[11] If a subject chooses the

---

[10] "[I]ntertemporal preference reversals can be attributed to hyperbolic discounting only if the options can be unambiguously ordered from any temporal perspective and if one does not gain additional information about their value following an initial decision. Few experiments satisfy these conditions" (Read et al. 2012, 179).

[11] These experiments have been implemented under two different designs. The within-subjects design asks the same participants to make each of the choices (the immediate and the distant). The between-subjects design asks one group to make the immediate choice and another group to make the distant choice. The groups are supposed to be the same except for the treatment. In general, each design has its strengths and weaknesses (Charness et al. 2012).

LL reward in the former case but the SS reward in the latter, that is classified as an *impatient* preference reversal. There are many technical problems with these studies (Spenger 2015). Perhaps the most important is that we do not observe actual reversal. What we observe is nonstationary discounting, but the experiments are unable to distinguish between time inconsistency and simple time-dependent preferences. If it is the latter, the individuals carry out their nonstationary plan. They are not time-inconsistent. Furthermore, there is an implicit assumption that time inconsistency can only take the form of impatient shifts. The individual makes a plan for LL but then ultimately shifts to SS. But patient shifts are also possible.

In recent research there have been experiments that elicit preferences by questioning participants over the passage of actual time, and not simply at a point in time as in the process just described. These are called "longitudinal" studies. A large majority of individuals do not actually switch over time: those who are patient with regard to the distant decision remain patient and those who are impatient remain impatient (Read et al. 2012). Relatedly, Halevy (2015) finds that only 10 percent of participants are actually time inconsistent in a longitudinal study. Furthermore, the ubiquity of impatient preference reversals is in doubt. The longitudinal experiments (Read et al. 2012; Sayman and Öncüler 2009) have found a very large number of shifts from SS to LL – that is, *patient* reversals – as the distant decision becomes more nearly immediate.[12] In fact, in two experiments conducted by Read and coauthors (2012) the numbers of impatient and patient reversals were roughly equal.

The psychological reasons for these "inverse preference reversals" are not clear at this time. One possibility is that for some people, the particular circumstances at the time of choice have changed. Another is that time periods relatively close to each other *and* to the present may be part of the agent's "extended present," in which larger is always preferred to smaller. In any event, these inverse reversal events are not consistent with hyperbolic discounting. Nevertheless, in what follows we will ignore, for the sake of argument, inverse preference reversals and take the hyperbolic phenomenon as genuine.

When the intertemporal discount rate is falling over time, true preference reversal can result. The apparent inconsistency of preference reversal

---

[12] Typically in preference reversal experiments the time to the smaller-sooner outcome varies but the delay between the two outcomes is fixed. The former constitutes the agent's (time) viewpoint.

is often used as an argument that a nonconstant rate of discount implies irrationality in more than just a formal sense. In other words, there must be something wrong with people who make plans and then abandon them. And if that is due to inconstant discounting, then there is also something wrong with such discounting. Although, as argued above, we do not believe this phenomenon is necessarily a reversal of preferences but rather might indicate different preferences over different time-stamped objects, we believe that it can be explained without reference to affective factors such as visceral temptation or impulsiveness.[13] To see this we must examine more closely the nature of decision-making for the farther future.

Beyond the issue of psychological time discussed earlier, there are many studies that effectively implicate longer-term discount rates as, at least in part, the result of cognitive "deficiencies" relative to an omniscient standard. The subadditivity model (Read 2001) has shown, both theoretically and experimentally, that the measured discount rate over a period of time taken as a whole is *lower* than the compounded average over the same period divided into component subperiods.[14] Thus, when a person prefers $50 today to $60 tomorrow (first interval) and $60 in a year and a day to $50 in a year (second interval), this "preference reversal" may be simply an artifact of looking at the year of delay as an undivided whole, despite the superficial appearance of declining impatience.[15] If the delay to the beginning of the second interval were broken down into subperiods – say, a decision each month for twelve months instead of one decision for the end of the year – the compounded average rate of discount for these subperiods together would be higher than for the period taken as a whole.

One possible psychological explanation is that when long periods are considered as a whole, the individual events (opportunities) comprising the periods lack salience.[16] Thus, the individual does not have to be compensated as much to wait, and the apparent discount rate will be lower. *If* there

---

[13] In general affective factors are "[a] term used in psychology for a feeling or emotion, particularly one leading to action" (Gregory 2004).

[14] The discount factor (δ) will decrease as the number of intervals into which a delay is divided increases. That is, the discount rate over an interval is greater when it is calculated in "installments" than when it is done in one operation.

[15] "First, subadditive intertemporal choice was observed in every experiment: when a delay was divided into three, the total discounting increased by an average of 40%. Second, there was no evidence of declining impatience: the amount of discounting was equal or lower for earlier intervals than for later intervals" (Read 2001, 24).

[16] On the other hand, "it is likely that the salience of a delay is increased by drawing attention to its parts. The imagined pain of two days waiting, for instance, might be increased if the days are contemplated separately rather than together" (Read 2001, 10).

is bias in not being attentive to all of the particulars in the anticipation of future periods, then the bias infects the long-run rate and not the short. The measured long-run rate is therefore "too low." But these results go further. In tests conducted to distinguish between the subadditivity effect and true declining impatience, evidence for declining impatience vanishes (Read 2001, 24). These findings suggest that the usual interpretation of the preference reversal phenomenon is not correct. It is not the consequence of an exceptional degree of impatience in the short term followed by a calmer, more "normal" degree of impatience in the longer term. Rather, it is the result of a tendency to pay too little attention to events, forgone opportunities, and changing circumstances within long stretches of anticipated time versus within smaller stretches of time.

Other models are more radical. One approach, consistent with the subjective evaluation of time differences discussed earlier, involves similarity models.[17] Similarity is based on the idea that sometimes the difference in payoffs or waiting times is not sharp. Either outcomes or delays may be regarded as "similar." For example, suppose an individual is faced with the option of $100 four years from now or $150 five years from now. While the individual may see a sharp difference between the amounts of money, she may see the delays as similar; $150 seems very different from $100, but four years does not seem that different from five years. If so, the similarity heuristic predicts that the individual will choose the larger amount. In calendar time, this is the LL reward. On the other hand, if the option is $100 today or $150 a year from today, the individual may see both differences as sharp; the difference between today and a year from now is very clear. In this case, the individual may choose the SS reward. In discounting language, she exhibits a seemingly higher rate of impatience in

Forgone opportunities that might not otherwise have been considered will be when the delay is more finely divided into subperiods.

[17] There are two main similarity models. In Rubinstein (2003) the individual first evaluates whether the amounts are similar and then evaluates whether the delays are similar. The method is lexicographic. Consider the standard choice between the smaller-sooner reward and the larger-later reward. If the answer to the amount-similarity question is "yes," then a "no" to the delay similarity question yields the smaller-sooner reward. If the answer to the amount question is "no," then a "yes" to the delay-similarity question yields the larger-later reward. If both the amounts and delays are similar, then she chooses according to some unspecified criterion. This could be standard exponential discounting. The text above follows the Rubinstein version. In Leland's (2002) model, if there is no determinate result on the similarity criteria, then the individual chooses randomly. When the similarity model yields a determinate prediction, it outperforms exponential discounting (the second-best predictor) as well as many variations of hyperbolic discounting in experimental results (Stevens 2016).

the shorter term than in the longer term. But the difference has nothing to do with discount rates. It is the result of a change from two dissimilar attributes in the earlier set of options to only one dissimilar attribute in the later set of options. The second choice does not necessarily reflect any affective difference; the difference is essentially a cognitive one. As the time horizon is pushed farther into the future, the range within which periods of calendar time are perceived as similar widens. Thus, the upfront one-year delay is more significant in terms of perception than the later one-year delay.

In principle, the similarity theory can also generate inverse preference reversals. If there is a clear dissimilarity between SS and LL in the less delayed frame but not much perceived difference in the times at which the rewards will be received, then the individual may choose LL. This can be seen as a willingness to wait in exchange for a certain amount of money per unit of time. If, in the more delayed frame, there is not much perceived difference between SS and LL, the individual may not be willing to wait. In fact, he may refuse to wait even though the trade-off between extra money and time is more favorable than in the less delayed frame.

Thus, as Rubinstein (2003) points out, much of the experimental evidence cited as support for hyperbolic discounting could equally well be interpreted as support for his similarity approach. Furthermore, Rubinstein has performed experiments that yield inverse preference reversals as described previously. Given the design of these experiments, these results can be explained by the similarity hypothesis but *not* by hyperbolic discounting.

The notion of similarity has been somewhat modified, or extended, by Manzini and Mariotti (2006). Their fundamental claim, supported by much psychological research, is that "the perception of events distant in time is in general 'blurred'" (Manzini and Mariotti 2009). Our ability to compare alternatives diminishes as the time horizon moves out. Therefore any intertemporal choice will have two components: traditional time preference *and* vagueness. The first is affective and the second is cognitive. As both options become more distant, intertemporal choice has less and less to do with standard time preference.

Options in the farther future may be difficult to distinguish in utility terms. In the vagueness theory (Manzini and Mariotti 2009), if individuals do not perceive a sufficiently large difference in utility to meaningfully distinguish between the options, a heuristic will be used to make the choice. The individual will simply choose either the reward that is sooner (one heuristic) or the reward that is larger (another heuristic). Since the utility of alternatives will be harder to distinguish when the decision concerns the more distant future, such decisions will tend to be a function of vagueness and the heuristic used, and not of time preference or time discounting. Instead of the standard preference reversal being interpreted as the result of more patient distant decisions, the vagueness theory suggests no such increasing patience or time-discounting inconsistency (Manzini and Mariotti 2009, 265).

The bottom line is that there is no good reason to privilege more distant (and more patient) rates of discounting if those rates are the result of a cognitive "bias." If someone chooses a larger reward between time t and $t + 1$ simply because they can't tell the difference between t and $t + 1$, then how can we say the inferred rate of discount is "better" or "more considered"? It is a rate of discount that's entirely a result of the individual's cognitive inability to distinguish between things. On the other hand, if we decide the agent's inability to distinguish distant time periods is normatively permissible – i.e., the agent is allowed to perceive time in this way – then we have preferences based on a vague predicate. As we saw in Chapter 3, specifically in the example of Jane's preference for a man with "a lot of hair," vagueness can generate an intransitive preference ordering. Therefore, the behavioral paternalist must either accept intransitive preferences or abandon the notion that more distant/patient rates of discounting are necessarily superior.

Intransitive Intertemporal Choices

In experiments performed by Roelofsma and Read (2000) in which subjects were asked to make pairwise comparisons of different amounts of money to be received at varying delays, more than half of the observed intertemporal choice patterns were intransitive, and 52 percent of subjects chose one of the intransitive choice rankings (p. 169). In this context, we do not mean the form of intransitivity associated with binary preference reversals such as those discussed previously (i.e., LL is preferred to SS when evaluated from one point in time, yet SS is preferred to LL when evaluated from another point in time). Here, we mean intransitivity among three or more objects of choice *even when evaluated at a single point in time* (i.e., *a* is preferred to *b* which is preferred to *c*, yet *c* is preferred to *a*).[18] While

---

[18] For example, Roelofsma and Read (2000, 163) asked subjects to rank the following four bundles, where the first component is the number of Dutch guilders and the second is the number of weeks' delay: (7, 1), (8, 2), (9, 4), and (10, 7). An intransitive pattern might

neither exponential nor quasi-hyperbolic discounting is compatible with intransitive choice patterns such as these, subadditive discounting, the similarity heuristic, and vague time preferences all are (Manzini and Mariotti 2009, 266–267).

Instead of looking at intransitive preferences such as these as the outcome of a breakdown in normative exponential discounting, we can understand them as resulting from people consistently pursuing reasonable rules or heuristics. Without the assertion of a norm of constant discounting, it is not clear why such behavior should be regarded as inconsistent at all. After all, if an individual continually and successfully applies the *same* *rule* in a series of choices, then the choices will all be consistent with that rule. To say that intransitive choices are not rational is, in the absence of showing that agents are demonstrably being harmed, simply to say that these choices are inconsistent with exponential discounting. But exponential discounting is merely a modeling norm, not a prescriptive one. There is nothing substantively irrational about following a particular rule unless the rule is somehow self-defeating. We turn to this question now.

Do Nonstandard Intertemporal Decision-Makers Suffer?

One of the difficulties in ascertaining whether individuals who display inconsistent time discounting, preference reversal, or intransitivities are harmed is the ambiguous nature of the standard of welfare. For example, persons with consistent but high rates of discount, *ceteris paribus*, will earn less income in their lifetimes than those who have consistent and low rates of discount. Any positive rate of time discount by definition involves the sacrifice of one dollar of future income for less than one dollar of present income.[19] Therefore, unless paternalists are willing to assert that zero discounting is the universally correct norm, maximization of lifetime earnings cannot be the appropriate standard. We can examine whether time-inconsistent agents earn less than time-consistent ones. But there is

---

have (7, 1) preferred to (8, 2) preferred to (9, 4) preferred to (10, 7), yet (10, 7) preferred to (7, 1).

[19] We are assuming, as is the practice in intertemporal trade-off experiments, that income is consumed when it is received. If a person could elect to receive the greater amount later and then borrow against this for present consumption, then she could maximize total lifetime income as long as there is someone else ready and willing to lend. But since the lending would presumably not be free (unless the lender had a perfectly coordinated preference for future consumption), there would still be some "penalty" for her positive time preference.

little direct evidence on the matter, and even if there were, it would not indicate who did better in terms of lifetime satisfaction of their goals. A pragmatic conception of rationality demands that the suspected "irrational" behavior be shown to have consequences deemed undesirable *by the agents themselves.*

Berg et al. (2010) survey the literature on the subject (which is very small) and do not find anything that sheds much light. In their own study of 881 participants, they find that time-inconsistent individuals earn substantially *more* than time-consistent ones across the forty time trade-off payoff options in the experiment. This is because the time-consistent individuals are, for whatever reason, *consistently more impatient* in the choices. Of course, this is not a *ceteris paribus* experiment. That would require comparing two groups of individuals with the same distant rate of discount (δ) but only one of which had present bias (β). However, if in the real world time-inconsistency is associated with other traits that increase performance, it would suggest that we do not fully understand the role of time inconsistency in decision-making. Along these lines, it is instructive to note that the time-inconsistent individuals also earned more on *risky* option decisions that had no time variation component, since they tended to be less risk-averse. Furthermore, in terms of this particular standard of performance, time-(in)consistency by itself is not sufficient to determine the consequences of behavior. Performance by this standard depends on the degree of impatience *overall*. Therefore, if time inconsistency is to be deemed irrational in more than a presumptive neoclassical sense, the comparison cannot be relative to just any time-consistent agent. It must be with a suitably patient time-consistent agent. Impatience *in whatever form* can depress lifetime earnings or wealth. Why single out inconsistency as the problem?

ENDOWMENT EFFECTS

Despite the pride of place the "endowment effect" has for some behavioral economists, its relevance to normative considerations is quite unclear. The experimentally observed phenomenon is really twofold: the gap between willingness to accept (WTA) and willingness to pay (WTP), and the consequent asymmetric willingness to trade (less willingness to trade what you already possess than to trade for what you do not). These are observed in many experiments. The normative implications are related to the cause of the gap, which has been in doubt for at least the last decade (Ericson and Fuster 2014). No judgment can be made about the rationality of the gap without knowing its cause.

In the neoclassical conception of economic rationality, there should be no WTA–WTP gap. Absent wealth effects, the maximum willingness to pay for something should be equal to the minimum willingness to accept payment for giving it up. However, in what sense is this symmetry an implication of rationality? Suppose that a person were willing to pay a maximum of $500 for a benefit she did not yet have. And suppose the same person were offered $501 to give up the same benefit and she refused. On the one hand, she is saying that the benefit is worth no more than $500; on the other hand, she is saying that it is worth more. This, as discussed in Chapter 3, is a primary violation of neoclassical rationality.

But is she really being inconsistent? This is where the causes of the phenomenon come into play. The abstract example as usually presented indicates that there are no other factors involved, except, of course, the mere possession of the benefit in the one case (WTA) and the absence of possession in the other (WTP). But wait. Then there *are* other factors involved in most or all cases; it's just that they are not regarded as normatively compelling. To understand this, and to see the confusion involved, we must take a look at the usual explanation for the gap phenomenon: loss aversion.

Loss Aversion as a Cause of Endowment Effects

In its original form, loss aversion is the idea that people value losses more than they value equal gains, with both losses and gains measured relative to their current position. The individual will therefore require more to give up a benefit they already have than they will pay to acquire it: WTA is greater than WTP. It is hard to see, however, what is "irrational" or even boundedly rational about this in itself. There are two valuations, but they are not, strictly speaking, inconsistent because the circumstances under which valuation is expressed in each case are different. These differences are regarded as unimportant by behavioral economists simply because loss aversion is inconsistent with *neoclassical rationality*.

The omission of loss aversion in standard theory makes good pragmatic sense primarily if the agents are under strong market pressure. When a loss of some benefit is not treated the same as a gain of that same benefit, the agent is not minimizing costs or maximizing gains. Suppose, for instance, that a firm were averse to losing a current revenue source due to a change in marketing tactics, even though the new marketing tactics would allow it to gain a new and greater revenue source. In perfect capital markets, such a firm would find itself the target of take-over agents who are not loss-averse.

Under standard neoclassical assumptions, the firm would be "irrational" to pursue this policy. And if it were pursued, the current decision-makers would accordingly be replaced. On the other hand, WTA–WTP gaps are typically identified in experimental conditions where strong market pressures are *not* present.[20] So why, in those circumstances, is such behavior less than rational? Loss aversion would then seem to be a taste variable no different from the nonpecuniary aspects of labor that economics has recognized from early on. Loss-averse agents happen to attach value to changes in wealth, with greater value attached to a loss than to the equivalent gain. Neither utility theory under certainty nor expected utility theory inherently specifies the carriers of value – these can be levels of wealth, changes in wealth, or something else entirely.[21]

Let us, nevertheless, assume for argument's sake that loss aversion is not characteristic of the fully rational agent; what then are the prescriptive implications?[22] A consistent application of the behavioral paternalist norm to move people in the direction of the standard neoclassical agent would mean that actual agents should end up in the same position in which they would find themselves if they were not loss-averse. But as we observed in Chapter 3, there would be more than one way to "fix" the loss-averse agent: by increasing their WTP, or by decreasing their WTA. Theory does not offer any particular reason to favor one over the other. Again for argument's sake, let us suppose that the higher value (WTA) is the "correct" valuation.[23] Now what follows?

To be more specific, suppose a worker would have willingly given up a maximum of $500 in wages (WTP) in exchange for better working conditions. Suppose the law nevertheless mandates these better working conditions (or mandates a default rule of better working conditions) and wages decline by $500. Now that the worker has these better working conditions, he perceives them as his starting point and won't give them up for less than $550 (WTA).

---

[20] Daniel Kahneman admits that the endowment effect is not present where there are strong market pressures *as well as* among the poor (2011, 297–298).

[21] Eyal Zamir (2014, 216–218) argues that loss aversion is not per se irrational, so policy ought to take it into account. In some cases this means that the law might possibly prevent "exploitation" of loss aversion by sellers who, for example, give the false impression that a product will not be available shortly when in fact it will. In this approach Zamir simply adds "loss aversion" to the tastes or characteristics that others might unjustly exploit.

[22] See, for example, Arlen et al. (2002). They describe the endowment effect as a departure from rationality.

[23] Hovenkamp (1991) argues that entitlements should be allocated to the party with the highest WTA in order to maximize wealth.

A behavioral paternalist might argue that the law has increased the worker's wealth because he now has something worth $550 that was previously worth only $500. But this argument is mistaken under loss-aversion theory, because the higher valuation attaches to the *giving up* of the endowed working conditions *and not the possession of them.*[24] Again: loss-averse agents attach utility to changes in wealth, not simply levels of wealth. Thus, in order for this utility value to be realized, individuals would have to give up the better working conditions, which of course is contrary to the purpose of the policy (and would actually reduce welfare rather than increasing it).[25]

Let us now suppose that there are other cases in which a behavioral economist would advocate use of the WTP norm in cost–benefit analysis. For example, in considering an anti-pollution law from a baseline of no regulation, the behavioral economist might believe that WTP has intuitive appeal.[26] However, this does not mean that she has now chosen the "rational" or bias-free norm. Behavioral economists argue that *both* WTA and WTP measures are distorted – in particular by framing and anchoring biases (Ariely et al. 2003; Kahneman et al. 1999). Should these manifestations of less-than-complete rationality be simply accepted? Or should the WTP measure be decontaminated? Presumably, we want to do the latter so as to adhere to the ideal of moving to outcomes that rational agents would desire. This requires quantitative estimates of each distortion in each context. Furthermore, it's worth noting that adopting WTP rather than WTA as the appropriate norm for "true" preferences would mean abandoning the case for many paternalist interventions, such as new labor-friendly default rules that offer workers additional contractual benefits. The alleged superiority of such rules rests on the implicit assumption that WTA is the right valuation.

Status Quo Bias as a Cause of Endowment Effects

Besides loss aversion, some have argued that status quo bias or inertia is either the primary cause or a main contributing cause of the WTA–WTP

---

[24] "[T]he main effect of endowment is not to enhance the appeal of the good one owns, only the pain of giving it up" (Kahneman et al. 1991, 197).

[25] Importantly, for cases such as the one discussed in the text, estimates of loss-aversion parameters from riskless choice do not exist. Furthermore, in risky choice there is also the matter of disentangling risk aversion (a conceded rational taste parameter) from loss aversion (a parameter of disputed normative status). See Ericson and Fuster (2014, 575).

[26] Obviously, the imposition of improved working conditions, as discussed previously, might be viewed as a gain from the original baseline. In that case the relevant norm is WTP. This is contrary to the paternalist rationale for employee-friendly regulation or defaults. It is not clear if there is a unique behavioral perspective here.

gap (Gilboa 2011, 23; Thaler 2015b, 154). Strictly speaking, status quo bias is not a mental preference for the existing endowment so much as a paralysis of choice – an unwillingness to take the better option and give up the inferior option already in one's possession. As such, it is more or less defined as "irrational." In actual cases where people seem to reveal a preference for what they have, there may be good reasons for this preference, such as greater information about the good possessed, transaction costs of trading, habit formation, and changes of tastes (Gilboa 2011, 24–27).

In any case, if status quo bias is the true explanation for the endowment effect, it casts doubt on the validity of paternalist nudges whose "sticking power" depends on it. Suppose a new default rule entitles workers to paid vacation time (presumably funded by lower wages). Now endowed with this new benefit, workers resist giving it up during contract negotiations. But why? Simply because the new rule is now the status quo. If status quo bias is indeed irrational, then the persistence of the new status quo offers no grounds for thinking the new rule is an improvement. To justify the new rule, behavioral paternalists need something other than status quo bias to explain the WTA–WTP gap.

Mere Ownership as a Cause of Endowment Effects

Finally, we consider the implications of a WTA–WTP gap explained by mere ownership. In this view, neither status quo bias nor loss aversion generates the gap. Instead, ownership in and of itself is sufficient to cause the individual to attach a higher value to something that he already owns (Morewedge et al. 2009). So here the actual having or possession of a good increases its value. Thus, if workers do not already have certain working conditions or benefits, they will value them more once they have them than when they are faced with the prospect of giving up wages to get them. There will be a WTA–WTP gap, not due to the excess pain of giving a benefit up (as with loss aversion) but from the positive increase in well-being the benefit confers. It might be thought, therefore, that mandating such benefits could increase value to the degree that the agent, for some reason, cannot anticipate that gain in formulating her WTP. However, if the mere ownership effect is deemed "irrational" or at least not normatively compelling, then to be consistent with the usual behavioral welfare standard, policymakers should *not* use it to justify mandates that create such a feeling of ownership.

On the other hand, it is hard to consider a true increase in value due to possession itself irrational. Possession or ownership may reflect important human values or lead to an association of the object with the individual's self-worth. If so, then once the agent possesses the object in question, WTA is the correct valuation. Any possible irrationality here is limited to the agent's failure to anticipate the jump in satisfaction that results from ownership. To our knowledge, the robustness and pervasiveness of this failure to anticipate has not been fully explored. But some experimental evidence does show that buyers who already own one unit of a good fully anticipate the ownership effect associated with the second unit (Morewedge et al. 2009, 949).

Contrary Evidence

It is often said that abundant evidence supports the existence of an "endowment effect." But what kind of evidence is it? Simply replicating previous studies is not additional evidence if those studies do not have adequate controls for confounding factors. It is important to remember that it is difficult to test a hypothesis without a fairly precise statement of what the hypothesis is. The hypothesis, as usually understood, is this: ownership alone is sufficient to affect willingness to trade and to accept payment (WTA). Stated in this way, the hypothesis does not distinguish among a number of plausible causes. In particular, it does not differentiate the *pure* ownership account discussed above from the conventional loss-aversion account, nor from status quo bias. In all of these cases the owner has a greater WTA than the nonowner's WTP, albeit for different reasons.

Plott and Zeiler (2005, 2007) test the endowment hypothesis by altering the standard experimental design to provide controls to eliminate defects in the elicitation process that might produce an illusory endowment effect. In other words, they seek to remove effects that are the result of experimental design rather than underlying behavior. They provide controls so as to provide incentives for subjects to report true valuations and to increase understanding of the valuation elicitation device. They also pay subjects for practice sessions and ensure anonymity to eliminate incentives to signal personal characteristics to others (e.g., the experimenters). In essence, they consider the union of all those factors that analysts have said might distort the experimental results. A representative outcome from their experimental work is:

The results strongly support the conclusion that experimental procedures have driven observed WTA–WTP gaps in price studies. When the procedures employed by Kahneman, Knetch, and Thaler [1991] were used, a statistically significant

WTA–WTP gap is observed. The median WTA was $4.50, whereas the median WTP was $1.50. When an incentive compatible mechanism was employed, training on the mechanism was provided, subjects engaged in paid practice rounds, and decisions were anonymous, all in an effort to control misperceptions, *no gap was observed.* Using these procedures, no statistically significant difference is observed. The median WTA was $5.00 and the median WTP was $5.00.

(Klass and Zeiler 2013, 38, emphasis added)

There has been argument and discussion about these results. Klass and Zeiler (2013, 46–53) review the discussion and answer criticisms. In our own view, their analysis constitutes a significant development in the growing realization that the previous experimental evidence on the endowment theory is inadequate.

Before concluding, it is also important to note that the experimental evidence we do have is for an "instant endowment effect." This means that the experimenters test for WTA–WTP gaps and reluctance to exchange within a few minutes after the subjects are given a mug or some other good (Ericson and Fuster 2014, 557). How these subjects react after they have possessed the good for some time (a day, week, month, or more) is unknown. Does the novelty of the gift wear off, or do they become more attached?[27] If they become more attached, what is the underlying causal basis? We simply do not know. In any real-world problem, it is unlikely that the opportunity to exchange or refuse to exchange would occur mere minutes after a gift or endowment.[28]

AFFECTIVE FORECASTING

In previous work (Rizzo and Whitman 2009b, 915–916, 929–931, 938–940) as well as earlier in this book, we have highlighted hot–cold empathy gaps and their use as a justification for cooling-off periods and waiting periods. But to examine empathy gaps more fully, we need to broaden our discussion to include affective forecasting. Affective forecasting refers to the individual's ability to predict their own affective (emotional) states under specific circumstances, such as how they will feel after suffering an injury, moving to a new city, acquiring a new possession, and

---

[27] We know of one study in which the period of ownership lasts more than a few minutes. In Strahilevitz and Loewenstein (1998) ownership lasts one hour. There seems to be an increased ownership-endowment effect in this study.

[28] An exception to this is arbitrage and some kinds of speculation. However, agents who engage in these activities are generally experienced traders who do not exhibit an endowment effect (List 2003, 2004, 2011).

so on. Hot–cold empathy gaps can be classified as a variety of affective misprediction, as they involve emotions affecting people's assessment of how much satisfaction or dissatisfaction will come from certain outcomes. Indeed, the *gap* in "empathy gap" technically refers to the difference between someone's anticipated satisfaction from something (when in a hot state) and the actual satisfaction from that thing (when in a cold state).

However, our interest in affective forecasting is not limited to empathy gaps. The idea that emotional individuals cannot think clearly about the consequences of decisions casts a general shroud of doubt over the reliability of individual decision-making, and thus lends support to privileging the judgment of experts instead. Concerns about poor forecasting can be used to justify a variety of paternalistic interventions. One example from securities law is the idea that "puffery" in prospectuses and other materials could have an emotional impact on potential investors, thus resulting in an inflated tendency to invest; the paternalistic solution would allow judges to consider not just the explicit information in such materials, but their likely emotional impact as well (Blumenthal 2005, 236).

Preferences can be technically biased if they are made on the basis of systematic misprediction of the relevant consequences. Our main discussion of alleged cognitive errors affecting beliefs will come in Chapter 5. But since the form of prediction involved here is self-prediction, that is, prediction about one's own future hedonic states and not about the external world, it seems best to discuss this separately.

The case of *impact bias* nicely illustrates some of the problems with analysis of affective forecasting in general. Impact bias is the tendency to overestimate the duration and intensity of positive or negative feelings in response to future events (e.g., Gilbert et al. 1998).[29] For example, people may overestimate the increase in the quality of life a renal transplant will bring, they may overestimate the unpleasant side effects of a drug, they may overestimate the happiness they will feel due to retirement, and so forth. In itself this might be of little consequence, but it has been claimed that accuracy in affective forecasting is a requirement of good decision-making (Loewenstein 2007). Clearly, however, this claim rests on the assumption that the decisions in question depend largely on hedonic consequences (as opposed to nonhedonic considerations) and also that the alternative courses of action are not all equally scaled up or down in hedonic terms. If faced with a decision to move to either Los Angeles or

---

[29] Sometimes the word "emotions" is used instead of feelings. In either case the impact bias involves conscious affective states directed toward certain events.

Chicago for a new job, the choice between the two options will not be affected by an equal overestimation of the hedonic consequences.

Despite a "substantial body of research [that has] examined . . . affective forecasts and has uncovered a variety of forecasting biases" (Wilson and Gilbert 2013, 740), the literature suffers from imprecision in a number of respects. These are not simply technical issues but affect whether the phenomenon in question should be considered a bias in either a technical or a consequential sense. The first problem is that in the experimental studies the *object* of affective forecasting is not always clear.

Impact Bias as Procedural Artifact?

The typical impact-bias experiment asks people "to imagine that an event has occurred and to rate how they will feel in general after a specified period of time. After the event has occurred and the period of time has elapsed, people are asked to rate how they feel in general without reference to the focal event" (Levine et al. 2013, 750). The problem should be clear. People are being asked how they *will* feel at a moment *where they are focusing on the particular forecasted event*, and then they are being asked how they actually do feel *in general* after the event occurs. Levine et al. (2012) hypothesize that the subjects interpret the first question as how they will feel *about the event itself* or while thinking about the event. And then they interpret the second question simply as how they feel *overall* after the event has occurred. Interpreting the questions this way makes a pseudo-impact bias almost a certainty. The emotional state of people's lives normally depends on more than the forecasted event, and thus some moderation of the specific event-related emotion is to be expected.

In a series of experiments as well as a meta-analysis of eighty-four previous studies, Levine et al. (2012) find that when ambiguity about the second question is eliminated, the impact-bias picture looks very different. First, explicit comparisons between predicted feelings about an event and realized feelings about that same event reveal "a high degree of accuracy" (2012, 15). Second, although they do not show a complete elimination of the impact bias, they do suggest that it is partly an artifactual consequence of a faulty experimental procedure.

Cognitive Feedback: Attention and Learning

The second critical problem with impact-bias analysis is that it assumes the main function of emotions is to constitute or reflect the value of outcomes.

From this assumption, it is a short step to analyzing affective forecasting errors solely in terms of nonoptimal decision-making. This is a mistake for at least two reasons. First, before there can be optimization there must be focused attention. Both current emotions and projections of future emotion have a role in focusing or getting the agent's attention. Second, the deviation of reward outcomes and their associated affective states from expectations is an important source of learning.

Focusing Attention. Optimization presupposes a limited world where preferences (objectives), alternative courses of action, and constraints are known and where, if there is uncertainty, it is reducible to risk. It is a world where the agent's problem is fully defined and all that remains is computation. In such a world, hedonic predictions serve mainly to facilitate the choice of an optimal course of action.

But where does the conception of the problem-situation itself come from? How does a person living in the real world ever come to cut his world down to size and represent a part of it as an optimization problem? This is where focus and attention play a crucial role. Exaggerated expectations of the hedonic value of a future event have a particular value in a world of uncertainty (Miloyan and Suddendorf 2015, 197). They heighten current emotions so as to direct the attention of the agent to an important matter (Lerner et al. 2015, 815).

The expectation of certain feelings (happiness, sadness, disgust, joy, and so forth) associated with a future event induces certain current emotions – whether conscious or not – that focus attention and place structure onto a problem situation. This attention is important "*before* you apply any kind of cost/benefit analysis to the premises, and before you reason toward the solution of the problem" (Damasio 1994, 173, emphasis in original). The process of structuring a problem involves at least these aspects:

1. Limitation of the information input to what is relevant;
2. Limitation of the inferences from that information to what is useful;
3. Reduction in the number of viable alternative courses of action;
4. Detection of the relevant components of future scenarios;
5. Categorization of factual knowledge into accessible types that enhance working memory.[30]

Furthermore, it is important to realize that although attention is directed toward something, it is also directed *away* from other issues and problems

[30] See Damasio (1994, 173–175, 197–198).

because the human capacity for attention is limited. In all of these ways, attention will produce a "stable playing field," or a stable conception of the problem situation. The emotions the agent experiences that are directed toward expected future states are thus not only markers for "the value of what is represented but also ... a booster for continued working memory and attention" (Damasio 1994, 198). In essence they make it possible to simplify a problem so that the agent can, at least in principle, apply cost–benefit reasoning in making her decision.[31]

Returning to the impact bias, we can now see the function of the asymmetry between the anticipated feelings and the actual feelings after the event has occurred. The anticipated emotion needs to be strong to generate attention and structuring. It must also take attention away from other problems. Once that function has been accomplished, the "exaggerated" effect can wear off and the agent can begin to adapt to her circumstances (Kwong et al. 2013, 44).

Learning from Falsified Expectations. The general lesson from "blocking experiments" (Tobler et al. 2006) is that associative learning does not occur without the falsification of hedonic expectations. The basic experimental design is straightforward. Suppose in pre-training of subjects, stimulus A is associated with a juice reward and B is not. Now take the unrelated stimuli X and Y, which are not associated with a reward individually, and pair them as follows: AX with a reward and BY with a reward. Blocking experiments show *no* increase in X's perceived pleasantness. This is because the reward *was expected* from its association with A; there is no added information. Learning is not a function of the mere association of a stimulus with a reward. On the other hand, when B and Y are paired and a reward is given there is an increase in Y's perceived pleasantness. This is because no reward was expected with B; there is thus a marginal increase in information. This *ex post* increase in information is the result of an *error* in the prediction of the reward, as the subject had not expected that B would not be accompanied by a reward. Learning is a function of the *unexpected* association of a stimulus and a reward. Thus the underestimation of

---

[31] "Assume all the powers already listed – logic, induction, and more than encyclopaedic knowledge: the philosophers' frame problem, roughly, is how to make use of just what we need from the vast store, and how not to retrieve what we don't need" (de Sousa 1987, 193). Further, de Sousa advances what he calls "New Biological Hypothesis 1," that is, "[t]he function of emotions is to fill gaps left by (mere wanting plus) 'pure reason' in the determination of action and belief, by mimicking the encapsulation of perception: it is one of Nature's ways of dealing with the philosophers' frame problem" (p. 195).

hedonic rewards increases the individual's ultimate learning about the hedonic value of a stimulus.

There can also be negative prediction errors when an expected reward is not given. In the previous example, if the pair *AX* for which a juice reward is expected is not followed by a reward, there will be a prediction error. The increase in pleasantness of *X* as a result of its association with A will become less and less until it is gone. Thus the overestimation of the hedonic reward ultimately results in learning that there is no reward. In each of these cases – positive and negative prediction errors – there is learning. Importantly, *when there are no prediction errors, there is no associative learning.*[32]

Falsified Expectations of Regret. Whether a person succeeds in attaining his goals or not, he may over- or underestimate how he will feel then. In particular, when individuals fail to achieve what they wanted or expected, they may feel regret or disappointment. Sometimes they will overestimate today how much regret they will have if they experience a failure tomorrow. On the other hand, perhaps surprisingly, after the satisfaction of attaining a goal wears off, they may feel regret that they did not strive for an even better but more difficult goal. In this case they may underestimate today how much regret they will feel if they succeed tomorrow. Does this misestimation of regret perform some learning function?

It is important, as we have seen, to clarify the object of an emotion. In experiments subjects were asked about their projected disappointment and regret in the event of an unsuccessful outcome, and then again after the unsuccessful outcome was revealed (Kwong et al. 2013). In these cases of failure people predicted more regret than they actually felt afterwards. They directed their exaggerated regret prediction toward *the means used* to achieve their goals.[33] They said, in effect, "I will regret not having tried hard enough or not having taken the right steps." This excess projected regret functions as motivation – at the outset of the attempt to attain a goal – to reevaluate the means used or to redouble one's efforts. In effect, it

---

[32] "Specifically, if the reward is better than predicted (positive prediction error), which is what we all want, the prediction becomes better and we will do more of the behavior that resulted in that reward. If the reward is worse than predicted (negative prediction error), which nobody wants, the prediction becomes worse and we will avoid this the next time around. In both cases, our prediction and behavior changes; we are learning. By contrast, if the reward is exactly as predicted (blue), there is no prediction error, and we keep our prediction and behavior unchanged; we learn nothing" (Schultz 2016, 24).

[33] Their predictions about regret with respect to outcomes, however, were fairly accurate.

can help to ensure that the most efficient means are used. In a world of uncertainty and complexity, overestimation can function as an attention-inducing and learning mechanism.

On the other hand, when the individual attains the same-as-expected or even better-than-expected outcomes, misestimated regret is directed toward *the goals themselves*. In this case, the individual underestimates the regret he will feel. The higher regret after success has the function of motivating the search for higher goals in the future.

It should be easy to see now that the traditional treatment of hedonic misprediction is one-sided and superficial. It does not recognize the logically and psychologically prior role of emotions and expectations of feelings in structuring a problem for decision-making. It assumes that the structure is just there or is obvious. It also confuses the expectation of *hedonic states* associated with a future event with the *whole value* of the event to the individual. Sometimes people want to do or avoid something for reasons that go beyond hedonic states, such as moral values or aspirational life goals.[34] When we examine the affective forecasting errors involved in impact bias, from the perspective outlined here, we can understand the epistemic function these errors serve. They promote learning both about the world and about the individual himself. Even if the errors produce some degree of static suboptimality with respect to decisions – after framing, learning, and structuring is accomplished – it is clear that trying to "debias" these decisions would short-circuit important decision-making processes.

CONCLUSIONS

In this chapter we have shown that the phenomena known as "preference biases" are far more complex than they are often portrayed to be. Sometimes more penetrating analysis shows that the evidence for their existence is weak. Other times they are (at least partially) artifacts of imprecise or misdirected questioning of subjects. And yet other times, evidence suggests they may function as adaptations to a broader set of behavioral and environmental factors than are normally considered.

Even more importantly, the normative analysis of biases is often arbitrary. Biases are typically demonstrated by showing inconsistencies in preferences and then choosing one set as normative. But alleging

---

[34] It is important to distinguish between feelings as constitutive of value and feelings as signals of other kinds of value. Simply because people may pay attention to the feelings produced by outcomes does not mean that such feelings are their exclusive concern.

inconsistencies does not in itself enable us to say which preferences are normative – particularly when other behavioral factors play a role in generating the behavior in question. For example, there is good evidence to suggest that both short- and long-run discount rates are "contaminated" and therefore neither has a clearly better claim to superiority. Or, as we'd rather say, *neither is contaminated; they just are what they are.* Agents do not typically exhibit pure neoclassical preferences. And this is not obviously a bad thing. In the real world, agents need not be worse off by their own lights when their behavior exhibits what outside observers would regard as bias.

5

The Rationality of Beliefs

Well done is better than well said.
—Benjamin Franklin, *Poor Richard's Almanack*

Human beliefs, like all other natural growths, elude the barriers of system.
—George Eliot, *Silas Marner*

In Chapters 3 and 4 we focused on the rationality of preferences. We now turn our attention to the rationality of beliefs, including the rationality of inference and learning. Since most inference decisions occur outside of a closed world of certainty, this will open up our analysis to decision-making under risk and uncertainty.

In our discussion of preferences, the overriding theme was that preferences need not conform to rigid models. We should countenance a much wider range of preferences, in both form and content, than economists have been inclined to accept. But does the same permissive attitude apply to beliefs? Preferences, after all, are creatures of the individual mind, subjective and idiosyncratic by their very nature. Beliefs, on the other hand, are *about the world*. They are either true or false. Surely, then, beliefs ought to be held to a stricter standard of rationality. Among other things, it seems obvious that beliefs should conform to basic rules of logic and probability, including Bayes' theorem.

Nevertheless, we will argue for a more permissive attitude towards beliefs. Much like our position on preferences, our position on beliefs is that economists, and to a lesser extent other social scientists, have become slaves to an exceedingly narrow conception of both the *function* and *operation* of beliefs. That conception reflects the desire for universally applicable and context-free modes of thought, rather than pragmatic tools that have evolved for specific circumstances and specific purposes.

In Chapter 3, we observed that it can be difficult to distinguish violations of preference axioms (completeness and transitivity) from violations of the rational-choice assumption. Violations of the former are easier to justify than the latter. Recognizing this, some behavioral paternalists now downplay concerns about nonstandard preferences and focus increased attention on errors in reasoning and information processing. Bernheim and Rangel, for example, propose a framework that would, among other things, "seek evidence that particular choices involve errors in processing factual information; we propose classifying those choices as 'mistakes' and excluding them from consideration" (Bernheim 2009, 293; see also Bernheim and Rangel 2007). In other words, as behavioral paternalism has evolved, it has come to rely increasingly on challenges to the rationality of beliefs rather than preferences.

To maximize the relevance to our ultimate task of evaluating paternalist policies based on behavioral economics, we will focus on some of the major cognitive "biases" of belief, inference, and learning that have been found in the literature. We need to look at these biases in considerable detail to evaluate their contextual or ecological rationality. The task is not an easy one because it involves going beyond the simple attractive parables that have been accepted by many behavioral economists as established facts. We question the existence, extent, and meaning of major cognitive biases. Our primary claim is that the standards by which certain cognitive behaviors have been labeled "biased" are inappropriate as criteria of rationality. Furthermore, the biases themselves are sometimes not clearly defined. Thus, it is often difficult to determine whether an alleged bias even exists.

We should note that not all of the alleged biases we address in this chapter have been deployed to justify specific paternalistic policies (yet). But they are relevant because challenging the ability of regular people to form and update rational beliefs has contributed to the general case against the efficacy of individual decision-making – and thus the case for corrective intervention.

As we saw in previous chapters, the historical development of criteria for rationality under certainty was mainly directed toward analytic concerns – specifically, how to put choice theory on a firm theoretical foundation. By contrast, when it came to the theory of rational choice under risk (subjective expected utility theory) and rational learning (Bayesian updating), the original concerns were not clearly identified as positive or normative (Anand 1995, 11). Early work by Allais (1953) cast doubt on the descriptive accuracy of subjective expected utility theory. However, it was not until Savage (1954) that the positive and normative aspects of the theory were clearly distinguished. In the past few decades, as time has passed and more and more positive violations have been discovered, economists have placed increasing emphasis on the normative status of expected utility theory (and the axioms and assumptions on which it is built).

The desirability of acting like an expected utility maximizer and Bayesian updater depends, from a pragmatic perspective, on showing that failure to do so will result in bad consequences to decision-makers from their own point of view. The establishment of these criteria as universal criteria for rationality of beliefs and choice under uncertainty will depend on whether, in the general or standard case, it can be shown that agents can better achieve their goals using this framework for decision-making and learning than not. We claim that this is not so.

THE FUNCTIONS OF BELIEFS AND LEARNING

In a pragmatic – and specifically economic – framework, the function of knowledge and learning is a derived one. Beliefs have a function. This function varies with the goals and constraints of the individual. The tools that people use to understand the world are and should be context-dependent.

The dominant assumption in economic theory, rarely stated explicitly, is that *beliefs are about truth-tracking*. In other words, the function of beliefs is simply to reflect the facts of the world as accurately as possible. Truth is instrumentally valuable because it guides decision-making. In the standard model, any divergence between one's beliefs and the truth has the potential to generate suboptimal decisions. Thus, correspondence with external truth is the sole criterion for rationality of beliefs.

We challenge the idea that the sole function of beliefs is truth-tracking. Beliefs can serve other functions. One such function, discussed extensively in Chapter 4, is focusing of attention on important matters that require cognitive attention. Relatedly, beliefs can provide a source of motivation to accomplish certain goals. Such beliefs are rarely stated explicitly in economic models as probability values or functions; instead, they are implicit in the values given to other things, such as the utility or disutility attached to certain outcomes (e.g., moving to Chicago or losing a limb), which is why we included them in our discussion of preference rationality instead of here.

Optimistic Beliefs

Evidence of the motivational value of beliefs comes from the literature showing that individuals with "optimism bias" – i.e., unrealistically positive beliefs about the future – actually tend to have higher rates of success in life on various measures. Sharot offers a survey of literature, which has shown that "other things equal, optimists tend to live longer and be healthier," to have longer survival times for HIV and cancer, and to "work harder and longer hours, which may account for their higher pay" (2011, R944, citing Puri and Robertson 2007). Varki (2009), among others, argues that optimistic illusions may have had adaptive value for early humans because it counterbalanced the fear of death and oblivion that came with the emergence of conscious foresight. In short, the "best" beliefs for attention, motivational, and even survival purposes may not be the most correct from the standpoint of truth.

Even when overoptimism appears to serve no offsetting function as in the previous discussion, it can be directly utility enhancing. This is an essential element in the theory of "optimal expectations" (Brunnermeier and Parker 2005). There is anticipatory utility associated with optimistic expectations. People like looking forward to good things and successes. Optimal expectations are "a set of subjective probabilities ... that maximize well-being" (Brunnermeier and Parker 2005, 1096). However, well-being is not maximized by ignoring the behavioral distortions (savings, investment) that will occur if expectations are not rational in the technical sense of consistency with objective probabilities. There are costs to fooling oneself. There is a trade-off between gains in anticipatory utility and the costs of behavioral distortion.

Is it *irrational* to hold beliefs for the satisfaction they provide even if there are costs? From the standpoint of inclusive rationality, it is not. We do not have grounds for dictating the kind of things people may have preferences about or even the costs that they are willing to incur to indulge them.

RATIONAL IRRATIONALITY

Going a step further, any kind of belief – not just an optimistic one – may provide someone with direct satisfaction; they make the person who believes them feel good in some way. Bryan Caplan (2000) dubs this phenomenon *rational irrationality* – a seemingly oxymoronic term that plays on the competing definitions of rationality. As Caplan puts it, "[i]f silly beliefs make you feel better, maybe the stickler for objectivity is the real fool. But this is why the term *rational irrationality* is apt: Beliefs that are irrational from the standpoint of truth-seeking are rational from the standpoint of individual utility maximization" (2000, 141).

Caplan argues that rationally irrational agents nevertheless respond to incentives. In other words, people will tend to indulge their cognitive biases less when the personal cost is high, and more when the personal cost is low. In the presence of weak incentives – i.e., minimal consequences from holding a false belief – the belief will be maintained, but greater consequences will tend to weaken it.

To expand the argument slightly, some beliefs may persist not because the agent strongly prefers that belief, but because *changing* one's beliefs – and doing so accurately – requires cognitive effort. Normal people often prefer not to exert effort. Just as with direct preferences for beliefs, preferences for not updating beliefs should also respond to incentives: greater consequences will tend to weaken resistance to updating unjustified beliefs. We should also note that in Caplan's model, the process by which beliefs get revised in the appropriate direction is essentially a "black box"; the mechanism is not specified. We believe the mechanism *could* involve adopting a more neoclassically rational means of updating beliefs based on full information – but not necessarily, because as we shall see, sometimes fast-and-frugal heuristics can actually outperform the neoclassical model.

Rational irrationality dovetails with our pragmatic perspective on beliefs. A pragmatically rational individual would not apply the same rules for formation and revision of beliefs regardless of context. Different contexts will create different consequences, and thus differing incentives for inference and learning. Again, the tools of rationality are context-dependent. (Rational irrationality will also play a key role in Chapter 8, on political economy, as the political sphere offers individuals notably weak incentives for correcting their cognitive biases.)

With these broader considerations in mind, we will now address some of the most prominent challenges to the rationality of beliefs.

RATIONAL VIOLATIONS OF CLASSICAL LOGIC

In everyday speech a person may say a particular statement is "logical" and mean that it makes sense or that, on the whole, it is reasonable to believe it. But the colloquial use of the terms "logic" and "logical" is too broad to be useful. Today, most philosophers think of logic as a narrower aspect of the reasoning process (Harman 2004, 46). Logic refers to the theory of implication and consistency among properties of propositions. When we make an argument, we may use logic to connect the propositions. When we construct a proof, we use logic but not necessarily in the traditional syllogistic fashion. As in geometry, we might construct a proof backwards – from conclusion to premise.

What happens when one belief implies a further statement? Must the agent submit to logic and believe the implied statement? Not necessarily and certainly not generally. The individual may find that the implied statement is completely implausible and therefore decide to reject the initial premise. This occurs often and is good reasoning. The rules of logic are constraints on the relation between propositions. They do not tell people what to believe, pure and simple. Thus, logic is not the whole of reason.

From a pragmatic perspective, the case for limiting the role of logic is even stronger. It is *uneconomic* for the agent who wants to attain his goals efficiently to worry about the consistency of all of his beliefs.[1] The inconsistency of an entire system of beliefs is likely to be vast. Most of the inconsistencies will also probably be irrelevant to the attainment of specific goals. As beliefs change, more inconsistencies may be added. Furthermore, no agent can be deductively thorough; that is, no agent can afford to draw out (logically) all of the implications of all the statements in which he believes. Much less can they all be kept in mind at the same time. Furthermore, an individual may have no *practical* reason to care whether a certain statement is true, is consistent with other beliefs, follows necessarily from certain premises, and so forth. The rules of logic are *constitutive* of a certain kind of argument or proof. It remains to be seen if that kind of mental operation is useful and appropriate in a given context. Thus, it remains to be seen whether it has prescriptive content.[2]

Logical Equivalence versus Informational Equivalence

Let us consider again Burkett's definition of framing invariance, which we previously considered in Chapter 3: "Neoclassical economists assume that all informationally equivalent descriptions of alternatives elicit identical choices" (2006, 140). Aside from the concerns we raised in Chapter 4, there is a question about the meaning of "informationally equivalent descriptions." As applied, it appears to mean logical equivalence. Two statements are logically equivalent if each can be derived from the other through logical deduction.

---

[1] On the role of economic considerations in rationality, see Rescher (1988, 1–18).

[2] The rules of inference "are rules that proofs must satisfy; not rules for reasoners to follow" (Harman 2004, 47).

But abstract logical criteria are not sufficient to understand real-world behavior. Logically equivalent statements used outside of logic classes or logic textbooks do not necessarily have the same semantic content. There may be "information leakage" from the selection of the particular frame which, in turn, can be received by those who interpret the frame (Sher and McKenzie 2006).

The act of selecting or interpreting a frame is logically prior to evaluation and choice. The frame can potentially convey implicit information that is relevant to the decision at hand.[3] Consider the description of a medical treatment. It can be offered to a patient as one that has a survival rate of p or a mortality rate of $(1 - p)$. Assuming that all the patient cares about is survival, does either of these logically equivalent statements convey different information – i.e., are they informationally equivalent? In normal everyday contexts, it appears that they are not. McKenzie and Nelson (2003) show that people select and interpret the different logically equivalent formulations when they are implicitly comparing the result to some norm or expected result. The p-description is more likely when the framer is conveying that the survival data is better than might be expected, that it may be better still if certain structural features in the world have changed, or that there is reason to believe that in the case at hand the degree of belief in a successful result is greater than the statistical frequency.[4] The selection of frame thus contains an informational message.[5]

Now, it is of course possible that the sender (whoever frames the decision) may inadvertently send an unintended message, or that the

---

[3] What we are discussing here often goes under the name "conversational implicature" and is associated with the philosopher Paul Grice. "Conversational implicatures are, roughly, things that a hearer can work out from the *ways* something was said rather than *what* was said" (Grandy and Warner 2017, 4).

[4] On the last point, Gigerenzer has emphasized the inappropriateness of simply applying relative frequencies to a single case (2002, 246–247).

[5] It would be a mistake to think that these considerations of communication and information transmission through frames are only important in the social sciences or perhaps in their less developed forms. In physics, as well, the frame is important. Two theories may yield, through deductions from their axioms or other assumptions, exactly the same empirical predictions. From a certain perspective they are equivalent theories. Yet the scientist may wish to keep both of them in his head because each, framed in its unique way, has the ability to suggest different new ideas. Richard Feynman stressed just this point: "So two theories [A and B] ... may be mathematically identical ... However, for psychological reasons, in order to guess new theories, these two things [A and B] may be very far from equivalent, because one gives a man different ideas from the other. By putting a theory in a certain kind of framework you get an idea of what to change.... [I]n theory A ... you will say, 'I'll change that idea in here.' But to find out what the corresponding thing is that you are going to change in [theory] B may be very complicated ... In other words, although they are identical before they are changed, there

receiver may infer the wrong message. But there is nothing irrational per se about this process. Inferring information from the way people present things is a natural and reasonable human behavior. Indeed, those who fail to do so will often be considered deficient. When a man asks his wife if he can go out drinking with his friends tonight, and she replies with a flat "Yeah, do whatever you want," he would be a fool to focus exclusively on the logical implications of that statement.

Wason Selection Test: Confirmation Bias?

The Wason selection test (Wason 1966) is a famous test of the ability of agents to think in terms of classical logic. In its original form, it was not connected to any pragmatic consideration; it was simply a test of the rules of "material implication." If that sounds unfamiliar to the reader, it is because it refers to the logic of conditional statements that have no relation to causality or other forms of explanation. Normally, if we say something such as, "If Mary is driving her car, she will be late," most people will think of the first part of this statement as bearing some causal or otherwise explanatory connection with the second part. This is not what is going on with material implication. The world of material implication is a rather austere world of abstract relations.[6]

Imagine four cards with two sides each, but the experimental subject can see only one side.[7] The subject is asked which cards need to be turned over to test the truth of the following rule:[8] *If there is a vowel on one side of the card, then there is an even number on the other side of the card.* Let the four cards display: *A* (vowel), *T* (consonant), *4* (even number), and *7* (odd number). Think about it before you read further.

The card that most obviously must be turned over is *A*. If there is not an even number on the other side, the rule is falsified. Less obviously, the only

---

are certain ways of changing one which look natural which will not look natural in the other" (1965, 168).

[6] "The deductive reasoning paradigm is focused on logical arguments ... To be scored as correct, participants in these experiments must assume the premises to be true, base their reasoning only on the premises (introducing no prior knowledge) and declare or produce as valid conclusions only statements which cannot logically be false given the premises. They must also accept the logician's interpretation of words in the English language such as *some, if, or,* and *not,* regardless of how such words are used in ordinary discourse" (Evans 2002, 979).

[7] In the selection task the subjects never get to turn over the cards. So they never see the other side.

[8] In other words, "only those cards needed" – the cards that are individually necessary and jointly sufficient to determine whether the statement is true for the cards presented.

other card that needs to be turned over is 7, because if a vowel appears on the other side the rule is again falsified. The other cards are irrelevant. We do not care what is on the other side of *T* – any letter or number is consistent with the rule. Similarly, the rule does not preclude a consonant or a number on the other side of *4*.[9]

If you got the wrong answers, don't worry: only 10 percent of university students got them both correct. The most common response was that the *A* card and the *4* card needed to be turned over. Each of these responses indicates a concern with *confirming* the rule, rather than with falsifying the rule as the logic of the problem seems to require. The putative mistake is called *confirmation bias*.[10] In trying to confirm the rule, the subjects seem to forget that even though a vowel on the other side of the *4* card would be consistent with the rule, the rule does not require a card with an even number to have a vowel. In general, it is not confirmatory instances that "prove the rule" but the absence of disconfirmations or falsifications. In the aftermath of the initial Wason test, it seemed as if the subjects were irrational. Wason and others equated lack of competence in abstract deductive reasoning with irrationality.

However, this result bears no obvious relationship to the fundamental question of pragmatic rationality: do people efficiently attain their goals? It is one thing for subjects in the role of disinterested observers (who have not taken logic classes) to get the answers to this abstract reasoning problem wrong. It is quite another thing to argue that this performance in the laboratory suggests problems with real-world decision-making where the issue is concrete and the individuals have at least a hypothetical interest in the outcome.

Gigerenzer and Hug (1992) adapted the selection task in a way that shows pragmatic reasoning is not necessarily concerned with abstractions. Suppose that subjects are given a rule: *if a previous employee gets a pension from a firm, then that person must have worked for the firm for at least ten years.* The subjects are divided into two classes. One is told to take the perspective of the employee, the other the perspective of the firm. Both groups are assigned to determine whether the rule has been violated. The subjects are given four cards, each representing one worker. The cards are labeled "got a pension," "worked ten years for the firm," "did not get a pension," and "worked eight years for the firm."

---

[9] This is true unless, of course, the subject interprets the "if" in the conditional as "if and only if" (the bi-conditional). In that case *all* of the cards would have to be turned over. In everyday life the context often makes the meaning clear.

[10] This is different from the kind of confirmation bias that refers to the tendency to seek verification and avoid falsification of one's preexisting beliefs.

From the standpoint of strict logic, the subjects should turn over "got a pension" and "worked eight years for the firm," as these are the only cards that could potentially reveal a rule violation. The subjects' assigned roles should not matter. But the actual results showed a difference. Those assigned to the employer role chose the logically correct cards by a margin of 70 percent to 0 percent, while those assigned to the employee role chose the other cards ("worked ten years for the firm" and "did not get a pension") by a margin of 64 percent to 11 percent.[11]

Why should the assigned roles make a difference? If the subjects were fully logical, or even similarly illogical, they would not. The assigned social roles seemingly triggered subjects to think in terms of detecting *cheating*. Cheating presupposes a "social contract" or economic exchange. This contract has two aspects: if I give you this, you give me that, *and* if I give you that, you give me this. Gigerenzer and Hug suggest that the statement of the rule in conjunction with the assignment of social roles activates a specific cognitive mechanism that informs economic transactions, among other kinds of social exchange.[12]

For the employer, the relevant cases for determining whether they have been cheated just happen to be correct from the perspective of the disinterested logician-observer. From the perspective of the employee, the other two cases are relevant. Both parties, however, are interested in whether their side has been denied a benefit despite incurring the cost, and also whether the other side has received a benefit without incurring the cost. For the employee the benefit is the pension and the cost is the work; for the employer the benefit is the work performed and the cost is the pension. Thus the same analysis predicts each party's behavior.[13] These results also conform to our pragmatic perspective on agent rationality, inasmuch as the parties attend to their respective interests. Whether classical logic is relevant to those interests depends on each party's particular situation.

Nonmonotonicity

Ordinary logic is monotonic. This means that deductive inference is "truth preserving." You cannot lose what you previously knew by engaging in the

---

[11] The percentages don't add up to 100 percent because those subjects who responded with any other pair are excluded.

[12] For an in-depth analysis of these issues from the perspective in the text see Fiddick et al. (2000).

[13] There were two other similar tests with the same result (Gigerenzer and Hug 1992, 19–24).

application of deductive reasoning. You can never unlearn something. Consider the following (Evans 2002, 983):

> If Ruth has an essay deadline to meet, she will work late in the library.
> Ruth has an essay deadline to meet.

Will Ruth work late in the library? Yes, or at least so we must conclude from what we have been given. Now suppose that the "test" is changed, and we are told:

> If Ruth has an essay deadline to meet, she will work late in the library.
> *If the library stays open, Ruth will work late in the library.*
> Ruth has an essay deadline to meet.

Is the new italicized statement simply a distraction? Is it irrelevant to the original inference? In an exclusively deductive universe, the italicized statement should be ignored. Nothing can be made of it by classical logic. It simply dangles there. We must conclude that Ruth will work late in the library.

But intuitively, that seems quite wrong. And it is, because monotonic logic is not the appropriate tool in the context. Ordinary people know it. What has gone wrong here is that the additional premise *suggests* additional possibilities. If the library does not stay open, she will not be able to stay. There is a possible constraint that the original syllogism did not mention. The inference of the original syllogism is now viewed as defeasible, and the purely deductive framework has been shattered. Therefore, in the new context, it would not be rational to insist, based on the rules of classical logic, on the original conclusion. Reason is more than logic.

This example also shows the limitations of classical logic in an open system that continually generates new data or evidence. Nothing scientific can be known with certainty precisely because the system is never closed, never complete. Therefore, the necessity with which a statement follows from other statements is an aspect of the relationship among propositions. It does not mean that the agent must *hold* the statement with certainty.[14]

---

[14] "It is one thing to say '*A*, *B*, and *C* imply *D*.' It is quite another thing to say, 'If you believe *A*, *B* and *C*, you should or may infer *D*.' The first of these remarks is a remark about implication. The second is a remark about inference ... Furthermore, a person who believes *A*, *B*, and *C* and realizes that *A*, *B*, and *C* imply *D* may also believe for very good reason that *D* is false. Such a person may now have a reason to stop believing one of *A*, *B*, or *C* rather than a reason to believe *D*" (Harman 2002, 173–175).

Wason Selection Test as Maximizing Expected Information Gain

In everyday life, premises and their deductive conclusions are only as useful as the truth of those premises. Although a conclusion may be validly deduced from false premises, this validity will normally not be of much use to the individual if the conclusion is false. Similarly, as we have seen, the statement that Ruth will study late in the library is a defeasible conclusion, as other factors may interfere. Therefore, it seems entirely reasonable from a pragmatic perspective that an individual will interpret the conditional more loosely: if Ruth has an essay deadline to meet, she is *likely* to study late in the library. Once this is admitted as a plausible interpretation of a conditional statement in everyday life, we can return to the Wason test and see that the traditional analysis has little to do with rationality outside of a logic class.[15]

Consider the familiar conditional hypothesis: if x is a swan, then x is white (Oaksford and Chater 2009, 78). First, let's treat this in the classic Wason manner – as a problem of falsifying a universal statement – and imagine four cards with words on them: *swan, not-swan bird, white,* and *not-white.* We can restate the rule: If *swan* is on one side of the card, then *white* is on the other. Turning over the cards *swan* and *not-white* is sufficient and necessary to test the conditional. But in cases such as this, people often turn over the *swan* and *white* cards. This is generally considered incorrect, but as we shall see, these *can* be the correct cards to turn over.

Take another look at the Wason selection test when the subjects construe the problem in an uncertain, or at least probabilistic, world.[16] It then becomes a problem of maximizing expected information gain (Oaksford and Chater 1996, 2009; McKenzie 2003). In the spirit of economizing on decision resources, subjects choose those cards to turn over that they *expect* will give them the most information bang for their efforts.

---

[15] For a discussion of why everyday reasoning is apt to be probabilistic (or at least defeasible) rather than strictly logical, see Chater and Oaksford (1999). More generally, they describe their method as "trying to explain cognitive performance in the laboratory in terms of the adaptive function of cognitive mechanisms in the real world" (p. 193).

[16] We do not mean to suggest that uncertainty can always be adequately handled by probability theory or even that in this case it is best handled by probability theory. See Politzer and Bonnefon (2009) for a discussion of this issue in the context of the information-gain approach. We are simply looking at this approach as an alternative *reasonable* framework that shows there is nothing hard and fast about the logicist solution in an open world.

An example will help us. We construe the initial rule as a conditional probability $P(white|swan)$, that is, the probability of x being white given that it is a swan. The conditional probability is assumed to be very high – let us say 0.9. This captures the spirit of the general rule in an uncertain world. We call this conditional probability the *dependence hypothesis* (H_D). It is labeled "dependence" because it states that the (high) probability a bird is white is dependent on the bird in question being a swan.

Now imagine an alternative possibility in which the conditional probability $P(white|swan)$ is equal to the base rate $P(white)$, that is, the probability of finding a white bird in the overall population. This means that the probability that a bird is white is independent of whether it is a swan or not. Let this equal 0.1 (that is, 10 percent of birds are white). This conditional probability is the *independence hypothesis* (H_I). A swan is no more or less likely to be white than is any other bird. In addition, the proportion of swans among birds is low; for illustration, suppose that the base rate probability of swans is 0.01 (that is, 1 percent of birds are swans).

The subject does not know which hypothesis is true and initially considers them equally likely. Thus, the subject considers it equally likely that whiteness is dependent or independent of swan-ness.

Notice what has happened here. The subject is not engaged in falsifying the rule. *It cannot be falsified by finding an exception.* After all, an exception is perfectly consistent with either hypothesis. Since we are confined to the sample of four cards by the nature of the experiment, the most the subject can do is choose between the alternative hypotheses before her.

Our subject must make her decisions as to which cards must be turned over with an eye to maximum *expected* information *gain*. The basic principles of expected information gain are quite intuitive. First, think of information gain as the difference between the prior uncertainty (measured by probability) and the posterior uncertainty about a hypothesis after turning over a card. The updating is performed using Bayes' theorem. Second, the expectation of information gain is the sum of the gains produced by the two possible card results (say *white* or *not-white* on the other side of *swan*), weighted by their probability of occurrence.

It turns out that for a wide range of parameters (including those we've chosen here), the subject's best choice is to turn over cards labeled *swan* and *white*, not *swan* and *not-white* as required by deductive logic. Rather than getting lost in the mathematics, we will make the intuitive argument. The argument turns on the relative rarity of both swans and white birds. When faced with a card that says *swan*, the subject has a great opportunity to test the hypotheses. Under the dependence hypothesis, the probability of seeing white is very high (0.9). On the independence hypothesis, it is low (only 0.1). Seeing white would be highly informative; it would shift the posterior probability toward the dependence hypothesis by a significant amount. For the same reason, seeing not-white would shift the posterior probability toward the independence hypothesis by a significant amount. Here, there is no difference in optimal behavior between the purely deductive and probabilistic cases.

Now consider turning over the *not-white* card. While this would be necessary for testing the deductive rule, it's not very helpful in the probabilistic case. The problem is that there are so many not-white not-swans out there – 89.1 percent of all birds, given our assumptions. Under either hypothesis, flipping the *not-white* card will almost always reveal a *not-swan*, resulting in a negligible information gain. Now, if this *not-white* card turned out to be a *swan*, that would result in a large information gain and dramatically boost the independence hypothesis – but this is unlikely to happen given the rarity of swans of any kind. Essentially, turning over the *not-white* card is gambling on a low-probability event – not-white swans – that will generate much information *if it occurs*. (Note that not-white swans are rare under both hypotheses.) If we weight the two outcomes of flipping the *not-white* card by their probability, the expected information gain is small.

Now let's consider turning over the *white* card. In the purely deductive case, this would be a mistake. But in the probabilistic world, it makes sense. If you've already got a bird known to be white, the population has already been narrowed down to a more informative class. If flipping *white* reveals a swan, which is substantially more likely under the dependence hypothesis than the independence hypothesis, that will result in a large boost to the dependence hypothesis. If flipping *white* reveals a not-swan, that is substantially less informative, though it slightly tips the scales toward the independence hypothesis. As with flipping the *not-white* card, there is a gamble involved. But for the *white* card, the chance of the gamble producing a large informative boost is better because swans constitute at least 1 percent and as much as 8.3 percent of the white birds. In addition, there will be some nontrivial gain of information no matter which outcome occurs.

Finally, for completeness, we should observe that flipping the *not-swan* card never generates any information gain. Here, as with flipping the *swan* card, optimal behavior in the purely deductive and probabilistic cases is the same.

Thus, we have a reasonable case, based on the maximization of expected information gain, for violating the logical answer to the Wason test and for choosing the most common answer that people give in this test, that is, to turn over the *swan* card and the *white* card. But have we not changed the test? The original test was a logical problem, and not a problem of statistical information gain – or so the experimenters intended.

This is an important point. We must distinguish between the *interpretation* of a problem and the *solution* of a problem. The interpretation of a problem is a higher-level decision that sets the parameters for a solution. We cannot assume that subjects in a laboratory experiment understand things the way that psychologists or economists want them to. The most obvious reason for a disjunction is that people in the real world tend to adapt to their circumstances. Certain types of problems arise in particular contexts. For example, in pragmatic contexts, conditional statements are often viewed not simply as "true" or "false" but as broad generalizations. It takes a good bit of arrogance to claim that interpretations and acquired skills that comport with the ecological structure of the subjects' ordinary world are "erroneous."

The rationality of a solution to a problem is subject to the interpretation of the problem given by the individual.[17] Even where the individual seems to interpret the problem the way the experimenter does, his failure to adapt normative intellectual tools to the task need not be a significant problem if that task is not the kind he usually needs to solve.

To conclude with a note of caution: Even if we are convinced that people in everyday life tend to grant certain statements only a relatively high probability, rather than the certainty assigned by experimenters, it does not follow that the Bayesian information-gain method described here is the only correct way to solve the Wason problem. However, as long as it can be seen as *a* reasonable way, our point has been made. Rationality does not require a uniquely correct solution to a problem. Furthermore, given the objections we'll be lodging against Bayesian updating later in this chapter, we should not be understood as saying that normal people actually solve the information-gain problem in Bayesian fashion, only that they may intuitively reason in a manner that is compatible with Bayesian updating in cases such as this.

THE CONJUNCTIVE EFFECT

One of the most frequently discussed examples of how people deviate from supposedly universal norms for rational inference is the famous "Linda

---

[17] Oaksford and Chater (1996, 384, second emphasis added) argue, "the purpose of rational analysis is to characterize the task participants *think* they have been assigned ... rational analysis characterizes how participants both interpret *and* solve a problem."

problem" (Tversky and Kahneman 1983). A hypothetical individual, Linda, is described in the following way:

Linda is 31 years old, single, outspoken and very bright. She majored in philosophy. As a student, she was deeply concerned with issues of discrimination and social justice, and also participated in anti-nuclear demonstrations.

After reading this description, the experimental subjects are asked to rank several propositions with respect to "probability," including the following three. (The designations A, B, and A∩B are ours, not presented to the subjects.)

Linda is active in the feminist movement (A)
Linda is a bank teller (B)
Linda is a bank teller and active in the feminist movement (A∩B)

Some 85 percent of subjects, *including statistically sophisticated ones*, rank A∩B over B. This is considered incorrect because the intersection (A∩B) is a narrower class than B. The class of *bank tellers* contains the class of *bank tellers who are active in the feminist movement*. So even if Linda is a bank teller active in the feminist movement, she is also a bank teller. Saying that the former is more likely than the latter is called the "conjunctive fallacy" because the probability of a conjunction of two events can *never* be higher than the probability of the least probable of those two events (referred to as "conjuncts").

Notice that the "correct" ranking of B and A∩B does not depend *at all* on the description of Linda provided. It is content-free. For example, an alternative problem with the same "correct" answer would go like this:

There is a woman named Linda. Rank the following propositions with respect to their probability. Linda is active in the feminist movement (A); Linda is a bank teller (B); Linda is a bank teller and active in the feminist movement (A∩B).

We could even get rid of gender and say, "There is a person X. Rank the following ..."[18] A tautology is, quite appropriately, a tautology.[19] The correct answer will never change in either the Tversky–Kahneman version or in our abbreviated versions. (The description might affect the ordering of A versus B, but it is irrelevant to the ordering of B versus A∩B, which is the question of interest.)

---

[18] When Tversky and Kahneman (1983, 305) reduced their description of Linda to "a 31 year old woman," the conjunction fallacy disappeared.
[19] Let A and B be any two events such that $P(B) < P(A)$, then $P(A∩B) \leq P(B)$. This is a tautology of probability.

The reason Tversky and Kahneman present a strictly irrelevant description of Linda is because they are applying a specific hypothesis about the cause of the conjunctive effect. They say that it is due to the subjects using the *representativeness heuristic* to assess probabilities.[20] In the subject's experience Linda's *description* makes her look more like a feminist than a bank teller. Thus she seems more like a feminist bank teller than simply a bank teller. So between the two possibilities presented here, the subject considers the feminist bank teller more "probable."

The alleged importance of this seeming violation of a simple rule of the probability calculus is that a "system of judgments that does not obey the conjunction rule cannot be expected to obey more complicated principles that presuppose this rule, such as Bayesian updating, external calibration, and the maximization of expected utility" (Tversky and Kahneman 1983, 313). So what is at stake here is whether individual inference under uncertainty conforms to the norms of the standard economic approach. To be clear, these norms are considered by their behavioral advocates to be highly prescriptive, even as they are not descriptive, of actual inferential judgments. But that is not all. These norms are thought of as the *uniquely* rational way to deal with uncertainty.

We will begin by discussing ambiguities in the interpretation of the Linda problem. When problems are themselves ambiguous, there is no necessity of a unique solution.

Conversational Norms and the Maxim of Relevance

In a world of uncertainty, people must make reasonable inferences about what other people mean by their behavior (Hilton 1995, 249). Before we can assess the rationality of subjects' responses, we must understand how they interpret the problem situation that experimenters present to them. What do the experimenters mean by what they are doing? In the Linda context, they are deliberately providing irrelevant information to the experimental subjects. The experimenters want the subjects to interpret

---

[20] The definition of the heuristic given by Tversky and Kahneman (1983, 295) is: "an assessment of the degree of correspondence between a sample and a population, an instance and a category, an act and an actor, or more generally between an outcome and a model. The model may refer to a person, a coin, or the world economy, and the respective outcomes could be marital status, a sequence of heads and tails, or the current price of gold." For a critical analysis centering on the vagueness and inadequacy of this definition for scientific purposes, see Gigerenzer (1996).

this as so much noise, but the subjects do not. In our view, they have very good reason not to.

The behavior of the experimenters violates the expected norms of conversational interaction (Grice 1989). Among these norms is the *maxim of relevance*, which says that in a cooperative setting, people assume that their interlocutors present them with the information required for current purposes and no more. Of course, these conversational norms are defeasible, but they do provide a first approximation to a reasonable method of inference for individuals in communicative relations with one another.

In the context of the Linda problem, the subjects' behavior might be characterized "as a case of content prevailing over form" (Crupi et al. 2008, 194). When a description is provided of Linda, reasonable agents have good reason to believe it is relevant to the solution of their putative problem, or else it would not have been provided. In what way might it be relevant? As even Tversky and Kahneman (1983, 311) admit, "The conjunction *feminist bank teller* is a better hypothesis about Linda than *bank teller*." It is unclear what exactly they mean by "better hypothesis." From which point of view is it better? Since it cannot be better from their perspective on the conjunction rule, this statement opens up the possibility that some other perspective might be reasonable.

Interpretation of Intersecting Events as Mutually Exclusive

Closely related to the linguistic argument is the possibility that subjects do not interpret the propositions in the Linda problem as the experimenters intend them to. Specifically, the format of the problem may suggest to subjects that the propositions are intended as mutually exclusive. In other words, the subject may read "Linda is a bank teller" to mean "Linda is a bank teller *and not active in the feminist movement*," and "Linda is active in the feminist movement" to mean "Linda is active in the feminist movement *and not a bank teller*."

Why are these natural interpretations? Because the parameters of the problem *suggest* mutual exclusivity. The subject is being asked to rank these three possibilities, and in everyday life it is common to rank things that are distinct, not overlapping. For instance, if a realtor asked you to rank potential homes that have "a pool," "a hot tub," and "a pool and a hot tub," you would probably assume the first home has no hot tub and the second has no pool. Indeed, the very presence of the third option – the one with both pool and hot tub – strongly suggests as much. If the first home also had a hot tub, or if its hot-tub status were unknown, surely the realtor would have said so.

Similarly, on seeing the contrast between the first two propositions, the subject may think, "Okay, so apparently Linda is either a feminist or a bank teller." And then upon seeing the third option, which has both together, the implicit assumption of disjointness seems confirmed: "Got it, Linda could be either a feminist, a bank teller, or both. The 'both' option is the last one." The both option is thus subtracted out of the first two.

Of course, once the options are interpreted as disjoint sets, the conjunction fallacy disappears. Any ordering is logically possible, but given the description of Linda, the most obvious ranking is feminist, then feminist bank teller, then bank teller. It seems very unlikely that a person with Linda's background would not be an active feminist, so the option that doesn't include that goes last.

Does the evidence support the mutual exclusivity interpretation? As it turns out, Tversky and Kahneman considered this possibility by replacing "Linda is a bank teller" with "Linda is a bank teller whether or not she is a feminist." We are not convinced this rewording is crystal clear. Even so, the rewording resulted in a 28 percentage-point drop in the error rate, almost a one-third reduction. Tversky and Kahneman (1983, 299) consider this result unimportant because a large error rate remained. We think that such a large reduction in the error rate suggests that a significant percentage of those committing the alleged fallacy were indeed interpreting the propositions as mutually exclusive.

Messer and Griggs (1993) find that a similar rewording ("Linda is a bank teller, regardless of whether or not she is also active in the feminist movement") resulted in a 21 percentage-point drop in the error rate. MacDonald and Gilhooly (1990) find that another rewording ("Linda is a bank teller who may or may not be active in the feminist movement"), along with a setup in which subjects were asked to make predictions about Linda's probable life in ten years rather than in the present, resulted in a 54 percentage-point drop in the error rate.

Dulany and Hilton (1991) took the novel step of simply *asking* experimental subjects how they interpreted the statement "Linda is a bank teller" after answering the Linda problem. The available answers were "Linda is a bank teller and she is not active in the feminist movement," "Linda is a bank teller and she is probably active in the feminist movement," "Linda is a bank teller and she is probably not active in the feminist movement," and "Linda is a bank teller whether or not she is active in the feminist movement." Notice that only the last of these four interpretations would not absolve the subject of having committed the conjunction fallacy. Dulany and Hilton found that while 52 percent of all subjects gave the supposedly wrong answer to the Linda problem, only 26 percent of them (i.e., half of those making the supposed error) chose the nonabsolving interpretation of the proposition.

Hertwig and Gigerenzer (1999) summarize the results of these and other studies on the question of mutual exclusivity by saying, "[w]ith few exceptions, the evidence reported so far indicates that at least some participants preserve the relevance maxim by drawing the T&not-F ['bank teller and not a feminist,' i.e., mutual exclusivity] implicature: Estimates range from 20% to 50% of participants" (p. 298).

Still, some (possibly large) fraction of subjects apparently commit the conjunction error without having assumed mutual exclusivity. As we will see, there are other possible explanations for this behavior. But here, we wish to emphasize the larger point: that subjects do not necessarily interpret problem situations according to the strict rules of classical logic. That is not a fault of the subjects; it is a fault of the analyst. In the real world, speakers do not always or even usually speak in strictly logical terms, nor do listeners assume they do. Communication is fundamentally a pragmatic endeavor, informed by the context at hand as well as the speakers' and listeners' prior experience. Some subjects – perhaps experienced test-takers – may have learned to set aside their outside experience when taking tests such as those administered by psychologists, but others will bring their experience with them.

Inductive Confirmation of Hypotheses

Setting aside subjects' interpretation of the propositions in the Linda problem, we now move on to their interpretation of the task itself. Tentori and coauthors (2013) suggest that subjects in Linda-type experiments may be solving what they believe to be an *inductive confirmation* problem. Inductive confirmation occurs where the probability of an event A given the evidence e, $P(A|e)$, is higher than the probability of A absent this evidence, $P(A)$. Confirmation is a function of increased support for a hypothesis rather than of its high probability in light of the evidence. Therefore, a relatively unlikely hypothesis can be "confirmed" or supported by relevant evidence.[21] In short, a subject who is looking for inductive

---

[21] Although there are a number of confirmation measures associated with increased support of a hypothesis, their differences do not seem important here. See Crupi et al. (2008, 185).

confirmation is focused upon *changes* in probability rather than *levels* of probability.

In the case of the Linda problem, subjects thinking in terms of inductive confirmation would ask which propositions are *most supported* by the evidence provided (the description of Linda). Any propositions involving feminism, including the joint feminist-banker proposition, would tend to be supported by that description. Meanwhile, the banker proposition (with no statement about feminism) would experience no such support. In terms of inductive confirmation, feminist-banker gets a greater "boost" from the evidence than banker, and so it is ranked higher. Of course, this is not how the experimenters *intend* for the subjects to interpret the problem, but it may be how they *actually* interpret the problem.

Distinguishing between the two hypotheses – representativeness heuristic and inductive confirmation – is no simple task, as they make essentially the same prediction. Tentori and coauthors conducted experiments designed to tease out the difference, and they report results they believe (a) support inductive confirmation while (b) falsifying representativeness. We do not find their approach persuasive with regard to (b), so we will not present their complete results here.[22] However, within these experiments, Tentori and coauthors had subjects perform a "confirmation task" in which they were provided with evidence and then asked to state how much the evidence strengthened or weakened a particular hypothesis. In general, the results showed that greater levels of confirmation were positively associated with greater occurrence of the conjunction fallacy.

For instance, in one experiment subjects were told that a man "O." is an expert mountaineer,[23] and then they were asked whether learning that "O." has a degree in violin performance strengthens or weakens the hypothesis that he gives music lessons. On a scale from −10 (maximally weakens) to +10 (maximally strengthens), subjects gave an average response of +5.6, representing a high level of confirmation. Meanwhile, a different group of

---

[22] Tentori et al. (2013) work on the assumption that the representativeness heuristic results from high perceived probability of the added conjunct (in the Linda case, being a feminist) given both the evidence (Linda's description) and the other conjunct (bank teller). They therefore conclude that a conjunction fallacy should be committed more often for an added conjunct that is obviously higher in probability (for example, that Linda has a pair of black shoes, as very many women do). Their experiments show that the conjunction fallacy happens far more often with an added conjunct that is supported by the evidence than for an added conjunct that is simply high in probability. However, we are not convinced that the representativeness heuristic must operate in this way, and thus we disagree that it would predict the latter kind of conjunction fallacy.

[23] In this scenario, "mountaineer" plays the same role as "bank teller" in the Linda problem.

subjects performed a conjunction-fallacy task based on the same scenario, and 67 percent committed the conjunction fallacy of saying "O. is an expert mountaineer and gives music lessons" is more probable than "O. is an expert mountaineer." The experiment included three other scenarios. Comparison across the four scenarios showed that occurrence of the conjunction fallacy was an *increasing function* of the level of confirmation – i.e., the higher the level of reported confirmation in a given scenario, the greater the occurrence of the conjunction fallacy in that scenario.

Furthermore, in a similar experiment using a within-subjects rather than between-subjects design, Tentori and coauthors found that subjects who saw a high level of confirmation were more likely to commit the conjunction fallacy.

Hertwig and Gigerenzer (1999) offer further evidence that we think supports the inductive-confirmation approach. They attempted to discover how subjects interpreted Linda-like problems by asking them to describe the problem as though they were explaining it to a non-native speaker of their language. They found that "most participants did not understand 'probability' in the sense of mathematical probability but as one of the many other legitimate meanings that are listed in, for example, the Oxford English Dictionary (e.g., meaning credibility, typicality, or *that there is evidence*)" (Gigerenzer 2002, 250–251, emphasis added).

To guard against these alternative interpretations, Linda-like problems can be framed in terms of frequency instead of probability – e.g., "There are 100 persons who fit the description above (i.e., Linda's). How many of them are . . ." (Gigerenzer 2002, 250). Multiple studies find that this alternate mode of presentation reduces the appearance of the conjunction fallacy dramatically – from percentages in the 80s (in the probabilistic presentation) to percentages below 20 (in the frequency presentation) (Gigerenzer 2002, 249, table 12.3).

These results suggest to us that the conjunction fallacy is largely a result of subjects interpreting the problem differently from how the experimenters intend. Instead of playing the intended apply-the-conjunction-rule game, they may be playing the choose-the-more-confirmed-hypothesis game. If so, then what appears to be an error is not one *relative to their game*, and the word "fallacy" is not appropriate. We find this explanation plausible. From the very outset of the problem situation, the subjects' attention is shifted away from a relative frequency interpretation of "probable." The presentation of the question in terms of a single individual, rather than a population of single individuals, tends to evoke other interpretations. If the participants in the experiment believe that the maxim of relevance is operative (why should they not?), they will be further reinforced in their conception that the meaning of "probable" *must relate to the evidence provided.* Apparently, this happened even with the statistically sophisticated participants in the Tversky and Kahneman (1983) study.[24] The idea of inductive confirmation, which uses the evidence in a clear and consistent way, is thus a good a candidate for the meaning of "probable."[25]

For both of the explanations of the conjunction fallacy that we have offered – seeing propositions as mutually exclusive, and interpreting probability in terms of inductive confirmation – it might be claimed that subjects are failing to interpret the question appropriately, and thus they are indeed making an error. But what is an "appropriate" interpretation cannot be definitively answered outside of a broader context. Ascertaining compliance with an abstract logical rule has little to do with how people solve problems of significance to them. Do they really need to know whether it is more probable that Linda is a bank teller or a feminist bank teller, in and of itself?[26] Subjects' interpretation of the problem is presumably driven by the real situations and contexts they have encountered in the world. In any case, as things stand now, the Linda problem is a tissue of ambiguities.

BAYES' RULE, BASE-RATE NEGLECT, AND BELIEF REVISION

Although we have touched on the issue of probability updating as an alternate explanation for the conjunction fallacy, we have been mostly discussing one static property of the probability calculus (the conjunction rule) promulgated as a criterion for rational thought. In this section we turn our attention in depth to what is often considered a *dynamic* property of probabilistic learning: Bayesian updating. The alteration of initial probabilities assigned to particular events in light of new information is

---

[24] Tversky and Kahneman (1983) interpret the prevalence of the "conjunctive error" even by statistically sophisticated participants as evidence of the stubbornness of the error. On the other hand, this can easily be seen to suggest that sophisticated individuals accept the maxim of relevance and are looking for an interpretation of probability that makes use of the evidence.

[25] However, it is not the *only* alternative. Another that makes sense but has not been as thoroughly investigated empirically is the degree of "verisimilitude." In the Linda case, for example, the supposedly irrelevant evidence is not irrelevant if the individual is interested in knowing the *whole truth* about Linda and not just that she is a bank teller. See Cevolani et al. (2010).

[26] "[O]ne might argue that the very task that we are asked to perform is not very natural: very seldom do we find ourselves ranking statements according to their relative likelihood" (Gilboa 2011, 37).

supposed to take place by means of the tautology variously called Bayes' theorem, rule, or identity. People who do not update their beliefs in a manner consistent with Bayes' theorem are typically deemed irrational.

Within the strict framework of assumptions from which Bayes' theorem is logically derived, the theorem is no doubt correct. But in practice, the issue is whether a mechanical and one-directional application of the theorem to experimental problems constitutes a necessary or sufficient criterion of rationality. As we shall see, it does not. Normative solutions to belief-revision issues cannot be a simple matter of plugging probabilities into a formula, however convenient that might be for those trying to discover errors in human reasoning.

Base Rates Are Not Necessarily Prior Probabilities

Let us begin with a standard example of a problem situation that requires Bayesian reasoning:

A cab was involved in a hit-and-run accident at night. Two cab companies, the Green and the Blue, operate in the city. You are given the following data: (i) 85% of the cabs in the city are Green and 15% are Blue. (ii) A witness identified the cab as a Blue cab. The court tested his ability to identify cabs under the appropriate visibility conditions. When presented with a sample of cabs (half of which were Blue and half of which were Green) the witness made correct identifications in 80% of the cases and erred in 20% of the cases. Question: what is the probability that the cab involved in the accident was Blue rather than Green?

(Tversky and Kahneman 1980, 62)

For Kahneman and Tversky, the normative solution is straightforward. We take Bayes' theorem off the shelf like so:

$$P(H|E) = \frac{P(H) \times P(E|H)}{[P(H) \times P(E|H)] + [P(\sim H) \times P(E|\sim H)]}$$

where H = the hypothesis that the cab involved in the accident was blue, E = the witness's testimony that the cab involved was blue, and ~H = the hypothesis that the cab was green. Now we plug in the numbers given to us by Tversky and Kahneman. First, we need the prior probabilities P(H) and P(~H). But what are they? Without argument, they assume that the base rates are the prior probabilities. Then the "new" evidence is the witness's testimony.[27] The witness's hit rate, *P(E|H)*, is assumed to be 0.80 and the

---

[27] We put the word "new" in quotations marks because when the data is all given simultaneously (as is usual in the experimentally constructed problems), the difference between prior evidence and new evidence is arbitrary.

false-alarm rate, $P(E|\sim H)$, is 0.20.[28] Thus, the normative answer is that the probability that the car involved in the accident is blue is approximately 0.41. For belief revision, this is the standard of rationality. Any departure from it ostensibly reveals an irrational deficit.[29]

The standard of rationality proffered here is not merely Bayesian statistics or even Bayes' theorem itself, but the designation of *base rates* as the relevant prior probabilities in accordance with Bayes' theorem. However, base rates are not prior probabilities unless the agent chooses to make them so (Levi 1983, 1996; Koehler 1996, 12–13). *Thus, base-rate neglect in itself cannot be a fallacy.*

In a Bayesian framework, all probabilities are conditional. The priors are conditional on everything the agent believes as background knowledge. This knowledge may include base rates, but not exclusively. In the subjectivist version of Bayesianism, *any* prior probability would be allowable. The rationality of Bayes' theorem begins *after* the agent has chosen his priors. Rationality does not inhere in the choice of priors; that is a subjective judgment.

Even if we think that base rates ought to have some role in establishing prior probabilities, it is not preordained what that role should be. For example, an agent might reasonably underweight or even ignore base rates if he believes that the base rate was established in a reference class that is too wide. The proportion of blue or green cabs in the town is wide. More interesting would be the proportion of blues and greens at night in the area of the accident. But even this could be perceived as not sufficiently relevant. The agent might wonder why we have not been told about each company's history of accidents. In view of all this data insufficiency, the agent could simply decide, as Levi (1983, 505) suggests, that his priors are 0.50 and

---

[28] More generally, these probabilities are known as "likelihoods."

[29] The reader who many not be accustomed to modeling human learning in terms of Bayes' theorem may find it distressing to find that this is the standard and that most people get the wrong answer. Why should it be *required* that rational agents be able to apply this mathematical relationship? After all, generations of students have had to learn this in college statistics courses. Are agents who do not take college statistics irrational as well as uneducated? L. Jonathan Cohen makes the perfectly valid point that there is no reasonable stopping point here. What other mathematical or statistical relationships should agents be required to know before their rationality can be established? As Cohen remarks, "[a]t best, these experiments would constitute a test of their subjects' intelligence or education, since the ordinary person might no more be expected to generate Bayes' theorem spontaneously than Bernoulli's" (Cohen 1981, 328). Bernoulli's theorem is essentially the law of large numbers applied to Bernoulli trials (events with a specified probability of success or failure). As the number of trials increases, the frequency of success in the trials approaches the probability of success in a single trial.

0.50. Were he to do this, the posterior probability that the car was blue would simply be 0.80. Notably, this is equal to the witness's hit rate. This is considered an error by Tversky and Kahneman, as it involves total base-rate neglect and the "confusion" of the hit rate with the posterior probability. The participant gets an undeserved *F*.

In any case, Tversky and Kahneman's term "base-rate neglect" is a misnomer. The decades-old literature on this problem shows that base rates are rarely completely neglected entirely, but typically they are "under-weighted" relative to the proposed norm (Koehler 1996). Therefore, what is at issue is quantitative and empirical: *how much* should historical base rates be weighted in forming priors?

The major problem, however, with the Tversky–Kahneman position on base-rate underweighting lies in its disregard for the pragmatic or ecological rationality of underweighting base rates relative to a mechanical application of Bayes' theorem. The experimental literature in this, as in many other areas, ignores reasonable expectations participants have developed and adapted to the real world. In the following analysis, let us imagine an agent-participant who lives in the real world and has coped with problems of belief formation and revision outside of the statistics classroom. Such an agent would not mechanically accept posted data and plug it into an equation.

Consider the case of a doctor who takes a job in a new clinic, where among other things she performs tests for sexually transmitted diseases. A significant number of her patients test positive for HIV. Now, if the doctor applied Bayes' rule using base rates from the national population – where the fraction of people with HIV is small – she would have to conclude that most of these are false positives. Fortunately, the doctor is smarter than that. She realizes her patients are probably not a random draw from the national population. They may have reasons for being worried about HIV and getting tested. So she adjusts her priors away from the base rates, and thus concludes that many of the positive test results are probably true positives. Now suppose that after working at the clinic for a few months, the doctor notices that the fraction of her positive-testing patients who exhibit symptoms of HIV infection (or who test positive on a "gold standard" test with a negligible false-positive rate) is even larger than she expected. In this instance, she might conclude that these results are due to chance – or she might suspect that even her adjusted priors fail to reflect her environment. Perhaps people in the clinic's neighborhood have a relatively high rate of risky behaviors and resultant HIV infections. Therefore, she adjusts her priors even further in the direction of greater HIV prevalence.

Nothing in this doctor's behavior is irrational. She is simply refusing to form her priors strictly on base rates. The larger point is that Bayes' rule is not unidirectional. You can plug givens into Bayes' rule to generate results, but you can also use results to revise the givens. Doing so may be ecologically rational in real-world situations.

Changing Causal Structure and Base-Rate Instability

The importance that we should attach to base rates depends upon perceptions about the stability of the underlying environment. To motivate this point, consider an example from Gigerenzer that does not strictly involve Bayes' rule:

> You live in a jungle. Today you must choose between two alternatives: to let your child swim in the river, or to let it climb trees instead. You use only one criterion for that choice, your child's life expectancy. You have information that in the last 100 years there was only one accident in the river, in which a child was eaten by a crocodile, whereas a dozen children have been killed by falling from trees. Just yesterday your neighbor told you that her child was eaten by a crocodile. Where do you send your child?
>
> (Gigerenzer 2002, 263)

If the parents were confident that the physical structure of the environment has not changed, they would simply treat the most recent death as one more data point, which would only slightly shift the likelihood of death at the river. However, the parents may not find the new computed risk useful. Perhaps the new data is not simply a random draw from the same static world as during the past 100 years, but rather a message that the river is different due to climate change, a change in pH of the water, or a change in the availability of the usual food sources. The parents will have to use their judgment to determine the perceived risk of danger at the river going forward.

Often researchers refer to this phenomenon or ones similar to it as cases of "unstable base rates." The base rates are unstable because agents find them unsatisfactory for one reason or another in the process of assessing risk. How do unstable base rates affect the usefulness of Bayes' rule?

Todd and Goodie (2002) perform a large series of simulations that vary the environment faced by "organisms" (computer agents) in two major respects. The rates of change in base rates and in cue accuracy are varied to produce thirty-six different environments.[30] Some environments are

---

[30] There is (again) the possibility of terminological confusion here. The terms "hit rate" and "cue accuracy" are used interchangeably or as the intuitive context varies. They are

relatively (un)stable in all respects while others have stable base rates and unstable environmental cues and vice versa. The idea is to see which rules for calculating posterior probabilities work best in each environment. The posterior probabilities were determined, in advance, by the simulations. So, for the purposes of the experiment, we know the "correct" results.

The study compared several methods of calculating posterior probabilities. For our purposes the key ones were: (1) Bayes' theorem; (2) complete base rate neglect (only the hit rate matters); (3) base rate underweighting (small adjustments in the weighting of the hit rate); and (4) base rates only. Averaging over the ten environments that were characterized by base rates that are much more unstable than cue accuracy, Bayes' theorem produced 74 percent accuracy in predicting posterior probabilities. However, base-rate underweighting was 73 percent accurate; even complete base-rate neglect was 72 percent accurate. Predictably, the results for environments with relatively stable base rates were different. Complete base-rate neglect performed poorly at 59 percent compared with Bayes' theorem at 74 percent. But even here an adjustment to allow for a small amount of weighting of base rates achieved a predictive accuracy of 66 percent.[31] Across all 36 environments, the standard Bayesian strategy had an accuracy rate of 73 percent compared with base rate underweighting at 69 percent. In short, the advantage of Bayesian updating over other intuitive strategies is small, particularly in relatively unstable environments.

False-Alarm Rates and Hit Rates May Not Be Independent of Base Rates

Another input into Bayes' theorem, the so-called false-alarm rate $(P(E|\sim H)$, may not be independent of the observed base rates and hence of Tversky and Kahneman's "prior probabilities." It is assumed in the standard story that the ratio of the hit rate to the false-alarm rate is independent of the base rates.[32] But this need not be so.

---

identical to $P(E|H)$, that is, the probability of observing the new evidence (E) given a particular hypothesis (H) or event. The new evidence is considered the cue.

[31] In intermediate cases where hit rates and base rates are unstable, all strategies perform less well. Nevertheless, base rate neglect and Bayes' theorem performed about the same (Todd and Goodie 2002, 218–219).

[32] This can be seen from the odds version of Bayes' Theorem: $P(H|E)/P(\sim H|E) = (P(H)/P(\sim H)) \cdot (P(E|H)/P(E|\sim H))$. However, in those cases where the hit and false-alarm rates are unlikely to move proportionally in the same direction, it is sufficient to think of them as each being independent (or not) of base rates. See Gigerenzer and Murray (1987, 169).

Let us return to the cab example. Recall that the data about witness reliability is derived from a testing sample with equal proportions of green and blue cabs. Assume, however, that at the time of the accident, the witness knew that the actual proportions were 15 percent blue and 85 percent green. It is unlikely that the reliability data (hit and false-alarm rates) would remain unchanged when the proportion of blue cabs is lower than in the test. To see this, we need a minimal theory of the witness. Signal detection theory points to the relevance of two factors (Birnbaum 1983). First, any witness (human or mechanical) operates along a *discriminal continuum* of perception. In this example it is assumed that there is a normal distribution of perceived signal strength emanating from "blueness" and "greenness." When the actual proportion of blues is low, the most common *error* the individual will make is the false alarm: saying blue when it is really green.

Second, the reasonable witness may respond to the lower proportion of blues by having a different *decision criterion*. In other words, since he can only say "blue" or "green," he must decide when the probability of blue relative to green is high enough to say "blue." If he wishes to minimize the sum of the two types of error, he will demand a stronger subjective signal impression before he says that the cab is blue. This second factor can be called the subjective factor. It goes beyond the strictly statistical (Bayes' theorem) issues. It will depend on the perceived *costs* of the different kinds of error – the miss rate and the false-alarm rate. If all errors are equally costly then the witness will simply minimize total errors. If, as seems plausible, calling a cab blue when it is not (thus leading to a guilty verdict) is worse than calling it green when it is blue, then the witness will raise the bar still further for saying "blue."

Looking back at Bayes' theorem, we can see that both of these changes will increase the posterior probability *toward the original witness hit rate (0.80)*. If we assume that the witness is minimizing the total number of errors, the induced changes due to a disproportionately low base rate of blues bring the posterior probability to 0.82 – close to the modal but "erroneous" response (Birnbaum 1983, 91; Gigerenzer and Murray 1987, 167–173).

Our claim here is not that the modal response is necessarily the optimum response, but that the standard analysis is simplistic. It assumes an implausible theory of the witness's discriminal abilities in an uncertain environment, as well as witness behavior that is completely invariant with respect to the decision criterion across all environments. More generally, there is no single correct or optimal result that is independent of the agent's decision-making preferences, such as the subjective costs associated with different types of error.

Magnification of Errors in a Noisy World

In the real world, people are not simply given base rates, hit rates, and false-alarm rates as they are in most experiments. They must try to calculate them from noisy data. The standard rules of combining probabilities multiplicatively as in Bayes' theorem may be normatively attractive in textbook scenarios where probabilities are error-free. When probabilities are assessed with error terms, the standard methods may lose their advantage. Specifically, when probabilities are combined multiplicatively, random errors are magnified relative to when they stand alone or are combined additively.

Juslin et al. (2009) compare the accuracy, in a noisy environment, of posterior probability estimates generated by either (a) Bayes' theorem or (b) linear additive estimation, a non-Bayesian alternative. Intuitively, an agent who uses linear additive estimation realizes that hit rates and false-alarm rates should affect their assessment of the posterior probability, but they perform the adjustment through simple addition and subtraction instead of multiplication and division.[33] In Juslin and coauthors' simulation, 10,000 probability arrays (priors and likelihoods) were generated to form 10,000 Bayesian inference problems. The posterior probabilities were computed using Bayes' theorem. Then noise was added to the constituent probabilities. So, we now have "true" posterior probabilities as well as noisy data from which they must be estimated.[34]

The key question is: would agents do better using Bayes' theorem on the error-laden probabilities, or using the theoretically "deficient" process of linear addition? It turns out that linear additive estimates fared *better* than Bayes' theorem in noisy environments. Furthermore, it did not much matter whether the weights applied were optimal or derived from actual behavior.[35]

---

[33] To be specific, the linear additive estimate of the posterior probability is set equal to $\alpha + b_1 \cdot P(H) + b_2 \cdot P(D|H) + b_3 \cdot P(D|\sim H)$ where α = constant; b_1 = weight for the prior probability (or base rate); b_2 = weight for the hit rate; and b_3 = weight for the false-alarm rate (Juslin et al. 2009, 868). Note that b_3 would typically be negative.

[34] The distribution of true probabilities was modeled as uniform, normal, or U-shaped (Juslin et al. 2009, 862).

[35] Optimal weights are derived from a linear regression of the participants' estimates of the actual probabilities. Behavioral weights are those that simply describe (rationalize) those estimates.

Noisy environments are quite common. They can be due to small samples from which the agent must estimate the relevant probabilities. They can be due to the limitations of memory or random errors in the processing of data. Simply to list these sources is to remind us that they are the rule rather than the exception.

Not All Base Rates Are Created Equal

One of the primary problems with a mechanical application of Bayes' theorem is that it implicitly assumes that all base rates are equally relevant or trustworthy. Statisticians realize that not all data sets are equally useful, relevant, or reliable. Is it possible that base-rate underweighting in the real world is a response to agents' broader understanding of the value of past data?

Recall that in Bayesian analysis all probabilities are ultimately conditional. Strictly speaking, we ought to condition base rates on the background knowledge of the agent. Welsh and Navarro (2012) explore the implications of different background factors that may, quite reasonably, affect the use of base rates. They argue that past and new data will be weighted by a *trust factor* as certain features of the data change (or are posited to change by the experimenters). These are location, age, source, and sample size. If the data has been collected at a different location from the one in which the probability assessment is to be made, trust will fall. For example, the proportion of black swans worldwide is not very relevant to the proportion in Australia. The oldness of data also reduces the weighting of the base rates. Perhaps the swan population has changed over time under selective pressure. The source of the data may also be a mystery. Who did the relevant research on swans? In most experimental problems the subjects are just told that the data is such and such. It appears to be the case, however, that data gathered by the agent is more trustworthy than data from a mysterious source. Finally, if the sample size is large, then it would seem reasonable to weight those probabilities more heavily than if the sample size were small.

In their experiments, Welsh and Navarro (2012) combined the first three factors into cover stories. The "high trust" story told the participants that the prior data (base rates) was recent and collected by the participant in the same location as the problem situation. The "low trust" story indicated that the prior data was old and collected by someone else in a different location. Base rates and new data were varied, as were the sample sizes for each kind of data. There were thirty-two different scenarios in total because in some cover stories only one or two high-trust variables were used.

As the experimenters added additional reasons not to trust the base rates, their measured weighting by participants declined substantially. Each single manipulation of the trust variables had a substantial effect (Welsh and Navarro 2012, 7). In these cases, the estimated posterior probabilities were closer to the proportion of relevant events displayed in the new data. This was true regardless of whether the base rate implied by the older data was high (75 percent) or low (25 percent).[36] Sample size also affected the trust variable, with a larger sample size increasing the weight of the base rates.[37]

Thus, while base rates are underweighted relative to the Bayesian criterion, the degree of the underweighting varies in systematic and reasonable ways. In real environments where issues of relevance and reliability are likely to be significant to agents, the propensity of experimental participants to discount given data is in line with a broadly rational approach to information updating.

We conclude that the mechanical application of Bayes' theorem is neither necessary nor sufficient for rational learning.[38] Nevertheless, it is important to reiterate that in our analysis of probability updating, we

---

[36] When the base rate was stipulated to be 75 percent the new data rate was 25 percent and vice versa.

[37] The authors separated sample size for special consideration. The effect of sample size is more difficult to interpret because the authors distinguished between actual and perceived sample size. The perceived sample size is hypothesized to be a logarithmic function of the actual size. Therefore, trust is positively related to the logarithmic transformation of sample size.

[38] Even in the absence of the ecological or contextual constraints on the application of Bayes' theorem discussed previously, a proponent of the general use of Bayesian conditionalization will find no comfort in the dynamic Dutch book argument. This argument purports to show that if the agent does not update his prior probabilities given new evidence in accordance with Bayes' theorem, a clever bookie could inflict losses on him. The usual demonstration involves a sequence of four bets. The bookie must know the direction and amount of the agent's deviation from the Bayesian conditionalization. Thus, the agent must fix beforehand exactly how he will deviate from Bayes' theorem at the very outset of the series of bets. In other words, he must follow a rigid rule of "erroneous conditionalization" before he knows of the existence of new evidence. Furthermore, what rule he will follow must be evident to the bookie *before* the agent follows it. Therefore, the requirement would seem to be that the agent *announce* all of this at the outset. In the final analysis, of course, whether this argument works depends on the institutional and cognitive assumptions made. It cannot be a general pragmatic defense of Bayesian conditionalization as the uniquely rational updating mechanism. See Vineberg (2011).

have not challenged the view that under *carefully specified and rather limited conditions*, Bayes' theorem will produce the "correct" answer. The problem is that the world in which agents make inferences and decisions does not mirror the abstract world of the theorem. In the real world people depart *and ought to depart* from the mechanical application of Bayesian updating.

AVAILABILITY BIAS AND FREQUENCY JUDGMENTS

Frequency judgments are estimates that individuals make about the relative or absolute frequency of specified events, such as types of accidents or death by particular causes. Although it would not constitute irrationality – by anyone's definition – for people merely to be ignorant about any particular frequency (do you know how many people die from drowning each year?), researchers have identified a systematic error that appears over many such estimates. Specifically, subjects tend to *overestimate low risks* and *underestimate high risks.*

This tendency, first identified by Lichtenstein et al. (1978) in a survey of students and members of the League of Women Voters, has since taken on a status close to an empirical law. The explanation typically given for this result is that people use the *availability heuristic* to answer these questions, meaning that people estimate frequencies based on how easily they can call examples to mind. The more easily examples can be called to mind, and the more vivid and memorable the examples are, the more they will be overestimated – so that, for instance, one man living to 100 despite bad habits is remembered, while the more typical cases of people with bad habits dying younger tend to recede (Cartwright 2011, 198).

Consider the types of questions typically used in studies of this type. In the general population, is the annual frequency of death from drowning greater than the frequency of death from appendicitis? Are there more suicides than deaths by electrocution? Or even: are there more words with *v* in the first position than with *v* in the third position? Most people do not know, and what is more, they do not care. Although answers to these questions may be highly relevant in a sociology or linguistics class, such population-level statistics are irrelevant to the lives and goals of ordinary people. What is relevant are the hazards that they face adjusted for their age and other temporal and local circumstances (Benjamin and Dougan 1997). Studies such as those of Lichtenstein et al. (1978), which posit unbiased estimation of *population figures* such as these as the test of "rationality," seem misguided from the outset.

Yet when economics students and nursing students were asked to estimate the frequency of deaths from various causes *in their own age cohorts*, the whole picture changed – in fact, the bias vanished (Benjamin et al. 2001).[39] The logic of this result is compelling. In a world of scarce resources, people have a tendency to learn what is in their interest to learn. The students, by and large, did not need to know population figures, but they did find it useful to have a decent idea of the hazards they actually face in their age groups. While their knowledge was far from perfect, they used the information they had efficiently to make close to unbiased estimates of deaths from various causes in their own age cohort. Additionally, the nursing students, who all had taken courses on individual and societal health issues, also had unbiased but better (i.e., lower variance) knowledge of the age-relevant deaths, as we might expect. Importantly, this study was able to replicate the findings of Lichtenstein with regard to the population-level data, thus suggesting that, to the extent the availability bias exists, it operates with respect to matters of little importance to the subjects. These results provide an example of the phenomenon of *rational irrationality*, discussed earlier.

To the extent that availability bias exists, the discussion above suggests that it might be confined to areas of little personal importance to individuals. We shall see more evidence later suggesting this is the case. However, there are serious theoretical and conceptual problems with this hypothesis that are far too often ignored. Both the phenomenon *and* its hypothesized cause are labeled "availability." This suggests that it is important to define the term precisely. Without a precise definition, we do not know what we are looking for or what mechanism can be assessed as its cause. Unfortunately, disappointment awaits us.

Pinning Down the Meaning of Availability

Let us first begin with the mechanism. In their original article on the subject, Tversky and Kahneman propose a definition of the availability heuristic:

---

[39] The world of empirical research is messy. There was a slight indication of overestimation of very low risks in the data. However, the authors surmise that this was most plausibly due to floor effects. In other words, since there cannot be negative deaths for any cause, the ordinary random component of estimation is "self-censored" at the low end so as to avoid the absurdity of a negative estimate (Benjamin et al. 2001, 45).

A person is said to employ the availability heuristic whenever he estimates frequency or probability *by the ease* with which instances or associations can be brought to mind.

(Tversky and Kahneman 1973, 208, emphasis added)

Generally this heuristic leads to accurate results because frequency and ease of retrieval are often highly correlated. But, we are told, this is not always the case. Ease may be correlated with factors other than frequency, and thus bias is possible. Ease of retrieval can be affected by such "irrelevant" things as the familiarity of instances (famous names in a list), the salience of events (seeing a house burn in contrast to reading about it), the recency of events (yesterday's airplane crash in contrast to one that occurred years ago), the "effectiveness of a search set" (trying to retrieve words with a given letter in the first position as opposed to the third position), the degree of abstractness of a concept (abstract entities are easier to retrieve than concrete ones – love versus doors, for example), the ease with which a general rule might generate instances (think of a mathematical generating function such as the number of combinations or permutations), the ease of imagining cases, and illusory correlations (as when "shifty" eyes are associated with deviousness). Of course, there are events of high availability on some of these criteria but of low availability on others. It is not clear what is supposed to happen to overall availability when evaluations on these criteria conflict. We understandably wonder how such a sprawling hypothesis can be tested.

Second, what are we trying to explain? As we have seen, the experiments have involved collecting data on subjects' assessment of the frequency or comparative frequencies of certain events. Then the analyst compares the pattern of estimates to their actual frequencies. If the estimates systematically deviate from the actual, this is seen as evidence of a bias *of some type*. The systematic deviation of estimated frequencies from actual frequencies is the phenomenon to be explained.[40] In the classic study of Lichtenstein et al. (1978), there was a bias with regard to population-level estimates – which, as we have noted, were of little personal importance to the subjects. Thus, the phenomenon itself is arguably of little interest from the perspective of pragmatic rationality.

Nevertheless, difficulties with the availability hypothesis can be seen even in terms of the problem situations proponents have devised for their experimental subjects. For example, consider the frequency with which

---

[40] Random deviation is not the issue, because people are not expected to have perfect knowledge of actual frequency distributions.

letters appear in the first versus third position of a word. Analysts assumed that it would be easier to recall words with a given letter in the first position than words with a given letter in the third position. For each of the tested letters (*K, L, N, R,* and *V*), the majority of subjects thought they were more likely in the first position (Kahneman and Tversky 1973).[41] It turns out, however, that *most* consonants are more likely in the first position, so the subjects' estimate does seem to be a good guess (Lopes and Oden 1991).[42] The letters tested in this experiment were atypical because *all* of the chosen consonants are actually more frequent in the third position.

In later work (Sedlmeier et al. 1998) the availability hypothesis was subjected to more rigorous testing. In order to account for original ambiguities in the formulation of the hypothesis, two measures of the ease of retrieval were used: (1) the actual number of instances retrieved and (2) the amount of time it takes to retrieve a single instance. Thus we have proxies for "availability-by-number" and "availability-by-speed" respectively. The subjects were assigned essentially the same letter position task as discussed earlier, with certain adjustments such as the use of more letters and the allowance for two-letter words in the German language. They were asked whether a certain letter was more likely in the first position or in the second position, and then they were asked to estimate the ratio of the two frequencies.

The experiment was designed to compare four hypotheses about how subjects answer these questions. Two were variants of the availability hypothesis. The third was the quite plausible "letter-class hypothesis." This is the idea that, in the absence of more specific knowledge, people assign to the specific letter the position frequency that a consonant or a vowel has in general. The fourth is the "regressed-frequencies hypothesis." This is the no-psychological-bias alternative. According to this hypothesis, subjects give estimates that reflect actual frequencies with an overestimate for those below the mean value and an underestimate for those above the mean value.

The results of the study were that, by three standard measures of fit, the regressed-frequencies hypothesis best explains the responses of the sub-

---

[41] This is a test of the participants' judgment about which position is most common and not their ability to actually retrieve instances in each category. This is a meta-cognitive process (Schwarz 1998, 88).

[42] Interestingly, Lopes and Oden (1991) observe that 60 percent of consonants are more likely in the first position, which is not far from the median estimate of 67 percent given by the participants in the original Tversky and Kahneman study (1974).

jects.[43] Thus the responses of the subjects were "roughly a monotonic function of actual proportions, with a regression toward the mean" (Gigerenzer et al. 2008, 1031). Subjects estimated the relative proportions of letter positions correctly, but with a tendency to move toward the mean percentage of the letters in the first position. The regression phenomenon is a consequence of the random estimation of errors that an imperfect, yet psychologically unbiased, measurement instrument (memory) produces.

Three important merits of this study over many others is that the availability hypothesis is much more precisely defined, a measure of availability is used that is based on the actual behavior of the subjects, and different hypotheses are confronted with each other and the data.[44]

Diagnosticity and Availability

In a series of experiments, Schwarz (1998) rejects the idea of a direct link from availability to estimation of frequencies. His claim is that availability is mediated by another factor, and by paying attention to that factor we can determine when the hypothesis holds and when it does not. In a response to the previous work in this field, he suggests that both availability-by-speed and availability-by-number are "content oriented," that is, they concern what comes to mind. However, availability is better understood as the *subjective experience* of accessibility independent of the number of recalled instances or their content. Does this recollection of ease or difficulty, by itself, affect judgment? Empirically, the subjective experience and the content usually go to together. Nevertheless, it is possible to disentangle the effects.[45]

Schwarz argues that ease by itself does not have a direct impact on frequency estimations. It must be mediated through the perceived "diagnosticity" of the experience – that is, whether the ease or difficulty in accessing memories is an informationally relevant experience. Perhaps it is due simply to extraneous and transient factors with no substantive bearing on the question posed. If so, the individual will discount the subjective experience. *Ease or difficulty in retrieving instances matters only when the*

---

[43] The three measures are: the root mean squared deviations of predictions from data, contrast analysis, and the proportion of choices falling into predicted intervals (Sedlmeier et al. 1998, 759).

[44] Gigerenzer (1998, 200–201) has alerted us to the scientific problems inherent in not comparing the hypothesis to plausible alternatives.

[45] The original work on availability confounded the content (including number of instances) with the subjective experience of ease.

subject has reason to believe that the experience is diagnostic. In other words, when the information content of availability (defined as ease) is high, it will be used. Otherwise, use of the heuristic will be inhibited.

Diagnosis of the experience as a source of knowledge can be affected when people are led to believe (correctly or incorrectly) that certain circumstances will make the retrieval task more or less difficult. For example, when subjects believed that ambient music would make retrieval of instances of their own assertive behavior more difficult, they reported higher self-assertiveness after being required to recall six (easy task) than twelve (hard task) examples of their assertive behavior (Schwarz et al. 1991).[46] The ease of the experience of recalling six – *against the perceived influence of the music* – was the dominant factor in self-assessment. On the other hand, when subjects believed that the ambient music made the task easier, they discounted ease. They reported higher self-assertiveness after recalling twelve rather than six examples. Ease was perceived as due to an extraneous factor. Thus the number and content of recalled examples was the dominant factor.[47]

The diagnosticity of availability can also be called into question by the subject's view of her own expertise in the knowledge domain (Schwarz et al. 1991). When people are asked to estimate the objective frequency of chronic diseases, they may base their answers on the ease or difficulty with which they can retrieve or generate instances – *but only if* they believe or are made to believe that they have some expertise in this area. Then ease or difficulty in recalling means something significant. Those who believed themselves to be knowledgeable made higher estimates when they recalled three examples (i.e., when the task felt easy) than when they recalled nine examples (i.e., when the task felt hard). The perception of expertise induced subjects to rely more on availability. On the other hand, subjects who did not think of themselves as knowledgeable made higher estimates when they recalled nine rather than three examples. The perception of lack of expertise caused subjects to discount availability. This is because availability in this case is likely to be a function of arbitrary or transient factors.

---

[46] This was a between-subjects study. Thus, it was not literally the case that the individuals first recalled six and then recalled twelve instances.

[47] The comparison is between the two treatments: when subjects believed the music would make retrieval of self-assertive instances more difficult and when they believed it would make retrieval easier. The effects of six compared with twelve are reversed between the two treatments. In the first treatment, ease (six) is important. In the second treatment, number (twelve) and content are important. (Note that the comparison of difficult versus easy, holding instances constant, could not be made because difficulty is related to the number of instances recalled.)

Finally, Rothman and Schwarz (1998) find that the use of the availability heuristic depends not only on the perceived diagnosticity of information but also on the perceived relevance of the task. The greater the personal interest subjects have in the question, the more they discount availability. Male students were asked to assess their personal risk for heart disease. Those who had a family history of heart disease appraised their own risk by the content of what they could recall. Students who did not have a family history of heart disease relied on the availability heuristic. Thus, those with a family history had a higher perception of risk when they could recall eight rather than three risk-increasing factors, which is the opposite of what the unmodified availability heuristic would predict. Although the former is perceived as the harder task, the content of their recollections dominated their assessment. On the other hand, those students without a family history had a *lower* perception of risk when they could recall eight rather than three risk-increasing factors. Being required to remember eight factors made the task seem harder, while being required to remember three made the task seem easier. In this case the ease of recall dominated assessment. "If I find it easier to recall personal risk factors, then I must be at high risk."[48] These conclusions are consistent with the study by Benjamin et al. (2001) discussed earlier in which risk-assessment bias disappears in an area of heightened self-relevance (age-cohort risks). And like that study, Rothman and Schwarz's results in the case of students without a personal interest in the task can be seen as another example of rational irrationality.

In summary, when individuals believe that their ease of memory retrieval is explained by transient changes in the environment or by their level of expertise, they discount availability as a source of knowledge. They also discount it when the risk or event in question is of personal significance. It is fair to conclude that these factors severely limit the cases in which the availability heuristic appears to be used, to the extent it is used at all.[49]

---

[48] Equivalently: "If I find it hard to recall eight personal risk factors, I must be at low risk."

[49] If the circumstances under which it does not apply are shown to be numerous and important, there is a temptation to use an "immunizing strategy" to save the day. This is what Kahneman (2011, 134–135) seems to have done in his recent book. In a nutshell, he says that Schwarz's research is an advance because it does indeed show when the hypothesis does not explain people's estimation of frequencies. But that is fine because it is under those circumstances that the conscious, analytical "System 2" takes over and inhibits the subject's tendency toward using the availability heuristic. Availability is thus transformed from an empirical phenomenon of presumably significant frequency to a *tendency*. We discuss the "Systems 1 and 2" approach in the Appendix to this chapter. However, it is important to realize that the discounting process referred to here need not be, and often is not, conscious (Oppenheimer 2004). This would seem to disqualify it as a System 2 process.

SALIENCE

Intuitively, "salience" is a concept closely related to availability. If we think of availability as either the ease or frequency with which something can be brought to mind, then salience might be considered *one* cause of availability. On the other hand, if salience means prominence in a person's consciousness or memory, then it is simply a name for the availability phenomenon. However salience is ultimately defined, it has been invoked both as an explanation and as a remedy for distorted judgments. For instance, the distortion of stock prices is sometimes attributed to an excess of salience (Fich and Xu 2018), while increased salience is proposed as a remedy for the deliberate shrouding of terms in consumer contracts (Bar-Gill 2014, 477–487). Unfortunately, this versatile idea is used far more than is warranted by its conceptual clarity.[50]

What is salience? One often-used definition comes from Thompson and Taylor (1982):

> Salience refers to the phenomenon that when one's attention is *differentially directed* to one portion of the environment rather than to others, the information contained in that portion will receive *disproportionate* weighting in *subsequent judgments.*
>
> (Taylor and Thompson 1982, 175, emphases added)

We have three concerns about this definition. First, it does not specify the causes of differentially directed attention. The definition assumes the existence of unspecified factors that cause differential attention, and then defines salience in terms of the consequences of such differential attention: disproportionate weighting. What we are interested in is the specific causes of differential attention – regardless of the name given to it.

The specific causes matter because, if the causes are unspecified, salience becomes a free-floating concept that can be deployed however the analyst pleases. Zywicki (2018, 448–449) documents, for instance, how salience has been used both to make predictions *and* to explain why those predictions failed to materialize. In the context of credit cards, Bar-Gill (2004) argued that consumers would tend to pay too much attention to annual fees and insufficient attention to interest rates and late fees (pp. 1402–1403), thereby making them vulnerable to "seduction by plastic." Bar-Gill therefore predicted that debit cards would be unable to compete

---

[50] "The concept of salience is an umbrella concept. It has been used to explain different constructs, grouped under a single conceptualization without any adequate cognizance and analysis of the existing diversities" (Guido 2001, 22).

effectively against credit cards, as debit cards' requirement of immediate payment means they cannot exploit consumers' inattention to long-term costs. As it turned out, in the following years debit cards reached and then surpassed credit cards in terms of transaction volume. How could that failed prediction be explained? Bar-Gill does so by asserting that salience "is fluid, evolving over time," and that while annual fees were salient before the early 1990s, during the 1990s interest rates became more salient (2012, 95). As Zywicki observes, this is a "just-so story" unsupported by any evidence of changing consumer awareness (2018, 449). The underlying problem here is that the causes of salience have not been identified, and this conceptual vagueness enables the telling of convenient stories in which the same supposed bias can explain any set of facts.

Second, implicit in Thompson and Taylor's definition of salience is the recognition that attention directed toward something is accompanied by attention directed away from something else (Kurzban et al. 2013). It is important to know what gets deemphasized when something else is emphasized. Given that it's impossible to pay attention to every aspect of one's environment, some differential attention seems unavoidable. At least in the short run, the individual presumably has an "attention budget" that must be allocated among different things. More attention must be paid to that which is perceived to be more relevant. How much differential attention, then, is sufficient to be considered pathological?

Third, and most importantly, the claim that salient information will be disproportionately weighted presupposes some standard of proportionate or optimal weighting. In certain narrow contexts, there is a clear standard for optimal weighting. For example, with respect to stock prices, there is a well-established model of relevant factors, and optimal weighting is measured relative to that model (Merton 1973). But a seemingly objective standard like this is not available everywhere. In ordinary consumer-choice situations, the normative standard will be related to the interests and hence the preferences of consumers. To know whether a consumer has placed disproportionate weight on a particular factor, we need to know the appropriate weight given to that factor according to the consumer's true preferences. For example, *how much* more important is one feature of a loan agreement relative to another? How much weight should be placed on a hotel's nightly rate versus the price of extras such as parking and wireless connections? How much relative weight should be placed on an internet service provider's price, convenience, storage capacity, and privacy policies?

Salience is often treated as a purely informational phenomenon, which is why we have included it in this chapter and not in Chapter 4. If salience relates only to how people form and update their beliefs, then its effects can be measured against the standard of "the truth." But as the previous examples demonstrate, salience is not strictly a matter of beliefs, but also of preferences. Consequently, the application of salience to "correct" decision-making failures raises many of the concerns discussed in previous chapters about models that impose a particular structure on the form of preferences. This becomes especially clear when we consider salience-based models that assume the agent is nominally *aware* of all relevant information, but some information is not vivid enough. What is the optimal degree of vividness for information the agent already has? The answer must depend on preferences.

Now let us consider why attention might be differentially directed. Among the many possible causes of the redirection of attention is the incongruity of the stimulus in the context (e.g., seeing a nutritious food advertised by someone who is smoking) or perhaps, more generally, a stimulus that is unexpected (e.g., news that a previously reliable drug is now considered risky).[51] Each of these factors, however, may be transient; incongruity can become old-hat over time. To complicate matters further, salience is not solely a property of the stimulus; it is the outcome of a process of interaction with an individual (Fiske and Taylor 1991, 249). People tend to notice what they are interested in or involved with. For any given objective measurement of the "salience" of a physical stimulus, the effective or actual salience will depend on the degree of individual interest. Thus, salience is not simply imposed from the outside world.

The second and third factors are interrelated. Since the new direction of attention toward one aspect of the environment usually means redirection away from another, how is the individual's overall judgment of an object affected? It may be a manipulator's or paternalist's intention to increase the weighting of certain characteristics at the expense of less important characteristics – that is, to effect optimal weighting. And yet the increase in weighting may be at the expense of factors particular individuals consider more important, thus creating distortions elsewhere in the decision problem.

Consider one prominent model, Bordalo et al. (2013), that illustrates some of these points. In their model, "rational" consumers are posited to value each attribute of a good (price and quality) "equally."[52] What does it

---

[51] On the effects of incongruity see Guido (2001, 47–50) and the references therein, and on the effects of the unexpected see Guido (2001, 50–53) and the references cited therein.
[52] See the critique of this model in Sugden (2015, 587–592).

mean to weight price and quality equally? In their mathematical model, it simply means that the variables in question (p and q) have the same coefficient. In reality, it's much less clear because quality, at least, often has no objective measure. Different agents could make different assessments of quality, and their tastes in this regard would manifest in the assessment of quality rather than its coefficient. Even if there were some objective measure of quality (for example, the purity of a drug), not all consumers would care about that quality to the same degree. Thus, it is already impossible to escape the subjectivity of preferences.

In Bordalo and coauthors' model, the agent's true preferences would manifest themselves in actual choices if no attribute were salient or if consumers were indifferent to salience. However, imperfectly rational consumers in the model are affected by the salience of the attributes. This aspect of perception results in distorted valuation of goods by consumers, which in turn results in choices that deviate from the optimal. Notice that in all of this, the objective measures of price and quality are assumed to be known by the agent, meaning that salience here is not a matter of beliefs or information processing. It is a matter of differential attention that causes the agent to put too much weight on one factor or the other. Thus, the only way to determine whether a real-world consumer made the mistake described by the model would be to know something about their preferences – specifically, the true weighting they should put on the relevant attributes. (Saying that the true weighting is equal weighting does not solve this problem for the reasons stated earlier.)

Salience, in the Bordalo et al. model, is a function of the deviation of a good's price or quality attribute from its rationally expected value, meaning the average value of that attribute over goods in a choice set – loosely, the set of all goods in the "same" category.[53] The good's price or a quality "stands out" to the degree that it differs from this mathematical expectation. Thus, the salience mechanism is quite simple and emanates from the environment, rather than from any interaction between the consumer and the environment. The particular interests and concerns of the consumer play no role; salience is strictly a function of the difference between actual and expected values of price and quality.

Taken as a whole, the setup of Bordalo et al.'s model reveals a significant lack of clarity and avoidance of some fundamental issues. If salience, as the evidence suggests, is the joint product of the stimulus and the consumer's

---

[53] It is odd to say that less-than-rational agents form rational expectations.

interests, then identifying rational preferences that are distinct from "salience-infected" preferences doesn't make sense. Differential attention is ubiquitous in human perception, as it should be. A rational standard must take account of differential attention that deviates from the optimal level of attention, but that cannot be done independently of knowing the consumer's true preferences. Therefore, the assumption that rational consumers attach equal weights to the product's attributes is not a harmless modeling assumption. It avoids the fundamental issue of discovering the true preference weights, which need not be equal. Finally, the vagueness of the causal process by which salience operates makes this sort of modeling inappropriate for policy purposes. At the very least we need a clearer conception of the causes of salience as well as, of course, a clearer definition of just what salience is.

OVERCONFIDENCE AND PROBABILITY JUDGMENTS

"Overconfidence bias" is a distortion in the evaluation of the accuracy of one's own knowledge.[54] It is not about the accuracy of that knowledge per se, but about what psychologists call "meta-cognition": How well do people know the accuracy of their own knowledge? This area of research is filled with dogma and naïve empiricism (Juslin et al. 2000), which we shall explore. Nevertheless, it is extremely important because the consequences of overconfidence are asserted, without much evidence, to be enormous.[55] The topic's importance requires us to look at overconfidence bias in considerable detail, from both the conceptual and the empirical perspectives. The conceptual and theoretical issues are messy partly because it is not clear what the normative standard is or should be. There is no escaping the statistical issues in the empirical analysis because much of what is called "overconfidence" is statistical artifact or otherwise difficult to interpret empirically.

The overconfidence literature in which we are interested relates to probabilistic knowledge, and specifically to the mismatch between subjective degrees of belief and observed frequencies. For example, in one common format, experiment subjects are presented with general knowledge questions such as these:

---

[54] The larger context of this bias is that people may be overconfident in their abilities more generally (as in driving skills, for example).

[55] "The significance of overconfidence to the conduct of human affairs can hardly be overstated" (Griffin and Tversky 1992, 432).

Which city has more inhabitants?
(a) Hyderabad (b) Islamabad
How confident are you that your answer is correct?
0.5 0.6 0.7 0.8 0.9 1.0
where 0.5 means you are guessing, and 1.0 means you are certain.

The experimenter will typically provide each subject with twenty to fifty questions and then tabulate the proportion that were answered correctly. This proportion will be compared with the *average* degree of confidence that she attached to her answers. Thus, an individual might have had an average degree of confidence of 70 percent but actually have answered only 60 percent of the questions correctly. This is interpreted as *overconfidence bias.*

Most of the time the questions are selected by the experimenters to differentiate among people – that is, to be difficult enough to separate high-knowledge from low-knowledge subjects. Thus, a number of "tricky" or difficult questions are deliberately included in the list given to participants. A bias toward error is built in. This is inconsistent with random sampling from a natural environment. However, more recently, questions have sometimes been chosen randomly from a well-defined category in the natural environment without an attempt to select the questions.

How to Make Guesses on Trivia Questions

Before focusing on the meaning of overconfidence, it's worth asking how people answer questions such as those used in overconfidence studies. If you were asked to decide which of two cities had the larger population, how would you do it? There are many possible methods, but some intuitive methods have been identified. One is the *recognition heuristic,* which simply means choosing a recognized option over an unrecognized one. If you've heard of one city and not the other, you choose the former. Another is the *Take the Best (TTB) heuristic.* This method involves searching sequentially through a sequence of cues that might predict the correct answer, with the cues ordered roughly in terms of their predictive accuracy.[56] For instance, if you recognize both cities, then you move on to other cues: whether the city is the capital of a country, whether it has a soccer team, and so on. As soon as you reach a cue that distinguishes between the two alternatives, the process stops.

---

[56] More exactly, the validity of a cue is the proportion of times the presence of the cue is associated with a higher value on the criterion than its absence is associated with.

Would a social scientist use these methods? Probably not. A typical approach would be to collect as much data as possible about cities and their populations, as well as possible correlates such as the cues noted earlier (capital or not, soccer team or not, etc.), and then run a regression to attach coefficients to the cues. The regression equation would allow you to make predictions about other cities. Of course, this approach would require a great deal of information and time to perform. And as it turns out, the gain from doing so could be small or even negative. The recognition heuristic and TTB, among other heuristics, can use less information and produce better decisions.

The key to grasping this surprising result is realizing that "bias" (ignoring apparently relevant information) is not the only source of error. There is also the variance of finite samples drawn from a population. When the regression equation estimated by sampling from a population reflects the true model, the deviations from it have an expected value of zero. This is what economists are thinking about when they say that there is no systematic bias. But this is not the end of the story. In our world, where there is genuine uncertainty regarding the true model, attempts to capture the fundamental underlying pattern and estimate the true relationship may also capture accidental patterns (due to variance). The more data from the sample the model seeks to fit, the greater will be this danger. There is a bias–variance trade-off. Especially in cases where the data is limited, the variance component of estimation will be very high (Gigerenzer and Brighton 2009, 117–120).

Ignoring some information can therefore reduce variance but often at the expense of more bias. In important cases, reducing variance – even with more bias – makes for superior predictions. We can see this phenomenon clearly in those cases where scientific models are complicated to obtain a good fit to all of the sample data but perform relatively poorly in out-of-sample prediction. From the agent's perspective, accounting for all the data *ex post* is not as important as prediction. And prediction may be enhanced by neglecting data or accepting bias.

Aside from being important on its own terms, the use of heuristics such as TTB will also play a role in helping us understand the overconfidence phenomenon.

Degrees of Confidence versus Subjective Probabilities

The most pressing question with regard to overconfidence is this: what sense can we make of the standard by which overconfidence is measured?

What is the meaning of perfect calibration (e.g., 70 percent average degree of confidence with 70 percent correct answers)?

The question that the participants in these experiments are being asked is their degree of confidence in the answers they give. Importantly, they are not explicitly asked the *probability* that their answer is correct. The allowed range begins with 0.5, which represents guessing. There is no need to interpret this as an assessment that conforms to the probability calculus. It could be simply the degree of potential surprise. If I cannot say that one answer is better than the other, then I would not be surprised if either were true. If I say that one answer is definitely true (call that 1) then I would assign a maximum of potential surprise to the other answer being the true one. Are the individuals expressing something of this sort when they assign a confidence number to their answer? If so, potential surprise is not a probability measure and as such we should not expect it to behave like one, that is, to have the same implications as probability assessments.[57] It is also quite possible that individuals interpret or intend the confidence assignments to be primarily ordinal. Therefore, 0.6 is more certain than simple guessing, 0.7 is more certain than 0.6 ... and 1.0 is more certain than 0.9 and the most certain it is possible to be. Again, this characterization of what the agents are doing does not necessarily follow the properties of the probability calculus. In general, the probabilistic interpretation is simply superimposed on the subjects' choices by the experimenter.

Subjective Probabilities and Objective Frequencies

Let us nevertheless assume for the purposes of discussion that the individuals are assessing subjective probabilities. As usual, a bias must be defined in relation to some standard. As we said, the literature on confidence has focused on the perfect calibration of subjective probabilities ("degrees of confidence") with actual objective frequencies. However, a subjective probability is a degree of belief in the occurrence of an event – a reflection of "the psychological sensation of an individual" about a single event (De Finetti cited in Galavotti 2001, xx). This assessment is based on "all of the information available to the individual and his own skill" (De Finetti

---

[57] For a general discussion of why the measure of potential surprise does not have the properties of the probability calculus, see Shackle (1961).

1974b, 16).[58] It is not in itself a prediction about the relative frequency of that event over a long series of trials.

In the typical experiment, an individual is being asked her degree of belief about the accuracy of her answer to a specific question. *She is not being asked what proportion of the questions she answered correctly.* Therefore, it is necessary to clarify the relation between the two – in particular, the relation between the average degree of confidence expressed over many questions and the proportion of the questions the individual answers correctly. On the assumption that the "degrees of confidence" should be interpreted as subjective probabilities, there is a theorem (an identity) that says that the average degree of belief will equal the mathematically expected proportion of correct answers.[59] This is a coherence relationship between the *explicit* individual subjective probability assessments and the *implied* expectation of the proportion of questions answered correctly. The implied expectation is called a "prevision" of the proportion and not a "prediction" (De Finetti 1974a, 69–74).[60] It is an *ex ante* subjective assessment made on the basis of the information the individual has at the time, and thus it cannot be regarded as a mistake.[61]

But, surely, the reader may respond: the individuals' mathematical expectation did not turn out to be correct; in fact, they implicitly overestimated the average number of correct answers. However, this would be a problem only if the individuals in fact made *predictions* based on their

---

[58] Operationally, the degree of belief is often treated as a betting quotient: the maximum amount an individual is prepared to pay for, say, a prize of $1 contingent on the occurrence of that event (Keren 1991). Usually, the amounts of money are kept small to avoid the problem of changing marginal utility of money confounding the revelation of the subject's assessment of probability. Unfortunately, this may lessen the seriousness with which people consider their bets.

[59] To see this, suppose the subject scores 1 for every correct answer and 0 for every incorrect answer. Her expected score on a question where her degree of belief is 0.7 is 0.7. Her expected score on a question where her degree of belief is 0.5 is 0.5. Her total expected score over both questions is $0.5 + 0.7 = 1.2$, and her expected average (expected score divided by number of questions) is $1.2/2 = 0.6$, which is also her average degree of belief. For a more general demonstration, see De Finetti (1964, 113–114).

[60] The degrees of belief assigned to the individual answers determine the assessments of subjective probability weights for the occurrence of zero correct answers, only one correct answer, only two correct answers, and so on – to all correct answers. The weighted average of these is the expectation of the overall number of correct answers. "Prevision" distributes our subjective probabilities over all of these possible alternatives.

[61] "Only if one came to realize that there were inadequacies in the analysis and the use of the original state of information which one should have been aware of at the time (like errors in calculation, oversights which one has noticed soon after, etc.) would it be permissible to talk of 'mistakes' in making a prevision" (De Finetti 1974a, 207).

implied expectations (i.e., their previsions). Oddly, most studies in this area do not ask subjects to estimate their overall frequency of correct answers directly. If they were asked to do so, they would presumably turn their attention to that question and make a separate (rather than simply an implied) prediction. And then, if they wished to be deductively thorough, they would revise their degree-of-belief assessments to make them consistent with the explicitly predicted overall frequency. Alternatively, they could simply tolerate the inconsistency.[62] Beliefs do not need to be coherent in the mathematical sense to be ecologically rational. Predicting a relative frequency is *not* what the participants in the experiments were doing. An implication from the prior assignment of degrees of confidence in individual answers is not the same as an explicit prediction of frequency.

This distinction between the *direct* prediction of a frequency and the expectation of that frequency *implied* by subjective probability assessments is not simply a subtle philosophical point. It is an empirical issue as well. The reason is that the mental processes involved in the two tasks are different. When each question is asked, a different knowledge base is activated. Accordingly, we need to think about the assessment of subjective degrees of belief and the accuracy of predictions separately.

When Is the Implied Expectation Consistent with the Actual Frequency?

To answer this question, we need a model of the process by which individuals assess their degrees of belief in the answers they have given. We adopt the Probabilistic Mental Model (PMM) of Gigerenzer et al. (1991). In this model there are two tasks: confidence and frequency. For each of these, there are three relevant factors: the target variable, the reference class, and the probability cues. Accordingly, in a confidence task about, say, determining which of two German cities is larger, the target variable is the number of inhabitants, the reference class is cities in

---

[62] De Finetti (1974a, 203) analyzes the case where the individual revises his judgments: "You might find that the [subjective] probabilities You [sic] have evaluated ... give ... a value which is greater the number of successes ... which in prevision seems to You reasonable. You then must ask yourself: 'have I given the p_i values which on the average are too large, or are the values which I thought of for the number of successes ... too low?' It is fairly difficult to answer this if the events are rather disparate, but when they are more alike, and especially if we know the frequency of other similar events, which have already been observed, it often happens that one places greater confidence in prevision of the relative frequency (under the assumption that it will remain close to that previously observed)."

Germany, and the probability cues are city characteristics that might help to predict population size.

When people answer questions from this particular reference class, they use something like the TTB heuristic described earlier: they draw on cues with perceived validity in distinguishing among the population sizes of cities – e.g., they might check whether the cities have soccer teams first, then whether they are state capitals, and so on. The degree of belief that the individual expresses in her answer reflects the perceived conditional probability of the decisive cue. If the perceived probability that the city is larger, given that it has a soccer team and the other does not, is 0.7, then that is the degree of confidence or belief.[63] When the perceived validity of the cues corresponds to their actual validity in a particular environment, the PMM is considered to be ecologically adapted.

In this type of test for overconfidence, there is also a frequency task. Here the target variable is the number of correct answers. The reference class is the set of general knowledge questions under equivalent testing conditions. Note that this is *not* the same reference class as in the confidence task. Instead of drawing on her personal knowledge about cities and demographics, the subject instead draws on her personal experience in tests similar to this one. The probability cues can be derived from the base rates of previous performance of such tests, the individual's self-perceived competence in general knowledge issues, or – *but by no means necessarily* – her mean confidence on the various answers. The important point is that the target, reference class, and probability cues are in general all different from those in the confidence task. In short, confidence and frequency are different problems with different solutions.

If the PMM is adapted to the confidence task, that is, if the cues have objective validity, *and* the questions are representatively sampled from the reference class of German cities, then measured overconfidence will tend to disappear. This means that the implied expectation will match the actual proportion of correct answers. Gigerenzer et al. (1991) asked West German students (before reunification) to determine which of two cities drawn from a random sample of major cities in West Germany had the greater population. The results showed a mean confidence of 70.8 percent and a frequency of correct answers of 71.7 percent. The crucial differences between this and many other studies are that the questions were taken

---

[63] When the two cities each have a soccer team, the individual proceeds to a second cue in the hierarchy. It may have a different perceived validity, and therefore the degree of belief assessed will be different.

from the participants' natural environment (that is, a knowledge domain familiar to them) *and* there was no deliberate selection of questions to differentiate among subjects. The questions were representative of the environment to which the subjects were adapted.

When Is the Implied Expectation "Overconfident" but the Frequency Judgment Accurate?

It is difficult to explain the coexistence of overconfident confidence judgments and accurate frequency judgments on the standard theory. They are supposed to be consistent with each other. However, this is not always the case empirically. The reason is again rooted in the different mental processes the individual uses to respond to each type of question. What is the background knowledge used to perform the confidence task versus the frequency task? What cue or cues will the individual use to make these estimates? With different knowledge bases and different cues, the implied expectation and the explicit prediction of the outcome could be different.[64]

If the PMM for the frequency task is adapted to the class of general knowledge questions and the particular set of questions asked in the experiment is representatively sampled from that class, the estimated number of correct answers will tend to be accurate. On the other hand, if the individual questions asked are selected to be tricky or harder than a representative draw from the class of "German cities," then the individual will exhibit "overconfidence" and the *implied* expected frequency of correct answers will be higher than the direct prediction and the actual outcome. In the series of experiments previously mentioned, Gigerenzer et al. (1991) asked German students to answer a set of *selected* general knowledge questions that had no particular connection to their natural environment. As before, they were asked to indicate their degree of confidence in the answers. The results here displayed the usual overconfidence. The mean confidence was 66.7 while the percentage of correct answers was 52.9. The interpretation is that the PMM regarding the confidence task is not well adapted.[65] On the other hand, when the participants were explicitly asked to predict the percentage of correct answers, they slightly *underestimated* it. They estimated 51.7. The difference between the predicted outcome and

---

[64] "*[I]t is senseless to speak of the probability of an event unless we do so in relation to the body of knowledge possessed by a given person*" (De Finetti 2008, 3, emphasis in original).

[65] The students applied a PMM adapted for an easier set of questions to a harder set. This is why the errors are biased toward overconfidence.

the percentage of correct answers was only 1.2. This means that on average the participants got one more question correct of the fifty questions asked than they predicted they would. The interpretation here is that the PMM with regard to the frequency task is adapted to the reference class of "general knowledge questions" even though the PMM for confidence tasks is not well adapted. The two tasks have different knowledge bases, and so we should not be surprised that they can produce different results.

Coherence or Adapted Frameworks?

The emphasis on the coherence of judgments across different areas of decision-making can lead us astray. We have seen this in relation to the pragmatic rationality of preference judgments that may fail to cohere – to be transitive, consistent, and so forth. The important issue before us now, from a pragmatic perspective, is whether the methods by which people make judgments in specific environments is adapted to those environments. If people are interested in predicting the frequency of some event (such as correct answers), how do they do it and how successful is that method? What are the conditions under which we should expect their judgments to be correct (aside from random errors)?

If individuals employ different PMMs to answer different questions and those models are adapted to the circumstances in which they are used, we should not worry about whether the judgments made in one area are perfectly consistent with those in another. Similarly, if people are misled in environments with which they have little familiarity because they apply the wrong PMM, then it seems absurd to call their decision-making "irrational" or "boundedly rational," as if there were a feasible world in which people would make correct predictions about alien environments. There is also the important matter of whether and to what extent people make systematic errors in circumstances *where the outcome matters in some practical way*, or whether we have simply discovered some possible truth about errors in playing games.[66]

---

[66] Even within the context of these games there may be no reason to worry about "overconfidence." Consider a simple example in which a subject is drawing balls from an urn. Black and white balls fill the urn in unknown but fixed proportions. Before each draw, the subject predicts the ball's color. Her prediction is made by reference to all of the data available before any prediction was made – there may have been some initial draws, some information about the person constructing the mix might be available, the composition of previous urns in this game may be known, and so forth. Let us say that the subject's degree of belief that the next ball is black is 0.6. Then she draws, with replacement, from

The Data: Extreme Format Dependence

We have discussed some fundamental conceptual difficulties with relative frequencies as a standard of subjective probability calibration. Nevertheless, let us abstract from these and ask the simple question: are people overconfident and to what extent? Unfortunately, the existing literature does not give us a useful answer. The answer depends on exactly how the question is asked ("the format"), the domain of questions, whether the data is adjusted for certain statistical problems, and even the characteristics of the participants studied. To anticipate our later policy discussion, the lack of robustness in these studies makes them difficult, perhaps impossible, to use in policy decisions.

The four major formats that have been used are:

1. Half-range format: *Does the population of Thailand exceed 25 million? Yes/No. How confident are you that your answer is correct (from 0.5 to 1.0)?*

The half-range format has been extensively studied. In the most comprehensive meta-analysis of which we are aware, Juslin et al. (2000) analyzed the data in fifty-one articles comprising ninety-five studies containing general knowledge questions asked in the half-range format. They sought, among other things, to test the ecological structure (or PMM) hypothesis (Gigerenzer et al. 1991). This says, as we saw in the previous section, that there should be much better calibration for questions chosen randomly from a natural environment ("representative sample") than for questions selected by experimenters to distinguish among the participants ("selected sample").[67] When Juslin and coauthors divided the studies into

the urn 100 times. She is not told whether these balls are white or black until the completion of all of the draws. Each time she draws from the urn, she predicts the color is black because on each draw it is more likely black than white. She assigns to that prediction her degree of belief 0.6, because there is no reason for that to have changed. After 100 draws, the black balls total sixty and white balls forty. Since she said black each time, she was correct 60 percent of the time. So what? Suppose she had assigned a degree of belief to a black draw at 0.8 and the observed frequency was still sixty–forty. She still would have said black each time and gotten 60 percent correct. In both cases the empirical outcome is irrelevant to the individual's purposes in guessing.

[67] There are subtly different variants of the ecological hypothesis. The essential element is that "[p]eople have knowledge of the statistical structure of real environments, allowing them to make inferences of probabilistic or statistical validity – which are true for most situations that may be encountered, but not all ... Accurate judgments can only be observed in humans when the sampling of items in the experimental tasks does not systematically deviate from the way these humans have sampled information in the

representative samples and selected samples, the mean subjective probability and proportion of answers correct in the selected studies were 0.73 and 0.64 respectively, indicating overconfidence. But in the representative studies, they were 0.73 and 0.72 (Juslin et al. 2000, 390, table 3), indicating close to zero overconfidence. These results support Gigerenzer and coauthors' PMM hypothesis. They are also consistent with rational irrationality, inasmuch as the agents who faced selected question sets were not in their natural environment and thus had little opportunity to overcome an experimentally constructed biased knowledge environment.

Some authors (Kahneman and Tversky 1996; Griffin and Tversky 1992) have claimed that this kind of result confounds the *hard–easy effect* with the assessment of a general overconfidence bias. The hard–easy effect is another finding of the overconfidence literature, which says that overconfidence is positively correlated with the difficulty of the task – i.e., subjects will display more overconfidence for harder questions, but less overconfidence (or even underconfidence) for easier questions. A representative sample not only reflects the individual's environment more accurately but, for the same reason, implies an easier set of questions. Therefore, representative samples will necessarily reduce the number of hard questions and thus reduce overconfidence. Even if this argument were correct, it would suggest that in ordinary real life, overconfidence is less pronounced and less likely than in the laboratory.

But further investigation finds that even the hard–easy effect dissolves (or nearly so) in representative samples. First, when comparing selected samples with hard questions (those with less than 70 percent correct answers) to representative samples with hard questions, Juslin et al. (2000) find that the mean overconfidence in the former is 0.10 and in the latter 0.05.[68] In other words, even controlling for difficulty, the results still support the ecological hypothesis.

Second, to capture any hard–easy effect more directly, it is useful to look at the regression line comparing over/underconfidence with the proportion of correct answers (see Figure 5.1). A significant hard–easy effect is captured when the slope is negative and steep, that is, as the proportion of

---

environment" (Winman and Juslin 2006, 412–413). In everyday life people use cues that with high probability allow them to make inferences about certain facts. Usually, for example, relative average temperature works to distinguish the latitude of cities, except where the two cities happen to be New York and Rome.

[68] Mean over/underconfidence is defined as the difference between the mean subjective probability and the proportion of answers correct. When the difference is positive, we have overconfidence. When it is negative, we have underconfidence.

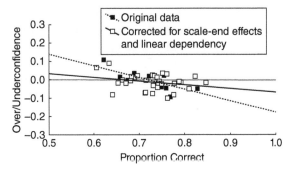

Figure 5.1 The remains of the hard–easy effect
Source: Juslin et al. (2000, 393)

correct answers increases we move from overconfidence to underconfidence. The flatter is the slope, the smaller is the hard-easy effect. When a
subset of the data, gathered from representative samples collected by the
authors, was corrected for two statistical problems (scale-end effects and
linear dependency), the slope of the regression line became much flatter. In
fact, the simultaneous correction of both problems resulted in a slope not
statistically different from zero (Juslin et al. 2000).[69] Again, this disappear-
ance of the hard–easy effect happened only in the representative samples,
not in the selected samples.

It is worth expanding on the two corrections that Juslin et al. (2000)
performed to find this result. The hard–easy effect can easily be generated
by random errors and scale-end effects. Even for the perfectly calibrated
subject, the association between confidence and proportion correct would
be subject to random variation. Assume that the subject's true degrees of
belief are revealed or made "overt" subject to random error. A true degree
of belief is one that would be assigned in the absence of "response errors"
caused by "chance variations in one's experiences, variability in feelings of
confidence given identical information, and unreliability in assigning a
numerical value to one's feelings" (Klayman et al. 2006, 159). The overt
degrees of belief are what we measure. So the highest true degree of belief
(around 1.0) will tend to be measured downward; it cannot be measured
upward because the scale ends at 1.0, and no random error can cause it to

---

[69] It is *possible* to have miscalibration even if the mean degree of belief is equal to the
proportion of correct answers. The hard–easy effect can exist without overconfidence in
the simple sense of *mean* miscalibration. In other words, in the half-range format the
difference between mean degree of belief and proportion of answers correct can be zero
while the calibration *curve* has a negative slope. In the data presented here we have
neither.

exceed 1.0. For other high true degrees of beliefs, it is *likely* that they also will be measured downward. Similarly, at the other end of the scale his true degrees of belief will tend to be measured upward because the scale ends at 0.5; no random error can cause it to fall below 0.5. The result is an apparent hard–easy effect: underconfidence at the high end of the scale (corresponding to easier questions) and overconfidence at the low end (corresponding to harder questions).

Furthermore, there is a response-error effect with regard to the measured number of answers that are correct. Sometimes, due to random factors such as the precise sample used and its proportion of tricky or contrary questions, an individual may answer fewer correctly than might be expected on the basis of his general familiarity with the area tested. The combined result of these response errors is to lower the measured subjective degrees of belief for the easy questions and raise them for the hard questions relative to perfect calibration, thus producing an apparent hard–easy effect without an underlying cognitive bias.[70] This is a matter of randomness, not a systematic failure in cognitive processing.[71]

2. Full-range format: *The population of Thailand exceeds 25 million. What is the probability that this proposition is correct (from 0 to 1.0)?*

In this format, the analyst separates the subject's answer from their confidence in the answer by converting to half-range format. For instance, an answer of 0.7 would be regarded as saying the statement is true while an answer of 0.3 would be treated as saying the statement is false, both with a confidence of 0.7.

The full-range format will necessarily show more overconfidence than the half-range format. Once again, if we postulate random response errors

---

[70] The apparent hard–easy effect will pivot around the mean of the half-range scale at about 0.75 – roughly the dividing line (proportion correct) that separates hard and easy questions in most studies.

[71] An important indication that the phenomenon is due to mean regression is that (1) if the analyst regresses subjective degree of belief against the proportion correct there is *overconfidence* in the difficult questions (proportion of correct answers is less than 70 percent) and underconfidence in the easy questions and (2) if the analyst regresses proportion of correct answers on subjective degree of belief there is *underconfidence* when the proportion correct is low and vice versa. This can be seen in the analysis of Dawes and Mulford (1996). See also Erev et al. (1994). More generally, "[g]iven two random variables X and Y with equal variance and less than perfect intercorrelation ... the variance of the estimates of X shrinks when plotted against fixed levels of Y, but the variance of the estimates of Y also shrinks when plotted against fixed levels of X" (Fiedler and Krueger 2012, 172).

as discussed earlier, their effect is to increase the appearance of overconfidence. The specific impact of the errors depends on the scale used. In the half-range format, these effects are felt near 0.5 and 1.0, with a pivot point around 0.75. In the full-range format, on the other hand, the effects occur near 0.0 and 1.0, with a pivot point around 0.5. These pivot points are where we would expect a crossover from measured underconfidence to measured overconfidence. As a result, the full-range format will tend to generate measured overconfidence over the 0.5–1.0 interval, whereas the half-range format will tend to generate underconfidence in the 0.5–0.75 interval and overconfidence in the 0.75–1.0 interval. In other words, the full-range format tends to induce measured overconfidence in all answers that are considered more likely than not. Indeed, the data shows that the full-range format consistently produces more measured overconfidence than the half-range format (Juslin et al. 1999). Of course, this has little, if anything, to do with systematic cognitive biases.

Overall, it seems fair to conclude that, once statistical effects and whether agents are adapted to the question environment are taken into account, there is not much evidence for overall overconfidence as cognitive processing bias in either the half-range or full-range format (Juslin et al. 1999).[72]

3. Interval production format: *Give the smallest interval for which you are .xx certain to include the population of Thailand. Between* _____ *and* _____ *inhabitants.* (The suggested level of confidence *.xx* is given by the experimenter.)

It is well known that the interval production format produces massive overconfidence (Klayman et al. 1999). But the effect is so format-dependent that the easiest debiasing technique is simply to ask questions in another format (e.g., the half-range discussed earlier). Furthermore, the results in this format are also heavily dependent on the *subformats* used to elicit responses. For example:

[O]ne can ask for a range that the judge is 90% sure contains the correct answer, or ask separately for a point with 5% chance of being too low and another with 5% chance of being too high, or ask for those two estimates plus a median estimate. The first will produce the most overconfidence; the last will produce the least.

(Soll and Klayman 2004, 311)

---

[72] With respect to findings with the two-choice question format, "some domains exhibit overconfidence and others underconfidence, but the net effect is small when representative sets of questions are sampled from multiple domains" (Soll and Klayman 2004, 311).

Specifically, for an interval of 80 percent, the first range format yielded a hit rate of 39 percent, and thus 41 percent measured overconfidence. The two-point format yields 23 percent measured overconfidence; the three-point format yields only 14 percent. When the last is adjusted for random variability effects, the number falls to 3 percent (Soll and Klayman 2004, 306, 308).

4. Interval evaluation format: *The population of Thailand lies between X and Y million. Assess the probability that the statement above is correct? 0%, 10%, 20% ... 100%.* (The *X* and *Y* are given by the experimenter.)

This is a relatively new format employed in the measurement of over-confidence. Instead of producing the interval that satisfies a given degree of confidence, the participant evaluates a given interval in terms of his degree of confidence that the target value lies within that interval. In principle, these are equivalent questions. Empirically, however, they elicit substan-tially different degrees of confidence. For example, if the experimenter asks the degree of confidence a participant has that the population of Thailand is between 25 and 50 million, the participant may say 90 percent. But if the experimenter asks what is the range of estimates of the population in which you would have 90 percent confidence that the true population is within that interval, he might get an answer such as 25–75 million.[73] In experi-ments such as this (Winman et al. 2004, 1171), the mean degree of overconfidence is about 75 percent higher for interval production than for interval evaluation. Nevertheless, mean "overconfidence" still appears with interval evaluation. If the calibration results pertained, for example, to interest rate forecasting, the intervals associated with a subjective probabil-ity of 1.0 would capture 100 percent of interest rates in the long run. Yet the average interval associated with 100 percent subjective probability captures only 50 percent of long-run interest rates – a big difference (p. 1174).

What all this format dependence ultimately means for an understanding of "overconfidence" phenomena is unclear. This is because there is no good theory to guide us in determining which measures are most relevant to pragmatic concerns. *In other words, we do not know which formats mirror the process by which real-world individuals evaluate their own knowledge and, most importantly, make decisions about significant matters.*

---

[73] For reference, the population of Thailand at the time of writing in 2019 is about 69 million.

Furthermore, many studies show considerable variation from overconfidence to underconfidence depending on the domain of questions asked and the gender of the participants (Soll and Klayman 2004, 310–311).

The Economics of Prediction: Trade-Offs

Psychologists have tried using many different models to explain the extreme format dependence in confidence studies. This is important because format dependence suggests that we do not understand the underlying phenomena very well. Yet all of these studies miss an essential point from the pragmatic perspective adopted in this book. Seeking to calibrate judgments of confidence with the frequency of correct outcomes is the application of an abstract normative standard divorced from the incentives that affect decisions in real life.

In the interval production format, Alpert and Raiffa (1982) showed that students produced intervals for unknown quantities at the 98 percent level of confidence for which the interval contained the answer only about 60 percent of the time. However, the normative standard is perfect calibration (Griffin and Tversky 1992, 431). This would imply a hit rate of 98 percent. Why do people not ensure the accuracy of the produced interval by choosing very wide intervals? This would be quite adaptive to the experimental task; it would produce high hit rates. Something is obviously holding them back. This is, presumably, the desire to be informative in producing the intervals (Yaniv and Foster 1995, 1997).

Suppose a person is asked the date of the first transatlantic flight.[74] If she were to produce a 95 percent confidence interval that the date is somewhere between 1900 and 1950, she would be certain to include the correct answer in the interval. But typically people will produce a narrower interval. The fifty-year interval is not very informative. It does not help the receiver to make a better decision than would be made without the judge's advice. Producers and receivers of such judgments usually want informativeness as well as accuracy. In a world of uncertainty, they cannot have both perfectly, which means there are trade-offs: to provide more informativeness, they have to sacrifice some accuracy. Individuals in experimental situations carry over the lessons learned in real life to their behavior in the experiment. They are accustomed to making accuracy–informativeness trade-offs, not to performing calibration tasks.

---

[74] The correct answer is 1919.

On the other hand, it would be possible for individuals to make accuracy–informativeness trade-offs consistent with a high degree of calibration. Such individuals, it is claimed, would display good meta-cognition. They would know just how much they do know; they would be neither overconfident nor underconfident.

However, neither experts nor novices seem to care much about calibration. McKenzie et al. (2008) compare the interval-production behavior of novices (people without expertise in the questions asked) and experts (people with such expertise). Experts provide intervals that are narrower in width and more accurate.[75] Nevertheless, *they are no better calibrated than the novices.* We might have expected that experts would have greater meta-cognition. What happened? Technically, the narrower intervals by themselves reduce the hit rate. The increase in accuracy increases the hit rate. For experts, the two offset each other and the calibration for both groups is the same: relatively low hit rates and hence poor calibration.

Let's examine the calibration criterion more closely. Under which conditions might it be a good proxy for the level of meta-cognition? It is a long-run standard, which means that it presupposes many trials from the *same* reference class – a class in which the structure producing the event in question is stable. This may not be hard to replicate in an experiment with the typical sets of knowledge questions. However, the long run of the real world is an extended period of actual time and the predictive intervals may not be all drawn from the same reference class with an unchanging structure. In this case, calibration does not measure meta-knowledge. It is not clear what it measures at all.

Even if we put this consideration aside, the incentives to produce calibrated results may be low in many real-world cases. Calibration will not be observable until some considerable time has passed, but informativeness will be obvious immediately and accuracy will be observed in short order relative to calibration (McKenzie et al. 2008). Therefore, it is rational for the producers of predictions not to care much about calibration when either short time horizons or defective incentive structures are in place.[76] This is not a decision-making problem. It may be a problem regarding the incentives faced by those making predictions.

---

[75] Perfect accuracy is defined as the absence of error. Error is the absolute value of the difference between the true value and the midpoint of the interval produced.

[76] It would be interesting to know the calibration of predictions in cases where producers and consumers of such predictions are in a long-term relationship.

If the incentives for good calibration are weak in the real world, it is worth asking what the incentives are like in the laboratory. The answer, it seems, is slim to none. The reason is that monetary incentives for calibration are extremely difficult to provide separately from incentives for accuracy. As Moore et al. (2015) explain:

> If you reward respondents for high hit-rates (getting the right answers inside their intervals) then clever respondents will make their intervals infinitely wide. If you reward respondents for providing narrower intervals, clever respondents will make their intervals infinitely narrow. If you try to reward both it becomes difficult to calibrate exactly how big this reward should be in order to perfectly counterbalance the incentive to increase hit rate, and the answer may depend on each respondent's subjective probability distribution.
>
> (Moore et al. 2015, 197)

Given these considerations, it is unsurprising that laboratory subjects don't perform well on calibration tasks. It is not clear they have any good reason to do so in the lab, nor do they have much experience in doing so outside the lab.

CONCLUSIONS

We have covered a wide range of cognitive operations and phenomena in this chapter – from the logical to the probabilistic. We have found that the literature on cognitive biases, vast though it is, tends to fail in one fundamental respect: recognizing the pragmatic and contextual nature of rational decision-making. The mistake that is constantly and consistently made is to equate rationality with an abstract system of thought unrelated to the purposes and plans of individuals in the environments in which they find themselves. In a related manner, the literature also fails to take into account the socially legitimate expectations of the participants in experiments that the researchers should not provide extraneous or misleading information. These are problems that go to the very heart of the "heuristics and biases" research program.

Our perspective, by contrast, recognizes that beliefs serve a purpose – and that purpose is not always truth-tracking. Beliefs can direct attention and provide motivation. Beliefs can be a source of direct satisfaction. Even when beliefs perform a primarily truth-tracking function, there is no uniquely correct way to form and revise beliefs in real-world environments characterized by uncertainty and change.

Most importantly, people in realistic contexts do not think like strict logicians and probability theorists – nor should they. While economists and psychologists are greatly concerned with the deductive consistency of beliefs, regular people need not share that concern. People acquire tools for different types of challenge in the wild, and they should not be expected to abandon all such tools when they enter the laboratory. In the study of beliefs, just as in the study of preferences, behavioral researchers have made the mistake of conflating their models with reality – and, when reality fails to conform to the model, judging it deficient.

APPENDIX TO CHAPTER 5: System 1 and System 2

Dual-system analysis, also known as "System 1" and "System 2" analysis, has become quite fashionable in popular presentations of the "heuristics and biases" literature as well as in the more technical psychological literature, largely due to the work of Daniel Kahneman. What is meant by System 1 and System 2, however, is not uniform. The popular rendition is probably an accurate statement of the technical perspective that reigned until approximately the turn of the twenty-first century. More recently, there have been important modifications of the dual-system (now generally called "dual process") framework.

We call the popular, but older, view the "received view" (Evans 2012). This view identifies System 1 cognitive processes and System 2 cognitive processes in terms of the aligned and dichotomous characteristics shown in Table 5.1.[77]

The received view dominates almost all of the popular discussion – and, unfortunately, some of the scholarly discussion, especially among behavioral economists. In particular, the picture that emerges in Kahneman's *Thinking, Fast and Slow* (2011) is the received view. System 1 is characterized as operating "automatically and quickly, and with little or no effort and no sense of voluntary control" (p. 20). System 2, on the other hand, "allocates attention to the effortful mental activities that demand it, including complex computations. The operations of System 2 are often associated with the subjective experience of agency, choice and concentration" (p. 21).

---

[77] Some dual-system theorists talk of *types* of processes rather than systems. In part this is to make clear that the processes do not constitute separate and identifiable physical brain systems. Although we agree, we nevertheless refer to System 1 and System 2 because this terminology is quite common in most of the behavioral economics and paternalism literature. We shall not, of course, change the terminology of the sources we cite or quote. Thus, there may appear to be some inconsistency in our use of terms.

Table 5.1 *"Received" view of dual-process theories of reasoning and higher cognition*

System 1 Processes	System 2 Processes
Unconscious, preconscious	Conscious
Rapid	Slow
Automatic	Controlled
Low effort	High effort
High capacity	Low capacity
Associative	Rule based
Intuitive	Deliberative
Contextualized	Abstract
Cognitive biases	Normative reasoning
Independent of cognitive capacity	Correlated with individual differences in cognitive capacity

Reprinted from Evans (2012, 117) with slight modifications.

System 1 processes are further characterized as automatic, autonomous, always on, relatively fast, effortless, productive of systematic errors in certain circumstances, not rule-following, and displaying lack of conscious access (Kahneman 2011, 21–57, 105). System 2 processes are characterized as deliberate, involving focused attention, conscious, minimizing effort, having a limited capacity especially with regard to working memory, rule-following, priority setting, and being the locus of self-control (Kahneman 2011, 21–41). Clearly, these lists constitute the received view.

Furthermore, the received view has come to dominate the policy discussion. Cass Sunstein, one of the main advocates of paternalistic public policy based on behavioral economics, describes System 1 as follows:

[It] works fast. It is often on automatic pilot. Driven by habits, it can be emotional and intuitive. It can procrastinate; it can be impulsive. ... It is a doer, not a planner.

(Sunstein 2014, 26–27)

There is also the suggestion that it has a short time horizon: "It wants what it wants when it wants it" (p. 26). On the other hand, System 2 is described in opposite terms:

[It] is more like a computer ... It is deliberative. It calculates. ... It thinks about probability, carefully though sometimes slowly. It does not really get offended. ... It insists on the importance of self-control. It is a planner as well as a doer; it does what it has planned.

(Sunstein 2014, 26–27)

While Sunstein recognizes that this is a simplification (p. 27), this characterization is what drives the entire book. The clear objective is to promote the twin ideas of an intuitive bias-generating system that operates costlessly,[78] and a corrective system based on deliberation that sometimes intervenes but at a high cost. However, neither Kahneman nor Sunstein clearly makes the distinction between the essential or universally present characteristics of specific processes within the two systems and those that are only sometimes associated with them.

WHAT IS THE FUNCTION OF DUAL-SYSTEM ANALYSIS?

Before we can evaluate the dual-systems construct, we must know what its function is. There are three plausible possibilities.

First, it might itself be a heuristic that helps us bring order to a large number of individual findings of the "heuristics and biases" literature. It can function as a metaphor or a "useful fiction" that substitutes for the more cumbersome invocation of technical processes (Kahneman 2011, 28–29). As such, it is an essentially backward-looking, and perhaps appealing, rhetorical summary of certain previous research.[79] On the basis of this previous research, Kahneman (2011) tells what has come to be a standard story. System 1, in certain circumstances, is bias-prone. These biases are generated automatically and without effort when the relevant stimulus is present. When the biases appear, System 1 is responsible for an initial cognitive state. In some cases an effortful System 2 will intervene and correct matters – although at other times it might create mistakes of its own. System 2 requires limited working memory capacity. Thus not all biases will be corrected.

An important issue, of course, is the selectivity of that summary and the usefulness of the selection criterion. As our discussion in Chapter 5 makes clear, there is much research that this classification omits in the course of setting up the dichotomy between automatic biases and effortful normative thinking. A reader who carefully followed Kahneman's simple constructs,

---

[78] Very little attention is paid to the cases where System 1 processes get things right, although there is acknowledgment that they do most of the time. See Sunstein (2014, 33) and Kahneman (2011, 24–25). This acknowledgment is undercut, however, by a research framework in which a premium is placed on discovering and confirming biases rather than successful adaptations.

[79] Kahneman (2011, 29) says that the systems' fiction appeals to the System 1 aspect of our minds. This is a curious claim, if you think about it: a fiction proving useful in terms of that very fiction.

System 1 and System 2, would be unaware of much of the literature we discuss in this book.

Second, the dual-systems construct might be a theory that makes falsifiable predictions. For example, it might predict that unconscious bias-generating processes are fast and conscious error-correction processes are slow.[80] However, it is persuasively denied by both advocates and opponents that it is a "theory" in this usual sense of the word. The characteristic terms are often imprecisely defined or inherently vague and with shifting of definitions across authors, so falsification tends to be difficult.[81]

Instead, it is claimed to be a "metatheory"– the third possibility – whose purpose is to "stimulate new research and accumulate supportive evidence," and that "such frameworks cannot be falsified by any specific instantiation or experimental finding." Falsification is a category that applies only to specific models within the framework (Evans and Stanovich 2013b, 263). Therefore, all of the intellectual action is ultimately in the testing of the specific, lower-level theories regarding processes and biases. If there is doubt about the adequacy of these theories, especially if they are not formulated for a relevant kind of rationality (that is, ecological or pragmatic rationality), then the systems construct can be unduly confining. It blinds us to possibly better theories outside its structure.

PARING DOWN THE CONSTRUCT

The received view has been significantly modified at the turn of the twenty-first century because of criticisms that key definitions are vague, attributes of the types of processing are not reliably aligned, the distinguishing attributes lie along a continuum and are not qualitatively different, and so forth. This is especially clear in the work of Jonathan Evans and Keith Stanovich, who have perhaps done the most to promote the dual-processes paradigm. In their current view, "the defining characteristic of Type 1 processes is their autonomy. They do not require 'controlled attention' which is another way of saying that they make minimal demands on working memory resources. Hence ... the execution of Type 1 processes is mandatory when the triggering stimuli are encountered and they are not

---

[80] Let it pass that many processes are a mix of conscious and unconscious elements and that the terms conscious and unconscious are not precisely defined (Evans and Stanovich 2013a, 227).

[81] This criticism is made by opponents of the dual-system construct (Karen 2013, 258) *and* is readily conceded by the advocates of dual systems (Evans and Stanovich 2013b, 263).

dependent on input from higher level control systems" (Evans and Stanovich 2013a, 236). All of the other Type 1 characteristics in Table 5.1 are considered mere imperfect "correlates" and not defining features.

The definition of Type 2 processing is not presented quite as directly, but "a key defining feature of Type 2 processing – the feature that makes humans unique – is cognitive decoupling: the ability to distinguish supposition from belief and to aid rational choices by running thought experiments" (Evans and Stanovich 2013a, 236).[82] This requires a significant amount of working memory, which is a scarce resource. In Evans and Stanovich's view, all of the other Type 2 characteristics are imperfect correlates of this key feature. An even more pared-down conception of the dual processes is given by Evans alone: "I suggest that the *only firm foundation* for the two types of processing is that one can bypass working memory [Type 1], whereas the other [Type 2] necessarily requires its use" (Evans 2012, 129, emphasis added). *To use working memory or not use working memory: that is the pared-down question.*[83]

And yet, it is difficult to see how the pared-down construct alone can do the work "required" by its most common uses. These uses require cheap production of errors and costly production of corrections.[84] These features require, in turn, much of what was in the received alignment view in Table 5.1. The sources of the cheap production of systematic errors seem to be not only unconscious processing and automaticity, but also intuitive-associative processing and the characterization ("contextualization") of events as ordinary or repetitive in a given environment when they are not. The costly correction of error seems to be explained by features of Type 2 processes that include high effort, consciousness (deliberateness), and slowness as well as other items in the second column. Its normative character – to the extent that Type 2 processes correct errors – seems to be a function of abstractness, a possible requirement of flexibility, and the character of the "correct" answers stipulated in experiments.

---

[82] "The important issue for our purposes is that decoupling secondary representations from the world and then maintaining the decoupling while simulation is carried out is *the defining feature* of Type 2 processing" (Stanovich and Toplak 2012, 9, emphasis added). This requires working memory.

[83] Working memory maintains information in focus for a short time so as to facilitate goal-directed behavior, including learning.

[84] "All of the different kinds of Type 1 processing (processes of emotional regulation, Darwinian modules, associative and implicit learning processes) can produce responses that are non-optimal in the particular context if not overridden" (Stanovich and Toplak 2012, 8).

LOOKING AWAY FROM THE BLINDING LIGHT

What is the harm of the received view beyond its theoretical equivocations? The received view diverts the reader's and scientist's attention from those processes that do not fit the standard alignment or constitute hybrids of these characteristics. Kruglanski and Gigerenzer (2011, 97–109) list several critical points that dual-process analysis does not help us understand:

1. Heuristics (usually associated with System 1) can be difficult to instantiate or access in particular environments; for example, the rely-on-the-expert heuristic is stymied by difficulty in identifying the expert.
2. Statistical rules (usually associated with System 2) such as base-rate incorporation can be easy to apply when information is presented clearly.
3. Higher processing capacity (associated with System 2) does not necessarily lead to the selection of more complex, deliberative rules. Easier, intuitive rules will be chosen if ecologically rational. For example, Take the Best or tallying will be chosen in preference to more complex methods of choosing in the appropriate environments.
4. Using less than all available information (associated with System 1) can, in appropriate environments, produce more accurate results than information-greedy methods. Therefore, the alignment of heuristics with second-best, error-prone judgments and complex statistical rules with rational judgments is an unproductive simplification.

We can go even further. If we think of the costly use of explicit working memory as a defining characteristic of System 2 processes, as Evans suggests, then we should see it in the context of research showing that System 1 processes use implicit or unconscious working memory.[85] This is because implicit working memory is a source of cheaper forms of flexible adaptation and learning in novel environments. These implicit processes can be *substitutes* for the use of explicit memory. For example, goal adoption and pursuit can be unconscious. Goals can be automatically set in motion. Nonconscious goal pursuit can activate the most important parts of working memory associated with executive control, which itself operates outside of consciousness (Hassin et al. 2009, 665–678).

---

[85] If we insist that *all* uses of working memory – conscious or unconscious – must be categorized as Type 2 processes, then we would have created a hybrid case that encompasses many of the other characteristics of Type 1. It is not clear what purpose this would serve, beyond saving the framework.

Furthermore, the pursuit of nonconscious goals is not tethered to inflexible means of attainment as is often thought. The means pursued can be *both* automatic and flexible (Hassin et al. 2009, 20–36). Nonconscious goal pursuit can also facilitate implicit learning in novel environments (Eitam et al. 2008, 261–267). Even unconscious reward cues can increase the successful updating of numerical information (Capa et al. 2011, 370–375).

Consider also the automatic-versus-controlled dichotomy. Working memory (involved in Type 2 processes) can be activated by unconscious information. An unconscious visual cue can be maintained for further use even in the presence of visual detractors normally expected to interfere with the retention of that cue. The suggestion, based on experimental work, is that "working memory may operate in a rather autonomous fashion independently of both conscious awareness and attention" (Soto et al. 2011, R912–R913). Inhibition of what are often thought to be automatic tendencies toward an initial response can be accomplished unconsciously and automatically (van Gaal et al. 2012, 1–15). The idea that controlled processes are needed to offset automatic processes is simplistic. Some automatic processes can offset other automatic processes.

Finally, even "controlled" activities such as driving, typing, and walking are not completely controlled. They have automatic components. For example, there are automatic processes involved in steering the car, touch-typing on a keyboard, and putting one foot in front of the other. These automatic components can be deliberately put into motion or stopped (Bargh 1994, 3). There are also specific "automatic" emotions – such as anger or sadness – that are shaped by controlled processes (Karen and Schul 2009).

To summarize: If we look away from the blinding light of the dual-systems perspective, we see many cognitive processes that look like hybrids. We also see unconscious processes that can correct the errors of other processes, whether the latter are conscious or unconscious. We see deliberate processes that have large automatic components. We have also seen that even the proponents of dual-system analysis have largely given up on the neat alignment of the characteristics attributed to System 1 and System 2 processes outlined in Table 5.1. And we have seen that the one remaining essential characteristic to distinguish the two systems – whether or not they use "working memory" – is alone insufficient to perform the function for which Kahneman and others have used the dual-systems framework. Finally, the use of working memory can be implicit, and as such it confounds the distinction between System 1 and System 2.

NORMATIVE CONSIDERATIONS

Before closing this Appendix, we must consider the normative aspects of System 2 cognitive processes. The first thing to note is that these processes are not considered invariably normative. System 2 processes can get things wrong (Kahneman 2011, 415), and so the criterion of normativity must lie outside of the dual-process analysis. In practice, the normative solutions to problems are constructed by the experimenters. *They* have a bias toward the solutions of statistical theory and standard logic. They present participants with intellectual problems rather than problems of living. Thus the tests are often not of the ecological or pragmatic rationality of agents' behavior, but of their knowledge of a formal learning apparatus. In general, what the received view calls System 2 processes are better equipped to handle this apparatus. It is no wonder, then, that System 2 processes are often thought of as normative. All this is now admitted by major advocates of the dual-system framework (Evans and Stanovich 2013b, 264).

A second normative issue is the claim that while System 1 processes are successful in everyday repetitive environments, System 2 processes are supposedly necessary to cope successfully with novel environments (Kahneman 2011, 416; Sunstein 2014, 33). On its own terms, this does not appear to be true on the basis of recent research (Eitam et al. 2011). But there is a more fundamental problem. To the extent that System 2 processing is identified with the standard economic agent (Sunstein 2014, 26–28), System 2 processing is at least being partially identified with standard statistical reasoning, including such apparatuses as expected utility theory. Unfortunately for the claim, that apparatus only works in repetitive risky environments where the structure of the underlying environment is unchanging and where agents know all of the consequences of their potential actions with definite probability distributions. This is not generally what is meant by a "novel" environment (Brighton and Gigerenzer 2012).

Despite the many warning signs that we should not identify System 2 processing with normative solutions, even a cursory look at the heuristics-and-biases literature reveals much to suggest a built-in bias on the part of experimenters and behavioral economists toward conceiving of normativity in intellectualistic System 2 terms.

CONCLUSIONS

Returning to the analytical functions of the dual-process construction, it is hard to see the construct adequately fulfilling any of its plausible purposes.

As a summary of past heuristics-and-biases research it may have had some merit, but only at the price of excluding research that does not fit the mold. As a framework leading to falsifiable predictions, it is often too slippery or vague in the hands of its users to make for a stable "target," and as a predictor of aligned characteristics it does not succeed. More importantly, however, as a stimulus to new research it blinds its adherents to new approaches and to hybrid processes that are part of the human repertoire of cognition. Finally, it is unhelpful as an aid to uncovering genuinely normative outcomes. In practice, the normative standards are the posited statistical or logical solutions to artificial problems created by experimenters. Therefore, those cases in which System 2 processes seem most tightly connected to normative solutions are not as significant as they may seem. Before we can evaluate the relative roles of the dual processes in producing rational behavior, we must refocus on agents in the actual environments in which they make decisions. The dual-systems construct, as usually applied, has diverted researchers from this task.

Deficient Foundations for
Behavioral Policymaking

The recognition of the insuperable limits to his knowledge ought indeed to teach the student of society a lesson of humility which should guard him against becoming an accomplice in men's fatal striving to control society.
—Friedrich Hayek, *The Pretence of Knowledge*

People should keep enthusiasm curbed in their lives. Always keep it. To not is unattractive. It's unseemly.

—Larry David, *Time*

Human decision-making is imperfect; on that much, we can all agree. Yet it is one thing to point out its imperfections relative to some standard, and quite another to implement policies that effectively correct them. In the preceding chapters, we have argued that the standards used by behavioral paternalists to specify fully rational decision-making are not, in general, persuasive. But in the chapters to follow, we will suppose for argument's sake that the behavioral paternalists are correct, at least to some degree: that people would be better off if well-designed policies nudged them closer to behavior consistent with neoclassical rationality.

Nevertheless, we will argue that policymakers and their academic advisors lack the *knowledge* required to design such policies in a fashion that would reliably achieve their stated goals. In that sense, the arguments of this and subsequent chapters constitute immanent criticism of behavioral paternalism.

A central claim of behavioral paternalists is that their approach is "evidence-based" (Thaler 2015b, 330–345). They claim to eschew ideology and simply advocate "what works" (Halpern 2015, 266–298). They say their policy recommendations rest on strong evidence provided by both behavioral economics and cognitive psychology. This decades-long research program has supposedly enabled them to discover how actual people behave rather than how hypothetical economic agents behave.

But just how adequate is such research for shaping policy? Imprecision and defects can be found in all research, so we are not arguing that the research underlying behavioral paternalism falls short of some perfectionist standard. That would be true, of course, but it would also be true of just about all research. Our argument is more specific. The policies recommended by behavioral paternalists rest critically on certain posited empirical facts or regularities about human behavior. As it turns out, some of these supposed facts have not actually been established with much confidence. Others, surprisingly, have not been addressed at all.

Most importantly, the crafting of behavioral paternalist policies depends not simply on the *existence* of phenomena such as the endowment effect or present bias, but on the *quantitative magnitudes* of such phenomena. These magnitudes are indispensable for answering such questions as: *How large* should sin taxes be? *How long* should cooling-off periods be? *How graphic* does a risk narrative need to be? *How much income* should people be defaulted into saving for retirement? *How difficult* should it be, in terms of time and effort, to opt out of default terms? All of these quantitative questions, raised automatically by any attempt to implement the policies in question, require quantitative inputs to calculate their answers. Research must therefore establish people's true preferences (whose better satisfaction is the *raison d'être* of behavioral paternalism), as well as the strength of the biases that impede them. The methods used by behavioral economists have not reliably estimated such quantitative magnitudes. Behavioral-economics research is therefore inadequate for the purposes that new paternalists have set for it.

This does not mean that the behavioral-economics research program is not worth pursuing or that, with suitable adjustments, no valuable insights can be had. Our aim is not to throw out the baby with the bathwater, but to highlight the limitations of existing research for policymaking purposes. Some of the limitations we point out in this chapter may be partially remedied by future research, and so this chapter's challenges may gradually become obsolete as time goes on. However, in Chapter 7 we will argue that many gaps in knowledge likely cannot ever be filled to the degree necessary. Chapter 7 will lay out in further detail the many kinds of knowledge that are necessary for successful paternalist interventions. For now, it is enough to emphasize the importance of establishing both the existence and the magnitude of the biases that support paternalist policy proposals. In this chapter, we highlight five key deficiencies in the underlying behavioral research:

1. Psychological findings are highly context-specific, and thus lack the generality required for policymaking.
2. Generalizing quantitative results from the laboratory to the real world is unreliable.
3. Most existing research does not account adequately for incentives and learning.
4. Most existing research does not consider small-group debiasing.
5. Most existing research does not adequately assess self-regulation and self-debiasing.

CONTEXT-SPECIFICITY OF PSYCHOLOGICAL FINDINGS

Daniel Kahneman claims that psychology offers "integrative concepts and mid-level generalizations, which gain credibility from their ability to explain ostensibly different phenomena in diverse domains" (2003, 144). However, Kahneman and behavioral economists tend to overestimate the generality of psychological findings. In fact, most psychological concepts, theories, and empirical results have a relatively narrow domain of applicability. Jerome Kagan has explored this important limitation of modern psychology:

[M]ost concepts refer to the behavioral or physiological reactions of animals and humans to specific situations, rather than to the relatively stable, inherent features of these agents ... As a result, many psychological concepts refer to phenomena that are necessarily influenced by the context. ... A frustrating consequence of the influence of local context is that few psychological concepts intended to represent a person's tendency to react in a certain way apply across diverse settings.

(Kagan 2012, 4)[1]

Context can have many meanings, which is part of the problem. In a strict sense, it refers to "the physical and social features of the setting ... and always the procedure that produced the evidence" (Kagan 2012, 14). In a broader sense, it refers to "the person's construal of the examiner, the task administered, [and] the expectation of what might happen" (Kagan 2012, 22).[2]

---

[1] "Three factors influence the probability that a particular behavior will be expressed. The properties of the brain and the individual's prior experiences are the most obvious. ... The local settings, the third influence, selects one behavior from an envelope that usually contains more than one possibility" (Kagan 2012, 9).

[2] One of the reasons Kahneman overestimates the generality of the heuristics-and-biases research findings is that the context is rarely specified, which gives the false impression that the biases are very general human traits. *But not explicitly specifying the context is not*

Contextuality of the Effect of Moods and Emotions

The problem of context can be illustrated by research on the effect of moods or emotions on risk-taking and other decision variables (Andrade and Chen 2007, 52–53; Winkielman and Trujillo 2007, 77, 82–85). Negative moods are often associated with individuals assigning higher subjective probabilities to unfavorable events. However, this does not necessarily mean that they engage in excessive risk avoidance.[3] In fact, they often appear to engage in *risk-seeking* behavior. Those who respond to negative affect in a risk-seeking way are those who perceive or expect a real chance to repair their mood by taking a risk. Those who don't expect such a likelihood, on the other hand, will be risk-averse so as to reduce their feelings of uncertainty. Obviously, this is already very context-sensitive, depending as it does on the subjects' perceptions about the efficacy of their actions. But the contextuality goes even further.

Moods and emotions need to be specified not just in terms of simple valence (i.e., whether the emotion is positive or negative), but also in terms of qualitatively different emotions: sadness, anger, fear, and so forth. Different qualitative moods, all of which are classified as "negative," will have different effects on behavior. Sadness may induce risk-taking while anxiety may induce risk aversion (Andrade and Chen 2007, 52–53). But these moods are also defined across six dimensions, all of which are highly context-dependent: pleasantness, anticipated effort, certainty, attentional activity, responsibility and control over self and others, and situational control (Smith and Ellsworth 1985, 813). Thus, any results we can derive from the literature on the effect of mood and emotions on decision-making are at a very low level of generalization. Nevertheless, behavioral economists have argued that decision-making under certain emotional or mood states are "red flags" for inferior choices along some dimension (Beshears et al. 2008, 1788). What the empirical results suggest is that the effect of emotions on the quality of decisions resists generalization.

Contextuality of Loss Aversion and Reference Points

Loss aversion is an extremely important idea in behavioral economics. A loss-averse individual has a tendency to focus on losses more than gains.

---

the same as varying the context and arriving at the same results. However, Kahneman has little interest in this limitation in practice (Ausch 2016, 35–39).
[3] We mean risk avoidance relative to the *objective* probabilities.

This asymmetrical focus is displayed as an asymmetrical weighting in actual decisions. It is usually claimed, on the basis of certain experiments, that losses are weighted approximately twice as much as gains of the same amount (Tversky and Kahneman 1992, 297–323). But people do not display loss aversion every time they are faced with a choice (Gal and Rucker 2018).[4] So, the first question has to be, *under what circumstances does loss aversion occur?* And second, *does it always occur with a 2:1 weighting?*[5] The history of economists searching for generalizable quantitative constants has not been encouraging.[6]

But perhaps the most important contextual question relates to the reference point from which a loss or a gain is defined. The reference point is subjective. As we saw in Chapter 4, the reference point need not be the subject's current endowment; it could be the subject's expectation of something in the future. The reference point is important because some paternalist policies hinge on manipulating the reference point. If the policymaker can induce the individual to focus on one reference point rather than another, the greater weighting of losses relative to that reference point can place a finger, as it were, on the individual's cost–benefit calculation. Consider, for instance, the decision of whether to save for retirement (or add to savings for retirement). If a person considers the status quo the relevant reference point, then the loss created by a decision to save will be seen as a reduction in present consumption. This will then be weighted twice as much as any longer-run gains (assuming the 2:1 ratio holds). As a result, there will be less saving than otherwise. However, if the person focuses on her *future* expected consumption, then the loss involved in *not saving* will be her expected investment returns – which will be weighted twice as much as the gains in present consumption from not

---

[4] "Our main conclusion is that the weight of the evidence does not support a general tendency for losses to be more psychologically impactful than gains (i.e., loss aversion). Rather, our review suggests the need for a more contextualized perspective whereby losses sometimes loom larger than gains, sometimes losses and gains have similar psychological impact, and sometimes gains loom larger than losses. In other words, the choice presented at the beginning of this article is a false one as it denied the audience the possibility of a contextual perspective. Rather, the question should have offered a fourth option: all of the above are true depending on the context" (Gal and Rucker 2017, 498).

[5] Walasek and Stewart (2015) find different loss-aversion parameters depending on the particular range of gains and losses people are exposed to. In one of four experiments they found the oft-cited parameter of 2 but in the other three they found parameters of 1 and 0.5 (reverse loss aversion – gains count more than losses).

[6] "[E]conomics contains no quantitative constants similar to Plank's constant, or the inverse square rule of universal attraction, or the Hubble constant – the value of which determines the size, age and ultimate fate of the universe" (Lipsey 2001, 172).

saving (again, assuming the 2:1 ratio holds).[7] As a result, there will be more saving than otherwise – or so the paternalists hope. We discuss the issue of retirement savings in greater detail in Chapter 7 and its Appendix. It is sufficient to say here, however, that conclusions regarding the effect of casting certain options as defaults (e.g., you're in the savings program unless you opt out) will be affected by what the individual considers the reference point. There is no general behavioral law that says that the default rule always serves as the subject's reference point.[8] The reference point resists generalization.[9] Yet many paternalist policy recommendations – including but not limited to those related to savings behavior – rest upon the implicit assumption that new default rules will necessarily shift the targeted individuals' reference points in the desired fashion.

Context-Specificity in Context

The examples of context-specificity given thus far are only illustrations. Similar stories could likely be told about most other cognitive biases. In previous chapters we have seen that whether people display overoptimism will vary according to the measure used; whether they violate elementary rules of probability depends on how they interpret the task environment; whether they discount the future hyperbolically depends on how they view the passage of time; and so forth. Furthermore, as in the Linda problem, the inference that people may be violating the laws of probability depends on the interpretation subjects give to the experimental problem.

The importance of the context-specificity of psychological research for policymaking is profound. Suppose policy aims at optimal intertemporal choices, including inducing people to save for their retirement in accordance with their true preferences. What rate of discount should be used? Studies vary widely depending on such factors as the goods exchanged (money, health, life-years), whether the experiment is based on real or hypothetical choice, the time range of the choice, and, perhaps most dramatically, the elicitation method (Frederick et al. 2002). Or suppose policy aims to correct for optimism bias via "scary" risk narratives, which

---

[7] As the reader can see, nothing has changed in these scenarios regarding the assumed profile of monetary costs and benefits of the decision to save (or not).

[8] There is a two-step process for the paternalist. First, identify the general reference point tendency – status quo, expectations, etc. Second, ensure that the manipulation makes the preferred option that reference point.

[9] For a review of the evidence suggesting various reference points, see Gal and Rucker (2018) and Marzilli Ericson and Fuster (2014).

supposedly activate availability bias. The strength of the optimism bias presumably depends on the risky activity in question (for example, smoking or bungee-jumping?), and the strength of availability bias presumably depends on the characteristics of the narrative (for example, is it presented as text, audio, or video?). For virtually any paternalist intervention, calibration of the policy will require the existence of research that specifically relates to the specific policy domain as well as the proposed remedy.

GENERALIZING QUANTITATIVE RESULTS FROM THE LAB TO THE REAL WORLD

The contextual nature of psychological findings leads naturally to the issue of the generalizability of experimental results to the real world. This is a broad topic that we cannot cover comprehensively, so we will instead focus on four aspects of the overall problem that are of special interest to us. First, we examine the unreliability of stated-choice experiments as predictors of actual choices. Our argument here is not that actual choices are necessarily the normative welfare standard, but that the properties, including biases, exhibited in stated-choice experiments do not necessarily manifest themselves in realistic situations. Second, we examine whether quantitative generalizability of effects is a reasonable expectation of laboratory experiments. Even where qualitative features – that is, the existence and direction of the effects – are generalizable, is the quantitative magnitude of those effects generalizable? Third, we examine the problem of replicability of results (or lack thereof). Fourth, we consider the potential mismatch between laboratory subjects and the general population. Together, these factors cast considerable doubt on whether findings from psychological research can be relied upon for policymaking.

Stated Choice and Revealed Choice

Most, though not all, behavioral research demonstrating biases of decision-making rests on hypothetical choice experiments. Two of the most popular methods are to elicit willingness to pay for a good in an open-ended way ("how much would you pay for . . .") or to give the subject a closed-ended choice of amounts they are willing to pay for a good ("which of these amounts is the most you would pay for . . ."). Even when subjects are paid for their participation in an experiment, the choice is not a real one; that is, they do not actually pay for the good in question. They do not bear the consequences of their choices. This fundamental fact bears upon whether the biased behavior exhibited in experiments manifests itself in the real choices people make. If hypothetical choice experiments deviate from actual choice situations in important ways – a phenomenon known as *hypothetical bias* – then the relevance of this kind of experimental evidence to policy is undercut.

There is no doubt that hypothetical bias exists,[10] although the full array of its causes remains unknown (Shogren 2005, 1005–1007). Meta-analyses show that the magnitude of the bias is considerable. List and Gallet (2001) find a mean ratio of hypothetical payment to actual payment of 3:1. Another meta-analysis conducted by Murphy et al. (2005) also finds a mean ratio of 3:1 in their general model. Further refinement shows a mean ratio of 2.6:1, although the results display high variance. Their results also show that the hypothetical bias ratio rises with the level of the subject's hypothetical willingness to pay. This suggests that the problem may be greater the more important the decision under analysis.

The upshot is that extrapolating the results of stated-choice experiments into the realm of actual behavior is fraught with difficulties, especially since most of the evidence on preference reversal (due to present bias) rests on stated-choice experiments. While the studies we have discussed do not specifically test for behavioral anomalies, they do test for the consistency of experimentally induced behavior with that in the actual world. Unfortunately, there is currently no general theory that explains the deviation of hypothetical behavior from actual behavior, nor are there generally successful methods to mitigate the bias (Loomis 2011, 363–364). Therefore, our ability to increase the accuracy of stated-choice studies as predictors of real-world choices is quite limited (Howard et al. 2015). As things stand now, they do not provide a reliable guide to choice in the real world.

Quantitative Generalizability

Perhaps the most succinct way to present our claim that the quantitative results of laboratory experiments do not generalize is to examine what the strong advocates of laboratory methods have said. Kessler and Vesterlund

---

[10] Hypothetical bias is defined and measured as the difference between willingness to pay as estimated from stated-preference surveys or models and the actual amounts as revealed by data collected in fieldwork or by other means. In these comparisons the choice scenarios are the same.

(2015, 394) argue that "the focus on quantitative external validity is misplaced" in most cases. Further:

> Few experimental economists would argue that the magnitude of the difference between two laboratory treatments is indicative of the magnitude one would expect to see in the field or even in other laboratory studies in which important characteristics of the environment have changed.
>
> (Kessler and Vesterlund 2015)

The methods used in this research are aimed at demonstrating the *qualitative* effects of certain treatments. For example, are particular bidders subject to the winner's curse bias, and if so, what is the effect of increasing the number of bidders and the amount of public information on the relative number of people subject to the bias? The object is not to make generalizations about the *amount* that they overbid, only the fact that they do overbid. Camerer (2015) agrees, adding that for *policy purposes* the generalizability of quantitative magnitudes to the relevant external setting is important.[11] Levitt and List (2007) provide many examples of social preferences in gift exchange, dictator, and other similar games that have been measured in lab experiments but that fail to generalize to the real world – either altogether or in quantitative magnitude.[12] Discount rates measured in the lab also fail to generalize to the real world (Frederick et al. 2002), as do endowment effects (List 2003).

Reproducibility

A more basic and general problem with psychological lab results is their failure to replicate. While the previous analysis takes for granted that laboratory results accurately reflect effects under the conditions of the experiments, there are troubling questions about their reproducibility, especially with respect to effect size.[13]

---

[11] "Of course, if the purposes of an experiment is to supply a policy-relevant answer to a particular external setting, then it is certainly important to ask how well the experimental setting resembles the target external setting to judge its [quantitative] external validity" (Camerer 2015, 254).

[12] We should note that social preferences are not necessarily irrational, even within the neoclassical model. But the deviation between social preferences as measured in the laboratory versus in the wild supports our general point about quantitative generalizability.

[13] "[I]t is typically important to have accurate estimates of the size of effects; it is rarely sufficient merely to know that an effect exists" (Schmidt and Hunter 2015, 515).

The Open Science Collaboration, a group of more than 125 psychologists, conducted replications of 100 experimental and correlation studies in three major psychology journals for the year 2008. There is no single standard of successful replications, but the results that are most important for our purposes are these: (1) only 36 percent of the replications showed a statistically significant effect in the same direction as the original study, and (2) the "mean effect size of the replication effects ... was half the magnitude of the mean effect size of the original effects ... representing a substantial decline" (Open Science Collaboration 2015, 943). The Open Science Collaboration's project has since been criticized on statistical grounds by Gilbert et al. (2016), who say that the project did not faithfully replicate the conditions of the original studies, and that the number of failed replications was in line with what would be expected from chance. Anderson et al. (2016) have replied, saying Gilbert et al.'s rebuttal depends on optimistic assumptions.

We don't know how this particular discussion will ultimately be resolved, but it is safe to say that the reproducibility of much psychological research is simply unknown. The dispute between Gilbert et al. and Anderson et al. is indicative of the scarcity of genuine attempts at replication. Furthermore, there are good theoretical reasons to suspect a replication problem exists – one of the foremost among them being *publication bias*: the tendency of statistically significant study results to get published, while statistically insignificant results remain in the so-called file drawer (Rosenthal 1979; Scargle 2000). Publication bias does not only imply that some nonexistent phenomena may get published; it also implies that real phenomena will be more likely to get published when the size effects are relatively large, as large effects have a better chance of clearing the bar of statistical significance. As a result, "replication efforts are likely to be more-reliable guides to the existence (and magnitude) of effects in psychology experiments than are the original studies" (Baker 2016).

In the first systematic, but limited, effort to replicate laboratory experiments in economics, Camerer et al. (2016) replicated eighteen studies published in the *American Economic Review* and the *Quarterly Journal of Economics* between 2011 and 2014. They found that 61 percent of the replications showed a statistically significant effect in the same direction as the original study. However, the mean effect size was 66 percent of the original magnitude. In most cases such a difference in magnitude (or a greater difference, as in the large study of psychology articles) will have a considerable impact on policy prescriptions.

In a more recent study, Camerer et al. (2018) examined twenty-one experimental studies mainly in social psychology and cognition that were published in the most prestigious general science journals, *Nature* and *Science*, between 2010 and 2015. They identified the most important statistically significant results in each. Each study was replicated in high-powered samples. A statistically significant effect in the same direction as the original was found in 62 percent of the studies. However, the mean effect size was only about 50 percent of the original.

If the quantitative results of laboratory experiments have not been reliably reproduced *even in the lab*, we can only be strengthened in our doubts about their generalizability to the real world.

The problem of replication, however, extends beyond laboratory experiments to empirical studies more generally. Ioannidis et al. (2017) surveyed both observation and experimental articles. Their data was drawn from 159 meta-analyses of 6,700 studies with over 64,000 estimates of economic parameters. The authors identify some of the root causes of reproducibility failures such as those discussed previously. The first is inadequate statistical power. The median power of these studies is 18 percent, far below the conventionally recommended 80 percent. Despite this, most studies report statistically significant effects. In fact, "even in areas of research without a single adequately powered estimate," an average of 44 percent of the parameter estimates are reported as statistically significant (p. F245).[14] When the power of a study is low, a greater proportion of statistically significant effects are not genuine. They are the result of chance and/or biases of various kinds. Furthermore, the effects that are genuine are

---

[14] Statistical power is defined as $(1 - \beta)$ where β is the rate of false negatives. Another way to see it is: power is the probability of correctly rejecting the null hypothesis when the alternative hypothesis is true, that is, when there are genuine effects. The higher the statistical power of a study, the more likely that these genuine effects will be discovered. The *lower* the power, the higher the probability of *accepting* the null hypothesis (and not accepting the alternative hypothesis) when there really is an effect. So many genuine effects will not be detected. Perhaps counterintuitively, low power also results in an increase in the probability that the effects claimed are not genuine, i.e., that they are false positives. *For any given level of statistical significance,* there will be a certain proportion of the discovered effects that are simply due to chance. Additionally, with low power (a high β) there will be many failures to detect genuine effects. The null hypothesis will be accepted too often. Thus the proportion of all effects found will be "biased" toward false positives compared with when β is low and more genuine effects are discovered. This means, for example, that a 5 percent significance level will be compatible with a greater probability of false positives when there is low power than when there is high power. For a general discussion see Kraemer (2013).

exaggerated in their magnitude (Ioannidis 2008).[15] The second cause of reproducibility failure is the collection of well-known biases such as publication bias, sampling bias, selection bias in the choice of data sets and econometric methods, misspecification due to extensive searching and prescreening of models to find effects, and so forth. Ioannidis et al. (2017, F253) estimate that low power and biases have resulted in average effects being exaggerated by a factor of two and that one-third of parameter estimates are exaggerated by a factor of four.[16]

The Population of Relevance

Most of the psychological and economics experiments on biases use students as test subjects. Most of the policy prescriptions developed by new paternalists apply to populations of which students constitute only a small fraction. Is this a problem? Obviously, the research on cognitive and preference biases is being used as the foundation for these policies. Therefore, the samples of students that are used must reflect the characteristics of the population targeted or affected by the proposed policies. Several factors are relevant here.

First, it is well known that student populations are more homogeneous than the general population. Thus, even a random sample of students is not equivalent to a random sample from the general population (Slonim et al. 2013, 44).

Second, are the students in the experiments representative of the student population from which they are taken? The answer seems to be *no*, at least in economics experiments (Slonim et al. 2013). There are biases of participation in experiments. Those who take part tend to be less wealthy, have more leisure time, have greater interest in economics-type tasks, have more prosocial preferences in the sense of volunteering time in general, and be

---

[15] The power of a study varies positively with the sample size, the statistical significance criterion, and the magnitude of the effect to be detected. Thus the greater the sample size, the larger the significance criterion, and the larger the effect to be detected, the higher the power.

[16] Schimmack et al. (2017) examined thirty-one laboratory studies in twelve articles cited in chapter 4 of Daniel Kahneman's book (2011) *Thinking Fast and Slow*. None of the studies were authored by Kahneman but they were favorably cited in support of the idea that the mind has a System 1 that draws intuitive, associative, but often erroneous connections. The median power of the studies was only 57 percent. Although all of the reported results were statistically significant at conventional levels, it is highly likely that at this degree of power many of these were false positives (Schimmack 2012). Kahneman (2017) has agreed that he placed too much reliance on studies with low power.

more patient than the population from which they are recruited. As many of these characteristics doubtless have some correlation with cognition and judgment, the participation biases suggest that we must be very careful in concluding that we have satisfactorily measured biases in the wider student population.

Third, do results from student samples plausibly gain generality when samples from a wider population also display the same behavioral characteristics? The answer is likely to be *no*. This is because the very same factors that produce participation biases in the student samples are likely to be operative in the samples from the wider population. This can make the sample from the wider population even less representative of that population than the sample from the student population is of that narrower population (Slonim et al. 2013, 46).[17]

Fourth, can we take laboratory evidence derived from student subjects who choose to participate in experiments and expect it to characterize the *subset* of the general population that is in need of being nudged or otherwise regulated (the "boundedly rational")? Of course the basic answer is again *no*. We cannot simply assume that the characteristics and behavior of one group travel to all others.[18]

FAILURE TO ACCOUNT ADEQUATELY FOR
INCENTIVES AND LEARNING

There is by now a significant literature on the effects of financial incentives on performance and, to a lesser extent, the effects of learning over time on the erosion of biases. We discuss some of this literature in this section. However, the fundamental research on which paternalist policy prescriptions are based rarely incorporates the lessons of incentives and learning in a significant way. The classic heuristics-and-biases research either did not

---

[17] This is because the *participants* in the sample from the general population will tend to look like the *participants* in the sample from the student population. Since the general population is more diverse than the student population, the participation bias will make the sample from the general population even less representative of its target than the sample from the student population with respect to its target. In short, the effect of the participation biases is likely to be understated in the student sample (Slonim et al. 2013, 46).

[18] "Efficacy [of a proposed policy in laboratory experiments] is no evidence whatsoever for effectiveness [in the actual real-world case] unless and until a huge body of additional evidence can be produced to show that efficacy can travel, both to the new population and to the new methods of implementation. . . .[E]fficacy is only one small piece of one kind of evidence" (Cartwright 2009, 133).

incorporate incentives for "good" performance at all or incorporated only trivial incentives.[19]

The absence of attention to learning was present from the start because of reliance on a "between subjects" methodology in which treatment groups are compared with one another in a one-shot test – such as, for instance, posing a problem situation described in two different ways to two different treatment groups, and then attributing any difference in the groups' aggregate behavior to a framing effect. Kahneman argues that the between-subjects design is the appropriate one for detecting biases because his purpose is to determine untutored or intuitive responses to "routine situations" (Kahneman and Frederick 2005, 281). But if his purpose is to measure responses to *routine* situations, then experiments with repeated exposure to a problem (as in a within-subjects design) would seem ecologically more valid.[20] In the real world people would, by definition, encounter routine situations many times and thus would have opportunities for learning.[21]

The effects of incentives can be divided into short-run effects and long-run effects. In the short run, the level of cognitive effort is variable. The standard prediction would be that stronger incentives lead to greater expenditure of cognitive effort. In the longer run, the stock of cognitive capital or cognitive ability is also variable. Accordingly, we would predict

---

[19] Even in those few cases where Kahneman and Tversky incorporated incentives, the opportunity cost of suboptimal behavior was low. When the experiments were redone to eliminate this problem, violations of expected utility theory, violations of Bayes' rule, and the susceptibility of agents to the Allais Paradox were dramatically reduced, and in proportion to increasing opportunity costs (Harrison 1994).

[20] In a within-subjects design many biases of normative omission such as base-rate neglect, duration neglect, and scope neglect do not appear. There may be a learning component here, but there also may be artifacts of the *experimental* setup that have nothing to do with learning. For example, Kahneman and Frederick (2005, 280–287) believe that by varying base rates, duration, and scope *within a given set of subjects*, the experimenter almost guarantees that there will be an effect, that is, the biases will not exist, because subjects will be explicitly faced with the nonnormative neglect. Their error will be obvious. However, learning cannot be simply ruled out, in part because the difference between learning and the experimental artifact is not clear-cut. When something becomes obvious it is because someone learned something.

[21] Thaler, on the other hand, seems to think that people get most of the routine judgments right and that the superficial intuitive judgments are made about the exceptional and relatively rare problems: "We do small stuff often enough to learn to get it right, but when it comes to choosing a home, a mortgage, or a job, we don't get much practice or opportunities to learn" (2015b, 50). But in these cases people often seek professional advice. See also the section "Small-Group Debiasing."

that given appropriate incentives and feedback, in the longer run people will learn to solve problems better or come closer to the normative standard.

Incentives: Clearing Away the Confounds

Our interest in incentives differs from that in much of the research in this area. In the psychological and economics literatures, there are substantial questions about whether performance on some task can be improved by experimenters adding a financial incentive to whatever other incentives people might have to complete a task. For example, can the performance of schoolchildren be improved by adding financial incentives for parents or the children themselves to the existing incentive structure? Similarly, what would be the effect of providing financial incentives to blood or kidney donors? These are issues of the optimal design of incentives.

In some optimal-design problems, financial incentives may crowd out other incentives based on motives of social approval and intrinsic psychological or moral satisfaction (Gneezy et al. 2011). If a person is being paid, say, to provide a kidney, he can no longer use the donation to display to himself or others his good moral character. The financial incentive has a hidden cost in the reduction or elimination of a nonpecuniary incentive (a "crowding out" effect). Therefore, it may appear as if the behavior is not subject to *financial* incentives or even that such incentives are perverse.[22] But financial incentives are not the real issue here, because our concern is with the broader question: *does actually bearing the burden of the normal negative consequences of biased behavior – whether financial, social, or intrinsic – tend to erode those biases?* Formulating the question in this way avoids focusing on cases in which the external (experimental) imposition of financial incentives distorts the natural context of decision-making.

We want to see whether marginal rewards in the relevant currency of the agent's concerns, *ceteris paribus*, have an impact on behavior. Suppose a person has been planning to donate blood but finds the process of the blood draw unpleasant. She may procrastinate, as a person with present bias tends to do. Let the nonpecuniary rewards to blood donation increase, while pecuniary rewards remain constant. Does present bias decrease? This is what we want to know. Unfortunately, we do not have direct evidence on this. We do know, however, that increased scrutiny of decisions by others

---

[22] It may be important in these cases to "pay enough or don't pay at all" (Gneezy and Rustichini 2000). Only if financial incentives are sufficiently high can they overwhelm the crowding-out effect.

tends to increase the incidence of prosocial behavior (Levitt and List 2007, 353), presumably by increasing the reputational reward. This would imply that the obstacles to prosocial behavior, including biased behavior such as procrastination, would be reduced by greater incentives. However, studies of social or intrinsic preferences usually involve the effect of introducing financial incentives into complex, multimotivated situations. Therefore, they do not provide a pure case to test the relevant nonpecuniary incentive effect on biases.

If we want to measure the effect of financial incentives, a good strategy would be to concentrate on cases where their pure effect can be assessed without interference from induced changes in other incentives.[23] Generally speaking, *most* of the biased behaviors paternalists are concerned about do not involve social preferences. They are cases of supposed decision-making failure in self-interested tasks or judgments. Therefore, isolating the effect of financial incentives can be useful.

Even in those areas where the individual is motivated primarily by financial incentives, there can also be hidden confounding factors in the form of *communication of negative information about the difficulty of the task*. Is an increase in reward for successful performance a signal from the employer or experimenter that the task is difficult? If so, this may attenuate the pure incentive effect of the reward. It is thus possible that there will *appear* to be little or no effect of financial incentives on behavior, including biased behavior.

Bremzen et al. (2015) conducted an experimental study to decompose the effects of financial rewards into (a) direct incentives to complete a task successfully and (b) the conveyance of information about the difficulty of the task. The principal in the joint task determines the wage rate and a bonus that he awards when the task is difficult. The principal knows whether the task will be difficult, but the agent does not. The agent, seeing what the principal has decided, chooses a level of effort to complete the task. The experimental results indicate a very strong pure incentive effect from the bonus payments, especially in the short run. However, in the longer run, as the agent realizes what is being communicated by the bonus

---

[23] "We argue that in settings where financial returns and 'doing the right thing' are at odds, the special features of the lab might preclude measurements of pro-social preferences to be directly applicable to other populations of people and situations. ... In situations where morality and wealth are not competing objectives, we expect that lab findings will be more readily generalizable than is the case for lab experiments that measure social preferences" (Levitt and List 2007, 351).

payments, there is an increasing negative effect of the "bad news" about the difficulty of the task.

This kind of problem does not exist when the benefits of avoiding biases are simply the natural consequences of decisions, such as when people incur too much debt, exercise too little, eat too much, or buy products impulsively that they later regret. The world imposes the costs and benefits, so to speak; there is no issue of interpreting the meaning of a principal's or experimenter's provision of incentives. So what is relevant for our purposes is the direct incentive effect purged of the information-communication effect.

From the foregoing discussion, we can see that it is important to avoid being sidetracked by crowding-out effects and bad-news information effects that might be interpreted as evidence that incentives do not affect biased behavior. They do not constitute such evidence.

There is also an unfortunate tendency in the literature to lump in prosocial preferences – and other types of other-regarding preferences – with departures from rationality in self-interested contexts. For example, the failure of an offeree in a one-shot ultimatum game to accept any small amount of money offered by the other player is treated as a violation of rationality on par with the failure of an agent to have transitive preferences; after all, more money is better than less. But this only appears to be a violation of rationality because economic models so often couple rationality with the pursuit of self-interest. There is nothing inherently irrational about a preference for punishing another player's selfish behavior (such as making a very low offer in the ultimatum game). From our perspective, other-regarding preferences are not *biases* for which we must investigate the effect of incentives. They are allowable preferences within the paradigm of inclusive rationality.[24]

Research on the effect of incentives does not speak with one voice; nor, given the diversity in the purposes of the experiments, should we expect it to. Confounding factors abound. The chosen standards of performance are not always the norms in which we are interested. Furthermore, in studies of short-run responses, the problems that the agents face may be too difficult; that is, they may exceed current cognitive ability. Thus, although there may be more effort expended, it does little good. A similar phenomenon exists when the problem is very simple; more effort will not increase performance because the maximum has already been reached. A few

---

[24] Of course, the effect of financial incentives on prosocial preferences is an interesting question in its own right.

studies even show *impairment* of performance with financial incentives.[25] This counterintuitive result can be explained, as we have suggested, by the crowding out of nonfinancial incentives and also by experimenters inadvertently sending a signal that the problem is very difficult.[26]

Incentive Effects

The heart of the issue, as we see it, is whether bearing the negative consequences of biased behavior decreases the prevalence of those biases in real-world settings. Our *presumption* – based on the evidence – is that biases are indeed eroded by bearing negative consequences, other things equal.

In Chapter 5, we introduced Caplan's notion of rational irrationality to describe the idea that people tend to indulge their cognitive biases less when the cost is high and more when the cost is low, and we included various examples supporting the phenomenon. More examples will be presented in Chapter 8. We are here slightly expanding the concept of rational irrationality; Caplan defines it primarily in terms of potentially biased beliefs, whereas we use "cognitive biases" to include nonstandard preferences as well.[27] In the latter case, higher costs of indulging a nonstandard preference (such as intransitive preferences) would tend to result either in greater effort to resolve the inconsistency *or* greater effort to resist acting upon it. Thus, rational irrationality (as we use the term) need not imply that agents will become neoclassically rational in their cognitive processes in response to stronger incentives, only that their *behavior* will change in the direction that indicates a lower *operative* level of bias. This might happen as a result of resolving preference inconsistencies, suppressing the urge to act on inconsistent preferences, adopting self-regulatory techniques, or even increasing another bias that tends to counteract the costly one.

A preliminary indication that costs can matter can be found in experiments showing that the effect of "normatively irrelevant" framing erodes

---

[25] See the studies cited in Kamenica (2012).

[26] Another explanation is that high incentives make people nervous ("choke") and thus impair performance. However applicable this might be in experimental situations, there is no evidence that it applies in real-world labor markets (Kamenica 2012, 434).

[27] Caplan does seem to foresee this expansion of the concept. Caplan (2000) presents a taxonomy of rationality that includes both belief rationality and preference rationality, but then he chooses to limit the scope of the article to belief rationality only (pp. 192–193).

under the pressure of scarcity. In such experiments, participants were divided into two income groups – higher than the median and lower than the median. The higher-income participants (the less income-constrained) were more likely to be susceptible to "framing illusions" than the lower-income groups, for whom scarcity was a more binding constraint.

Consider the experiment conducted by Thaler (1985, 206). In a hypo-thetical beer-on-the-beach scenario, people were asked their maximum willingness to pay for a beer. In one treatment, the beer was to be obtained from a fancy resort hotel; in the other, from a run-down grocery store. It turned out that people said that they were willing to pay more for the same beer in the fancy resort case than in the run-down grocery case. In theory, this difference in willingness to pay is deemed irrational, inasmuch as the beer is the same regardless and will be consumed on the beach, not in the place where it was purchased. When the experiment was repeated (Shah et al. 2015) while dividing the participants by income constraint, it was found that there was no statistically significant difference in willingness to pay between the two kinds of stores for the lower-income (i.e., more income-constrained) group.

We do not interpret this result as showing that lower-income people are more standardly rational by temperament or character; this seems highly unlikely. What seems more likely is that for lower-income people, the *subjective opportunity cost* of money is higher. When they spend an extra dollar on something, what they give up is more important to them than to those with higher incomes. To exaggerate, the low-income person gives up some eggs for breakfast while the higher-income person gives up some chewing gum. Thus, the cost of succumbing to so-called irrelevant framing does seem to affect its incidence.

The difference between the two groups is also reflected in their thought processes. In a later study (Shah et al. 2015, 404), participants in a redo of the beer-on-the-beach scenario were asked what went into their thinking about willingness to pay. The higher-income participants were more likely to think in locational terms ("the fancy hotel") while the lower-income participants thought about trade-offs or opportunity costs.

Cost also seems relevant when the coin of the realm is calories. Partici-pants in one treatment were primed to think of a daily caloric budget and in the other a weekly caloric budget. Then they were asked to rate how fattening a large order of french fries is on a scale of 1–11. Nondieting subjects thought the fries were more fattening when primed with the daily frame than when primed with the weekly frame. Dieting subjects, on the other hand, exhibited no such framing effect. A natural interpretation of this result is that participants who are committed to dieting experience a higher subjective opportunity cost of succumbing to framing effects – the extra unwanted weight.

Becker and Rubinstein (2004) examine the use of public bus services in Israel after a spate of suicide bombings on buses. Their hypothesis was, broadly speaking, that the greater the cost of one's fears in terms of reducing the consumption of the terror-infected good (bus rides), the more agents will expend effort to control those fears. The putative cognitive bias in play here is availability bias – the tendency to overestimate the likelihood of a terrorist act based on recent events.

Since Becker and Rubinstein could not measure fear directly, they sought to measure the effect on the consumption of the terror-infected good. They found that frequent or more intensive users of buses were not affected at all by the terror threat, while all of the reduced consumption was on the part of low-frequency users. This differential impact conforms to the rational application of more effort to reduce fear when there is greater value from doing so.[28] Thus it appears that when the opportunity cost of riding on the bus is relatively high, the operative bias disappears.[29]

Surveys of previous research also support the importance of incentives. In the area of judgments and decisions, our major concern here, incentives made a positive difference in 54 percent of the studies (fifteen out of twenty-eight) in the sense that mean performance was closer to the normative standard, and in many other cases where the mean performance was not affected the variance around the normative standard was reduced (Camerer and Hogarth 1999).[30] Furthermore, Hertwig and Ortmann (2001) find a positive effect of incentives in about half of the ten studies that (a) employed financial incentives, (b) systematically studied their effects relative to nonpayment or other payment schedules and conditions, and (c) had a clear normative standard.[31] Furthermore, "the positive effect of financial incentives on performance is more often found in repetitive

---

[28] While Becker and Rubinstein give the impression that this is done in an explicit or conscious way, this is not essential to their theory. Debiasing can be automatic or implicit, as we will see later in the chapter.

[29] A natural alternative is that more intensive bus users have lower income, and thus don't really have viable alternatives to the bus. However, the intensive or frequent users have a higher price elasticity of demand, as measured before the terrorism, which implies they must have alternatives – at least as a group.

[30] A reduction in the variance of results around the normative prediction is also consistent with the survey of Smith and Walker (1993).

[31] There were forty-eight studies that *simply* employed financial incentives, but that in itself was not sufficient to test the hypothesis of an effect on normative performance.

task experiments than in single-shot task experiments" (Lee 2007, 647). This suggests that *we cannot see the full effect of incentives in the short run.* We therefore move to some of the longer-run studies that incorporate repetition and thus the potential for learning.

Learning and Experience

Research on the effect of learning on the incidence of behavioral biases is still in its early stages. One of the major problems with assessing learning is that plausible learning periods are usually much longer than the duration of an experiment, which is usually only about an hour (Levitt and List 2007, 359). Nevertheless, progress has been made, especially in field experiments. In a sports card trading experiment, List (2003) found that endowment effects in the form of deviations of willingness to accept from willingness to pay were largely eliminated after trading experience. Similarly, undertrading (another symptom of the endowment phenomenon) dissipates after six months of trading experience (List 2011). To avoid confounding the experience effect with a self-selection effect, List (2011) and List and Millimet (2008) randomly assigned participants to the experience treatment of the experiment. Again, experience seemed to erode GARP violations in the first case,[32] and the endowment effect in the second.[33] Relatedly, Castillo et al. (2008) suggest that it is not experience per se that erodes nonstandard behavior, but experience in *competitive* markets. Interestingly, they find that those working in competitive labor markets act in accordance with expected utility theory and hence do not exhibit loss aversion (one of the claimed causes of the endowment effect).[34] Obviously, this result casts doubt on the behavioral rationale for assigning worker-friendly default terms in labor markets.

Learning and Errors

To say, as we did earlier, that people learn from experience does not fully capture what learning requires. In this section we argue that learning often

---

[32] The Generalized Axiom of Revealed Preference is a requirement for consistent choice and the existence of a standard utility function.

[33] In a study of market behavior in rural Ethiopia, 98.5 percent of farmers and 81.8 percent brokers originally had at least one GARP violation. After market experience, these percentages fell to 73.1 percent and 58.3 percent respectively. See Cecchi and Bulte (2013).

[34] Castillo et al. (2008) are not able to distinguish between sorting of individuals into a particular market and experience in that market.

requires error. While not desirable in themselves, errors are catalysts for learning. Modern associative learning theory rejects the idea that mere contingency and contiguity of a stimulus with its reward are sufficient for operant learning, i.e., learning about the consequences of one's actions.[35] Instead, learning is induced by errors in the prediction of a reward given a stimulus.

When a smaller reward is expected than actually occurs (positive reward-prediction error), predictions are revised upward in the direction of the surprise. On the other hand, when a larger reward is expected than actually occurs (negative reward-prediction error), predictions are revised downward (Schultz and Dickinson 2000, 495).[36] The process continues in either case until the prediction errors approximate zero.[37] This process is constituted by both indirect learning and direct learning. In the case of direct learning, attention is focused on the stimulus whether or not a reward is associated with it; that is, the individual learns to pay attention. This prepares the individual for action in the event of a possible reward. In the next period, if there are reward-prediction errors, indirect learning takes hold. Positive reward-prediction errors directly produce an increase in the associative strength and increased movement toward (or consumption of) the reward. Negative reward-prediction errors directly produce a decrease in associative strength and decreased movement toward (or consumption of) the reward. In each case the effect is proportional to the degree of reward-prediction error. However, it is not simply the magnitude of the prediction error in physical units that determines the effect, but the marginal utility of the reward (Stauffer et al. 2014). Thus, all else constant, the more valuable the reward, the greater the behavioral response.

---

[35] Broadly speaking, there are two kinds of learning: classical conditioning (Pavlovian learning) and operant learning. The former is learning about stimuli and what they may predict. Pavlov's dog salivates at the sound of a bell that typically accompanies a sausage. He does not do anything to bring about his reward. The latter is learning about the consequences of actions. The individual learns what operations he must perform to get the reward (Schultz 2015, 854–855). We are concerned here only with operant learning.

[36] The evidence from the studies cited in the text is both neurological and behavioral. The former consists in measuring dopamine neuron responses to prediction errors. The latter consists in correlating the choices made with the brain activity. Much of the evidence comes from animal models (monkeys, rats, and mice). However, the same dopamine neuron patterns have been observed in hundreds of neuroimaging studies of the human brain (Schultz 2015, 871).

[37] "In realistic situations, rewards may be unstable, which results in frequent prediction errors, continuous updating of predictions, and correspondingly variable behavior. Thus learning of a single stable reward is a special case of, and formally equivalent to, the general process of updating of reward predictions" (Schultz 2015, 868–869).

Many of the experiments showing the updating effects of reward-prediction errors are examples of "model-free learning," meaning that the agents understand only the reward feedback and then expect what they have just experienced to happen in the future.[38] People sometimes determine their behavior in this simple way. In such cases, individuals update their expectations, which were based on prior reinforcement, in accordance with the present reward attained. They show no understanding of the structure of the environment. When their goals or something in the environment changes, they wait for reward feedback before they change their behavior. By contrast, more sophisticated "model-based learning" involves an understanding of the structure of the environment. The predictions individuals make in this case are not simply responses to immediate rewards; they derive from a broader understanding of the causal mechanisms at work. For example, they will know that even if an action is followed by a reward, it may be a low-probability consequence and hence that action should not necessarily be repeated. They also understand how to change behavior when their goals change.

Reward-prediction errors change behavior in a model-based context as well as in a model-free context (Sambrook et al. 2018). Recent research has shown that when model-free actors encounter many negative prediction errors, they switch to model-based predictions (Wunderlich et al. 2012, 421). They may find it is worth shifting to a more complex and costly method to avoid more cases of unrewarded behavior. Relatedly, the neurological processes generated by prediction errors can support the making of neural connections that result in constructing models of the environmental structure (Sharpe et al. 2017).

The case of biased heuristics seems to fit within model-based learning. Individuals may make predictions that are implications of an inappropriate model of the environment, and as a result they make reward-prediction errors. For example, people may overestimate the value of a change in life circumstances because they fail to account for hedonic adaptation, as in the case of impact bias. The issue is whether they learn to correct for such biases as they experience negative reward-prediction errors. A simple reinforcement process would tell them something about the specific case at hand, and thus they would adjust their expectations without generalizing the lesson to other cases or contexts. (For instance, upon moving to a new city, they might realize they had overestimated the impact the move would

---

[38] For an overall discussion of model-free learning and the contrast with model-based learning, see Sambrook et al. (2018).

have on their satisfaction and therefore correct their thinking about that subject, while failing to correct their general tendency to overestimate the impact of other life changes.) However, as we noted earlier, as model-free prediction errors mount, people switch to theory-based predictions, meaning they try to learn more about the structure of the world. This enables them to adjust prospectively to new situations and not simply react to current rewards. These learning processes are all error-driven.

Policy Implications of Learning and Incentives

When interpreting the research on learning and incentives, we must keep in mind that better performance on normative tasks in the laboratory is not equivalent to showing that good performance on these tasks is necessary for ecologically rational behavior. The "focus on coherence criteria (e.g., logical consistency, rules of probability) over correspondence criteria, which relate human performance to success in the real world (e.g., speed, accuracy, frugality)" (Hertwig and Ortmann 2001, 396) suggests that many of these experiments are testing the effect of incentives on individuals becoming *approximate or asymptotic neoclassical agents*. But as we have argued throughout this book, that is neither necessary nor sufficient for success in real-world environments. Furthermore, it is not necessary for individual agents to be "rational" in the consistency sense for markets to display efficiency, that is, for prices to converge to competitive levels where consumer–producer surplus is maximized (e.g., List and Millimet 2008).

From a policy perspective, biases have been blamed for suboptimal decision-making in many areas. However, only to the extent that these "biases" are, in fact, not adaptive in the real world does the particular focus in current research on the effect of incentives have much policy significance. In those cases, given the insufficient attention paid by paternalists to the short- and long-run effects of actually bearing the burden of mistakes, policy prescriptions based on laboratory findings will doubtless need reassessment. This is not only because the particular biases at issue may not survive incentives and learning, but also because their quantitative extent may well be altered under these learning conditions.

SMALL-GROUP DEBIASING

Organizations often use small groups to make important decisions. Individuals may consult others, including expert advisors, before making decisions. Couples may make decisions that affect each of them in some collaborative fashion. In matters of importance, the frequency of atomistically individualistic decision-making is probably low. Yet behavioral economists and new paternalists usually conceive of decision-making, and most importantly error-making, as being done by solitary individuals. Here we inquire about the comparative adherence to standard rationality norms for individual and group decisions.

By "small groups" we usually mean two to four, sometimes five or six, but rarely more, individuals who make decisions by majority vote or consensus.[39] In the experiments under consideration, financial incentives are used to motivate finding the "correct" solutions to standard decision problems posed in the economics and psychology fields. Normally, either each member of the group will receive an actual reward for good performance or a group(s) will be randomly selected to receive a reward divided equally among the members.[40] Therefore, individuals bear the consequences of group decisions, and because the groups are small, each individual has a measurable impact on the final decision. It is important to note that in all of the studies in this section, group decisions are more than an aggregation of individual decisions. In other words, the analysts are not simply subjecting individual decisions to majority or unanimous decision rules. Individuals are allowed to discuss the issues involved and change any tentative decisions they may have made before arriving at the group decision. The discussion aspect of the process appears to have a greater role in generating rational group decisions than any "magic" of aggregation (Baillon et al. 2015). Finally, the results we discuss here are highly task-oriented and contextual. Thus, we are not arguing that groups never display the "biases" often attributed to individuals by behavioral research.[41] Nevertheless, there are many tasks for which the performance of individuals and groups differ substantially, meaning the implications for policymaking of the neglect of group decision-making may be considerable.

---

[39] While the optimum group size for accuracy of decision-making is unknown, it is definitely not the case that the larger, the better. While the optimum size will be quite sensitive to the kind of task and the assumed conditions, two simulation studies place the range of optimum sizes at fifteen or fewer. See Kao and Couzin (2014) and Galesic et al. (2015).

[40] In order to avoid the dilution of incentives in the group case (as well as other problems), the same reward given to one individual acting alone is given to each individual in the group acting jointly.

[41] "Although groups tend to outperform individuals in many domains, groups also can fall prey to the same heuristic-based biases found at the individual level" (Kerr and Tindale 2004, 634).

Small Groups and Task Performance

Groups perform better than individuals in standard "intellective" tasks, that is, those with a clear evaluation criterion. We now consider some of the most discussed of these.

Conjunctive Effect. For example, in the Linda problem (discussed in Chapter 5), which is usually interpreted as testing the ability of individuals to understand an elementary rule of probability called the "conjunction rule," college undergraduates fail to grasp that it cannot be more probable that Linda is a bank teller who is also active in the feminist movement than that she is a bank teller with no further description. In fact, some 85 percent think that the former is more probable than the latter (Tversky and Kahneman 1983).

A subsequent study (Charness et al. 2010) produces a smaller error rate, but 58 percent of undergraduates did make the conjunctive error. When incentives were introduced, the error rate fell to 33 percent. When students were tested in pairs (without incentives), the error rate declined to 48 percent; in trios, it declined to 27 percent. Adding incentives to the groups, the error rates fell to 13 percent and 10 percent respectively. Small groups with incentives only infrequently made the conjunction error.

Wason Selection Test. Another example is the Wason selection task (also discussed in Chapter 5), a test of the ability of individuals to engage in abstract deductive reasoning in order to test the truth of a conditional rule of the form, "If p then q." Individuals correctly solve this kind of problem at only an 11 percent rate, but groups of four individuals have a 50 percent solution rate (Maciejovsky and Budescu 2007).

First-Order Stochastic Dominance. One basic test of standard rationality in the context of decision-making under risk is whether agents adhere to first-order stochastic dominance in their choice or ordering of lotteries. For example, suppose an individual is asked to choose between the following two risky prospects:

X: 0.4 probability of a $10 gain and 0.6 probability of a $3 gain
Y: 0.5 probability of a $11 gain and 0.5 probability of a $3 gain

Regardless of the shape of his utility function, he should choose the lottery that is stochastically dominant. This is the lottery that has a higher probability of a larger prize for every prize level.[42] To illustrate, for X the probability of winning more than \$3 is 0.4 and the probability of winning more than \$10 is zero. For Y the probability of winning more than \$3 is 0.5 and the probability of winning more than \$10 is 0.5. Y stochastically dominates X and, by the axioms of expected utility theory, should be chosen.

In a study that compared individuals with groups of three, the violation of stochastic dominance occurred for 24 percent of individuals but only 9 percent of groups, although for groups of two the difference was not statistically significant (Charness et al. 2007).[43] In another study (Baillon et al. 2015) of groups of three, 64 percent of the groups (deciding by majority vote) satisfied stochastic dominance while only 42 percent of individuals did.

Probability Assessment.   Groups of three also make more accurate judgments than individuals in an evaluation of the risks associated with dying of different medical causes (Sniezek and Henry 1989). They also have narrower 99 percent confidence intervals with respect to the range of possible risk estimates associated with each cause. The degree of their *over*confidence in the accuracy of their estimates declined by 24 percent relative to individuals.

Probability Matching.   Schulze and Newell (2016) showed that groups of four avoid matching their bets on an outcome in a repeated choice problem to its probability (frequency). Consider a virtual ten-sided die with three red and seven green sides. The die is "tossed" by a computer fifty times. The participants in this experiment make a series of fifty bets at the outset and are rewarded if they select the correct color that comes up on the computer screen at each toss. They are instructed to maximize their earnings. What is the best strategy? A moment's thought tells us to bet on green *every time*. Then we are virtually guaranteed to get it right on

---

[42] More precisely, "Gamble A has first-order stochastic dominance over gamble B if for any outcome x, A gives at least as high a probability of receiving at least x as does B, and for some x, A gives a higher probability of receiving at least x." See Stochastic Dominance (n.d.).

[43] The study was also a test of the relative ability of individuals and groups to follow Bayesian rules for updating probabilities. The agents learned what probabilities to assign to the gamble outcomes on the basis of a prior stage in which they were exposed to simulated card draws. Groups were more Bayesian.

70 percent of the tosses. No other rule can do as well. Nevertheless, 35 percent of individuals do probability matching; that is, they guess green 70 percent of the time. In contrast, *none* of the groups engage in probability matching. Furthermore, when the performance of individuals is divided into the first, second, third, and fourth best, there is no significant difference between the group performance and that of the best individual performers. In these groups, it appears that the best ideas came out on top.[44]

Small Groups and Preference Biases

Myopic Loss Aversion. This is the tendency of individuals who evaluate their portfolio often (myopia) and who disproportionately weight losses more than gains (loss aversion) to invest less in risky assets (Thaler et al. 1997). However, when teams of three subjects did the investing, those who were prompted to check their portfolios often invested just as much as those individuals who were prompted to adjust their portfolios significantly less often (Sutter 2007).[45] In another study of investment behavior (Rockenbach et al. 2007), teams of three people were considerably more likely to adhere to the basic principles of "portfolio selection theory" than were individuals. Teams chose the investment option with both higher expected value and lower variance more often (73 percent) than did individuals (56 percent).[46] Most of the teams implemented their decisions by majority vote, although in this case there was sometimes an implicit individual veto of shouldering excessive risk.

Present Bias. In a study of husband–wife intertemporal decision-making in rural China, husbands were found to be individually more impatient than wives (Carlsson et al. 2012). Although the basic purpose of the study was to reveal the relative influence of husbands and wives in joint decision-making, the evidence showed that, when made jointly, decisions

---

[44] The groups were allowed to discuss their decisions before making them.

[45] Teams who evaluated portfolios more often were also subject to myopic risk aversion compared with teams who did so less often; they invested less than the latter teams. However, the point is that the team-quality of the decision *attenuates the bias* relative to individual decision-making under the same constraints and incentives.

[46] Overall, there were no statistically significant differences between individuals and teams in their adherence to the axioms of expected utility theory.

were less impatient than those made by husbands or wives alone.[47] While the participants were both jointly and individually impatient, there was only a slight present bias for joint decisions. A more extensive study of sixty-four real-life couples making intertemporal decisions with time horizons from one month to two years found that for all delays, decisions made by couples were more patient than decisions made by individuals (Abdellaoui et al. 2013). Furthermore, the joint decisions were more patient than decisions by either member of the couple taken individually. This means that the joint decision was not the result of mere aggregation or compromise between the two individuals; it was likely the emergent outcome of a discussion process between them. While the level of patience does not directly measure present bias, these results are relevant because high levels of impatience are frequently associated with time inconsistency (O'Donoghue and Rabin 2015) and greater short-run patience attenuates the effects of time inconsistency.

In perhaps the best study of the time consistency of group decisions, Denant-Boemont et al. (2017) compared the intertemporal decisions of five-member randomly selected groups with those of individuals over an eight-week period. Importantly, this experiment examined time inconsistency in the only theoretically appropriate way – by following decision-makers over time. This longitudinal study allowed people actually to reverse a previous decision between smaller-sooner and larger-later rewards. Decisions were incentivized by a randomized procedure where the probability of getting a significant reward (based on choices within the experiment) was 20 percent. Decisions were made on the basis of majority voting after a long sequence of information exchange, and all group members would share the rewards equally. The results show that groups were more patient and highly time-consistent. The decision process brings about a convergence of decisions to a standard neoclassical outcome.

SELF-REGULATION

In this section we use the terms "self-regulation" and "self-debiasing" to denote the full range of strategies that individuals may use to reduce the

---

[47] The decisions in this field experiment were made under very significant economic incentives (on average equivalent to two days' pay), so participants had an incentive to reveal their actual preferences.

impact of biases on their behavior.[48] We gave examples of several such strategies in Chapter 1; now we will be more specific. Strategies for self-regulation can broadly be classified as cognitive, environmental, and directly behavioral (Encyclopedia of Mind Disorders 2016). We have discussed this categorization extensively in previous work (Whitman 2006, 7–9; Rizzo and Whitman 2009b, 944), but here a short summary will do. *Cognitive* strategies involve "changing one's thoughts or beliefs about a particular behavior" (Encyclopedia of Mind Disorders n.d.). Common cognitive strategies include:

- Making resolutions and commitments, such as resolving to follow a new diet or committing to a new exercise regime.
- Adopting self-management techniques, such as counting to ten when in a heightened emotional state or facing temptations.
- Using mental accounts and budgets, which can help to keep spending in certain categories (such as entertainment) from exceeding certain limits, while permitting "guilt-free" indulgence within those limits. The prevalence of such techniques has been well established (Heath and Soll 1996; Thaler 1985; Wertenbroch 1998).
- Establishing personal rules that govern when and where indulgences are allowed or prohibited, such as only drinking while eating out, only having desserts on weekends and special occasions, and so on.

Environmental strategies involve "changing times, places, or situations where one experiences problematic behavior" (Encyclopedia of Mind Disorders 2016). Common environmental strategies include:

- Structuring of one's home or work environment to make targeted activities more costly, such as by removing cigarettes from the home and placing tempting foods in hard-to-reach or hard-to-notice locations.
- Setting up automatic money transfers from checking to savings accounts.
- Avoiding people, places, and situations that tend to trigger one's weaknesses, such as bars and restaurants.

Behavioral strategies involve "changing the antecedents or consequences of a behavior" (Encyclopedia of Mind Disorders 2016). Common behavioral strategies include:

---

[48] The meaning given to the term "self-regulation" in the broader psychological literature is "the general process by which people adopt and manage various goals and standards for their thoughts, feelings, and behavior, and then ensure that these goals and standards are met" (Fujita 2011, 353).

- Adopting internal incentives schemes, such as rewards for meeting weight-loss goals. This includes the phenomenon of self-gifting (Mick 1996; Mick and DeMoss 1990; on the efficacy of such schemes, see Bandura and Schunk [1981] and Bandura and Perloff [1967]).
- Enlisting social support in maintaining commitments. This can include joining organizations such as Alcoholics Anonymous and Weight Watchers, as well as simply advertising one's goals to family and friends.

The cognitive–environmental–behavioral classification does not capture the full variety of self-regulation. In addition to different strategies, there are different *modes* of implementation. Self-regulation can be conscious, deliberately focused on a specific goal, and thus costly in terms of cognitive effort, or it can be automatic and therefore far less costly. Furthermore, and perhaps most surprisingly, behavior that has often been considered indicative of the existence of biases – such as systematic misprediction of own-behavior, mental accounts, the sunk-cost "fallacy," and so forth – may actually constitute aspects of self-regulation.

Context-Dependence of Self-Regulation

As we saw in the section "Context-Specificity of Psychological Findings," the results of psychological research are highly contextual. This point deserves special emphasis with respect to self-regulation. Even a cursory examination of self-regulatory behaviors such as those mentioned earlier reveals the importance of context (Duckworth et al. 2016; Aldao 2013). Implementation of strategies will depend on such factors as the time of day, whether one is at work or at home or on vacation, who is in the individual's social space, and the special character of the occasion (wedding, anniversary, or birthday). Special occasions can relieve some of the costs of denying oneself indulgences without creating a precedent for breaking a resolution to diet or follow a study routine. Avoidance or modification of the physical or appetitive environment is a proactive and fairly standard form of self-regulation. For example, a person can take a different route home with no bars or avoid certain restaurants with an unlimited dessert buffet. This is often a lower-cost option than encountering the temptation and resisting it by pure psychic effort. Associating with people who are good at pursuing their long-term goals without being deflected by short-term rewards can have a significant self-regulatory effect (Fitzsimmons and Finkel 2010). Those addicted to drugs do much better when there is a change in their physical as well as social environment (Duckworth et al. 2016, 44–45).

Another set of contextual factors involves the characteristics of the actors themselves. Sometimes, for example, there are important gender differences in the form of self-regulation used (Nolen-Hoeksema and Corte 2004). Age also matters: older children have considerably greater self-control capacities than younger children (Mischel et al. 1989). More broadly, some strategies will assuredly be more effective for some individuals than others.

Much of this escapes the purview of laboratory experiments. In an attempt to produce results of general applicability, many experiments are devoid of relevant context (Loewenstein 1999). Familiar cues are omitted and individuals are treated as abstract agents. And yet this attempt at generality results in an impoverished and narrow view of self-regulation. Consider that it is impossible in a laboratory experiment to avoid facing the prescribed choice. The participants cannot say, "No. I would never face that temptation. I would change or modify the situation." Even more restrictive is the practice in many experiments of giving the participants specific instructions about what self-control device to use. Sometimes participants are told to push certain emotions away so that they won't feel them, not to think about their feelings, or to act in such a way that if there were other people in the room they would not detect one's true emotions (Aldo 2013, 161). The results of such experiments are not very informative. In natural environments, people choose their own regulatory strategies. These will be a function of personal characteristics, contextual demands, and opportunities present.[49]

Not all laboratory experiments, however, fail to see the contextual nature of self-regulation. In particular, one interesting strain of the literature shows context-dependency in the effect of temptation. Consider a tempting dessert such as a chocolate cake. Does the presence of a chocolate cake increase the probability of a person deviating from her diet? Will she lose self-control? Or is it possible that the presence of the chocolate cake will increase her resolve to diet? Surprisingly, it is not a foregone

---

[49] "In most psychological studies of self-control, participants are thrust into situations that they have not anticipated and for which they have not had an opportunity to plan their responses. In their everyday lives, however, people have the opportunity to anticipate events and can choose to enter into those that are amenable to their goals and to avoid those that are not" (Fujita 2011, 359).

conclusion that she is more likely to cheat on her diet. It all depends on context. Let's see how and why.

The usual behavioral story about temptation, as formalized in a number of models, is as follows: tempting objects or cues activate hedonic impulses. Self-control consists largely in impulse resistance.[50] Since self-control is cognitively costly, temptations reduce the probability that an individual will pursue her overriding or long-term goals. However, if we explore the cognitive processes involved, we see that the effect of the chocolate cake depends on context in the broad sense of the word. Although we cannot go into great detail, we can summarize the basic factors.

First, temptations have direct and indirect effects. The direct effects of increasing the probability of succumbing to short-term temptations are emphasized in standard analyses. But temptations can also indirectly activate higher priority or long-term goals (Fishbach et al. 2003). People exercise *counteractive self-control* in the presence of temptation (Myrseth et al. 2009).[51] Temptations can activate long-term goals through their experienced association with these goals and by inducing a reconception of the tempting object. For example, when an individual thinks of her internal conflict at a high level of construal, the option becomes transformed (Fujita and Carnevale 2012). Now it is a momentary hedonic pleasure versus a healthy diet and long life. This reconception is itself a form of self-control because it makes the tempting object less alluring and the long-term goal more valuable. Higher-level construal and counteractive self-control are more frequent when the individual has been more successful at self-control, as evidenced by her personal history, and when the subjective degree of importance she attaches to long-term goals is high.

Second, cognitive load can also be helpful to self-control (Van Dillen et al. 2013). Traditionally, behavioralists have seen cognitive load as an impediment to self-control, such as when a person with a demanding deadline approaching eats more junk food or relapses into smoking. Nevertheless, cognitive load at an *earlier stage* in the full hedonic development of a temptation may decrease the selective attention paid to a temptation. Consider that a person who is "keeping busy" may barely notice a chocolate cake in front of her or, more importantly, may not

---

[50] Self-control is a form of self-regulation. "Self-control is one of these specific regulatory challenges – promoting one's abstract and distal goals when they are threatened by competing concrete and proximal goals" (Fujita 2011, 353).

[51] It is important to note that when the direct and indirect effects of temptations are equal, they cancel out, and thus there is effective self-control.

process the temptation sufficiently to evoke actual cravings. It takes cognitive resources to process hedonic value. Thus, cognitive load can reduce the allure of temptations and thereby facilitate self-regulation if it occurs early in the process or before the stimulus is encountered.

Third, the character of the temptation itself can affect the likelihood of self-control. A really delicious-looking and readily available chocolate cake is more likely to evoke overriding goals such as good health or weight reduction and thus self-control than a mediocre-looking and not very available chocolate cake (as in a simple photograph of the cake). A higher level of temptation can generate more self-control because the individual's long-term goals are perceived as more threatened.[52] Paradoxically, a lower level of temptation may make the individual more vulnerable (Kroese et al. 2011; Geyskens et al. 2008). These results suggest that, contrary to Thaler and Sunstein's (2003) speculative discussion of dessert location in a cafeteria line, a more available and outrageously delicious-looking cake may ultimately be *less* tempting than one not so prominently placed.

Environmental and personal characteristics provide the context in which self-regulation is exercised. Even something as superficially simple as the allure of a chocolate cake depends on the context. Obviously, these mechanisms of self-control are not always effective. Nevertheless, to the extent that behavioral economists are oblivious to such factors, they will not look for them and will not attempt to include them in their models. The result will be an underestimation of self-regulation and an overestimation of bias.

Automaticity of Much Self-Regulation

There is good theoretical reason and empirical evidence to support the claim that much self-regulation, including self-control, is automatic or, as it is also called, implicit. By "automatic" and "implicit," we mean that it is spontaneous, unconscious, and effortless. It does not utilize cognitive resources such as working memory to any significant degree.[53]

---

[52] This does not mean that the stronger the temptation, the more likely self-control will be successful. The optimum degree of temptation from the perspective of long-term goals is somewhere between weak and extremely strong, that is, an intermediate level (Trope and Fishbach 2005, 539).

[53] "Unlike explicit self-control operations, implicit operations are far less resource dependent and thus may be relatively more resistant to the detrimental effects of stress or mental and physical fatigue" (Fishbach and Shah 2006, 830).

Unfortunately, most of the psychological research conceptualizes self-control as deliberate, conscious, and a heavy consumer of cognitive resources (Muraven and Baumeister 2000). Following this lead, behavioral economics also models self-control as deliberate and costly (Gul and Pesendorfer 2001, 2004). Restricting attention to this form of self-control biases the analyst toward observing self-control failures to a greater degree than would otherwise be the case.[54]

The theoretical presumption in favor of automatic self-regulation derives from the costliness of deliberate self-regulation. It is difficult to see how people could achieve their goals to the great extent they do if all goal pursuit required conscious regulation. There is simply too much potential interference out there for every step along the path to be guided by a costly deliberate process.

There is a significant empirical literature (de Ridder et al. 2012) on the degree to which self-control tendencies or traits are associated with the avoidance of "bad" behaviors (such as drug addiction) or the furtherance of "good" behaviors (such as dieting). The traits in question include characteristics such as the general impulsiveness of the individual, whether the individual is more interested in the present than in the future, how quickly the person loses his or her temper, and so forth.[55] A meta-analysis of 102 studies of self-control found that self-control traits were largest and most strongly associated with automatic behaviors, whereas the association of self-control traits with controlled behaviors was small. Those with high self-control traits were more likely to exhibit automatic than deliberate self-control. They tended to form good routines or habits rather than engaging in continual deliberate and costly self-control (de Ridder et al. 2012).

Many of the examples of self-control discussed in previous and subsequent sections can be activated and implemented implicitly.[56] In particular, automatic processes include the redirection of subjective attention

---

[54] One reason for this is that successful self-controllers tend to routinize their behavior or form habits over time (even if they start out with deliberate efforts). Another related reason is more general: the higher the imputed costs of self-control, the more often actual applied self-control will not be sufficient to overcome the pull of immediate satisfaction. Therefore, if the analyst ignores automatic behaviors and if the cost of deliberate self-control is high, the analyst will simply see a failure of self-control.

[55] The traits were assessed by questionnaires and the behaviors were assessed either by observation by third parties or by questionnaires, depending on the particular study.

[56] "We argue that explicit and implicit self-control modes operate in tandem and follow the same basic principles" (Fishbach and Shen 2014, 455).

away from temptations, physical avoidance of environmental cues, and perceiving events or filtering information in a "biased" way (see section "Biases as Self-Regulation"). Most important, however, may be the spontaneous and asymmetric reevaluation of long-term benefits compared with short-term benefits mentioned in the section "Context-Dependence of Self-Regulation." This is counteractive self-control.[57]

Standard economics is particularly ill-equipped to deal with the process of automatic counteractive self-control. Most choice problems are conceived as the agent maximizing an objective function. In the more recent extended versions, designed to accommodate behavioral insights, an extra constraint is added: self-control. This is costly impulse control – the deliberate application of cognitive effort to resist temptations. But the modeled agent's perception of the problem, and thus the framework of decision, is itself static.[58] The agent takes the parameters of the problem, including the costs and benefits assigned to outcomes, as given. By contrast, a central idea of counteractive self-control is that the individual spontaneously *revalues* the costs and benefits of resisting temptation. Rather than drawing on his limited supply of willpower, the agent reconceptualizes the problem he faces. The benefits of long-run goals such as dieting or not smoking are revised upward while the benefits of giving in to temptation remain the same or are revised downward. This process is initiated *after* a particular goal conflict has been identified (either consciously or implicitly). What may appear to be the operative decision framework really just identifies the problem; it is only a tentative construct. The actual framework is a revision that results from a self-control process.

Of course, not all cases of counteractive self-control are successful. People still give in to temptation. However, unless this form of self-control is acknowledged, it will appear as if the initial framework is permanent, and therefore the only way to deal with a conflict among goals is to use up costly resources (i.e., willpower). Yet people are more creative than that; they can break out of the static problem.

Biases as Self-Regulation

Ainslie (2012) argues that what is often called "self-control" is the outcome of a within-person intertemporal bargaining process. The critical element

---

[57] There have been several surveys of the research on automatic self-regulation and self-control. See, for example, Fitzsimons and Bargh (2004) and Fishbach and Shen (2014).

[58] Israel Kirzner has stressed the importance of changes in the framework of decision for economic theory in a series of books beginning with *Competition and Entrepreneurship* (1973).

in this process is the agent's understanding of the significance of an act of resisting or yielding to temptation. Does yielding presage future defections from long-run value-maximizing decisions? Does resisting predict future avoidance of impulsive short-run choices? When looked at in this way, the intertemporal decision process is *recursive*. What the individual does today will depend on his prediction of the impact of today's decision on his future decisions. This idea will be familiar to lawyers as the precedential value of a judicial or legislative action (Rizzo and Whitman 2003, 546–547). A seemingly benign decision today may open the floodgates to bad decisions in the future. For the individual, simply eating an extra dessert today may lead to consuming extra desserts in the future. The individual who decides to resist says, "If I cheat on my diet today, I predict that I will cheat on future dates when I have the same decision before me. Therefore, I will not cheat today." This individual reevaluates his current decision by bundling the future flows of larger later rewards and opposing them to the short-run benefits of impulsive eating.[59] On the other hand, if the individual yields to temptation, he may seek to limit the precedential value of the particular decision by characterizing it as "special" in some way – "It was my birthday," for instance. Of course, such strategies might involve *ex-post* rationalization, but if they are believed, they will preserve the individual's credibility in self-signaling. Thus, self-deception can be an element in a self-regulatory strategy.

Within this analytical framework, behaviors and beliefs that are allegedly irrational or less-than-rational can be seen as part of self-regulation (Ainslie 2005). Consider the individual who pays high interest on her credit card rather than drawing down a savings account, even though the savings account yields an annual return that is a fraction of the credit card's interest rate. This is an example of keeping mental accounts that from a traditional economic perspective makes no sense since money is fungible. It would be less expensive to spend the same amount of money from the savings account. And yet people consciously do this. Why? In the presence of impulsive consumption spending, mental accounts can accomplish two things. First, they place a "tax" – the higher credit card rate of interest – on this activity, thereby reducing its frequency and extent. Second, they create a certain discipline in maintaining the farsightedness of saving decisions by refusing to deplete the savings

---

[59] The bundled benefit profiles of similar decisions in the future will be discounted at a much lower rate than the hyperbolic spike rate because the bundled benefits occur with delay from the standpoint of today's decision.

account. Accordingly, the credit card spending needs to be understood *in conjunction* with the savings decision made feasible by these mental accounts. A theory that seeks to explain the credit card decision as present bias and tries to measure the extent of that bias – while ignoring the functional role of mental accounts – necessarily overstates the individual's overall degree of present bias.[60]

Similarly, a recurrent but puzzling phenomenon is the lower rate of discount individuals apply to options between smaller-sooner and larger-later when the amounts of each increase proportionately. This is known as the "magnitude effect" (Burkett 2006, 208). It makes no sense in terms of the theory of quasi-hyperbolic discounting that individuals would become more patient as the amounts of both rewards become larger. Patience in the quasi-hyperbolic model depends solely on the delay to the initial reward. But this seeming contradiction is due to the theory's inadequate treatment of self-regulation. People can safely indulge in impulsive behavior for "pocket change." However, they quite reasonably want to isolate the behavior in this case from circumstances in which large sums of money (or other large rewards) are at stake. The magnitude effect accomplishes that.

Finally, sometimes "excessive" risk-taking from the perspective of the agent may be a problem. The individual's self-regulatory response to excessive risk-taking may take the form of just those anomalies that behavioral economists call biases. The related phenomena of endowment effects, loss aversion, and status quo bias can all function as caution-inducers. In a truly uncertain world, the *opportunity cost* of departing from the current situation is not always clear. A relatively easy measure of success or failure is to treat the status quo as the reference point. A neoclassical actor, on the other hand, would judge changes relative to the next-best opportunity forgone. When an individual faces the opportunity to depart from the status quo, he can ask himself, "Is this a gain or loss compared with where I am now?" or he can ask himself, "How sure am I that the change will be the best possible change?" Focusing on the second question outside of a small world of calculable risk is a very unnerving task. It is not unreasonable to think that individuals may want to restrain themselves from impulsively plunging into decisions based on highly

---

[60] Angeletos et al. (2001) find that a high level of present bias is necessary to explain the observed rate of credit card borrowing but a low discount rate is necessary to explain long-run wealth accumulation. This is consistent with the view expressed earlier regarding mental accounts as a self-regulation mechanism.

speculative opportunity-cost comparisons.[61] This would be the function of applying extra negative weight to losses and extra positive weight to the current endowment or status quo position.[62] In such an approach, losses relative to an easily observable baseline will count for more than hard-to-see forgone opportunities for gain.[63]

Self-Regulatory Processes Mistaken for Agent Naïveté

In a very influential study, Della Vigna and Malmendier (2006) attempt to calculate present bias on the basis of observed consumer behavior in purchasing gym memberships. There are three basic phenomena they seek to explain: (1) Gym members who purchased monthly memberships paid considerably more per visit than they would have if they had purchased on a single-visit or ten-visit basis. In fact, 80 percent of monthly members would have done better purchasing the ten-visit bundle. On average they lost about $600 over the first year. (2) A survey of gym members (not those observed in the purchasing data) shows that members go to the gym about half as often per month as they expected to. (3) There is a lag of more than two months between the last visit a person makes to the gym and the point at which he cancels the monthly membership.

Before we discuss Della Vigna and Malmendier's interpretation of these facts, it is important to understand the possible functions served by a monthly (or yearly) contract. The most relevant for our purposes here is that when individuals exhibit present bias, gyms will charge a membership fee along with a below-marginal-cost price (free) for each visit. When individuals are sophisticated – that is, they know perfectly their degree of present bias – this arrangement functions as a commitment device. It

---

[61] This issue can be pushed back yet another step: to follow a strategy of covering opportunity costs, the individual must be adequately confident that she has assessed the true opportunity costs. What is the "optimal" amount of deliberation required to assess that in cases of true uncertainty? This is not well defined. Therefore, the individual may easily second-guess herself if things do not turn out well and thus feelings of regret at the *ex post* outcome may be hard to avoid (Ainslie 2005, 267).

[62] The so-called sunk-cost fallacy can be understood in a similar way. This is the case when individuals do not abandon a plan simply because of the desire to "save" previously invested resources. However, this "bias" can serve the function of counteracting impulsiveness leading to the premature abandonment of a plan when staying the course is the better option. See Eswaran and Neary (2016).

[63] On the other hand, traders who are experienced tend not to display the endowment effect. See List (2003).

lowers the cost of going to the gym at the moment of decision when they may not feel like exerting the effort to go. On the other hand, if people are naïve with respect to their degree of present bias, the arrangement can serve as an "exploitation" device because people will buy memberships that make sense only for a larger number of visits than they actually make. Based on this framework and the data above, Della Vigna and Malmendier compute a present-bias parameter of 0.7.[64] This indicates that individuals are partially naïve and that the commitment device is at least in part an exploitation device.

Our primary concern is whether this analysis adequately accounts for self-regulation. Unlike laboratory studies, which take place largely without real-world context and thus without the cues that trigger self-regulation, this study is derived largely from observations of real-world behavior. Nevertheless, it seems to misconstrue the nature of the self-regulatory process. The analysis is fundamentally static, and thus the crucial observations that individuals plan to go to the gym more than they actually do and that they delay canceling inappropriate contracts are interpreted as partial naïveté. Indeed the individuals may be naïve to begin with, but does that explain where things end? To answer *yes* would seem implausible. Consider that the people in this study were new gym members and therefore likely inexperienced. Do they continue to overestimate their self-discipline – and hence overestimate their number of trips to the gym – after a year or more, even though they now see that they are paying more and going less?

Instead of looking at overestimation as a simple error due to naïve present bias, Ali (2011) constructs a plausible model in which the decision-maker's awareness of his self-control problems is something *acquired gradually* as a result of learning that his estimates of gym use are overly optimistic. Thus, the degree of self-awareness is not modeled as exogenous as it is in Della Vigna and Malmendier. Why should we expect inexperienced individuals to know how much self-discipline they will have in going to the gym? The only way they will find out is by getting feedback on their initial optimistic expectations. And this will not happen all at once. Inevitably there will be a period during which they will be paying for visits they do not use. The more patient they are about learning, the longer this period

---

[64] The expected cancelation delay is critical in computing the parameters. The delays of 60 and 120 days observed in the data are rationalized by $\delta = 0.9995$ and $\beta = 0.7$ (Della Vigna and Malmendier 2006, 114).

will be. Patience in acquiring the knowledge necessary for self-regulation can be confused, ironically, with present bias.[65]

Our argument is not that people will necessarily become perfectly sophisticated after this process.[66] Rather, we claim that the method used by Della Vigna and Malmendier to estimate present bias does not account for learning that can lead to more effective self-regulation. They assume that all of the delay by infrequent gym users, from the time of initial membership to the time at which they switch to per-visit payment, is the result of present bias. But, as Ali suggests, there is no reason to do that. Individuals will take time to learn about their self-control problems and therefore about the optimal manner of paying for gym visits. Thus, self-regulation is underestimated and present bias is overestimated. Once again, the reliability of quantitative estimates of behavioral parameters is called into question.

Even if we exclude the possibility that overestimation of the number of gym visits may be indicative of a dynamic learning process, optimistic expectations of success in attaining a goal have been shown to function as a self-control mechanism (Zhang and Fishbach 2010). When people attempt to achieve a goal beset with obstacles, such as transient temptations, they tend to become *more* optimistic about the likelihood that they will achieve the central goal. This goal could be dieting, studying, or exercising. In the case of exercise, the optimistic expectations are likely to be manifested in overestimation of the number of gym visits they will make. While visiting the gym frequently is only an intermediate goal, ultimate goals such as good health and attractive physique will take time to attain and monitoring them may not be feasible in the short run. Thus, overestimation of an intermediate goal has instrumental value. A higher standard is set, and the individual works harder to achieve it. While the accuracy of their

---

[65] "[T]here are numerous reasons to believe that decision makers may begin with optimistic priors and learn slowly, and findings in the field are consistent ... Moreover, when a decision maker makes choices in an environment in which he has had little prior experience, he has to simultaneously learn about how tempted he is by different choices in that setting and the payoffs of different actions" (Ali 2011, 863).

[66] Ali (2011) discusses the necessary and sufficient conditions for full sophistication. However, when learning fails to get to this point, it is likely that the agent will be underestimating rather than overestimating his future self-control. If an originally optimistic planning agent is not sufficiently *patient* about learning, he will stop experimenting at some point short of optimal learning. This is because the benefits of learning about self-control are in the future and the costs are in the form, say, of the present extra cost of gym visits due to not canceling the monthly contract. Thus, people will choose too many or too rigid commitments relative to the optimum.

predictions is compromised and this may be costly (paying not to go to the gym), it can be a perfectly reasonable expenditure of resources to combat the effects of temptations or other diversions from central goals.

Lastly, let us return to the possibility of consumers using memberships as a way of altering their future behavior – i.e., as a kind of commitment device. A gym membership reduces the *marginal* cost of visiting the gym to zero, thereby reducing the future disincentive to exercise. To see whether this self-imposed incentive works as planned, we would need to compare the frequency of visits for members versus per-visit users (and we would also need to control for selection effects). Unfortunately, the authors report that data on attendance by per-visit users is not available (Della Vigna and Malmendier 2006, 697).

Significance of Underestimating the Extent of Self-Regulation

New paternalists have suggested various ways of offsetting lack of self-regulation generally and lack of self-control in particular. One of the most popular is the "sin tax" (O'Donoghue and Rabin 2006). Such a tax is designed to deal with goods or activities that generate present benefits but also future costs. The "sin goods" are often perceived to be tempting or viscerally attractive: potato chips, chocolate cakes, or cigarettes. Faced with such temptations, people exhibit present bias. They discount the future costs relative to the immediate benefits very highly – much more highly than they would discount the same future costs relative to benefits that accrue before the present but not immediately. This is considered suboptimal from the individual perspective. If a tax were imposed on the sin good, some of its immediate attractiveness would be eliminated and the individual would consume less, thus reducing the burden placed on his future selves. But how high should the tax be? Too high a tax would impose a needless penalty on the consumption. Accordingly, the tax should vary in accordance with the actual *degree* of present bias. Since present bias is usually thought to be due to a lack of self-regulation or self-control, what is at issue is the amount of each exercised by consumers. To the extent that the behavioral framework of analysis ignores the varieties of self-control discussed here, self-control is likely to be underestimated and the tax will be excessive (Whitman 2006, 11–12).

Consider a case where individuals exercise self-control but it is "invisible." This could be because self-control has taken the form of asymmetric revaluation of the immediate benefits and future costs of the sin good. The immediate benefits are revalued downward and the future costs are revalued upward (Fishbach et al. 2010), as discussed earlier. The process is usually automatic and takes place as the individual becomes aware of the goal conflict but before the very moment of choice. The present-bias discount rate will not necessarily be affected by this process. Since the decision to consume depends on the discount rate *and* the time profile of perceived benefits and costs, self-control could be manifested in either an adjustment in present bias *or in the profile of costs and benefits*. The standard sin-tax models treat the profile as simply given. In these models, the *only* indicator of self-control is the present-bias parameter. Attempting, in effect, to eliminate or reduce the bias through corrective taxation will be nonoptimal if the profile is subject to change.

Self-Regulation and the Opportunity Costs of Executive Function

If self-regulation resources are indeed scarce, as they are treated in much of the behavioral literature, then individuals face an allocation problem: how should these scarce resources be deployed? After all, a person typically faces multiple different tasks that require the application of self-regulation. The automatic processes of self-regulation discussed earlier can ease this burden. Nevertheless, when there are competing demands on the use of conscious executive functions – i.e., focus, vigilant monitoring, and self-control – then allocating more of these resources to one task will leave less for other tasks, at least in the short run. There is an opportunity cost of their use, and the subjective feeling of effort or fatigue in using them can serve as a signal of that opportunity cost (Kurzban et al. 2013). This implies that paternalistic interventions that successfully direct cognitive resources toward targeted areas also pull resources away from others.

An implicit assumption behind some paternalistic interventions is that they will *augment* people's scarce cognitive resources in some way. But it is equally plausible that they will simply divert cognitive resources from other things. For instance, a sin tax is supposed to make the sinful temptation more costly and thus easier to resist. But is this really so? The temptation does not cease to be tempting, after all. The now-greater cost increases the need to resist it, and therefore pulls away cognitive resources that would have been deployed elsewhere. Consider the case of a lawyer studying for the bar exam, which we introduced in Chapter 2. If a higher cigarette tax induces her to use greater cognitive resources on resisting her cravings to smoke cigarettes, she will presumably have fewer resources left for focusing on studying. It is not obvious that this intervention has made her better off.

At a minimum, there is an opportunity cost in terms of alternative uses of the diverted cognitive resources.

A similar concern applies to policies that purport to increase the salience of product attributes that consumers might otherwise neglect. Graphic images, "typical use" product disclosures, and risk narratives can all be understood as devices for manipulating salience. Such policies are ostensibly justified because boundedly rational individuals do not "adequately" perceive all of the relevant attributes of a product *even if* they are revealed by the firm. As we discussed in Chapter 5, however, it may not be possible for a consumer to attend to every attribute that may be important now or later, because attention is limited. Salience of one attribute may crowd out the salience of another. Not everything can be put front and center. If the paternalist policies in question do not augment the attention budget of individuals, the reasonable probability of crowding out and wearing off must be faced. These policies represent, in their essence, attempts to manage the scarce attention budget of the individual, reallocating attention from one thing to another. There is no guarantee that the new allocation of attention is better than the old one.[67]

Unfortunately, this discussion is and must be speculative, as we are not aware of any behavioral research that specifically addresses whether interventions supplement rather than divert cognitive resources. Yet the answer to that question bears directly on whether such interventions can confidently be predicted to improve consumer welfare, all things considered.

CONCLUSIONS

In a survey of the literature on the use of technical research by policy actors, Bogenschneider and Corbett (2010) identify twelve criteria by which the usefulness of research is evaluated for policy purposes. Among those, three stand out as having critical significance for the behavioral and cognitive research we have discussed in this chapter. They are:

Definitiveness: Results are clear.
Generalizability: Results are applicable to the jurisdictions or populations of interest to the policymaker.
Policy Implications: The links between results and policy are clear.

(Bogenschneider and Corbett 2010, 33)

---

[67] Spiegler (2015, 407–410) offers an intriguing model in which product-use disclosure in the presence of fixed attention budgets causes a reduction in consumer welfare.

Unfortunately for behavioral paternalism, the research displays serious deficiencies with regard to these criteria. First, it is hard to claim that the results are clear-cut. When incentives, learning, group debiasing, and self-regulation have not been adequately assessed, it is not clear which results we can confidently export to the world of public policy. Second, generalizability is uncertain because the results are highly contextual, the rate of reproducibility is unknown and possibly quite low, and the populations studied do not necessarily resemble those targeted by policy. Finally, the link between results and policy recommendations is far from clear. What appear as biases may in specific contexts actually be debiasing techniques. And the failure of quantitative results to generalize opens the real possibility of overcompensating for perceived biases.

Recall our introductory remarks that the claims in this chapter constitute immanent criticism. Even if we agreed that the standard rationality norms of neoclassical and behavioral economics provided an appropriate basis for prescribing public policy, the tools that real people use to achieve their goals and to shape their own behavior are multifarious and resistant to description by simple models. To craft policies that help agents reduce their biases, we still need reliable scientific knowledge about how, when, and where those biases operate, their strength in real-life settings, the extent to which agents learn about and correct biases on their own, and so on. These questions are still largely unanswered, although we can hope that future research will begin to fill in the blank spaces. In Chapter 7, however, we will discuss the kind of knowledge that we cannot reasonably expect will be generated by the scientific process.

7

Knowledge Problems in
Paternalist Policymaking*

> It is a standing topic of complaint, that a man knows too little of himself. Be it so: but is it so certain that the legislator must know more? It is plain, that of individuals the legislator can know nothing: concerning those points of conduct which depend upon the particular circumstances of each individual, it is plain, therefore, that he can determine nothing to advantage.
>
> —Jeremy Bentham, *An Introduction to the Principles of Morals and Legislation*

> But a little reflection will show that there is beyond question a body of very important but unorganized knowledge which cannot possibly be called scientific in the sense of knowledge of general rules: the knowledge of the particular circumstances of time and place. It is with respect to this that practically every individual has some advantage over all others because he possesses unique information of which beneficial use might be made, but of which use can be made only if the decisions depending on it are left to him or are made with his active coöperation.
>
> —Friedrich Hayek, *The Use of Knowledge in Society*

What constitutes a "good" paternalist policy intervention? And what sort of evidence would be sufficient to show it is justified? Behavioral economists emphasize the importance of evidence and social scientific research in making the case for any given intervention. Sunstein and Thaler say interventions "should be designed using a type of welfare analysis, one in which a serious attempt is made to measure the costs and benefits of outcomes (rather than relying on estimates of willingness to pay)" (Sunstein and Thaler 2003, 1166). The phrase "rather than relying on estimates of willingness to pay" refers to the fact that, in the behavioral perspective, the market choices of consumers cannot be fully trusted, which means that reliable knowledge of

---

* Some sections of this chapter, as well as the general shape of the argument, are adapted from Rizzo and Whitman (2009b).

what people want must come from elsewhere – presumably, behavioral research. Sunstein further emphasizes the need to "rely on evidence rather than intuitions, anecdotes, wishful thinking, or dogmas" (2014, 3).

In short, broad intuitions and generalizations about human nature, even those grounded in behavioral research, are not enough to justify paternalist interventions. The burden of proof is higher than that. There must be good reason to believe that an intervention will indeed result in genuine welfare improvements – that the costs will exceed the benefits, properly measured, taking into account all people affected by the policy. This burden must be met by each intervention in its specific context. The question, then, is whether policymakers possess the knowledge needed to meet that burden – or if not, whether they can acquire it.

In Chapter 6 we examined several ways in which the existing research in psychology and behavioral economics is not sufficient for good policy-making. But we acknowledged that future research could alleviate those deficiencies. As our scientific knowledge about human behavior grows, so should our ability to craft well-designed paternalistic interventions – or so it would appear.

However, scientific knowledge is not the only kind of knowledge relevant to policy. There is another type of knowledge that lies largely beyond the reach of academics and policymakers: the particular details of time and place that affect the preferences, constraints, and choices of individuals. Following Friedrich Hayek (1945), we will call this kind of knowledge "local knowledge." In the case of scientific knowledge, a suitable body of experts may legitimately claim to have the best and most recent knowledge available. But when it comes to local knowledge, individuals have insights and perspective unavailable to outside experts. They have access to their inner selves and circumstances in a way that outsiders typically do not.

Some local knowledge is tacit – that is, not easily expressed in words or conveyed to others. Tacit knowledge is often embodied in behaviors that may be unconscious, and often these behaviors are automatically induced by context and environmental cues. In Chapter 6 we saw that much, perhaps most, self-regulation is of this type. Self-regulation can also differ from person to person in myriad ways, and it is not always visible to the outside observer.

Furthermore, as Ainslie (2001) has argued, behavior should not be viewed in isolation but as part of a wider complex of behavior. Actions that may appear "biased" in themselves may actually reflect attempts to debias another type of behavior – or at least may serve that function. How an entire behavioral system operates also differs from person to person and context to context. Local knowledge is complex, idiosyncratic, and diffuse. As such, it defies attempts to collect it all in one place.

It is true, of course, that sometimes individuals lack knowledge of themselves. They may be unaware of their own biases. For this reason, behavioral economists sometimes claim that outside experts have better knowledge than individuals about their psychology. However, even this kind of knowledge is typically unavailable to outsiders in the specific form needed. Behavioral economists may have scientific knowledge of a certain kind of bias that afflicts many people or the "average" person. But they do not typically know how much any particular individual is affected by a given bias, the extent to which the individual has become aware of her own bias, and the ways in which she may have attempted to compensate for it. The best the expert can hope for is population-level or group-level summary statistics, not the specific contextual knowledge needed to guide and correct individual behavior. As we shall see, this kind of knowledge is necessary to craft welfare-improving policies for the population as a whole. As a result, paternalist policymakers face a severe, and possibly insurmountable, *knowledge problem.* They do not and often cannot possess the kind of knowledge needed to craft policy interventions that reliably improve human welfare.

The title of this chapter is inspired by the "knowledge problem" identified by Friedrich Hayek in the mid-twentieth century as the primary impediment to socialist central planning (Hayek 1945). Socialists of the era often argued that central planners could effect a more rational organization of economic activity than could the private market, *provided* that planners possessed all the relevant knowledge about resource endowments, production processes, and individual preferences. Hayek argued, in essence, that the socialists had *assumed away the problem.* The most important problem that any economic system must solve is mobilizing and using knowledge that "never exists in concentrated or integrated form but solely as the dispersed bits of incomplete and frequently contradictory knowledge which all the separate individuals possess" (Hayek 1945, 519). In Hayek's view, a key virtue of markets was their ability to create incentives for individuals to act upon local knowledge that was beyond the reach of socialist planners. We suggest that a very similar (though not identical) problem hobbles "paternalist planners" who would intervene to improve individual choices.

The knowledge problem of central planning arose in large part because socialists had been seduced by simple economic models created by mainstream economists. Models of general competitive equilibrium, based on "given" endowments, technologies, and preferences, suggested the possibility of directly calculating optimal economic arrangements from the information provided. But in reality, such information is not "given" to anyone in its totality, and no general model can fully capture the full range and variability of the world it is intended to model. Similarly, we believe paternalists have been misled by simple models devised by both neoclassical and behavioral economists. While these models can be enormously useful in understanding specific aspects of human behavior, no one model can encompass *all* of the relevant factors governing choice. Even the most sophisticated behavioral models account for at best two or three interacting biases, affecting one or two types of behavior, and calibrated based on a narrow range of parameter values. In short, we should not mistake simple models for a simple world.

In Chapter 6 we saw that the factors that allegedly cause deviations from formal neoclassical standards are highly context-dependent. Crucially, these factors vary from place to place, time to time, and circumstance to circumstance; they also vary with the experimental method of eliciting the particular bias. Thus, not only is rational behavior highly contextual, but all attempts to debias putatively less-than-rational conduct are also highly contextual. From a policy perspective, "contextual" is a synonym for "contingent on local and personal knowledge."

For the sake of argument, we will assume that the scientific generalizations of the behavioral paternalists – the existence of present bias, reference-dependent preferences, base-rate neglect, and so forth – are well supported, despite the concerns we've expressed in earlier chapters. Nevertheless, they are not sufficient to support the creation of policies that reliably increase the welfare of individuals. The primary reason is that the operation of biases in the real world is heavily dependent on local and personal circumstances. It is peculiar that behavioral economists have not fully appreciated this point, as sensitivity to context is one of the most important lessons of their work. But conveniently, the simplified behavioral view of the world does not allow "too much" context dependency, as that would impede the creation of *generally applicable* policies that can confidently be predicted to improve well-being. A full appreciation of the importance of local and personal knowledge makes paternalist policymaking extremely difficult and often infeasible.

A TYPOLOGY OF KNOWLEDGE REQUIREMENTS

Chapter 6 suggested several types of knowledge that paternalist planners need in order to design successful interventions. Now we will attempt a more complete typology of the many types of knowledge required.

Knowledge of True Preferences

If paternalists genuinely wish to make people better off in terms of their own preferences ("as judged by themselves," to use the popular phrase in the literature), then it is necessary to identify what those true preferences are. Only with such knowledge can they hope to push behavior in the right direction.

True preferences must be distinguished both from actual choices and from mental preferences at the very moment of choice. They are the preferences that individuals supposedly have "before" behavioral distortions or biases take effect. In an important sense, the concept is counterfactual. These are the preferences that *would* determine choice in a sanitized or bias-free environment. Operationally, the analyst must somehow undo or abstract from the effects of cognitive and preference biases on the choices at hand; what is left is the manifestation of true preferences. Of course, purifying preferences in this manner implies having a complete list of all biases that might affect choice – a list we do not have.

A key difficulty here is that the evidence of most biases – particularly those relating to the violation of preference axioms – comes from inconsistent behaviors that imply underlying inconsistencies of preference, such as: (a) having more than one rate of discount for intertemporal trade-offs; (b) having a willingness to pay that differs from willingness to accept, even when wealth effects should be negligible; (c) making different choices under different framings of the same situation; or (d) making different choices when influenced by different emotional states. In the early chapters of this book, we challenged the idea that such inconsistencies *necessarily* indicate irrationality. We argued that people may justifiably have unresolved inconsistencies in their preferences – or even no preferences at all. But here, we continue to suppose (as in Chapter 6) that the behavioral paternalists are right to assume that true preferences exist and that they are fully consistent in the ways required by neoclassical rationality norms.

Even so, a knowledge problem remains: which among the inconsistent preferences expressed are the "true" ones? Which of the chooser's inconsistent choices better represents their underlying welfare *as they see it*? As we argued in Chapter 3, inconsistencies can be resolved in more than one way. The inconsistency itself provides no evidence as to the true underlying preferences. Let us return to some key examples, this time emphasizing the knowledge aspect of the problem.

Present Bias. If a subject exhibits two different rates of time-discounting, one less patient and one more patient, either the former or the latter could

be designated as the correct rate. Behavioral paternalists such as O'Donoghue and Rabin (2003, 2006) and Gruber and Köszegi (2001) have
assumed that the more patient rate is the correct one, but that is only an
assumption. We have offered reasons in earlier chapters (especially Chapter 4) to think that more patient rates of discount, not just the less patient
ones, may be "infected" by biases or errors of reasoning or perception.
Once all sources of bias and error have been "cleansed" from the choice
process, the true preference that emerges might correspond to the more
patient rate, the less patient rate, or some rate of discount *in between* them.

To complicate matters further – and to support our claim that paternalist planners have been misled by grafting simple models onto a complex
world – actual behavior may not resemble the simple binary process of
discounting represented by quasi-hyperbolic discounting, which only
requires two different rates of time-discounting. As we have noted before,
quasi-hyperbolic discounting was adopted in large part for its analytical
tractability, and recent research suggests that real behavior may better
approximate truly hyperbolic discounting (Bleichrodt et al. 2016). This
means a subject may have a very short-term discount rate, a short-term
discount rate, a medium-term discount rate, a long-term discount, an
extremely long-term discount rate, and so on (Ainslie 2001, 210 n. 29,
214 n. 21; Angeletos et al. 2001, 50). If finding true preferences means
identifying a single normative rate of discount, truly hyperbolic discounting means the paternalist planner will be faced with numerous different
discount rates with no objective means of choosing among them.

Framing Effects. Framing effects, used to justify (among other things)
labor-friendly default terms in employment contracts, can also be resolved
in more than one way. If Frame A' leads to choice A, while Frame B' leads
to choice B, which of these two choices better represents the subject's true
underlying preferences? The inconsistency itself provides no guidance in
answering the question.

Take the specific case of vacation time in employment contracts. Behavioral arguments suggest that employees will make different contractual
demands based on whether the default rule is "no paid vacation" or "two
weeks' paid vacation." Specifically, the latter default will induce them to
demand more vacation time because opting out of the paid vacation will be
perceived as a loss (thereby triggering loss aversion). Assume this is
correct. Keep in mind that wages and other benefits will most likely adjust
downward to compensate for the increased cost of paid vacation, so this is
not a simple matter of employees preferring more leisure time to less; it's a
matter of trade-offs among types of compensation. So now the question is

which package of wages and benefits best represents the typical employee's *true* preferences. How much are they willing to give up in exchange for two weeks of paid vacation? We cannot simply ask how much vacation time workers have in fact negotiated for, because *by hypothesis*, how much they negotiate for is a function of the frame.

To make the matter more difficult, it would not be enough to know employees' true preferences regarding two weeks of paid vacation versus none. There is nothing special about two weeks. Thus, we would need to know their true rate of trade-off between vacation and wages/benefits for each marginal unit of vacation time, which presumably is not constant. The first day of vacation is probably more valuable than the twentieth; how much more valuable, we do not know.

The concerns we raise here are not specific to vacation time. They apply generally to most if not all cases of new default rules designed to take advantage of framing or endowment effects.

Hot and Cold States. To take one more example, if individuals made different choices in a "hot" state (angry, fearful, aroused, etc.) than they would in a "cold" state (sober, calm, reflective), the inconsistency may constitute evidence of an underlying bias, which paternalists might wish to correct by instituting cooling-off periods for certain options. But to correct people properly, we need to know their true preferences – that is, the value they *really* place on those options. As in the previous examples, there is more than one way to correct the inconsistency: we could induce people to consistently behave as their "cold" preferences would dictate, or consistently behave as their "hot" preferences would dictate, or consistently behave in some intermediate fashion that reflects a balance of hot and cold considerations.

To see this point clearly, we must recognize the relevance of "hot" preferences. From the behavioral paternalist perspective, the agent "ought" to be making decisions with carefully contained emotion. Nevertheless, hedonic considerations may, and often do, underlie preferences. The pleasure one gets out of a purchase of (say) a fancy new car is a legitimate part of the benefit of the purchase, and this pleasure ought to be considered when making the decision. What is *not* acceptable in the behavioral framework, however, is for emotions or hedonic factors to affect the decision-making process itself.

At first glance, this seems a clear enough distinction. However, consider a teenager who is very sexually attracted to another person. This strong emotion is *constitutive* of the preference. It makes her rationally willing to incur greater costs to satisfy the preference than if the sexual attraction were weaker. So far, there is no violation of normative decision-making. However, if somehow the very same emotion were to distort the cost–benefit calculation prior to the decision, something would be amiss. There-fore, we must surgically separate the effect of emotion on preferences from its effect on the calculation. Only by doing so can we isolate the chooser's true underlying preferences – but such information seems unknowable to anyone but the individual herself, and maybe not even to her.[1]

Behavioral paternalists have typically assumed that behavior in a "cold" state hews closer to true preferences than behavior in a "hot" state. It is not clear, however, why decisions made in the cool state are normatively preferred to those made in the hot state. One possible reason to privilege cold-state decisions is that hot-state decisions are likely to be followed by regret. However, regret can be induced by many things. Suppose the sexual encounter was not as satisfying as expected; that could be a cause for regret. Suppose one acquired a sexually transmitted disease; that also could be a cause for regret. Analytically, we can distinguish between regret caused by incorrect expectations and regret caused by corrupted decision-making, but that does not help us empirically. Furthermore, regrets can also be triggered by decisions made in a cold state; a person who chooses to abstain may later regret not having lived more spontaneously, taken greater chances, and acquired more exciting memories. To sort all of this out and "purify" preferences, we would need extensive empirical evidence about the magnitude of different sorts of regret.

Let us assume away this problem as well. Assume the chooser regrets her previous decision because in the *ex post* cool state she views the cost–benefit calculation differently; she would not have made the same decision about the sexual encounter if she had been in a cool state at the time. A paternalist observing this situation might say that it is better to side with the cool decision-maker over the hot decision-maker. By the standard of the cool decision-maker, the decision to have sex (or whatever other tempting action) was not worth its costs, despite the fact that just the opposite is true by the standard of the hot decision-maker.

---

[1] See George Loewenstein (2000, 429): "[I]t would clearly be suboptimal to make decisions that ignore visceral factors. Visceral factors do affect the marginal utility of different activities: eating is more pleasurable when one is hungry, and sex is more pleasurable when one is aroused. ... Clearly, welfare maximization lies somewhere between the two extremes of making decisions that ignore visceral factors and treating visceral influences as no different from any other influence on tastes."

The situation now moves to yet another level of complexity. Did the hot decision-maker *know* she would later regret her decision? In other words, is she sophisticated in her bias? If so, then she may reason in this way: "I know I will regret this in the morning because then I will be in a cool state. But it is totally worth it. My cool self is such a bore. I am always choosing the 'safe' way. Perhaps I need to take some risks and live a little." If the harm of hot decision-making is the disutility of the *ex post* regret, and if the hot decision-maker foresees it, then the original action does not necessarily violate traditional rational standards. To add even greater complexity here, even if the hot-state decision-maker might account for her future regret *incompletely*, and therefore she makes some errors, they will not be as many as if she ignored future regret entirely.

Our point here is not to challenge the claim that hot-state bias exists; in this chapter, we are assuming for argument's sake that the paternalists are correct about that. We are, however, challenging the claim that paternalist policymakers could know what the true preference looks like when stripped of all bias. And knowing the true preference is a necessary input into deciding the correct policy intervention.

We should emphasize that our challenge goes beyond the illustrative example. We are not aware of any proposed cooling-off periods for sexual activity (although the new rules universities have developed to ensure consent for sexual activity, prompted by the Obama administration's interpretation of Title IX of the Education Amendments of 1972, might unintentionally serve that function as well). But cooling-off periods have been proposed for a variety of consumer purchases, and they could be proposed for many other activities as well. Similar concerns would apply in all such cases.

Stepping back from these specific biases and policy areas, we can draw some general conclusions. For most if not all paternalist policy proposals, paternalist planners need to know true preferences. Ascertaining that knowledge will require confronting multiple candidates for true preference (all of which may be contaminated by bias), finding a way to "cleanse" these candidates of bias to reveal the underlying truth, delving deep enough to reconstruct an entire range of marginal valuations, measuring and comparing types of regret, and so on. Moreover, given the context-specific nature of behavioral findings – discussed in Chapter 6 – these questions would need to be answered empirically for each potential area of regulation. It would not be enough to answer them for one type of purchase or activity and then apply the empirical findings across the board; true preferences will differ depending on the context.

Knowledge of the Extent of Bias

For policy purposes, it is not sufficient to know people's true preferences. It is also necessary to know the extent of the bias (or set of biases) that causes decisions to deviate from true preferences. A large bias will justify some interventions that a small bias will not, and the size of the bias will also affect the optimal degree of intervention. Only by knowing the extent of bias can the policy be calibrated to the appropriate strength: the size of a sin tax, the length of a cooling-off period, the height of barriers to opting out of defaults, and so on.

Again, we focus our discussion through specific examples.

Present Bias. The extent of present bias matters for a variety of paternalist proposals, but most notably for sin taxes and retirement-savings defaults. There have, of course, been many attempts to measure the extent of present bias. To be specific, the research has found estimates for both the long-term rate of discount (which behavioral paternalists take as the normative standard) and the short-term rate of discount (which they regard as the deviation). Taking the paternalists' normative assumptions as given, the difference between the former and the latter would be the extent of bias. In a review of the literature, Frederick et al. (2002) find that "[t]here is extraordinary variation across studies, and sometimes even within studies" in estimates of discount factors (p. 393). Even using different, but nevertheless standard, econometric techniques on the same data set can generate wide variation in estimates (p. 385). Overall, there is "spectacular disagreement among dozens of studies that all purport to be measuring time preference" (p. 389). Often it is not even clear that what is being measured is the rate of time preference because of the plethora of confounding factors. Even the most recent work has not come to any consensus on how to measure time preference empirically (Cohen et al. 2016).[2]

It might be argued that the widely varying existing estimates are good enough; we can simply take their mean or median value. However, it turns out that optimal policies can be highly sensitive to small differences in parameter values. In a theoretical exercise, O'Donoghue and Rabin (2006, 1838) provide a striking example of the sensitivity of their sin-tax model to parameter estimates:

---

[2] "Even among the community of researchers who believe that the discount function framework is fruitful, there is no consensus about how we should measure the discount function" (Cohen et al. 2016, 45).

If half the population is fully self-controlled while the other half [of] the population has a very small present bias of β = 0.99, then the optimal tax is 5.15%. If instead the half [of] the population with self-control problems has a somewhat larger present bias of β = 0.90 – which is still a smaller present bias (larger β) than often discussed in the literature – the optimal tax is 63.71%.

Thus, a mere 9 percentage-point shift in one parameter (from β = 0.99 to β = 0.90) results in a twelvefold increase in the optimal tax. This means we would need to measure the degree of present bias not just accurately, but also *precisely*, in order to properly calibrate the tax. (Note as well that O'Donoghue and Rabin's model depends on the fraction of the population subject to present bias – an issue we will address later.)

The sensitivity issue arises in other contexts as well. Laibson et al. (1998) perform calculations to estimate the value of defined-contribution (DC) savings plans to people with different levels of present bias. They find that the gross value of a DC plan to a twenty-year-old high school graduate varies from 28 percent of his current annual consumption for β = 1 (i.e., no present bias), to 71 percent for β = 0.85, to 99 percent if β = 0.8. For β = 0.60, the impatience factor derived from some experimental evidence, linear extrapolation suggests that "the true hyperbolic [excessive impatience] effect is two to three times as large as the effects reported above" (p. 165). The sensitivity of these values to the present-bias parameter suggests that policies relating to retirement savings, and justified by the need to correct present bias, should be similarly sensitive.

Now recall our earlier observation that actual behavior may resemble truly hyperbolic discounting rather than quasi-hyperbolic discounting. This means that a single individual could have many different rates of discount, depending on the type of decision being made.[3] Assume that, somehow, policymakers have ascertained the "true" rate of discount that is normatively preferred. Even so, the extent of bias must be measured as the difference between the true discount rate and the operative discount rate. This means that the extent of bias will differ substantially *for the same individual* depending on circumstances. Indeed, if the true discount rate is neither the highest nor the lowest exhibited by a given person, it follows that the person will be present-biased in some cases *and* future-biased in other cases. Knowledge of the *entire bias profile* is thus a necessary component for crafting policies to correct temporal bias.

---

[3] For example, if a person chooses between t_2 and t_3 he may have a different rate of discount than if he chooses between t_5 and t_6 or between t_{10} and t_{11} and so forth. Each will have its own rate of discount.

To take one example, an optimal fat tax would need to be larger when someone is buying food for immediate consumption (e.g., at a convenience store), smaller when buying food for less immediate consumption (e.g., at a grocery store), and perhaps even negative – i.e., a subsidy – when buying food for very distant consumption (e.g., for a wedding next summer). Alternatively, policymakers could adopt a single fat tax that applies in all these situations. Such a tax would yield errors of both undertaxation in cases where rates of discount are relatively high and overtaxation in cases where they are relatively low. The policymaker would have to balance these effects against each other in order to calculate the optimal single-valued tax, which again requires knowing the entire profile of discount rates.

Status Quo Bias. Interventions in the area of retirement savings are also sometimes justified based on status quo bias. Status quo bias also matters for other types of paternalist intervention, insofar as any default rule (including a new one) has the potential to induce status quo bias, whether or not status quo bias was used to justify the new default. The *extent* of status quo bias matters because it affects both whether to implement a new policy (a weak status quo bias might not be enough to justify intervention) and how much to facilitate opting out (because status quo bias may unduly privilege the new default position).

In their seminal study of status quo bias, Samuelson and Zeckhauser (1988) find that the status quo bias differs in magnitude across tasks and alternatives – from substantial effects to small effects – and this variability persists even if we focus on only the statistically significant effects (pp. 15–17, tables 1a–c). These differences could be due to contextual factors, inherent variability of the bias, or difficulties in measurement technique; we suspect all three. Furthermore, it can be difficult to distinguish true status quo bias from the effect of both decision costs and the costs of implementing decisions, which naturally tend to favor sticking with the status quo for purely rational reasons.

Samuelson and Zeckhauser also find that status quo bias is negatively correlated with the strength of the individual's preference for a neutrally presented alternative – that is, the greater one's preference for the alternative, the smaller the status quo effect (1988, 8). Thus, the extent of the bias likely depends on the default rule. When choosing among default rules, then, policymakers must have knowledge of how large the status quo bias is likely to be for any given default they may adopt.

In the case of default enrollment in savings plans, for instance, Choi et al. (2003) found that the generally low returns on default allocations led to offsetting effects: "[w]hile higher participation rates promote wealth accumulation, the low default savings rate and the conservative default investment fund undercut accumulation," and in their sample, the two effects were approximately equal in magnitude (p. 2). So, in the aggregate, these individuals were in no better position than before, although some individuals' positions were improved and others were made worse. On the other hand, the further the default is from the optimal position, the weaker will be the status quo bias keeping people there. Ironically, a clearly inappropriate default might do a better job of encouraging people to act upon their true preferences. We will have much more to say on default enrollment in the Appendix to this chapter.

Hot and Cold States. After ascertaining the "true" preferences of people whose decisions are affected by their emotional states, the policymaker must next determine how much people's emotions cause them to deviate from optimal decisions. In other words, we need to know the *strength* of the bias. Yet a moment's reflection tells us that the impact of emotional states differs from person to person and situation to situation. Not all "hot" states are the same; anger, hunger, and excitement are different things. As George Loewenstein, one of the first authors to address this topic, recognized, whether any given decision will constitute a hot state that generates suboptimal behavior "depends on a wide range of influence," including "how recently a drive was satisfied and on the presence of arousing stimuli" as well as "the interaction of situational factors and construal processes and on internal psychobiological factors" (1996, 281). Different contexts will trigger the individual to different degrees.

The crafting of policies to correct behavior that has been unduly influenced by emotional states requires extensive knowledge of all these factors – and how they are correlated with the activities to be regulated. Waiting periods, for instance, will have different consequences as the context varies; the impact will be more beneficial in some circumstances and more costly in others. That means waiting periods must be domain-specific. Even if a rule is aimed at a particular domain (say, car purchases), ensuring that the rule is beneficial all things considered requires knowing the relative frequency of all relevant contextual factors that individual might encounter in that domain. In addition, the policymaker should consider the duration or rate of dissipation of hot states, as affected by numerous contextual factors, in calculating the optimal length of the cooling-off period.

The problems discussed here might seem to be a shortage of Hayek's "scientific knowledge," which can potentially be remedied by future research. Yet the research in this area is already quite extensive, and it demonstrates the importance of microcontextual factors. Scientific generalizations themselves cannot ascertain the myriad local and personal circumstances that differ from person to person and context to context. Even small differences in methodology will therefore elicit different responses from subjects. The very nature of local knowledge is to resist generalization. Yet generalizability is what is needed when using research to calibrate policy.

Knowledge of Self-Debiasing and Small-Group Debiasing

Chapter 6 discussed self-debiasing and small-group debiasing extensively, so here we will limit ourselves to discussing their implications for policymaking. The short answer is that self-debiasing and small-group debiasing affect the extent of bias *in real-world behavior*, as distinct from laboratory behavior. If the extent of bias matters for policy, the extent of debiasing must also matter. The longer answer is that policies designed to correct biases can interact with existing debiasing strategies in complex ways – possibly augmenting such debiasing, but also possibly unraveling it.

To demonstrate the first point, consider the case of a sin tax designed to correct present bias that ostensibly leads to excessive consumption. To the extent that the behavioral framework ignores the varieties of self-control discussed in Chapter 6, actual levels of self-control are likely to be underestimated and the tax will be excessive (Whitman 2006, 11–12). Similarly, consider a type of purchase that could be affected by one's affective state (i.e., a hot state). People who wish to avoid such purchases may deliberately avoid places and situations where those temptations exist. When they do put themselves in temptation's way, it can reflect a deliberate exception they allow themselves as part of an intrapersonal bargain or other self-control scheme; that trip to the car dealership might have been planned months in advance as a reward for "good" behavior. The existence of such self-control schemes reduces the initial justification for cooling-off periods and also should affect their length. But how common are such self-regulatory efforts, and how successful are they in terms of individuals' own goals? This we do not know.

Self-regulation is complex and much of it is not obvious. Consider an overweight individual with a propensity to eat junk food. Imagine that she often stays away from restaurants that serve junk food but occasionally indulges herself. Does she need the help of a paternalist? Should her indulgences be taxed or should she be nudged away from junk food on those occasions? A person who has made an intrapersonal bargain to abstain, but also to reward her "present self" with some tasty junk food from time to time, may not require a correction. Or, if she does to some extent, the paternalist would have to know in which respects this bargain has broken down and to what extent it is inadequate. To tax the present-self reward would tend to unravel the bargain, thereby potentially putting the agent in a worse condition than before.

Now consider the possibility that some individuals exercise self-control that is "invisible." This could be because self-control has taken the form of asymmetric revaluation of the immediate benefits and future costs of the sin good. The immediate benefits are revalued downward and the future costs are revalued upward (Fishbach et al. 2010), as discussed in Chapter 6. The present-bias discount rate will not necessarily be affected by this process. Since the decision to consume depends on the discount rate *and* the profile of benefits and costs, self-control could be manifested in either an adjustment in present bias *or in the profile*. But the standard sin-tax models treat the profile as simply given; the *only* indicator of self-control is the present-bias parameter. Attempting to offset the bias through corrective taxation may be deleterious if the profile is subject to change. Moreover, attempts to measure the extent of operative bias based strictly on measurements of present bias will *necessarily* neglect this form of self-regulation.

As we have emphasized, self-debiasing is by its nature context-dependent. People adopt resolutions, commitments, mental budgets, and internal reward-and-punishments schemes whose application depends on social cues, location, time of day and time of year, type of activity, and so on. They structure their personal and work environments to avoid triggers they know are especially tempting or troublesome *given their particular preferences and psychology*. When people rely on family members to influence their choices – which the small-group debiasing literature indicates can be an effective strategy – they may do so only with respect to certain kinds of choices they find especially challenging. Even purely cognitive strategies – those that operate entirely within the mind of the individual – often rely on environmental cues chosen by the individual. Lab experiments almost by definition cannot capture this kind of idiosyncratic self-regulation, and even field experiments can capture it only in summary fashion. Yet without such knowledge, paternalistic interventions cannot be calibrated to the correct level of bias.

Nevertheless, let us suppose that policymakers manage to discover the actual level of operative bias, taking into account both self-debiasing and small-group debiasing. Yet even this is not sufficient, because debiasing can be affected by the policies in question. External and internal forms of control can function as substitutes; as a result, increasing one may diminish the other. Fishbach and Trope (2005) present experimental evidence that this is the case. In one study, they offered students the opportunity to take a diagnostic test described as either "interesting" or "boring." They found that students primed to consider the test "boring" evaluated the expected value of the test more highly than did students primed to consider the test "interesting" (p. 261), suggesting that the students applied counteractive self-control to offset the greater cost of taking a boring test. However, that effect only occurred when the experimenter was *not present* to witness the students' decision about whether to take the test. When the experimenter was *present* for that decision, the effect disappeared (p. 261). These results support the substitutability of external control (in the form of social monitoring) and self-control. Students appeared to reduce their self-control effort when they knew external pressure would be present.

In a similar study, Fishbach and Trope looked at students' evaluation of the importance of studying. Students who were primed to think about distractions to studying (such as film and television) rated the importance of studying *more highly* than did students who hadn't been primed to think about such distractions (2005, 262). This result is consistent with the exercise of counteractive self-control. However, this result only occurred for students who had also *not* been primed to think about parental expectations regarding their study habits. By contrast, among students who *had* been primed to think about parental expectations, the difference disappeared: they rated the importance of studying about the same regardless of whether they had been primed to think about distractions (p. 262). Once again, the results suggest that the presence of external controls – in this case, the pressure of parental expectations – substituted for the exercise of self-control.

External controls come in various forms. Some external controls are private, as in the case of parental expectations or the moderating influence of small groups. Other external controls may be imposed by the state, such as those recommended by paternalists. Both types of external control can substitute for self-control, and they may substitute for each other as well (although we are unaware of any studies on this question). The policy-relevant point is that the imposition of any given paternalist intervention could suppress self-control and, quite possibly, private external control as well. To calibrate policy correctly, then, we would need to know the magnitude of these effects for each proposed policy intervention. One simplifying assumption would be that private debiasing efforts are fixed, so that any policy-induced debiasing simply adds to them. Then it would "simply" be a matter of calibrating policy to close the remaining gap between actual and ideal behavior. But the evidence does not support this assumption. Another simplifying assumption would be that private debiasing is reduced in a manner that perfectly offsets policy-induced debiasing. In that case, the policymaker could ignore private debiasing and correct for the uncorrected baseline level of bias. But for any outcome between these poles, it is crucial for the policymaker to know precisely *how responsive* private debiasing is to policy-induced debiasing.

To summarize, the paternalist who wishes to craft welfare-improving policies needs to know the extent of self-control being exercised by people "in the wild." But to know that, the paternalist also must know the social-pressure context of people whose behavior has been targeted for change. And finally, the paternalist must know how both social pressure and self-control efforts will change in response to the policies enacted. To the extent that paternalistic interventions tend to depress or unravel people's efforts at self-regulation, the case for such interventions is diminished.

Knowledge of Dynamic Impacts on Self-Regulation

In the preceding discussion on substitution between self-control and external control, we implicitly assumed a static problem in which the individual adjusts (possibly unconsciously) to changes in the level of external control. The individual's underlying capacity to engage in self-control remained unchanged. However, it is possible that increases in external control, including control provided by paternalist interventions, will have a dynamic effect on the capacity for self-control. Predicting such effects is necessary for the crafting of policies that are beneficial in the long term.

Psychologists often argue that people's capacity for self-regulation is a scarce resource that can be depleted by frequent use (Baumeister 2006). As a result, when people have to exercise self-control, their subsequent efforts at self-control will tend to be less successful. Thus, after performing an initial task requiring the exertion of self-control, people are more likely to "spend money impulsively ... [,] show higher levels of aggressive responding ...[,] drink more alcohol even when anticipating a driving test ... [,] perform inappropriate or uncontrolled sexual behaviours," and so on (Baumeister 2006, 1776). In short, self-control is like a "fund" that can be drawn down. To the extent this is the case, policymakers need to know whether any given intervention will supplement self-control resources (thereby freeing them to be used elsewhere) or instead divert them to the activity targeted by policy (thereby creating an opportunity cost in terms of other uses of self-control). As discussed in Chapter 6, there is little research on this question. Opportunity costs of diverted self-control ought to be considered as part of the cost–benefit analysis.

If paternalist interventions augment rather than divert self-control resources, then they might seem to be an unqualified improvement. In the long run, however, the capacity for self-control does not seem to be fixed. Infrequent use of self-control can result in reduced capacity for self-control (Baumeister 2006, 1779–1786). More frequent use of self-control can increase it. If self-control is like a fund in the short run, it is more like a muscle in the long run.

Consider an illustrative experiment (Gailliot et al. 2007, 283–286) in which researchers measured subjects' motivation to avoid the expression or appearance of prejudice toward homosexual and obese people. Not surprisingly, some subjects were more motivated in this regard, others less. Then both groups were asked to write about a day in the life of a homosexual or obese person without resorting to using stereotypes. After-ward, they were asked to solve anagrams, an unrelated problem. Both of these tasks involved exerting a degree of self-control. Consistent with the scarce self-control theory, the less motivated subjects tended to do worse on the anagram task than the more motivated ones. For these subjects, the first task required a greater level of effort, thereby depleting their self-control fund more.

However, the same subjects were also asked to practice unrelated self-regulatory activities (controlling their daily speech activities) for two weeks before being tested a second time. The results showed that the subjects' performance on the second task (solving anagrams) improved. Thus, practice at unrelated self-control appeared to increase self-regulatory cap-acity. More importantly, however, this improvement was observed *only* in the group of subjects who had displayed low motivation to avoid the appearance of prejudice – in other words, those for whom the first task (writing an essay without stereotypes) had been more costly in terms of self-control. Together, these results support the idea that exerting self-control, while diminishing one's ability to engage in further self-control in the short run, can also increase the capacity for self-control in the longer run. Those who were not motivated to avoid stereotypes seemed to gain self-control resources during the two-week unrelated exercise period, and thus there were more resources left over than before to solve the anagrams.

If self-regulatory capacity is indeed like a muscle, it follows that pater-nalist interventions that reduce the need for present self-control can reduce the capacity for future self-control. And as the experiment just described indicates, that reduced capacity may be felt in areas unrelated to the regulated domain. As a result, the paternalist's optimization problem will change over time. The optimal policies for the present will not necessarily be optimal in the future; stronger interventions will be called for if people's capacity for self-control weakens. Some of those future interventions could be in different policy domains. More importantly, these future adverse impacts – on both behavior and policy – ought to be taken into account when calculating which policy is best for the present.

Knowledge of Counteracting Behaviors

We will consider two types of counteracting behavior in this section. The first occurs when individuals respond to a policy with a related behavior that counteracts the intended effect of the policy. The new behavior may compensate for or offset a positive behavior, or it may substitute for the negative behavior. Such counteractive behavior tends to occur as a consequence of narrowly targeted interventions that are designed to correct specific errors in decision-making. This strategy is central to the behavioral paternalist paradigm. But targeting is not always a simple matter. There is always a question of how broadly or narrowly to frame an intervention. If the intervention is too broad, it will "correct" behaviors that needed no correction. But if it is too narrow, it will open the door for substitution effects and compensatory behaviors. We illustrate with two examples, retirement-savings defaults and sin taxes.

Retirement-Savings Defaults. An illustration of compensatory-substitution effects comes from the attempt to improve savings behavior by enrolling people in retirement-savings plans by default. Suppose that a new default rule successfully increases an individual's retirement savings. Does it follow that they are better off savings-wise? Not necessarily, because the individual may compensate by incurring greater debts or saving less in other ways. We show in the Appendix to this chapter that there is a great deal of offsetting behavior in the form of both withdrawals of money from the plans and additional debt outside of the plans.

Sin Taxes. Sin taxes provide a straightforward illustration of the substitution problem. Any given sin tax will apply to a specified set of targets. Ideally, a sin tax for food would target all "unhealthy foods with short-run temptations." But that is too vague for policy. As a result, the tax will most likely target a narrower class of foods, such as those with high sugar or calorie content. Sometimes the target is even more specific. In recent years several cities and other jurisdictions have imposed so-called soda taxes – that is, taxes on sugar-sweetened soft drinks. If we interpret these taxes as paternalist taxes rather than simple revenue-raisers, the substitution effects become important. The objective is to induce consumers to shift away from these drinks and toward something more healthful. Reducing obesity and its related consequences is usually what paternalists have in mind.[4] Does a tax on sugar-sweetened drinks induce healthful substitutions?

Let us assume, as seems likely, that the main substitution is toward artificially sweetened drinks. The effect of artificially sweetened drinks on weight is unclear. The scientific literature provides support for all three possible effects: reduced weight, no effect, and increased weight (Peters and Beck 2016). Obviously, the tax only makes sense on paternalistic grounds if the first is true. Our conclusion, which we will explain shortly, is that the current evidence "does not consistently demonstrate that ASBs [artificially sweetened beverages] are effective for weight loss or preventing metabolic abnormalities" (Borges et al. 2017).

These results nicely illustrate the problem of counteracting effects. Theoretically, i.e., if everything else is held constant, the replacement of a sugary product with an artificially sweetened product that yields no energy should result in the loss of weight. But people do not live in an everything-else-held-constant world. The theoretical potential for weight loss will be realized only if the artificially sweetened beverages are actually used in the right way.[5] But "evidence that use of NNS [nonnutritive sweeteners] in free-living individuals results in improved weight loss or maintenance is lacking" (Mattes and Popkin 2009, 9).

Then there are the troubling studies showing that low-calorie sweetener use actually is associated with heavier weight "even after accounting for diet quality and weight and body size at the time of low-calorie sweetener use assessment" (Chia et al. 2016, 9).[6] The mechanisms responsible for the

---

[4] "There is convincing epidemiological evidence linking SSB [sugar sweetened beverage] consumption to increased risk of overweight and obesity and type II diabetes" (Borges et al. 2017, 1).

[5] "Taken together, the evidence summarized by us and others suggests that if NNS [nonnutritive sweeteners] are used as substitutes for higher energy yielding sweeteners, they have the *potential* to aid in weight management, but whether they will be used in this way is uncertain" (Mattes and Popkin 2009, 10, emphasis added).

[6] "Although the hypothesis that consuming low-calorie sweeteners contributes to weight and fatness has been previously investigated ... the present study takes advantage of the extensive data in the BLSA [Baltimore Longitudinal Study of Aging] up to 28 years of longitudinal observations on body composition and low calorie sweetener consumption found in all food products, not just diet soda" (Chia et al. 2016, 9).

counterintuitive effects are not yet clear. One possibility is that decreased energy intake in one area may induce compensatory consumption of calories elsewhere. These effects can take place through conscious and unconscious mechanisms. The sensation of sweetness can unconsciously stimulate the appetite, and the individual may explicitly consider himself free to eat fries with a diet soda but not with a sugar-sweetened drink. Thus, "when sugar-reduced foods and beverages were consumed as part of the habitual diet, no significant change in body weight was observed. This was due to energy compensation: fat and protein intakes were both higher on the sugar-reduced diet, when compared to the regular diet" (Markey et al. 2016, 2146).[7]

Accordingly, a tax on sugary beverages will not necessarily improve health, as we must account for substitution effects. Of course, the paternalist might respond that we also need taxes on the unhealthy substitute products, but this is difficult if the substitution occurs in the *quantity* consumed of otherwise healthful products. Furthermore, we have only considered dietary substitution and not other possible lifestyle changes. There may be further compensatory effects between diet and exercise when "improved" diets are externally incentivized. Compensatory reductions in exercise may occur to return the individual to the previous level of subjective utility. Thus, it is easy to imagine a whole web of taxes, subsidies, nonprice constraints, and nudges to deal with this complex of related behaviors.

As these two examples suggest, it can be difficult to design an intervention that targeted individuals cannot circumvent. Biases can find other avenues of expression. At a minimum, substitution effects and compensatory behaviors indicate that some policies will not be as effective as hoped. More importantly, they mean that policy designers must pay close attention to another dimension of their interventions – breadth – and they need reliable knowledge to guide their choices in this respect. But the greater the breadth, the greater the chance that behavior in no need of correction will also be discouraged. At the same time, the argument that behavioral paternalism is modest becomes weaker.

The second type of counteracting behavior occurs as a consequence of behavioral manipulations creating more than one psychological effect.

---

[7] The diet did result in a significant reduction in sugar, and a *ceteris paribus* model predicted that the individuals would lose weight. However, it "had no significant effect on body weight, BP [blood pressure], fasting serum glucose or lipid concentrations, which was in part due to energy balance compensation" (Markey et al. 2016, 2147).

These effects need not be rooted in biases of any sort and may include standardly rational responses. We consider two examples: nutritional nudging and social marketing campaigns.

Nutritional Nudging. Perhaps a tax on sugar-sweetened beverages or other unhealthful food items can be avoided by simply posting calorie or other nutritional information at the point of purchase. Perhaps these postings will cause people to order food with lower caloric content. Unfortunately for advocates of this policy, there is almost no evidence that it is effective. A recent systematic review of menu labeling policies (VanEpps et al. 2016) finds that only three of sixteen studies conducted in a real-world restaurant setting show unambiguous evidence of decreased caloric impact. In a sense, this is the bottom line. Nevertheless, it will be useful to examine this in greater detail.[8]

Despite appearances, this is a complex issue for behavioral paternalists because it is important to distinguish between the standard ("rational") effect of increased knowledge and the behavioral effect of salience. Accordingly, Shimokawa (2016) discusses three effects that together comprise the overall reaction to calorie postings. First, people may learn from calorie postings that they have underestimated the calories in the food they usually order; this is expected to result in reducing caloric intake. Second, people may learn that they have overestimated calorie content; this is expected to result in increasing caloric intake. Obviously these two effects can partially or fully offset each other in the aggregate. Each of these is the result of learning what was not known before. There is nothing behavioral here, as standard economics has no problem accounting for changed behavior because of new knowledge.[9] Third, people may have their attention to calories switched on, *without learning anything new*, through a salience

---

[8] One of the most rigorous studies (Bollinger et al. 2011) does find a reduction in the purchase of calories at Starbucks after calorie postings. The reduction is 6 percent per transaction. A rough estimate that 25 percent of all calories are consumed at chain restaurants and a mere assumption that the same 6 percent reduction takes place at all chain restaurants implies a 1.5 percent daily reduction in calories. Further research cited by the authors suggests that a permanent reduction in caloric intake of such a magnitude will result in a decrease in body weight by no more than 1 percent. They then say that this might be an understatement. But the reasons given are speculative, as they admit.

[9] In an analysis of the effect of unit-price information, Russo and Leclerc (1991) found that listing unit prices in one place *greatly reduced comparison time* relative to simply putting unit-price tags under a product on the shelf. Thus, costs were reduced. This seems analogous to the calorie-posting issue where the information is readily accessible in one place (in contrast, for example, to looking up the caloric content on a fast-food chain's website).

effect. If behavioral economics has any special role to play here, it must be through this mechanism.

To isolate the salience effect, the analysis must control for learning. This was accomplished by asking people about the calorie content of the group of snacks they had chosen before and after seeing the calorie posting. Some underestimated or overestimated the calories, but some had reasonably good guesses beforehand and thus learned nothing from the posting. As predicted, the underestimators decreased and the overestimators increased their calorie purchases.[10] So, posting can actually increase caloric choices when people believe that they had been inadvertently "dieting" all along. But what about those who had learned nothing – those who might have been affected by pure salience? Of the two component studies that were undertaken in this research, only one yielded a statistically significant result for salience. In that study the effect of salience was to *raise* caloric choices. Most behavioralists assume that if the calorie content of food is made highly accessible at the moment of purchase, individuals will reduce their intake. But this does not follow. Such a conclusion would require that people really want to diet and that lack of salient information is what "prevents" them from doing so. On the other hand, Loewenstein (2011, 680) speculates that some, especially low-income, individuals may seek to get the most calories per dollar. Therefore, if this is the case, salience simply encourages them in that direction.[11]

Another variety of behavioral nudges that has been promoted to increase the consumption of healthful foods is position manipulation. This originated with the fanciful discussion of item placement along a cafeteria line in Thaler and Sunstein (2003). The articles seeking to test the hypothesis that positioning matters can be divided into those that vary proximity or distance and those that vary order. The former either impose costs on individuals who might choose "unhealthy" foods by placing them in more distant locations or reduce costs of more healthful foods by placing them in more convenient locations. Strictly speaking, these positional variations do not test nudging (in the sense of costless reframing of the same choice situation) because they alter the relative effort costs of obtaining different

---

[10] We do not know if all of the calories purchased were actually consumed. Of course, they may not have been.

[11] "[O]ur results suggest that the ineffectiveness of calorie posting may be explained mostly by the saliency effect rather than the LOE [learning overestimation] effect. That is, although the learning [underestimation] effect significantly reduces calorie purchase, the effect of calorie posting can be insignificant or even positive mostly due to the calorie-increasing saliency effect" (Shimokawa 2016, 117).

foods. The latter category – those that vary order – are purer tests of the nudging hypothesis. In a recent review of the literature on positional effects, Bucher et al. (2016) analyze fifteen articles comprising eighteen studies that meet basic quality criteria.[12] Sixteen of these studies concluded that positional changes do affect food choice *in the very short run*.[13] In one case, the effect was simply for one pass through the cafeteria line (Wansink and Hanks 2013).

What is there about position that would lead us to believe that food choice could be so manipulated? If we exclude the studies that changed relative costs, the answer might be salience. But salience is an under-analyzed concept. It is very easy to confuse salience with novelty.[14] This is important because novelty is inherently transient while salience need not be. It does seem reasonable that if individuals are unaccustomed to seeing food in a particular order or seeing prominent calorie postings, these factors might have a temporary effect. Whether this effect persists will depend on what exactly is capturing attention: salience or novelty. In many actual cases salience and novelty are simultaneously present. In experiments designed to distinguish their effects it was found that salience alone is not sufficient to capture and bind attention. On the other hand, novelty is sufficient to do so (Horstmann and Herwig 2016, 2015).[15]

---

[12] The quality of the studies available in this literature is not high. Based on widely accepted quality criteria of the Academy of Nutrition and Dietetics (2016), research is classified as "negative," "neutral," or "positive." Using these criteria, Bucher et al. (2016, 2254) say that "[o]f the eighteen studies that were included, only one received a positive quality rating, with fourteen studies being assessed as neutral and three as negative, because the study procedures were not described in detail and several validity questions could not be answered clearly."

[13] None of the studies examined (and no others to date) adequately assess longer-term consequences. "There is a lack of research investigating long-term outcomes of positional interventions, and it is not clear whether changes in product order or distance would have sustained effects" (Bucher et al. 2016, 2260).

[14] One example of the failure to distinguish salience and novelty can be found in Bollinger et al. (2011, 118). The authors infer an increase in salience due to calorie postings because there was a statistically significant increase in the importance that consumers attach to calorie content after the implementation of a posting requirement in Seattle on January 1, 2009. However, the measurement was taken on January 30, 2009, while the postings were still novel. And the *quantitative* significance of an increase in the importance rating from 3.5 to 4.2 (on a scale of 1 to 7) is unknown.

[15] Experiments were "conducted to evaluate the discrepancy-attention link in a [visual] display where novel and familiar stimuli are equated for saliency … Results show … salience … did not prioritize items in the display. The results thus reinforce the notion that novelty captures and binds attention" (Horstmann and Herwig 2016, 69). See also Horstmann and Ansorge (2016).

When we disentangle the rational and behavioral processes induced by calorie postings, we find that the induced novelty process is likely the dominant factor. The information effect is weak because people largely know which foods are fattening. Food positioning, on the other hand, has at best very short-run effects because the psychological process at work is novelty – and a position can be novel only for a short time.

Social Marketing Campaigns. These are campaigns designed to harness availability or salience to control targeted behaviors such as smoking and alcohol consumption. Most of the research on the behavioral effectiveness of social marketing campaigns is superficial because it has been confined to "one-time exposure to a single message studied in isolation" (So et al. 2017, 5). Nevertheless, over time the messages induce further psychological processes in addition to those desired by the advocates of such campaigns. There is good research suggesting that the effectiveness of such advertising over time is limited by tedium (So et al. 2017; Bornstein 1989). At first, repetition of a message or class of messages has an increasing effect in discouraging the target behavior, but after a few repetitions, this will cease and subsequently reverse. Thus there is an inverted U-shaped response curve (Reinhard et al. 2014, 127).[16] The precise psychological mechanisms responsible for this are in dispute. One possibility is that repetition can become boring and thus the messages may be ignored. Another possible mechanism is that continued repetition may arouse suspicion about the motives of the source and thus the accuracy of the message.

Another factor to consider is the "boomerang effect" (Byrne and Hart 2009). This is an unintended consequence in which attitudes toward the targeted negative behavior become *more* favorable and the frequency of that behavior is increased. Such effects are not uncommon in the case of campaigns based on inducing fear as well as in other emotion-manipulation messages (Emery et al. 2014, 278–282). The boomerang effect has been seen in campaigns to reduce smoking, alcohol consumption, and illicit drug use.

Psychological reactance is a specific type of boomerang effect that occurs when people feel that their freedom or autonomy has been threatened. Their response is to increase the targeted negative behavior as a way of

---

[16] In the area of smoking cessation ads, Reinhard et al. (2014, 127) conclude: "The results provided strong evidence for the predicted inverted U-shaped relationship between message repetition [and] attitudes toward smoking: with rising repetition (i.e., two, three, and five repetitions), the negative attitudes toward smoking first increased and then decreased when repetition reached an excessive level (i.e., seven repetitions)."

reasserting control. There is little research on this phenomenon, but there is some support for its occurrence in the aftermath of the soda tax approval in Berkeley, California (Debnam 2017) and in an experimental study (Arad and Rubinstein 2017).

Whether any or all of these effects are present in a particular case will depend on many contextual factors (Byrne and Hart 2009). Specifically, these include the mode of communication and the degree to which the messages combine fear with awareness or instruction. There are also individual differences that will produce different responses, including general cognitive and processing ability. Does the receiver interpret the message as intended? Does she process certain aspects of the message while ignoring others? Gender is also likely to be important; males are more likely to react in the opposite of the intended direction. The history of the individual's experience with the targeted behavior can be important as well. For example, those who are heavy drinkers are prone to increase their drinking when faced with ads urging abstinence. When individuals do not believe that they are competent to reduce a certain behavior (as many who have failed to diet or abstain from smoking might be), fear may induce a boomerang effect.

The kind of boomerang phenomena that affect social marketing campaigns could affect other policies that rely on the use of availability or salience to induce behavior, including risk narratives and graphic images. Overall, determining the quantitative effects of risk messages will be difficult, but they can prove important in calibrating the correct paternalist policy.

Knowledge of Bias Interactions

Most behavioral studies deal with one bias at a time (Fang and Silverman 2006). Analytically, this is convenient because the distortion in behavior or cognition relative to a norm is clear-cut. Empirically, if the bias is shown in a particular context to have a statistically significant effect on behavior or on the incidence of economic costs, the study will be considered to have academic merit.

However, the demands of policy are more severe. In addition to knowing the magnitude of the effect in isolation, the policymaker needs to know how the bias interacts with other biases in the context in which the proposed policy is to be applied. Because biases can reinforce or offset each other, policies that would improve welfare by correcting a bias *if that were the only bias present* may in fact reduce welfare *when multiple biases are in play*. As Besharov (2004) has pointed out, this problem is analogous to the second-best problem in the study of market failure. To take one example, negative externalities (such as air pollution from the burning of fossil fuels) can lead to too much consumption, while a degree of monopoly power (such as that created by OPEC in the petroleum industry) can lead to too little consumption. When both market imperfections are present, theory alone cannot say whether consumption is too high, too low, or just right; any of these are possible. Furthermore, correcting one imperfection – say, by implementing a policy to reduce the power of OPEC – could actually exacerbate the other problem. Consequently, the optimal policy requires detailed knowledge about *both* market imperfections as well as how they interact. The same kind of detailed knowledge is required in the case of interacting biases. Consider the following plausible examples:

1. Some people may have a propensity, due to present bias, to save too little. On the other hand, they may exhibit *projection bias*; that is, they assume their future consumption needs will be the same as current needs, or they do not accept the inevitability of death, or they plan for too long a retirement (Fang and Silverman 2006; Kopczuk and Slemrod 2005). Depending on the magnitudes of these biases, they may be saving too much, too little, or just the right amount.

2. A smoker believes that the health risks of smoking are higher than they really are (Antoñanzas et al. 2000; Viscusi 1990). He also exhibits present bias. If we simply assume that he has rational expectations of the health risks but discounts them with a present-bias factor, then he will smoke too much. On the other hand, the degree of his overestimation of health risks can offset the degree of his present bias such that his smoking is optimal, or even less than optimal. (In fact, as we have seen earlier, a person employing counteractive self-control may revalue the costs of an activity – conceiving them as higher than they really are – in order to reduce the temptation to smoke.) We can go further by introducing a third bias. Suppose he also exhibits "optimism bias"; that is, he believes that he is specially protected from the risks other people in his circumstances face. This bias would reduce or eliminate the significance of his overestimate of the health risks to the population in general. What does he believe *his personal health risks* are? In order to estimate the net result of these factors, we would need reliable estimates of the magnitude of all three biases as well as a reliable model of how they interact. Such evidence is not available.

Similar reasoning applies, *mutatis mutandis*, to the case of over-weightness and obesity. If and to the extent that potential overeaters *overestimate* the health risks of their behavior, that factor can offset their present bias.

3. This example is presented in Besharov (2004). An agent must decide how much effort to expend on a project with immediate costs and delayed benefits. Present bias tends to reduce the amount of effort the agent applies. Yet the same person also exhibits overconfidence in the efficacy of her efforts, causing her to overestimate the future benefits of the project. And she also experiences *ex post* regret, that is, dissatisfaction from exerting low levels of effort. The latter two biases will tend to increase the agent's level of effort. Thus, depending on the relative magnitudes of the biases, the agent may apply too much, too little, or optimal effort.

4. Salience, in the presence of the standard array of cognitive biases, may be hyper-distortionary. Remember that to make a piece of information salient is to focus attention on it, that is, to draw it out of the background of other information in some simple and direct way. This does not in itself change how information is processed; it simply makes it more likely that it will be processed (or at least that is the hope). For example, if mandated "typical usage" disclosure for credit cards causes consumers to focus on penalties for late payment, in effect the policy nudges them to focus on an unfavorable future possibility. When individuals overestimate the disutility they will experience from such eventualities (impact bias), they will overweight this negative attribute of the agreement. This effect may be reinforced by the tendency to overestimate the probability of events that have been made more salient (availability bias). Interest rates can be made to look high or low depending on what they are compared with (anchoring bias). Thus, inducing consumers to focus on interest rates may be distortionary, diverting excessive attention from other product attributes that can and should be considered. None of these distortions is certain to occur. Nevertheless, we cannot simultaneously recommend disclosure because people are less than perfectly rational and then proceed to assume that people will process the "saliently" disclosed information rationally or as intended.

These examples suggest the complexity of bias interactions. Such complexity cannot be ignored in crafting policies. A paternalist who knows only one of the interacting biases – indeed, anything less than the full set of interacting biases – will wish to implement policies that are not properly calibrated and might even push behavior in the wrong direction relative to the optimum.[17] The previous examples also strengthen the view of Ainslie (2015, 2012), discussed previously, that in particular contexts observed biases may actually constitute conscious or unconscious methods of offsetting other biases.

At a minimum, then, a paternalist policymaker needs to know the magnitude of all biases interacting in a given context. But that is not enough. The policymaker also needs to know how the biases interact, i.e., how a change in the operative level of bias A will affect the operation of bias B. Or to put it another way, the policymaker must possess a functioning model of the entire system. Only with such a model could the policymaker possibly choose the right type of policy and calibrate it appropriately. Yet such a model is far beyond anything that we have yet seen in the behavioral literature, except in stylized theoretical models such as the one used by Besharov (2004) to illustrate the third example shown here. For empirical work, such a model would need to be validated independently of its constituent biases.

Interestingly, the existence of multiple biases has already been treated in the behavioral paternalist literature – but as a feature rather than a bug. This treatment appears in proposals for risk narratives and graphic images. Both of these are part of a larger public policy program whose explicit purpose is to *use some biases to counteract other biases* (Loewenstein 2012). The same principle is at work in social marketing campaigns designed to improve individual behavior. In the case of risk narratives and graphic images, the phenomenon to be corrected is optimism bias, and the tool to correct it is availability bias or salience. The paradigmatic case is smokers whose optimism supposedly causes them to underestimate their personal likelihood of suffering bad health consequences, and who therefore need to be jolted out of their delusions by a harrowing tale or frightening image.

How effective should we expect such narratives and images to be? Keep in mind that the goal here is not simply to get people to stop smoking. Old-fashioned paternalism, of course, is not concerned with the optimal amount of smoking. But behavioral paternalism supposedly is. So, the

---

[17] Even in cases where multiple biases move individuals in the same direction, they may have different implications for policy. Therefore the quantitative magnitudes of each one are still relevant. See Fang and Silverman (2006) and Rizzo and Whitman (2009b, 952–953). More generally, see Grüne-Yanoff (2015).

purpose of risk narratives from a behavioral perspective is to enable people to satisfy their *true* preferences – which, given the pleasures of smoking, does not imply complete abstinence for all individuals.[18] To know whether that goal is advanced by risk alerts, we first need to know the quantitative effect of such an alert on the assessment of personal risk and the behavior of individuals. However, there is little research on the effect regarding the assessment of personal risk. As we have seen, the sheer quantitative effect of such risk-alerting or fear-inducing campaigns is difficult to predict and will vary widely with respect to different groups.

And yet it would not be enough to know how much the messages reduced smoking unless somehow we already knew the optimal level of smoking. Lacking that, the paternalist policymaker would need to know how frightening an image or story must be to precisely offset the effect of the present bias that ostensibly causes the smoking. Yet these biases are not even measured in the same units! And we have yet to take into account any other biases that might be involved – such as impact bias, which can cause people to overestimate the disutility of adverse future events such as reductions in health (Loewenstein and Ubel 2008). All things considered, the case of risk narratives and alerts only underscores the severe knowledge impediments that can arise from multiple interacting biases.

But how prevalent is the multiple-biases phenomenon? The empirical evidence is scarce on this point. There are hardly any empirical estimates of the correlation of biases with each other. Nevertheless, one study of stock market investors (Kudryavtsev et al. 2013) found an extremely high and statistically significant correlation among five standard biases (specifically, the disposition effect, herding, availability heuristic, the gambler's fallacy, and the hot-hand fallacy). Again, such simultaneous biases can induce offsetting behaviors in particular circumstances. Suppose an individual owns a stock that has risen to a new high in a buoyant overall stock market. The disposition effect (the tendency to sell stocks that have gained value while holding onto losers) may lead him to sell it, while the availability heuristic triggered by an overall rising market may lead him to buy more of it. Similarly, the hot-hand fallacy may induce him to buy more of what he has made a profit on because he is on a roll. But the gambler's

---

[18] There is a nonzero optimal amount of smoking. This is due to several factors. First, there are pleasures and some other benefits derived from smoking. Second, most of the mortality risk due to smoking can be avoided by stopping in one's mid-thirties. See Lucas (2013, 234–235) and the sources cited therein. There is also obvious heterogeneity given the differences in individuals' valuation of the benefits of smoking.

fallacy suggests that the market's rise to a new high will be followed by a fall – and thus that he should sell.

Furthermore, there are now about 175 cognitive biases identified in the psychological and behavioral economics literature.[19] There is little agreement or data on how many people or how many decisions are affected by these biases. On the one hand, Kahneman and Frederick (2005) suggest that biases are typically present in routine or everyday situations, which evoke the casually intuitive mode of decision-making.[20] On the other hand, Thaler (2015a, 50) claims that in unfamiliar areas such as choosing a college or planning for retirement individuals have the least opportunity to practice and learn. Therefore they are more likely to make biased decisions in these cases. Regardless of how this is sorted out, the more *widespread* are the biases within their applicable domains (even with zero correlation), the greater the probability that they will overlap in the population.[21] Thus it may be the case that the more decisions or types of decisions are "behavioral," the less behavioral economics will be able to say about policy in an unambiguous way.

Knowledge of Population Heterogeneity

In the paternalist planner's ideal world, policies would only have to target a single individual. They would be chosen precisely to correct that one

---

[19] List of Cognitive Biases (n.d.).

[20] "The between subjects design, in contrast, mimics the haphazard encounters in which most judgments are made and is more likely to evoke the casually intuitive mode of judgment that governs much of mental life in routine situations" (p. 281). This position is vital to justify Kahneman's use of the between-subjects methodology because the implicit assumption is that learning over time or with greater experience is not relevant. In everyday situations people have presumptively already learned all they can. But Kahneman has not been consistent. He has also said that biases don't typically affect routine situations; rather, they mainly affect unfamiliar or unique situations (Kahneman 2011, 416).

[21] Let P(A) and P(B) equal the probability that a given person will have bias A and bias B, respectively. If A and B are independent, implying a correlation of zero, then the probability of having both A and B is $P(A)*P(B)$. This is increasing in both P(A) and P(B), which means that as the prevalence of these biases increases in the population, the prevalence of the intersection (overlap) also increases. That is holding independence (and thus zero correlation) constant. Now, what if the correlation is positive? That implies more overlap for any given prevalence levels for A and B. The probability of the intersection is given by $P(A)*P(B|A)$ and also $P(B)*P(B|A)$. If correlation is positive, $P(B|A) > P(B)$ and $P(A|B) > P(A)$. That is, knowing A is present increases the likelihood B is present and vice versa. On the other hand, if correlation among biases is negative, then overlap will tend to be lower.

person's biases. In many abstract models of paternalism, it does seem as though only one person would be affected by the policy; this is the peril of the "representative agent" models so often used by economists. In other models of paternalism, there is a hint of diversity – such as in O'Donoghue and Rabin's sin-tax model, which effectively assumes the existence of two types of agent: rational and irrational. Similarly, Camerer et al. (2003, 1212) assume the public can be divided into two groups, "those who make errors" and "those who are fully rational." Nevertheless, in these approaches the rational agents are all the same, and the irrational agents are all the same.

The reality, of course, is that people are heterogeneous. Any paternalist intervention will therefore have disparate impacts across the affected population. To craft welfare-improving policies with diverse targeted populations, the paternalist planner must have extensive knowledge of the *distribution of relevant characteristics over the affected population.* And what are the relevant characteristics? Everything we have discussed thus far in this chapter. People will exhibit heterogeneity with respect to their true underlying preferences; the extent of their targeted biases; their exercise of self-debiasing, as well as the form of such debiasing; their tendency (or not) to let external control substitute for self-control; their tendency to engage in counteracting behaviors; their susceptibility to the weakening of self-control "muscles"; and the set of biases that interact in determining their behavior.

It is difficult to fully describe how formidable is the knowledge barrier here. To get a sense of the problem, imagine that one characteristic – say, true preferences – is represented by a single parameter. Over a whole population, this could be represented by a frequency distribution. If we're lucky, it's a simple bell curve; otherwise, it could be bimodal, highly skewed, or discontinuous at some point. Now let's introduce a second characteristic – say, extent of bias. This parameter, too, may be represented by a distribution over the population. To represent the full interaction between these two characteristics, we would need a bivariate distribution, which could be visualized as a probability "surface" (a curve in three-dimensional space) over many different characteristic pairs. If the two characteristics are not independent – and there's every reason to think they won't be – then knowing the two univariate distributions is not enough to construct the bivariate distribution. Research would be required to discover the shape of the entire bivariate "surface." To introduce more characteristics, we would need a multivariate distribution, which normal people cannot even visualize. In short, each additional characteristic exponentially increases the knowledge burden.

Furthermore, some characteristics don't take the form of a single, easily quantifiable parameter. Methods of self-regulation are particularly notable in this regard. The ways that people try to alter their behavior (consciously and unconsciously) are endlessly idiosyncratic, which means that seeing self-regulation as a single dimension of difference is misleading. Numerous dimensions of behavior are captured in just this one category.

Perhaps it isn't clear why paternalist planners need to know entire distributions of characteristics, rather than just (say) the mean, median, or modal characteristic. An illustration will help to make the point. Suppose, unrealistically, that *only one* characteristic is relevant to the impact of policy: the extent of bias. Suppose a new policy targets a correction at the mean level of bias. How will this affect the welfare of individuals? For people with higher levels of bias, the correction will not be enough, although some correction is better than none. For people with lower levels of bias, the correction will be excessive relative to the ideal correction, although they might still be better off than with no correction at all. For people with sufficiently low (or zero) levels of bias, the correction will make them worse off than they were before. And for people with a bias *in the opposite direction* of the average individual's, the correction will actually be an anti-correction – exactly the opposite of the correction they needed. In short, any policy will create both winners and losers, with the specific magnitudes of gain (or loss) differing from person to person.

To judge whether the policy is a net gain relative to the status quo or alternative policies, then, the policymaker must weigh all the gains and losses.[22] It would not be sufficient to know that the winners outnumber the losers, because the average gain and average loss will not necessarily be the same. And even calculating the average gain or average loss presupposes knowing the constituent gains or losses that contribute to the average – or in other words, the whole distribution. (In terms of probability theory, finding the expected value or mean would involve integrating over the probability density function multiplied by a gain/loss function.)

To make matters more complex, the gain or loss to an individual is not a monotonic function of the distance between their own bias and the average population bias (that was targeted by the policy). People's reactions to policies can display discontinuities and other confounding behaviors. For instance, as discussed in the earlier section on extent of bias, a very large difference between a default rule and someone's ideal outcome can actually

---

[22] Whether the size of these gains and losses ought to be measured using willingness to pay (WTP) or willingness to accept (WTA) is another vexing issue with no clear answer.

generate *optimal* behavior; this happens because a large discrepancy can do a better job of motivating opt-outs. Imagine that we line up the potential "losers" in order of the distance between the default and their ideal. What happens as we walk down this line of people away from the default? At first, the per person loss will increase as we get further away from the default, because these people are defaulted into an increasingly less preferred outcome. But then, as we start to reach those individuals who are motivated to opt out, the loss will drop or even disappear. To do a proper cost–benefit analysis of the new default, the paternalist would need to know the shape of the whole loser distribution – and particularly where in that profile people start to opt out. (And we haven't yet discussed the shape of the winner distribution.)

As this example demonstrates, even when there is only one policy-relevant characteristic, the paternalist policymaker needs to know the whole distribution of that characteristic. If we introduced more characteristics, the policymaker would need to know the shape of the multivariate distribution. The task seems insurmountable.

One tempting response to this challenge is to say policy only needs to induce better behavior *on the margin*. For instance, we don't have to calculate the optimal sin tax; we only need to know that it's greater than zero. We don't have to know the optimal default rate of savings; we just need to know that people should save something rather than nothing. We don't have to know the optimal cooling-off period, only that a small waiting period is better than none at all. But this response is mistaken for at least three reasons. First, if there are multiple interacting biases, then the policymaker cannot justifiably assume that even a small marginal "correction" will actually move people in the right direction. The theory of the second-best demonstrates that the marginal intervention can exacerbate errors resulting from other biases.

Second, a policy based on the average person does not affect only the average person; even a small marginal change can induce gains and losses throughout the distribution of affected people. For example, even a small sin tax affects all purchasers of the targeted product, including people far from the average (e.g., anorexics and the extremely obese). A cooling-off period, too, will affect everyone who might wish to buy the product in question. Even changing a default rule while allowing opt-outs can be highly complex, as we have seen. To predict the welfare impact of a "small" change in the default rule for retirement contribution – say, from zero contribution (unless you opt in) to a minimal contribution (unless you opt out or increase the contribution) – it's necessary to ask how the new default will affect not only the targeted individuals who otherwise wouldn't save at all, but everyone who would have opted in and might have chosen a higher or lower contribution.

Third, the shape of the distribution can affect whether the mean is a meaningful measure of population behavior. For a highly skewed distribution, the mean, median, and mode can differ substantially. To take one example, consumption of alcohol is dramatically skewed, with the top decile of drinkers consuming more than 50 percent of all alcohol (Ingraham 2014). The *mean* American drinker drinks at least fifteen times as much as the *median* drinker.[23] A sin tax aimed at the behavior of the mean drinker would be much higher than necessary for well over half the population, while a sin tax aimed at the behavior of the median drinker might well be zero. But let's suppose the authorities impose a "small" sin tax to split the difference. Whom will the tax affect the most? There is evidence that moderate drinkers are actually more responsive to an increase in the price of alcohol than heavy drinkers (Mast et al. 1999, 217). Thus, those whose behavior needs the least correction could be those most affected by the intervention.

Another response to the heterogeneity challenge is to suggest that, perhaps, people are not that heterogeneous after all. However, ample evidence supports the claim that behavioral and cognitive biases are *not* uniform in the population. Mitchell (2002) cites at least 100 studies on this point, showing that behavioral phenomena (including cognitive biases) differ in the population along such dimensions as educational level, cognitive ability (as measured by, for instance, performance on the Scholastic Aptitude Test), cognitive mindsets or dispositions, cultural differences, age differences, and gender differences (pp. 94–95, 140–156). These correlations of cognitive bias with group characteristics should not, of course, be taken to imply uniformity of bias within any given group (e.g., educated white women). Substantial within-group differences presumably exist as well. The correlations do, however, strongly indicate that substantial variation exists in the population.

To take a specific example, consider the heterogeneity of responses to the current food environment – fast-food restaurants, easy availability of junk-food snacks, added sugar and salt in processed foods, and so forth. This

---

[23] The actual number may be much higher. The average weekly consumption in the fifth decile is 0.14 drinks per week; the average weekly consumption in the sixth decile is 0.63 per week; the median value lies somewhere between these two. The mean consumption for the whole population is 9.833. Thus, the mean-to-median ratio must lie between 15.6 and 70.2. (Calculation based on figures in Ingraham 2014.)

environment is shared by many people who do not become obese, and there is much individual variability in the response to what some people consider a "weight-promoting environment." Blundell et al. (2005) outline many psychobiological differences among people that determine whether the environmental stimuli result in obesity or not. These factors are often quite complex, but in general terms, "susceptibility [to weight gain] can be identified at various levels – genetic, physiologic and metabolic, behavioral and psychological" (p. 615). The implication of this widely accepted perspective is that the availability of fattening or junk food has different effects on different people. (We should also observe that a high level of responsiveness of one's weight to the food environment is not *necessarily* a result of bias.)

Aside from the heterogeneity of tendency toward weight gain, there is heterogeneity in the *effects* of weight gain on health. One measure of health consequences is the estimated number of life years lost due to some behavior. By this measure, there is notable heterogeneity across various demographic groups. There have been at least fifteen studies as of 2014 comparing the body mass index (BMI) for black men or women compared with their white counterparts. All report a weaker BMI–mortality relationship for blacks compared with whites (Jackson et al. 2014). In one influential study (Fontaine et al. 2003), an increase in mortality was not noticed until a BMI of 37 or 38 for black women and 32 to 33 among black men. Small increased mortality effects begin for white women at about a BMI of 26 and for white men at a BMI at about 28. (For comparison, official thresholds for overweightness and obesity are 25 and 30, respectively.) In none of these groups do substantial effects become noticeable until the person becomes technically obese with a BMI of at least 30, and in some groups a much higher BMI. So, those who are merely overweight are not in the same situation regarding years of life lost.

Of course, this data has its limitations. The effects of a poor diet may not show up in a comparison of BMIs and increased mortality. But our point is not to say that some groups have no cost of eating poorly; it is to say that the costs may be different. If they are different, then the rational cost–benefit balance will be struck differently by different people. And we should point out, again, that race-correlated differences are merely a loose indicator of how much variation may occur across a diverse population.

THE EMPIRICAL SEARCH FOR TRUE PREFERENCES

In our typology of paternalist knowledge requirements, the first and most significant item was knowledge of true preferences. In recent years there have been some serious attempts to meet the challenge of true-preference identification and to provide policymakers with some guidance about how the knowledge problems might be solved. We discuss the two most notable ones here.

Augmented Revelatory Frame Approach

Jacob Goldin (2015) has developed two related approaches to solving the knowledge problem that are within the behavioral revealed preference framework. We discuss one of them in detail. His approach concentrates on ascertaining the true preferences of those agents whose choices vary according to the frame in which the options are presented. For example, if the default for an employer-sponsored retirement-savings program is automatic enrollment, some agents will be enrolled who would *not* be enrolled under the traditional opt-in frame. These agents are called "inconsistent." By contrast, "consistent" agents will opt out of the default when necessary to choose in accordance with their preferences. These agents will make the same decisions regardless of the frame.

With this distinction in mind, Goldin's goal is to estimate the true preferences of those who are inconsistent. These agents' choices are affected by the frame. And since the frame is viewed as a possible instrument of policy – such as automatic enrollment or not – the object is to nudge individuals in the direction of their true preferences.[24] More specifically, the goal is to maximize the number who end up with the option they prefer. Unless there are substantial transaction costs involved in opting out, the consistent agents need no help. However, the inconsistent do need help. But what are their preferences? To find out we need to find a *neutral frame*, that is, one that will reveal true preferences because it removes the effects of the distorting frames. Then we must subject a random sample of the relevant population to a series of decisions:

- First: Ascertain the choices agents make in the neutral frame. For example, they can be required to make an active choice. From this we compute the percentage that truly favors enrollment. We call this the average preference of the population. Assume, for illustrative purposes, this is 60 percent.
- Second: Ascertain the fraction of the choosers who are consistent. We subject the same sample as above to the two nonneutral

---

[24] By assumption or definition the frame affects choices but does not affect preferences.

frames – automatic enrollment and the traditional opt-in. The consistent are the sum of those who opt out of these frames in the direction of their active choice; these are agents who would choose against any nudge if warranted by their preferences. Assume this is 70 percent.

- Third: Ascertain the average preferences for those who are consistent, say, the percentage favoring enrollment. Assume this is 75 percent.
- Finally, we are in a position to compute the average preferences of the inconsistent and thus to design the frame (nudge) correctly. The formula is:

$$\frac{\text{average preference of population} - (\text{fraction consistent} \times \text{average preference of consistent})}{\text{fraction inconsistent}}$$

The logic of the formula runs like this. Since we know that of the *entire population* 60 percent prefer enrollment, and we know that of the *consistent* (who are 70 percent of the whole) 75 percent prefer enrollment, we conclude that the *inconsistent* must have a much lower proportion in favor of enrollment because a mere 30 percent of the population must bring the whole population average down to 60 percent. With these numbers, it turns out that only 25 percent of the inconsistent prefer enrollment. The nudge is then decided on this basis. In this example, because most of the inconsistent prefer not to be enrolled, the nudge ought to be the traditional default: the agent is out of the plan unless he signs up.

Obviously, the arithmetic of the formula is not at issue. Our purpose in working through these details is to emphasize *the distinction between the use of "given" information and the problem of acquiring it in the first place.* Although the claimed advantage of Goldin's approach over previous efforts is that it focuses on the preferences of the inconsistent as the only determinant of the nudge, nonetheless we are required to find the average true preferences of the population as a whole *and* of the consistent agents as well in order to ascertain the preferences of the inconsistent.

The method depends crucially on understanding the mechanisms of the biases operative in the nonneutral frames and in the so-called neutral one as well. Goldin's illustration simplifies the knowledge problem to the point of assuming it away. Let us begin with the neutral frame. Unless we have a genuinely neutral frame, we cannot estimate the true average preferences of the population. If a truly neutral frame is available, then we have to wonder why paternalists don't simply advocate that frame to begin with. But set that concern aside. In the illustration, the neutrality of the frame is relative to the particular nudge being contemplated: a change in the default rule from opt-in to opt-out. In the putatively neutral frame, individuals are required to make an active choice. But are they free of biases there?

Presumptively, they are not. The rationales for default effects include present bias, loss aversion, implicit recommendation effects, choice complexity, and so forth. It is quite likely that the absence of a default will work to neutralize some effects (such as anchoring and implicit recommendation effects) but not the others. At the very least, the policymaker must know which effects will and won't be neutralized. Consider that an active chooser may be subject to present bias in some yet-to-be-determined degree; this would contaminate the choices of the consistent and inconsistent agents alike. If the options are too complex, then that complexity (now unaided by a recommendation effect) is still there in the neutral frame. Choosers may choose a seemingly "simple" option such as zero contribution with the intention of revisiting the choice after further research or contemplation. Thus, again, choices may not reveal true preferences. In the neutral frame, what is the reference point that loss-averse agents focus on? Obviously, this can affect their choices.

The nonneutral frames are suspect as well. The conditions under which people make these choices is assumed to be a behavioral frame – in other words, a characteristic of the choice situation that does not affect preferences even as it affects choices. Suppose, for example, the default serves as an implicit recommendation from a trusted source for a decision that individuals find complex. Then the default lowers information costs, which means that people will change their choices because their knowledge has changed. Thus the agents who appear to be inconsistent are not, as their optimal position rationally depends on the default. The attempt to find their true preferences amid their changing choices is chasing a mirage.

The upshot is that the formula Goldin provides is only a tool of mental organization. To fill in the terms, the analyst needs to understand the mechanisms of all the biases at work in the specific context under discussion, just as we have suggested in our typology of knowledge requirements. This investigation must go beyond the mere presence of biases to assess their magnitudes. For example, suppose defaults function as pure anchors *and* as implicit recommendations. To what extent are the different choices made between the frames an expression of a change in knowledge or a biasing of true preferences?

Finally, we should point out that Goldin's task is greatly simplified by positing an objective function in which the *number* of individuals who wind up with the option they prefer is maximized. A more natural, if less tractable, objective would be to minimize the welfare cost of errors or to maximize the consumer surplus of the individuals affected by the policy. That means we would need to know the gains and losses for the people differentially affected by the policy. For example, some individuals may prefer to be in a retirement-savings program more intensely than others prefer to stay out; some individuals may suffer a larger loss than others from waiting too long to enroll. This can become quite complicated (Bernheim 2015). And yet it is important, because even in the simplified example above it can change the recommended nudge from the traditional opt-in to automatic enrollment (or vice versa).[25]

Unified Behavioral Revealed Preference

In Chapter 3, we cited Bernheim and Rangel's (2007) work that explicitly assumes individuals are endowed with well-behaved lifetime preferences. But in more recent work, Bernheim (2016) largely abandons the traditional behavioral search for true preferences. The notion of an inner neoclassical agent who is free of all biases and has well-formed and coherent preferences does little work in Bernheim's new approach. Indeed, Bernheim adopts a general view of preferences that is largely compatible with our own notion of inclusive rationality. Preferences are constructed in the sense that agents aggregate many aspects of their experience both to determine the pros and cons of an option and to weigh them. The preferences are created *de novo*; they do not preexist the choice in any literal way.[26]

---

[25] The second method Goldin explores is called the "Demographic Extrapolation Approach." Here the analyst first divides a random sample of the relevant population into as many demographic groups as possible. Then he must manipulate the frame at issue (automatic enrollment or not) to identify the consistent choosers under each frame. From this we have the consistent choosers in each demographic group and can identify their choices, which are assumed to be identical to their preferences. It is assumed that the preferences of the *inconsistent* choosers within each demographic group are identical to the preferences of the consistent choosers in the same demographic groups. The nudge can then be based on the imputed preferences of the majority of the inconsistent. Again, the central knowledge problem here is to purify the sample from all of the biases that can "contaminate" the preferences of the consistent choosers. If, for example, they are all affected by present bias, then the assumption that their choices reveal preferences will fail on behavioral grounds. This requires a comprehensive understanding of biases and their interactions. Behavioral economists do not have this.

[26] "According to this view, I aggregate the many diverse aspects of my experience only when called to do so for a given purpose ... I cannot simply access an aggregate sensation that is already part of my subjective experience, or consult an overall preference ordering that

In Bernheim's revised view, most of what behavioral economists consider biases or distortions are treated as normatively valid ways of seeing
the array of options – if the perspective of the agents is to carry weight. For
example, what is called present bias is simply an aspect of decision-making
that differentially values rewards because of their immediacy. To argue that
it is a *bias* is to arbitrarily privilege the distant perspective over the
immediate perspective. Generalizing this view across other "biases," Bernheim concludes that many perspectives or frames can be relevant to the
welfare of individuals as they see it, and not simply to the determination of
their choices.

In many respects, we find Bernheim's new position congenial. However,
Bernheim allows one major exception to his skepticism about biases:
"characterization failure." This occurs when the individual misunderstands
the options available or the consequences of choosing an option.[27]
Observed choices under these conditions are not considered welfare-
relevant; that is, they do not provide evidence of welfare enhancement.
Therefore, from a normative perspective they can be ignored.

Importantly, Bernheim believes that characterization failure can be
identified *without* ascertaining true preferences of individuals. But this is
not precisely true. The relevance or importance of any given misunderstanding or lack of knowledge depends upon what the individual is trying
to achieve. Suppose, for example, people misunderstand the concept of the
variance of expected returns with regard to an asset they are contemplating
buying. This would seem to be a characterization failure. However, perhaps
the individual is risk-neutral and is looking for the asset with the greatest
expected return. In such a case, the so-called characterization failure would
be irrelevant. Furthermore, if the asset were being considered for reasons
other than pecuniary benefit, then again characterization failure would be
irrelevant. What is true, however, is that the economist need not know the
agent's preferences *exactly*. So long as the particular lack of knowledge is
relevant to the set of plausible underlying preferences – for example, it's
plausible that many individuals are risk-averse – we can characterize
choices under these conditions as having problematic welfare relevance.

While abandoning the task of identifying (unique) true preferences,
Bernheim's new behavioral welfare economics does rely on the idea of a

---

resides inside of my head, because neither of these aggregates exist until I am called upon
    to deliberate and aggregate" (Bernheim 2016, 20). See also Rizzo (2014).
[27] This idea is similar to Carl Menger's concept of "imaginary wants." See Menger
    (1981, 120).

set of welfare-relevant preferences. The set includes any preferences expressed in any choice situation or framing thereof, aside from characterization failure. For instance, if the individual chooses A under Frame A' and B under Frame B', but never chooses C, then for welfare purposes, the individual's most preferred set is {A,B} but not {A,B,C}.[28] In one respect, this is an obvious way to go if the behavioral standard of true preferences is viewed as essentially arbitrary. But notice that, generally speaking, the set of welfare-relevant preferences will not be consistent in the usual sense that "if A is preferred to B, B will never be preferred to A." Different frames will elicit different choices, and when a fairly large array of frames is considered relevant to welfare, they will all be deemed worthy of respect by the economist. So the welfare standard need not be internally consistent.[29] We will call this the "multiple preferences" approach.

Bernheim's behavioral welfare economics is in many ways less ambitious than its predecessors. By adopting a more inclusive attitude toward preferences, it substantially reduces the scope for paternalist interventions and thus the associated knowledge problems. But in the remaining areas where Bernheim's approach does countenance paternalist interventions, it does not solve the knowledge problem so much as it exchanges one set of problems for another. Let us begin with the notion of characterization failure. It is no doubt true that, generally speaking, people may misunderstand the problem or set of options before them. And yet in practice we must identify such misunderstandings in specific cases. Misunderstanding is often the result of imperfect attention and memory (as well as imperfect knowledge). However, as Bernheim recognizes, there are difficulties in observing the *processes* of attention and memory independently of the actual decision outcome. We do not have sufficient scientific foundations to go this route (Bernheim 2016, 37–41, 49). Practically speaking, therefore, whether people are deemed "sufficiently" attentive in a problem situation may depend on whether they make the choice the paternalist considers correct.

Even when people fail to use some of the available information, they will not always send a clear signal of an error that would unambiguously qualify as a characterization failure. We could, of course, simply question

---

[28] We are using the term "frame" in both its narrow sense as choice architecture and in an expansive sense of the biases that may affect choices in a given situation.

[29] Nevertheless, Bernheim must rule out the possibility that within a finite set of options there is no maximal option. Within *each frame* there must be a best choice. Thus cyclic preferences within a frame cannot be welfare-relevant (Bernheim 2016, 58).

people about their decision-making to determine if they know what is going on. Aside from the costs involved in doing so, this type of investigation privileges explicit over implicit (or tacit) knowledge.

Perhaps we can put all of these complications aside and simply provide people with information if it is potentially relevant to a decision and then go on our way.[30] However, the characterization-failure approach is fundamentally a static one. As we have seen in Chapter 4, errors generate learning processes. Any sensible policy would have to weigh the consequences of present mistakes against the value of longer-term learning. Thus, while characterization failure may be a necessary condition for paternalistic intervention, it is surely not a sufficient condition even when it is properly identified.

Another major difficulty is that Bernheim's multiple-preferences welfare standard is not entirely consistent with his general philosophy, which rejects the preexistence of well-defined preferences. According to the multiple-preferences view, preferences may not be well defined because they vary across frames and other normatively relevant behavioral factors. But *within* each frame, Bernheim assumes they are well defined. In effect, all of the ill-defining noise is put in the lap of the frame. The problem is that the same frame may elicit different responses from individuals in different contexts. This is because the frame itself may not be the only factor contributing to the choice.[31] A frame may be exogenously set, but it also must be interpreted by the targeted individuals in the context of their specific circumstances of time and place. If more than one choice is possible for each given frame, then the evaluation of welfare consequences becomes more complex. We would have multiple frames and multiple choices within each frame. To know whether this is or is not significant obviously cannot be settled by assumption. It requires the economist to have an understanding of the psychological mechanisms at work. Bernheim does not believe we have this understanding. Indeed, he designed his alternative approach to avoid such issues.

---

[30] Even here the welfare consequences are not certain. With regard to financial education, for example, "the effects ... on the quality of decisionmaking are far from obvious, given that it may influence behavior through indoctrination, deference to authority, social pressure and the like" (Bernheim 2016, 51).

[31] As long as we do not know the circumstances in which a particular frame affects choice and in which it does not (or the circumstances in which a bias is present and in which it is not), we do not have sufficient understanding to know whether the effects of a change in framing are due (solely) to the frame or something else.

Setting these difficulties aside, how does a standard of multiple preferences work in application? An example is provided in Bernheim et al. (2015), which examines the case of employer-sponsored 401(k) retirement plans. Bernheim and coauthors begin with a model based entirely on the costs of opting out of a default (say, nonenrollment) as the only explanation for the tendency to stick with the default. The "as-if" costs that must be assumed in order to rationalize this default effect are implausibly high. Therefore, they move on to other models that involve psychological biases of one form or another. Rather than pruning decisions made under biases as not reflecting genuine welfare, Bernheim's strategy is to accept them *all*. For example, a decision made under the influence of present bias truly affects the individual's welfare. She is better off when she incorporates this "bias" in her decision-making and either fails to enroll or simply procrastinates before enrolling.

For simplicity, let us divide the various factors that seem to rationalize a particular behavior – such as enrolling (or not) in an employer-sponsored retirement program – into two categories: endogenous and exogenous. (This is our terminology, not Bernheim's.) The endogenous factors are internal to the decision-maker: present bias with naïve or sophisticated actors, anchoring, and the degree of attention. The exogenous factors are those imposed or planned by the policymakers, typically as part of the frame: automatic enrollment or active sign-up enrollment, forward-looking or con-temporaneous decision frames,[32] and inattention- or attention-generating frames. Ultimately what we want to know is the value to the agents of a proposed change in the default frame, for example, to automatic enrollment. Because we do not have a unitary-preference welfare standard, we will not have a unique estimate of that value. For each welfare-relevant frame, we will have a minimum and maximum estimate of the value of the change.[33] Then we ascertain the global minimum and maximum value *across all of*

---

[32] A forward-looking decision frame is one in which a decision made today is not imple-mented until later. A contemporaneous decision frame is one in which the present decision is implemented immediately.

[33] Bernheim uses equivalent variation as the value measure. Suppose the consumer is notionally or actually shifted by policy to a new option (enrollment in a retirement plan). We must calculate two variations: first, the minimum amount of money that could be taken away from the consumer so that she unambiguously chooses not to enroll; second, the largest amount of money that could be taken away from the consumer such that she unambiguously chooses to enroll. This gives us the upper and lower limits respectively of the value of the policy within a particular frame. The equivalent variation is estimated by simulations in conjunction with the parameters of the fitted model. Needless to say, perhaps, there are many unobvious and heroic identifying assumptions that must be made to estimate all of this.

the frames.[34] Finally, we multiply these values by the number of people affected. Thus the answer to our question about the value of the proposed policy will be of the form "at least $X but not more than $Y." In principle, the range can be large and one or both of the values can be negative.

The most obvious consequence of this approach is that instead of fitting one model to the data and estimating the welfare consequences of a change in policy, the economist must fit several models and derive a number of welfare estimates. This involves making many assumptions in order to estimate such parameters as present bias, degree of naïveté, and opt-out costs. There are many moving parts, as even a perusal of Bernheim et al. (2015) will show. It is true that the economist can avoid identifying *unique* true preferences, but instead she must make numerous empirical estimations through fitting various models to a specific set of data.

In summary, Bernheim's approach simplifies or eliminates certain knowledge problems by accepting the welfare relevance of most standard biases. On the one hand, this is a conceptual improvement over the usual behavioral approach. On the other hand, it also encounters knowledge problems inherent in constructing and fitting *multiple* models for each application of the framework. This replaces the search for true preferences with the search for a range of normatively acceptable preferences. There is a heavy empirical burden here.

THE PRACTICALLY INSURMOUNTABLE
KNOWLEDGE PROBLEM

Let us recap our typology of knowledge requirements for successful behavioral paternalism. Policymakers working in this area would need to discern:

- True preferences of targeted people as well as other affected people;
- The extent of bias that prevents attainment of those preferences;
- Self-debiasing and small-group debiasing methods used by affected people, including how those methods will adjust to new policies;
- Dynamic effects of new policies on people's capacity for self-control;
- Counteracting behaviors that may offset the impact of interventions;
- Other biases that may affect choices and how they interact with the targeted bias;
- The distribution of all of the above over the affected population.

---

[34] Excluding, of course, those frames that involve characterization failure.

Behavioral paternalists display a great deal of confidence in their agenda, which they say is based on solid research in psychology and economics; as Richard Thaler emphasizes, it is "evidence-based" (2015b, 338). And indeed, a great deal of research has been done. But we suggest that the knowledge requirements listed here are insurmountable. This is true for three reasons. First, the sheer volume of knowledge required is simply too vast. Second, the knowledge must be acquired at a high level of specificity. The context dependence of behavioral phenomena means that knowledge of one domain of human activity cannot easily be transferred to another. It is true that the *general form* of a phenomenon may occur across many different domains – but that's not enough, because policymaking requires knowledge of *specific magnitudes*, and those magnitudes will assuredly differ.

Third, and most importantly, much of the required knowledge simply lies beyond the reach of researchers. It consists of subjective attitudes, perceptions, beliefs, and tastes. It includes personal strategies whose application depends on the idiosyncratic environments, routines, and social contexts of countless individuals. The factors that allegedly trigger biases are highly context-dependent, varying from person to person, place to place, time to time, and circumstance to circumstance; they also vary with the experimental method of eliciting the particular bias. Rational behavior is contextual, ostensibly irrational behavior is contextual, and attempts to correct irrational behavior are contextual. In a policy environment, "contextual" means "contingent on local and personal knowledge."

It might seem that we have erected a knowledge burden so high that it rules out all social scientific research. But that is not true. It is entirely possible to conduct research that identifies general patterns and phenomena, and the behavioral literature has done just that. However, the knowledge burden for policymaking is much higher. If behavioral paternalism is to clear the high bar its own creators have set for it – to provide an evidence-based policy program that reliably improves personal welfare from the perspective of the individual – then its practitioners need to have the vast body of knowledge we have discussed. For most proposed interventions, they do not have it.

APPENDIX TO CHAPTER 7: Retirement-Savings Defaults

Shifting from default nonenrollment to default enrollment in retirement-savings plans has taken on iconic status among behavioral paternalists. Some even regard this default shift as the paradigmatic case of behaviorally justified paternalism. For that reason, we will devote an appendix to examining this issue more closely.

Given the prominence of this proposal, it is odd that so little attention has been paid to the question of who should implement it. Should employers adopt the new default voluntarily, or should government require all employers to do so? Obviously, the latter raises concerns that the former does not. To clarify our position, we have no opposition in principle to employers – or even government in its capacity as an employer – choosing a new default rule, provided that employees are properly notified. When the new default is adopted voluntarily by employers, there remains room to move away from the new default when and if circumstances warrant – for instance, if it produces unintended consequences or if a different default makes most sense for a particular employer or set of employees. We do, however, challenge the *behavioral justification* behind shifting to an opt-out default. Genuine behavioral biases may not be fully or even largely responsible for the observed effects that opt-out defaults have on savings behavior, inasmuch as classically rational factors play a significant role. Furthermore, to the extent that genuine behavioral effects are involved, it is unclear that the new default always improves welfare.

The fundamental difficulty with many behavioral analyses of policy-created default changes is that they are satisfied with showing some effect – specifically, an increase in enrollment – when people are automatically enrolled in an employer-sponsored retirement plan, irrespective of the cause of that effect. The increase in enrollment is measured relative to what would happen under an alternative rule, either (a) default nonenrollment, also known as opt-in enrollment, or (b) active choice, meaning the individual is required to explicitly choose between enrollment and nonenrollment. For example, Beshears et al. (2006) find that in one medium-sized US chemical company, 401(k) participation rates among those automatically enrolled were 35 percentage points higher than for those voluntarily enrolled (95 percent versus 60 percent) after three months of employment. At twenty-four months, the difference was 25 percentage points. Choi et al. (2004) find in one large US company that the difference between those automatically enrolled and those voluntarily enrolled was 30 percentage points (85 percent and 50 percent) after twenty-four months.[35] However, neither the data from Beshears et al. nor that from Choi et al. is from a nationally representative sample. Butrica and Karamcheva (2012, table 3) find, in a nationally representative survey, that the difference between the enrollment rate of those under the traditional default and those under automatic enrollment is about 10 percentage points (67.3 percent and 77.1 percent respectively). When other factors are controlled for in a regression analysis, the effect of automatic enrollment is reduced to a 7 percentage-point advantage (Butrica and Karamcheva 2012, table 5). Of course, there are limitations of this data as well.[36] Nevertheless, there is reason to believe that the very large increase in enrollment suggested by often-referenced studies may be an exaggeration of the true magnitude.

Data issues aside, two questions seem relevant at this point. First, to what extent is this effect due to behavioral factors, rather than factors that are understandable from the standpoint of either neoclassical or inclusive rationality? And second, does this effect constitute a *welfare improvement* over opt-in enrollment or active choice? Many older and more popular analyses simply assume or superficially argue that welfare has increased simply because more people are enrolled. Certainly this is true of the claims of Thaler and Sunstein (2008b), Thaler (2015b), and certain "nudge" partisans (Halpern 2016). In general, even among the technical studies of retirement-savings defaults, relatively few analyze welfare effects in any depth.

---

[35] Under active choice, Beshears et al. (2009) find that enrollment rates are closer to automatic enrollment rates than voluntary enrollment. At twenty-four months' tenure active choice produced about 65 percent enrollment, while automatic enrollment produced 80 percent. At thirty-six months the figures were about 75 percent and 85 percent respectively.

[36] For a discussion of the relative advantages and disadvantages of their data set, see Butrica and Karamcheva (2012, 7–9, ns. 6, 12).

SEARCHING FOR A MECHANISM

To answer both questions, we must examine the causes of the "stickiness" of the default rule in this particular case. *What is the mechanism that produces the default effect?*

At the outset, we should note that the usual analysis of defaults is distorted by three factors – conceptual and empirical. First, there is an essentially arbitrary assumption that the long-run perspective is the only normatively appropriate standard. We have challenged that assumption in previous chapters. We must therefore be careful to separate the explanation of a phenomenon from its welfare evaluation. For example, present "bias" could play a role in explaining the phenomenon even if we do not consider it a bias in the normative sense. Similarly, the greater valuation of losses compared with gains, characteristic of loss aversion, is not necessarily a bias rather than a legitimate taste variable. Accordingly, there could be enrollment effects due to present bias or loss aversion – without implying that one default is necessarily better than another.

Second, it is important to distinguish between rational and behavioral mechanisms of influence. Simply because a policy has been advocated by behavioral paternalists does not mean that it has its desired effect through bypassing or superseding irrational processes. In particular, we argue that defaults operate primarily by communicating an implied recommendation from employers to employees. In a world of complexity, limited knowledge, and uncertainty, there is nothing particularly nonrational about accepting advice. In fact, advice-seeking and advice-taking are ubiquitous and part of the market for information broadly understood.

Third, it is not adequate to test hypotheses about the causes of default effects simply by fitting models of particular biases to sample data. In essence, analysts using this approach are content to observe that default effects are *consistent* with an alleged bias-driven explanation, even though other factors might be able to explain the same effects. Given the difficulties of sharply separating biases (Beshears et al. 2015, 5), there is a great deal of room for the effects of biases to intermingle both with each other and with relatively straightforward knowledge problems, as we shall see. Therefore, it is important to assess the logic and plausibility of particular biases in specific contexts.

Our analytical strategy is to examine the various explanations that have been proffered for the existence of default effects, assess their relative plausibility, and then examine the behavior of several agent types to better understand which actors may be affected by given mechanisms. Each of these parts of the analysis will have implications for welfare.

THE PARADE OF EXPLANATIONS

We take our list of seven possible explanations from Choi (2015, 170–171). With the exception of the first, these explanations have generally been considered "biases," but as we shall see, the behavioral bases of default effects have been exaggerated. We argue that the consequences (favorable and unfavorable) of changes in defaults typically occur through inclusively rational, rather than behavioral, mechanisms. The primary mechanism involves induced alterations in the *effective knowledge base* of decision-makers. We consider alternative possible mechanisms, but we find they are not adequately supported by the evidence.

Complexity of the Decision Task

We start with the explanation we find most compelling. Many financial decisions such as saving for retirement, especially at the distance of several decades, are complex in at least two ways. The first is the properties of the investment vehicle(s), including likely performance under conditions of radical uncertainty about the future. The second is the appropriateness of the investment in terms of the individual's preferences, circumstances, and opportunity costs.

It is well documented that large numbers of Americans have serious shortcomings in their ability to make financial decisions (Lusardi and Mitchell 2014). Compound interest, risk diversification, and the effects of inflation are poorly understood. And these deficiencies are just the beginning of the knowledge needed to (literally) optimize retirement decisions. None of this should be surprising. Lusardi et al. (2009) conducted a study using surveys, focus groups, and in-depth interviews to determine the causes of nonparticipation in a retirement-savings program. About 40 percent of the respondents admitted that they did not have "enough knowledge" (p. 216).[37] As might be expected, the problem of financial illiteracy seems to be more acute among low-income than high-income groups (Tang and Lachance 2012, 126).

---

[37] In this study there was no statistically significant difference between high- and low-income employees (p. 217).

Rational agents, whether neoclassically or inclusively rational, will need and seek assistance in making these decisions. In many areas of life people do not solve technical problems without assistance. This is part of the established role of doctors, lawyers, and tax preparers, to mention a few. Factors that reduce the complexity of such decisions at little cost to the decision-maker are unambiguously welfare-enhancing in any rational framework. Greater financial literacy and access to information make for better decision-making.[38] Defaults may constitute a cheap and effective way of communicating rough knowledge to individuals with inadequate financial literacy. When a default is set *positively*, that is, when the automatic option is an action, it may be perceived by choosers as a recommendation from the default setters. When a default is set *negatively*, that is, when the automatic option is a nonaction, this too may be perceived as a recommendation from default setters, albeit a weaker signal than in the positive case.[39] Accordingly, we have good reason to believe that automatic enrollment has been perceived by employees as a recommendation to be enrolled in the 401(k) program (McKenzie et al. 2006).

Many of those who choose the default do so because of their lack of knowledge *and* because the recommendation implicit in the default simplifies the problem. In one field study (Brown et al. 2012), 35 percent of respondents asked to choose a retirement plan said that they did not have enough information to make a choice about retirement options. In that same study about 33 percent said they believed the default option constituted an implicit endorsement. Two studies conducted by Agnew and Szykman (2005) found that 20 percent and 25 percent of low-financial-knowledge participants chose the default, while only 2 percent and 4 percent respectively of the high-knowledge participants chose the default. Furthermore, Löfgren et al. (2012) provide evidence in a different context that in choices made by knowledgable individuals, there is no statistically significant difference in the choices under different default rules or lack

---

[38] Do people with a greater propensity to save and invest endogenously acquire more financial knowledge? Or does financial knowledge have a causal relationship to better decision-making? Instrumental variable and field experiment approaches suggest it has an independent causal influence and is large (Lusardi and Mitchell 2014, 27–33).

[39] McKenzie et al. (2006, 417, 419) found that when the human-resources staff had chosen enrollment in a 401(k) plan as the default, 89 percent of the experiment's participants inferred that enrollment was the recommendation. On the other hand, when the default was nonenrollment, 49 percent treated that as the recommendation. There is, however, some contrary evidence indicating that negative defaults are treated as conveying no recommendation (Tannenbaum and Ditto 2011).

thereof.[40] In a meta-analysis of fifty-eight studies of defaults in various contexts, Jachimowicz et al. (2018) find that endorsement is a major channel of causation in the increased likelihood that people will choose a default.

Recommendations from trusted sources can help reduce the complexity of decision-making in two ways. First, they help the individual *interpret* the information she has at hand – whether to be in the savings plan and what investment vehicles to use. Recommendations from perceived experts are a standard part of information gathering and interpretation in the modern world, as we have already stated. Second, recommendations can act as *surrogates* for complex information, as has been demonstrated in energy-saving decisions (Houde 2014). Each of these changes in the information context will produce a tendency on the part of decision-makers to *deliberately* choose the default. In the first case, with their improved appreciation for the information at hand, decision-makers may decide that their optimal decision conforms to the default in whole or in part (it may differ in the exact level of savings contribution). In the second case, decision-makers may simply use the recommendation as an information surrogate and therefore deliberately choose the default.[41] The difference between these two groups is a matter of degree depending on just how much knowledge about the options individuals have. Both groups have been counted in behavioral evidence of the success of automatic enrollment. Both effects, however, are certainly inclusively rational and, we would argue, even standardly rational adjustments to the reduction in complexity.

In recent years, automatic enrollment has become the dominant default in employer-provided retirement savings plans, now accounting for 60 percent of such plans (Plan Sponsor Council 2018). However, an additional factor has reduced the complexity of decision-making during the same period: the increased availability of investment advice in the workplace from both employers and the mutual-fund companies with which they contract. Automatic enrollment and explicit investment advice have grown together, so it is not easy to sort out the individual influences on behavior.

---

[40] This was a study of the choices made by experienced environmental economists regarding whether to purchase carbon offsets for their air travel to a conference. There was no statistical difference between active choice, a carbon-offset default, and no-offset default.

[41] This is not much different than the case in which people defer to their doctor about some complicated medical issue about which they have no independent knowledge. Most observers would say this is rational if the patient has reason to believe that the doctor is competent.

Between 2013 and 2014, the percentage of firms with 401(k) plans offering online investment guidance grew from 56 percent to 69 percent; the percentage offering phone access to financial advisors rose from 35 percent to 53 percent; and the percentage offering third-party investment advice rose from 44 percent to 49 percent (Aon Hewitt 2015, 14). According to the consulting firm Callan LLC, in 2015, 36 percent of large firms offered one-on-one consultations while 42 percent did in 2017. In 2015, about 9 percent offered "financial wellness" programs coupled with online tools, and by 2017, 17 percent did (Tergesen 2018).[42] We conclude that both the implicit recommendation of automatic enrollment and, to some extent, increased explicit advice have decreased complexity costs.

Anchoring on the Default's Characteristics

Anchoring is different from the recommendation effect, in that people simply focus on an outcome (enrollment) or a number (contribution rate) because it is made salient in some way and not because they believe it is recommended by a trustworthy source. In almost all cases it will be difficult to distinguish between these two explanations, in part because anchoring itself is a symptom of deficient knowledge (if the agent knew what she wanted, the anchors would be irrelevant) and also because anchors are usually suggested or created by "official" sources (employers, benefits departments, etc.).

However, it would be possible to distinguish if there were no default enrollment involved in the study. Goda et al. (2014) conducted such a field experiment, which assessed the response of university employees to general retirement information and different projections of retirement income. Three parameters were varied in successive treatments: illustrative additional savings per pay period, hypothetical retirement age, and assumed annual rate of return during accumulation. All these were presented in as neutral a way as possible to avoid endorsement effects. Higher illustrative contribution amounts did result in additional savings, but they were not focused on the illustrative amounts and in fact were considerably less. Thus, anchoring did not appear to occur here. Strangely, if anchoring occurred by the focus on a higher hypothetical retirement age, it was associated with individuals contributing more, not less, to the retirement program. Finally, the variation of assumed annual rates of return had no

---

[42] These two studies are not directly comparable because they use a different sample of firms to arrive at the percentages.

statistically significant effect. Overall, this evidence does not support the existence of economically meaningful pure anchoring effects.

"Biased" Subset of Contribution Possibilities

Closely related to the anchoring explanation is the argument that individuals are prone to consider only a subset of contribution rates salient to them. Again, this is related to the "imperfection" of knowledge. Perfect neoclassical agents would consider the continuum of options, although thinking of a subset might seem normal to inclusively rational individuals.

This "consideration set" may be determined by a rounding heuristic (such as multiples of five) as well as other salient points such as the employer's full-match point (Choi et al. 2002, 94). If we add to this the presumed salience of the status quo (either zero contribution or the automatic enrollment contribution rate), we have a bounded consideration set. Because the status quo is disproportionately likely to appear in the consideration set, this may lead to a tendency to stick with the status quo (Choi 2015, 171). There is almost no evidence supporting this causal chain in the retirement-savings context. Furthermore, from a theoretical point of view, it does not tell us why, of all of the disproportionately represented options, the status quo is the most compelling rather than (say) the 5 percent option, another point very likely to appear in consideration sets.

Unawareness of Default Implementation

It is possible that individuals are not aware that they have a choice of retirement programs and therefore they stick with the default because they don't realize they can opt out (Brown et al. 2012). In other words, they do not realize that the default is simply a default. It is not clear whether any significant number of people fall in this category. What is clear is that this is simple ignorance rather than a bias and thus it can be remedied without recourse to manipulating the default.

Loss Aversion

At one time loss aversion was considered an accepted fact, but increasingly since the turn of the century doubts have been raised and the phenomenon is now seen as quite complex (Gal and Rucker 2018). Nevertheless, it is still often held responsible for the stickiness of the traditional default of nonenrollment in 401(k) savings plans (e.g., Thaler 2015b, 313–314).

The argument is based on the twin ideas that individuals consider the "safe" status quo of nonenrollment as their reference point and that they weight losses relative to that reference point more heavily than equal-sized gains. Thus, individuals will worry that participation in a retirement fund carries the risk of losses. And since losses count perhaps twice as much per dollar as gains, they are inclined to do nothing.[43]

Loss-aversion arguments tend to be weak. As we have argued in Chapters 4 and 6, there are serious conceptual and empirical problems with loss aversion and the related endowment effect. We have also expressed serious doubt that the asymmetrical treatment of gains and losses, an essential characteristic of loss avoidance, ought to be considered a bias from the perspective of inclusive rationality instead of a taste variable. In what follows, we ignore these points and apply other arguments to the retirement-default case. There are two fundamental issues. First, reference dependence does not necessarily give rise to asymmetric valuation of losses and gains at all, much less in the standard 2:1 ratio. Second, the reference point for gains and losses is not necessarily the status quo. Many states, both actual and counterfactual, can potentially serve as reference points, including an expected state (Higgins and Liberman 2018). When the reference point is higher than the status quo (for instance, if one's reference point contribution level is higher than the status quo or default contribution level), then the consequence of loss aversion is not to create stickiness of the status quo but to impel movement away from it because the status quo will be coded as a loss. We discuss each of these in turn because we want to go beyond simply fitting default patterns to the loss-aversion hypothesis (as is typical in the literature) toward a more detailed examination of the plausibility of the hypothesis itself.

Psychological research has shown that many reference points are not accompanied by a greater valuation of losses over gains. Increased sensitivity in the vicinity of the reference point can be associated with no valuational asymmetry or even with greater valuation of gains (Gal and Rucker 2018; Higgins and Liberman 2018). This may be the case when the reference point is what would have happened otherwise (a counterfactual state),[44] what a peer group is doing (social comparisons), or an

---

[43] On the other hand, if they perceive the gains to be more than twice as large as losses then loss aversion will not prevent them from enrolling. This is more likely to be the case the larger the period over which the retirement plan is evaluated.

[44] A person may feel disappointment, even if he gains relative to the status quo, if he could have chosen an alternative that turned out even better. Relative to the counterfactual gain, the actual outcome is seen as a loss.

all-or-nothing goal. In recent years expected states have also been considered as reference points, and this has created significant complications in determining the effect of loss aversion on behavior (O'Donoghue and Sprenger 2018).

The determination of the appropriate reference point is difficult. Reference points are not directly observable in the usual data that is available (Hack and Bieberstein 2015, 34–37). Often they are inferred from risky behavior under the *assumption* that loss aversion is the appropriate model. Thus, if the agent engages in risk-preferring behavior above a certain point and risk-averse behavior below it, the inflection point is assumed to be the reference point. Alternatively, survey or other experimental evidence might be used to more directly establish the appropriate reference point. In all of this, the evidence is mixed, but one conclusion is clear: the reference point is highly contextual (O'Donoghue and Sprenger 2018). And, we might add, it is not necessary that all agents in the same situation have the same reference point. For example, Baillon et al. (2017) found that about 30 percent of the subjects used a status quo reference point while 26 percent used an expectations-based reference.[45] Moreover, people might have multiple reference points simultaneously (Higgins and Liberman 2018, 527–528; O'Donoghue and Sprenger 2018).[46] The specification of the reference point is important because it defines the losses (and gains) toward which loss-averse individuals supposedly attach their asymmetric weighting, and thus it affects their behavior.

We are unaware of any direct evidence regarding the reference point specifically in the retirement-default case. The usual assumption is that it must be the status quo, and for the traditional default framing, that would be nonenrollment. This is by no means necessary or the only plausible assumption. Alternatively, someone's reference point might be the expectation of future enrollment. Those who believe that the time is not currently right but will be soon may fall in this group. Furthermore, naïve present-

---

[45] Another 30 percent used a MaxMin reference point. This means that in a comparison of two prospects, individuals assess the minimum outcome of each and choose the maximum of these two as their reference point. If MaxMin were used in the real world rather than in an experiment, the individual would have to forecast the minimum and the maximum, which would make MaxMin an expectations-based referent. The remaining subjects in the study used other reference points.

[46] It is also not at all clear that reference points found in one area also operate in other areas of decision-making (O'Donoghue and Sprenger 2018). Therefore, evidence of loss aversion from laboratory experiments or even field studies from, say, labor-market decisions may or may not be applicable to personal financial decisions.

biased individuals who procrastinate but believe they will enroll later may also fall in this group.[47] If expected enrollment is the reference point for gains and losses, then loss aversion *itself* does not work in the direction of inhibiting enrollment. One possibility is that the status quo is coded as a loss relative to a reasonably expected gain over a period of time. Applying typical assumptions about the behavior of loss-averse agents, the individual will be risk-preferring so long as the status quo is below the reference point. Loss aversion thus makes enrollment *more* likely in this case. We can also imagine someone with a moving reference point, which corresponds to the status quo for some period of time and *then* jumps to expected enrollment. Yet another possibility is that someone may have a *stochastic* reference point; perhaps the individual is not sure that he will enroll later, or the reference point might be either the loss if he enrolls or the gain if he enrolls. In these cases the equilibrium can get complicated (O'Donoghue and Sprenger 2018), but it is still the case that the individual will be more likely to enroll when the reference point is above the status quo.

Even if the status quo is a relevant reference point, it may not be the only one (Koop and Johnson 2012). Suppose, for example, an individual has two reference points: the status quo and the goal of providing for her retirement. The status quo is nonenrollment in a retirement plan. Thus, in accordance with loss aversion, she weights the probability of loss, should she enroll, more heavily than the equal probability of gain. This may inhibit enrollment. However, with respect to her retirement goal the status quo is already a loss or, at least, a nongain. The more confident she is that she will not lose (as she takes the longer-run perspective), the more the second reference point will come to dominate her decision. This reference point will encourage signing up as she will be risk-preferring in perceived losses.[48]

The scenarios discussed here are not intended as a definitive analysis of the decision-making in this area. Nevertheless, they are hard to dismiss because loss aversion is an underdetermined concept. It has numerous moving parts that must be assessed and calibrated. This accounts both for

---

[47] "Ordinarily people take the status-quo as the reference point ... It has been plausibly argued, however, that this assumption pertains only, or primarily, when people expect the status quo to be maintained" (Zamir 2014, 8).

[48] This example is based on a close analogy with investment managers who have been shown to consider both the status quo percent and a target performance rate in their decision-making. They incorporate the two referents in the way indicated in the example here (Sullivan and Kida 1995).

its flexibility and for the ability of researchers to protect it from falsification. It is relatively easy to attribute numerous nonstandard behaviors to loss aversion if the only standard is plausibility. Thus, we conclude that attributing default stickiness to loss aversion is unwarranted in view of the current state of the evidence.

Present Bias

Default effects can be either temporary or quasi-permanent. For illustration, consider Choi's (2004) study. Choi finds that enrollment under an opt-in default rises dramatically, from 10 percent at three months to about 50 percent over a period of eighteen to twenty-four months, and it continues to rise afterwards to 60 percent at thirty-six months and 65 percent at forty-eight months (Choi 2004). Obviously, there is a continuum of behavior here, but for simplicity, let us think in terms of two dichotomous types. The first type is individuals who delay for up to forty-eight months before eventually signing up for their retirement program. These are considered "procrastinators" because it is assumed by behavioral economists that the true preference of these individuals is to sign up *immediately.* The second type is those individuals who "never" sign up but would participate under auto-enrollment. (We say "never" in quotes because it's conceivable they would eventually sign up given enough time.) These individuals might be called "long-term passives," as they passively accept the default for an indefinite period of time. The supposed explanation for the behavior of both of these groups is present bias.

The evidence of present bias in this area usually results from fitting a model incorporating present bias to a data set in which some individuals do not enroll in a 401(k) program immediately or at all (Bernheim et al. 2015). An alternative explanation for their behavior, transactions costs in implementing the enrollment decision, can usually and correctly be dismissed as requiring preposterously high costs. And yet it is troubling to rely on fitting a model to data when direct evidence that present bias affects financial decisions or money flows is lacking, as we have argued in Chapter 6. The most recent and sophisticated empirical tests indicate that the evidence for present bias in decisions regarding money now or money later is weak (Augenblick et al. 2015).[49] Moreover, Bradford et al. (2017) conducted a wide-ranging study in which they investigated the connection

---

[49] "[I]n the domain of money we find virtually no evidence of present bias" (Augenblick 2015, 1071).

between retirement savings and present bias (as represented by the short-run discount factor β). The authors did not find any statistically significant relationship. They did, however, find a statistically significant relationship between the *long-run* discount factor (as represented by δ) and retirement savings. This suggests that individuals consider this decision as fundamentally one of sacrificing nearer-term consumption (say, a portion of one's next paycheck) for far-future consumption, and *not* one of immediate sacrifice – meaning that present bias is irrelevant in this context.[50] The focus on immediacy in the manifestation of present bias is supported by Balakrishnan et al. (2017), who find that present bias affects decisions where the front-end delay is zero and *not* where it is fourteen or twenty-eight days. (A front-end delay is the delay from the moment of decision until the earliest money payment.) When people make a decision about how much to contribute to a 401(k) plan, the decision takes effect only after a delay – usually one month. Because present bias applies only to *truly immediate* costs or rewards, contributions to 401(k) programs do not qualify. However, we should note that all of these studies have relied on the assumption of quasi-hyperbolic preferences, meaning the individual only has two rates of discount, one that applies to immediate costs and benefits and one that applies everywhere else. In Chapter 4, we have argued that actual discounting may follow a true hyperbolic pattern characterized by many different discount rates, and there is evidence to support this (Bleichrodt et al. 2016). If so, then we cannot rule out the possibility that some kind of present bias affects financial decisions even when the immediate present is not involved. The difficulty, as we have argued, is that the presence of multiple rates of discount makes it especially problematic to designate any one rate as the "correct" one. If we nevertheless designate some intermediate-valued rate of discount as correct, hyperbolic discounting actually implies *future* bias rather than present bias for decisions involving long enough time horizons. In any case, behavioral economists have focused near-exclusively on quasi-hyperbolic discounting as their model of present bias, and *that* model is largely irrelevant to the case of retirement savings for the reasons already discussed.

However, present bias may be relevant in this area not because of any effect on the valuation of money flows, but because of the cognitive

---

[50] Referring to retirement saving, Bradford et al. (2017) remark that "it often involves tradeoffs between strictly future periods (e.g., less net income in next month's paycheck compared to monthly income in retirement years hence), so these outcomes are expected to be influenced by δ more than by β" (p. 123).

(disutility) costs of decision-making.[51] Present bias is about *utility flows* (O'Donoghue and Rabin 2015, 273–274).[52] Employees face a complicated decision about whether and when to enroll as well as what savings contribution to make, as we have seen. The cognitive cost of considering options and reaching a decision is immediate, while the benefits of enrolling are in the future. Present-biased agents seek to put off the immediate cognitive burden: "Let me think about this tomorrow." If they are naïve about their propensity to delay in this manner, they will continue to do so in every period and thus fail to sign up, although they continue to believe that they will one day enroll. Strictly speaking, this mechanism is static – i.e., the same analysis applies for every possible present – and therefore an agent who procrastinates in the first period will procrastinate *forever*. We will analyze this possibility later. But naïve present bias cannot provide a *complete* explanation when the effect is temporary, i.e., when individuals do eventually sign up. So we must ask: *is the fact that many agents eventually opt in explained by their learning about their own bias and then reducing it, or by their learning more about the situation context (including their preferences and the investment options available)?* It would seem to be due to both because the processes are interrelated. When they cannot be distinguished, learning looks like procrastination.

Procrastination tends to be self-limiting as some agents come to realize that it is now or never. Unless they break out of their previous naïve framework, they will never sign up. Discarding this framework is motivated and constituted by perceiving that the entire future stream of benefits is at stake (Ainslie 1992). This is consistent with the more general view – and with our extension of Caplan's notion of rational irrationality (2000) – that the greater the perceived costs of "indulging" biases, the more individuals will become aware of and challenge them. When the individual himself reframes the retirement-savings problem, that spells the end of procrastination.

Moreover, as time passes knowledge can grow quite independently of present bias. It takes time to process bits of information into usable knowledge about what to do in one's own situation. People need time to

---

[51] The cost of coming to a decision must be distinguished from the cost of *implementing* a decision. The former is usually not in the main financial, although it could be if the individual is willing to pay an expert to make the decision for him. The latter is quite low here and does not play an important role in the default effects.

[52] We emphasize that none of the following discussion should be interpreted as suggesting that those who enroll will not go through with or procrastinate in their plans to save their decided-upon amount, at least not due to present bias.

contemplate what decision they want to make: to enroll or not, what investment vehicle to use, and what their contribution level should be. Part of this process occurs in consultation with others. As we have seen in Chapter 6, the erosion of present bias occurs when decisions are made in couples, in groups, or in consultation with others. This form of decision-making is not instantaneous. Decisions about retirement savings are likely to be made after a period of discussion and consultation.

Furthermore, the growth of knowledge reduces effective present bias even if the individual's propensity for such bias remains unchanged. Recall that present bias is the "overweighting" of decision-making costs. If decision-making costs were zero, there would be no effective present bias and hence no procrastination. If the individual's decision costs fall due to greater financial literacy or the provision of more (or less, but more concise) information, the overweighted cost of this factor will fall. If the individual gains better financial knowledge about the likely returns over a long period of time from retirement savings (e.g., learning about the "magic of compound interest"), then their perceived benefits from decision-making will rise, and so there will be less procrastination.

Now let us turn to the case of "permanent" passive defaulting. This case is particularly difficult to explain by procrastination because *it is difficult to distinguish the effect of the overweighting factor from the disutility of the decision itself.* The latter is a subjective magnitude and we are not aware of any attempt to measure it directly. If the complexity of the decision perceived by the individual is great enough, the disutility will be large without overweighting. Therefore the individual will not make the decision to enroll. This could last quite a while until there is some exogenous change. It may look like procrastination in the sense of a present-bias effect, but it need not be. Merging these two effects into one and calling it "procrastination" is not warranted by the evidence.

Regardless of the position one takes on these issues, to the extent that defaults are treated as recommendations from trusted sources they reduce complexity costs by increasing the availability of a knowledge surrogate, as we have discussed. Because of their one-size-fits-all nature, defaults are not perfect substitutes for the individual's own knowledge and personalized optimization, but they may be perceived as good enough by agents who perceive high decision-making costs. Like the temporary procrastinators, the long-term passives can be expected to be reduced in number by the recommendation effect of automatic enrollment. But there is nothing particularly "behavioral" going on here – or at least no more so than at any other time when an individual acts on a specialist's advice. The advice in the 401(k) case is communicated in a novel way, but advice it is.

In short, endogenous changes in agents' framing of the costs of their own behavior can dissolve procrastination. This is an aspect of counteractive self-control. The growth of knowledge or the provision of a knowledge surrogate (recommendation, endorsement, advice) can also reduce effective present bias and thus reduce or eliminate procrastination. The long-term persistence of default effects theoretically can be the joint consequence of present-bias overweighting *and* the unobserved disutility of decision-making. However, behavioralists have not sorted out the degree to which overweighting (a putative bias) versus the mere cost of deciding the best course of action (not a bias) is responsible for default stickiness.

Overview of Bias Explanations

Our review of the various explanations of the stickiness of the traditional nonenrollment default has shown that proffered explanations based on cognitive bias are either implausible or lack adequate supporting evidence. Furthermore, even if we were to grant these explanations credence, most of them would not result in default stickiness in the absence of knowledge deficiencies. The recommendation effect of defaults greatly reduces the complexity of decision-making either directly or indirectly, thereby making it easier for some agents to optimize while encouraging others to default deliberately.

Anchoring on the default's characteristics is difficult to distinguish from inadequate knowledge and the recommendation effect, but to the extent that we can, it does not seem operative. Biases in the consideration set, even if they exist, do not necessarily point in the direction of status quo stickiness. Unawareness of default implementation is not a bias and is subject to elimination through greater information. In addition to having little empirical support, these three explanations are only rarely cited by behavioral economists as explanations for retirement-savings behavior.

Loss aversion, although more frequently cited by behavioral economists in this area, is not an adequate explanation because we do not know the appropriate reference point and whether valuation around that point really is greater for losses than gains. It is also possible for loss aversion to encourage, rather than discourage, the decision to enroll in this case. Finally, any impact of present bias – the most frequently cited explanation among behavioral economists for the stickiness of retirement-savings defaults – will tend to decline as the complexity of decision-making is reduced, inasmuch as present bias does not affect the willingness to save (i.e., financial flows) but the willingness to make decisions (utility flows).

Overall, the success of automatic enrollment in increasing the number of 401(k) participants is likely not primarily due to the overcoming of cognitive biases. It is more likely due to the direct or indirect reduction of knowledge deficiencies through implicit advice (or "information leakage") from the auto-enrollment default and increased provision of information by employers. To the extent that supposed biases are indeed involved, the channel seems to be *through* the reduction in decision costs that comes with reduced complexity of decision-making.

GENERAL WELFARE EFFECTS

How does a shift to automatic enrollment affect welfare? The most important factor to keep in mind is that most behavioral explanations for the stickiness of defaults are not adequately supported by the evidence. We have emphasized the effect of defaults on the knowledge base of individuals. With the exceptions noted below, the mechanism or channel of effects is inclusively rational. Therefore most of our analysis of welfare will focus on how the complexity of the decision problem is altered by automatic enrollment. We divide our discussion into four basic cases corresponding to different types of agents affected by automatic enrollment. They are: learners, deliberate defaulters, marginal optimizers, and passive (behavioral) defaulters. We do not claim that these groups are mutually exclusive, as there may be some overlap among them. We introduce them as useful types for categorizing the potential effects of adopting automatic enrollment.

Learners

This consists of two subgroups, both of which include individuals who would have delayed enrollment under the traditional rule. First, there are *bias learners*, i.e., those whose learning under the traditional rule is primarily about their own tendency to procrastinate and then reframing their decision. Second, there are *context learners*, i.e., those whose learning under the traditional rule is primarily about their preferences and investment options. The bias learners likely gain from accelerated enrollment, insofar as they would likely have enrolled earlier if they fully understood their biases to begin with. The context learners might gain, but they also could lose if acceleration is not optimal, that is, if they have immediate financial needs that warrant a delay in participating or participation at a significantly different rate. There may of course be some overlap between these groups. In both groups, learning would seem to be cut off by automatic enrollment.

Deliberate Defaulters

This group consists of people who are essentially pure advice-takers. They use the implicit recommendation provided by automatic enrollment as a surrogate for particular knowledge of what is best for them. Although their choices are not perfectly optimized to their circumstances, their behavior is nevertheless inclusively rational under the circumstances of a complex decision. They conform to the default because they explicitly defer to those whom they believe are better informed. Whether they are better off depends on the relative appropriateness of the implicit advice of enrollment compared with the implicit advice under the previous frame (presumably, nonenrollment).

Marginal Optimizers

The willingness of individuals to accept the implicit advice of the default as a surrogate for personal knowledge is not unlimited, nor is it completely exogenous. Among other things, it may depend on the specifics of the advice. For example, if the automatic-enrollment contribution rate were 15 percent, many who deliberately defaulted at a 3 percent rate would balk and opt out. They might now find it in their interest to optimize – choosing some contribution rate less than 15 percent – because the opportunity cost of not deciding has risen. For some, even at 3 percent, the difference between their guessed-at optimum and the default might also be large and thus induce them to optimize. If it were mainly present bias that prevented them from optimizing previously under an opt-in default, then this would be an improvement.[53] However, note that in this category of

---

[53] To the extent that present bias is normatively irrelevant, then individuals overweight the costs of decision-making. If this overweighting is solely responsible for their not optimizing, then the effective decision costs under opt-in are illusory from the social perspective. They were not making an economically appropriate decision to balance the costs and

effects, the welfare gain is produced by an inferior, not superior, default.[54] These individuals are motivated to optimize precisely because of the *wrongness* of the default.

On the other hand, there may be some who *would* have optimized under the opt-in default but who now choose not to optimize because the auto-default is close enough to their guessed-at optimum contribution level. For instance, they might have opted in at a contribution level of 5 percent under the traditional rule, but upon seeing a 4.5 percent contribution under auto-enrollment, they accept the default rather than optimize. This case is ambiguous with regard to welfare. They certainly save on decision-making costs, but they also run the risk of a less appropriate decision. It is difficult, even for the individuals involved, to say which consequence predominates.

Passive Defaulters

Although there is much talk about passive agents, there is little discussion of what constitutes their "passivity." There seem to be three different kinds of passive agents: the genuinely indifferent, those who have no preferences (incomplete preferences), and those who are still overwhelmed by the complexity of the decision despite the knowledge effects of auto-enrollment. Empirically, it is difficult to distinguish among these. It can also be difficult to distinguish empirically between deliberate defaulters and passive defaulters. How much knowledge they have and to what extent their conformity with the default is conscious or implicit are obviously critical to a determination.

Since it is passive defaulters who are of primary interest to behavioral economists, let us suppose that we can distinguish this group. Are they better off because of automatic enrollment? The first two kinds of passives are neither better nor worse off provided we adhere to a subjective theory of welfare. Whether the third category is better off depends on how well default enrollment, including its associated contribution level, matches up

---

benefits of coming to a 401(k) decision. They "should" have been optimizing. On the other hand, if the individuals under opt-in were not present-biased, then they made an appropriate cost–benefit calculation not to optimize. In this case under auto-enrollment they are induced to optimize by the greater inappropriateness of the default and so they are worse off.

[54] Carroll et al. (2009) argue that with sophisticated and highly time-inconsistent (present-biased) employees, the optimal policy is to set an extreme default contribution rate to induce optimizing. See also Choi et al. (2003) and Samuelson and Zeckhauser (1988).

with employees' unobserved true preferences. Some individuals will be better off and others worse off relative to this standard.[55] The more heterogeneous the optimal savings preferences, the greater the probability that auto-enrollment will create mismatches. "Required" active choice might be the superior regime in this case (Choi et al. 2009, 1672).

Summary of Welfare Effects

We have discussed four categories of agents and how they are affected by automatic enrollment. Among *learners*, it is plausible that those who take time to learn about their biases and then debias themselves (the *bias learners*) would gain from the acceleration of their enrollment. However, those who are learning about their preferences and the options available (the *context learners*) could lose if earlier enrollment is not optimal given their situation and preferences. There is no simple way to distinguish these cases empirically.

Deliberate defaulters, those who use the default recommendation either as an element in their own knowledge of the options or as a surrogate for personal knowledge, are likely to gain. However, this is a rational effect – informational leakage from the default. Moreover, there may be some losers here: those for whom the new default's implied recommendation is worse than the old default's implied recommendation.

The group of behavioral or *passive defaulters* may or may not gain overall. It will depend on whether they have "true preferences" at all, as well as whether the default contribution rate is too high or too low. If the default contribution level is closer than nonenrollment to their true preferences (if they have them), they are likely to gain. This is the group that has received the most attention from behavioral paternalists.

Among *marginal optimizers*, those who are induced to optimize are probably better off, although they do lose from having to incur decision-making costs, while those who are induced to stop optimizing are probably worse off, although they do gain from avoiding decision-making costs. Note that the benefits for the induced optimizers depend on a rational response to a significantly *inappropriate* default.

Therefore, the only groups that unambiguously gain through a behavioral mechanism or channel are pure bias learners,[56] and passive defaulters

---

[55] Are people better off if they do not know they are? It is hard to argue that this is the case while maintaining a subjectivist welfare standard.

[56] That is, their learning is about their biases and not simply about the options available and whether they are desirable or not.

who have true preferences consistent with enrollment at more or less the default rate. Neither group is easily identified empirically for the reasons we have discussed. Thus the *behavioral* benefits of automatic enrollment, under the caveats discussed earlier, are limited to a much smaller subset of those affected than is ordinarily assumed.

Distributional Considerations

The previous analysis has shown that certain types of decision-makers may gain and others lose under automatic enrollment. Furthermore, the gains in most cases are not through behavioral mechanisms but through inclusively or even standardly rational mechanisms. In this section we parse the distributional effects along some different dimensions.

Recent empirical work has shown that low-income employees are more susceptible to the influence of defaults than high-income employees. They are much less likely to opt out of the default contribution rate. Beshears et al. (2016) sought to answer the question of whether they are less likely to opt out because the default is more consistent with their preferences than for the higher-income group, or because – for some reason – defaults are stickier for them. The authors conclude that the defaults are stickier for the low-income group.

What they found has important distributional implications. First, the difference between income groups in their probability of staying at the default, despite having a different target contribution rate, is 7.1 percentage points two years after hire.[57] Thus, the low-income group is more likely to stay at an "inappropriate" contribution rate than the high-income group. Second, this is true *even though* the low-income individuals' target rate is much more strongly influenced by the default than is that of the higher-income group.[58] Third, the differential stickiness of

---

[57] A "target contribution rate" is the rate that individuals would eventually end up with if given an indefinitely long period of time to switch. It is not, *strictly speaking*, their "optimal" rate because some individuals might never switch; even with unlimited time, the benefits of opting out in terms of reaching one's optimum may not be worth the costs of opting out. The target contribution rate is estimated on the basis of those who do in fact opt out, their characteristics, and their constant probability of opting out.

[58] Target rates can be influenced by the default for reasons explained in the previous note. At one of the companies studied, when the default changed, the fraction of the low-income group with the old default fell by 14 percentage points more than for the high-income group; the fraction with the new default was higher by 21 percentage points.

the default is seen at every level of the target rate, whether below or above the default.[59] We conclude from this data that the error-generating feature of defaults is likely to be greater for lower-income groups than for higher.

Other things equal, when employers are matching the contributions of employees, automatic enrollment will increase total compensation costs to employers because of the additional enrollees. In the absence of increased employee productivity, employers will therefore need to make compensating adjustments. They have used two methods. First, firms with auto-enrollment have lower matching rates, even after controlling for other relevant factors (Butrica and Karamcheva 2015a, 20). Their match rate is 8.2 percentage points lower (or 12 percent of the average) than for plans with opt-in enrollment. The *maximum* match rate is also 0.38 percentage points lower for opt-out plans than for opt-in plans (or 11 percent of the average).[60] Second, firms with automatic enrollment on average have default employee contribution rates (which tend to be sticky) that do not take advantage of the full employer match (Butrica and Karamcheva 2015a, 12). Together, these two methods of adjustment keep the aggregate costs to employers constant (Butrica and Karamcheva 2015a, 2012).[61] This must mean that the total employer retirement contribution is redistributed, rather than increased, as a consequence of automatic enrollment itself. Although some employees will receive more compensation by taking greater advantage of matching contributions,

---

[59] Beshears et al. (2016) say that this behavior is consistent with anchoring but also consistent with other explanations. Our interpretation is that it is unlikely to be a case of pure anchoring because the defaults are not perceived as being set arbitrarily or randomly; they are deliberately set by employers. In addition, since low-income groups have lower levels of financial literacy (Tang and Lachance 2012), they would seem to be more susceptible to the implicit advice of defaults. Two of the seven possible explanations – among which Beshears et al. cannot distinguish – are consistent with our emphasis on limited knowledge and recommendation effects. See the summary of their paper, which was presented at the Joint Meeting of the Retirement Research Consortium on August 6–7, 2015 (Beshears et al. 2015, 5).

[60] The match rate is the percentage of each dollar of employee contributions that is matched by the employer, e.g., 50 percent. The match ceiling is the limit on employee contributions as a percentage of total salary that will be matched (e.g., contributions matched up to 6 percent of salary). The maximum match rate is determined by the match rate and the match ceiling. It is computed as (match rate · match ceiling)/100. Thus, if the match rate is 50 percent and the match ceiling 6 percent, the maximum match rate is 3 percent (Butrica and Karamcheva 2015a, 7).

[61] It is also possible that overall wages or other forms of compensation or their rate of increase would adjust downward. At present there is no evidence of this.

others will lose because of the lower matching rates and lower default contribution levels.[62]

Unintended Consequences: Offsetting Behavior

The default contribution rate under automatic enrollment is sometimes set lower than the rate at which those who voluntarily enroll contribute. Among the reasons for this is to discourage certain people from opting out of enrollment altogether because the default savings rate is too high. Therefore, it can happen that although more people participate under automatic enrollment, the average amount saved can be lower than under the traditional opt-in or active choice.[63] This corresponds to the behavior of the marginal optimizers we described earlier, who may choose not to optimize because the default contribution rate is close enough to their guessed-at optimum. In the first nationally representative survey of older employees (ages 55–69), Butrica and Karamcheva (2015b) conclude that those auto-enrolled have lower total contribution rates by 1.6 percentage points, even allowing for employer contributions, than voluntarily enrolled employees. This difference is more pronounced at the bottom earnings quintile (3 percentage points) and second earnings quintile (almost 3 percentage points).

Furthermore, automatic enrollment is negatively associated with the probability of continuing to make contributions over time. Those still enrolled in their plans are 17 percentage points less likely to continue making any contributions at all than those voluntarily enrolled (Burke et al. 2015, 24, 27). In other words, they stay enrolled but reduce their contributions to zero.

Perhaps the most dramatic unintended consequence of automatic enrollment is the large offsetting asset decumulation by those automatically enrolled in the US Army's civilian Thrift Savings Plan (Beshears et al.

---

[62] If the total compensation of some workers is increased at the expense of others, employers might adjust *relative* wages or other forms of relative compensation to offset this. To our knowledge this has not been researched.

[63] "401(k) participants' average savings rates have fallen in recent years. Among plans Aon Hewitt administers, the average contribution rate declined to 7.3 percent in 2010, from 7.9 percent in 2006. The Vanguard Group Inc. says average contribution rates at its plans fell to 6.8 percent in 2010, from 7.3 percent in 2006. Over the same period, the average for Fidelity Investments' defined contribution plans decreased to 8.2 percent, from 8.9 percent. Vanguard estimates about half the decline 'was attributable to increased adoption of auto-enrollment'" (Tergesen 2011).

2017). After four years, the effect of automatic enrollment on increased net wealth was offset by an average of 48 percent due to increased debt (including auto loans but not mortgages).[64] In other words, while they increased their wealth in retirement savings, they simultaneously decreased their wealth by taking on more debt. Furthermore, increased debt accounted for more than 100 percent of the increased contributions by employees alone; that is, the net increase in wealth induced by automatic enrollment was entirely attributable to the matching contributions by employers induced by automatic enrollment (Beshears et al. 2017, 21).[65] To the extent that additional debt offsets the gains from increased retirement savings, it weakens the case in favor of default enrollment.[66] Another study (Beshears et al. 2018) of a large firm

---

[64] This percentage and those to follow are calculated from entries in tables 2 and 4 of Beshears et al. (2017). If we look at debt exclusive of both auto loans and mortgages (which Beshears et al. [2017] call D1), increased debt offset increased net wealth by 16 percent, or 35 percent of the increase in employee contributions. However, the increase in D1 is not statistically significant, whereas the increase in debt including auto loans (D2) is.

[65] Our presentation here is substantially less optimistic than Beshears et al.'s (2017) presentation of their own results, so we ought to address the difference. Although Beshears et al. use three different measures of debt, they focus their discussion on debt exclusive of both auto loans and mortgages (D1; see previous note). The increase in this measure of debt did not achieve statistical significance, and the authors highlight this result. We, however, think debt including auto loans (D2) is the better measure. The essence of the argument for favoring D1 over D2 is that a car is also an asset; to a first approximation, buying a car with a loan means acquiring an asset and a liability with equal value, so they cancel out. However, we prefer D2 for three reasons. First, a car is a mixture of consumption and investment, and the higher the rate of depreciation, the more consumption-like and less asset-like it becomes (as Beshears et al. admit). Second, in cases where employees would have purchased a car under either default rule, the car cannot be counted as an *increase* in assets resulting from the opt-out default. In such a case, if there is an observed increase in auto-loan debt, the employee must have (to some extent) increased their debt rather than reducing consumption in response to the new default. For example, they might have put a lower down payment on the car than they would have under the opt-in default. Third, and closely related to the last point, an increase in car-loan debt (and thus D2) does not necessarily correspond to an increase in car-buying (whether more employees buying cars or employees buying higher-valued cars). Because money is fungible, other forms of consumption can be financed by means of an auto loan. Expanding the size of one's car loan might simply be the cheapest or most convenient means of storing one's debt, irrespective of the purpose for which the added debt is incurred. Consequently, D1 and D2 are not clearly distinguishable.

[66] As Beshears et al. (2017, 1) put it, "[t]he implicit presumption among those adopting automatic enrollment has been that the incremental contributions are financed by decreased consumption. ... [T]he possibility that the incremental contributions are funded by other asset accounts or debt ... would work against the purpose of automatic enrollment." However, there is a possible argument that additional debt is not a genuine concern because such debt might well be paid out of future (preretirement) consumption

that introduced automatic enrollment in 2005 compared the behavior of individuals who enrolled in the retirement plan voluntarily with those who were enrolled automatically. Eight years after enrollment there was "leakage in the form of outstanding loans and withdrawals [from the plans] that are not rolled over into another qualified savings plan ... offsetting approximately 40% of the potential increase in savings from automatic enrollment" (p. 1). It may be tempting to add 40 percent and 48 percent and conclude that almost nine-tenths of the effects of automatic enrollment are offset. However, these studies are of different groups of people and we are not sure how the results generalize to the entire population. And yet the lesson is clear. Previous studies of the effects of automatic enrollment examined the choices of individuals narrowly, focusing solely on increases in enrollment and retirement savings. They did not account for what standard portfolio theory tells us is a decision on several margins. If people are eased into savings behavior that is not entirely the result of deliberate choice, they may compensate for that elsewhere.

Why do people engage in the kind of offsetting behaviors discussed here? We can only speculate, but one obvious answer is that they are being defaulted to behaviors that don't really match their underlying preferences. Support for this possibility can be found by looking at the consequences of automatic enrollment in a somewhat different setting. The State Universities Retirement System of Illinois offered employees a choice of three retirement plans, all of which would replace Social Security, and their decision (or lack of decision) was irrevocable (Brown et al. 2016). Clearly this is an extremely important set of options. If no decision were actively made, the individual would be automatically enrolled in the Traditional Plan – a nonportable defined-benefit pension plan. The study investigated, among other things, the frequency with which people regretted either their choices or what they had allowed to be chosen by default. Holding the plan constant, people were

---

and thus not necessarily offset gains in terms of retirement savings. We have not found any behavioral paternalists making this argument, but we anticipate and reply to it here. First, while it is certainly possible for debt to be funded by reduction in future (but preretirement) consumption, it is also possible for debt to be maintained or rolled over long enough to affect retirement. Second, maintaining debt for any period of time means paying interest, and the interest paid must to some extent offset the gains from appreciation of retirement savings. If the interest rate on debt is greater than the growth rate on savings, as is often the case, then interest payments on debt will *more* than offset gains on the same amount of money in retirement savings. Third, even if debt and interest are paid off before retirement, the funds used to do so will not necessarily come out of future (preretirement) consumption; they may come out of other accounts or assets that would otherwise have lasted into retirement.

more likely to regret an option if they were defaulted into it than if they had actively chosen it. Specifically, 59 percent of those who had been automatically enrolled in the Traditional Plan regretted it, while 43 percent of those who had actively chosen the Traditional Plan regretted the choice. When the question was phrased in terms of "strong regret," 17 percent of those automatically enrolled regretted it while 7 percent of active choosers regretted their decision. Admittedly, stated regret is not an ideal indication of welfare loss. But the fact that this study held constant the plan involved means that the *differences in regret* are not due to something specific to the plan itself, but more likely to the mismatch between the plan and the preferences of the individuals created by the default system.

THE ROLE OF GOVERNMENT

The role of government in this area has been indirect. Automatic enrollment became easier after the passage of the Pension Protection Act in 2006, which created safe harbors so that individuals defaulted into particular investment vehicles would be highly unlikely to sue their employers. In itself, this does not tell us why employers began to shift to automatic-enrollment defaults. But one possibility was that it enabled them to increase the benefits of highly paid employees without violating nondiscrimination provisions of the Internal Revenue Code. The Internal Revenue Code defines maximum contribution rates for highly compensated employees as a function of the contribution rate of lower-paid employees. By gathering up lower-paid employees in the 401(k) retirement plan, automatic enrollment created the opportunity to offer higher benefits to the highly paid (Butrica and Karamcheva 2012, 2–3).[67] Burke et al. (2015, 2) cite national survey data that 20 percent of plan sponsors said improving nondiscrimination test results was their *primary* reason for adopting automatic enrollment. There is also little doubt that since most employees do want to be enrolled eventually, automatic enrollment provides a small convenience to them. Whether employers have been motivated by beneficence or the ability to attract employees or some other consideration is not of critical importance, although most economists will be rightly skeptical that the transition to automatic enrollment occurred because of the firms' desire to use behavioral tools to accomplish "social welfare goals."

---

[67] This has been noted in advice blogs for small businesses. See Mirpuri (2016).

Automatic enrollment is not mandated in the United States at this time. This is good. The benefits of automatic enrollment and of the default rate of savings vary with the conditions of particular firms and the characteristics of their employees. In fact, Choi et al. (2009) argue that when preferences are heterogeneous, active choice is optimal. In effect, this means that employers should simply ask employees what their preferences are as a requirement for starting the job. A similar conclusion is drawn by Carlin et al. (2013), who emphasize the welfare-reducing aspect of defaults when preferences are heterogeneous, planners' knowledge of them is deficient, and the economic stakes are high. It is also important to recognize that it is not simply the welfare of employees that is at stake. The employer–employee relationship is two-sided. As we have said, the total compensation offered to employees will not necessarily be increased by automatic enrollment. Legal requirements in this area will create rigidities inconsistent with optimal distribution of compensation in accordance with productive contributions, employee needs, and profit maximization.

CONCLUSIONS

Behavioral economists overreach when they confidently attribute the increase in 401(k) participation after automatic enrollment to countering biases by creating sticky defaults that people passively accept. Much of the increase in participation is likely attributable to improved information and the recommendation effect of the new default. Biases such as anchoring, limited salient options, and loss aversion do not seem as plausible in this context. While present bias may be operative with regard to decision-making costs, its importance is diminished as decision complexity is reduced. Since automatic enrollment improves the information position of agents, it reduces the complexity of decision-making. Thus, even if employees overweight initial decision costs due to present bias, the impact of this bias is substantially reduced due to the fall in decision costs.

Policy-oriented behavioralists are also mistaken in suggesting that the welfare effects of automatic enrollment are unambiguously positive to all groups. There are heterogeneous effects, especially in the class of former optimizers and, in general, when the knowledge of the planners is poor. There are distributional effects within the category of retirement benefits. In addition, there are also a number of substantial unintended consequences, including increased consumer debt and early withdrawal of retirement savings. These have been ignored in previous research because of the narrow focus on 401(k) activity.

Behavioralists are also likely mistaken in claiming that the greater use of automatic enrollment observed in recent years is a consequence of private paternalism. The appearance of such may be the result of an excessively loose or vague concept of paternalism – a topic we will address directly in Chapter 10. Employers in the United States are not currently required to provide an automatic-enrollment default. They are still maximizing profits and engaging in mutually advantageous bargains with their employees. How likely is it that they have suddenly become benevolent paternalists under the influence of behavioral economics?

Finally, we have to wonder why so much attention has been focused on automatic enrollment versus other options. Given the evidence that information and recommendation effects play a significant role in explaining default stickiness, why not advocate explicitly providing the information and recommendations in question?[68] Such messages could be provided in the presence of either the traditional default or active choice. Changing the default rule seems a very indirect way of conveying messages that could be provided directly, especially since implicit messages can easily be misunderstood. We surmise that the focus on automatic enrollment derives from the presence of other (or additional) motives – specifically, the desire to increase retirement savings *irrespective* of whether that is what any particular individual truly wants.

---

[68] Behavioral paternalists often advocate providing information in other contexts, so it is odd that so little attention is given to information here. We address the question of whether providing information is genuinely paternalistic in Chapter 10.

8

The Political Economy of
Paternalist Policymaking*

Politics. *n*. A strife of interests masquerading as a contest of principles. The conduct of public affairs for private advantage.

    —Ambrose Bierce, *The Devil's Dictionary*

[T]he typical citizen drops down to a lower level of mental performance as soon as he enters the political field. He argues and analyzes in a way he would readily recognize as infantile within the sphere of his real interests. He becomes a primitive again.

    —Joseph Schumpeter, *Capitalism, Socialism, and Democracy*

In Chapters 6 and 7, we argued that policymakers do not and most likely cannot possess the knowledge needed to craft paternalistic policies that reliably improve human welfare. Nevertheless, real-world policymakers face tremendous pressure to take action, to legislate, to attempt to solve problems even in imperfect ways. The question, then, is what kind of paternalistic policies we can reasonably expect policymakers to create.

Camerer and his coauthors say that their strategy of "asymmetric paternalism" offers "a careful, cautious, and disciplined approach" (2003, 1212) to crafting paternalistic policies. Zamir (2014) exemplifies the behavioral paternalists' optimism about the political process:

Policymakers weigh the options in a more detached and calm manner, based on objective, general statistics. The various inputs to the legislative, administrative, and judicial processes, coupled with the decision-makers' cumulative experience, are likely to result in a sensible assessment of the relevant factors.

    (Zamir 2014, 222–223)

---

* Portions of this chapter, particularly in the section "Public-Choice Paternalism in Practice," were adapted from Rizzo and Whitman (2009b).

Yet policymakers' lack of truly *relevant* knowledge guarantees that the paternalists' vision of well-informed and cautious policymaking is literally impossible. In the rough-and-ready world of practical politics, policy is shaped in a maelstrom of idealism, activism, ignorance, time constraints, power struggles, and special-interest pressures. It would be genuinely shocking for real-world policies to resemble those imagined by hopeful academics.

Behavioral economists have provided reasons to believe individual behavior is not always optimal, and is sometimes deeply flawed. We have argued in earlier chapters that they have overstated the extent of such flaws, and understated the extent of self-correction; nevertheless, it's reasonable to believe some flaws persist. So, if we simply compared *imperfect* private decision-makers to *perfect* public decision-makers, the debate would be over: we would have to approve of state paternalism. But in so doing, we would commit what Harold Demsetz dubbed "the nirvana fallacy," in which any discrepancy between "the ideal and the real" is deemed sufficient to justify government intervention (1969, 1). The problem, of course, is that however bad the status quo may be, the intervention could be worse. A fair accounting demands that we consider the possibility of government failure.

The reader may notice many of the arguments in this chapter apply not only to paternalist policymaking, but to policymaking in general. Thus, they represent a general reason to resist legislation and regulation whether it is paternalist or not. This is true, with two caveats. First, the government-failure arguments we present here do not provide a *conclusive* reason to oppose all policymaking, but rather a justification for downgrading the expected benefits of any given policy. Even so, the expected benefits might still be great enough to justify the costs. Second, we argue that paternalistic policies are particularly vulnerable to the dysfunctional processes identified by the government-failure literature. The primary reason is that the subject matter of paternalism lends itself to moralistic attitudes and prejudices that reinforce some of the worst aspects of the political process.

RATIONAL AND IRRATIONAL MECHANISMS OF GOVERNMENT FAILURE

The field of public choice economics has developed a framework for understanding why state interventions so often do turn out worse. In this chapter, we apply that framework to paternalist policies. First, we show how policymakers who are fully rational (in the neoclassical sense) face incentives to adopt undesirable paternalist policies. Second, we show how policymakers who are cognitively biased, often in the same ways that regular individuals are alleged to be, may adopt even worse policies. In all of this, "policymakers" should be understood to include all people involved in the making of policy, including voters, legislators, bureaucrats, and judges.

Given that we have argued in previous chapters that many alleged biases may not be biases at all, that acting upon them might sometimes be rational, and that people have various means of controlling their biases when necessary, we need to justify why here – in the public policy context – we are seemingly changing our tune. What justifies our invocation of cognitive biases to explain government failure?

Our answer is twofold. First, we are to some degree offering an imma- nent critique: *if* and *to the extent that* people have genuine and significant cognitive biases, then we should expect those biases to affect public policy. Thus, any justification for paternalist policy that refers only to the biases of people in the private sector and not the public sector is incomplete at best. When genuine biases exist, they will operate in both arenas. Implementing effective paternalist policies – in light of all the relevant philosophical and empirical concerns – is an exceedingly difficult task. The presence of operative biases in the public sphere suggests that policymakers will not rise to that task. Behavioral paternalists could respond by arguing that cognitive biases are *not* really that severe and therefore should not have deleterious effects on policymaking – but to do so, they would also have to abandon much of their case for paternalist intervention in the first place.

Second, the public sector is rife with spillover effects, also known as externalities. Government policies automatically affect thousands of people who did not choose them. People making political choices – including voters, legislators, regulators, and judges – rarely, if ever, bear the full benefits and costs of their actions.

Why are externalities a problem? There are two distinct but related reasons. One reason is that any activity, rational or not, will naturally constitute greater cause for concern when the consequences spill over onto others. There is nothing inherently irrational about enjoying loud music late at night, but it still matters whether the music is played in a sound- proof room or blasted to the entire neighborhood. Likewise, it matters whether the effects of alleged biases fall primarily on the decision-makers or on the population as a whole. For instance, suppose someone is affected by optimism bias that makes them willing to take greater risks. On an individual level, as we've indicated in earlier chapters, it's not clear this

constitutes irrationality; it could reflect the individual's unusual preferences, or perhaps a positive mindset that is conducive to their overall life
success despite greater exposure to risk. But on a social level, if that
optimism results in policies that expose the whole body politic to greater
risk, that fact is worrisome whether the optimism is rational (for the
individual) or not. Others may not share the individual's risky preferences.

The other reason to be concerned about political externalities is that, as
economists have long recognized, externalities affect incentives. When
activities have external costs, people tend to do too much of them; when
they have external benefits, people tend to do too little of them. In the
context of cognitive biases, the presence of externalities implies that people
will tend to indulge their biases more than they would if they bore the full
consequences. The phenomenon of *rational irrationality* – first introduced
in Chapter 5 – implies that *biases are less likely to be corrected in the public
sphere*, because the incentives for their correction are usually far weaker.

Recall that rational irrationality, as we use the term, means that people
will tend to indulge their cognitive biases less when the personal cost is
high, and more when the personal cost is low. As we will see later in this
chapter, the personal cost of being *ill-informed* about politics is vanishingly
small for most people. The same goes for the personal cost of being
cognitively biased about politics. Suppose a voter chooses to train her mind
to avoid cognitive errors and biased thinking on political matters; what will
be her reward? In all likelihood, the same public policies will be enacted as
would have been enacted if she had done nothing to curb her irrational
tendencies. Given the low personal stakes, the odds are that she won't
bother trying. As Caplan argues, "Irrational beliefs probably play a role in
all human activities, but politics makes the 'short list' of areas where
irrationality is exceptionally pronounced" (2007, 115).

Ample evidence supports the claim that people indulge their irrationality more when it comes to politics. Somin (2016) offers a summary of the
evidence, which includes, among other things, the fact that "political
partisans not only reject new information casting doubt on their beliefs
but sometimes actually respond by believing in them more fervently"; that
"most citizens tend to discuss political issues only with those who agree
with them" rather than seeking out alternative viewpoints; that "committed
Republicans and Democrats both prefer media that align with their partisan proclivities"; that "those with the strongest ideological views and
relatively high cognitive ability tend to be the most biased in their assessments of empirical evidence"; that "people tend to reason more carefully
and logically when they know in advance that they will have to explain

their conclusions to well-informed people who do not necessarily share their preexisting views"; and most tellingly, that "even otherwise mathematically sophisticated people grossly misinterpret statistical data on political issues in ways that fit their preexisting ideological views" – an effect that, notably, does *not* occur with similar statistical data about nonpolitical matters (Somin 2016, 94). All of these behaviors make little sense from a pure truth-seeking perspective, but make perfect sense if people gain psychic satisfaction from holding certain views without particular concern for their truth.

Legislators, unlike voters, may cast decisive votes on a regular basis. That may give them a stronger incentive to control their cognitive biases than voters. But unbiased legislators with biased constituents have an incentive to behave as their constituents would like them to – that is, to reflect their biases. Viscusi and Gayer (2015) observe that cognitive biases are likely to affect policy both "because policymakers are also human and because public pressures incorporate these biases" (p. 977). As a result, cognitive biases can become embedded in our public institutions rather than, as we might hope, getting weeded out.

Furthermore, legislators and regulators still face strong externalities despite their choices more often being decisive. They face relatively low costs for making poor regulatory decisions that affect other people, whereas private citizens face relatively high costs for making poor personal decisions that mainly affect themselves. As a result, private decision-makers have stronger incentives than public decision-makers to acquire information and work to overcome their behavioral biases (Viscusi and Gayer 2015, 979). In other words, only a small portion of the bad consequences of an ill-chosen law or regulation are likely to fall on the legislator or regulator who supported it. Most effects fall on the public.

In addition, officeholders cannot expect to hold office forever. Eventually they will retire or be removed from office, making them less likely to experience long-run consequences from the policies they support. This would be true even if policymakers were perfectly rational, but irrationality amplifies the effect. Officeholders have little reason to curb their own irrational tendencies if the benefits of self-correction will largely fall on future officeholders rather than themselves.

Finally, we should emphasize that when we use the terms "bias" and "irrationality" to describe the behavior of political actors, we do so for simplicity (and consistency with the behavioral literature). Some of the biases in question might be totally reasonable from the standpoint of inclusive rationality – particularly once we allow for beliefs that serve functions other than truth-tracking. In the discussion of each so-called bias that could affect policymaking, we will endeavor to explain how it might be broadly rational given the goals and incentives of political actors. The fact that a given cognitive bias can be construed as individually rational does *not* imply that it will have socially beneficial consequences in the political process.

But before we show how cognitive biases can lead to government failure, we need to understand how even standardly rational decision-making can do so. That is the subject of the first half of this chapter.

RATIONAL IGNORANCE

The underlying condition that sets the stage for government failure is *rational ignorance* – the fact that most voters are ignorant about most matters of public policy most of the time, not because of any moral or intellectual failing on their part, but simply because the costs of becoming informed outweigh the expected benefits (Downs 1957, 149). In general, people have a strong incentive to become informed about decisions that directly affect their own lives – what clothes to wear, jobs to seek, romantic partnerships to pursue, and so on. In these areas, they can expect their own choices to be decisive. In politics, however, the incentive to become informed is far weaker. Becoming educated about policy issues might allow you to cast a better-informed vote – but inasmuch as a single vote is vanishingly unlikely to swing the outcome of an election, the benefit of that education is vanishingly small. So why bother?

Numerous studies affirm that voters often lack even the most rudimentary knowledge of political issues, such as being able to name the three branches of the federal government or identify which party currently controls Congress, to say nothing of complex matters of economic policy or foreign affairs. Somin (2016, 17–46) offers an excellent summary of the breadth and depth of voter ignorance.

There is every reason to expect people to be rationally ignorant about paternalist policies as well. As we have seen in the preceding chapters, the factual issues involved in crafting paternalist policies can be radically complex – so much so that even dedicated academics and policymakers cannot reasonably expect to grasp them all. Even from the experts, the best we can hope for is that they will have a sense of their own ignorance, perhaps from reading a book such as this one. But the typical voter cannot be expected to grasp even that much. Not only do most voters know little about these matters, *they don't know what they don't know.*

For example, the typical citizen has *some* knowledge about the relationship between diet, exercise, and obesity. Out of an interest in their personal health, they have an incentive to gain a minimal level of knowledge (though, to be sure, some fail to absorb even that much). Guthrie et al. (1999), for instance, report that "American consumers show fairly high levels of awareness of the relationship between their diets and serious chronic diseases such as heart disease and cancer" (p. 245), and over 95 percent "agree that being overweight is a health problem" (p. 250). Even casual attention to the news suffices to make them aware that the country faces an obesity "epidemic," which many experts seem to think deserves action. According to an AP-NORC survey, 75 percent of Americans believe "being overweight or obese is an extremely or very serious health problem for people in this country" (Tompson et al. 2012). But that, we suspect, is about the limit. Exceedingly few voters will have even considered – much less possess actual knowledge of – the distribution of the population over different levels of body mass index (BMI), the efficacy of various policies in affecting that distribution, the potential for interaction among various policies, and the potential disadvantages of those policies.

Fewer still will have grappled with the sticky *conceptual* and *analytical* issues relating to obesity control, many of which we have discussed earlier in this book: whether some individuals may have genuine preferences that would justify being obese, whether experts can ascertain people's "true" preferences to determine the optimal balance between health and enjoyment, and so forth. These are difficult matters to sort through, and for typical citizens, there is simply no gain from doing so. Some will remain agnostic. Others will simply defer to what they regard as expert opinion: there is an "ideal" range for BMI, too many people exceed it, end of story. And as we shall see later in this chapter, some will indulge their own biases without concern for the facts.

We could tell a similar story about every other realm of paternalist policy, from retirement savings to labor contracts: even the so-called experts don't know as much as they need to know to craft good policy (as demonstrated in Chapter 7), and the vast majority of voters know even less. This is the ever-present background radiation that pervades all policy-making, and paternalistic policy is no exception.

CONCENTRATED BENEFITS, DIFFUSE COSTS

How does rational ignorance affect the incentives of policymakers, particularly legislators? It enables them to pass legislation – on a wide range of topics, including paternalism – knowing that most of their constituents will be unaware they even did so. Even those voters who are relatively well informed will often have insufficient knowledge to determine whether the policy in question is well designed and effective; many will lack the tools to even think clearly about the matter.

Furthermore, political issues nearly always come bundled together in the form of candidates and platforms. As a result, voters cannot easily reward or punish their representatives for *specific* pieces of legislation, especially when they regard the issue in question as relatively unimportant compared with "big ticket" issues such as abortion, gay rights, immigration, and criminal justice. Hence, legislators can be confident that their choices about paternalistic policies – as in so many other areas – will go unnoticed and ignored by most voters.

But not everyone will remain ignorant. Special interests who are heavily affected by paternalistic laws will have a strong incentive to become informed and to organize themselves to influence them. Some of these interests may resist paternalistic laws. Tobacco companies and restaurants are obvious examples – although, as we shall see later, sometimes they may actually support paternalist laws for subtle reasons. Other interests clearly stand to benefit from paternalistic laws. Examples include financial-services firms that would benefit from laws pushing citizens to invest more of their income, and makers of products such as milk and bottled water that compete with disfavored products such as sugary sodas. These special interests will attempt to influence the legislative process in their favor via lobbying, research support, publicity, and campaign contributions.

The intense involvement of special interests combines with the ignorance and indifference of the rest of the population to create the well-known dynamic of *concentrated benefits and diffuse costs* (Olson 1965). That is, legislators have an incentive to support legislation that concentrates benefits on small but highly interested parties (i.e., special interests), while spreading the legislation's costs thinly over the rest of the population. By doing so, they gain the support of the former with little fear of punishment by the latter.

To be fair, gains to special interests sometimes align with gains to the general public, and in such cases we may observe concentrated benefits and diffuse *benefits*. If we suppose that citizens need to drink more water, for example, then the influence of bottled-water sellers could in theory push policy in the right direction. However, it is unlikely that even these "publicly aligned" special interests will care about all the detailed information relevant for the crafting of policy. They will be well informed about precisely those aspects of legislation that will tend to affect their bottom line – not the abstract question of how to weigh health against other values, or the reliability of the empirical research they use to support their position. These parties cannot be expected to support a "careful, cautious, and disciplined approach" to paternalist policymaking.

SELF-INTERESTED REGULATORS

Bureaucrats in regulatory agencies are not immune from the logic of concentrated benefits and diffuse costs. When it comes to regulatory rule-making, special interests have a far stronger incentive to become informed and organized than diffuse groups such as consumers and taxpayers – a point made by George Stigler (1971), among others. The goals of regulated industries will therefore tend to be advanced by the agencies that regulate them – a phenomenon that, in its most extreme version, has been dubbed "regulatory capture."

Bureaucrats' own self-interest can also influence regulatory outcomes. William Niskanen has argued that bureaucrats can be modeled as trying to maximize the budget (or discretionary budget) of their agencies (Niskanen 1971, 1991). However, Niskanen notes that the size of an agency's budget is actually a *proxy* for the real things that a bureaucrat may desire, such as "salary, perquisites of the office, public reputation, power, patronage, output of the bureau, ease of making changes and ease of managing the bureau" (Simard 2004, 407, quoting Niskanen 1971, 38); aside from the last two, Niskanen says, these goals are all correlated with larger budgets. Simply put, bureaucrats have poor incentives to advocate policies that shrink their power and influence, such as choosing *not* to intervene in places where they have the authority to do so, whereas they have strong incentives to do the opposite. Administrative agencies rarely have reason to admit that something is *not a problem* or *not enough of a problem to justify regulation*.

As an example of Niskanen's argument, Viscusi and Gayer offer their own work on the so-called energy-efficiency gap. The energy-efficiency gap refers to evidence that consumers don't make energy-efficient purchases – of durable appliances, for example – because they "underestimate the future cost savings stemming from an energy-efficient product compared to the weight they put on future savings in other market settings" (Viscusi and Gayer 2015, 982). Regulators have relied heavily upon this alleged bias to justify regulations. For instance, when the Department of Transportation performed a cost–benefit analysis of fuel-economy mandates for passenger cars and light trucks, they estimated benefits of $521 billion versus costs of just $177 billion. Of that $521 billion in benefits, $440 billion (85 percent) came from the correction of alleged consumer irrationality (Viscusi and Gayer 2015, 984). Without the supposed benefits from correcting irrationality, the regulations would not have passed the cost–benefit test. Yet Viscusi and Gayer offer a variety of other explanations for the energy-efficiency gap in consumer purchasing; for instance, it could represent "a rational response to high sunk costs and uncertainty over future conservation savings" (Viscusi and Gayer 2015, 982). They ultimately conclude that "[t]aken as a whole, the literature on the energy-efficiency gap does not provide strong, credible evidence of persistent consumer irrationality" (p. 984). So why did the Department of Transportation – and other agencies, including the Department of Energy and the Environmental Protection Agency (Gayer and Viscusi 2013, 257–262) – choose to rely on weak evidence for consumer irrationality in this area? Niskanen's theory suggests an answer: that doing so allowed the agencies to increase their power and influence, while equally or more plausible readings of the evidence did not.

BOOTLEGGERS AND BAPTISTS

Thus far, we have implicitly assumed that special interests have only a *financial* interest in the outcome of legislation (paternalistic or otherwise). But that is not necessarily so. Some special interests have ideological, religious, or moralistic motives for trying to affect policy. These "true believers" can play a key role in advancing legislation and regulation, especially when they work in concert with typical rent-seeking special interests. Bruce Yandle coined the phrase "Baptists and bootleggers" to describe the surprising coalitions that can form to support legislation:

Durable social regulation evolves when it is demanded by both of two distinctly different groups. "Baptists" point to the moral high ground and give vital and vocal endorsement of laudable public benefits promised by a desired regulation. Baptists flourish when their moral message forms a visible foundation for political action. "Bootleggers" are much less visible but no less vital. Bootleggers, who expect to profit from the very regulatory restrictions desired by Baptists, grease the political machinery with some of their expected proceeds. They are simply in it for the money.

(Yandle 1999, 5)

Although the Baptist–bootlegger dynamic can arise in many areas of legislation and regulation, Yandle's coinage was originally inspired by paternalistic laws – specifically, state laws banning the sale of alcohol on

Sundays. Such laws were supported by Baptists, who applauded any effort to restrict consumption of the demon drink, and bootleggers, who bene-fited from restricting competition from legal sellers of alcohol one day of the week (Yandle 1983, 13).

The Baptist–bootlegger dynamic continues in the present day. Consider the state and federal laws that maintain the "three tier" system of alcohol regula-tion, which guarantees liquor distributors (also known as wholesalers) a privileged role in the industry. By law, most alcohol in the United States *must* go through a distributor that is neither a producer nor a retailer. Distributors collect substantial markups while transferring liquor from the former to the latter. Publicly, the lobbying arm of the alcohol wholesaling industry defends its privileged position on grounds of preventing the sale of alcohol to minors, collecting taxes, and ensuring the safety of alcohol products. In the early 2000s, when intrastate shipping of wine directly from wineries to consumers threatened to weaken the three-tier system, alcohol wholesalers formed coali-tions with conservative organizations including "the National Association of Evangelicals, Phyllis Schlafly's Eagle Forum, Gary Bauer's American Values, and Concerned Women for America" to oppose it (Smith and Yandle 2014, loc. 1628–1629, citing Wiseman and Ellig 2007).

The original Baptists were, of course, *actual* Baptists – a religious group inclined to support paternalism for moral reasons. They exemplified the "old paternalism," which paid no particular regard to the preferences of the targeted parties. At the risk of stating the obvious, paternalism has a strong historical link to religion. The notion that maintaining one's personal health constitutes a moral obligation has a long pedigree in Christian thought (Rizzo 2005, 816–818) as well as other religious traditions. At least three of the seven deadly sins – lust, gluttony, and sloth – directly relate to matters of personal conduct that have often been targeted by paternalistic laws. Even when religion plays no explicit role in justifying paternalistic laws, its influence on popular attitudes about personal con-duct is not hard to discern.

Religious paternalism does not wield as much influence as it once did, but its place has been filled by public health advocacy. One prominent example is the Center for Science in the Public Interest (CSPI), which publishes studies on the health consequences of various foods and drinks – and also lobbies for laws to restrict these items, such as the Sugar-Sweetened Bever-age Tax Act (Center for Science in the Public Interest 2014). Unlike the original Baptists, CSPI has no religious agenda. But like the Baptists, it pays little attention to the question of what consumers really want. In that sense, the activists at CSPI and similar organizations are still old-school paternalists. They share many of the same implicit attitudes about personal health and related matters that animated religious paternalists in the past.

Here, we suggest that *new* paternalists – those drawing their support from behavioral economics – may also fill the Baptist role in Yandle's model of policymaking. Their arguments provide the justificatory "fig leaf" for policies that traditional special interests (i.e., bootleggers) support for more cynical reasons. We are not, however, suggesting that the new paternalists fill this role deliberately. As Smith and Yandle suggest, Baptist–bootlegger coalitions need not be deliberate, but can arise simply from the alignment of policy goals (2014, loc. 280).

The new paternalists have not entirely replaced the old, of course. Old-school paternalists still exert some influence on policy. We can therefore expect to see the emergence of "Baptist–Baptist–bootlegger" coalitions – that is, coalitions of both old paternalists (coming from a religious or moral perspective) and new paternalists (coming from a behavioral perspective), as well as the usual financially motivated special interests. Such tripartite coalitions will tend to make paternalistic policymaking especially durable – and inclined toward expansion – because the policies in question can rely on support from multiple sources.

In practice, the distinction between the "Second Baptists" (behavioral paternalists) and "First Baptists" (moralists) may be difficult to see. When activists champion policies to reduce consumption of unhealthy foods, and they point to such foods' adverse health consequences as justification, are they new or old paternalists? The only way to know would be to interrogate them as to why the health effects matter: "Do you believe that living a healthier lifestyle is *inherently* or morally better? Or do you believe that people who consume these goods are irrationally deviating from their *own* desire to live healthier lives?" Such questions are rarely posed, and even if they were, they might not elicit clear and honest responses. Old paternalists may wish to downplay their moralistic judgments and emphasize scientific-sounding reasons instead, leading them to adopt the language of behavioral economics. The more sophisticated behavioral paternalists thus lend credibility to the moralists who held paternalistic positions all along, thereby enhancing their influence in the political process.

PUBLIC CHOICE PATERNALISM IN PRACTICE

Yandle's original Baptist–bootlegger coalition is one example of how paternalistic legislation can be shaped by special-interest pressures (as well as moralistic thinking). Here, we present three more illustrative cases.

The Definition of Overweightness and Obesity[1]

Overweightness and obesity are typically defined in terms of body mass index, which is determined by the ratio of one's weight to one's squared height.[2] A BMI of at least 25 and less than 30 is classified as overweight, and a BMI of 30 or greater as obese. These thresholds derive from recommendations by the World Health Organization (WHO) and the National Institutes of Health (NIH), adopted in 1997. However, these definitions have little or no scientific basis. Both the WHO and NIH claim to have based them on evidence of higher mortality among people with BMI levels above these thresholds, but the research they cited did not substantiate this claim (Oliver 2006, 22). For example, the NIH report relied on the work of nutritionist Richard Troiano, even though his work did not support the claim of higher mortality for people exceeding these thresholds. Troiano found that increased mortality does not become evident "until well beyond a BMI level of 30," and that the difference in mortality does not become statistically significant until BMI reaches 40 or more (Oliver 2006, 23). Prior to 1997, the BMI thresholds for overweightness and obesity had been higher: overweightness required a BMI of at least 27.8 (for men) or 27.3 (for women), and obesity required a BMI of at least 31.1 (for men) or 32.3 (for women) (Kuczmarski 2007, 38). The new, lower thresholds increased the number of Americans classified as overweight or obese by more than 35 million overnight (Kuczmarski and Flegal 2000). What motivated the WHO and NIH to adopt the new recommendations? We cannot say for sure, but we can venture an educated guess. The WHO report, which heavily influenced the NIH's later decision to change the BMI thresholds, "was drafted and written under the auspices of the International Obesity Task Force (IOTF)," an organization "primarily funded by Hoffman-LaRoche (the maker of the weight-loss drug Xenical) and Abbott Laboratories (the maker of the weight-loss drug Meridia)" (Oliver 2006, 28–29). These companies stood to benefit from more people being qualified for coverage of their products by private and governmental health insurance. Yet the involvement of the WHO and NIH, both organizations associated with unselfish advocacy of public health, provided cover for the private interests involved. The process has every hallmark of a classic Baptist–bootlegger coalition, with public health advocates playing Baptist to the pharmaceutical sector's bootleggers.

---

[1] The analysis in this section first appeared in Rizzo and Whitman (2009b, 715–717), which also drew on the work of Oliver (2006, 23–29, 47–51).

[2] In metric units: kilograms and meters squared.

Regulation of Cigarettes and Vaping

The tobacco regulatory regime that arose from the Master Settlement Agreement (MSA), adopted in 1998 by state attorneys general and leading tobacco companies, is a case study in Baptist–bootlegger regulation. The MSA, which resolved a series of lawsuits against tobacco companies to reclaim smoking-related health expenditures under Medicaid, effectively cartelized the tobacco industry. At the center of the agreement was "the promised payment of $206 billion by the four participating cigarette companies to the participating states" (Adler et al. 2015, 32). The tobacco companies agreed to raise prices in order to fund the payments, thereby passing along their cost to consumers. In fact, it seems the benefits of cartelization *more* than compensated for the settlement cost, as US domestic tobacco revenues and profits actually rose relative to pre-MSA levels (Sloan et al. 2004).

This whole scheme would have collapsed if new entrants to the tobacco industry, unencumbered by the MSA, could have undercut the incumbents' higher prices and claimed market share. To forestall this possibility, "the MSA provided that for every percent of market share over 2 percent lost by a participating cigarette manufacturer, the manufacturer would be allowed to reduce its payments to the states by 3 percent, *unless each participating state enacted a statute to prevent price competition from non-participating manufacturers* (which each state did)" (Adler et al. 2015, 32, emphasis added). Thus, the MSA incentivized the states to protect the market position of the leading tobacco companies, while punishing smaller firms that were not even defendants in the lawsuits. With no fear of competition, these incumbents could raise prices with impunity – while sharing the profits with money-hungry state legislatures.

The bootlegger angle here is obvious: both tobacco companies and state governments stood to benefit financially. Yet the entire bargain was struck under the banner of public health. Anti-smoking advocates – the Baptists in this scenario – cheered the lawsuits that made the MSA possible. To be sure, the motivation was not purely paternalistic, as protection of both secondhand smokers and taxpayers' pocketbooks played a leading role. Still, the attitude that smoking is simply an unwise choice for the smokers themselves assuredly buttressed the case.

The underlying paternalist motivations for the MSA, and the tobacco regulations it fostered, have been exposed again by the more recent push to regulate or ban e-cigarettes, also known as "vaping" devices. Vaping involves the inhalation of nicotine-infused vapor. Because the vapor does not contain the combustion products that are the primary cause of health harms, it minimizes the risk posed by cigarette smoke. While e-cigarettes may not be entirely free of risk, there is good reason to believe they constitute a far superior alternative to regular cigarettes from a health perspective. A report from Public Health England, a division of the UK's Department of Health, found that "[w]hile vaping may not be 100% safe, most of the chemicals causing smoking-related disease are absent and the chemicals which are present pose limited danger," and concluded that e-cigarettes are "around 95% safer than smoking" (McNeill et al. 2015, 12).

Concrete evidence of health harms from e-cigarettes is scant and mostly speculative, focusing on the chemicals and nanoparticles in the vapor fluid (Raloff 2014). For example, one study found that e-cigarette vapor contains higher levels of formaldehyde than regular cigarettes (Jensen et al. 2015). But this occurs only when there is too little liquid or too much heat, conditions that also result in vapor with a highly unpleasant taste. Under conditions more like those typical for actual vaping, little or no formaldehyde could be detected (Morris and Khan 2016, 18). In general, toxic substances in e-cigarettes appear at "much lower levels than those in conventional cigarettes" (Britton and Bogdanovica 2014, 7).

Genuine health harms from e-cigarettes may yet be found.[3] But thus far, and to the best of our knowledge, no study has shown genuine and systematic health problems among direct users of e-cigarettes, to say nothing of secondhand users. Secondhand vaping is likely much safer than secondhand smoking because 85 percent of secondhand smoke from regular cigarettes is side-stream smoke – i.e., the smoke that comes from the tip of a lit cigarette – while e-cigarettes do not produce side-stream vapor (McNeill et al. 2015, 65). Thus, the only vapor released into the environment is the vapor exhaled by the user. In a technical review of the available data on the chemistry of electronic cigarettes, Igor Burstyn (2013, 1) concluded, "[e]xposures of

---

[3] Shortly before this book went to press, evidence of some genuine harms from vaping began to emerge – specifically, a lung condition affecting over 500 e-cigarette users, and killing at least seven, over a six-month period. The causes are not yet clear. However, early investigation suggests the condition is associated with vitamin E acetate, an additive included in black-market vaping capsules. The recency of the problem, despite vaping products having been on the market for over a decade, suggests the problem is not inherent to all vaping. Although we await further research, at the moment these cases do not substantially change our position. Problems of black-market quality control do not provide a case for further regulating the legal e-cigarette market; indeed, such regulations could drive more business to the black market. Furthermore, the resulting rush to regulate e-cigarettes in ways seemingly unrelated to the present crisis – such as banning flavored capsules despite zero evidence that flavors caused the condition – is illustrative of the problem of action bias in the public sphere, as discussed later in the chapter.

bystanders are likely to be orders of magnitude less [than those to direct users], and thus pose no apparent concern."

Yet the absence of evidence has not stopped anti-tobacco advocates and anti-smoking organizations from pushing for vaping regulations and bans immediately; the mere suggestion of possible harms is sufficient. To take just one example, the website for the United States' Action on Smoking & Health (ASH) presents a series of unknowns – not proven harms – related to e-cigarettes, and then concludes that "while the safety of e-cigs remains in doubt, they should be s [sic] treated like cigarettes" (Action on Smoking and Health n.d.). Other abstinence-focused organizations, such as the Campaign for Tobacco-Free Kids and the Truth Initiative, have also supported regulation of e-cigarettes in a manner similar to that of regular cigarettes.

In May 2015, a year after the US Food and Drug Administration proposed new regulations on e-cigarettes, a coalition of "31 health and medical groups including the American Academy of Pediatrics, the American Academy of Family Physicians and the American Heart Association" sent a letter to the president urging the federal government to finalize the regulations (Sifferlin 2015). Although the letter to the president emphasizes the health risks associated with e-cigarettes, no such risks are cited, aside from observing a recent increase in "calls to poison control centers involving exposures to e-cigarettes and liquid nicotine" (AAFP 2015). These are, of course, only calls – not verified injuries or deaths. The number of such calls was 3,783 in 2014, while the total number of calls to poison-control centers annually is more than 2 million (Safe Kids Worldwide 2013). As evidence for policy goes, this is weak sauce – and if better evidence had been available, the letter's authors surely would have cited it.

The primary strategy that "Baptists" use to support vaping regulation is fear, especially the fear that e-cigarettes could provide a gateway to regular cigarettes. Yet there is good evidence that e-cigarettes provide a substitute for regular cigarettes (Britton and Bogdanovica 2014, 24; Zhu 2017). Based on UK survey data, Public Health England finds that vaping "is not undermining, and may even be contributing to, the long-term decline in cigarette smoking" (McNeill et al. 2015, 9). Even the American Cancer Society has grudgingly admitted that e-cigarettes could prove useful for smokers who wish to quit and have rejected Food and Drug Administration (FDA)-approved methods (Boyles 2018). As weak as the evidence for direct health harms from e-cigarettes is, the evidence of harm to nonsmokers is essentially nonexistent. The case of e-cigarettes thus lays bare the paternalistic motivation behind tobacco regulation in general.

Now we turn to the bootleggers. Who stands to benefit financially from restriction of e-cigarettes? The obvious answer is the makers of regular cigarettes, which could lose revenues and cartel power if their consumers choose to vape instead of smoke. Not surprisingly, in 2014 Reynolds American Inc. "recommended to the Food and Drug Administration in a 119-page submission that the agency ban the use of vapor electronic cigarettes," while both Altria and Lorillard recommended somewhat less aggressive regulation (Craver 2014). The Reynolds brief naturally relied on public health arguments to support its position – despite the fact that the company had recently launched its own e-cigarette brand, Vuse.

Ultimately, the FDA chose not to ban e-cigarettes outright, except for children under 18. In new rules issued in May of 2016, the FDA required that all new tobacco products introduced to the market after February 7, 2007 – in other words, the period during which most e-cigarettes became available – to submit applications for FDA approval (McGinley and Dennis 2016). Onerous regulations such as these naturally weigh more heavily on small companies and start-ups than on large established firms. Going through a lengthy and costly FDA approval process poses little difficulty for firms such as Reynolds and Altria that already have entire divisions devoted to regulatory compliance, while newer and smaller businesses can find the same regulations insurmountable. Greg Conley, president of the American Vaping Association, predicted that the proposed regulations could shut down "99% of the small businesses in the vaping industry" (Villarreal 2015). Even if Conley's statement is an exaggeration, the direction of the effect is more than plausible.

Thus, the bootlegger angle in supporting the initial regulation of e-cigarettes seems straightforward. However, the landscape may have changed since then. Despite having initially supported the new regulation, Altria and other tobacco companies later backed legislation that would have rolled back the very same rule (Lipton 2016). The reasons for the about-face are unclear. The most obvious explanation is that the leading tobacco companies now have their own e-cigarette brands and related products. But this explanation is not satisfying, as the established tobacco companies should benefit from regulations that disproportionately hamper their small competitors. Indeed, when the FDA (under new leadership) unexpectedly announced a delay in the implementation of the new rules – along with a new stance focusing on harm reduction – stock prices for the leading tobacco companies immediately tumbled (Lovelace 2017). Another possible explanation is that, in light of the evidence that e-cigarettes can help people stop smoking, the large tobacco companies wish to claim the moral high ground both as a public relations strategy and as a defense against potential future legislation and litigation (Sweanor 2018).

In any case, tobacco companies are not the only bootleggers with a stake in the regulation of e-cigarettes. Insofar as e-cigarettes provide a means of quitting smoking, they pose a threat to other quitting methods: nicotine gum, patches, inhalers, and lozenges. The makers of these products, such as pharmaceutical giant GlaxoSmithKline (GSK), have also put their weight behind proposed e-cigarette regulations. "In their comments to the FDA, GSK contended that e-cigs are 'recreational' and 'have not been proven to help smokers quit.' (GSK's products, on the other hand, are described as 'medicine,' but appear to be no more effective at helping smokers quit.)" (Adler et al. 2015, 34). The company advocated regulating e-cigarettes in the same manner as regular cigarettes (Adler et al. 2015, 34).

Finally, it's worth noting that in order for the FDA to regulate e-cigarettes, it had to "deem" them to be a "tobacco product," because that is what the FDA has legislative authority to regulate. Yet e-cigarettes do not, in fact, contain tobacco. Vaping fluid contains nicotine, which is usually extracted from tobacco, but no other parts of the tobacco plant are included. Nicotine can in principle be produced in other ways; for instance, other members of the nightshade family (including tomatoes and eggplants) contain some level of nicotine (Siegmund et al. 1999), and nicotine can even be synthesized in the lab (Myers 2007, 192). The use of the tobacco plant is simply the most economical way to obtain pure nicotine. Given these facts, the FDA's decision to deem e-cigarettes a "tobacco product" is far from obvious on definitional or scientific grounds – but it is fully consistent with Niskanen's theory that bureaucrats seek to maximize their power and influence rather than social welfare.

Given its institutional incentives, the FDA's new deregulatory stance, adopted under a new FDA commissioner who will probably last only as long as the current administration, may not stand the test of time. Indeed, even under the current leadership, the FDA's harm-reduction approach seems to be morphing into a more aggressive posture, including a ban on flavored e-cigarettes in all retail locations that admit minors, proposed bans on menthol cigarettes and flavored cigars, and proposed caps on the nicotine content of traditional cigarettes (Grier 2018).

USDA Nutritional Guidelines

In 1992, the US Department of Agriculture (USDA) released a now-famous diagram of the composition of a healthy diet: the Food Pyramid. The chunky layers of the pyramid corresponded to different categories of food – carbohydrates, fruits and vegetables, dairy, proteins, and fats and oils – with the size of each layer corresponding to the recommended number of servings. In 2005, the USDA replaced the Food Pyramid with a new illustration: MyPyramid, in which the chunky layers were replaced with wedges and wordy explanations removed. In 2011, the USDA replaced MyPyramid with MyPlate, a circular diagram with four of the food groups represented by shapes that were almost, but not quite, the shape of pie pieces – plus an extra circle on the side for dairy.

In each case, essentially the same parties took part in building the illustration. The Harvard School of Public Health's "Nutrition Source" website observes that, in addition to input from USDA scientists and nutrition experts, "Intense lobbying from a variety of food industries also helped shape the pyramid and the plate" (Harvard n.d.). The lobbyists involved in drafting the USDA's Dietary Guidelines for Americans, which provided the basis for the pyramids and MyPlate, included the "National Dairy Council, the United Fresh Fruit and Vegetable Association, the Soft Drink Association, the American Meat Institute, the National Cattlemen's Beef Association, the Salt Institute, and the Wheat Foods Council" (Harvard n.d.). Nestle (1993) lists twenty-four lobbying organizations and seven firms with an interest in affecting food and nutrition policy (p. 487).

The evidence of special-interest involvement appears in the diagrams themselves, as well as in the underlying guidelines. For example, although a 1977 federal nutrition report recommended reducing consumption of meat, over the years the recommendation evolved toward a recommended number of servings of meat – which could easily be understood as a *minimum* (Nestle 1993, 489). By the time the Food Pyramid was released in 1992 after intense lobbying pressure, Nestle adds, "it had actually increased the upper range of the meat recommendation; its text calls for daily consumption of an amount equivalent to five to seven ounces rather than the six ounces recommended in 1990 *Dietary Guidelines*" (pp. 492–493).

In our previous examples, the Baptists and bootleggers worked largely in the same direction, though not necessarily in a coordinated fashion. In the case of government nutrition guidelines, their positions appear to have been more directly opposed, with the resulting recommendations reflecting a compromise of sorts. Luise Light, one of the nutritionists on the panel that created the USDA's original food pyramid – a version that was never published – describes the process of creating the final version as one in which agricultural interests trumped nutritional science:

For instance, the Ag Secretary's office altered wording to emphasize processed foods over fresh and whole foods, to downplay lean meats and low-fat dairy choices because the meat and milk lobbies believed it'd hurt sales of full-fat products; it also hugely increased the servings of wheat and other grains to make the wheat growers happy. The meat lobby got the final word on the color of the saturated fat/cholesterol guideline which was changed from red to purple because meat producers worried that using red to signify "bad" fat would be linked to red meat in consumers' minds.

(Light 2004)

Light describes some of the notable differences between the unpublished food pyramid and the final version. The number of recommended servings of fresh fruits and vegetables fell from 5–9 to 2–3, while the recommended servings of whole-grain breads and cereals rose from 3–4 to 6–11. (The recommendation for fruits and vegetables eventually rose to 5–7 through the efforts of an anti-cancer campaign by the National Cancer Institute.) Light further notes that white-flour baked goods, which the experts had placed at the pyramid's peak for items to be eaten sparingly, had been moved to the pyramid's base (Light 2004). Light says that she "vehemently protested" the revised pyramid, but "[t]o my amazement, I was a lone voice on this issue, as my colleagues appeared to accept the 'policy level' decision" (Light 2004). The final version was published over her objections.

If Light's version of events is correct, then ultimately it appears that the USDA's nutritional guidelines still fit the Baptist–bootlegger model. Nutritionists motivated by a genuine desire to improve public health were willing to support a weakened (and, in Light's view, dangerous) set of industry-backed recommendations because, presumably, they considered them better than no recommendations at all.

In presenting this story, particularly Light's account, we do not intend to take a position on the correctness of any specific dietary recommendations. In recent years, many have begun to reevaluate the conventional wisdom that emphasizes caloric restriction and reduced fat intake, instead arguing for restriction of carbohydrates and greater consumption of protein and fat – a position most commonly associated with the names John Yudkin, Gary Taubes, and Robert Atkins (Leslie 2016). If these authors' position is true, then it could be that the meat and dairy lobbies deserve less blame, and the grain and sugar lobbies more blame, for American obesity. We do not feel qualified to weigh in on this debate, except to observe that there exists plausible evidence in support of both sides (see, for instance, Hall [2017], Hall et al. [2016], and Hall et al. [2015] in defense of the traditional view; and Miller et al. [2017], Chiu et al. [2016], and Johnston [2014] supporting the alternative view). We are inclined to agree with Denise Minger's conclusion that "*Anyone who's certain they're right about everything in nutrition is almost definitely wrong. Our understanding of diet and health is still too young for anyone to have all the answers*" (Minger 2014, 53). Our purpose here is to shine a light on the *process* by which government nutritional guidelines have been created, which stands in sharp contrast to the humble, cautious, and disciplined approach imagined by behavioral paternalists. Real-world political outcomes reflect a push-and-pull between high-minded and cynical interests. Genuine controversies in the field of nutritional science make it even easier for those interests to manipulate the regulatory process with a veneer of scientific backing for their positions.[4] If that process somehow yielded optimal nutritional guidelines, coincidence and good luck would have to get most of the credit.

PUBLIC SECTOR IRRATIONALITY

In the remainder of this chapter, we will argue that cognitive biases identified by behavioral economists – including some that have been used to justify paternalist interventions – will tend to affect public policy for the worse. Policymakers are subject to cognitive biases just as regular people are, and we should expect those biases to manifest in policy choices.

Thus far, behavioral economists have paid little attention to this concern. Berggren (2012) examined all articles on behavioral economics in the top ten economics journals over a ten-year period (2000–2009). He found that 20.7 percent (sixty-seven of 323) of the articles made policy recommendations, and of those, 95.5 percent (sixty-four of sixty-seven) "do not contain any analysis at all of the potential problems with cognitive limitations and biases of policymakers" (Berggren 2012, 200). Still, a handful of authors have given greater attention to how cognitive biases can affect public policy – specifically, Viscusi and Gayer (2015), Tasic (2009, 2011), Lucas and Tasic (2015), and Hirshleifer (2008) – and we will draw heavily on their insights.

We wish to emphasize again that, in discussing the impact of cognitive biases on policymaking, we are not abandoning our position that many so-called biases may be inclusively rational, nor our position that real people can often self-regulate and control their own biases. Our claim is that people are far *less likely* to control their biases (whether inclusively rational or not) in the public sector, while the ill effects of such biases will

---

[4] Scheall et al. (2018) argue that there is yet another mechanism at work. In an effort to arrive at official dietary guidelines, agencies of the federal government have over the past forty years short-circuited the normal course of scientific research and exchange. The result has been that tentative (and ultimately misleading or inadequate) theories about the link between diet and heart disease were promulgated as scientific fact. We would add that any system of policy nudges or sin taxes designed to improve health necessarily requires an official position on these scientific matters. Furthermore, we suggest that a general policy of paternalism encourages the short-circuiting of the scientific process so as to arrive at official standards, not only in nutritional science but possibly in other areas as well.

spill over to the general public. For more on the reasons why, see the discussion at the beginning of this chapter under the heading "rational and irrational mechanisms of government failure."

TYPES OF BIAS THAT AFFECT POLICYMAKING

But how, specifically, will cognitive biases affect policymaking? While policymakers and everyday citizens are both human, and thus will be subject to the same kinds of biases, the biases that matter most in private decisions are not necessarily those that matter most in public policy – although there is some overlap. In what follows, we discuss several biases that we suspect will hinder the crafting of effective paternalist legislation.

We hasten to add, however, that this is one of the more speculative sections of this book. Behavioral political economy is at a very early stage of development, and little attempt has been made to test for the operation of specific biases in the political context. Given our previous objections to the facile application of behavioral concepts with inadequate attention to context, it would be inconsistent for us now to argue that the same concepts will apply to politics in precisely the way we imagine. Rather, our aim is to show that the possible role of behavioral biases on policymaking ought to be taken seriously – and therefore we ought to reject the asymmetrical perspective that pays attention only to the flawed choices of private decision-makers and not to those of public ones.

Action Bias

When disaster strikes, politicians react. From high-profile terrorist attacks to the latest mass shooting, the immediate response is nearly always a demand for action, often with little regard for efficacy or unintended consequences. The 9/11 terrorist attacks led to the passage of the PATRIOT Act and the initiation of two foreign wars. Omar Mateen's 2016 murder spree in an Orlando nightclub led to immediate demands for background checks that would deny guns to anyone on the government's no-fly list – a list of people who *might* have terrorist ties, even if they've never been convicted or charged with anything, and lacking any due process or procedure for getting one's name struck from the list.

Behavioral economists will recognize these events as instances of *availability bias* – the tendency of people to judge the likelihood of categories based on memorable examples. The latest terrorist attack or mass shooting is taken as indicative of the prevalence and characteristics of such events in general. We are more interested, however, in how they exemplify *action bias*, which Patt and Zeckhauser define as occurring when "[d]ecision makers ... weight the direct effects of choices above side effects, or ... redeploy resources to produce a positive impact in the 'action' realm while slighting losses in the realm from which they are taken" (2000, 45). Tasic (2009) argues that regulators afflicted with this particular bias "would be likely to respond to a new problem with a new regulation, even though inaction or the removal of a previous regulation may be the better response," and therefore "overreaction is a familiar phenomenon following a crisis" (p. 425).

While reactions to crises are the most obvious political applications of action bias, it can also manifest in more mundane situations. Political observers often judge politicians by the quantity of their output – for instance, when they malign a Congressional cohort as "do-nothing" or "the least productive Congress" in modern history (Quinn 2014), without regard to the quality of legislation passed. Legislators often tout the number of bills they have sponsored or cosponsored as a measure of their activity. And particularly when something is perceived to be a pressing social issue, such as obesity or (in the wake of the 2008 financial crisis) predatory lending, the pressure is on for legislators and regulators to *do something*. That pressure tends to suppress concerns about the wisdom of whatever *something* has been proposed.

Patt and Zeckhauser apply action bias to the realm of environmental policy, listing several features of environmental policy that encourage the tendency to take action with less than full concern for efficacy and side effects:

First, the consequences of actions are often uncertain, with long time lags and periods of latency until effects are felt. Second, the impacts often come from others' choices, or from the contributions of many parties. Third, there are no effective markets in which we can see how goods are valued, and no markets for wagers (such as a stock market) to help gauge probabilities. Fourth, bright lines, such as nondegradation and zero risk, facilitate demonstrations of impact. Fifth, our objective functions are rarely clear. Sixth, unlike in many domains, such as business, where resources flow to better decision makers, the environment offers few strong incentives for consistent decision making.

(Patt and Zeckhauser 2000, 47)

Notably, almost every item on this list applies to paternalist policymaking as well. Let us take them in turn:

Uncertain consequences with long delays. Given the many factors that can influence the outcome of paternalist policies – including potential unraveling effects, learning and unlearning effects, offsetting behavior, and interaction among biases – there is little doubt that paternalistic policies will have uncertain consequences that play out over time. To take just one example, new labor-friendly default terms in employment contracts would not immediately affect all workers in the labor market unless they retroactively applied to existing contracts. It would take even longer to collect data on how contracting parties actually responded – such as how often workers opted out of the new default, how much employers adjusted wages and other forms of compensation, and so on.

Impacts Resulting from Others' Choices and Multiple Parties. How paternalistic policies work will depend on the initial legislation, regulations written to implement the legislation, enforcement of those regulations, compliance by regulated parties (such as employers in the case of new defaults for labor contracts, or food stores in the case of sin taxes), and of course the responses of the targeted individuals. In addition, the impact of interventions aimed at assisting one side of a market, such as consumers or employees, will be mediated by the reactions of the other side of the market, such as producers or employers (Spiegler 2015). Multiple parties help to diffuse blame for unsatisfactory consequences if such consequences should ever become apparent.

Lack of Effective Markets to Value Goods. In the environmental context studied by Patt and Zeckhauser, this refers to the absence of clear market prices for some environmental amenities. But it applies to paternalist policies because, if behavioral economists are right, consumers' "true" valuations of goods and services are not necessarily reflected in market prices. For instance, behavioral arguments imply that the prices of tempting goods and services, such as fattening foods or risky forms of entertainment, have been distorted by cognitive biases and thus cannot be trusted – which is why sin taxes and risk narratives are allegedly needed to correct them. Even if true valuations are indeed reflected in prices, paternalistic policies are passed on the assumption that they are not. Hence *by their own hypothesis* the paternalists lack the assistance of markets to determine the value of goods and services.

Presence of Bright-Line Rules to Demonstrate Impact. This is the only factor listed by Patt and Zeckhauser that doesn't clearly apply to paternalism – although it might. What they mean is that certain attractive (though not necessarily efficient) goals such as "zero emissions" naturally encourage taking regulatory action because progress toward them is easily measured.[5] Now, as we have argued throughout this book, the *purported* goal of

---

[5] We do not believe that all bright-line rules have the unfortunate effect that Patt and Zeckhauser (2000) indicate. Some bright-line rules can have the salutary effect of limiting action rather than encouraging it. A better term for what Patt and Zeckhauser intend would be "simplistic goals."

behavioral paternalism – better satisfaction of people's true preferences – is neither simple to define nor easy to measure. However, the paternalist policy arena does offer plenty of simplistic and superficially attractive goals: reducing measured obesity and overweightness, reducing consumption of unhealthy or risky goods and services, increasing the rate of savings, and so on. If these become the operative goals, despite their lack of theoretical justification, they will make legislation and regulation that much more attractive.

Lack of Objective Functions. The purported objective function of behavioral paternalist policies is the better satisfaction of people's true preferences. But as we emphasized in Chapter 7, these true preferences are largely inaccessible to policymakers; we cannot see inside people's brains or directly measure their all-things-considered life satisfaction. In addition, many paternalist policies will tend to produce "winners" and "losers" – that is, some people will benefit from the intervention while others will suffer from it. A sin tax, for instance, may help some people exercise greater self-control – but other people who need no such help will have to pay more for goods they enjoy. There is no unambiguous way to weigh these effects against each other – especially without the guidance of market prices. The absence of an objective function makes it harder to demonstrate the negative consequences of policies, and it also encourages policymakers to rely on simplistic goals such as those discussed earlier.

Lack of Strong Incentives for Consistency in Decision-Making. This factor would seem to be true of legislative and regulatory policy in general, whether paternalistic or not. Rational ignorance, the logic of concentrated benefits and diffuse costs, and the presence of externalities throughout the public sector all point toward weak incentives for efficacy or consistency. To put it simply, if policies create poor results or conflict with other policy goals, who will be held to account? The political process offers plenty of opportunities for those responsible to dodge responsibility by simply ignoring results, deflecting blame onto others, or no longer holding office. In the context of paternalism, policymakers could (for example) face minimal consequences for implementing a supposedly optimal sin tax and later raising the tax above the optimal level simply to raise revenue.

Policymakers' action bias is not necessarily irrational. This is true for a couple of reasons. First, policymakers may be responding rationally to an ignorant and irrational public that assumes taking action is desirable. Hirshleifer in particular draws attention to the public's flawed assumptions that can push regulators to take action. When the public demands that government do something to solve a problem, the implicit assumption is that there is something worthwhile to be done; furthermore, the very act of proposing a solution can send a spurious signal that the solution is indeed worthwhile. "Voters who do not analyze proposals deeply react to this signal credulously" (Hirshleifer 2008, 864).

Second, the political process can be seen as a principal–agent problem in which politicians are the agents responsible for advancing the interests of the public. Given the deep uncertainty about whether most policies (paternalistic ones included) are truly effective, the agents have an incentive to do whatever they can to prove they are at least trying – i.e., exerting effort. As Patt and Zeckhauser put it:

> From the waiter who stops by the table to ask whether everything is okay, to the politician who files a bill he can report to his constituency even though it is sure to lose, agents are continually trying to make their actions evident, because principals often have difficulty discerning consequences. An agent who stands idly by and lets good things happen will reap much less reward than one who takes action and gets associated with something good.
>
> (pp. 62–63)

So why classify action bias as a bias at all? Patt and Zeckhauser say that it can be rational or irrational, depending on the chooser's reasons. The less rational form of action bias typically involves an excessive willingness to attribute causality to one's own actions, thus allowing one to take internal credit for good outcomes, and also to experience a greater sense of control (Patt and Zeckhauser 2000, 65). Even this mental process might be deemed broadly rational, once we allow for beliefs that have direct utility to the believer.

From a public policy perspective, it matters little whether action bias is rational, irrational, or a combination of both. Because policymakers' incentives don't necessarily align with the public interest, the public can suffer from ill-considered policies that result from politicians' and bureaucrats' desire to take action on perceived social ills.

Overconfidence and the Illusion of Explanatory Depth

Overconfidence, the tendency to overrate one's own knowledge or competence, has been alleged to exist in a wide variety of contexts. In Chapter 5, we addressed the most frequently discussed type of overconfidence, the tendency to overestimate the accuracy of one's knowledge. More broadly, overconfidence refers to overestimation of one's abilities in general, whether in terms of knowledge, competence, or other traits. Behavioral economists claim to have identified overconfidence in a wide range of domains, from consumer behavior to declarations of war (Malmendier and Taylor 2015, 6).

To the extent that overconfidence is a real phenomenon, there is good reason to think it will be prevalent in the public sector. As difficult as it may be to understand oneself, understanding a whole society constitutes an even greater challenge. Social science is difficult in large part because it involves considering not just the behavior of one individual, but the behavior of many individuals with diverse characteristics, as well as how they interact. In this kind of environment, policymakers will tend to have insufficient information – and, as we argued in Chapter 7, paternalist policymaking is no exception. Yet policymakers afflicted by overconfidence will tend to assume that their information is better and more reliable than it is (a phenomenon called *overprecision*), and that their ability to craft effective policies is greater than it is (a phenomenon called *overestimation*). Together, these tendencies lead policymakers to overreact in the formation of policy – that is, to support policies even when their costs exceed their benefits (Maor 2012). We also surmise that a form of selection bias could encourage overconfidence in the political arena: overconfident people might be disproportionately attracted to a profession with the capacity to "save the world" or remake society.

Overconfidence effects can be exacerbated by the complexity of good paternalist policymaking. Paternalist policies involve complex chains of cause and effect with numerous and heterogeneous actors both within and outside of government. As discussed in the context of action bias, the consequences of paternalist policies are characterized by uncertainty and long delays, both of which impede the learning processes that could lead to more accurate and reliable beliefs. As Ghaffarzadegan and coauthors observe, "[i]n complex systems with long delays and a large degree of uncertainty, overconfidence is especially likely given the difficulty that policymakers have learning about their own performance and capabilities" (2011, 26).

Hirshleifer, in discussing how overconfidence affects regulation in general, draws attention to regulators' insufficient appreciation for existing and potential market solutions to problems. Even economists, Hirshleifer says, sometimes do not fully internalize "the richness of adaptation of economic institutions" (2008, 864). This blind spot has special importance in the context of paternalism. Earlier in this book, we drew attention to the wide variety of strategies people have for "debiasing" their own perceived shortcomings: resolutions, precommitments, self-rewards and self-punishments, environmental structuring, mutual support groups, and so on. The point is not that these private solutions are perfect, but that they reduce the relative strength of the justification for regulation, as they indicate that problems have already been at least partially addressed. The presence of overconfidence among policymakers suggests that they may pay too little attention to such private solutions.

A variant of overconfidence likely to manifest in public policy is the illusion of explanatory depth (IOED), Rozenblit and Keil's (2002) term for the fact that "[m]ost people feel they understand the world with far greater detail, coherence, and depth than they really do" (p. 522). Based on a series of studies probing the depth of people's knowledge of complex phenomena, they conclude that "knowledge of complex causal relations is particularly susceptible to illusions of understanding" (p. 522). This kind of knowledge, which they call *explanatory* knowledge, is distinct from other forms of knowledge, such as factual knowledge (e.g., world capitals), knowledge of procedures (e.g., cooking recipes), and knowledge of narratives (e.g., recalling the plot of a movie). Rozenblit and Keil find that the IOED is stronger with respect to explanatory knowledge than other types of knowledge. Note that explanatory knowledge is exactly the sort of knowledge required for policymaking.

Tasic applies the IOED to policymaking, dubbing the result "the illusion of regulatory competence" (2009). He points out several factors that make market regulation especially vulnerable to the IOED. First, markets exhibit causal relationships that are typically characterized by some degree of randomness. Second, while we may be able to predict patterns of behavior and directions of effects, "our ability to predict the magnitude of effects is very limited."[6] Third, "our knowledge is reduced to a few large and visible effects, while there are many other causalities that we cannot reliably predict" (Tasic 2009, 9). The same factors apply just as strongly to paternalistic regulation aimed at correcting the irrational behavior of individuals – especially since such behavior often takes place within a market context.

At the risk of oversimplifying, the IOED could be dubbed the "a little knowledge is a dangerous thing" bias. It afflicts people who are inclined to *think* they really understand a complex phenomenon – a belief driven, at least in part, by the appeal of simple intuitive theories. One of Rozenblit and Keil's suggested explanations for the IOED is "a tendency on the part of laypeople and cognitive scientists to assume that *intuitive theories* are a powerful component of our knowledge systems" (2002, 525, emphasis added). A slightly different explanation is that the IOED arises from the

---

[6] We discuss this issue in Chapter 6.

use of simple causal stories that, despite their limitations, nevertheless "have some efficacy and do provide a *rush of insight*" (2002, 525, emphasis added).

"Intuitive theories" and "rushes of insight" are the stock-in-trade of behavioral economics, at least as it has been marketed to both policy-makers and the general public. Concepts such as status quo bias, empathy gaps, and the endowment effect have instant intuitive appeal as policy levers, and proponents of behavioral paternalism have been quick to propose *seemingly* simple and straightforward policy applications – often in domains where the effects have not yet been explored, such as using new contractual defaults to trigger the endowment effect in labor-market contracts. The paradigm of behavioral paternalism could hardly be better designed to trigger the illusion of explanatory depth.

The facile character of behavioral paternalists' policy recommendations weighs against one potential defense against overconfidence: that policy-makers can rely on experts with a better understanding of the subject matter. Unfortunately, experts are not immune to overconfidence. Angner (2006) makes the case that economist-experts are susceptible to overconfidence for a variety of reasons. Among other reasons, Angner points out that the overconfidence effect is not restricted to the ignorant; it has been found among experts and educated people as well, and in many different domains. Thus economists will be vulnerable to overconfidence simply "because they are like everyone else" (Angner 2006, 7).

Frequent and clear feedback could exert some discipline on economic advisors' confidence levels . . . if only such feedback were forthcoming. But, Angner notes, economists acting as experts often do not receive much clear feedback about outcomes (2006, 10). Koppl (2018) observes that when the subject matter is "complex, uncertain, indeterminate, or ambiguous, feed-back mechanisms may be weak or altogether absent" (p. 203). Economic predictions tend to be vague and feedback ambiguous – two features that encourage confirmation bias and hindsight bias (Angner 2006, 11, citing Rabin 1998, 28, and Fischhoff 2001, 547). Thus, two other biases tend to impede the correction of overconfidence among economic experts. We will simply add that paternalist policies are no different from other economic policies in this regard. Knowing whether interventions have in fact made individuals better off "by their own lights" is inherently imprecise and ambiguous, and the goal only becomes precise and unambiguous via oversimplification – for example, assuming that everyone's true preference is to eat healthily or achieve the expert-recommended body mass index.

As with action bias, overconfidence is not necessarily irrational. From the self-interested perspective of policymakers and their economic advisors, it may represent an optimal response to the incentives they face. Laboratory and field studies have provided evidence that overconfidence increases perceptions of competence, thereby leading to higher status (Anderson and Brion 2010). Politicians who project confidence about their proposals may have a greater likelihood of getting them passed. If they can get credit for their legislative accomplishments while dodging or minimizing negative consequences, overconfidence (whether in appearance or reality) makes strategic sense. Likewise, economic experts who display confidence may have a better chance of landing advisor jobs, gaining media attention for their work, and enhancing their public image. They may also experience direct satisfaction from the feeling of "being right" and having an impact on the world. We will simply emphasize again that behavior which is optimal for policymakers is often very different from behavior that would be optimal for the public.

One factor that may mitigate overconfidence among experts and professional policymakers is the impact of small-group decision-making, which we observed in Chapter 6 can improve the performance of individuals in their private-sector decisions. To the extent that policymakers also make decisions in groups, such as committees, caucuses, and task forces, such groups could dampen or eliminate overconfidence. On the other hand, the concept of groupthink (Janis 1972) implies that groups can also have a negative impact on the quality of decisions, especially when accountability is low – as we have argued is typically the case in public policy.

One last question about overconfidence and the IOED: are we committing the same error? After all, we too are taking intuitively appealing concepts (action bias, overconfidence, and so on) and applying them to subject matter where often they have not yet been fully studied (policymaking). This is a fair response, as there are undoubtedly many aspects of both behavioral economics and policymaking that the two of us don't fully understand. But in our defense, we are taking the more modest position. We are not using behavioral research to justify new interventions; *we are using behavioral research to warn against the facile use of behavioral research*. Ignorance and uncertainty recommend greater caution in advocating new policy interventions.

Confirmation Bias

Confirmation bias refers to seeking and overweighting information that tends to support beliefs and positions one already has, while avoiding and underweighting information that tends to disconfirm those beliefs and positions. Confirmation bias is thought to occur in many areas of human endeavor; if this is true, we should not be surprised to find it operating in the public sector. To appreciate how confirmation bias can affect policymaking, it is useful to think chronologically, i.e., in terms of how a policy comes into being and how it evolves over time.

In the early stages, new policies will naturally be championed by interested parties. Among those interested parties will be academics and other experts who have advanced theories that tend to justify the new policies; these are the "Second Baptists" of the Baptist–Baptist–bootlegger coalitions we discussed earlier. Lucas and Tasic argue that such experts "may cherish certain beliefs because of the material and psychological benefits of doing so" (2015, 254). The material benefits come from the professional and reputational rewards from playing a significant role in the public sector and having legislation passed based upon one's own work. The psychological benefits include the greater self-esteem that comes from doing popular and influential research. By contrast, there are few rewards for experts who back off from their publicly stated positions, acknowledge weaknesses in their research, or recognize when their recommendations have yielded unfavorable outcomes.

As these material and psychological benefits suggest, confirmation bias may have a rational basis. The experts have self-interested reasons to play up further research that supports their position while downplaying research that challenges it. The rational reasons may be girded by a capacity for self-delusion that obstructs the ability of experts to correctly interpret new evidence. As with previous biases, it matters little whether rational or irrational forces play the larger role, as the result is the same: academics and other experts will tend to push policies based on their theories without adequate attention to counterarguments and shortcomings of their research. Lucas and Tasic focus on paternalism, in particular, to illustrate how the biases of experts can affect their positions. Public health advocates tend to focus on health concerns to the exclusion of other relevant factors such as autonomy, and they are particularly inclined to downplay the notion that people may rationally sacrifice some health in exchange for other things they value (Lucas and Tasic 2015, 254).

Whatever benefits accrue to experts from having their work manifested in policy are magnified when their work has broader applicability. As Mitchell has shown, "[b]ehavioral law and economics scholars simplify and overgeneralize findings on human cognition and rationality to make these findings seem simultaneously important and simple enough to be incorporated into legal policy" (2002, 72). Simple and intuitively appealing solutions have a better chance of making their way into law. To the extent that experts are vulnerable to confirmation bias, they will tend to ignore evidence indicating that their conclusions cannot be so easily generalized.

Once enabling legislation has been passed – or reinterpreted – to grant regulators the authority to enact paternalistic policies, they too become vulnerable to confirmation bias. Lucas and Tasic observe that "paternalistic intervention allows bureaucrats to assert greater control over market exchanges and enhance their power" as well as to "enhance their self-esteem and reputations" (2015, 255). In conducting their own research, regulators will tend to privilege results that support the mission to which they have already committed themselves – a tendency amplified by the fact that regulators are often self-selected to believe in the importance and efficacy of regulation. Tasic (2009) draws together several factors that contribute to regulators' interventionist bias, and his summary is worth quoting in full:

> [T]hose who choose to become, say, financial regulators are likely, *ceteris paribus*, to believe that such regulation is necessary. Whatever beliefs initially motivate this conviction may be reinforced cognitively by the selective perception and retention of information that confirms the initial belief (confirmation bias), in what Jeffrey Friedman (2006, drawing on cognitive research in Lord, Ross, and Lepper 1979 and Lodge and Hamill 1986) has called a "spiral of conviction." Similarly, at the affective level, Ziva Kunda (1987) has demonstrated that people confirm their beliefs through "motivated reasoning" (cf. Lundgren and Prislin 1998). These cognitive and affective sources of growing confidence in one's initial beliefs, in turn, may be reinforced by "motivated skepticism," which is to say emotional resistance to counter-arguments (Johnston 1996; Zuwerink and Devine 1996; Taber and Lodge 2006).
>
> (Tasic 2009, 425)

Thus, the empowerment of agencies with the job of intervening in a particular area creates a dynamic that will tend to increase the perceived need for such intervention. To the extent that academics and other experts continue to exert influence on the regulatory process, we can expect the confirmation biases of regulators and experts to reinforce each other.

Earlier in this chapter, we offered Viscusi and Gayer's work on energy-efficiency mandates as a possible example of Niskanen's theory of self-interested bureaucrats as a source of regulatory activity. But this example may better illustrate the susceptibility of bureaucrats to confirmation bias. Recall that regulators for the Environmental Protection Agency (EPA) and the Department of Transportation (DOT) relied on cost–benefit analysis in which the lion's share of benefits from the proposed regulations came from consumer irrationality in purchasing decisions – despite weak evidence of such irrationality. The willingness of the regulators to rely on weak evidence and dismiss alternative explanations of consumer behavior could reflect confirmation bias in action. In the same vein, Viscusi and Gayer also point to the FDA's proposal to require graphic warnings on cigarette packs despite the lack of any good evidence that such warnings would be effective. In fact, the US Court of Appeals for the DC Circuit overturned the FDA's proposal because there was not "a shred of evidence" that the graphic warnings would reduce the prevalence of smoking (Viscusi and Gayer 2015, 1002–1003). "Thus, a regulatory intervention intended to alter behavior in effect ignored the behavioral evidence on its likely efficacy" (p. 1003). Confirmation bias is an obvious explanation, although we cannot rule out rational self-interest on the part of regulators as well.

These examples come from existing regulatory agencies that have latched on to behavioral research to support their existing missions. But behavioral paternalists do not merely wish to inject behavioral thinking into existing regulatory agencies. They have proposed the creation of whole new domains of regulation. In the United Kingdom, their work contributed to the creation of the Behavioural Insights Team, also known as the "nudge unit," a government group (now partly privatized) whose *raison d'être* is to find public sector applications of behavioral research. In the United States, behavioral research provided the impetus for President Obama's Social and Behavioral Sciences team. What are the odds that groups such as these would *not* find justification for their existence? To the extent that new agencies and divisions are created with the express purpose of using behavioral research to shape policy, we should expect them to be especially vulnerable to confirmation bias.

Availability and Salience Effects

The *availability heuristic* refers to assessing the frequency or importance of an event by "how easily examples of the event can be called to mind" (Jolls and Sunstein 2006, 204). While it is sometimes referred to as a bias, the availability heuristic can be a quite sensible shortcut for people who lack the time or motivation to find reliable information on a topic, as is often the case with voters, as well as politicians appealing to such voters. Nevertheless, the heuristic can lead to errors in assessment, as easily recalled examples may distract from better and more complete information.

When decision-makers "ignore relevant information that remains implicit and therefore 'off screen'" (Lucas and Tasic 2015, 217), that is a prescription for bad policy. What remains "off screen" often needs to be front and center. In the case of paternalistic policy, the problems that supposedly demand correction are obvious, easily recalled, and often vivid: morbidly obese people, spendthrifts living in poverty because they didn't save for retirement, impulsive buyers who purchase fancy sports cars they can't afford, and so on. (As we will see later, these images are also *prototypes*, which affect people's attitudes toward the larger groups they are meant to represent.) The downsides of intervention are more abstract and harder to visualize: people forced to pay a bit more for dessert or forgo treats they would have enjoyed, people who end up saving somewhat less because they accept the default investment option, consumers who pay more for goods to cover the hidden costs of regulation – and these are the *simplest* of the potential costs. Given the relative ease with which the paradigmatic cases that favor paternalism come to mind, the availability heuristic will tend to support legislation and regulation without enough attention given to the factors that argue against it.

Interestingly, Cass Sunstein himself – along with coauthor Timur Kuran – has drawn attention to political problems arising from the availability heuristic. Kuran and Sunstein posit the existence of *availability cascades*, a process "through which expressed perceptions trigger chains of individual responses that make these perceptions appear increasingly plausible through their rising availability in public discourse" (1998, 685). In other words, as a perceived problem receives increasing levels of public attention, more people decide the problem must be significant – and as more people decide the problem is significant, the problem receives yet more public attention. The resulting feedback loop can dramatically overstate the real size of the problem. The process can be kicked off, or amplified, by "availability entrepreneurs" who "attempt to trigger availability cascades likely to advance their own agendas" (Kuran and Sunstein 1998, 687).

Kuran and Sunstein document various historical instances of (what they deem to be) availability cascades. Although they focus on cascades relating to the regulation of risk, they also cite McCarthyism, the Civil Rights Movement, the feminist movement, and ethnic and religious separatism, among many others (1998, 688–689), and many of them occurred in the public sector. Paternalist cascades are also not hard to imagine. Indeed, the explosion of popular books and articles about human irrationality – including Sunstein and Thaler's *Nudge*, Ariely's *Predictably Irrational*, and Kahneman's *Thinking Fast and Slow* – has helped generate growing support for the belief that normal people cannot be trusted to make good decisions and need the government's assistance. The visibility of obese people, and others who *seem* to have made poor decisions, has provided a salient reference point in building this consensus. Sunstein and Thaler appear to meet Kuran and Sunstein's definition of availability entrepreneurs.

As suggested by the preceding paragraph, availability is closely related to – though analytically distinct from – the concept of *salience* (Kuran and Sunstein 1998, 706). Behavioral researchers claim that certain aspects of an environment or choice situation will tend to capture a person's attention more than others, and these aspects will tend to carry greater weight in decision-making and belief formation.[7] In Chapter 5, we argued that salience has been too loosely defined in the literature, with inadequate attention to the question of what factors contribute to salience (or lack thereof). However, much that is attributed to salience can as easily be explained by the standard economic notion of information costs. Some aspects of a situation, such as the immediate and concentrated effects of a policy, can be ascertained at lower cost than others, such as the indirect and long-term effects of a policy. Consequently, we should expect voters and even "expert" policymakers to pay more attention to the former than the latter. To the extent that salience correlates with information costs, it will tend to amplify the policy role of information available at lowest cost. Hirshleifer notes that "the costs of a regulation, though widely incurred, are often far less salient than the exceptional wrongdoings that incited it. . . . So we expect planners to underestimate the costs of unexpected side effects of regulation" (2008, 859).

Although Hirshleifer focuses on financial regulation – his phrase "exceptional wrongdoings" refers implicitly to the Enron scandal and the 2008 financial crisis – we can apply the same argument to paternalist policy. Salience effects can lead to *opportunity-cost neglect* – a tendency to pay insufficient attention to what is forgone when making a choice (Lucas 2015). When buying a product, for instance, consumers tend to focus on the characteristics of the item in front of them, rather than what else they could buy (Lucas 2015, 267). The product that is the focus of attention is more salient than all the other (more abstract and diffuse) things that might be done with the money. Fortunately, in the private sphere, the consequences of a failure to consider opportunity costs fall primarily on

---

[7] "Availability and affect are processes internal to the individual that may lead to bias. The external equivalent of these processes is salience, whereby information that stands out, is novel, or seems relevant is more likely to affect our thinking and actions" (Samson 2014).

the individual consumer. But in the public sphere, opportunity-cost neglect can induce policymakers to ignore or downplay hidden regulatory costs that affect other people.

For instance, cooling-off periods can be expected to lead to a greater frequency of returns (possibly with unseen damage), and thus an increase in the cost of doing business. But the higher cost will most likely be hidden in the final price of the products, making the increase largely invisible to consumers – and that's *after* the law has been passed. *Before* passage, the higher cost due to regulation is entirely hypothetical, as well as spread out among many future consumers. The expected beneficiaries of the law, on the other hand, are relatively easy to picture and thus more salient to most policymakers. Opportunity-cost neglect will tend to ease the passage of paternalistic interventions (indeed all interventions) that create diffuse and hidden costs. This is an insight that precedes modern behavioral economics, having been stated as early as 1848 in Frederic Bastiat's famous essay *What Is Seen and What Is Not Seen*.

Affect and Prototype Heuristics

The *affect heuristic* refers to the general tendency to rely on subjective feelings about the goodness or badness of things in making judgments and decisions about them. More loosely, the affect heuristic means allowing one's emotional reactions to guide choices. Tasic (2011) and Lucas and Tasic (2015) draw attention to the *intentions heuristic*, a special case of the affect heuristic, which refers to the tendency to judge the goodness or badness of actions based on the perceived intent of the person acting. When an act is perceived to be motivated by good intentions, we are more inclined to assume the act produces desirable results.

There may be a rational basis for the intentions heuristic, inasmuch as good intentions probably lead to better results on average than bad intentions. For political actors who lack strong incentives to seek out better information, the affect heuristic can be a useful shorthand. Nevertheless, the heuristic may also cause people to neglect other relevant factors such as "the evidence of real effects, trade-offs and unintended consequences of a policy" (Tasic 2015, 8).

Behavioral paternalists have highlighted people's tendency to let emotions drive their decisions to justify policies to curb emotional decisions on the part of consumers – for instance, they have used the hot–cold empathy gap to justify cooling-off policies. Yet the incentive to subjugate emotion to reason is arguably even weaker in the public sector. Voters have little to gain from resisting their gut reactions on political issues. Politicians and regulators, in addition to indulging their own emotional reactions, also have a rational incentive to track voters' emotions. When voters judge policies by the intentions that motivated them, that reduces legislators' incentive to pay attention to other relevant information. Given that paternalistic laws are universally marketed under the banner of making people better off – in other words, based on the intentions behind them – the intentions heuristic should be especially pronounced in this arena.

The affect heuristic is closely connected to the *prototype heuristic*. A prototype, as the term is used in the literature, is a representative example of a class or category. It may be defined by the average values of salient properties for members of the class (Kahneman 2003, 1463), or it may simply be what comes to the agent's mind, perhaps as a result of recent or spectacular instances. Decision-makers will often rely on their attitudes about prototypes to make choices regarding whole classes. This is where the affect heuristic comes into play, as the affective response to the prototype often transfers over to the class as a whole (Kahneman et al. 1999, 206). Prototypes can provide a rough-and-ready judgment tool for broadly rational people with limited information, particularly when the individual rewards for acquiring better information are minimal – as they typically are in the public sphere.

The question, then, is what sort of prototypes play into discussions of paternalist policies. Two types of prototypes seem relevant: prototypes of targeted individuals, and prototypes of paternalist policies. With regard to the former, the prototypes will tend to be spendthrifts, drug addicts, morbidly obese people, and other archetypes of out-of-control behavior. To be fair, behavioral paternalists have emphasized the prevalence of "bad" choices even among the most typical members of society, not just extreme cases such as these. But extreme cases naturally come more easily to mind; if we wish to imagine "the problem of overweightness," we are more apt to think of the obese than the mildly overweight. Negative attitudes toward the prototypical groups will tend to support intrusive policies that affect larger categories of people, despite the existence of much variation within these groups.

With respect to policies, it is possible that some voters and legislators will think of unfavorable policy prototypes such as alcohol prohibition, which produced famously bad outcomes. To that extent, they will tend to be biased against paternalism. However, behavioral paternalists – particularly Sunstein and Thaler – have worked hard to promulgate *new* prototypes that evoke more favorable attitudes, such as cafeterias displaying fruit more prominently than desserts, or employers opting their employees into retirement-savings programs with the ability to opt out (Thaler and Sunstein 2003; Sunstein and Thaler 2003). They have actively popularized the term "nudge," which naturally evokes more positive associations than "push" or "shove." We will have much more to say about the role played by these policy prototypes in Chapter 9, but for now, we'll note that such examples have been chosen for their seeming innocuousness: they are both drawn from the private sector, and they both have notably low costs of opting out. Yet not all paternalist policies have these characteristics. To the extent that behavioral paternalists have succeeded in altering the prototypes of paternalist policy, they have created conditions that will tend to support all manner of interventions – including ones that are substantially more intrusive.

Present Bias and Hyperbolic Discounting

We have discussed *present bias*, usually characterized as a result of *hyperbolic discounting*, extensively in previous chapters. It is probably the most common justification for paternalistic interventions. Whatever its incidence in ordinary individual decision-making, we should expect to find present bias operating more often in the public sector – especially since legislators and regulators also have *rational* reasons to focus on the present over the future.[8] As a result, they have an incentive to support policies with immediate benefits and delayed costs. Some paternalist policies fit that criterion. On the benefit side, politicians who support them can expect to gain credit for taking action to solve pressing problems such as obesity and insufficient savings. When and if the chosen policies generate unexpected costs through unintended consequences and side effects, those costs will occur at a substantial delay – after the policies have been implemented and results measured. (And if results are never measured, so much the better.) Politicians can be expected to behave in this manner even if fully rational, but present bias – to the extent that it results in an even higher rate of time discounting – will tend to amplify the effect. Present bias might also result in policy preference reversals, such as committing to keeping a sin tax at a

---

[8] Strictly speaking, present bias (or hyperbolic discounting) means *inconsistent* time-discounting, not simply *high* time-discounting. However, behavioral paternalists' *concerns* about present bias seem to be driven primarily by the present rate of discounting being relatively high in comparison with the long-term rate.

low (supposedly optimal) level, but raising the tax later in response to short-term revenue needs.

Some paternalistic interventions might work in the opposite direction – that is, promising long-run benefits that justify their initial costs. For instance, a fat tax might generate political opposition from the usual opponents of tax hikes – causing politicians who supported it to suffer, despite the policy's (supposed) long-term benefits in terms of health and obesity control. Yet that is the sort of policy that present bias will tend to discourage. In other words, present bias in the political process will tend to discourage exactly the kind of policy that behavioral paternalists favor. Of course, we have argued throughout this book that sin taxes (and most other paternalist policies) are likely ill-advised. If so, then present bias in the political process could have the salutary effect of helping prevent some bad paternalist policies. In general, present bias will tend to discourage policies with upfront costs, irrespective of their long-run effects, and to encourage policies with upfront benefits, irrespective of their long-run effects. That may be good or bad in any given case, depending on the size and direction of the long-run effects.

As explained in previous chapters, we don't necessarily agree with characterizing agents as having a "present bias" simply because they display inconsistency in their intertemporal preferences and choices. But if the paternalists *do* believe that present bias is a problem for private decision-makers, then they ought to be concerned about present bias among public decision-makers as well, especially given that policymakers have much weaker incentives than private individuals to correct or contain their own biases.

We will have more to say about the impact of present bias on policy-making in Chapter 9.

CONCLUSIONS

Even if policymakers (including voters) were perfectly rational, there would be good reason to doubt that democratic government would generate well-designed paternalist policies. The diffusion of responsibility and accountability inherent in our form of government creates poor incentives for people to become well informed and to demand policies that genuinely track the public interest. Instead, legislators and bureaucrats will tend to promote laws and regulations that garner the support of highly motivated parties, including moralists and activists who want to promote values that others may not share, experts and academics who wish to see their research make an impact, and special-interest groups that stand to benefit financially from paternalistic laws.

If policymakers are subject to the same cognitive biases that behavioral economists attribute to regular people, we should expect the policymaking process to be even worse. Such biases are *more* worrisome in the public sector than the private sector, because the public sector offers far worse incentives for people to curb their irrational tendencies and numerous opportunities to indulge pleasing beliefs and prejudices at low cost. Furthermore, poor decisions in the public sector almost by definition affect large numbers of people who have little or no input into them; in other words, government policy is rife with externalities. As a result, we should expect paternalist (and other) policymaking to suffer from the effects of action bias, overconfidence, the illusion of explanatory depth, confirmation bias, availability bias, and other cognitive limitations.

Although we have considered both rational and irrational contributors to government failure separately, it's worth taking a moment to consider how they interact. Behavioral economics indicates that certain types of argument will be more likely to succeed in the political sphere: those that emphasize the urgent need for taking action; those that downplay complexity and emphasize simple solutions; those that flatter people's current beliefs and attitudes; those that rely on easily recalled and vivid illustrations of alleged problems; and those that emphasize the benevolent goals of the policies in question. Given these tendencies, we should expect the highly motivated parties mentioned earlier to exploit them to advance their agendas. Activists, academics, experts, and industry lobbyists have strong *rational* incentives to craft their policy proposals so as to maximize their appeal to *irrational* voters and legislators.

This interaction suggests what Hirshleifer calls the *psychological attraction theory of regulation*, which suggests that "regulation is the result of psychological biases on the part of political participants and regulators, and the evolution of regulatory ideologies that exploit these biases" (2008, 869). Once these regulatory ideologies, heavily informed by behavioral paternalism, take hold, they contribute to an overall environment that is conducive to the passage of yet more paternalist interventions. Hirshleifer's theory "predicts a general tendency for overregulation, and for rules to accrete over time like barnacles, impeding economic progress" (2008, 870). This concern about the tendency of present interventions to encourage further interventions is the subject of Chapter 9.

9

Slippery Slopes in Paternalist Policymaking*

> Indeed the safest road to hell is the gradual one – the gentle slope, soft
> underfoot, without sudden turnings, without milestones, without
> signposts ...
>
> —C. S. Lewis, *The Screwtape Letters*

> The blank form of an inquiry daily made is—'We have already done this; why
> should we not do that?' And the regard for precedent suggested by it, is ever
> pushing on regulative legislation. ... Not precedent only prompts this
> spread, but also the necessity which arises for supplementing ineffective
> measures, and for dealing with the artificial evils continually caused. Failure
> does not destroy faith in the agencies employed, but merely suggests more
> stringent use of such agencies or wider ramifications of them.
>
> —Herbert Spencer, *The Man versus the State*

Behavioral paternalists often distinguish their views from harder forms of
paternalism by emphasizing the moderate character of their proposals.
Jolls and Sunstein (2006) frequently refer to their proposals for debiasing
behavior through law as a "middle ground" between laissez-faire and more
heavy-handed paternalism (pp. 208, 216), one that is a "less intrusive, more
direct, and more democratic response to the problem of bounded rationality" (pp. 200–201). Sunstein and Thaler (2003) characterize their "libertarian paternalist" approach as a "relatively weak and nonintrusive type of
paternalism" that in its "most cautious forms ... imposes trivial costs on
those who seek to depart from the planner's preferred option" (p. 1162). In
short, leading behavioral paternalists claim we can attain significant
improvements in individual welfare with relatively small interventions that
do not substantially restrict liberty or autonomy.

---

* This chapter was previously published, with some important differences, as Rizzo and
Whitman (2009b).

In this chapter, we argue that behavioral paternalism's vulnerability to slippery slopes makes the claim to moderation unsustainable. Despite the sometimes poor reputation of slippery-slope arguments, a body of literature to which we have contributed has rehabilitated slippery-slope reasoning by examining the specific processes by which slippery slopes occur and the circumstances under which slippage is most likely (Ikeda 1997; Rizzo and Whitman 2003; Schauer 1985; Volokh 2003; Walton 1992). The insights of this literature suggest that behavioral paternalist policies are particularly subject to expansion. We argue that this is true even if policymakers are rational (in the neoclassical sense). But perhaps more importantly, we argue that the slippery-slope threat is even greater if policymakers share the behavioral and cognitive biases attributed to the people their policies are supposed to help. Consequently, accepting behavioral paternalist policies creates a risk of accepting, in the long run, greater restrictions on individual autonomy than have been acknowledged. Inasmuch as behavioral paternalists claim to be interested in preserving autonomy,[1] this surely must be taken into account as a cost to be balanced against any possible gains from their policies.

Not all behavioral paternalists make the claim to moderation. Sarah Conly (2013) is the best example; she explicitly argues that Sunstein and Thaler's "nudging" approach does not go far enough. Bhargava and Loewenstein (2015) also advocate going beyond soft paternalism, arguing that "insights from [behavioral economics] have the potential to expand this toolkit and more aggressively address the underlying causes of problems" (p. 397). And, as we have noted before, even some of the earliest proposals for behavioral paternalism did not fully respect individual choice; for instance, consumers typically lack the ability to "opt out" of sin taxes and cooling-off periods. It appears that some behavioral paternalists have already gone a fair distance down the slope. In this chapter, we will lay out some of the reasons why this development is not surprising – and why further slippage is likely.

In Chapter 1, we expressed our intention to rely primarily on conceptual and consequentialist arguments against behavioral paternalism, while leaving the autonomy or freedom-based arguments to the philosophers (despite our admitted sympathy for such arguments). However, in the context of slippery slopes, we cannot entirely ignore questions of freedom and

---

[1] For example, Sunstein and Thaler (2003): "To borrow a phrase, libertarian paternalists urge that people should be 'free to choose.' Hence we do not aim to defend any approach that blocks individual choices" (p. 1161, footnote omitted).

autonomy. We do not claim to offer a philosophical defense of these values. But inasmuch as at least some behavioral paternalists *do* care about freedom and autonomy while claiming that moderate interventions pose little danger to them, it is worthwhile to evaluate that position. In a sense, we are sticking to our consequentialist approach, but we are considering potential incursions on individual autonomy among the possible consequences. To the extent that behavioral paternalists (and our readers) do care about personal liberty, such consequences should be taken into account.

Even for those who do not particularly care about autonomy for its own sake, slippery slopes are still cause for concern. This is true for two reasons. First, there is a consequentialist case in favor of autonomy: that autonomous individuals can be trusted to seek their own best interests conditional on their preferences and beliefs, and *therefore* policies that interfere with their autonomous decisions will tend to make them worse off. It is this position, of course, that behavioral paternalists have challenged most directly. However, the preceding chapters of this book have offered many reasons to doubt that conclusion. Once we accept a more inclusive notion of rationality, it becomes clear that many actions *alleged* to be counter to people's own interests, as they see them, can be justifiable within a broader framework. Furthermore, individuals have privileged access to their own preferences and beliefs, which puts them in a better position to satisfy them. Even when individuals are afflicted by biases, they have superior knowledge of their own attempts at self-correction. To the extent that we have rehabilitated the idea that individuals can usually be trusted to advance their own interests, interventions that threaten their autonomy also threaten their well-being.

Second, as we have emphasized in earlier chapters, implementing effective paternalistic interventions depends crucially on proper calibration of policy variables. In other words, we should not implement just any paternalistic policy; we would need to implement the *right* policy, informed by relevant knowledge about preferences, extent of biases, and so on. Yet slippery-slope argumentation suggests that even optimally calibrated policies may not be stable, but instead set in motion forces that will lead to more extensive intervention irrespective of the initial calibration. In short, slippery slopes make well-crafted paternalistic intervention difficult to maintain.

We will begin by exploring slippery-slope arguments in general and explaining why they are more valid than commonly supposed. Next, we will discuss the relationship of slippery slopes to gradients and show how such gradients inhere in the behavioral paternalist framework. Then, following the pattern of Chapter 8, we consider paternalist slopes that can occur *even if policymakers are fully rational*, and then paternalist slopes resulting from policymakers who are *not fully rational* (in the neoclassical sense). We conclude by offering rejoinders to arguments against slippery-slope analysis in the paternalist context.

THE LOGIC OF SLIPPERY SLOPES

The term "slippery slopes" is shorthand for two related phenomena: slippery-slope *arguments* and slippery-slope *events*. A slippery-slope argument (SSA) is an argument about how the acceptance of one argument (regarding a decision, act, or policy) may lead to the acceptance of other arguments (regarding other decisions, acts, or policies). It describes "a 'process' or 'mechanism' by which accepting the initial argument and making the initial decision raise[s] the likelihood of accepting the later argument and making the later decision" (Rizzo and Whitman 2003, 544).

In this sense, a slippery-slope argument can be characterized as a *meta-argument*: an argument about arguments, and specifically, how some arguments ease the acceptance of others. Although this is true of any slippery-slope argument, it has special importance given the specific manner in which behavioral paternalism has been advanced by its leading proponents. We will argue not just that their proposed policies create slope risks, but also that their *rhetorical strategy itself* creates slope risks. We refer to this rhetorical strategy as the "paternalism-generating framework."

We use the word "risk" deliberately. SSAs do not describe inevitabilities, but simply an increased probability of unfavorable outcomes. "A slippery-slope event (SSE) refers to the actual manifestation of the events (decisions, acts, or policies) described in the SSA" (Rizzo and Whitman 2003, 545). If an SSA provides a highly persuasive cautionary tale, it may help to avert an SSE – possibly by persuading people to oppose the initial policy. Thus, an SSA could be correct and yet the corresponding SSE is never observed (p. 545). Indeed, that is part of our hope in writing this chapter.

Slippery slopes may, in principle, involve only one actor – say, a Robinson Crusoe decision-maker. Crusoe might, for example, start by accepting an argument about the value of relaxation and end up accepting an argument in favor of serious laziness (perhaps because there is, along the way, no clear dividing line between the two). Most slippery slopes, however, involve more than one actor. To take one illustrative example, which is not strictly paternalistic but has a paternalist dimension, suppose the government requires emergency rooms to take all patients regardless of ability to pay. As a result, people engage in activities with greater health risks, such as drinking heavily or riding motorcycles without helmets. In response to those greater risks, as well as greater public exposure to them, the government subsequently passes laws to control those risks, such as mandatory health insurance and mandatory helmet laws. In this story, there are at least two sets of actors involved: the policymakers who adopted the policy and the people affected by it. Importantly, the later policymakers may differ from the original policymakers.

That most slippery slopes involve multiple actors is a point that bears emphasis, as critiques of slippery-slope reasoning often miss it. A slippery-slope skeptic might simply say, "We'll do the right thing today, and then resist doing the wrong thing tomorrow." The problem is that the composition of "we" can change. The policymakers who create the initial policy are not necessarily the same policymakers who will consider a subsequent policy, nor are they coextensive with the people affected by their policies. The initial policymakers do, however, make decisions that affect the environment in which future policymakers will act.

It is therefore useful to clearly distinguish the various actors involved in a slope process. We concentrate on five groups: *policymakers* such as politicians, bureaucrats, judges, and voters; *targeted agents*, that is, those people whose actions are to be controlled or influenced; *rent-seekers*, or those who seek regulations for their own private, but not necessarily monetary, gain; *moralists*, who seek regulations to advance their vision of good personal behavior; and finally, *experts* such as scientists and economists who support policies with their research and advice. (The last three groups are respectively the bootleggers, First Baptists, and Second Baptists discussed in Chapter 8.)

Authors in the slippery-slope literature have also emphasized that there is no *single* slippery-slope phenomenon. Instead, there are various processes or mechanisms by which slippery slopes can occur (Rizzo and Whitman 2003; Volokh 2003). These processes are the key to understanding the "logic" of how one argument or policy can lead to another.

GRADIENTS AND VAGUENESS IN BEHAVIORAL PATERNALISM

As various slippery-slope analysts have recognized, slippery slopes flourish in the presence of a gradient or continuum (Lode 1999, 1477–1482; Rizzo and Whitman 2003, 557–560; Volokh 2003, 1105–1114). When arguments or policies are connected by a series of small (perhaps infinitesimally small) steps, the absence of a sharp line between different cases eases the process of moving from one to another.

Gradients typically result from the vagueness of a key term. For example, there is no precise number of years that separates a "child" from an "adult"; there is no specific IQ that separates the "mentally able" from the "mentally retarded." Though we may choose an arbitrary dividing line for a particular purpose (e.g., 18 years for legal majority or 70 IQ as the dividing line between able and retarded), there is nothing inherently right about it. People on either side of the line may be virtually indistinguishable. We call this *continuity vagueness* because it exists in the presence of a continuously measurable variable, such as IQ or age.

On the other hand, *similarity vagueness* exists when measurement is impossible or irrelevant, or when it depends, at least in part, on imprecise components. We might say, for instance, that a butter knife is similar to a steak knife, a steak knife similar to a dagger, a dagger similar to a sword, and (perhaps) a sword similar to a gun. Similarity relationships are inherently vague because similarity is not precisely definable; it is intuitive and elusive (Rouvray 1992).[2] A judgment of similarity can be based on both objective and subjective (or impressionistic) components along many dimensions.

The existence of a gradient created by vagueness, whether from continuity or similarity, does not necessarily lead to a slippery slope. It is sometimes possible to resist the slope, perhaps by standing firmly on an arbitrary distinction. But the existence of a gradient makes defending a given position harder than it would otherwise be, because no specific line can be defended in principle. And in the presence of similarity (rather than continuity) vagueness, even drawing an arbitrary line can prove difficult. Corner et al. (2011) find experimental evidence supporting the idea that slippery slopes result from a psychological process involving the reappraisal of category boundaries in the presence of conceptual vagueness.

Movement along a gradient is especially likely in the context of precedent-based decision-making, as in a common law judicial system. Given that no two cases are exactly alike, precedent can operate only if

---

[2] "In spite of there being manifold examples of similarity about us, this does not mean that the concept is either easy to comprehend or to define. In fact, the concept is remarkably elusive, and it is fair to say that the concept cannot be defined in any absolute sense. However we may choose to define the similarity of two entities or events, there will always be some arbitrariness associated with whatever measure we adopt" (Rouvray 1992, 580).

decision-makers rely on judgments of continuity or similarity. If there are relatively sharp lines between classes of case, the slippery-slope threat from precedential decision-making is small. But in the presence of a gradient, the slippery-slope threat is larger, as a sequence of "close" cases that differ only slightly can provide a bridge between cases that differ substantially.

Judicial decision-making is especially vulnerable to gradients because of judges' tendency "to place a premium both on drawing non-arbitrary, rationally defensible lines and on maintaining a coherent, consistent body of case law within a particular jurisdiction" (Lode 1999, 1494). Legislators and regulators, on the other hand, can more easily impose arbitrary distinctions. But legislative and regulatory decision-making is not immune to slipping on gradients, for at least three reasons.

First, the fact that legislators *can* impose arbitrary lines does not necessarily mean they *will*. Their political incentives can militate against taking unambiguous stands that create clear winners and losers, and their interests may be better served by ceding discretion to bureaucrats or judges. Gary Bryner points out that "[m]ost regulatory laws, however, give little guidance to agencies for the substance of their regulations and for the way in which the burdens they impose are to be distributed ... Some laws provide competing objectives that give administrators broad latitude" (1987, 7).

Second, as discussed at length in Chapter 8, legislators and bureaucrats are subject to the pressures of lobbying by interest groups, including both rent-seekers and moralists. Such groups may have an interest in pushing for small changes that gradually move policy along the gradient (Lode 1999).[3] Importantly, these groups may not share behavioral paternalists' deference to the subjective preferences of targeted agents.

Third, once an initial policy is in place where no policy existed before, it often becomes politically cheaper than before to propose extensions to that policy. There are at least three reasons for this:

1. The creation of an initial policy may involve incurring certain fixed costs, such as setting up an administrative agency to implement the policy. As a result, the added cost of extensions to that policy will be reduced – a process that Volokh (2003) refers to as a "cost-lowering slippery slope" (pp. 1039–1051). To illustrate, the administrative cost

---

[3] "[P]eople with power and influence also may stand to gain economically from taking steps down the slope. In addition, they may think that it is better from a moral point of view to take such steps" (Lode 1999, 1513).

to collect a $1.25 tax per unit differs little from the cost to collect a $1.00 tax per unit, but the administrative cost to collect a $1.00 tax per unit is substantially greater than the cost to collect zero tax per unit.

2. The attitudes of policymakers – voters, politicians, regulators, and judges – may change after the initial policy step, because even rational actors are subject to the "is–ought heuristic." The is–ought heuristic indicates that a rule or law, once in place, provides *evidence* that this type of intervention is acceptable (Volokh 2003, 1081). This effect is especially likely when it is costly to evaluate policy. Therefore voters and politicians rationally look to existing policies for signals of policy desirability.

3. Policymakers may be affected by the improved political position of an interest group that has a victory under its belt. It may, with good reason, appear to be more likely to win victories in the future (Volokh 2003, 1122–1123). Politicians want to hear "winning ideas" so they can claim to have made legislative accomplishments, which means interest groups with recent victories will be more likely to be persuasive. Together, these three factors (and possibly others) can make the legislative process susceptible to slipping down gradients.

The existence of a gradient does not, in itself, tell us in which direction the sliding (if any) will go. In principle, we could imagine a slippery slope that leads toward less paternalism rather than more. However, there are various factors that tend to impart an interventionist direction to the slope. The cost-lowering effect of incurring fixed costs, the attitude-shifting dynamic of the is–ought heuristic, and the empowerment of interest groups are among those reasons. Gradients create fertile ground for those processes and others to operate.

How Behavioral Paternalism Creates New Gradients

The behavioral paternalist paradigm, as presented by its leading advocates, relies on discarding sharp distinctions in favor of gradients. Specifically, those advocates reject standard distinctions between choice and coercion and between public and private action. Sunstein and Thaler (2003) minimize the importance of the distinction between paternalism in the private and in the public sectors (p. 1162). In explaining their concept of "libertarian paternalism," they say that the distinction between libertarian and nonlibertarian paternalism "is not simple and rigid" (p. 1185). Moreover, they explicitly state that libertarian and nonlibertarian paternalism lie on a continuum: "[t]he libertarian paternalist insists on preserving choice, whereas the non-libertarian paternalist is willing to foreclose choice. But in all cases, a real question is the cost of exercising choice, and here there is a continuum rather than a sharp dichotomy" (p. 1185).

Sunstein and Thaler thus present us with a gradient on which choice is characterized by low costs of escaping the prescribed course of action, while coercion corresponds to higher costs of escape. Who imposes the costs of escape and how these costs are imposed are treated as unimportant questions. This is by no means the *only* way to frame the issue of freedom versus coercion, but it is the one the leading paternalists have advanced. To see how this framework operates, it will be useful to consider the specific order and manner in which they have presented their proposals (most of which we have already discussed).

Sunstein and Thaler begin their analysis with a low cost-of-exit point on the continuum: the seemingly innocuous question of where sugary desserts are placed in a cafeteria line (Sunstein and Thaler 2003, 1164; Thaler and Sunstein 2003, 175). No options are completely blocked, although the costs of exercising some of them are raised, however slightly.[4] This is presented as a pure case of "libertarian paternalism."[5] Their next example, with somewhat higher costs of exit, is the automatic enrollment of employees in retirement-savings programs with the ability to opt out (Sunstein and Thaler 2003, 1172–1173). So far there is no mention of coercion, by government or anyone else.[6]

Further along the gradient is the suggestion that a legal mandate on employers to adopt automatic enrollment may be consistent with "libertarian goals," and that implementing such a mandate "would respect the freedom of employees to choose, and . . . would be libertarian in that sense" (Sunstein and Thaler 2003, 1176). That the freedom of employers is restricted goes unmentioned. Nevertheless, the state has now entered the

---

[4] Specifically, a customer who puts fruit on his tray and then sees cake that he prefers will have to put back the fruit.

[5] As Daniel Klein points out, the use of the term "libertarian" in this context serves no analytical function, since it would be equally libertarian for private restaurant owners to eliminate desserts from the menu altogether; they have no obligation to provide desserts in any form to their customers (2004, 266).

[6] Again, the word "libertarian" serves no analytical function here, since it would be equally libertarian for employers to require their employees to join a savings plan with no exit option, or even to pay lower wages and invest money on employees' behalf.

picture in a way that is ever so tentative – a relatively small intervention that is not explicitly advocated, but simply mentioned as a possibility.

Still further along the continuum of coercion lie default or framing rules, such as a legal presumption of "for-cause" rather than "at-will" termination, minimum vacation time, and other labor-friendly terms in labor contracts. Sunstein and Thaler claim that some amount of paternalism is "inevitable" (2002, 1174) in such cases, but that is not necessarily true, because assignment of a default rule does not require either paternalistic intent or state intervention. Rather, the law could merely accept the results of customary practice; what is recognized by the law need not have been created by it. Defaults can also evolve through competitive interaction in the marketplace, in response to the needs of both buyers and sellers; indeed, this is likely the source of most customary expectations ratified by law. The imposition of a new default rule effectively *shifts transaction costs* (that is, the costs of negotiating agreements) from those who would depart from customary practice to those who would follow it.[7] How far such interventions to alter contractual defaults take us along the continuum of costs depends upon the ease of opting out.

The next step along the continuum, however, is to impose *additional* transaction costs instead of merely shifting them. For example, Sunstein and Thaler offer the Age Discrimination in Employment Act (ADEA) as another example of libertarian paternalism (2003, 1186–1187). The ADEA allows employees to sign a "knowing and voluntary" waiver at retirement of age-discrimination protections. For the waiver to be valid, however, it must meet a series of requirements, including consultation with a lawyer, a twenty-one-day waiting period, and a seven-day revocation period. Further, consulting a lawyer is costly for the employee, and the rest of the requirements are burdensome to the employer (p. 1187).[8]

Yet further along the continuum is legislation that creates new defaults that can be waived, but *only under conditions set by the state*. One example is the Fair Labor Standards Act, discussed in Chapter 1, which imposes a

---

[7] When the default is at-will termination, those who prefer for-cause termination will have to initiate a negotiation for different terms. If a paternalistic law changes the default to for-cause termination, then those who prefer at-will termination will have to initiate a negotiation for different terms. Negotiations are costly. Therefore, the paternalistic law shifts the negotiation costs from those who prefer for-cause termination to those who prefer at-will termination.

[8] Sunstein and Thaler (2003): "[T]he ADEA goes beyond the inevitable minimum level of paternalism by imposing those barriers, which significantly raise the burdens of waiver" (p. 1187).

maximum number of hours per week. In order to waive the forty hours per week maximum, workers must receive time-and-a-half pay for the extra hours; they cannot waive the maximum number of hours for any lower rate of pay. Here, the default rule is not merely a default, because it expressly prohibits certain exchanges. Similarly, Sunstein and Thaler point to the Model Employment Termination Act, which replaces at-will with for-cause termination. This right can be waived by agreement – but only if the employer agrees to provide a severance payment (equal to one month's salary for every year of employment) in the event of a not-for-cause termination. Of this policy, Sunstein and Thaler say that it is "less libertarian than it might be. But freedom of choice is nonetheless respected" (2003, 1187). Yet freedom of choice is *not* fully respected; the employer and employee are prohibited from arriving at contracts with "at-will" termination and no severance payment.[9]

Once we reach the point of actually restricting the terms of voluntary agreements, the movement along the continuum is straightforward: either increase the cost associated with opting out, further restrict the terms of agreements, or both. Here, for instance, Sunstein and Thaler back mandatory cooling-off periods, during which consumers would be allowed to return purchased items (such as cars) without penalty (2003, 1187–1188). For this policy, they do not even mention the possibility of consumers waiving the requirement (even if doing so might earn a price discount).

At the far end of the continuum lie outright bans on certain activities. Sunstein and Thaler embrace this conclusion: "Almost all of the time, even the non-libertarian paternalist will allow choosers, at some cost, to reject the proposed course of action. Those who are required to wear motorcycle helmets can decide to risk the relevant penalty, and to pay it if need be" (2003, 1189–1190).

Notice that the same argument would place outright prohibition of alcohol, drugs, or anything else on the same spectrum. You are free to do anything you want, says the argument, if you're willing to incur the cost of potential imprisonment. At this end of the continuum, we find, lies genuine hard paternalism. In Sunstein and Thaler's words:

A libertarian paternalist who is especially enthusiastic about free choice would be inclined to make it relatively costless for people to obtain their preferred outcomes. (Call this a *libertarian* paternalist.) By contrast, a libertarian paternalist who is

---

[9] Employees might wish to make such agreements if the alternative is lower wages or unemployment. Ruling out some contract options means that some contracts won't be made at all.

especially confident of his welfare judgments would be willing to impose real costs on workers and consumers who seek to do what, in the paternalist's view, would not be in their best interests. (Call this a libertarian *paternalist*.)

(Sunstein and Thaler 2003, 1185–1186, emphasis in original)

Movement along a paternalist continuum should come as no surprise when the two ends of the continuum depend on which word is italicized, as well as on the subjective confidence of the policymaker in his welfare judgments. Although Sunstein and Thaler stop short of explicitly endorsing bans, they fit within the proffered framework.

It bears emphasis that the sequence of steps we've outlined – from nudging (changing the order of cafeteria items) to pushing (imposing costs on those who deviate from the state's preferred terms of contract) to shoving (ruling out some terms entirely) to controlling (banning some activities altogether) – is not our creation. Sunstein and Thaler present the same proposals in approximately the same order, to demonstrate the existence of a continuum.

We have focused on Sunstein and Thaler's work because they are admirably explicit about their belief in a paternalist continuum. But the same pattern can be observed in Camerer et al. (2003), who also structure their proposals in order from the seemingly innocuous to the fully intrusive. They summarize the progression as follows: "We focus on four types of policies: (1) default rules; (2) provision or re-framing of information; (3) cooling-off periods; and (4) limiting consumer choices. This list is ranked roughly in increasing order of departure from pure asymmetric paternalism—i.e., the increasing 'heavy-handedness' of the policy" (p. 1224).

Again, we see that leading behavioral paternalists believe that soft and hard paternalism can be connected by a series of small steps. Like Sunstein and Thaler, Camerer et al. (2003) present public and private, and coercive and noncoercive, paternalistic activities alongside each other with little or no recognition of when they are crossing the line from one to the other. They describe their position as "asymmetric paternalism," meaning a form of paternalism that helps irrational agents while imposing negligible costs on fully rational agents. Yet in discussing asymmetrically paternalistic regulations that operate by requiring the provision of information, they offer state occupational licensing as an example (p. 1237). Unless they mean a form of licensing that merely requires the unlicensed to reveal that fact (a form of licensing for which we are hard pressed to find a single example), the "asymmetrically paternalistic" classification is completely mistaken because significant costs are imposed on rational agents. Licensing requirements typically coerce both service providers and clients by preventing them from engaging in voluntary transactions – but the authors do not mention this.

Some may object that the existence of a gradient from soft to hard paternalism is just a fact, and that behavioral paternalists cannot be faulted for pointing it out. But the gradient in fact *results* from the conceptual framework that behavioral paternalists have adopted and urge the rest of us to adopt. The main problem with the framework, in our view, is that it defines freedom of choice (and libertarianism) in terms of costs-of-exit, *without any attention to who imposes the costs and how*. To see how this framework is misleading, consider two cases: (1) a person who has voluntarily chosen to live many miles from the nearest convenience store, which considerably increases the cost of buying a Twinkie; and (2) a state tax of ten cents on the same Twinkie. In the Sunstein–Thaler framework, the former is more coercive than the latter simply because of the higher cost. The fact that the cost in the former case is self-imposed, and in the latter case state-imposed, does not enter the discussion.

An alternative framework, one that is more consistent with the typical usage of words such as coercion and choice,[10] would focus on whether rights of person and property are abridged by a given policy. In this framework, a restaurateur's decision about dessert placement and a government's decision about whether to allow helmetless motorcycle riding simply would not be on the same continuum. The former is private and noncoercive, the latter public and coercive. This is the sort of framework that behavioral paternalists encourage us to reject in favor of theirs.

How Behavioral Paternalism Exploits Existing Gradients

In addition to creating new conceptual gradients, behavioral paternalism also exploits gradients that already exist as a result of theoretical or empirical vagueness.

Hyperbolic and Quasi-Hyperbolic Discounting. We have already discussed hyperbolic preferences several times in this book. In particular, we have highlighted the non sequitur of showing that an individual has multiple inconsistent rates of time-discounting and then assuming that one of these rates must be their "true" rate of time-discounting. We have also

---

[10] And certainly more consistent with the way self-described libertarians use these words – a relevant observation when the framework is dubbed "libertarian paternalism."

drawn attention to the extreme difficulty of identifying the true rate of intertemporal discounting, even if we assume such a thing exists. Here, we will take the argument a step further.

On a theoretical level, behavioral economics provides no clear *standard* by which to determine what is the correct normative level of discounting – despite the fact that behavioral economists have repeatedly favored more patient rates of discount (e.g., O'Donoghue and Rabin 2015, 276). The implicit normative standard is exponential discounting, which merely requires a constant rate of discounting over time; this is no help when it comes to choosing among multiple internally consistent rates of discounts that are inconsistent with each other. And as we have seen in Chapter 4, there is little reason to believe that longer-term rates are free of bias. Thus, the very notion of basing policy on "true" rates of time-discounting is inherently vague.

On an empirical level, we have seen that there are multiple measures of both short-term and long-term rates of discount. The research does not appear to be converging on a clear answer as to what people's true long-term and short-term rates of discount are.[11] On the contrary, it appears that actual behavior has features of true (rather than quasi-) hyperbolic discounting, which means each individual may have a gradient of discount rates. Discount rates also differ across individuals and demographic groups (Soman et al. 2005, 354), raising questions about whose discount rate (or rates) ought to be privileged by law.

In short, the target rate of time discount involved in any attempt to "help" agents with hyperbolic preferences is *inherently vague*. We do not know where "reasonable" impatience ends and "excessive" impatience begins. There is no sharp dividing line between them. There is little promise that future research will resolve these questions. This vagueness itself is sufficient to create a gradient. There is no clear line to resist the gradual creep of higher savings requirements, higher fat taxes, and the like.

Framing and Context-Dependence. As we have discussed often in this book, people are subject to what behavioral economists call context-dependence: how they choose among two or more options depends on seemingly irrelevant aspects of how the situation is described. The phenomenon of context-dependence underlies various behavioral paternalist proposals. All of Sunstein and Thaler's proposals for new contractual defaults, for example, rely on the difference between willingness to pay

---

[11] See discussion in Chapter 4.

and willingness to accept, which is a form of context-dependence (p. 1181).[12]

The problem with context-dependence is similar to that of hyperbolic discounting. The behavioral paternalist argument relies on an internal inconsistency to justify intervention – but as we have argued before, there is no valid and convincing basis for choosing which behavior represents the individual's "true" preference. There is no theoretically correct answer to this question, as Sunstein and Thaler (2003) admit: "If the arrangement of the alternatives has a significant effect on the selections the customers make, then their true 'preferences' do not formally exist" (p. 1164). In the absence of a true preference as the correct standard, what standard should be used? Sunstein and Thaler decline to answer that question: "We are not attempting to say anything controversial about welfare, or to take sides in reasonable disputes about how to understand that term" (2003, 1163, n. 17). This is the very definition of vagueness.

Given the absence of a clear standard courtesy of behavioral economic theory, the answer to the "what standard" question will depend on policymakers' own particular notions of welfare and well-being, as well as the weight they attach to autonomy. Notably, behavioral economics does not necessarily place *any* weight on autonomy, despite Sunstein and Thaler's obeisance to the value of individual choice. Policymakers who adopt the behavioral paternalists' approach need not share their belief in choice. The behavioral paternalist paradigm places them on a gradient from policies that only mildly restrict choice to policies that restrict or abolish it.

Emotional Responses. Some paternalist policies are meant to operate by manipulating people's emotional responses to information or other stimuli. Jolls and Sunstein's (2006) risk-narrative proposal is the best example of this approach. Recall that in this proposal, policy would attempt to correct optimism bias by requiring producers of dangerous products to "provide [to consumers] a truthful account of consequences that resulted from a particular harm-producing use of the product" (p. 212). The tendency of people to take narratives more seriously than statistical information is characterized as a form of availability bias. A narrative has a greater capacity to grab someone's attention on an emotional level.

---

[12] "A default rule might create a 'pure' endowment effect. It is well known that people tend to value goods more highly if those goods have been initially allocated to them than if those goods have been initially allocated elsewhere. And it is well known that, in many cases, the default rule will create an initial endowment effect" (Sunstein and Thaler 2003, 1181).

For risk narratives to be effective, they have to be sufficiently frightening or visceral. And therein lies the problem: there is no objective line between "not frightening enough" and "too frightening." Jolls and Sunstein admit that excessively frightening narratives could be counterproductive, inducing too little risk-taking, and their response is telling: "Of course there are line-drawing problems here, but the basic point is straightforward" (p. 214). Line-drawing problems are, of course, the telltale sign of a gradient. What is the right level of emotional response needed to qualify a decision as rational? As an empirical matter, there is simply no way to know whether customers who engage in a risky activity are doing so rationally – with a full understanding of the risks – or have simply not been exposed to a sufficiently scary narrative. The gradient goes from missing narrative to mildly compelling narrative to worst-case-scenario narrative. Courts of law asked to adjudicate "insufficient narratives" claims under Jolls and Sunstein's proposed law could easily, if guided by precedent-based decision-making, slide down the gradient.

The gradient could even cross the threshold between truth and falsehood. Although the policy description above specifies a "truthful account," there is no particular reason, in theory, to think a truthful account provides the appropriate visceral response to approximate a rational assessment of risk. Sunstein and Thaler (2003) themselves state that truthful information can, in cases, be harmful: "In the face of health risks, for example, some presentations of accurate information might actually be counterproductive, because people might attempt to control their fear by refusing to think about the risk at all" (p. 1183). If too much information is a bad thing, then policies that require withholding information could be justified on the same grounds as policies that require providing narratives. And if withholding information can be the correct choice, it might also be appropriate to lie – if such lies do a better job of pushing people toward what policymakers think is in their best interests.

What Jolls and Sunstein propose, then, is a movement from a bright-line liability rule that requires truthful statistical information, to a vague liability rule that requires generating the "correct" level of emotional response – with no objective means, in theory or evidence, of determining what is correct.

SLIPPERY SLOPES WITH RATIONAL POLICYMAKERS

In this section we will analyze "rational" slippery-slope processes, i.e., those in which the choices of experts, policymakers, moralists, and rent-seekers are rational in the standard economic sense of the term. Only the choices of the targeted agents are subject to cognitive or behavioral biases. We adopt this approach to show that behavioral paternalist policies have an expansive tendency *even if* policymakers are somehow immune to the biases that behavioral paternalists ascribe to most people.

In some cases, the slope process may be driven by decision-making heuristics, and some of these heuristics might be characterized as less than fully rational. In this section, however, we only invoke those heuristics that can easily be characterized as rational responses to scarcity of information and time. We will discuss three major categories of rational slippery slopes: altered incentive slopes; authority and simplification slopes; and expanding justification slopes.

Altered Incentives Slopes

Sometimes acceptance of an initial policy can induce unintended or unexpected changes in the behavior of target agents, thereby creating an incentive for policymakers (either the same policymakers or later ones) to enact further policies to control or correct the new behavior. The unintended consequences may occur because of the interaction of the targets' biases, the crowding out of the targets' self-regulatory behaviors, and the substitution between targets' personal inputs, all of which can impede attainment of the paternalists' goals.

Bias Interactions. In Chapter 7, we introduced the idea that multiple biases can interact; some biases may partially offset others. As a result, if one bias is corrected by policy while another is ignored, the latter bias may create new problems or worsen existing ones. In the earlier discussion, our focus was on showing that policymakers must have knowledge of bias interactions in order to craft welfare-improving policies. But here we focus on the resulting slippery-slope potential: if paternalist interventions create or exacerbate other behavioral problems, policymakers will have incentives to engage in further interventions.

To take the example from Besharov (2004) discussed in Chapter 8, overconfidence can offset present bias when it comes to decisions about whether to pursue projects that involve future rewards. Overconfidence effectively inflates the potential rewards in a manner that (partially or completely) cancels out their deflation due to present bias. Now, suppose a new paternalist policy successfully corrects overconfidence related to projects with future rewards. Given that the biases had previously offset each other, reducing overconfidence could exacerbate the effect of present bias, resulting in agents who are unwilling to take enough risks. If policymakers observe that unintended result, they may then take additional action aimed at correcting the present bias.

Another example is provided by fat taxes and cigarette taxes. An implicit assumption in these policy proposals is that the higher prices will be experienced by the current self – the one that is subject to the temptations of overeating and smoking. If, however, the targeted agents have access to credit, then they can "offload" the increased financial burden to their future selves (Whitman 2006, 12). To put it another way, there can be an interaction between present bias in eating/smoking decisions and present bias in savings decisions. An attempt to correct the former can therefore exacerbate the latter, which will give policymakers added incentive to regulate savings decisions.

If cognitive and behavioral biases interact in a simple manner – as in the simple paired interactions just described – then there may be a natural stopping point to the slippery slope. Corrective legislation in area A leads to a problem in area B, and thus to corrective legislation in area B, and the process ends. But if, as we suspect, cognitive and behavioral biases interact through a complex web of effects, then the process need not have a stopping point. Each corrective intervention leads to problems that potentially justify yet more interventions.

Crowding Out of Self-Regulation. Bias interaction, as previously described, can create slopes wherein intervention in one area creates incentives for policymakers to intervene in other areas. Here, we consider a process by which intervention in one area creates an incentive for further intervention in the same area.

The effect occurs because the initial policy turns out to be ineffective or counterproductive for some reason, and therefore the same motivation that justified the initial interventions can justify further interventions. As Volokh (2003) has noted, policymakers will often cite the need to enforce an existing policy as a reason for enacting new policies (pp. 1051–1056). More broadly, enactment of a policy generally involves a commitment to achieving certain goals; as long as those goals remain unachieved, policymakers have the incentive to intervene further. In the case of behavioral paternalist legislation, we think this effect is most likely to arise from the crowding out of self-regulation.

In previous chapters, we have discussed the various means people use to control their own cognitive and behavioral problems (as they perceive them). Examples include making resolutions and commitments, using mental budgets, imposing self-reward and self-punishment schemes, creating self-imposed constraints, and deliberately exposing themselves to external social controls from family, friends, social groups, and organizations. We have also highlighted the role of counteractive self-control, by which people reconceptualize objects of temptation in order to prioritize their highest-level goals. Most importantly, we have drawn attention to the experimental studies by Fischbach and Trope (2005), which have shown that the imposition of some forms of external control can cause individuals to engage in less counteractive self-control. (See Chapter 6 for elaboration of this point.)

In short, individuals may treat external control and self-control as functional substitutes, which has important implications for paternalist policymaking. Suppose a policymaker decides to place a tax on a "bad" activity or a subsidy on a "good" activity. Insofar as the new policy is perceived as a form of external control, the evidence suggests that targeted agents will respond by decreasing their level of self-control. This means that if such results are difficult to anticipate, as they will be for rationally ignorant policymakers, the initial policy will later be found insufficient. Then arguments will be made for increasing the subsidy or tax and expanding the degree of paternalistic intervention. The changing behavior of the target agents generates a new round of incentives for policymakers to intervene.

There is a close analogy here to the economic literature on public goods and externalities. Economic theory indicates that an increase in the amount of state funding for a public good (say, maintenance of a public park) can lead to an offsetting decrease in the amount of private funding for the same good (Abrams and Schitz 1978; Bergstrom et al. 1986; Bernheim 1986). Similarly, Buchanan (1969) has argued that a tax on a negative externality (his example is the noise nuisance created by someone's barking dogs) can decrease the degree to which the nuisance creator takes into account costs to others, such as his neighbors, when deciding how much nuisance to create (Buchanan 1969). In a sense, the state-imposed tax diminishes the self-imposed tax. The same point applies in the context of paternalist policies designed to correct "internalities" created by conflict between one's present and future selves: we can expect that individuals will reduce the extent of their self-regulation (Whitman 2006, 12–13).

To the extent that paternalistic policies reduce self-regulation, they will tend to produce unsatisfactory results relative to expectations. That disappointment sets the stage for further intervention. In theory, it would be possible for behavioral paternalists to resist further intervention on the grounds that *outcomes* are not the issue. They have admitted that (for instance) it is not intrinsically irrational to place greater value on hedonic pleasures than on long-term health. The problem, they claim, is that people commit errors in the implementation of their own preferences. So, if a paternalistic policy has counteracted those errors, and yet behavior hasn't changed, that could be judged as a policy success; whatever "bad" behavior remains must correspond to people's true preferences. But this response seems unlikely. It seems more likely that if initial interventions fail to produce the expected results on concrete goals such as reducing obesity, increasing savings, reducing debt burdens, and so on, that will provide the impetus for more aggressive intervention.

In this regard, we should observe the key role that can be played by shifting majorities in democratic politics. If behavioral paternalists and their allies all shared a single attitude – one that privileges people's own true preferences over those of outsiders, and that favors the preservation of freedom of choice whenever possible – then the same majority that supported the initial intervention could be counted upon to oppose subsequent interventions, on essentially the grounds discussed previously. But as the slippery-slope literature emphasizes, each step in the process of intervention can be supported by different coalitions with different rankings of policies (Volokh 2003, 1041–1043; Rizzo and Whitman 2003, 563–567). Upon the perceived failure of the initial intervention, perhaps some of the original supporters will oppose further action. But others will favor additional intervention; recall that some behavioral paternalists are already on board with harder paternalism. They will be joined by moralists who never cared much about individual preferences to begin with, rent-seekers who expect to gain from more intrusive policies, and bureaucrats in newly created agencies who see the opportunity to expand their power and influence. Still other political actors will support further intervention out of the simple belief that it is good practice to carry through on policy commitments rather than abandoning them.

Indeed, we have already seen how the failure of soft interventions to generate expected results can lead the supposed experts to get behind more aggressive intervention. In a *New York Times* op-ed, George Loewenstein (a behavioral economist) and Peter Ubel (a physician and behavioral scientist) observe that mandatory calorie posting at restaurants has had little impact on eating choices – and immediately jump to the conclusion that policy needs to increase the relative price of unhealthy foods to have a real impact (Loewenstein and Ubel 2010). In their analysis, the justifiability of the policy goal of reducing overweightness and encouraging better health is simply taken as given. The remainder of the op-ed considers a number of other policy arenas in which, they suggest, the failure of a behavioral "nudge" provides grounds for more aggressive intervention.[13]

Substitutability of Personal Inputs. Much as external and internal self-control can be substitute inputs in the attainment of one's goals, different forms of personal activity can also be substitute inputs. For instance, the goal of reducing one's weight can be served by two activities: eating healthily and exercising regularly. Following Fishbach and coauthors (2006), we will refer to the larger goal as the "superordinate goal" and the inputs as "subgoals." To the extent the individual views the subgoals as substitutes, greater attainment of one subgoal will lead to a reduction in the other subgoal.

Now suppose that some form of external control leads to greater attainment of a subgoal. For instance, suppose a fat tax helps the individual to improve her diet, and this might seem to be an improvement (from a paternalist perspective). However, she might also reduce her effort toward other subgoals, such as exercise. The overall effect on the individual's weight could be negligible or even positive. As a result, policymakers have reason to intervene further – by increasing the fat tax, or subsidizing gym memberships, or perhaps even resorting to food bans and exercise mandates.

The above reasoning follows even in a straightforward rational-choice framework, given personal preferences that regard healthy eating and frequent exercise as substitutes in the maintenance of weight. But if targeted agents are susceptible to a myopic focus on subgoals, rather than focusing on the superordinate goal, this makes the substitution effect even more likely.[14] When a person is focused on the *subgoal* of eating more healthily, she is likely to interpret the effect of the fat tax as progress toward

---

[13] Loewenstein and Ubel pitch their position in terms of the limits of behavioral economics, and thus how neoclassical economics can sometimes provide superior solutions. But they do not actually repudiate behavioral economics, as they assume the choices people are making are indeed flawed and need correction. What they really mean is that the sort of policy interventions that typically come from neoclassical economics, such as changing relative prices, can be more effective than the "nudges" often advocated by behavioral economists.

[14] "The degree to which individuals interpret subgoal attainment in terms of progress or commitment depends on their attention to the relatively concrete subgoal in comparison to the corresponding, relatively abstract superordinate goal ... In the course of pursuing multiple goals (e.g., weight loss and food enjoyment), partial fulfillment of a focal goal suggests to the individual that other objectives are somewhat neglected, further motivating disengagement from that goal" (Fishbach et al. 2006, 233).

the primary goal of good health. Then, in a world of multiple goals and a desire to maximize overall utility, she may shift away from exercise to the pursuit of other, unrelated goals – such as the relatively neglected goal of watching television.[15]

If the individuals affected by the tax are relatively myopic, insofar as their focus is mainly on the subgoal of reducing the junk or fat content of their diet, this research suggests that they will cut back on other health-producing activities such as working out. Whether a tax on the fat content of food actually promotes better health will be affected not only by the impact on fat intake but also by the impact on complementary activities. It is not a foregone conclusion that the net effect will be positive. Indeed, if individuals are being "compelled" to reduce fat intake by a tax when they have no operative interest in doing so, then it is likely that their main focus will be on the subgoal, meaning the substitution effect is more likely.

More generally, when there are multiple inputs to an overarching goal, paternalistic policies that increase input to that goal can decrease the other input, thereby making the policy less effective or even counterproductive. As a result, policymakers may be tempted to engage in further interventions.

Authority and Simplification Slopes

Substantial deference to authority is inherent in the application of behavioral paternalist ideas to public policy. This is because the complexities, vagueness, and indeterminism of their analysis raise the costs of decision-making on the part of voters, politicians, and bureaucrats. The locus of effective decision-making will then quite reasonably shift to experts ("authorities") or to simplifiers of technical ideas who may have agendas of their own. As Volokh puts it, "[t]he more complicated a question seems, the more likely it is that voters will assume that they can't figure it out themselves and should therefore defer to the expert judgment of authoritative institutions" (2003, 1082).

There will thus be a tendency for policy to slide away from the values of the targeted agents themselves toward those of outsiders regarded as

---

[15] "On the other hand, when the focus is on the superordinate goal, the same level of successful attainment highlights commitment to that overall goal ... For example, when the goal to have an attractive figure is highly accessible, an initial success at losing weight strengthens the commitment to this goal as well as related activities toward that end (e.g., working out)" (Fishbach et al. 2006, 233).

authorities. Although it may seem as though shifting effective decision-making to experts is the right thing to do in difficult cases, this is not always true. It is especially unlikely to be true in the case of behavioral paternalist policies because, as we have argued earlier, the underlying standards and information needed to craft welfare-improving policies are *fundamentally* vague and indeterminate. The experts themselves have, at best, only a tenuous grip on the values of the targeted agents, which limits the direct applicability of their paternalistic theories to policy. Thus, there will be a tendency for the experts to reify their own values, and to simplify their own theories, in order to make more definite policy recommendations. We offer two examples of how this has already occurred in the behavioral paternalist literature.

First, there has been a notable tendency in the behavioral paternalist literature to resolve internal conflict in favor of the expert's preferences. Consider the previously mentioned assumption, on the part of analysts trying to calculate optimal sin taxes, that the appropriate normative rate of time discounting is the longer-run rate (that is, the one that applies when all costs and benefits lie in the future).[16] This assumption is offered without argument, but the choice is probably not arbitrary. It reflects, no doubt, certain intellectual middle-class values – not coincidentally, the values of many experts. A similar presumption underlies the assumption that, between decision-making in a "hot" state (of fear, anxiety, arousal, etc.) and decision-making in a "cool" state (calm and sober), the latter must better represent an agent's "true" preferences (Loewenstein 2000; Sunstein and Thaler 2003, 1188).[17]

The underlying values of the new paternalists are also revealed in their more "casual" statements of their positions. Thaler and Sunstein, along with many others, think that Americans are too fat. Too fat by what standard? As Thaler and Sunstein (2003) recognize, consistent behavioral paternalism requires that the standard be the *overall* preferences of the targets themselves. Obviously, these preferences involve a certain balancing of health risks, attractiveness, enjoyable food, avoidance of unpleasant physical exertion, and so forth – all in the context, of course, of ultimate certain death. Yet their evidence for the proposition that Americans are too fat is simply that Americans' weight has increased despite the health

---

[16] See Gruber and Köszegi (2001, 1287) and O'Donoghue and Rabin (2003, 187).
[17] "The essential rationale [for cooling-off periods] is that under the heat of the moment, consumers might make ill-considered or improvident decisions" (Sunstein and Thaler 2003, 1188).

consequences: "Given the adverse effects obesity has on health, it is hard to claim that Americans are eating optimal diets" (p. 176). This is a complete non sequitur. There are costs of being overweight; no one is denying these.[18] But there are benefits of indulgence as well. In a later paper Sunstein and Thaler seem to recognize the subjectivity of the cost–benefit balance:

> Of course, rational people care about the taste of food, not simply about health, and we do not claim that everyone who is overweight is necessarily failing to act rationally. It is the strong claim that all or almost all Americans are choosing their diet *optimally* that we reject as untenable.
>
> (Sunstein and Thaler 2003, 1168)

What does "optimal" look like? Even if everyone acted in a manner fully consistent with their "true" preferences, there would surely be some people who qualified as overweight or obese. People would still die of weight-related illnesses, so the mere fact of such illnesses does not constitute evidence of suboptimal diets.

As we argued at length in Chapter 4, when the evidence reveals a conflict between competing preference orderings within the individual, neither theory nor evidence provides a reliable basis for favoring one preference ordering over another. Yet the behavioral paternalists do not hesitate, when making policy recommendations, to choose among the competing preferences. They claim to have found policy interventions that will make targeted agents better off according to the *targeted agents'* own preferences, when in fact they have found evidence of internal conflict in the target agents' preferences and then resolved the conflict in favor of the *experts'* preferences. The error in reasoning is subtle enough not to be detected by most nonexperts (and perhaps not even by the experts themselves).

What creates the slippery-slope potential here is the veneer of scientific objectivity. It is the simplified argument, not the original and more sophisticated one, that becomes reified in policy. Yet the simplified form of the argument can justify far more than the initial intervention, especially if the experts are appointed to agencies and commissions tasked with implementing it. If simple observations – that people weigh more than they used to, that they don't save as much as we think they should – are taken as *ipso facto* evidence of suboptimal choices, then further intervention will surely follow.

---

[18] There is, however, some doubt as to how overweight one must be for the ill-health effects to occur. See the discussion in Chapter 8 on the definition of overweightness and obesity.

Second, behavioral paternalists have tended to elide important qualifications of their own arguments. Consider the rule for asymmetric paternalism proposed by Camerer and coauthors (2003, 1219). If some fraction of the public p is irrational, irrational people will receive a per capita benefit of B, and rational people will suffer a per capita cost of C, then the policy is justified if

$$pB - (1 - p) C > 0$$

(We have simplified their model slightly to exclude implementation costs and profits to firms.) The rule corresponds to a set of justifications: if the benefit (B) to irrational people is large enough, *and* the cost to rational people (C) is small enough, *and* the ratio of irrational to rational people is high enough, then the policy is justified. Notice, however, the shorthand explanation the authors offer:

> Such policies are appealing because, even possessing little information about the frequency of consumer errors, as long as we think p is positive—as long as we can get even the truest believer in consumer rationality to concede that some agents, some of the time, exhibit bounded rationality—we can conclude with some confidence that the policy is on net beneficial.
>
> (p. 1219)

This explanation is wrong. Given their own criterion, it is not sufficient for the fraction of irrational people to be positive; it must also be true that the ratio of benefits (B) to costs (C) is greater than the ratio of rational to irrational persons. To the authors' credit, in the very next paragraph they clarify the principle (pp. 1219–1220). We have less confidence, however, that policymakers internalizing the asymmetric paternalism criterion will be so careful. Instead, they could easily draw out a simpler principle: *a policy is beneficial as long as there exist some irrational people.* This is a case of a broader justification substituting for a narrower one (or alternatively, a stripping away of important qualifications). Even if the initial policymakers do not employ this broader principle, subsequent policymakers may well infer it.

To compound this problem, however, even the narrower, initial criterion is itself a significant simplification, in that it imagines that the population can be cleanly divided into rational and irrational groups. In reality, irrationality presumably exists on a spectrum, with people being subject to varying degrees of irrationality. Thus, the proportion of people significantly benefiting from a policy may be smaller than the "irrational" category's size would suggest. Behavioral paternalists have already felt the need to elide such complications in order to explain their approach to *intellectuals.* We should not be surprised if much greater simplifications occur when policies are being sold to voters and politicians and implemented by bureaucrats.

Expanding Justification Slopes

An effective means by which a proponent can argue for a new policy is to show that the accepted justification for an existing policy also provides the foundation for a new one. This is rational in most circumstances because policymakers, especially voters, lack the ability, time, energy, and motivation to analyze each policy proposal on its own merits. They will be rationally ignorant about most proposals. Therefore, if a new policy is seen as a small extension of an existing policy, decision-makers will tend to defer to the perceived rationales behind existing policies, or will at least not strongly resist new policies based on them. This tactic is especially effective in the presence of a gradient, since that makes it easier to find policies whose distance from existing policy is sufficiently small. Volokh refers to this phenomenon as the "small change deference heuristic" (2003, 1108).

When a new policy is advocated using the rationale of an older policy, the rationale for the old policy must be reconstructed. Reconstruction is not simply a replication of the arguments historically produced at the time of the original discussions. Rather, it is an *interpretation* or *rationalization* of the original arguments based on current understanding of the meaning or function of certain policies. Since most people are not historians, it is this reconstruction that is most relevant to current decisions. A given law may function to promote a particular goal, whether or not that was in fact the goal that led to the law's passage. If decision-makers assume the existing law is (all things considered) justified, then a similar law with a similar function may also be deemed a good idea. Again, this assumption is natural in the context of rationally ignorant decision-makers.

How does the reconstruction of the rationales behind older policies work? Slippery-slope theorists have noted a tendency for complex principles to be simplified in the process of rationalizing existing rules and policies. Frederick Schauer refers to this tendency as the "bias in favor of simple principles" (1985, 372). Lode quotes Justice Cardozo, who observes that "[t]he half truths of one generation tend at times to perpetuate themselves in the law as the whole truth of another, when constant repetition brings it about that qualifications, taken once for granted, are disregarded or forgotten" (Lode 1999, 1516). Volokh draws attention to the process of simplification in the policy realm: "Sometimes, the debate about a statute will focus on one justifying principle ... But as time passes, the debates may be forgotten, and only the law itself will endure; and then advocates for future laws B may cite law A as endorsing quite a different justification" (2003, 1089).

We have already seen the simplification process at work in the previous subsection, when considering the tendency of experts to simplify their own theories. Now we will consider how simplification occurs more broadly, regardless of who does it. There are at least three possible patterns by which justifications expand in the process of reconstructing them.

Substituting Broader for Narrower Justifications. A relatively narrow justification J1 leads to the adoption of policy P1. Later, in reconstructing the origin of P1, observers conclude that some broader justification J2, which is sufficient to justify *both* P1 *and* P2 (the new policy proposal), was the real reason for P1's adoption. The authority conferred on J2 by the existence of P1 thus increases the likelihood of P2 also being adopted.

In the context of behavioral paternalism, an example of this phenomenon is provided by the substitution of outsiders' preferences for those of targeted agents. The *initial* (i.e., behavioral paternalist) argument is that government can help advance the targeted agents' own "true" preferences. This argument, honestly applied, can only justify a limited set of policies. The initial justification, however, is easily replaced with the simpler and broader argument that government can help advance the target agents' welfare according to some exogenous or "objective" definition of the good. That justification obviously supports much greater intervention.

As we have seen, the experts themselves have already taken the first step in the simplification process by choosing between the many competing preferences of the target agent, without any basis for doing so. It is not hard to believe that nonexperts will make the same simplification and take it even further. They might, for instance, follow Sunstein and Thaler's lead in seeing direct evidence of the "need" for intervention in the form of low savings rates, high obesity rates, and so forth. According to the sophisticated behavioral paternalist justification, these are not sufficient to demonstrate suboptimal choices according to agents' subjective preferences. But we cannot assume that future voters, politicians, and bureaucrats will infer the sophisticated justification from existing policies, especially when even the supposed experts are inconsistent in their support for that justification.

Paring Multiple Justifications Down to One. The initial policy P1 is adopted based on the joint support of two justifications, J1 and J2. Later, in reconstructing the origin of P1, observers focus on the most obvious or salient justification J1 while ignoring the supporting role of J2. This increases the likelihood of adopting policy P2, which is supported by J1 but not J2.

Nonpaternalistic justifications can interact with paternalistic ones to support policies that would not succeed with one justification alone. Earlier, we suggested that socialization of health costs creates a greater incentive to regulate lifestyle choices (such as smoking, overeating, and riding a motorcycle without a helmet) on grounds of protecting the taxpayers' pocketbooks. This situation is not *strictly* paternalistic because it is the interest of others that provides the justification. Such arguments, however, can play a supporting role. A lifestyle restriction that saves tax dollars *and* allegedly induces better individual choices stands a greater chance of passage.

The slippery-slope risk arises from the possibility that lifestyle restrictions will later be reinterpreted as having arisen largely or entirely as a result of paternalist concerns. If so, then other policies – those that lack the buttressing justification of saving taxpayer dollars – naturally follow. While such policies might not have been supported initially, the *is–ought* heuristic can lead rationally ignorant policymakers to assume the paternalistic justification is solely (not just jointly) sufficient. If autonomy-based objections were not enough to block the existing policy, why should they block the newly proposed extension?

Stripping Justifications of Their Qualifications. An initial policy P1 is adopted with the support of justification J, with significant qualification Q (which specifies some circumstances where J would not apply). Later, in looking back, observers note J but fail to consider the importance of Q. This increases the likelihood of adopting policy P2, which would fail under J-with-Q, but is supported by J unlimited by Q.

We have already seen an example of this phenomenon, in Camerer and coauthors' criterion for asymmetric paternalism. In summarizing their own criterion, they left out an important proviso about *how many* people must be irrational to justify intervention and relied instead merely on the *existence* of irrational people. But let us consider a more concrete example of how qualifications may get stripped away.

Earlier, we discussed Jolls and Sunstein's concept of risk narratives, and we pointed out how risk-narrative laws might be vulnerable to slipping down a gradient defined by the subjective degree of scariness of the narrative. Now consider how that gradient might even cross the threshold between truth and falsehood. Although Jolls and Sunstein's policy description specifies that producers should expose consumers to a *truthful* account of harm-causing use of a product, there is no particular reason, in theory, to think a truthful account provides the appropriate visceral response to approximate a rational assessment of risk. Sunstein and Thaler themselves state that truthful information can, in cases, be harmful: "In the face of health risks, for example, some presentations of accurate information might actually be counterproductive, because people might attempt to control their fear by refusing to think about the risk at all" (2003, 1183). If too much information is a bad thing, then policies that require withholding information could be justified on the same grounds as policies that require providing narratives. And if withholding information can be the correct choice, it might also be appropriate to lie – if such lies do a better job of pushing people toward what policymakers think are their best interests. In short, it is not hard to imagine that the justification for risk narratives could be stripped of its *truthfulness* qualification, thereby setting the stage for expansion of the policy into the realm of legally required untruth or withholding of the truth. Indeed, behavioral economics even supplies an argument for that expansion.

Application to Smoking Bans

The expansion of justifications does not take place in a vacuum. The activities of targeted agents, policymakers, experts, moralists, and rent-seekers interact to alter the terms of the public debate. In addition, justificatory expansion can interact with other slope processes. To show these interactions, we offer the example of smoking bans.

The original Surgeon General's report on the dangers of smoking (US Department of Health, Education and Welfare 1964) generated demand for various kinds of legislation to reduce the incidence of smoking, including higher cigarette taxes, health warnings, and bans on tobacco advertisements on television. Such direct paternalistic efforts, however, had their political limits. Attention then turned increasingly to the dangers of secondhand smoke. To be clear, concerns about secondhand smoke are not strictly paternalistic, inasmuch as secondhand smoke can potentially harm bystanders. There is a subtle aspect of paternalism involved, inasmuch as many anti-smoking regulations limit the ability of individuals to *voluntarily* expose themselves to secondhand smoke as customers or employees of restaurants and bars. Nevertheless, in the early stages, justifications based on the protection of nonsmokers played the primary role in justifying further legislation, such as bans on smoking in public buildings, with paternalistic justifications playing at most a supporting role.

It became increasingly clear, as further studies were published, that smoking restrictions in public spaces had the additional effect of reducing primary smoking (Jha 1999, 51–53; Campaign for Tobacco-Free Kids 2006). These results could be regarded as simply a "side effect" of a policy whose primary goal was to curtail harm to others. But to the extent that this was seen as a benefit, the paternalistic aspect of the smoking bans became more prominent. As the political demand for smoking restrictions grew, the emphasis shifted from protecting nonsmokers to protecting smokers, that is, to the paternalistic aspect of public-smoking restrictions. As James Colgrove and Ronald Bayer (2002) put it:

> But it was precisely because restrictions on public smoking had important effects on smoking itself that many public health activists gave such emphasis to broadening the range of prohibitions. It would have been impossible to ignore the fact that measures initially pursued in the name of protecting nonsmokers had secondary benefits—restricting smoking itself—that far outweighed the contribution associated with limiting exposure to ETS [environmental tobacco smoke].
>
> (p. 953)

For example, the CDC now "strongly" recommends public-smoking bans on two grounds: the reduction of workplace exposure to secondhand smoke *and* the decrease in daily smoking or increased rates of cessation among smokers (Hopkins et al. 2000, 5).[19] Going further, anti-smoking advocates now emphasize reduced cigarette consumption almost exclusively, with little reference to protecting third parties:

> *More stringent* clean indoor air laws are associated with decreased smoking prevalence and cigarette consumption and a higher proportion of quitters ... *Comprehensive* [emphasis added] public clean air laws have the potential to reduce prevalence and consumption rates of the entire population (including nonworking and non-indoor-working smokers) by about 10 percent. Additionally, clean air regulations may contribute to a changing social norm with regard to smoking by altering the perceived social acceptability of smoking. Because of changes in social attitudes and the need to smoke in less hospitable places, smokers may be induced to attempt to quit or not initiate.
>
> (Bonta 2007, B1–B2)

Thus, laws whose initial purpose was to protect bystanders were *reinterpreted* as a means of protecting people from themselves. Their benefits

---

[19] Hopkins et al. (2002): "Smoking bans, effective in reducing exposure to ETS, also can reduce daily tobacco smoke consumption for some tobacco users and help others quit entirely" (p. 5); "Smoking bans and restrictions" are "[s]trongly recommended" (p. 6, table 2).

were measured not in terms of fewer nonsmokers being diagnosed with smoking-related conditions, but in terms of less smoking overall (Gruber and Köszegi 2001, 1289).[20]

This history provides an example of the first simplification pattern described earlier, in which a policy initially justified in terms of one policy is later interpreted as having a different justification – one that can justify further interventions. Or we may see it as an example of the second pattern, in which multiple justifications are whittled down to one. Either way, the stage is set for further legislation that is difficult if not impossible to support based on the initial justificatory foundation. Proposals and legislation designed to ban outdoor smoking at, say, beaches have minimal health value for nonsmokers.[21] A further step in this direction is the growing movement to restrict smoking in apartment-style housing (Giles et al. 2007, 8).[22] The latest step – discussed at length in Chapter 8 – is the campaign against vaping, despite scant evidence of harm to the vapers themselves and essentially zero evidence of harm to bystanders. Although there is still some reference to the bystanders justification, paternalistic concerns now do the heavy lifting.

Note that expanding justifications do not tell the whole story of anti-smoking regulation. The combined effect of anti-smoking laws has been to "undercut[] the social support network for smoking by implicitly defining smoking as an antisocial act" (Glantz 1987, 747). In addition, such laws have restricted the ability of nonsmokers to accommodate smokers by exposing themselves voluntarily to secondhand smoke that is not especially harmful (Grier 2017). Consequently, an "attitude-altering slope" (Volokh

---

[20] Gruber and Köszegi show that, on the assumption that smoking in different areas is complementary, if it cannot be regulated in the home, it should be "overregulated" outside in, say, restaurants and bars. This will cause a reduction in smoking in the home. Thus, the shift in justificatory emphasis noted earlier is a rational adjustment to data showing the interrelation of the two areas of smoking. If smoking is very inconvenient (costly) outside of the home, some people may stop smoking altogether.

[21] See, for example, Giles et al. (2007): "Oakland [Cal.] said last month that smokers could no longer light up at bus stops and ATMs. Down the coast in Calabasas, smoking in public places, including the street, has been illegal for over a year" (p. 8).

[22] Belmont, Cal., has banned "smoking in apartment blocks and shared houses ... In Maine ... officials say that 40 percent of all shared residential buildings are now smoke-free" (p. 8). This issue has now been raised with regard to co-op apartments in New York City. Some smoke from one apartment may seep into another apartment. One solution is to ensure that the smoke pathways are sealed. Whose obligation it is to pay for this is contested. Should it prove expensive, a case could be made that smoking at home should be restricted. The justification will then have *both* paternalistic and harm-to-others aspects (Hope 2007, 1).

2003, 1077–1082) has buttressed the expanding justification slope, as more nonsmokers now feel entitled to have smoke-free environments provided for them (even when the health risks are negligible).

On Experts versus Ordinary People

Experts, and more broadly intellectuals such as the readers of scientific and law journals, naturally respond to sophisticated argumentation. The complex interaction of multiple justifications is their favored milieu, the drawing of distinctions their stock in trade. Some of the claims of this section might, therefore, seem anti-intellectual or unfair, because we are discussing the *misinterpretation* of the behavioral paternalists' arguments, rather than the behavioral paternalists' actual arguments. Why can't the experts simply reject the simplification, distortion, and expansion of their justifications for policy?

The answer is twofold. First, intellectuals cannot always control the development of their own ideas. Many ordinary people, whose job is not the careful parsing of sophisticated arguments, nevertheless affect the policy process. These ordinary people include voters, of course, but in varying degrees other public decision-makers, such as politicians, bureaucrats, and some judges. The point is not that such people are stupid, but that they are rationally ignorant. They act based on simplified versions of arguments because they do not have the time, energy, or motivation to explore the sophisticated versions. In short, *simple is easy; complex is hard.*

Second, decision-making takes place in a social context. The fact that some people will recognize certain distinctions as relevant does not mean that others will. The decision-makers who create a policy are not necessarily the people who enforce it, interpret it, or consider extensions of it. We therefore need to keep in mind Bernard Williams's distinction between "reasonable distinctions" and "effective distinctions." The former are distinctions for which a reasoned argument can be made, whereas the latter are distinctions that can be defended "as a matter of social or psychological fact" (Lode 1999, 1479). The social and psychological facts, in a world of rational ignorance, often point toward simplification of both theory and fact.

SLIPPERY SLOPES WITH COGNITIVELY
BIASED POLICYMAKERS

Thus far, we have described slippery-slope processes generated by behavioral paternalism on the assumption that policymakers behave rationally (in the neoclassical sense).[23] In this section we drop that assumption. We now assume that the policymakers are no different from the targeted individuals. To the extent that ordinary people exhibit biases, policymakers presumably do as well. We argue that such biases would generate even greater slippery-slope potential.

Given that we have argued in much of this book that alleged biases are not necessarily irrational, we ought to justify our shift in argumentative strategy. Our reasons were laid out in Chapter 8 on political economy, but we will summarize them again here. First, we are offering an immanent critique. If behavioral paternalists believe that cognitive biases really do cause poor decision-making, they must also confront the issue of biased policymakers. Second, the public sector is rife with externalities. While biased decision-making in the private sector primarily affects the person deciding, biased decision-making in the public sector necessarily affects us all. And inasmuch and insofar as private decision-makers face the consequences of their own biases, they have an incentive to control their biases that is largely lacking in the public sector (an application of Caplan's notion of rational irrationality). We therefore think people are more likely to exhibit biases in the public sector than in their private affairs.

Furthermore, many of the biases we will consider could be inclusively rational for the individuals who exhibit them – while nevertheless having deleterious consequences for public policy. Beliefs that people hold because they are pleasing in some way, whether or not they track the truth, are especially notable in this regard. At some risk of repeating ourselves, for each bias that we consider, we will also explain (briefly) why it might qualify as inclusively rational.

We should also highlight, again, the speculative character of this kind of argument. The cognitive limitations we discuss have not been tested in the particular slippery-slope contexts addressed here. Furthermore, we have not undertaken a systematic analysis of *every* specific bias that has been identified by behavioral science and how it might affect the political process.[24] This would prove to be a very difficult task, since the effects of these biases often run in opposite directions, have different degrees of importance, and interact with each other. Finally, it is not clear in any

---

[23] We also assumed that the experts and rent-seekers are rational.

[24] There are just too many. See Krueger and Funder (2004, 317, table 1). The authors present forty-two errors or biases identified since 1985; they consider it a partial list. A more up-to-date Wikipedia list identifies at least 185 biases (List of Cognitive Biases, n.d.).

given situation that policymakers will exhibit the *same* biases as targeted agents. It is conceivable that they could have offsetting biases.

Nevertheless, we have chosen to analyze what we believe are the most relevant cognitive limitations in public affairs, many of which were chosen for emphasis by Daniel Kahneman (2003) in the revised version of his Nobel lecture.

Action Bias, Overconfidence, and Confirmation Bias

Three categories of bias discussed in Chapter 8 on political economy can naturally extend to slippery slopes as well. Because the extensions are fairly obvious, we will keep the discussion brief.

Action bias, in addition to encouraging initial paternalistic interventions, has the potential to encourage subsequent interventions as well. As long as the problem does not appear to have been solved by the initial intervention, policymakers will feel pressure to take further action. To the extent that initial interventions create unintended consequences, including the exacerbation of other perceived problems through the interaction of cognitive biases, action bias will support intervention in those areas as well.

Overconfidence, too, lends support to both initial and subsequent interventions. When early interventions do not lead to expected results, overconfident policymakers do not necessarily conclude that the regulated activity is beyond their competence to understand and correct. The related *illusion of explanatory depth* can lead policymakers to think that they truly grasp the reasons why previous actions did not produce the desired results, as well as the additional measures that could "plug the holes" and improve outcomes. Together, these effects will tend to encourage further intervention.

Both action bias and overconfidence are buttressed by *confirmation bias*, which will tend to dissuade policymakers from changing their minds and altering course. Rather than concluding that their previous interventions were mistaken or based on weak analysis, policymakers affected by confirmation bias will tend to think the results – such as they are – actually support their prior beliefs, and therefore more aggressive action in the same vein is needed to achieve the desired results.

Action bias, overconfidence, and confirmation bias may be inclusively rational for policymakers who benefit in the eyes of the public from appearing active, decisive, and firm in their beliefs. But what is rational for the individual policymakers can have deleterious consequences for the public.

Present Bias and Hyperbolic Discounting

In Chapter 8 we discussed various reasons that policymakers tend to have short time horizons with regard to the policies they support. They might no longer hold office when future costs and benefits of their policies occur. Insofar as voters have imperfect memories, they might fail to fault policymakers for the ill effects (or credit them with the good effects) of policies they championed. Both of these effects give fully rational policymakers an incentive to discount future consequences. But if policymakers are also hyperbolic discounters, there is yet another reason they will tend to discount the future: because they apply *especially* high rates of discount when some costs or benefits are in the present (or near future).

How does this worsen slippery-slope risks? Slippery-slope events are by definition sequences that play out over time: policy A's adoption now leads to policy B's adoption later, leading to policy C's adoption yet further in the future. Hyperbolic discounting implies that when policymakers are faced with a policy proposal that is appealing in the present, but which creates a danger of bad policies being adopted further down the line, they will be inclined to focus on the former at the expense of the latter. In short, they will be less cognizant of slippery-slope risks.[25]

For instance, policymakers might be tempted to create a small fat tax, on grounds that it will induce marginally "better" eating decisions. Opponents might argue that adopting a small fat tax will create a danger of a larger fat tax in the future, as future policymakers – having already incurred the costs of creating a tax-collection mechanism – see the opportunity to increase tax revenues and fund special-interest constituencies. If they are hyperbolic discounters, the policymakers will not take this risk seriously enough, even if they recognize it as real.

Similar to hyperbolic discounters in the private sector, policymakers may exhibit time inconsistency: the tendency to make commitments and promises and then break them when the moment of choice arrives. They might, for instance, repeatedly express a willingness to take measures to fight budget deficits in the future, while nevertheless passing bloated budgets and incurring large debts in the present. Note that critics of

---

[25] See Herbert Spencer: "But the 'practical' politician who, in spite of such experiences repeated generated after generation, goes on thinking only of proximate results, naturally never thinks of results still more remote, still more general, and still more important than those just exemplified" (1981 [1884], 43).

slippery-slope arguments will sometimes claim to be able to resist the urge to adopt bad policies in the future. The idea is that we can do the right thing today and resist doing the wrong thing tomorrow (Volokh 2003, 1029–1030).[26] They might, for instance, promise to keep fat taxes relatively low (and linked to scientific evidence about the extent of present bias). The existence of time inconsistency bears directly on the plausibility of promises to do the right thing in the future even in the face of temptation.

Hyperbolic discounting is not necessarily irrational; we have argued for the inclusive rationality of seemingly inconsistent time-discounting in prior chapters. Nevertheless, it can have unfortunate consequences in public policy, just like fully consistent but high levels of time-discounting, by encouraging the tendency of policymakers to give little consideration to the long-term consequences of their policies on the general public.

Availability and Salience

In Chapter 8 we discussed how availability and salience may influence policy by directing policymakers' attention to problems that loom large in their imagination, with insufficient attention paid to costs and unintended consequences. Here, we argue that availability and salience can also affect policy through the framing of policy choices. *Narrow framing* arises, in large part, because immediate and concrete effects tend to be more psychologically accessible (available or salient) than remote and abstract ones.

The concreteness of specific problems – such as a perceived low savings rate, the readily observed expansion of waistlines, the rising costs of healthcare, and so forth – will tend to focus policymakers on immediate policy choices without regard for more distant consequences. As Daniel Kahneman (2003) puts it, in the context of purely private decision-making, "[t]he problem at hand and the immediate consequences of the choice will be far more accessible than all other considerations, and as a result decision problems will be framed far more narrowly than the rational model assumes" (p. 1460). There is no reason to think policymakers can counter this tendency any better than private citizens, and both rational ignorance and rational irrationality imply that they will be worse at countering it. Availability and salience are, in a sense, mental shortcuts for people with limited time and cognitive resources. In that sense, they are inclusively

---

[26] "The slippery slope argument, opponents suggest, is the claim that 'we ought not make a sound decision today, for fear of having to draw a sound distinction tomorrow'" (Volokh 2003, 1029–1030).

rational. When the potential ill effects of relying on these shortcuts are concentrated on the chooser, as is generally true in private choices, there is at least an incentive to seek out better information and possibly adopt a broader framing of the situation. In the public sector, the diffusion of control and responsibility make the narrower framing likelier to prevail.

Narrow framing leads decision-makers to consider choice-options simply as they arise, framed by present circumstances, the crisis of the moment, and perhaps the activities of moralists and rent-seekers. Their actions will often be ad hoc solutions to particular problems, and the narrow framing produces a tendency not to see important interrelationships. In Kahneman's words again, "[t]he decision of whether or not to accept a gamble is normally considered as a response to a single opportunity, not as an occasion to apply a general policy" (p. 1459). For example, the interaction of biases may be ignored. This means the problem is not simply one of discounting long-term effects, but also of discounting effects that occur through longer and more complex chains of causality.

Narrow framing will tend to enhance every variety of slope we have discussed so far, because all slopes occur in part from a failure to take a global perspective on policy. Altered incentives slopes, for instance, occur because policymakers tend to focus on one issue at a time – in this case, a single cognitive or behavioral bias, or a single means of correcting a bias. Simplification and distortion slopes occur because policymakers enact policies to address a specific problem, while failing to see how the new policy could empower experts and rent-seekers to advance less desirable policies in the future. To the extent that narrow framing inhibits policymakers' awareness of such possibilities, it exacerbates the slippery-slope risk.

Moreover, as we have emphasized repeatedly, slippery slopes are most likely to occur in the presence of a gradient. Movement along gradients is assisted by a narrow focus on two very close or similar cases, where the second case is considered to have a certain characteristic such as acceptability simply because the first did as well. A gradient slope is easier to resist when policymakers consider the whole spectrum of possibilities rather than two similar policies or cases at a time.

Framing and Extremeness Aversion

Framing effects can, as explained in Chapter 3, result in violations of the axiom of independence of irrelevant alternatives. In other words, the choice between two options can be affected by whether a third option is present or not. We suggest that such effects – specifically, the *extremeness aversion* identified by Itamar Simonson and Amos Tversky (1992) – can increase the likelihood of initial passage of behavioral paternalist policies and ease the movement along the slope to harder paternalism.

Extremeness aversion refers to the finding that "the attractiveness of an option is enhanced if it is [presented as] an intermediate option in the choice set and is diminished if it is [presented as] an extreme option" (Simonson and Tversky 1992, 281). For instance, Simonson and Tversky found that experimental subjects choosing between a low-end camera and a medium-quality camera split about equally between the two options – but when they were also presented with a high-end camera, they became substantially more likely to choose the medium-quality camera (p. 290). Although we can imagine consumers being exploited by firms that manipulate extremeness aversion to boost sales, we can also see an inclusively rational logic to extremeness aversion. It is a heuristic that naturally appeals to consumers for whom extreme options (the *very worst and cheapest* camera, versus the *very best and most expensive* one) are often not desired. In a market context, where no single firm can unilaterally frame the choice, opportunities for exploitation are naturally limited – and consumers also have a built-in incentive to police their own choices.

But with the inherently low individualized stakes in the political context, cognitive heuristics can have a more dysfunctional effect. Specifically, consider how the behavioral paternalists' rhetorical device of positioning their proposals as the "middle ground" exploits, perhaps inadvertently, the phenomenon of extremeness aversion. In advocating their favored "soft" paternalism, they make a point of introducing "hard" paternalism for contrast. Camerer et al., for instance, say:

> For those (particularly economists) prone to rigid antipaternalism, the paper describes a possibly attractive rationale for paternalism as well as a careful, cautious, and disciplined approach. For those prone to give unabashed support for paternalistic policies based on behavioral economics, this paper argues that more discipline is needed and proposes a possible criterion.
>
> (2003, 1212–1213)

Similarly, Jolls and Sunstein say their approach "adopts a middle ground between inaction or naive informational strategies, on the one hand, and the 'insulating' strategies of heightened liability standards or outright bans, on the other" (2006, 216). Thus, in characterizing the choice between two policies, absence of paternalism and their own proposals, behavioral paternalists make a point of introducing a third option, hard paternalism, that should – in theory – be irrelevant to the choice between the first two.

More formally, we may characterize the alternatives in terms of a supposed trade-off between autonomy and welfare. "Anti-paternalism" (AP) is characterized by high autonomy and (ostensibly) low welfare. At the other extreme is "hard paternalism," (HP), characterized by low autonomy and (ostensibly) high welfare.[27] "Soft paternalism" (SP) lies somewhere in between. If policymakers are affected by extremeness aversion, the deliberate presentation of SP as the middle ground can make policymakers more inclined to implement SP.

Furthermore, extremeness aversion can be exploited to move policy further down the slope toward harder paternalism. The mechanism works through the introduction of another policy – let us call it "soft paternalism plus" (SP+) – that is intermediate between the newly adopted SP and HP. The latter two options now constitute the extremes of comparison, making those policymakers affected by extremeness aversion more favorably disposed toward the new middle ground of SP+. If SP+ is adopted, that becomes a new endpoint when another intermediate policy, SP++, is introduced. The middle ground continues to move toward the paternalistic extreme. Notice that this process is eased by the presence of a gradient, which guarantees the existence of intermediate policies.

To illustrate concretely, consider again the expansion of anti-smoking restrictions, this time in the context of air transportation. (Again, this policy arena is not strictly paternalistic, though it has a paternalistic dimension, and we present it primarily to illustrate how this slippery-slope process can operate.) If we think of public-smoking restrictions as occupying a continuum of costs to smokers, we can see how the middle ground moves by steps along this continuum. Initially, when smoking was restricted in only minor ways or in few places, the costs to smokers of the restrictions were relatively small.

One of the first smoking restrictions, mandated by the Civil Aeronautics Board in 1973, was simply to separate smokers and nonsmokers in separate sections on airplanes. As a middle ground between an outright smoking ban and laissez-faire, this seemed to be a reasonable low-cost policy option. Then this became the "laissez-faire" position. In 1988 the Federal Aviation Administration (FAA) imposed further costs upon smokers when the agency banned smoking on all scheduled domestic flights under two hours in duration. These two hours of abstention became a middle ground between the mere separation of passengers and the higher costs imposed

---

[27] We do not agree that hard paternalism will in fact lead to higher welfare; this is, however, how the trade-off seems to have been characterized by behavioral paternalists.

by abstention for many hours. This middle-ground position imposed somewhat larger costs that most smokers could still presumably tolerate. With that as the new left end of the spectrum, the FAA in 1990 banned smoking on all scheduled domestic flights. In 2000, the US Department of Transportation extended the ban to all US international flights. The airplane ban was complete. But not all airports are smoke-free yet; that is the express goal of the American Nonsmokers' Rights Foundation (2017).[28]

Behavioral paternalists offer a policy framework that emphasizes the middle ground, not just in specific policy areas such as smoking regulation, but as a general perspective. Yet the middle ground is not a stable place; what constitutes the middle ground is a function of which policies have already been adopted. To the extent that the behavioral paternalists' middle-ground argument is successful and policymakers adopt policies on this basis, there is a potentially powerful dynamic at work.

Affect and Prototype Heuristics

In Chapter 8 we introduced the affect and prototype heuristics to show how negative feelings about people targeted by interventions (morbidly obese people, spendthrifts, etc.) as well as positive feelings about policymakers' intentions (they want to "help people help themselves") and proposed interventions (they are "mere nudges") can increase the likelihood of adopting paternalist policies, irrespective of their true costs and benefits. The slope potential of these heuristics should also be clear, as they will ease the way for both initial and subsequent interventions.

But here, we take the analysis a step further. The prototype heuristic is also the root of the phenomenon known as *extension neglect*. Sometimes called quantitative neglect, this is the tendency to ignore the quantity or extent of something when determining how much to value it. The behavioral literature claims to find extension neglect in many different contexts (Kahneman 2003, 1463–1466). For example, when asked to determine their willingness to pay for wildlife preservation or other public goods, respondents tend to ignore quantitative dimensions; in one experiment, subjects' willingness to pay to save migratory birds from drowning in an oil pond was more or less the same for 2,000 or 200,000 birds saved (pp. 1463–1464).[29] In this case, the prototype driving these valuations might be

---

[28] The history is recounted in Bonta (2007).

[29] Another example of extension neglect is duration neglect. When asked to rate the degree of discomfort of a colonoscopy, people will ignore the length of time the procedure takes,

the image of a single bird dying in a pool of oil; the image does not account for the *number* of birds that might be spared this fate.

For our purposes here, the most important feature of a prototype is that it is "extensionless." A prototype is an *exemplar*; it is not the set of all instances. The size of the set can grow without the exemplar changing, and thus an increase in the extensional (that is, quantitative) aspect of the class is neglected in the prototype (Kahneman 2003, 1464).[30] Yet it is the prototype that affects actual decision-making.

If policymakers are also subject to extension neglect as a result of using prototypes in the evaluations of policy, they will be more susceptible to slippery slopes. As we have seen, behavioral paternalists such as Sunstein and Thaler have highlighted certain representative policies, such as cafeteria placement of fruit and dessert and default enrollment in 401(k) programs, as prototypes of their new approach to paternalists. Their case for paternalism always begins with one of these cases, before gradually extending to cases that are less purely "libertarian." As laid out earlier, the analysis moves from the prototypical (low cost-of-exit) cases, to legal presumptions that can be waived only under general conditions set by the state, to working-hours limitations that can be waived only for time-and-a-half overtime, to mandatory cooling-off periods for consumer purchases that cannot be waived at all. The progression proceeds in terms of greater costs of opting out by the putative beneficiaries. In addition, and rarely mentioned by Sunstein and Thaler, the progression can also proceed in terms of greater costs imposed on employers, sellers, and other parties. The phenomenon of extension neglect suggests that policymakers will tend to pay insufficient attention to this kind of policy expansion because their attitudes are anchored by the new prototypes.

In our earlier discussion of the gradients created and exploited by behavioral paternalism, we found it reasonable to blame information costs for policymakers' potential insensitivity to incremental changes. The introduction of prototype analysis and extension neglect, however, suggests the possibility that these quantitative or extensional features will be ignored entirely. Policymakers will tend to focus on the prototype (the seemingly simple cafeteria placement or 401(k) issues), and their affective response to

concentrating only on the "representative" moments of peak and end (Redelmeier and Kahneman 1996, 3).

[30] "Other things equal, an increase in the extension of a category [e.g., the number of birds in the previous example] will increase the value of its extensional attributes [the total number of birds saved], but leave unchanged the values of the prototype attributes [the value of the representative bird]" (Kahneman 2003, 1464; bracketed remarks supplied).

further policies will be determined in part by their positive response to the prototype. Therefore, approval of the initial, least intrusive policies will increase the likelihood that more intrusive policies will be adopted through the interplay of the prototype and affect heuristics.

In Chapters 6 and 7, we noted that the behavioral paternalists' paradigm is one that trusts policymakers to make careful, nuanced calculations of costs and benefits (Sunstein and Thaler 2003, 1166)[31] – calculations that depend on both the extent and degree of cognitive biases. Even the application of a simple model such as Camerer et al.'s "asymmetric paternalism" criterion to specific policies depends crucially on a quantitative variable, the *fraction* of people considered irrational. A better version of the criterion would also account for heterogeneity in the *degree* of irrationality. This, too, is a quantitative variable. If policymakers are subject to extension neglect, we should not be surprised to find them ignoring both of these variables, as well as the many others we catalogued in previous chapters.

Extension neglect may be inclusively rational. It is yet another means of economizing on mental resources by using a simple rule of thumb. It especially makes sense for individuals whose relevant goal is feeling good about themselves (say, by donating to a wildlife fund), because the psychological need in question does not really depend on the quantitative value (the number of birds saved). In personal affairs, extension neglect might often work just fine – and when it doesn't, there is a built-in self-interested incentive for agents to resist it. But in the public sphere, where incentives for self-correction are weak at best, we can expect voters and other policymakers to focus on their emotional reactions to policies – in the form of the affect and prototype heuristics – with insufficient attention to the relevant quantitative variables.

Extension Neglect in the Calculation of Optimal Sin Taxes. The taxation of immediate-gratification goods provides a more specific example of how extension neglect may enhance slippery-slope processes. From the behavioral paternalist perspective, the issue is not merely reducing consumption of immediate-gratification goods, but reducing it to an *optimal level.* Under an optimal paternalist policy, people would still eat junk food and smoke cigarettes, but to an optimal degree. The relevant quantitative variables for

---

[31] "First, programs should be designed using a type of welfare analysis, one in which a serious attempt is made to measure the costs and benefits of outcomes ... Second, some results from the psychology of decisionmaking should be used to provide ex ante guidelines to support reasonable judgments about when consumers and workers will gain most by increasing options" (Sunstein and Thaler 2003, 1166).

designing the policy would include the extent of people's irrational impatience, the distribution of impatience levels across consumers, the fraction of the public that is tempted by any particular taxable good, and so forth.

How does a nonexpert policymaker deal with these quantitative complexities? If he uses the heuristics discussed in this section, his approach will largely be to ignore them. The most psychologically available pictures are the prototypes of a compulsive cigarette smoker or obese junk-food consumer – that is, persons with little willpower who seek immediate gratification and endanger their future health. *How many* such people there are, and *how much* correction each of them needs, will likely have little influence on policymaking. Prototypes, by definition, contain no reference to the distribution of attributes within the relevant class. The affect or evaluation evoked by the prototype will be, presumably, a generalized disapproval of junk-food consumption and smoking with little or nothing in the way of quantitative distinctions.

Suppose an expert produces a policy paper with specific estimates relating to impatience, willpower, and optimal tax rates, and *mirabile dictu*, it is adopted by the policymakers. Will matters stand there? This seems unlikely. To the extent that policymakers, especially voters, deal with the issue through prototype and affect heuristics, with their resulting quantitative neglect, constraints to limit further taxes are quite loose. The reasoning follows a simple path: "People smoke cigarettes and eat junk food, thereby endangering their health. Health is good; that which endangers it is bad. Perhaps they should be taxed until they stop." This is counter to the behavioral paternalists' theory, but behavioral paternalists do not control the policy process. The behavioral paternalists have offered no effective bar to sliding beyond their modest proposals, and the dynamics of cost-lowering slippery slopes – especially in the presence of a gradient, as in this case – will tend to encourage such sliding.

THE PATERNALISM-GENERATING FRAMEWORK

As presented in the behavioral literature, framing does not result from the deliberate choices of the decision-maker; instead, it is an aspect of decision-making that is *passively accepted* (Kahneman 2003, 1459).[32] It is the result of unconscious processes whereby the conscious mind sees options or

---

[32] "The basic principle of framing is the passive acceptance of the formulation given" (Kahneman 2003, 1459).

events with particular features accentuated; framing alters "the relative salience of different aspects of the problem" (p. 1458).

Here we suggest that the particular way in which behavioral paternalists (most notably Camerer et al. and Sunstein and Thaler) have framed the issue of paternalism gives rise to an inherently expansionist dynamic. If rationally ignorant and boundedly rational policymakers accept the behavioral paternalist approach, they will have accepted a paternalism-generating framework. Thus future policymakers, or the same policy-makers in future situations, will tend to see more opportunities for paternalistic intervention than they otherwise would.

The public policy framework produced by behavioral paternalists directs policymakers' attention to intrapersonal preference conflicts, that is, conflicts between operative preferences (choosing the sugary dessert) and longer-term and supposedly more important preferences (maintaining good health). The framework then labels as paternalism any plan that alters the decision problem with the intent of improving welfare. Therefore, if there is to be any solution to the target's problem, paternalism is inevitable. Thus, the decision problem is framed not as "whether or not paternalism is desirable," but as "what form of paternalism shall we have?" Sunstein and Thaler, for example, urge us to "abandon the less interesting question of whether to be paternalistic or not, and turn to the more constructive question of how to choose among the possible choice-influencing options" (2003, 1166).

To the extent that policymakers accept behavioral paternalists' framing of the problem of intrapersonal preference conflict, they shall be led to produce all manner of paternalistic schemes. Yet it is far from necessary to look at matters in this way. An alternative perspective, which steers clear of the behavioral paternalist framework of trying to extricate people exogenously from decision contexts in which they cannot promote their own welfare, is available to us (Gul and Pesendorfer 2001, 2004).

People subject to temptation assign utility not only to individual options, but also to decision problems or sets of options that they will face in the future. Thus, a person may assign a higher utility to a decision problem that omits a certain tempting, but ultimately welfare-reducing, alternative. As a result – and as we have emphasized earlier – they will deliberately make choices to structure their decision contexts. A vegetarian who still likes the taste of meat may prefer not having meat on a restaurant's menu. A dieter may raise the cost of less-preferred options by placing treats on a high shelf where they can be reached only with increased effort. People may announce their intent to lose weight to their friends, thus suffering embarrassment if they do not. Other market participants may offer them controlled options to make a profit. This could include restaurants with no unhealthful options, or with the sweets placed in less tempting locations, or with especially good fruit alternatives. Recently, manufacturers have sold portion-controlled bags of cookies or chips to help individuals with self-control problems (Peters 2007, C1). With a framework such as this in mind, the mere existence of intrapersonal preference conflicts would not necessarily suggest the need for paternalistic intervention.[33]

In this alternative framework, the policymaker or analyst is first led to search for ways in which individuals or markets might control their choice sets. Then, if she sees no such methods in operation, she will inquire as to whether people's supposed preference to behave differently is true or merely cheap talk. People may fail to restrain their choices because they have no real interest in doing so. Only when the analyst is satisfied that the issue is the prohibitive costs of private control does the discussion of government paternalism begin.

Therefore, the behavioral paternalist approach is expansive not only in the sense that adoption of specific policies today will make the adoption of more intrusive policies more likely in the future, but also because their basic framework of analysis frames the overall issue as one in which some form of paternalism is either "inevitable" or the first solution to be considered. This is what we call a *paternalism-generating public policy framework*. If policymakers accept this framework, they will be led by the framing to produce more and more paternalistic policies. In Chapter 10 we will have more to say about the alternative paternalism-resisting framework.

REJOINDERS TO BEHAVIORAL PATERNALIST RESPONSES

In their book *Nudge*, Sunstein and Thaler recognize the slippery-slope objections to their policies, and offer three responses. We reply to their responses here.

Sunstein and Thaler's (2008) first response is that the slippery-slope argument "ducks the question of whether our proposals have merit in and of themselves." They say if the initial interventions are worthwhile, then we

---

[33] To be more precise, paternalistic intervention would be considered only when its costs are lower than the lowest of the following: self-control, self-commitment, and market choice-restriction costs.

should "make progress on those, and do whatever it takes to pour sand on the slope" (p. 237).

Our claim is not that slippery slopes are the *only* objection to behavioral paternalism. In previous chapters, we have questioned the direct merits of paternalist interventions. The slippery slope is an *additional* argument against behavioral paternalism.

The idea that we should "make progress" on the initial interventions, and then do what we can to "pour sand" on the slope, is a variant of the usual (and, we think, hackneyed) response to all slippery-slope arguments: that we can simply "do the right thing now, and resist doing the wrong thing later." But if the slope argument is correct, there is a causal (albeit probabilistic) connection between initial interventions and later ones. Saying we should move forward on those initial interventions is akin to saying we should do something because it promises present benefits while ignoring the potential costs in the future. Ironically, it is just this sort of error in private decision-making that behavioral paternalists think cries out for correction. *The slope risk must be counted among the costs of the initial intervention.*

Furthermore, how should we "pour sand" on the slope? Aside from invoking the term "libertarian," Sunstein and Thaler offer no suggestions. We will do so in Chapter 10. Our suggestions involve, among other things, rejecting their paternalism-generating framework in favor of a paternalism-resisting one.

Sunstein and Thaler's second response is that their "libertarian condition" limits the steepness of the slope. They say their proposals are "emphatically designed to retain freedom of choice" (p. 237).

In short, they are relying on the "libertarian" part of libertarian paternalism to do the work of resisting paternalist slopes. But as we have seen in this chapter – in the section "How Behavioral Paternalism Exploits Existing Gradients" – their redefinition of "libertarian" actually encourages the slope. They recognize no sharp line between noncoercive (libertarian) and coercive (nonlibertarian) policies, just a smooth gradient. And also as we have seen, their proposals do *not*, in fact, preserve freedom of choice in all cases. They have proposed or supported numerous policies (such as mandatory time-and-a-half overtime pay and cooling-off periods) that rule out certain options altogether, all under the rubric of libertarian paternalism.

It is also simply implausible to think the mere word "libertarian" will create a bulwark against further interventions. Even if Sunstein and Thaler themselves genuinely care about freedom of choice, they cannot control the application and transformation of their own ideas. They will not be in charge of all future legislation. As we have emphasized throughout this chapter, the creation of policy is a social process that involves multiple decision-makers, many of whom may not share their alleged concern with freedom of choice.

Sunstein and Thaler's third response is to insist that in many situations, "some kind of nudge is inevitable," because there will always be default rules and contexts that frame choices in certain ways (p. 237).

It is one thing to have defaults, quite another to choose them with paternalist goals in mind (Mitchell 2005, 1259–1260).[34] Traditional contract law sets defaults in line with the customary expectations of the parties in question. Defaults can be set to minimize transaction costs, or to avoid unintended inferences of information. Defaults can also arise through a decentralized market process that responds to the needs of both buyers and sellers. In other words, it is entirely possible to have default rules without paternalism. Behavioral paternalists who insist on paternalistic means of choosing defaults are, in effect, saying other processes for selecting defaults ought to be overruled so as to privilege what they (the experts) believe are better decisions. They would purposely shift opting-out costs onto those who wish to deviate from the experts' preferred outcomes.

If behavioral paternalism were truly inevitable, it would hardly be necessary to argue for it. Clearly, Sunstein and Thaler believe they are offering something beyond the inevitable. Moreover, they present their position in a manner that seems designed to ease the transition from the inevitable to the more intrusive. They explicitly reject any sharp line between changing defaults and raising costs in other ways. Again, their very own next step, in discussing default rules, is to suggest *raising the cost of exercising exit options*, and then to endorse *eliminating some options altogether*.

CONCLUSIONS

Slippery-slope arguments are often treated dismissively, sometimes even consigned to lists of logical fallacies as a form of spurious reasoning. Without doubt, some writers do deploy slippery-slope arguments in a casual and imprecise way by simply asserting that *seemingly attractive*

---

[34] "But not all default rules are equally paternalistic or paternalistic in the same way, and . . . it does not follow from libertarian principles that the central planner should choose the default rule that enhances the welfare of affected individuals" (Mitchell 2005, 1259–1260).

policy A will lead to *clearly awful policy B*. But this error does not mean all slippery-slope arguments are invalid. Rather, it means that we should pay attention to the specific processes – often probabilistic rather than deterministic – that connect one policy to another, as we have sought to do in this chapter.

The slippery slope is a broad category, and many different mechanisms and processes fall under its umbrella. As such, it can be difficult to describe all slippery slopes in summary form. Nevertheless, certain features characterize many, though not all, types of slope. In particular, slopes tend to occur in the presence of vague and ill-defined concepts – what we have called *gradients.* Consequently, the same features of behavioral paternalism that are problematic on a *conceptual* level also raise concerns on a *pragmatic* level. In the earlier chapters of this book, we argued that the theoretical and empirical foundation of behavioral paternalism is fundamentally vague. It relies on distinctions that often fail to hold up under scrutiny, and that in any case cannot be reliably identified in practice. Policies based on such unstable moorings are almost bound to drift from their original justifications, because the justifications were weak and imprecise to begin with.

Another common feature of slippery slopes is the presence of multiple and diffuse decision-makers, many lacking in accountability for outcomes. When accountability is lacking due to diffuse responsibility, delayed consequences, and unclear objectives, decision-makers will typically display both rational ignorance and rational irrationality. Whatever cognitive biases are present in the private sector will tend to be magnified in the public sector, thereby creating the room necessary for the gradual drift of policies away from their initial purposes as well as the purposeful movement of policy under the influence of moralists and rent-seekers.

If behavioral paternalists genuinely care about personal autonomy, as some claim, then they ought to take slippery-slope concerns more seriously than they have thus far. And if behavioral paternalists care about the implementation of thoughtful and well-designed policies, as virtually all of them claim, then they should worry about how slope processes could warp their nuanced justifications and well-intentioned plans. To ignore the risk of slippery slopes is to commit an error that behavioral paternalists often caution against: focusing on present gains at the expense of future (and uncertain) losses. To repeat: the slope risk must be counted among the costs of the initial policy intervention.

What, then, can be done to avoid, or more realistically to *minimize*, the danger of paternalist slopes? We have suggested some of the answers in this chapter. They involve, among other things, rejecting the paternalism-generating framework suggested by behaviorally minded thinkers, and adopting instead a paternalism-resisting framework. Such a framework would emphasize the distinction between voluntary and coercive action, as well as the distinction between private and state action. We leave the full description of that framework to Chapter 10.

10

Common Threads, Escape Routes, and
Paths Forward

In the eyes of an economist, my students were "misbehaving." By that I mean that their behavior was inconsistent with the idealized model of behavior that is at the heart of what we call economic theory.

—Richard Thaler, *Misbehaving: The Making of Behavioral Economics*

Sure as I know anything, I know this—they will try again. Maybe on another world, maybe on this very ground swept clean. A year from now, ten? They'll swing back to the belief that they can make people . . . better. And I do not hold to that. So no more running. I aim to misbehave.

—Capt. Mal Reynolds, *Serenity* (Joss Whedon)

At the end of *Pinocchio* – the final ending, not the earlier death by hanging – the Blue Fairy rewards the puppet for his (recent) good behavior by turning him into a real boy. The Disney film features a similar ending. But the novel features something the film does not: the boy's puppet body collapsed over a chair. When Pinocchio sees the lifeless puppet, he says to himself with "great complacency," "How ridiculous I was when I was a puppet! And how glad I am that I have become a well-behaved little boy!" (Collodi 2016, 145). It's unclear what meaning Carlo Collodi attached to this ending, but to us it feels like a threat: fail to behave as a good child, and you may return to being a puppet.

In this final chapter, as we bring the strands of our argument together, we hope to reveal an alternative to the puppet view of human nature. In both economics and public policy, we should treat humans as creatures whose complexity makes them, not bad puppets, but real people.

Over the previous nine chapters, we have presented a gauntlet of challenges to behavioral paternalism, and the extended exploration of each one on its own may have obscured the bigger picture. Here, we hope to unite these challenges with renewed emphasis on the links that hold them together. Then we consider several possible routes by which behavioral paternalism might be rescued from our critique. We conclude by offering some recommendations on a better path forward for both academics and policymakers.

COMMON THREADS

We began this book with an extended critique of the neoclassical model of rationality, which behavioral economists have rejected as a positive model of human behavior but nevertheless have accepted as a normative standard. We argued that the assumptions of that model – including complete and transitive preferences, indifference to framing, consistency with classical logic and probability theory, and Bayesian updating of beliefs – constituted arbitrary restrictions on "proper" behavior by real people. While these assumptions might be useful in constructing mathematical models, they are not useful as an ideal standard against which to measure the desirability of real behavior. In place of this "puppet" rationality, we offered our preferred notion of inclusive rationality.

The rest of the book could easily be read as a series of "even if" arguments: *even if* we accept neoclassical rationality as true rationality, behavioral science has not advanced far enough to answer a number of crucial questions for policymaking, such as the generalizability of behavioral results across different contexts and the applicability of laboratory results in the wild. *Even if* we had better research on those questions, policymakers would face practically insurmountable local and personal knowledge gaps that would hobble attempts at crafting paternalist policies that are effective and cost-benefit justified. *Even if* we could acquire such knowledge, policymakers have little incentive to do the hard work of crafting good policies, especially when interested parties (such as rent-seekers, moralists, and bureaucrats) can tilt the legislative and regulatory process in their favor – and so much the worse if policymakers are afflicted by any of the cognitive biases attributed to regular people. And *even if* we set all of these concerns aside, behavioral paternalism creates the risk of a slippery slope toward more extensive and intrusive policies that go beyond what has been justified by theory and evidence, resulting in ever greater restrictions on individual choice.

The "even if" reading is a valid, and intended, one. But we believe there is also a unity to the arguments. Each argument sets the stage for the next, and some common threads run through them all.

The Complexity of Inclusive Rationality

The first common thread is the complexity of inclusive rationality. Unlike neoclassical puppets, real humans are not black boxes that simply accept inputs and yield outputs. There is a process by which people form their preferences and seek to achieve them, and that process is embedded in time. Take a snapshot, and people may appear to be making errors. But look at them over time, in real environments and contexts, and a nuanced tapestry of behavior emerges. Inclusive rationality manifests itself in experimentation, trial and error, resolutions and commitments, structuring of our environments, demand for market-provided solutions, and cooperation with other people, among many other strategies.

These matter to the next phase of the argument, because it is in just these areas that the state of behavioral science is most often deficient. And the more context-specific are people's strategies, the more difficult it becomes to gather policy-relevant knowledge. People often adopt strategies that depend intimately on local and tacit knowledge of their inner selves and their environments. The heterogeneous and idiosyncratic ways in which inclusive rationality manifests resist attempts to summarize them in usable form. The inevitable scarcity of knowledge in this regard leads directly to the next phase of the argument, as policymakers who lack necessary knowledge – but who are nevertheless charged with doing something – will tend to rely on unjustified assumptions and "folk wisdom" instead, leading to poorly designed interventions as well as the threat of more when the initial interventions appear to fail.

The Indeterminacy of Welfare Criteria

The second common thread is the indeterminacy of behavioral paternalist welfare criteria. Behavioral paternalists, unlike old-style paternalists, say they wish to advance people's own interests *as judged by themselves*. That is, they believe the proper goal of paternalism is to advance individuals' own preferences, values, and goals, not those of a third party. But they also assume that *there must be a well-defined answer* to what is in someone's best interests, which we can discern if we just look hard enough. Despite the substantial evidence from behavioral economics that people's actual preferences are not necessarily complete and transitive, and despite admitting that well-defined and stable preferences may not formally exist, behavioral paternalists still seem to think of people as neoclassical agents "deep down inside."

That implicit (and occasionally explicit) assumption ripples through their analysis and our critique. When confronted with cases wherein people exhibit inconsistencies of choice, the behavioral paternalists "fill in" what seem to be appropriate (i.e., consistent and well-defined) preferences. Thus, they assume the superiority of more patient rates of time-discounting to less patient ones, of cool-state preferences to hot-state preferences, and (sometimes) of willingness to accept over willingness to pay. We have dubbed this the non sequitur at the heart of behavioral paternalism. This non sequitur makes knowledge problems seem more tractable than they really are, because it allows analysts to substitute their own judgments rather than confront the indeterminacy in the data. To take one specific example, if it is deemed acceptable to favor more patient rates of discount over less patient ones, then it becomes unnecessary to confront the problem of identifying the "true" discount rate from the wide range of discount rates that real people display across time and over different contexts.

The apparent willingness of behavioral paternalists to favor some expressed preferences over others also colors the policy debate. They lend the veneer of science to what are in fact subjective judgments, giving policymakers the cover they need to implement policies based on prejudices and moralistic attitudes, such as the universal desirability of conventional virtues such as patience, moderation, and temperance. Once assumptions of this nature become embedded in policy, they help to justify further interventions with even weaker justifications in behavioral science.

The Role of Incentives and Learning

A third common thread is the role of incentives and learning in the operation of inclusive rationality. In the world of puppet rationality, there is little room for people to learn about themselves, to discover their own weaknesses and foibles, or to find ways to shape and correct their own behavior. Why not? Because the work has already been done, instantaneously and costlessly, by assumption. Their preferences are fully formed and comprehensive, evaluating and ranking all objects of choice in the present and future in all possible states of the world. Their beliefs about all matters, significant and trivial, are complete, unambiguous, and fully consistent with one another. Real people, on the other hand, have better things to do than ensuring the comprehensiveness and consistency of all their mental states. Forming and discovering one's preferences takes time and effort, as does rationalizing all of one's beliefs. Consequently, real people with scarce mental resources must decide how best to use them. Their process of discovery will always be ongoing and incomplete, responding to their personal needs and wants as well as the demands of their environment.

These points might seem to be the territory of behavioral economists, given their emphasis on the limits of human cognition. Yet many behavioral economists – particularly those of the paternalist stripe – package this observation with a heavy burden of normative judgment: *that real people compare unfavorably to ideal neoclassical puppets.* Along with this judgment comes a blindness to the fundamental rationality of economizing on mental resources, as well as how the economizing process makes people responsive to incentives. Thus, they observe failures of "rationality" in the laboratory – where subjects are faced with unfamiliar choices in context-free environments and often with trivial stakes – and then generalize these results to the real world. What this approach misses is how often people alter their behavior, including their alleged biases, in response to stronger incentives in real-world environments. In this book, we have seen numerous demonstrations of rational irrationality, the responsiveness of seemingly irrational behavior to costs and benefits. We have also seen many examples of ecological rationality, the adaptive quality of decision-making processes in real-world environments. Both of these show the capacity of real people to learn and respond to incentives when the incentives are strong enough.

Incentives and learning also matter for the proper calibration of policy. Without knowledge of how quickly people learn and how effectively they respond to incentives, we cannot calibrate policies to give them the optimal amount of correction (which might well be none at all). The lack of such knowledge once again sets the stage for policymaking driven by unjustified assumptions and popular prejudice. We might hope for policymakers who resist these temptations. But incentives matter for policymakers, too, and their incentives are relatively poor in this regard. Most policymakers – including voters – face few negative consequences of indulging unjustified biases and prejudices about their fellow citizens. Indeed, legislators have strong incentives to reflect their constituents' biases, not to correct them, and to show evidence of their productivity in office, whether or not the resulting policies achieve their promised results.

The Rush to Policy

A final common thread is what we call the rush to policy: the tendency to seek policymaking relevance for behavioral research, despite the inadequacy of existing research for that task. At the conceptual and philosophical level, behavioral paternalists have yet to grapple adequately with the thicket of thorny issues that arise in trying to identify people's true preferences. They have not yet managed to fill in the gaping chasm between *identifying inconsistencies among individual preferences* on the one hand and *choosing which preferences to favor* on the other. They have also not yet grappled with the evidence indicating that fast-and-frugal non-Bayesian heuristics can perform better in real-world environments. They have hardly begun to fill the gaps in knowledge required to craft policies that reliably improve human welfare by their chosen standard. Yet these gaps in the research have not prevented behavioral paternalists from confidently recommending policy interventions.

The reality of behavioral policymaking stands in sharp opposition to the rhetoric. Behavioral paternalists have frequently emphasized the need for evidence-based policy (Thaler 2015b, 338) that should be implemented in a cautious and disciplined manner (Camerer et al. 2003, 1212). Their confident tone often suggests that it is anti-paternalists who eschew evidence and rely on gut instinct for policymaking. To paraphrase the Bible, they behold the mote in the anti-paternalists' eyes while neglecting the beam in their own. Consider this telling passage from Sunstein that purports to recognize the need for better evidence:

> With respect to errors, more is being learned every day. Some behavioral findings remain highly preliminary and need further testing. There is much that we do not know. Randomized controlled trials, the gold standard for empirical research, must be used far more to obtain a better understanding of how the relevant findings operate in the world. Even at this stage, however, the underlying findings have been widely noticed, and behavioral economics, cognitive and social psychology, and related fields have had a significant effect on policies in several nations, including the United States and the United Kingdom.
>
> (Sunstein 2014, 11–12)

Notice the speed of the transition from the need for cautious collection of more research to a congratulatory discussion of policy impact. If the need for better research were taken seriously, surely the "significant effect on policies in several nations" would be cause for concern, not approbation.

The willingness of behavioral paternalists to cheer on policy interventions despite the insufficiency of supporting research leads us to worry that they have indeed become the unwitting "Second Baptists" in an emerging Baptist–bootlegger coalition, wherein special interests, old-school moralists, and new-school behavioralists combine their energies to support paternalistic interventions. In the real world of legislation and regulation, caution and discipline take a back seat to expediency and political opportunism.

ESCAPE ROUTES

We believe the challenges presented in this book, taken together, present a formidable barrier to most forms of behavioral paternalism. We don't wish to claim that no paternalist policy could ever pass muster, but we do believe that most will fail, and even seemingly innocuous policies are more difficult to justify than they appear on first blush.

Given the case against behavioral paternalism, how might behavioral paternalists respond? We will now consider a series of potential "escape routes," i.e., analytical or argumentative strategies that could potentially rescue behavioral paternalism from our challenges. Some of these responses have already been made by behavioral paternalists. Others we haven't seen made yet, but they could be made eventually, and so we try to anticipate them here.

Revert to Objective-Welfare Paternalism

We have claimed that behavioral paternalism relies on an *untenable welfare standard*: the ideal of the neoclassical economic agent, whose preferences are comprehensive and internally consistent. This welfare standard is *unpersuasive*, because people may quite reasonably lack preferences that meet its requirements; and also *indeterminate*, because it does not provide a means of resolving the internal inconsistencies in people's actual choices and preferences. Empirically, even if we concede that people have true preferences somewhere deep within themselves, we lack a reliable means of determining the content of those true preferences.

Facing this challenge, one simple path forward for paternalists would be to adopt an alternative welfare standard. But what should it be? In principle, the behavioral paternalist might support the goal of maximizing long-term wealth and health, irrespective of the individual's willingness to trade off these goals against other goals such as spontaneous enjoyment and gustatory pleasure. Although health and wealth are the goals that come up most often in the literature, the paternalist could identify other supposedly objective values as well, such as bonding with family and friends, engaging with one's community, or flourishing in one's career. (To the extent that these values conflict with each other, the paternalist would need to specify the welfare-maximizing trade-offs between them.) We will call this the *objective-welfare* strategy, as it relies on a definition of welfare that is independent of the subjective judgments of the people involved.

Some behavioral paternalists already seem to have objective welfare in mind when they justify intervention by pointing to people making choices that clearly harm their long-run health or wealth. Further evidence comes from those behavioral paternalists who have explicitly defined optimal behavior using long-term rather than short-term rates of discount.[1] On the other hand, many behavioral paternalists emphasize their commitment to a subjective standard of welfare and explicitly reject objective-welfare standards (see especially Conly 2013, 102–103). We have not found any behavioral paternalists who have *unambiguously* adopted an objective-welfare standard, although some have come close.[2] Would doing so insulate them from our critique?

The first thing to notice about the objective-welfare strategy is that it constitutes *an abandonment of the new paternalism and a reversion to the old.* Paternalism itself is nothing new; moral and political authorities have long claimed the right to manipulate people's behavior for their own good. What makes behavioral paternalism distinctive is its seemingly novel justification for paternalism: making people better off "as judged by themselves." It claims to generate policy recommendations based on what individuals really value subjectively. If behavioral paternalism now reverts to a notion of objective welfare, it ceases to be truly different from the older style of paternalism that disregarded the preferences of people targeted for

---

[1] This raises the question, however, of why they allow any time-discounting at all, aside from the level justified by objectively measurable risk of death or other risks.

[2] Kahneman et al. (1997) claim that experience (hedonic) utility is a superior measure of well-being to decision utility (that which guides choice). They sometimes refer to experience utility as "objective happiness." The normative standard that comes out of this discussion is the maximization of total lifetime experience utility. Since *total* utility is not time-dated (p. 393), this means the maximization of the sum of experience utility derived at different points in time *without discounting*. They do not unambiguously recommend that this standard be applied: "Our analysis applies to situations in which a separate value judgment designates experienced utility a criterion for evaluating outcomes" (p. 377). Thus, presumably when government or policymakers make the required value judgment, it would be acceptable to use this as a normative standard for policy. This is what we would call objective welfare, because hedonic consequences are only one class of consequences of behavior and because zero discounting of utility does not generally reflect people's preferences. Loewenstein and Ubel (2008) note the difficulties with both decision utility and experience utility. Nevertheless, they conclude, "whether it comes to government policies that influence individual decisions or policies that directly affect people's situations, the ideal welfare criterion will involve a hybrid consideration of both decision utility and experience utility" (p. 1808). How or by whom the balance is to be struck is clouded in the ambiguities of "deliberative democracy" (p. 1807).

correction. True, it might offer some new ideas about the policy levers by which people's behavior might be manipulated, but it offers nothing new in terms of justification. Meet the new boss, same as the old boss.

We believe behavioral paternalists have distanced themselves from objective welfare for good reason. We reject the notion of a Platonic ideal of "the good life." Instead, we believe that individuals define the good life for themselves. In taking this position, of course, we're wading into deep philosophical waters – and as we said at the start of this book, philosophy is not our comparative advantage. We will therefore keep our argument on this point brief. From our perspective, the very idea of objective welfare is implausible. No such thing as "welfare" exists until an individual mind comes into being. The individual mind generates values, desires, and preferences (typically through interaction with many other minds). And as it turns out, different minds can generate very different values, desires, and preferences. People are idiosyncratic; they want different things. And despite the many wants they have in common, they want the same things to a different extent. We see no plausible grounds for stepping outside of the mind to define what is good for it. The human mind determines what is good for itself. It seems incredibly peculiar, at best, to support a standard of the mind's well-being that may be rejected (indeed, often *is* rejected) by the mind itself. We can say all of this without positing – as both neoclassical and behavioral economists have done – that the mind must decide what is good for itself *in a complete and fully consistent fashion*. Rather, the mind's determination of what is good for itself is an ongoing process.

But again, we are not philosophers. For a more complete philosophical defense of subjective welfare versus objective welfare, we recommend Conly (2013, 102–112), who has addressed these questions more directly than behavioral paternalists with academic homes in psychology or economics.

Putting our economist hats back on, does objective-welfare paternalism effectively dodge the other challenges posed in this book? The answer is a partial yes – especially with respect to challenges relating to subjective knowledge. If we don't care about the individual's preferences, whether idealized or actual, then we don't need to identify them. We don't have to worry about anyone's true willingness to trade off long-term health and wealth against other goals. We don't have to isolate their "true" rate of time discount. We needn't concern ourselves with their genuine weighting of desires expressed in hot states versus cold ones. Questions of this kind disappear.

The objective-welfare paternalist also has the advantage of referencing simple and observable outcomes to judge the success of their policies. If longer life is the undisputed goal, then we can judge the policy's success by reference to calculated life expectancy. Likewise for the goal of greater retirement savings: just see how much people are saving.

Nevertheless, many challenges remain. To the extent that objective-welfare paternalists wish to draw on behavioral insights to manipulate behavior, they will have nearly as much need for reliable research as subjective-welfare paternalists. For any given behavioral phenomenon they wish to exploit or counteract, they need to know the specific contexts in which it occurs, whether it generalizes from the lab to the real world, and how it interacts with other behavioral phenomena. And unless their standard of objective welfare is entirely one-directional (e.g., "it is always better to have more health, no matter the cost"), they need to know the extent of these behavioral effects as well. Using an objective definition of welfare obviates some knowledge problems, but by no means all.

Furthermore, even an objective-welfare paternalist must be concerned with political economy: how their well-intentioned policy agenda can be twisted to serve the ends of interested parties. They must also take into account the risk of slippery slopes, unless they implausibly believe that *any* additional intervention will necessarily further their objective goals.

Appeal to Obviousness

According to this line of argument, there are some cases in which people are obviously making mistakes, and/or some interventions that will obviously make them better off. We've heard this rebuttal often when talking to others in conversation about our research. The basic idea is that, as fellow humans, we know we make errors. And looking around us, it's clear that some people are erring *very badly*.

In a sense, this approach asks us to set aside all the careful research and analysis that has been done by, among others, behavioral economists. Do we really need academic studies to know that some people are too fat, some gamble themselves into poverty, and so on? The research, such as it is, merely provides further evidence of what we already knew.

This argument reminds us, again, of some behavioral paternalists' tendency to justify their policies by pointing toward people who are clearly making choices that harm their long-run health and wealth. So, one interpretation of the obviousness argument is that the speaker actually has an objective standard of welfare in mind. If so, our responses are laid out in the previous discussion.

Another interpretation is that the speaker still embraces subjective welfare but believes it is relatively easy to identify mistakes relative to that standard – at least in some cases. When we see so many people making poor decisions, the facts speak for themselves. We observe behaviors that are irrational on their face.

Our response is that the bare facts *do not* speak for themselves. When we think they do, we are typically projecting our own preferences onto other people who may not share them. Eating, gambling, smoking, and countless other "indulgent" behaviors have benefits that must be weighed against costs. The correct weighting of those benefits and costs is unavoidably subjective. For some people the optimal result will involve worse health, lower lifetime wealth, and other seemingly undesirable outcomes. We cannot, therefore, simply observe irrational behavior and know it as such. Rationality and irrationality are defined relative to subjective preferences that are typically unobserved and often unobservable.

If irrational behavior can be observed simply and directly, then why have behavioral paternalists spent so much time citing and explaining the behavioral literature on biases and heuristics? We believe it's because they wish to have a *scientific basis* for paternalism, rather than rely on vague intuitions and moral judgments. They want some assurance that they are not simply indulging longstanding biases against those whose behavior is regarded as weak, unpleasant, deviant, or indulgent. Behavioral economics promised to provide that scientific foundation. Specifically, the systematic violation of neoclassical rationality norms suggested a rigorous basis for the claim that people make genuine and systematic mistakes according to their own preferences.

But now we have ventured well beyond the realm of the obvious. Obvious facts tell us very little about whether the choices we see are subjectively optimal. To continue with the obesity example, it's obvious many people are obese and suffer the health consequences – but that's where the obviousness ends. To make the scientific argument stick, the behavioral paternalists must grapple with the forbidding conceptual and philosophical challenges that arise from identifying welfare with the neoclassical rationality norms.

Sunstein, in particular, has tried to meet these challenges. But in doing so, he sometimes falls back on obviousness, relying on numerous examples of supposed decision failures that *seem* to be even simpler than obesity. In a 2015 article, Sunstein directly responds to our challenge to the use of neoclassical rationality as a welfare standard: "Whitman and Rizzo assume far too close a link between the neoclassical axioms, and in particular the problem of inconsistency, and the welfarist arguments for nudges. Recall the seven cases with which I began" (2015, 518). His counterargument here is not immediately clear; *why* is the link not as close as we say? Sunstein does not explain. However, the "seven cases" to which he refers suggest an appeal to obviousness. We will therefore quote his list in full:

1. Jones is asked to make a choice between two identical radios. One costs more. He chooses the more expensive one.
2. Jones orders fish tacos at a restaurant. He used to like fish tacos, but he hasn't recently. (He forgot that fact; he ordered them out of habit.) He doesn't enjoy the fish tacos.
3. Jones often gets lost driving to local restaurants. He has a poor sense of direction. His girlfriend gets him a GPS, and he no longer gets lost. He's glad he has the GPS.
4. Jones is asked to make a choice between two health insurance plans. One dominates the other: It is better along several dimensions and worse along no dimension. Jones chooses the dominated plan.
5. Jones is buying a car. The first option costs very slightly less than the second but has terrible fuel efficiency, so much so that after 6 months, the second option would save him money. (He expects to own the car for at least 5 years.) He likes the two cars the same. He chooses the first option, because he pays no attention to the fuel economy of the cars.
6. Because he is busy and inattentive, Jones, who is poor, is often late paying his credit card bills. If he received text messages from his credit card company, he would make his payments on time. His credit card company does not send him text messages.
7. Jones fails to sign up for a retirement plan. He is aware that his employer has such a plan, and he thinks that enrolling would be an excellent idea, but he keeps thinking that he will sign up next month. Next month turns out to take a while. He does not start saving for 5 years.

(Sunstein 2015, 517–518)

Some of these examples are quite trivial (does our country really face a fish taco problem?), while others are more serious. It's also unclear whether *any* of them involve genuine paternalism, a question we'll address later in this chapter. But what all of these examples have in common, by virtue of being hypothetical, is that they simply *assert* the facts of the matter, including the subjective mental facts.

We know the two radios are identical for Jones – with no differences in search cost, convenience, delivery time, etc. – because the example says so. We know that Jones ordered the fish tacos out of habit (and not for some other reason), and also that he didn't enjoy them, because the example says so. We know he's happy with his GPS because the example says so. We know he likes the more and less fuel-efficient cars equally well because the example says so. We know the text-message reminders would indeed cause Jones to pay his bills on time, even though he is poor, because the example says so. We know one health insurance plan dominates the other – with all relevant dimensions of quality taken into account – because the example says so.

In short, these examples are obvious because their presentation gives us privileged access to the subjective mental states of the chooser while assuming away all possible caveats and qualifications. They also evoke familiar experiences such as forgetfulness and procrastination, which lend support to the feeling of obviousness. But the real world of actual paternalist proposals is substantially more complicated.

Sunstein continues: "To be sure, we can complicate those cases in such a way as to make the welfare assessment more difficult. But some cases are easy, and difficult cases present an opportunity for better thinking, not for skepticism about the whole project" (2015, 518).

We suggest that these examples are only simple because they are made so by construction. In the real world, we cannot read each other's minds, which complicates matters substantially. And "better thinking" has not yet answered the challenge of finding a welfare standard that does not rely on the neoclassical rationality axioms. Sunstein's response amounts to a confident assurance that really smart people will eventually find a solution to these problems; it is not itself a solution.

Moreover, we believe that Sunstein has mistaken a conceptual problem for an empirical one. Despite denying a close link between his notion of welfare and the neoclassical axioms, he does not offer an alternative definition of welfare. Instead, he implies that the conceptual challenges can be answered by better empirical research and analysis that will eventually reveal people's true welfare, whatever that might be. As an example of the kind of research he favors, he cites Goldin's (2015) approach to "discerning" the preferences of inconsistent choosers (i.e., people whose choices are affected by default rules). The key assumption behind Goldin's approach is that inconsistent choosers must have underlying "true preferences." By citing Goldin's approach, Sunstein implies that he, too, assumes the existence of such true preferences – despite having repeatedly emphasized that such preferences may not exist. Therefore, Goldin's approach cannot save behavioral paternalists from the dilemma of finding a proper welfare standard.

Suppose, nevertheless, that we follow Sunstein in treating the preferences of inconsistent choosers as an empirical rather than conceptual issue. Thus, we assume true preferences exist and we try to identify them using

Goldin's method. We highlighted some difficulties with Goldin's method in Chapter 7. Most importantly, Goldin implicitly assumes a problem situation in which there is only one operative bias, rather than multiple biases (as well as rational inference of information), involved. And even if Goldin's approach were successful in identifying the true preferences of inconsistent choosers, it would only apply to a small fraction of situations: choice among default rules when a "neutral" frame untainted by bias is also available, where there are no concerns about choosing among multiple opt-out frames (e.g., contribution levels for savings plans), and so on. And even in this narrow set of cases, we are far beyond the outer bounds of obviousness.

In short, behavioral paternalists who rely on an appeal to obviousness wish to evoke a broad and vague intuition shared by many of their readers – that flawed people are constantly making obvious and correctable mistakes – while also claiming the mantle of rigorous and evidence-based policymaking. They cannot have it both ways.

Shift the Burden of Proof

In *Why Nudge?*, Sunstein offers what is probably his most complete defense of behavioral paternalism. In the process, he presents his own version – often an admirably persuasive version – of the leading arguments against his position, and then explains why he finds these arguments lacking. In responding to welfare-based arguments against paternalism, which he says should be taken "extremely seriously" (2014, 22), he offers the following summation:

> In many contexts, the objections to paternalism depend on strong empirical assumptions, involving extreme optimism about private choosers and extreme pessimism about public officials, that *do not always hold*. It follows that there is *no sufficient abstract or a priori argument against paternalism*, whether hard or soft.
>
> (Sunstein 2014, 22, emphasis added)

Later, Sunstein adds:

> Each of those objections must be taken seriously. But none of them supports an *across-the-board barrier to paternalism*, whether hard or soft.
>
> (Sunstein 2014, 113, emphasis added)

The rhetorical strategy here is to define the burden of proof so that your intellectual opponent cannot possibly meet it. In this case, Sunstein asks that opponents of behavioral paternalism offer a "sufficient abstract or a priori argument against paternalism" or "an across-the-board barrier to paternalism." In other words, it is not enough to offer an array of theoretical, conceptual, and empirical arguments against behavioral paternalism (as we have in this book). Rather, we must offer a broad and comprehensive argument that is sufficient to *decisively rule out any form of paternalism whatsoever*.

Sunstein sets a lower burden for paternalists. The rhetorical strategy becomes clear when he says, "[t]he strength of the objections to paternalism depends on the particular form that paternalism takes. The objections are weakest when it is soft and limited to means. Especially in such cases, there are many opportunities for improving welfare without intruding on freedom of choice" (2014, 133). In other words, Sunstein's defense focuses on justifying the weakest of interventions, and even there he need only suggest that opportunities for improvement exist. His position seems to be that if just one intervention survives the challenges we have laid out, then behavioral paternalism will be judged a success.

In considering Sunstein's argumentative strategy, we detect an even subtler shifting of the burden of proof. As suggested by the second quotation earlier, Sunstein takes each objection to paternalism one at a time, and then he argues that certain categories of paternalist intervention escape that objection. In other words, Policies A and B might be immune to Objection 1, while Policies C and D are immune to Objection 2, and Policies E and F are only mildly vulnerable to Objection 3. So, none of these objections constitutes an "across-the-board barrier" to paternalism, *even if each policy stumbles on at least one objection*.

Not surprisingly, we reject this burden of proof. We do not claim that any one of our objections, taken in isolation, decisively rejects every possible paternalist intervention. We do not even claim that our objections *taken in combination* are decisive against all paternalist interventions. We are willing to admit there could be a paternalist proposal – one that is sufficiently nonintrusive, is based on strong research, poses minimal knowledge problems, and so on – that clears all the hurdles and passes an honest cost–benefit test. We don't expect this book to provide a conclusive argument that ends all future debate on paternalist proposals.

So, what do we expect? First, we hope to have convinced the reader that behavioral paternalism is far more problematic than typically portrayed, and therefore we should have a generalized resistance – though not necessarily decisive resistance – to new paternalist incursions. We should not rule out all such interventions, but we should view them with great skepticism. Second, with respect to any specific paternalist proposal, we should ask whether it can survive the gauntlet of objections laid out in this book. Many proposals will clear some of these hurdles, but we suspect relatively few will survive them all. Some proposals will stumble at the level of basic theory and concept. Others will fail on grounds of insufficient knowledge. Others will simply fail the cost–benefit test, especially once political risks are taken into account. Simply put, we aim to establish a *presumption* against paternalist intervention.

Loosen the Definition of Paternalism

Earlier, in response to the obviousness argument, we questioned whether any of the examples in Sunstein's list actually involves paternalism. Is GPS really a form of paternalism? Sunstein thinks so. In fact, GPS is one of his favorite examples, and not just when it's a gift. He even calls GPS an "iconic nudge" that should be seen as "a form of means paternalism," and one that paternalists should seek to build upon (Sunstein 2015, 61–62).

GPS is, of course, almost always self-adopted; people "impose" it upon themselves. Not knowing the fastest route from A to B, they seek out information and then act upon it. Is consulting a map also a form of paternalism? A map does, after all, simplify the territory that it depicts in order to ease the process of finding things.

But GPS is not the most trivial example of alleged paternalism. According to Sunstein, a restaurant providing a low-calorie menu for its customers is (or can be) a paternalist nudge (2014, 2). According to Thaler, giving someone accurate instructions on how to get to the subway is a form of paternalism (2015b, 324). Text-message reminders from doctors (Thaler 2015b, 342) and credit card companies (Sunstein 2015, 518) are also apparently paternalism. Bumpy lane markers on the highway may also constitute a form of paternalism (Thaler 2015b, 325), at least to the extent they aim at helping the driver herself rather than other people on the road. As Sunstein and Thaler see it, any time someone gives helpful advice, provides useful information, or gives a friendly warning, that's paternalism. The paternalist bar seems to be remarkably low.

What is gained by defining paternalism so broadly that it includes numerous everyday activities that few, if any, had previously regarded as paternalism? Broadening the definition of paternalism goes hand in hand with the previous strategy of shifting the burden of proof. Shifting the burden means the behavioral paternalist need only find one, or perhaps a few, proposals that pass muster in order to declare victory for behavioral paternalism. Defining paternalism downward ensures that at least some proposals do, in fact, seem to be justified. To oppose paternalism full stop, we would have to oppose dozens of commonplace activities that most of us engage in from time to time – either as providers or recipients.

In this context, it is difficult to avoid engaging in a semantic debate. We find Sunstein and Thaler's definition of paternalism absurdly expansive in comparison with how most people use the term. There exist many alternative terms that could describe the anodyne activities they have classed as paternalism, such as "helpfulness," "good customer service," "ergonomic product design," and "responsiveness to consumer demand." Lumping these in the same category with the more intrusive activities commonly called paternalism obscures more than it enlightens.

To confuse matters further, Sunstein and Thaler often substitute the word "nudge" in place of paternalism. "Nudge" is a nontechnical word in the English language. It can have various shades of meaning. Sunstein and Thaler have created a technical meaning, but they sometimes shift between the technical meaning and the everyday meaning. The technical meaning requires a bias. The technical nudge must operate at a psychological level to counteract a bias such as the tendency to procrastinate. On the other hand, a nudge in everyday life can be a simple reminder – an alarm clock, a note in a calendar, etc. It can also be guidance of some kind, such as a map or a GPS device. These might be called "rational nudges" because they require no biases for their effectiveness. The casual shifting between the technical and everyday meanings makes it appear as if nudges in the technical sense are everywhere and the only issue is to implement the right ones.

But now let us set the semantics aside. We want to focus on the characteristics that distinguish innocuous interventions from more problematic ones, irrespective of the label attached. Here are several factors, often overlapping and highly correlated with each other, that will help us to distinguish the harmless activities from more troubling ones:

Self-Imposed versus Other-Imposed. Most people don't have GPS forced on them; they ask for it, in the form of vehicles and smartphones, and then use it voluntarily. Self-help groups and self-help books are also self-imposed. As we have discussed extensively in earlier chapters, these are among the many strategies that people use to shape their lives and, in some cases, to control their perceived biases. From the perspective of inclusive rationality, strategies of this kind are well within the range of rational behavior. They prove that people do, in fact, try to correct their own flaws and acquire better habits. They indicate that laboratory-derived measures of bias do not necessarily generalize to real-world behavior, because they do not capture the full range of human activity including self-correction. As such, self-imposed strategies constitute good reasons to be skeptical of more intrusive interventions imposed by others.

Invited versus Uninvited. Some interventions are delivered by others, but only by invitation. Text-message reminders are often invited, such as when a doctor's office asks if you're willing to provide your cell phone number for this purpose. When people visit financial planners and nutritionists, they are explicitly asking for advice. Likewise when restaurant patrons ask the waiter for a recommendation from the menu. Invited strategies overlap substantially with self-imposed ones, and in some cases they may be identical; for instance, self-imposed attendance at a support group may also be a way to request advice. Like self-imposed strategies, invited nudges strongly indicate the chooser's desire to make better choices and awareness of mechanisms that may help. They argue against more intrusive interventions, not for them.

Competitive versus Monopolistic Environment. Some interventions take place in a competitive environment, meaning individuals have the option to choose among different providers of interventions or nudges. In the restaurant business, different restaurants offer different menus. Some have health-conscious sections, some have low-price sections, some have a vegan section, some even have deliberately "sinful" sections. If customers don't like a given restaurant's menu, including its nudge-like elements, they are free to go elsewhere. Similarly, in the labor market, numerous employers exist, and they can and do offer different processes for enrollment in savings plans (and other human-resources policies). Some may have opt-in enrollment, others opt-out, others explicit choice. It is true, of course, that employees may have fewer choices among employers than customers have among restaurants; nevertheless, these transactions are still characterized by some degree of competition. By contrast, the government and legal system are essentially monopolistic. Citizens who don't like their rules and interventions – including default rules, waiting periods, sales restrictions, and so on – cannot choose another provider of government and laws without disclaiming their citizenship and/or moving to another jurisdiction. We ought to be more skeptical of interventions provided in a monopolistic environment than those provided in a competitive one.

Coercive versus Voluntary. Some interventions are coercive, in the sense of using compulsion or threats of force, while other interventions do not foreclose options. Sin taxes – supported by Cremer et al. (2012), O'Donoghue and Rabin (2003, 2006), and Gruber and Köszegi (2001) – provide a clear example, as they prevent people from concluding voluntary exchanges without also surrendering some money to the state. They foreclose options by reducing the budget set of consumers, meaning they cannot afford as much (with the same income) as they could without the tax. Cooling-off periods – supported by Camerer et al. (2003) and Thaler and Sunstein (2003) – also coerce, as they foreclose the option of concluding a final sale immediately. Needless to say, outright bans such as those supported by Conly (2013, 149–181) are coercive. Violators of any of these rules could be subject to punishment by the state.

Sunstein and Thaler have repeatedly emphasized their preference for noncoercive forms of paternalism – hence the heavy weight they place on shifts in default rules and provision of information. But as we have laid out extensively in Chapter 9, their notion of coercion is flawed. They define coercion (or its opposite, which they style as "libertarianism") in terms of the cost of exercising choice, *without reference to who imposes the cost and how*. By this odd definition, self-imposed costs – such as banning ice cream from your home, or choosing to live far away from liquor stores and bakeries – would constitute a form of coercion.

Defining coercion in terms of the cost of exercising choice creates a smooth gradient between softer and harder paternalist policies, which Sunstein and Thaler immediately exploit by presenting a range of interventions that play on the gradient. The best example is labor-friendly default terms in employment contracts, which in principle could be noncoercive. Yet then they discuss how the cost of opting out of the default could be raised via increasingly onerous requirements, such as filling out long waiver forms, consulting a lawyer first, attending a mandatory counseling session, and so on. Such modifications *do* constitute coercion insofar as they unnecessarily, and avoidably, limit the ability of parties to a contract to reach voluntary agreements contrary to the default rule.

Finally, it is worth noting that even some seemingly noncoercive interventions, such as new default rules, actually coerce people by preventing them from choosing their own default rules. For instance, imagine a new legal rule that requires employers to have opt-out rather than opt-in retirement plans. This rule respects the freedom of choice of *employees*, but it does not respect the freedom of choice of *employers*, who may wish to have a different default rule. In addition to coercing employers, this approach also replaces what had been a competitive environment (different employers choosing different default rules) with a monopolistic one (the government choosing one default rule for everyone).

Public versus Private. This distinction closely parallels the previous two distinctions, so we will keep the discussion short. While there are certainly exceptions, public interventions are often both coercive and monopolistic, inasmuch as they tend to foreclose options through the threat of legal punishment, and they typically allow little if any means of choosing a different "provider." Private interventions, on the other hand, tend to be noncoercive – and when they are coercive, the coercer can be criminally charged. (If someone steals your donuts and forces you to exercise, he can be charged with theft and assault.) In addition, the private sector is typically characterized by markets and polycentric institutions. If you don't like the paternalistic interventions of your church, college, family, or support group, you have the option of leaving them.

Note that behavioral paternalists have often obscured the distinction between public and private. When making their case for paternalism, they almost always begin with private mechanisms, such as GPS in our cars and cafeteria lines that place fruit before desserts. In this regard, it's worth noting that there is nothing coercive about either of those situations. Honda can choose to make GPS navigation standard in all its vehicles, or none of them; if you don't like it, you can choose a different car dealer. A cafeteria can display desserts, hide them, or ban them altogether; if you don't like it, you can find a different place to eat.[3] What makes this acceptable is *not* that every automaker and restaurant will necessarily make the "best" choice, but that they cannot force their choice on anyone else, and consumers are free to negotiate with other providers for services that better satisfy their needs.

Informative versus Manipulative. We will spend more time on this distinction, as behavioral paternalists frequently point to providing information as a quintessential paternalist nudge – one that many listeners will find unobjectionable.

Everyone knows that relevant information is helpful for making choices. This is why we have instruction manuals, hazard warnings and symbols, product ratings on Amazon, service ratings on Yelp, and – yes – mandatory legal disclosures in cases where providers are unlikely to provide them voluntarily. Even fully rational individuals (that is, individuals without any biases) can make poor decisions if they don't know the facts. A wide range of disclosures, both voluntary and mandatory, can potentially provide people with the information they need to make better decisions. We didn't need behavioral economics to tell us this; mainstream neoclassical economics told us so.

---

[3] This is true even for government cafeterias, at least to the extent that consumers may choose to eat elsewhere. A prison cafeteria would raise a host of other concerns, of course.

We find it peculiar (at best) to treat mere provision of information as necessarily paternalistic. But set that aside. The substantive question relates to the justification for providing information. From the perspective of inclusive rationality, the focus would be on the *accuracy of messages* – both in content and in interpretation. When more than one presentation is available, some presentations might yield more accurate interpretations than others. In this vein, Hoffrage and Gigerenzer (1998) have emphasized conveying information in ways that receivers interpret as intended; for instance, people seem to grasp frequencies correctly, while misinterpreting probabilities. (This is not necessarily a failure of rationality, as the unintended interpretation may be perfectly justifiable under standard conversational norms; the *mis*interpretation is only relative to the intended message.)

By contrast, behavioral paternalism offers the possibility of conveying information in ways that purposely manipulate people toward desired behaviors, irrespective of how they interpret the information. For example, risk narratives and graphic images on products are justified on the basis of *salience* – how noticeable or arresting the information is – rather than the accuracy of the receiver's interpretation. Such narratives and images might even trigger incorrect or excessively pessimistic assessments of risk. This is fine, from the paternalistic perspective, provided that it pushes people in the desired direction, possibly by offsetting some other bias (such as optimism or present bias). Notice that these interventions are recommended in cases where consumers already possess the relevant information – but because it hasn't motivated them to change their ways, paternalists posit that salience must have distorted their choices.[4]

To take another example, there is good evidence that the impact of default rules is largely attributable to information and recommendation effects; people make inferences from the default rule. But rather than advocating a default rule that minimizes inadvertent information leakage, or advocating the provision of free information and advice (such as through investment seminars), most behavioral paternalists favor using the default rule as a direct device for channeling people toward "better" choices.

---

[4] Without an independent measure of the degree of salience and its effect on behavior, invoking lack of salience as an explanation for particular choices is not a true explanation but ad hoc speculation. To our knowledge, those who invoke salience in a policy context do not have such a measure.

Yet another example is provided by the Food and Drug Administration's stance with respect to truthful information about tobacco products. When a Swedish maker of snus, a form of smokeless tobacco, petitioned to modify the warning label on its product to say that it carries "substantially lower risks to health than cigarettes," the FDA rejected the petition even though the claim is true given current medical knowledge. Why? The primary concern seems to have been that "labels that indicate lower risk may tempt people, particularly young people, to use tobacco products that they might not have tried otherwise" (Tavernise 2015). We don't know whether any behavioral paternalists weighed in on this particular issue, but it is indicative of how providing truthful information, even that which is clearly relevant to some consumers, takes a back seat when the regulatory focus is on changing behavior.

In short, behavioral paternalism has a complicated relationship with the truth. Truthful disclosures may be useful from a paternalist standpoint . . . but not necessarily. To judge whether a given piece of information is desirable, the paternalist must have some notion of how the targeted agent should behave, all things considered. Then information can be delivered – or obscured – in the manner most likely to nudge the agent in the supposedly correct direction.

Concerns of this nature should give us pause when considering informational interventions *based on paternalist motives*. While we would not wish to rule out all possible interventions aimed at providing information to decision-makers, we ought to be highly skeptical about proposals driven by this kind of goal-directed rather than accuracy-directed reasoning.

Let us return to the question of how paternalism is defined. Obviously, definitions are to some extent arbitrary. Behavioral paternalists are free to define paternalism as they like, and to persuade others to adopt their definition. But why have they done so in the way they have? One possibility, as we've suggested, is that it's part of a rhetorical strategy to make it easier to claim success for behavioral paternalism. But it is more than that. A broader definition of paternalism, one that encompasses dozens of everyday acts of voluntary noncoercive helpfulness, serves to ease opposition to further interventions by framing them all as essentially the same thing: "We're already doing paternalism all the time, so why not do a little bit more?" And with the relevant distinctions sufficiently obscured, the "little bit more" can involve movement toward interventions that more often fall on the wrong side of those important distinctions: other-imposed, uninvited, monopolistic, coercive, public, and manipulative.

Rely on the "Libertarian Condition"

Sunstein and Thaler repeatedly and emphatically state their desire to keep paternalism relatively limited. Their term "libertarian paternalism" is meant to emphasize maintaining freedom of choice, while their term "nudge" emphasizes the mild nature of their proposals. When confronted with the possibility of harder forms of paternalism taking hold, they insist that they have no such intentions, that their proposals are "emphatically designed to retain freedom of choice," and that the "libertarian condition" will help prevent more intrusive policies (Thaler and Sunstein 2008, 240). Thaler says that "we have no interest in telling people what to do," but apparently this is "a point that critics of our book seem incapable of getting" (2015b, 325).

We are the critics in question. We have partially responded to this claim in Chapter 9, but we will reiterate and expand our responses here.

First, while Sunstein and Thaler have vowed not to cross the line into restricting freedom of choice, not all behavioral paternalists have done so. Some of the most prominent proposals in this area do restrict freedom of choice. For multiple examples, see the earlier discussion on the distinction between coercive and voluntary interventions.

Second, even while voicing support for freedom of support, Sunstein and Thaler have helped to construct an intellectual framework that undermines support for freedom of choice. Freedom of choice plays no important role in the theory itself. As behavioral paternalist arguments take hold in political, legal, and regulatory circles, there is no particular reason to think they will be bound by Sunstein and Thaler's "libertarian condition."

Third, even in their own works, Sunstein and Thaler fail to consistently support freedom of choice. Often this happens because they focus exclusively on the freedom of choice of particular groups such as customers and employees, while ignoring the freedom of choice of other groups such as sellers and employers. Thus, a rule *mandating* that sellers or employers offer certain terms or adopt certain defaults will be characterized as preserving or even expanding freedom of choice, despite the prohibitions and conscriptions placed on other parties. Mandatory risk narratives such as those suggested by Jolls and Sunstein (2006) – which go beyond the mere provision of accurate information – also fall into this category.

Other times, freedom of choice is restricted in ways unrecognized or minimized by Sunstein and Thaler. One example is the Model Employment Termination Act, which recommends replacing "at-will" with "for-cause" termination. The for-cause requirement could be waived, but only in exchange for a mandatory severance payment equal to a month's salary if the employee is terminated without cause. Note that this rule would *rule out* any contract in which an employee waives for-cause termination entirely or for a smaller severance payment. Sunstein and Thaler admit that this is "less libertarian than it might be," yet still conclude that "freedom of choice is nonetheless respected" (Sunstein and Thaler 2003, 1187). We have to conclude that their notion of freedom of choice is not very robust. Although Sunstein and Thaler do not explicitly support every policy they offer as an illustrative example of "libertarian paternalism," the presence of coercive policies on the list should make us skeptical about the ability of the "libertarian condition" to protect freedom of choice.

How did Sunstein and Thaler come to include a variety of choice-restricting policies under the libertarian umbrella? Again, we think the answer lies in their peculiar definition of coercion and libertarianism in terms of the cost of exercising choices, rather than who imposes the costs and how. For more on this, see the section "Loosen the Definition of Paternalism" as well as Chapter 9.

Fourth, even if we limit ourselves to interventions that do not restrict freedom of choice, such as shifting of default rules without any additional burdens on opting out, mere satisfaction of the "libertarian condition" does not mean that these interventions are justified. The promise to limit interventions to choice-preserving ones may forestall concerns about a slippery slope, but it does not allay other concerns. Specifically, behavioral economists still have not offered a welfare criterion for determining that some defaults are better than others (see Chapter 3). They also haven't yet filled the many gaping holes in the research (see Chapter 6), nor have they satisfied the basic knowledge requirements for conducting a convincing cost–benefit analysis (see Chapter 7). These objections apply even to interventions that appear minimal and that preserve freedom of choice.

Finally, there is the slippery-slope argument. As we argued throughout Chapter 9, claims to moderation cannot always be sustained. Initial interventions can create conditions that encourage further interventions. Among other things, initial interventions tend to create expectations for policy success to be judged in terms of measurable outcomes. Thus, if small and nonintrusive interventions – sold to policymakers on grounds that small nudges can produce substantial effects – eventually produce disappointing outcomes, policymakers feel pressure to strengthen the policy to achieve the promised results. Policymakers also tend to draw upon the leading justifications of earlier interventions to justify later interventions, while stripping away the qualifications (such as the freedom-of-choice requirement) and supporting justifications (such as spillover effects on other people) that accompanied the initial policy. The tendency of soft interventions to encourage harder ones can be exacerbated by the same biases that behavioral economists have warned us about, including over-confidence and confirmation bias on the part of policymakers. Incentives and behavioral effects work together in the political arena to support movement toward more intrusive interventions. We cannot expect mere words and promises to hold the line against these forces.

The slippery-slope argument can be overstated, of course. We don't wish to imply that the slope is inevitable, only that the risk exists. That risk ought to be included in any *ex ante* cost–benefit analysis of smaller interventions.

Invoke the Inevitability of Choice Architecture

In their early work on the subject, Sunstein and Thaler frequently say that some form of paternalism is inevitable.[5] This is true, they say, because the way in which decisions are framed unavoidably affects the choices people make. They regard this argument as a crucial part of their case against anti-paternalism: "But in an important respect the anti-paternalist position is incoherent, simply because there is no way to avoid effects on behavior and choice" (2003, 1182).

While it is true that the framing of decisions (including default rules) can affect choices, it is *not* true that frames must be chosen with the goal of influencing people's choices for their own good – the key element of paternalism. Therefore, paternalism per se is not inevitable. Recognizing this point, Sunstein is more careful in later work. Rather than saying paternalism is inevitable, he says that *choice architecture* is inevitable (2015, 14).[6] Choice architecture is his term for the entire set of background features of choice situations that may influence decisions, whether or not

---

[5] For example, they say that "a form of paternalism cannot be avoided" (Sunstein and Thaler 2003, 1166), that the "conceptual heart" of their article "asks whether a form of paternalism is inevitable" (2003, 1166), that "our emphasis has been on the inevitability of paternalism" (2003, 1174), that "some form of paternalism verges on the inevitable" (2003, 1177), and that "[t]he inevitability of paternalism is most clear when the planner has to choose starting points or default rule" (2003, 1184). "The inevitability of paternalism" is also the name for a whole section of the article (2003, 1182).

[6] However, Sunstein sometimes lapses into less careful language; for example: "my basic conclusion is that the welfarist objections to paternalism have no force when some kind of paternalism is inevitable" (2015, 121).

anyone deliberately tries to exert such influence. His point is that how things are framed always has effects on decisions, "whether or not they are intentional or the product of any kind of conscious design" (2015, 21).

This is an important concession. If paternalism is inevitable, it's pointless to discuss whether or not to be paternalistic, and instead we should focus on how and *how much* to be paternalistic. But in fact, only choice architecture is inevitable. That means we can ask about other ways, besides paternalistically, that choice architecture might be chosen.

Even this wording may be too narrow, as "chosen" implies a level of intentionality. In many cases, choice architecture may evolve over time in response to the needs of interacting people, in much the same way that language and manners evolve. As Friedrich Hayek suggested, such evolved institutions "of human action but not of human design" may embody tacit knowledge that central planners often cannot access. It would be a mistake, then, to assume that undesigned choice architecture is simply arbitrary or random. Here is one simple example: goods displayed in public view in a store, particularly those with price tags, are available for sale to anyone who can afford the price. When this rule is violated, merchants will usually say so explicitly ("Display items not for sale"). This simple default rule, a kind of choice architecture, minimizes confusion and eases communication between potential buyers and sellers. As far as we know, this practice was never explicitly chosen by anyone.

Consider a more detailed example: the case of refunds and exchanges. In the United States, there is no general legal rule requiring merchants to let customers return goods for a refund or exchange. Although there are some exceptions, especially with regard to door-to-door sales, for most transactions merchants are free to make all sales final (Ben-Shahar and Posner 2011, 115–116). Fourteen states require merchants to publicly disclose their rules for refunds and exchanges, with a default refund requirement that applies otherwise; in the remaining thirty-six states, the consumer's ability to get a refund or exchange is entirely a function of the seller's policy, without even a requirement to post the policy (FindLaw n.d.). Yet in actual practice, *refunds and exchanges are the operative default.* As Ben-Shahar and Posner observe, despite differences among retailers with regard to time periods, restocking fees, and so on, "the core right to withdraw, at least for stores selling new goods, seems virtually universal" (2011, 120). Consumers *assume* goods can be returned in good condition during a reasonable period, unless sellers explicitly say otherwise. How did this near-universal default come to be? We surmise that it arose from frequent interactions between merchants and customers wherein customers requested (or demanded) refunds, merchants responded in various ways, and practice eventually settled on a policy generally agreeable to both. Of course, incentives provided by profit maximization and competition surely contributed to the process. Yet profit maximization does not directly dictate the answer to the question; in principle, given high enough costs of allowing refunds and weak enough demands from consumers, profit maximization could have dictated an all-sales-final policy. A competitive process of discovery was therefore required to yield the outcome we observe. Tacit knowledge is embodied in the de facto default rule.

Furthermore, the usual default rule is suspended in a number of familiar cases, undergarments and perishable foods being well-known examples. In these cases, most customers are aware that refunds cannot be taken for granted, even if the merchant hasn't said so explicitly. These goods presumably differ from other goods because the goods in question "depreciate" quickly after sale or use. What all of these cases together suggest is an ongoing *market for default rules*. If all-sales-final were the universal default, we might suspect that consumers aren't thinking carefully and sellers are simply taking advantage of them. But the variation of default rules tells a different story – one in which market default rules are responsive to the needs of both buyers and sellers. As Vernon Smith argues, "[t]here is a sense in which ecological systems, whether cultural or biological, must necessarily be, if not already, in the process of becoming rational: they serve the fitness needs of those who unintentionally created them through their interactions" (2005, 144).

Even when defaults are chosen deliberately rather than evolving, there exist ways to decide among default rules that do not necessarily involve paternalism. Here are a few possibilities:

- Defaults may be chosen in line with conventional expectations. This has the advantage of not surprising or confusing people who have become accustomed to the usual rules. In addition, conventional expectations have likely been shaped by the evolutionary process described earlier. Oftentimes legal rules appear to have been set in this way: by imitating common practices that have come to be expected.
- Default rules may be chosen in a minimalistic fashion – i.e., assuming that people are not making promises or exchanges unless they explicitly consent to them. This would rule out, for instance, a default rule that assumes for-cause termination, as that constitutes an additional promise on top of the simple agreement to exchange labor for

compensation. (Note that this approach would produce the opposite of conventional expectations in the case of refund and exchange policies.)

- Defaults may be chosen in line with the goal of minimizing transaction costs, which usually would mean minimizing opt-outs. Although Sunstein and Thaler say that minimizing opt-outs might provide a rule of thumb for maximizing welfare (2003, 1195), this is not necessarily the case (Goldin 2015, 248–251). Yet even if minimizing opt-outs doesn't maximize welfare directly, it could still be a reasonable approach if it grounds expectations: people know that defaults are chosen in this way.

- Defaults could be chosen to minimize how much choosers infer from the rule. In other words, people are more inclined to infer advice or information from some defaults (or framings) than others. The idea would be to choose the default rule that is least likely to cause such inferences, thereby avoiding or reducing problems of "information leakage." This approach could be paired with explicit provision of information or advice.

We don't necessarily advocate any of these approaches. Our strong suspicion is that all of them have impacted the evolution of default rules in the real world. Which approach to default-setting makes most sense could easily depend on details of context – such as whether the default rule takes place in a market setting, whether choosers are familiar with the choice situation, and whether the transaction is simple or complex.

In much of the behavioral paternalist literature, the implicit assumption about existing default rules and choice architecture is that they have been selected either arbitrarily or exploitatively. Our perspective, rooted in inclusive rationality, suggests instead that default rules and choice architecture arise from the interaction of real people in specific contexts. If we are correct, then newly imposed default rules don't merely fill unavoidable gaps at zero cost, as would be true if one default were as good as any other. They displace existing defaults, chosen by market participants, with new defaults chosen by the paternalists. Even if market participants can freely opt out of the new defaults, the new rules place an additional burden (though hopefully a small one) on choosing the market default. That burden takes the form of disappointed expectations, transition costs of adjusting to the new rules, and potentially higher transaction costs of opting out. To justify imposing such costs, behavioral paternalists have the burden of proof to demonstrate that their alternative is clearly better – a burden they have not met.

Let us now return to the inevitability of choice architecture. We have been arguing that even if choice architecture is inevitable, *paternalistic* choice architecture is not, and that selecting choice architecture paternalistically carries unacknowledged costs. But suppose this argument is wrong. Even so, the inevitability argument only goes so far. It means that *in some cases* we have no alternative but to act paternalistically. Behavioral paternalists have advocated or suggested all manner of interventions that go far beyond the inevitable, including cooling-off periods, sin taxes, default rules with nonwaivable terms, and outright bans. Retreating to the inevitability position avoids the burden of defending some of the most troubling interventions under consideration.

Focus on the Irrational Subset of the Population

Behavioral paternalists sometimes emphasize that even if most people are broadly rational, there surely exists some fraction of the population that is not. The goal, then, is to find interventions that target this irrational fraction while imposing negligible costs on those who are rational.[7] We call this the "irrational subset" argument.

The Achilles heel of this approach is the knowledge problem, as it relies on a highly simplified model of population heterogeneity (a topic we discussed at much greater length in Chapter 7). It assumes just two classes of people, the rational and the irrational, with uniformity within each class. Further, it ignores the possibility of multiple interacting biases. The reality is far more complex. Biases, even when they are genuine, exhibit a range of values from extreme to mild, and some people at the other end of the spectrum may exhibit the reverse bias (for example, extreme future orientation rather than extreme present orientation). Some people may exhibit what seems to be rational behavior because of multiple biases that offset or balance each other to some degree. Complexity of this nature confounds attempts to identify a well-defined "irrational" group to target with intervention. Yet knowing the relative size of the rational versus irrational parts of the population is a critical parameter for determining whether the supposedly negligible costs of the policy for rational people are indeed negligible when taken in total (and weighed against the gains for the irrationals). Even if we ignore the supposedly rational actors, it is not even

---

[7] For example, Camerer et al. (2003, 1219) say that "a policy is *asymmetrically paternalistic* if it creates large benefits for those people who are boundedly rational ... while imposing little or no harm on those who are fully rational."

clear that a single intervention could successfully address the failures of the irrational actors when such people may exhibit different types and degrees of bias. The intervention that fixes one irrational group's bias could easily exacerbate another group's bias.

Aside from the knowledge problem, the irrational subset argument does not solve any of the most basic conceptual challenges we have laid out – such as, for instance, distinguishing true biases from nonstandard preferences, or finding a means of identifying "true" preferences from inconsistent behavior. Furthermore, the modest and moderate interventions supported by the irrational subset argument are still vulnerable to the political manipulations and slippery slope processes that we outlined in Chapters 8 and 9.

Finally, even in the best of circumstances, the irrational subset argument would only justify a narrow range of policies – specifically, new default rules with very low costs of opting out. More ambitious policies impose unavoidable and potentially high costs on people who are rational, as well as those who aren't irrational in precisely the manner assumed by paternalist planners.

Rely on Extreme Cases

If you want to demonstrate the irrationality of human beings, one very simple strategy is to point to extreme cases: drug addicts whose actions destroy their lives, compulsive gamblers who lose everything they have and more, morbidly obese people who cannot even leave their homes. It is hard to believe that such people are acting rationally, even by the most permissive definition.

In these cases, perhaps we can safely indulge our intuition that their biases are truly damaging in terms of their own well-considered well-being, and if only they could see their situation globally they would truly wish to behave differently. Even so, we have severe doubts about whether behavioral paternalist policies would do these individuals much good. How much difference would the "nudges" advocated by behavioral paternalists make in such extreme cases? Would a small or even a large sin tax really induce the morbidly obese to shape up, or would the tax simply deplete their bank accounts? Would graphic warning labels on heroin make a difference to the dedicated heroin addict, despite heavy-handed criminal penalties that apparently do not? One of the most salient features of hard cases such as these is how unresponsive they are to even strong incentives. As economists who believe in the power of incentives, we have to believe they are at least *somewhat* responsive to rewards and punishments – but in cases of this kind, the elasticity of behavior seems remarkably low. Recall, for instance, the research suggesting that the heaviest drinkers are those least responsive to alcohol taxes (Mast et al. 1999, 217).

Ideally, we might want to design one set of rules for the truly extreme cases and another for the rest of us. But this raises two related concerns, one abstract, the other more concrete. The abstract concern is the difficulty of distinguishing the two classes, because there is no clear dividing line between those who have genuinely self-destructive tendencies and those who just have unusually indulgent preferences. Even if we're happy deeming some people "clearly irrational," a smooth gradient connects them to everyone else. The more practical concern is whether it would be dangerous to empower some agency to decide who qualifies as sufficiently rational and who does not, with no objective way to distinguish them, and then apply different rules to each group.

In any case, behavioral paternalists do not usually focus on the extreme cases. Their focus is not on demonstrating that a small minority of individuals make truly poor decisions, but on establishing that the *bulk of humanity* does so. Thaler and Sunstein (2008), for instance, like to compare regular people to Homer Simpson.[8] It seems unlikely that the policies that would prove most helpful to the great majority of society are the same as those that would be helpful in the most difficult cases.

One thing we can say with confidence is that existing paternalistic laws forbidding the use of certain addictive drugs have turned out to be wildly ineffective and incredibly destructive (Miron and Zwiebel 1995; Csete et al. 2016). If behavioral paternalists take up the cause of rolling back drug prohibition in favor of softer paternalist measures, we will happily applaud them. Though we have our doubts about the efficacy of those softer measures, we have no doubt about the harms of the harder ones. In the existing literature, however, behavioral paternalism has almost always been deployed to advocate more intervention, not less.[9]

---

[8] "One of our major goals in this book is to see how the world might be made easier, or safer, for the Homers among us (and the Homer lurking somewhere in each of us)" (Thaler and Sunstein 2008, 22). "Self-control problems can be illuminated by thinking about an individual as containing two semiautonomous selves, a far-sighted 'Planner' and a myopic 'Doer.' You can think of the Planner as speaking for your Reflective System, or the Mr. Spock lurking within you, and the Doer as heavily influenced by the Automatic System, or everyone's Homer Simpson" (p. 42).

[9] The major exception seems to be Thaler and Sunstein (2008, 215–226) in the chapter "Privatizing Marriage." The chapter "Privatizing Social Security" (pp. 145–156) advocates allowing people to choose among investment vehicles for their Social Security funds, but does not go so far as to advocate allowing them to opt out of the Social Security system entirely.

Treat Behavioral Paternalism as a Toolbox

Not long ago, one of us had a conversation with a friend who was a Republican state legislator. When he learned about the topic of our book – the case against "nudge" – he expressed surprise and a bit of disappointment: "I thought Thaler was my spirit animal!" On further prodding, it became clear that our more conceptual concerns about behavioral paternalism, such as its problematic standard of welfare, were not even on his radar. His attraction to behavioral paternalism was simple: it promised a new set of tools, seemingly simple and low-cost ones, that could be used to achieve goals such as getting people to save more and eat better.

We refer to this as the "toolbox" position, and we suspect it is very common among nonacademics who know about behavioral paternalism (and who almost always call it "nudge"). In essence, this position sets aside questions about welfare standards and, more broadly, the justifications for government action. *Why* should the state try to get people to save more, or eat healthier food, or whatever? The justification might come from new paternalism (people are behaving badly even by their own standards), old paternalism (some behaviors are objectively better than others), the interests of other people (we need to reduce state spending on health and retirement programs), or something else entirely. But whatever the goals might be, the toolbox position simply takes them as given. Behavioral paternalism merely provides advice on how to achieve them.

The toolbox position avoids some of our conceptual challenges to behavioral paternalism. It does not refute those concerns; it simply does not engage with them. But we would encourage anyone tempted to use this toolbox to examine their goals more carefully. Why are these appropriate goals for the state? If the answer relies on better satisfaction of people's own preferences, then all of our conceptual challenges apply with full force. If the answer is that some goals are inherently worth achieving, then the standard arguments against old-style paternalism may apply. If the answer is serving the interests of others, then our responses to the "fiscal externalities" argument (see the section "Invoke Fiscal Externalities") may apply.

As with the appeal to objective welfare, the toolbox position must also grapple with other challenges we've laid out in this book, particularly those that relate to the successful implementation of the policies in question, including deficiencies of the underlying research, lack of relevant knowledge, unintended consequences, and political risks. For more detail, we refer the reader to our responses to the objective-welfare strategy.

Invoke Fiscal Externalities

Although some choices might seem to affect only the person who makes them, they actually burden other people by increasing taxpayer expenditures on healthcare and retirement programs (such as Medicaid, Medicare, and Social Security in the United States and single-payer healthcare systems in other developed countries). For example, if a person experiences higher medical expenses as a result of smoking, and those costs are partially or completely covered by public programs, then arguably the choice to smoke harms the public at large, and therefore the state is justified in trying to reduce smoking. Furthermore, the existence of a public subsidy might actually encourage more of the harmful behavior – a phenomenon known as moral hazard – which provides an additional reason to try to restrict the behavior. This is known as the "fiscal externalities" argument (Browning 1999).

As we observed in Chapter 1, the fiscal externalities argument is *not* paternalistic. It is based on the interests of third parties, not on the supposed interests of the people whose behavior is targeted by policy. It is therefore somewhat outside the scope of this book. However, we have encountered the fiscal externalities argument often when discussing behavioral paternalism, so we will at least sketch a response here.

The first thing to note is that the fiscal externalities argument does not require irrationality in any way. It justifies discouraging *any* activity that could potentially increase the tax burden via the welfare state. Any number of commonplace activities meet this criterion. For example, most sexual activity – even when done in a relatively safe way – creates some risk of sexually transmitted diseases and related healthcare costs. Sexual activity also creates the risk of childbearing, which involves substantial health costs that may be partially borne by the taxpayers (and some fraction of the resulting children may end up being net tax burdens to the state). Sports, sun exposure, travel, and countless other activities also have some impact on health costs. If and to the extent the public covers healthcare costs, the fiscal externalities argument effectively transforms *all* of these seemingly private choices into matters of public concern. We see this happening now.

However, for at least some of these activities, the impact on public expenditures is opposite to what is usually supposed. Smokers undoubtedly incur higher average health expenditures than nonsmokers per year of life. On the other hand, they also tend to have shorter lives, and shorter lives mean lower health expenditures. Multiple studies in various countries have concluded that the latter effect dominates the former, whether looking at healthcare costs alone (Leu and Schaub 1983; Barendregt et al. 1997; Van

Baal et al. 2008) or including pension costs as well (Viscusi 1994; Tiihonen et al. 2012). In other words, smokers actually save taxpayers money – which means the fiscal externalities argument would suggest encouraging smoking rather than restricting it. Lifetime health expenditures also appear to be lower for obese people than for the nonobese, and for the same reason: higher annual spending is offset by fewer years of spending, again due to greater mortality (Van Baal et al. 2008). The fiscal externalities argument would therefore suggest encouraging obesity as well.

Although we have not found similar studies on other health-related behaviors, it would not be surprising to find this result duplicated in such areas as highway accidents and occupational safety hazards. Additional years of life, especially at the end at life, come with added health costs. Anything that tends to reduce those years will have a salutary effect on the public purse, which should at least partially offset any higher health costs incurred before death. A variety of "anti-nudges," designed to get people to make worse decisions that lighten the burden on the state, might be justified along these lines. The fiscal externalities argument does not imply that *every* activity that reduces life years should be encouraged and every activity that increases them should be discouraged – but it does imply that the fiscal gains from lost years of life must be taken into account. In some cases, that might imply promoting rather than limiting certain "bad" behaviors. If proponents of the fiscal externalities argument are unwilling to grasp this nettle, they have the burden to explain why not. They cannot simply invoke the notion of fiscal externalities when it supports the policies they want and ignore it when it doesn't.

Our main concern about the fiscal externalities argument, however, is that it allows the state to create circumstances that then justify further interventions – specifically, interventions that tend to infringe on personal choice. In Chapter 9, we offered this dynamic as a classic example of a slippery slope in action: a public policy partially socializes health costs, and then those health costs provide the rationale for limitations of personal choice – even if the people targeted had no role in the creation of the initial policies. We have seen publicly funded emergency rooms used to justify motorcycle helmet laws; we have seen the welfare state used to justify tighter immigration restrictions. In fact, this process was identified as early as the 1700s by Adam Smith (1976 [1776]), who observed that the Poor Law of England – which required each parish to support indigent people within its borders – fomented support for laws restricting the free movement of labor. This is not a favorable dynamic for preserving freedom of choice.

But there is an alternative way to think about the matter. The individuals whose behavior creates spillover costs for the public do not unilaterally cause the spillover. The spillover results from the *joint* actions of individuals and the state: the individual's choice *and* the public policy. It's true that no costs would spill over on the public if the individual made different choices about smoking, eating, drinking, and so on. It's also true that no costs would spill over on the public if the state adopted different health, education, and welfare policies. When X (free choice) and Y (welfare policy) jointly cause Z (spillover costs), there's no good reason to place the blame on X alone. If fiscal externalities provide an argument for limiting freedom of choice, by the same token they provide an argument for limiting the welfare state (which, to be clear, does not necessarily mean eliminating it).

But we would go a step further. It is a known fact that normal people engage in indulgent, risky, and costly behaviors from time to time. This fact was easily foreseeable when cost-spreading welfare policies were first adopted; the behaviors in question predated the policies. It was also foreseeable that such policies might induce some degree of moral hazard. Yet democratic governments chose to adopt these policies anyway. For that reason, our instinct – which we concede others may not share – is to say the polity as a whole bears moral responsibility for the resulting spillover effects. If those consequences are not acceptable, then it makes sense to limit payouts in some way. To target the individual behavior instead effectively scapegoats a specific group of people rather than accepting collective blame for collectively chosen policies. And doing so creates a genuine risk of slippery slopes that we find deeply troubling.

But some readers may not agree with these arguments. So let us suppose that in principle it is acceptable for the state to target behaviors associated with fiscal spillover effects. Even so, supporters of the fiscal externalities position must still face the possibility that their argument would support "anti-nudges" to reduce lifespans. And they must also face the gauntlet of practical challenges that we have laid down relating to insufficient context-specific knowledge, unintended consequences, counteractive behaviors, political opportunism by rent-seekers and moralists, and many more. Not all of these challenges will apply in the same way or to the same degree as they do to the behavioral paternalist position, of course, but many will continue to be relevant.

RECOMMENDATIONS

In light of the arguments in this book, how should academics and the general public think about behavioral economics, paternalism, and public policy? We have several recommendations.

Replace Puppet Rationality with Inclusive Rationality

One possible conclusion is that we should reject behavioral economics in its entirety and revert to the neoclassical approach – one that largely rejected paternalistic thinking. But that would be far too simplistic. It would be a mistake to cling tightly to sterile models of human behavior that have no room for inchoate preferences, self-discovery, trial and error, and self-regulation.

While the simplified models of neoclassical theory may still be useful for particular purposes and contexts, they cannot provide a panoptic picture of human decision-making. They cannot capture the full depth and complexity of human choice. This is true in general, but particularly with regard to normative analysis. Reliance on formalistic models carries the distinct danger of measuring real humans relative to the model – and judging them deficient when they depart from it. This is a failing of both neoclassical and behavioral economics.

The alternative is inclusive rationality, which encompasses all manner of strategies people use to shape their own behavior and interpret the world around them. They do not necessarily follow strict rules of choice and belief revision, nor do they have fixed and invariant preferences. They do not strictly operate within the conceptual framework provided by a model, like puppets performing on stage; instead, they are capable of stepping outside the model, reconceptualizing it, and framing their own decisions in new ways. They are thus able to see their own behavior, judge it, and potentially act to change it. Inclusive rationality has layers.

This does not mean humans can never be irrational. In principle, it is possible to make serious and systematic errors in seeking one's goals. But in practice, outside observers often lack the evidence to "convict" any given behavior of irrationality. There are simply too many subjective variables for outsiders to make that kind of judgment in particular cases. What looks like irrationality from the outside may reflect internal motives and understandings that are fully available only to the person who has them. Intellectually, agnosticism is often called for. Practically, we should give individuals the benefit of the doubt when making judgments about their own interests.

Reject the Paternalism-Generating Framework

Here is one lesson we have learned from behavioral economics: how decisions are framed can make a difference. A frame can highlight some aspects of a problem while downplaying others. Behavioral paternalists have framed human behavior and public policy in a particular way. Specifically, their framework encourages us to see humans as hapless bumblers ("Homer Simpsons"), and to see public policy as an unbiased source of helpful corrections. This framework has its roots in the "heuristics and biases" research program, which naturally channels scholars toward seeing in human behavior evidence of errors rather than practical functionality, hidden wisdom, or nonstandard preferences.[10] As we have seen, the behavioral paternalist paradigm also frames any attempt to correct errors – indeed, any act of advising or helping another person – as a form of paternalism. In this framework, the only remaining questions for policy are *how* and *in what ways we should be paternalistic*. It is thus a paternalism-generating framework.

But there is an alternative, paternalism-resisting framework available. We discussed this framework in Chapter 9, but we will reiterate it here. In this framework, we would not begin by seeking evidence of errors, but by seeking understanding. The work of Gerd Gigerenzer and his associates provides a template for how such a research program would operate. In their research we see considerable evidence for the functionality, even superiority, of cognitive processes that deviate from the neoclassical model. A paternalism-resisting framework would also take a more permissive attitude toward preferences that appear inconsistent and incomplete, and would then ask how people with such nonstandard preferences would approach the world. That inquiry naturally leads to exploration of people's diverse and idiosyncratic strategies of self-management, as well as how markets, families, clubs, and other voluntary associations can assist in the process. Behaviors that look like departures from rationality, such as mental budgets and self-imposed constraints, begin to look more like solutions. In this framework, many fewer opportunities for legal and regulatory correction would present themselves.

---

[10] Vernon Smith argues that the language employed in the heuristics-and-biases research program tips the analysis toward a perspective critical of real behavior: "Thus, 'errors' in the sense of deviations from the SSSM [standard socioeconomic science model] predictions, are referred to in the psychology and behavioral science literature as 'cognitive errors,' meaning mistakes as deviations from what 'should be' observed. This description implicitly accepts the undoubted and un-doubtable 'truth value' of the SSSM as a representation of optimality, and therefore those subjects are indeed making mistakes transparently contrary to their own rational best interest" (2005, 145, with slight changes to quotation marks).

The paternalism-resisting framework would also direct attention to how policymakers' incentives will not necessarily line up with the interests of the governed. But that is the subject of our next recommendation.

Have Reasonable Expectations of Policymakers

Behavioral paternalists offer an alluring vision of public policy that is evidence-based, cautious, and disciplined. We cannot help but note the irony of such optimistic aspirations coming from scholars who have also highlighted the phenomenon of optimism bias. In Chapters 8 and 9, we have presented what we consider a more realistic model of political behavior. In the presence of both rational ignorance and rational irrationality, we cannot reasonably expect policymakers – including voters, legislators, regulators, and judges – to collect the best evidence from the behavioral sciences, to analyze every issue carefully, to curb their own biases, to stand on nuanced distinctions, to resist the influence of rent-seekers and moralists, and to craft well-designed and targeted interventions. We should not expect policies to resemble carefully calibrated and finely tuned machines; we should expect them to be blunt instruments.

Our claim is not that policymakers are somehow worse or less rational than anyone else. On the contrary, they are like everyone else. What differs is their environment. In the private sector, the costs and benefits of decisions are for the most part concentrated on the decision-makers themselves, giving them strong incentives to experiment with the many strategies for self-management included within inclusive rationality. In the public sector, such incentives are frequently nonexistent or, worse, point in the wrong direction. Policymakers have ubiquitous opportunities to indulge wrong-but-pleasing beliefs and attitudes without serious consequence – and often with political benefits.

A realistic perspective on policy does not gloss over these concerns in the way we have seen so often in the behavioral paternalist literature. It puts them front and center. No analysis of a paternalist proposal should be regarded as complete unless and until it considers how the proposal will look after it has gone through the political sausage factory.

Maintain Important Distinctions

One hallmark of the behavioral paternalist literature has been its indifference to distinctions that economists and other social scientists usually take seriously. We have seen various examples in this chapter in our discussion of paternalistic escape routes – particularly the routes that involve loosening the definition of paternalism, relying on the "libertarian criterion," and invoking the inevitability of choice architecture. Behavioral paternalists explicitly represent soft and hard paternalism as lying on a smooth continuum, with scant recognition of anything that might represent a discontinuity or inflection point on that continuum. The general approach has been to treat paternalism as ubiquitous, inevitable, and indistinguishable across domains.

By contrast, we recommend keeping important distinctions clearly in view. We laid out these distinctions earlier in this chapter: self-imposed versus other-imposed, invited versus uninvited, competitive versus monopolistic, informative versus manipulative, coercive versus voluntary, and public versus private (the last two distinctions being the most important). Even if these distinctions don't provide absolute barriers against undesirable paternalism, they can at least focus our attention on the most troubling features of paternalist proposals – and, we hope, help us to resist them. When we cross these lines, we should know that we are crossing them.

Why have behavioral paternalists tended to obscure rather than highlight these important distinctions? We think it is in part a rhetorical strategy designed to soften resistance to their agenda. But rhetoric aside, we also suspect they resist such distinctions because – from the paternalist perspective – they seem arbitrary. There might be "bad" interventions on the right side of these lines and "good" interventions on the wrong side. Strictly respecting the distinctions we have drawn therefore creates the risk of both over- and under-inclusion. It would allow some forms of paternalism they may not like, such as religious colleges' strict moral codes of conduct and Walmart's decision to bar controversial movies from its shelves. And it would disallow some forms of paternalism they might favor, such as difficult-to-waive terms in labor contracts and intrusive product warnings that go far beyond the merely informational. The behavioral paternalists would rather evaluate all (supposedly) paternalistic interventions by means of cost–benefit analysis.

But we contend that the distinctions we have offered are *not* arbitrary. They are strongly correlated with the ability of individuals to accept wanted interventions and to reject unwanted ones. They also provide a bulwark against supposedly objective cost–benefit analysis that – given the fundamental indeterminacy of paternalist welfare standards – will tend to embody the subjective judgments and prejudices of those empowered to make decisions on others' behalf. In addition, maintaining important distinctions helps us to resist slippery slopes created by the inherent vagueness of central concepts of behavioral paternalism.

To be sure, the distinctions we've laid out are not always perfectly clear. Zoom in close enough, and even the sharpest line will start to look fuzzy. If we look carefully, we can find gray areas between public and private, between coercive and voluntary, and so on. But the existence of gray areas does not render these distinctions meaningless or useless. Moreover, behavioral paternalism would replace these occasionally vague standards with even vaguer standards – ones that admit countless boundary cases and vast tracts of gray. We would stand on distinctions that offer a higher degree of certitude rather than trust the overconfident assurances of paternalist social planners.

A BETTER PATH FORWARD

In his classic essay *On Liberty*, one of the earliest statements of anti-paternalism, John Stuart Mill (1989 [1859]) argued:

[The individual] cannot rightfully be compelled to do or forbear because it will be better for him to do so, because it will make him happier, because, in the opinions of others, to do so would be wise, or even right. These are good reasons for remonstrating with him, or reasoning with him, or persuading him, or entreating him, but not for compelling him, or visiting him with any evil in case he do otherwise.

(p. 13)

Mill's position has come to be known as the Harm Principle: the idea that we are justified in coercing people only for the purpose of preventing harm to others. We think there is still much to recommend the Harm Principle as a guideline for both individual behavior and public policy. But behavioral paternalists have called the Harm Principle into question. Conly explicitly rejects it, saying that coercion is indeed justified to prevent people from harming themselves. Sunstein also rejects the Harm Principle – but with the added twist of observing that the Harm Principle simply doesn't speak to the many ways in which people's behavior may be influenced without coercion (Sunstein 2014, 4–5, 14–15).

We have already discussed our many objections, both rhetorical and analytical, to behavioral paternalism in general and Sunstein's approach in particular. But we wish to conclude on a more positive note. For Mill's statement does not only tell us what we cannot do; it also suggests what we *can* do: remonstrate, reason, persuade, and entreat. In other words, when we believe others may be making mistakes that harm their well-being, we are free to tell them so. We may even beg and plead if the situation warrants. The advantage of this approach is that it offers potentially useful information and perspective while still respecting people's right to choose for themselves. After all, they probably have information and perspective on their own lives that outsiders lack.

To some extent, behavioral researchers have presented their insights as self-help advice. Thaler and Sunstein's *Nudge* and Dan Ariely's *Predictably Irrational*, for instance, often read this way. When they avoid policy advocacy, these authors often sound like friendly voices offering helpful suggestions for better living. The nice thing about advice is that it can be heeded or ignored, as the reader pleases. If the popularizers of behavioral research had always stayed within such bounds, we likely would not have spent a decade of our careers responding to their claims.

That people sometimes buy self-help books is illustrative of the fact that many people do wish to improve their choices. They also write to advice columnists and ask friends and family for help. We don't intend to denigrate these activities. On the contrary, we see them as part of the broader fabric of inclusive rationality. Rationality does not have to mean instantaneous perfection, or any of the other restrictive meanings that economists have attached to it. It means seeking to better achieve one's subjective goals and values, whatever they may be. Some amount of experimentation and trial and error is to be expected. Advice can assist in the process, as can personal resolutions, social commitments, structuring one's environment, and all the other tools of self-management we have discussed in this book. Where paternalists see evidence of the problem, we see evidence of the solution.

Behavioral economists and psychologists have produced a great body of insights on how human beings make decisions. While many of these insights are not as solid as we've been led to believe, they have nevertheless advanced our knowledge of the human mind. Our exploration of behavioral paternalism has forced us to question ideas and concepts that we once thought unassailable. We have, among other things, become more acutely aware of the failings of the neoclassical model of preferences and beliefs – which in turn drove us toward the notion of inclusive rationality that we have presented in this book. Therefore, we should not be understood as rejecting the whole of behavioral economics.

What the discipline does need, however, is a strong dose of *humility* – particularly for those behavioral researchers looking for policy applications of their work. It is jarring, to say the least, to see social scientists pointing out the errors of private individuals – and then failing to consider that social scientists and policymakers are also subject to error. It is frustrating to see behavioral researchers demonstrating the complexity of real decision-making processes – and then ignoring that complexity when recommending regulatory corrections of those very processes. It is simply baffling to see behavioral economists showing how real behavior deviates from neoclassical norms – and then insisting that behavior must conform to those norms or else be judged deficient. Our hope is that, equipped with greater humility, greater respect for nonstandard preferences, and greater awareness of the surprising functionality of real-world behavior, behavioral researchers will be less inclined to approach humanity from a position of presumed superiority, like puppet masters correcting the behavior of errant puppets. Instead, they will approach them as fellow human beings doing the best they can, trying to improve their own choices, and offering friendly advice on how others might do the same.

References

AAFP (2015). https://timedotcom.files.wordpress.com/2015/05/2015_04_28_obama.pdf

Abdellaoui, M., L'Haridon, O., & Paraschiv, C. (2013). Do couples discount future consequences less than individuals? Université de Rennes 1 Working Paper 2013-20. Université De Rennes 1.

Abrams, B. A., & Schitz, M. D. (1978). The "crowding-out" effect of governmental transfers on private charitable contributions. *Public Choice*, *33*(1), 29–39.

Academy of Nutrition and Dietetics. (2016). *Evidence analysis manual: Steps in the academy evidence analysis process*. Chicago, IL: American Dietetic Association. Retrieved from www.andeal.org/vault/2440/web/files/2016_April_EA_Manual.pdf

Achourioti, T., Fugard, A., & Stenning, K. (2011). Throwing the normative baby out with the prescriptivist bathwater. *Behavioral and Brain Sciences*, *34*(5), 249.

Action on Smoking and Health. (n.d.). E-cigarettes and the fight against tobacco. Retrieved from https://ash.org/programs/e-cigarettes-the-fight-against-tobacco

Adler, J. H., Meiners, R. E., Morriss, A. P., & Yandle, B. (2015). Bootleggers, Baptists, and e-cigs. *Regulation*, 30–35. Retrieved from https://object.cato.org/sites/cato.org/files/serials/files/regulation/2015/3/regulation-v38n1-3.pdf

Adriani, F., & Sonderegger, S. (2014). Evolution of similarity judgements in intertemporal choice. Centre for Decision Research and Experimental Economics, School of Economics, University of Nottingham, Discussion Papers 2014-06. Nottingham, UK: University of Nottingham.

Agnew, J. R., & Szykman, L. R. (2005). Asset allocation and information overload: The influence of information display, asset choice, and investor experience. *Journal of Behavioral Finance*, *6*(2), 57–70.

Ainslie, G. (1992). *Picoeconomics: The strategic interaction of successive motivational states within the person*. Cambridge, UK: Cambridge University Press.

(2001). *Breakdown of will*. Cambridge, UK: Cambridge University Press.

(2005). Précis of breakdown of will. *Behavioral and Brain Sciences*, *28*(5), 635–650.

(2012). Pure hyperbolic discount curves predict "eyes open" self-control. *Theory and Decision*, *73*(1), 3–34.

(2016). The cardinal anomalies that led to behavioral economics: Cognitive or motivational? *Managerial and Decision Economics*, *37*(4–5), 261–273.

Aldao, A. (2013). The future of emotion regulation research capturing context. *Perspectives on Psychological Science*, 8(2), 155–172.

Aldred, J. (2003). The money pump revisited. *Risk Decision and Policy*, 8(1), 59–76.

(2007). Intransitivity and vague preferences. *Journal of Ethics*, 11(4), 377–403.

Alexander, B. (2010). *Curb Your Enthusiasm's* Larry David. *Time*. Retrieved from http://content.time.com/time/magazine/article/0,9171,1993876,00.html

Ali, S. N. (2011). Learning self-control. *Quarterly Journal of Economics*, 126(2), 857–893.

Allais, M. (1953). L'extension des théories de l'équilibre économique général et du rendement social au cas du risque. *Econometrica*, 29(2), 269–290.

Alpert, M., & Raiffa, H. (1982). A progress report on the training of probability assessors. In D. Kahneman, P. Slovic, & A. Tversky (Eds.), *Judgment under uncertainty: Heuristics and biases*, 294–305. Cambridge, UK: Cambridge University Press.

American Nonsmokers' Rights Foundation. (2017). 100% Smokefree U.S. Retrieved from https://no-smoke.org/wp-content/uploads/pdf/100smokefreeairports.pdf

Anand, P. (1995). *Foundations of rational choice under risk*. Oxford, UK: Oxford University Press.

Anderson, C., & Brion, S. (2010). Overconfidence and the attainment of status in groups. IRLE Working Paper No. 215-10. *Institute for Research on Labor and Employment*. Retrieved from http://irle.berkeley.edu/files/2010/Overconfidence-and-the-Attainment-of-Status-in-Groups.pdf

Anderson, C. J., Bahník, S., Barnett-Cowan, M., Bosco, F. A., Chandler, J., Chartier, C. A., . . . & Zuni, K. (2016). Response to comment on "Estimating the reproducibility of psychological science." *Science*, 351(6277), 1037.

Andrade, E. B., & Cohen, J. B. (2007). Affect-based evaluation of regulation as mediators of behavior: The role of affect in risk taking, helping and eating patterns. Available at SSRN: https://ssrn.com/abstract=928926

Angeletos, G. M., Laibson, D., Repetto, A., Tobacman, J., & Weinberg, S. (2001). The hyperbolic consumption model: Calibration, simulation, and empirical evaluation. *Journal of Economic Perspectives*, 15(3), 47–68.

Angner, E. (2006). Economists as experts: Overconfidence in theory and practice. *Journal of Economic Methodology*, 13(1), 1–24.

Antoñanzas, F., Viscusi, W. K., Rovira, J., Braña, F. J., Portillo, F., & Carvalho, I. (2000). Smoking risks in Spain: Part I – Perception of risks to the smoker. *Journal of Risk and Uncertainty*, 21(2–3), 161–186.

Aon Hewitt. (2015). *Hot topics in retirement*. Retrieved from www.aon.com/attachments/human-capital-consulting/hot-topics-retirement-2015.pdf

Arad, A., & Rubinstein, A. (2018). The people's perspective on libertarian-paternalistic policies. *Journal of Law and Economics*, 61(2), 311–333.

Ariely, D. (2008). *Predictably irrational: The hidden forces that shape our decisions*. New York: Harper.

Ariely, D., & Wertenbroch, K. (2002). Procrastination, deadlines and performance: Self-control by precommitment. *Psychological Science*, 13(3), 219–224.

Ariely, D., Loewenstein, G., & Prelec, D. (2003). "Coherent arbitrariness": Stable demand curves without stable preferences. *Quarterly Journal of Economics*, 118(1), 73–106.

Arkes, H. R., Gigerenzer, G., & Hertwig, R. (2016). How bad is incoherence? *Decision, 3*(1), 20–39.

Arlen, J., Spitzer, M., & Talley, E. (2002). Endowment effects within corporate agency relationships. *Journal of Legal Studies, 31*(1), 1–37.

Arrow, K. J. (2012 [1951]). *Social choice and individual values.* New Haven, CT: Yale University Press.

(1959). Rational choice functions and orderings. *Economica, 26*(102), 121–127.

Arrow, K. J., & Debreu, G. (1954). Existence of an equilibrium for a competitive economy. *Econometrica: Journal of the Econometric Society, 22*(3), 265–290.

Augenblick, N., Niederle, M., & Sprenger, C. (2015). Working over time: Dynamic inconsistency in real effort tasks. *Quarterly Journal of Economics, 130*(3), 1067–1115.

Aumann, R. J. (1962). Utility theory without the completeness axiom. *Econometrica, 30*(3), 445–462.

Baillon, A., Bleichrodt, H., Liu, N., & Wakker, P. P. (2015). Group decision rules and group rationality under risk. www.aurelienbaillon.com/research/papers/pdf/group.pdf

Baillon, A., Bleichrodt, H., & Spinu, V. (2017). Searching for the reference point. Erasmus School of Economics, Erasmus University Rotterdam, The Netherlands, working paper. Available at https://personal.eur.nl/bleichrodt/Baillon_Bleichrodt_Spinu_2017_05_23.pdf

Baker, M. (2016). Psychology's reproducibility problem is exaggerated – say psychologists. Retrieved from www.nature.com/news/psychology-s-reproducibility-problem-is-exaggerated-say-psychologists-1.19498

Balakrishnan, U., Haushofer, J., & Jakiela, P. (2017). How soon is now? Evidence of present bias from convex time budget experiments. NBER No. w23558. National Bureau of Economic Research.

Bandura, A., & Perloff, B. (1967). Relative efficacy of self-monitored and externally imposed reinforcement systems. *Journal of Personality and Social Psychology, 7*(2), 111–116.

Bandura, A., & Schunk, D. H. (1981). Cultivating competence, self-efficacy and intrinsic interest through proximal self-motivation. *Journal of Personality and Social Psychology, 41*(3), 586–598.

Barendregt, J. J., Bonneux, L., & van der Maas, P. J. (1997). The health care costs of smoking. *New England Journal of Medicine, 337*(15), 1052–1057. Retrieved from www.nejm.org/doi/full/10.1056/NEJM199710093371506

Bargh, J. A. (1994). The four horsemen of automaticity: Awareness, intention, efficiency, and control in social cognition. In R. S. Wyer, Jr. & T. K. Srull (Eds.), *Handbook of social cognition: Basic processes; Applications,* 1–40. Hillsdale, NJ: Lawrence Erlbaum Associates.

Bar-Gill, O. (2004). Seduction by plastic. *Northwestern Law Review, 98*(4), 1373–1434.

(2012). *Seduction by contract.* Oxford, UK: Oxford University Press.

(2014). Consumer transactions. In E. Zamir & D. Teichman (Eds.), *The Oxford handbook of behavioral economics and the law,* 465–490. Oxford, UK: Oxford University Press.

Bastiat, F. (1995). *Selected essays on political economy.* Edited by G. B. de Huszar. Irvington-on-Hudson, NY: Foundation for Economic Education. Retrieved from www.econlib.org/library/Bastiat/basEss1.html

Bates, C. (2018). Tobacco control and the tobacco industry: A failure of understanding and imagination. Retrieved from www.clivebates.com/tobacco-control-and-the-tobacco-industry-a-failure-of-understanding-and-imagination/

Baumeister, R. F., Gailliot, M., DeWall, C. N., & Oaten, M. (2006). Self-regulation and personality: How interventions increase regulatory success, and how depletion moderates the effects of traits on behavior. *Journal of Personality, 74*(6), 1773–1802.

Becker, G. S. (1965). A theory of the allocation of time. *Economic Journal, 75*(299), 493–517.

(2007). Libertarian paternalism: A critique – Becker [Blog post]. Retrieved from www.becker-posner-blog.com/2007/01/libertarian-paternalism-a-critique–becker .html

Becker, G. S., & Rubinstein, Y. (2004). Fear and the response to terrorism: An economic analysis. http://citeseerx.ist.psu.edu/viewdoc/download?doi=10.1.1.556.5346& rep=rep1&type=pdf

Bell, D., Raiffa, H., & Tversky, A. (1988). *Decision making: Descriptive, normative, and prescriptive interactions.* New York: Cambridge University Press.

Benjamin, D. K., & Dougan, W. R. (1997). Individuals' estimates of the risks of death: Part I – A reassessment of the previous evidence. *Journal of Risk and Uncertainty, 15*(2), 115–133.

Benjamin, D. K., Dougan, W. R, & Buschena, D. (2001). Individuals' estimates of the risks of death: Part II – New evidence. *Journal of Risk and Uncertainty, 22*(1), 35–57.

Ben-Shahar, O., & Posner, E. A. (2011). The right to withdraw in contract law. *Journal of Legal Studies, 40*(1), 115–148.

Berg, N., Eckel, C., & Johnson, C. (2010). Inconsistency pays? Time-inconsistent subjects and EU violators earn more. MPRA Paper 26589. Munich, Germany: University Library of Munich.

Berggren, N. (2012). Time for behavioral political economy? An analysis of articles in behavioral economics. *Review of Austrian Economics, 25*(3), 199–221.

Bergstrom, T., Blume, L., & Varian, H. (1986). On the private provision of public goods. *Journal of Public Economics, 29*(1), 25–49.

Bernheim, B. D. (1986). On the voluntary and involuntary provision of public goods. *American Economic Review, 76*(4), 789–793.

(2009). Behavioral welfare economics. *Journal of the European Economic Association, 7*(2–3), 267–319.

(2016). The good, the bad, and the ugly: A unified approach to behavioral welfare economics. *Journal of Benefit–Cost Analysis, 7*(1), 12–68.

Bernheim, B. D., & Rangel, A. (2007). Behavioral public economics: Welfare and policy analysis with nonstandard decision makers. In P. Diamond & H. Vartiainen (Eds.), *Behavioral economics and its applications,* 7–77. Princeton, NJ: Princeton University Press.

Bernheim, B. D., Fradkin, A., & Popov, I. (2015). The welfare economics of default options in 401(k) plans. *American Economic Review, 105*(9), 2798–2837.

Besharov, G. (2004). Second-best considerations in correcting cognitive biases. *Southern Economic Journal, 71*(1), 12–20.

Beshears, J., Choi, J. J., Laibson, D., & Madrian, B. C. (2008). How are preferences revealed? *Journal of Public Economics, 92*(8), 1787–1794.

(2009). The importance of default options for retirement saving outcomes. In J. Brown, J. Liebman, & D. A. Wise (Eds.), *Social Security policy in a changing environment,* 167–199. Chicago, IL: University of Chicago Press.

(2018). *Potential vs. realized savings under automatic enrolment.* TIAA Institute Research Dialogue No. 148. TIAA Institute.

Beshears, J., Choi, J. J., Laibson, D., Madrian, B. C., & Wang, S. Y. (2015). Who is easier to nudge? Paper presented at the 17th Annual Joint Meeting of the Retirement Research Consortium, Washington, DC. Retrieved from www.nber.org/programs/ag/rrc/rrc2015/papers/7.3%20-%20Beshears,%20Choi,%20Laibson,%20Madrian,%20Wang.pdf

(2016). *Who is easier to nudge.* Unpublished. Retrieved from http://scholar.harvard.edu/files/laibson/files/who_is_easier_to_nudge_2016.05.27.pdf

Beshears, J., Choi, J. J., Laibson, D., Madrian, B. C., & Skimmyhorn, W. L. (2017). Borrowing to save? The impact of automatic enrollment on debt. Unpublished manuscript. Retrieved from https://scholar.harvard.edu/files/laibson/files/total_savings_impact_2017_12_06.pdf.

Bhargava, S., & Loewenstein, G. (2015). Behavioral economics and public policy 102: Beyond nudging. *American Economic Review, 105*(5), 396–401.

Binmore, K. (2009). *Rational decisions.* Princeton, NJ: Princeton University Press.

Birnbaum, M. H. (1983). Base rates in Bayesian inference: Signal detection analysis of the cab problem. *American Journal of Psychology, 96*(1), 85–94.

Blais, B., & Dion, S. (Eds.). (1991). *The budget-maximizing bureaucrat: Appraisal and evidence.* Pittsburgh, PA: University of Pittsburgh Press.

Bleichrodt, H., Gao, Y., & Rohde, K. I. (2016). A measurement of decreasing impatience for health and money. *Journal of Risk and Uncertainty, 52*(3), 213–231.

Blumenthal, J. A. (2005). Law and the emotions: The problems of affective forecasting. *Indiana Law Journal, 80,* 155–238.

Blundell, J. E., Stubbs, R. J., Golding, C., Croden, F., Alam, R., Whybrow, S., … & Lawton, C. L. (2005). Resistance and susceptibility to weight gain: Individual variability in response to a high-fat diet. *Physiology & Behavior, 86*(5), 614–622.

Bogenschneider, K., & Corbett, T. (2010). *Evidence-based policymaking: Insights from policy-minded researchers and research-minded policymakers.* New York: Routledge.

Böhm-Bawerk, E. von (1959 [1889]). *Capital and interest: Positive theory of capital,* Vol. 2. Translated by G. D. Huncke. South Holland, IL: Libertarian Press.

Bollinger, B., Leslie, P., & Sorensen, A. (2011). Calorie posting in chain restaurants. *American Economic Journal: Economic Policy, 3*(1), 91–128.

Bonnie, R. J., Stratton, K., & Wallace, R. B. (2007). *Ending the tobacco problem: A blueprint for the nation.* Washington, DC: National Academies Press.

Bonta, D. (2007). Clean air laws. In R. J. Bonnie, K. Stratton, & R. B. Wallace (Eds.)., *Ending the tobacco problem: A blueprint for the nation,* 423–434. Washington, DC: National Academies Press.

Bonta, D., & Permanente, K. (2007). Appendix B: Clear air laws. In R. J. Bonnie, K. Stratton, & R. B. Wallace (Eds.), *Ending the tobacco problem: A blueprint for the nation,* B1–B9. Washington, DC: National Academies Press.

Bordalo, P., Gennaioli, N., & Shleifer, A. (2013). Salience and consumer choice. *Journal of Political Economy, 121*(5), 803–843.

Borges, M. C., Louzada, M. L., de Sá, T. H., Laverty, A. A., Parra, D. C., Garzillo, J. M. F., . . . & Millett, C. (2017). Artificially sweetened beverages and the response to the global obesity crisis. *PLoS Medicine, 14*(1), e1002195.

Bornstein, R. F. (1989). Exposure and affect: Overview and meta-analysis of research, 1968–1987. *Psychological Bulletin, 106*(2), 265–289.

Boyles, S. (2018). ACS: E-cigarettes OK for smoking cessation . . . with caveats. *MedPage Today*. Retrieved from www.medpagetoday.com/pulmonology/smoking/71315

Bradford, D., Courtemanche, C., Heutel, G., McAlvanah, P., & Ruhm, C. (2017). Time preferences and consumer behavior. *Journal of Risk and Uncertainty, 55*(2–3), 119–145.

Bremzen, A., Khokhlova, E., Suvorov, A., & Van de Ven, J. (2015). Bad news: An experimental study on the informational effects of rewards. *Review of Economics and Statistics, 97*(1), 55–70.

Brighton, H., & Gigerenzer, G. (2012). Are rational actor models "rational" outside small worlds? In S. Okasha & K. Binmore (Eds.), *Evolution and rationality: Decisions, co-operation and strategic behavior*, 84–109. Cambridge, UK: Cambridge University Press.

Britton, J., & Bogdanovica, I. (2014). *Electronic cigarettes*. Public Health England. Retrieved from https://assets.publishing.service.gov.uk/government/uploads/system/uploads/attachment_data/file/311887/Ecigarettes_report.pdf

Broome, J. (1999). *Ethics out of economics*. Cambridge, UK: Cambridge University Press.

Brown, J. R., Farrell, A. M., & Weisbenner, S. J. (2012). The downside of defaults. NBER No. onb12–05. National Bureau of Economic Research.

(2016). Decision-making approaches and the propensity to default: Evidence and implications. *Journal of Financial Economics, 121*(3), 477–495.

Browning, E. K. (1999). The myth of fiscal externalities. *Public Finance Review, 27*(1), 3–18.

Brunnermeier, M. K., & Parker, J. A. (2005). Optimal expectations. *American Economic Review, 95*(4), 1092–1118.

Bryner, G. C. (1987). *Bureaucratic discretion: Law and policy in federal regulatory agencies*. Oxford, UK: Pergamon Press.

Buchanan, J. M. (1954). Social choice, democracy, and free markets. *Journal of Political Economy, 62*(2), 114–123.

(1969). *Cost and choice*. Chicago, IL: Markham.

(1979). Natural and artifactual man. In J. M. Buchanan (Ed.), *What should economists do?*, 93–112. Indianapolis, IN: Liberty Fund.

(1982). Order defined in the process of its emergence. *Literature of Liberty, 5*(4), 5–18.

(2005). Afraid to be free: Dependency as desideratum. In W. F. Shughart & R. D. Tollison (Eds.), *Policy challenges and political responses*, 19–31. Boston, MA: Springer.

Buchanan, J., & Brennan, G. (1985). *The reason of rules: Constitutional political economy*. Cambridge, UK: Cambridge University Press.

Bucher, T., Collins, C., Rollo, M. E., McCaffrey, T. A., De Vlieger, N., Van der Bend, D. ... & Perez-Cueto, F. J. A. (2016). Nudging consumers towards healthier choices: A systematic review of positional influences on food choice. *British Journal of Nutrition*, *115*(12), 2252–2263.

Burke, J., Hung, A. A., & Luoto, J. E. (2015). Automatic enrollment in retirement savings vehicles. RAND Labor & Population Working Paper. RAND Corporation.

Burkett, J. P. (2006). *Microeconomics: Optimization, experiments, and behavior*. Oxford, UK: Oxford University Press.

Burstyn, I. (2013). *Peering through the mist: What does the chemistry of contaminants in electronic cigarettes tell us about health risks*. Philadelphia, PA: Department of Environmental and Occupational Health, School of Public Health, Drexel University.

Buss, F. T., & Rüschendorf, L. (2010). On the perception of time. *Gerontology*, *56*(4), 361–370.

Butrica, B., & Karamcheva, N. (2012). *Automatic enrollment, employee compensation, and retirement security*. Boston, MA: Center for Retirement Research at Boston College.

(2015a). Automatic enrollment, employer match rates, and employee compensation in 401(k) plans. *Monthly Labor Review*, *138*, 1–33.

(2015b). *The relationship between automatic enrollment and DC plan contributions: Evidence from a national survey of older workers*. Center for Retirement Research at Boston College.

Byrne, S., & Hart, P. S. (2009). The boomerang effect: A synthesis of findings and a preliminary theoretical Framework. *Annals of the International Communication Association*, *33*(1), 3–37.

Camerer, C. F. (2015). The promise and success of lab-field generalizability in experimental economics: A critical reply to Levitt and List. In G. R. Frechette & A. Schotter (Eds.), *Handbook of experimental economic methodology*, 249–295. Oxford, UK: Oxford University Press.

(2000). Prospect theory in the wild: Evidence from the field. In D. Kahneman & A. Tversky (Eds.), *Choices, values, and frames*, 288–300. New York: Russell Sage Foundation.

Camerer, C. F., & Hogarth, R. M. (1999). The effects of financial incentives in experiments: A review and capital-labor-production framework. *Journal of Risk and Uncertainty*, *19*(1–3), 7–42.

(1999). The effects of financial incentives in experiments: A review and capital-labor-production framework. *Journal of Risk and Uncertainty*, *19*(1–3), 7–42.

Camerer, C. F., Issacharoff, S., Loewenstein, G., O'Donoghue, T., & Rabin, M. (2003). Regulation for conservatives: Behavioral economics and the case for "asymmetric paternalism." *University of Pennsylvania Law Review*, *151*(3), 1211–1254.

Camerer, C. F., Dreber, A., Forsell, E., Ho, T. H., Huber, J., Johannesson, M., ... & Heikensten, E. (2016). Evaluating replicability of laboratory experiments in economics. *Science*, *351*(6280), 1433–1436.

Camerer, C. F., Dreber, A., Holzmeister, F., Ho, T. H., Huber, J., Johannesson, M., ... & Altmejd, A. (2018). Evaluating the replicability of social science experiments in Nature and Science between 2010 and 2015. *Nature Human Behaviour*, *2*(9), 637.

Campaign for Tobacco-Free Kids. (2006). Smoke-free laws encourage smokers to quit and discourage youth from starting [Press release]. Retrieved from www.tobaccofreekids.org/research/factsheets/pdf/0198.pdf

Canadian Cancer Society. (2016). *Cigarette package health warnings: International status report.* Retrieved from www.cancer.ca/~/media/cancer.ca/CW/for%20media/Media%20releases/2018/CCS-international-warnings-report-2018—English—2-MB.pdf?la=en.

Capa, R. L., Bustin, G. M., Cleeremans, A., & Hansenne, M. (2011). Conscious and unconscious reward cues can affect a critical component of executive control. *Experimental Psychology, 58*(5), 370–375.

Caplan, B. (2000). Rational irrationality: A framework for the neoclassical-behavioral debate. *Eastern Economic Journal, 26*(2), 191–211.

(2007). *The myth of the rational voter.* Princeton, NJ: Princeton University Press.

Carlin, B. I., Gervais, S., & Manso, G. (2013). Libertarian paternalism, information production, and financial decision making. *Review of Financial Studies, 26*(9), 2204–2228.

Carlsson, F., He, H., Martinsson, P., Qin, P., & Sutter, M. (2012). Household decision making in rural China: Using experiments to estimate the influences of spouses. *Journal of Economic Behavior & Organization, 84*(2), 525–536.

Carroll, G. D., Choi, J. J., Laibson, D., Madrian, B. C., & Metrick, A. (2009). Optimal defaults and active decisions. *Quarterly Journal of Economics, 124*(4), 1639–1674.

Cartwright, E. (2011). *Behavioral economics.* New York: Routledge.

Cartwright, N. (2009). Evidence-based policy: What is to be done about relevance? *Philosophical Studies, 143*, 127–136.

Castillo, M., Petrie, R., & Torero, M. (2008). Rationality and the nature of the market. Available at SSRN: https://ssrn.com/abstract=1265015

Cecchi, F., & Bulte, E. (2013). Does market experience promote rational choice? Experimental evidence from rural Ethiopia. *Economic Development and Cultural Change, 61*, 407–429.

Center for Science in the Public Interest. (2014). Support the SWEET Act. Retrieved from http://action.cspinet.org/ea-action/action?ea.client.id=1927&ea.campaign.id=34422

Centers for Disease Control and Prevention. (2000). Strategies for reducing exposure to environmental tobacco smoke, increasing tobacco-use cessation, and reducing initiation in communities and health-care systems: A report on the recommendations of the task force on community preventive services. *Morbidity and Mortality Weekly Report, 49*(RR-12).

Cevolani, C., Crupi, V., & Festa, R. (2010). The whole truth about Linda: Probability, verisimilitude, and a paradox of conjunction. In M. D'Agostino, F. Laudisa, G. Giorello, T. Pievani, & C. Sinigaglia (Eds.), *New essays in logic and the philosophy of science*, 603–615. London, UK: College Publications.

Charness, G., Karni, E., & Levin, D. (2007). Individual and group decision making under risk: An experimental study of Bayesian updating and violations of first-order stochastic dominance. *Journal of Risk and Uncertainty, 35*, 129–148.

(2010). On the conjunction fallacy in probability judgment: New experimental evidence regarding Linda. *Games and Economic Behavior, 68*(2), 551–556.

Charness, G., Gneezy, U., & Kuhn, M. A. (2012). Experimental methods: Between-subject and within-subject design. *Journal of Economic Behavior & Organization, 81*(1), 1–8.

Chater, N., & Oaksford, M. (1999). The probability heuristics model of syllogistic reasoning. *Cognitive Psychology, 38*(2), 191–258.

Chesterley, N. (2017). Defaults, decision costs and welfare in behavioural policy design. *Economica, 84*(333), 16–33.

Chia, C. W., Shardell, M., Tanaka, T., Liu, D. D., Gravenstein, K. S., Simonsick, E. M., ... & Ferrucci, L. (2016). Chronic low-calorie sweetener use and risk of abdominal obesity among older adults: A cohort study. *PloS One, 11*(11), e0167241.

Chiu, S., Bergeron, N., Williams, P. T., Bray, G. A., Sutherland, B., & Krauss, R. M. (2016). Comparison of the DASH (Dietary Approaches to Stop Hypertension) diet and a higher-fat DASH diet on blood pressure and lipids and lipoproteins: A randomized controlled trial. *American Journal of Clinical Nutrition, 103*(2), 341–347.

Choi, J. J. (2015). Contributions to defined contribution pension plans. *Annual Review of Financial Economics, 7*, 161–178.

Choi, J. J., Laibson, D., Madrian, B. C., & Metrick, A. (2002). Defined contribution pensions: Plan rules, participant choices, and the path of least resistance. *Tax Policy and the Economy, 16*, 67–113.

(2003). Optimal defaults. *American Economic Review, 93*(2), 180–185.

(2003). For better or for worse: Default effects and 401 (k) savings behavior. In *Perspectives on the economics of aging* (pp. 81–126). University of Chicago Press.

Cohen, J. D., Ericson, K. M., Laibson, D., & White, J. M. (2016). Measuring time preferences. NBER No. w22455. National Bureau of Economic Research.

Cohen, L. J. (1981). Can human irrationality be experimentally demonstrated? *Behavioral and Brain Sciences, 4*(3), 317–331.

Colgrove, J., & Bayer, R. (2002). Science, politics, and ideology in the campaign against environmental tobacco smoke. *American Journal of Public Health, 92*(6), 949–954.

Collodi, C. (2016). *Pinnochio* [E-reader version]. (Original work published 1883)

Conly, S. (2012). *Against autonomy: Justifying coercive paternalism.* Cambridge, UK: Cambridge University Press.

(2013). *Against autonomy: Justifying coercive paternalism* [Kindle edition]. Cambridge, UK: Cambridge University Press.

Corner, A., Hahn, U., & Oaksford, M. (2011). The psychological mechanism of the slippery slope argument. *Journal of Memory and Language, 64*(2), 133–152.

Costello, F. (2009). How probability theory explains the conjunction fallacy. *Journal of Behavioral Decision Making, 22*(3), 213–234.

Costello, F., & Watts, P. (2014). Surprisingly rational: Probability theory plus noise explains biases in judgment. *Psychological Review, 121*(3), 463–480.

Cowen, T. (1991). Self-constraint versus self-liberation. *Ethics, 101*(2), 360–373.

Craver, R. (2014). Reynolds American wants FDA to ban vapor e-cigs. *Winston-Salem Journal*, September 7. Retrieved from www.journalnow.com/business/business_news/local/big-tobacco-makers-want-fda-to-ban-vapor-e-cigs/article_77b131f5-540d-5f02-927c-733bac751529.html

Cremer, H., De Donder, P., Maldonado, D., & Pestieau, P. (2012). Taxing sin goods and subsidizing health care. *Scandinavian Journal of Economics*, *114*, 101–123.

Crupi, V., Fitelson, B., & Tentori, K. (2008). Probability, confirmation, and the conjunction fallacy. *Thinking & Reasoning*, *14*(2), 182–199.

Csete, J., Kamarulzaman, A., Kazatchkine, M., Altice, F., Balicki, M., Buxton, J., . . . & Hart, C. (2016). Public health and international drug policy. *The Lancet*, *387*(10026), 1427–1480.

Damasio, A. (1994). *Descartes' error: Emotion, reason and the human brain*. New York: Avon Books.

Dawes, R. M., & Mulford, M. (1996). The false consensus effect and overconfidence: Flaws in judgment or flaws in how we study judgment? *Organizational Behavior and Human Decision Processes*, *65*(3), 201–211.

De Finetti, B. (1964). Foresight: Its logical laws in subjective sources. In H. Kyburg & H. Smokler (Eds.), *Studies in subjective probability*, 93–158. New York: John Wiley.

   (1974a). *Theory of probability: A critical introductory treatment*. Translated by A. Machi & A. Smith. Chichester, UK: J. Wiley.

   (1974b). The true subjective probability problem. In C.-A. Von-Holstein (Ed.), *The concept of probability in psychological experiments*, 15–23. Dordrecht, Netherlands: Springer.

   (2008). *Philosophical lectures on probability*. Berlin, Germany: Springer-Verlag.

de Ridder, D., Lensvelt-Mulders, G., Finkenauer, C., Stok, M., & Baumeister, R. F. (2012). Taking stock of self-control: A meta-analysis of how self-control affects a wide range of behaviors. *Personality and Social Psychology Review*, *16*(1), 76–99.

de Sousa, R. (1987). *The rationality of emotion*. Cambridge, MA: MIT Press.

Dean, M., Kıbrıs, Ö., & Masatlioglu, Y. (2017). Limited attention and status quo bias. *Journal of Economic Theory*, *169*, 93–127.

Debnam, J. (2017). Selection effects and heterogeneous demand responses to the Berkeley soda tax vote. *American Journal of Agricultural Economics*, *99*(5), 1172–1187.

Debreu, G. (1954). Representation of a preference ordering by a numerical function. *Decision Processes*, *3*, 159–165.

DellaVigna, S., & Malmendier, U. (2006). Paying not to go to the gym. *American Economic Review*, *96*(3), 694–719.

Demsetz, H. (1969). Information and efficiency: Another viewpoint. *Journal of Law and Economics*, *12*(1), 1–22.

Denant-Boemont, L., Diecidue, E., & l'Haridon, O. (2017). Patience and time consistency in collective decisions. *Experimental Economics 20*(1), 181–208.

Desvousges, W. H., Johnson, F. R., Dunford, R. W., Hudson, S. P., Wilson, K. N., & Boyle, K. J. (1993). Measuring natural resource damages with contingent valuation: Tests of validity and reliability. In J. A. Hausman (Ed.), *Contingent valuation: A critical assessment*, 91–164. Amsterdam, Netherlands: North-Holland.

Dorausch, M. (n.d.). Studies reveal health risks of e-cigarettes. Retrieved from www.iflscience.com/health-and-medicine/studies-reveal-health-risks-e-cigarettes

Downs, A. (1957). An economic theory of political action in a democracy. *Journal of Political Economy*, *65*(2), 135–150.

Duckworth, A. L., Gendler, T. S., & Gross, J. J. (2016). Situational strategies for self-control. *Perspectives on Psychological Science, 11*(1), 35–55.

Dulany, D. E., & Hilton, D. J. (1991). Conversational implicature, conscious representation, and the conjunction fallacy. *Social Cognition, 9*(1), 85–110.

Eitam, B., Hassin, R. R., & Schul, Y. (2008). Nonconscious goal pursuit in novel environments: The case of implicit learning. *Psychological Science, 19*(3), 261–267.

Elster, J. (1984). *Ulysses and the sirens: Studies in rationality and irrationality* (Rev. ed.). Cambridge, UK: Cambridge University Press.

Emery, S. L., Szczypka, G., Abril, E. P., Kim, Y., & Vera, L. (2014). Are you scared yet? Evaluating fear appeal messages in tweets about the tips campaign. *Journal of Communication, 64*(2), 278–295.

Encyclopedia of Mind Disorders. (n.d.). Self-control strategies. Retrieved from http://www.minddisorders.com/Py-Z/Self-control-strategies.html

Erev, I., Wallsten, T. S., & Budescu, D. V. (1994). Simultaneous over- and under-confidence: The role of error in judgment processes. *Psychological Review, 101*(3), 519–527.

Ericson, K. M. M., & Fuster, A. (2014). The endowment effect. *Annual Review of Economics, 6*(1), 555–579.

Ericson, K. M. M., White, J. M., Laibson, D., & Cohen, J. D. (2015). Money earlier or later? Simple heuristics explain intertemporal choices better than delay discounting does. *Psychological Science, 26*(6), 826–833.

Eswaran, M., & Neary, H. M. (2016). The evolutionary logic of honoring sunk costs. *Economic Inquiry, 52*, 835–846.

Evans, J. (2002). Logic and human reasoning: An assessment of the deduction paradigm. *Psychological Bulletin, 128*(6), 978–996.

Evans, J. S. B. T. (2012). Dual process theories of deductive reasoning: Facts and fallacies. In K. J. Holyoak & R. G. Morrison (Eds.), *The Oxford handbook of thinking and reasoning*, 115–133. Oxford, UK: Oxford University Press.

Evans, J. S. B., & Stanovich, K. E. (2013a). Dual-process theories of higher cognition: Advancing the debate. *Perspectives on Psychological Science, 8*(3), 223–241.

(2013b). Theory and metatheory in the study of dual processing: Reply to comments. *Perspectives on Psychological Science, 8*(3), 263–271.

Fang, H., & Silverman, D. (2006). Distinguishing between cognitive biases. In E. J. McCaffery & J. Slemrod (Eds.), *Behavioral public finance*, 47–81. New York: Russell Sage Foundation.

Ferguson, A. (2010). Nudge nudge, wink wink. *Weekly Standard*, April 19. Retrieved from www.weeklystandard.com/nudge-nudge-wink-wink/article/433737#!

Fernandez-Villaverde, J., & Mukherji, A. (2002). *Can we really observe hyperbolic discounting?* Unpublished manuscript, University of Pennsylvania. Retrieved from http://economics.sas.upenn.edu/~jesusfv/hyper2006.pdf

Feynman, R. P. (1965). *The character of physical law*. London, UK: Cox and Wyman.

Fich, E. M., & Xu, G. (2018). Are market reactions to M&As biased by overextrapolation of salient news? Available at SSRN: https://ssrn.com/abstract=2996714 or http://dx.doi.org/10.2139/ssrn.2996714

Fiddick, L., Cosmides, L., & Tooby, J. (2000). No interpretation without representation: The role of domain-specific representations and inferences in the Wason selection task. *Cognition, 77*, 1–79.

Fiedler, K., & Krueger, J. I. (2012). More than an artifact: Regression as a theoretical construct. In J. I. Krueger (Ed.), *Social judgment and decision-making*, 171–189. New York: Psychology Press.

Finch, C. (1993). *Jim Henson: The works; The art, the magic, the imagination*. London, UK: Random House.

FindLaw. (n.d.). Customer returns and refund laws by state. Retrieved from https://consumer.findlaw.com/consumer-transactions/customer-returns-and-refund-laws-by-state.html

Fischhoff, B. (2001). Learning from experience: Coping with hindsight bias and ambiguity. In J. S. Armstrong (Ed.), *Principles of forecasting: A handbook for researchers and practitioners*, 543–554. Boston, MA: Kluwer.

Fishbach, A., & Shah, J. Y. (2006). Self-control in action: Implicit dispositions toward goals and away from temptations. *Journal of Personality and Social Psychology*, *90*(5), 820–832.

Fishbach, A., & Shen, L. 2014. The explicit and implicit ways of overcoming temptation. In J. W. Sherman, B. Gawronski, & Y. Trope (Eds.), *Dual-process theories of the social mind*, 454–467. New York: Guilford Press.

Fishbach, A., & Trope, Y. (2005). The substitutability of external control and self-control. *Journal of Experimental Social Psychology*, *41*, 256–270.

Fishbach, A., Friedman, R. S., & Kruglanski, A. W. (2003). Leading us not into temptation: Momentary allurements elicit overriding goal activation. *Journal of Personality and Social Psychology*, *84*(2), 296–309.

Fishbach, A., Dhar, R., & Zhang, Y. (2006). Subgoals as substitutes or complements: The role of goal accessibility. *Journal of Personality and Social Psychology*, *91*(2), 232–242.

Fishbach, A., Zhang, Y., & Trope, Y. (2010). Counteractive evaluation: Asymmetric shifts in the implicit value of conflicting motivations. *Journal of Experimental Social Psychology*, *46*(1), 29–38.

Fiske, S. T., & Taylor, S. E. (1991). *Social cognition* (2nd ed.). New York: *McGraw-Hill*.

Fitzsimons, G. M., & Bargh, J. A. (2004). Automatic self-regulation. In R. F. Baumeister & K. D. Vohs (Eds.), *Handbook of self-regulation: Research, theory, and applications*, 151–170. New York: Guilford Press.

Fitzsimons, G. M., & Finkel, E. J. (2010). Interpersonal influences on self-regulation. *Current Directions in Psychological Science*, *19*(2), 101–105.

Fontaine, K. R., Redden, D. T., Wang, C., Westfall, A. O., & Allison, D. B. (2003). Years of life lost due to obesity. *JAMA*, *289*(2), 187–193.

Frazão, E. (Ed.). (1999). *America's eating habits: Changes & consequences*. Washington, DC: US Department of Agriculture, Economic Research Service.

Frechette, G. R., & Schotter, A. (2015). *Handbook of experimental economic methodology*. Oxford, UK: Oxford University Press.

Frederick, S., Loewenstein, G., & O'Donoghue, T. (2002). Time discounting and time preference: A critical review. *Journal of Economic Literature*, *40*, 351–401.

(2003). Time discounting and time preference: A critical review. In G. Loewenstein, D. Read, & R. Baumeister (Eds.), *Time and decision: Economic and psychological perspectives of intertemporal choice*, 13–86. New York: Russell Sage Foundation.

Friedman, J. (2006). Democratic competence in normative and positive theory: Neglected implications of "The nature of belief systems in mass publics." *Critical Review*, *18*(1–3), i–xliii.

Friedman, M., & Savage, L. J. (1948). The utility analysis of choices involving risk. *Journal of Political Economy*, 56(4), 279–304.

Fujita, K. (2011). On conceptualizing self-control as more than the effortful inhibition of impulses. *Personality and Social Psychology Review*, 15(4), 352–366.

Fujita, K., & Carnevale, J. J. (2012). Transcending temptation through abstraction: The role of construal level in self-control. *Current Directions in Psychological Science*, 21(4), 248–252.

Gailliot, M. T., Plant, E. A., Butz, D. A., & Baumeister, R. F. (2007). Increasing self-regulatory strength can reduce the depleting effect of suppressing stereotypes. *Personality and Social Psychology Bulletin*, 33(2), 281–294.

Gal, D., & Rucker, D. D. (2018). The loss of loss aversion: Will it loom larger than its gain? *Journal of Consumer Psychology*, 28(3), 497–516.

Galavotti, M. C. (2001). Subjectivism, objectivism and objectivity in Bruno de Finetti's Bayesianism. In D. Corfield & J. Williamson (Eds.), *Foundations of Bayesianism*, 161–174. Dordrecht, Netherlands: Kluwer.

Galesic, M., Barkoczi, D., & Katsikopoulos, K. (2015). Can small crowds be wise? Moderate-sized groups can outperform large groups and individuals under some task conditions. Santa Fe Institute Working Paper. Retrieved from www.semanticscholar.org/paper/Can-Small-Crowds-Be-Wise-Moderate-sized-Groups-Can-Galesic-Barkoczi/af4e27a5367125b9fcab3da57ad418949edcd87d/pdf

Gass, R. H., & Seiter, J. S. (2015). *Persuasion: Social influence and compliance gaining*. 4th ed. Boston: Allyn & Bacon.

Gayer, T., & Viscusi, W. K.(2013). Overriding consumer preferences with energy regulations. *Journal of Regulatory Economics*, 43(3), 248–264.

Geyskens, K., Dewitte, S., Pandelaere, M., & Warlop, L. (2008). Tempt me just a little bit more: The effect of prior food temptation actionability on goal activation and consumption. *Journal of Consumer Research*, 35(4), 600–610.

Ghaffarzadegan, N., Lyneis, J., & Richardson, G. P. (2011). How small system dynamics models can help the public policy process. *System Dynamics Review*, 27(1), 22–44.

Gifford, A., Jr. (2002). Emotion and self-control. *Journal of Economic Behavior & Organization*, 49, 113–130.

Gigerenzer, G. (1996). On narrow norms and vague heuristics: A reply to Kahneman and Tversky. *Psychological Review*, 103(3), 592–596.

(1998). Surrogates for theories. *Theory & Psychology*, 8(2), 195–204.

(2000). *Adaptive thinking: Rationality in the real world*. Oxford, UK: Oxford University Press.

(2008). I think, therefore I err. In *Rationality for mortals: How people cope with uncertainty*. Oxford, UK: Oxford University Press.

(2015). *Simply rational: Decision making in the real world*. Oxford, UK: Oxford University Press.

Gigerenzer, G., & Brighton, H. (2009). Homo heuristicus: Why biased minds make better inferences. *Trends in Cognitive Science*, 1, 107–143.

Gigerenzer, G., & Hug, K. (1992). Domain-specific reasoning: Social contracts, cheating and perspective change. *Cognition*, 43, 127–171.

Gigerenzer, G., & Marewski, J. N. (2015). Surrogate science: The idol of a universal method for scientific inference. *Journal of Management*, 41(2), 421–440.

Gigerenzer, G., & Murray, D. J. (1987). *Cognition as intuitive statistics*. Hillsdale, NJ: Lawrence Erlbaum Associates.

Gigerenzer, G., Hoffrage, U., & Kleinbölting, H. (1991). Probabilistic mental models: A Brunswikian theory of confidence. *Psychological Review, 98*(4), 506–528.

Gigerenzer, G., Hertwig, R., Hoffrage, U., & Sedlmeier, P. (2008). Cognitive illusions reconsidered. In C. R. Plott & V. L. Smith (Eds.), *Handbook of experimental economics results*, Vol. 1, 1018–1034. Amsterdam, Netherlands: Elsevier.

Gilbert, D. T., Pinel, E. C., Wilson, T. D., Blumberg, S. J., & Wheatley, T. P. (1998). Immune neglect: A source of durability bias in affective forecasting. *Journal of Personality and Social Psychology, 75*(3), 617.

Gilbert, D. T., King, G., Pettigrew, S., & Wilson, T. D. (2016). Comment on "Estimating the reproducibility of psychological science." *Science, 351*(6277), 1037.

Gilboa, I. (2011). *Making better decisions: Decision theory in practice*. Chichester, UK: Wiley-Blackwell.

Giles, J., Coghlan, A., & Geddes, L. (2007). Anti-smoking groups accused of distorting the science on the risks of heart attack. *New Scientist, 196*(2629), 8.

Gintis, H. (2016). *Individuality and entanglement: The moral and material bases of social life*. Princeton, NJ: Princeton University Press.

Glaeser, E. L. (2006). Paternalism and psychology. *University of Chicago Law Review, 73*(1), 133–156.

Glantz, S. A. (1987). Achieving a smokefree society. *Circulation, 76*(4), 746–752.

Gneezy, U., & Rustichini, A. (2000). Pay enough or don't pay at all. *Quarterly Journal of Economics, 115*, 791–810.

Gneezy, U., Meier, S., & Rey-Biel, P. (2011). When and why incentives (don't) work to modify behavior. *Journal of Economic Perspectives, 25*(4), 191–210.

Goda, G. S., Manchester, C. F., & Sojourner, A. J. (2014). What will my account really be worth? Experimental evidence on how retirement income projections affect saving. *Journal of Public Economics, 119*, 80–92.

Gokhale, J., Kotlikoff, L. J., & Neumann, T. (2001). Does participating in a 401(k) raise your lifetime taxes? NBER No. 8341. National Bureau of Economic Research.

Goldin, J. (2015). Which way to nudge: Uncovering preferences in the behavioral age. *Yale Law Journal, 125*, 226–270.

Grandy, R. E., & Warner, R. (2014). Paul Grice. In E. N. Zalta (Ed.), *The Stanford encyclopedia of philosophy*. Retrieved from http://plato.stanford.edu/archives/spr2014/entries/grice/

(2017). Paul Grice. In E. Zalta (Ed.), *The Stanford encyclopedia of philosophy*. Stanford, CA: Metaphysics Research Lab, Stanford University. Retrieved from https://plato.stanford.edu/archives/win2017/entries/grice

Green, H. J. (1971). *Consumer theory*. Harmondsworth, UK: Penguin.

Gregory, R L. (Ed.). (2004). *The Oxford companion to the mind*, 2nd ed. Oxford, UK: Oxford University Press.

Grice, H. P. (1989). *Studies in the way of words*. Cambridge, MA: Harvard University Press.

Grier, J. (2017). We used terrible science to justify smoking bans. *Slate*, February 13. Available at https://slate.com/technology/2017/02/secondhand-smoke-isnt-as-bad-as-we-thought.html

(2018). Scott Gottlieb's FDA is moving toward a stealth ban on cigarettes and cigars. *Reason*, November 26. Available at http://reason.com/archives/2018/11/26/got tlieb-fda-vape-cigar-cigarette-ban

Griffin, D., & Tversky, A. (1992). The weighing of evidence and the determinants of confidence. *Cognitive Psychology*, 24(3), 411–435.

Grimm, P. (2010). Social desirability bias. In *Wiley international encyclopedia of marketing*. In J. Sheth, N. Malhotra, & L. L. Price (Eds.), 258. Oxford, UK: Wiley-Blackwell.

Gruber, J., & Köszegi, B. (2001). Is addiction "rational"? Theory and evidence. *Quarterly Journal of Economics*, 116(4), 1261–1303.

Grüne-Yanoff, T. (2015). Why behavioural policy needs mechanistic evidence. *Economics and Philosophy*, 32(3), 1–21.

Guido, G. (2001). *The salience of marketing stimuli: An incongruity–salience hypothesis on consumer awareness*. Boston, MA: Springer Science & Business Media.

Gul, F., & Pesendorfer, W. (2001). Temptation and self-control. *Econometrica*, 69(6), 1403–1435.

(2004). Self-control and the theory of consumption. *Econometrica*, 72(1), 119–158.

(2008). The case for mindless economics. In A. Caplin & A. Schotter (Eds.), *The foundations of positive and normative economics*, 3–39. Oxford, UK: Oxford University Press.

Guthrie, J. F., Derby, B. M., & Levy, A. S. (1999). What people know and do not know about nutrition. America's eating habits: Changes and consequences. In E. Frazão (Ed.), *America's eating habits: Changes & consequences*, 243–290. Washington, DC: US Dept. of Agriculture, Economic Research Service.

Halevy, Y. (2015). Time consistency: Stationarity and time invariance. *Econometrica*, 83(1), 335–352.

Hall, K. D. (2017). A review of the carbohydrate–insulin model of obesity. *European Journal of Clinical Nutrition*, 71, 323–326.

Hall, K. D., Bemis, T., Brychta, R., Chen, K. Y., Courville, A., Crayner, . . . & Yannai, L. (2015). Calorie for calorie, dietary fat restriction results in more body fat loss than carbohydrate restriction in people with obesity. *Cell Metabolism*, 22(3), 427–436. Retrieved from https://doi.org/10.1016/j.cmet.2015.07.021

Hall, K. D., Chen, K. Y., Guo, J., Lam, Y. Y., Leibel, R. L., Mayer, L. E., . . . & Ravussin, E. (2016). Energy expenditure and body composition changes after an isocaloric ketogenic diet in overweight and obese men. *American Journal of Clinical Nutrition*, 104(2), 324–333. Retrieved from https://doi.org/10.3945/ajcn.116.133561

Halpern, D. (2015). *Inside the nudge unit: How small changes make a big difference*. London, UK: W. H. Allen.

(2016). *Inside the nudge unit: How small changes can make a big difference*. London, UK: Random House.

Hands, D. W. (2015). *Normative rational choice theory: Past, present, and future*. Unpublished. Available at SSRN: https://papers.ssrn.com/sol3/papers .cfm?abstract_id=1738671

Harman, G. (2002). The internal critique. In D. M. Gabbay (Ed.), *Handbook of the logic of argument and inference: The turn towards the practical*, 171–186. Amsterdam, Netherlands: Elsevier.

(2004). Practical aspects of theoretical rationality. In A. Mele & P. Rawling (Eds.), *The Oxford handbook of rationality*, 45–56. Oxford, UK: Oxford University Press.

Harrison, G. W. (1994). Expected utility theory and the experimentalists. *Empirical Economics, 19*, 223–253.

Harsanyi, J. C. (1982). Morality and the theory of rationality choice. In A. Sen & B. Williams. (Eds.), *Utilitarianism and beyond*, 39–62. Cambridge, UK: Cambridge University Press.

Harvard University T.H. Chan School of Public Health. (n.d.). "Healthy Eating Plate." www.hsph.harvard.edu/nutritionsource/healthy-eating-plate/13/.

Hassin, R. R., Bargh, J. A., Engell, A. D., & McCulloch, K. C. (2009). Implicit working memory. *Consciousness and Cognition, 18*(3), 665–678.

Hassin, R. R., Bargh, J. A., & Zimerman, S. (2009). Automatic and flexible: The case of nonconscious goal pursuit. *Social Cognition, 27*(1), 20–36.

Hausman, D. M. (2000). Revealed preference, belief, and game theory. *Economics and Philosophy, 16*(1), 99–115.

Hayek, F. A. (1945). The use of knowledge in society. *American Economic Review, 35*(4), 519–530.

(1948). *Individualism and economic order*. Chicago, IL: University of Chicago Press.

(1955). *The counter-revolution of science*. Glencoe, IL: Free Press.

(1975). The pretence of knowledge. *Swedish Journal of Economics, 77*(4), 433–442.

Healthy eating plate & healthy eating pyramid. (n.d.). Retrieved from www.hsph.harvard.edu/nutritionsource/pyramid-full-story/

Heath, C., & Soll, J. B. (1996). Mental budgeting and consumer decisions. *Journal of Consumer Research, 23*(1), 40–52.

Henley, D. E., Denneny, J. C., Hassink, S. G., Foti, M., Salvatore, F. R., Hansen, C. W., ... & Henry-Crowe, S. T. (2015). Open letter, April 28. Retrieved from https://timedotcom.files.wordpress.com/2015/05/2015_04_28_obama.pdf

Herrnstein, R. J., Loewenstein, G. F., Prelec, D., & Vaughan, W., Jr. (1993). Utility maximization and melioration: Internalities in individual choice. *Journal of Behavioral Decision Making, 6*(3), 149–185.

Hertwig, R., & Gigerenzer, G. (1999). The "conjunction fallacy" revisited: How intelligent inferences look like reasoning errors. *Journal of Behavioral Decision Making, 12*(4), 275–305.

Hertwig, R., & Ortmann, A. (2001). Experimental practices in economics: A methodological challenge for psychologists?. *Behavioral and Brain Sciences, 24*(3), 383–403.

Heukelom, F. 2014. *Behavioral economics: A history*. Cambridge, UK: Cambridge University Press.

Higgins, E. T., & Liberman, N. (2018). The loss of loss aversion: Paying attention to reference points. *Journal of Consumer Psychology, 28*(3), 524–532.

Hilton, D. (1995). The social context of reasoning: Conversational inference and rational judgment. *Psychological Bulletin, 118*(2), 248–271.

Hirshleifer, D. (2008). Psychological bias as a driver of financial regulation. *European Financial Management, 14*(5), 856–874.

Hoffrage, U., & Gigerenzer, G. (1998). Using natural frequencies to improve diagnostic inferences. *Academic Medicine, 73*(5), 538–540.

Hope, B. (2007). Latest hot co-op topic: Secondhand smoke. *New York Sun*, December 6, 1–3. Retrieved from www.nysun.com/real-estate/latest-hot-co-op-topic-second hand-smoke/67569/

Hopkins, D., Briss, P., Harris, J., Ricard, C., Rosenquist, J., Harris, K., Husten, C., McKenna, J. W., Sharp, D. J., Woollery, T. A., Sharma N., & Pechacek, T. (2000). Strategies for Reducing Exposure to Environmental Tobacco Smoke, Increasing Tobacco-Use Cessation, and Reducing Initiation in Communities and Health-Care Systems: A Report on Recommendations of the Task Force on Community Preventive Services. Morbidity and Mortality Weekly Report: Recommendations and Reports, 49(RR-12), I–11.

Horstmann, G., & Ansorge, U. (2016). Surprise capture and inattentional blindness. *Cognition, 157,* 237–249.

Horstmann, G., & Herwig, A. (2015). Surprise attracts the eyes and binds the gaze. *Psychonomic Bulletin & Review, 22*(3), 743–749.

(2016). Novelty biases attention and gaze in a surprise trial. *Attention, Perception, & Psychophysics, 78*(1), 69–77.

Houde, S. (2014). How consumers respond to environmental certification and the value of energy information. NBER No. w20019. National Bureau of Economic Research.

Houthakker, H. S. (1950). Revealed preference and the utility function. *Economica, 17*(66), 159–174.

Hovenkamp, H. (1991). Legal policy and the endowment effect. *Journal of Legal Studies, 20*(2), 225–247.

Howard, G., Roe, B. E., Nisbet, E. C., & Martin, J. (2015). Hypothetical bias mitigation in choice experiments: Effectiveness of cheap talk and honesty priming fade with repeated choices. Available at SSRN: http://papers.ssrn.com/sol3/papers.cfm? abstract_id=2697573

Huber, J., Payne, J. W., & Puto, C. (1982). Adding asymmetrically dominated alternatives: Violations of regularity and the similarity hypothesis. *Journal of Consumer Research, 9*(1), 90–98.

Ikeda, S. (1997). *Dynamics of the mixed economy: Toward a theory of interventionism.* London, UK: Routledge.

Ingraham, C. (2014). Think you drink a lot? This chart will tell you. *The Washington Post*, September 25. Retrieved from www.washingtonpost.com/news/wonk/wp/2014/09/25/think-you-drink-a-lot-this-chart-will-tell-you/?utm_term=.7ef5a29da02d

Ioannidis, J. P. (2008). Why most discovered true associations are inflated. *Epidemiology, 19*(5), 640–648.

et al. (2017). https://academic.oup.com/ej/article/127/605/F236/5069452

Iowa Right to Life. (n.d.). Post abortion syndrome. Retrieved from www.iowartl.org/get-the-facts/abortion/post-abortion-syndrome

Isaac, A. G. (1998). *The structure of neoclassical consumer theory.* EconWPA No. 9805003. EconWPA.

Jachimowicz, J., Duncan, S., Weber, E. U., & Johnson, E. J. (2018). When and why defaults influence decisions: A meta-analysis of default effects. Available at SSRN: https://ssrn.com/abstract=2727301 or http://dx.doi.org/10.2139/ssrn.272 7301

Jackson, M. O., & Yariv, L. (2014). Present bias and collective dynamic choice in the lab. *American Economic Review, 104*(12), 4184–4204.

Janis, I. L. (1972). *Victims of groupthink: A psychological study of foreign-policy decisions and fiascoes.* Boston, MA: Houghton Mifflin.

Jehle, G. A., & Reny, P. J. (2011). *Advanced microeconomic theory.* Harlow: Financial Times.

Jensen, R. P., Luo, W., Pankow, J. F., Strongin, R. M., & Peyton, D. H. (2015). Hidden formaldehyde in e-cigarette aerosols. *New England Journal of Medicine, 372*(4), 392–394. Retrieved from www.nejm.org/doi/full/10.1056/NEJMc1413069?query=featured_home&

Jha, P. (1999). *Curbing the epidemic: Governments and the economics of tobacco control.* Washington, DC: World Bank.

Johnston, B. C., Kanters, S., Bandayrel, K., Wu, P., Naji, F., Siemieniuk, R. A., ... & Mills, E. J. (2014). Comparison of weight loss among named diet programs in overweight and obese adults: A meta-analysis. *Journal of the American Medical Association, 312*(9), 923–933. Retrieved from http://doi:10.1001/jama.2014.10397

Johnston, L. (1996). Resisting change: Information-seeking and stereotype change. *European Journal of Social Psychology, 26*(5), 799–825.

Jolls, C. (1998). Behavioral economic analysis of redistributive legal rules. *Vanderbilt Law Review, 51*, 1653–1677.

(2011). Behavioral economics and the law. *Foundations and Trends in Microeconomics, 6*(3), 173–263.

Jolls, C., & Sunstein, C. R. (2006). Debiasing through law. *Journal of Legal Studies, 35*, 199–241.

Joram, E., & Read, D. (1996). Two faces of representativeness: The effects of response format on beliefs about random sampling. *Journal of Behavioral Decision Making, 9*(4), 249–264.

Juslin, P., Wennerholm, P., & Olsson, H. (1999). Format dependence in subjective probability calibration. *Journal of Experimental Psychology: Learning, Memory, and Cognition, 25*(4), 1038–1052.

Juslin, P., Winman, A., & Olsson, H. (2000). Naive empiricism and dogmatism in confidence research: A critical examination of the hard–easy effect. *Psychological Review, 107*(2), 384–396.

Juslin, P., Nilsson, H., & Winman, A. (2009). Probability theory, not the very guide of life. *Psychological Review, 116*(4), 856–874.

Kagan, J. (2012). *Psychology's ghosts: The crisis in the profession and the way back.* New Haven, CT: Yale University Press.

Kahneman, D. (2003). Maps of bounded rationality: Psychology for behavioral economics. *American Economic Review, 93*(5), 1449–1475.

(2011). *Thinking fast and slow.* New York: Farrar, Straus & Giroux.

(2017). Re: Reconstruction of a train wreck: How priming research went off the rails [Blog comment]. https://replicationindex.wordpress.com/2017/02/02/reconstruction-of-a-train-wreck-how-priming-research-went-of-the-rails/comment-page-1/#comments

Kahneman, D., & Frederick, S. (2005). A model of heuristic judgment. In K. J. Holyoak & R. G. Morrison (Eds.), *The Cambridge handbook of thinking and reasoning*, 267–293. Cambridge, UK: Cambridge University Press.

Kahneman, D., & Tversky, A. (1996). On the reality of cognitive illusions. *Psychological Review*, *103*(3), 582–591.

Kahneman, D., Knetsch, J. L., & Thaler, R. H. (1991). Anomalies: The endowment effect, loss aversion, and status quo bias. *Journal of Economic Perspectives*, *5*(1), 193–206.

Kahneman, D., Wakker, P. P., & Sarin, R. (1997). Back to Bentham? Explorations of experienced utility. *Quarterly Journal of Economics*, *112*(2), 375–406.

Kahneman, D., Ritov, I., & Schkade, D. (1999). Economic preferences or attitude expressions? An analysis of dollar responses to public issues. *Journal of Risk and Uncertainty*, *19*(1), 203–235.

Kamenica, E. (2012). Behavioral economics and psychology of incentives. *Annual Review of Economics*, *4*(1), 427–452.

Kao, A. B., & Couzin, I. D. (2014). Decision accuracy in complex environments is often maximized by small group sizes. *Proceedings of the Royal Society B: Biological Sciences*, *281*(1784), 20133305. Retrieved from http://dx.doi.org/10.1098/rspb.2013.3305

Katz, L. (2014). Rational choice versus lawful choice. *Journal of Institutional and Theoretical Economics*, *170*(1), 105–121.

Keinan, A., & Kivetz, R. (2008). Remedying hyperopia: The effects of self-control regret on consumer behavior. *Journal of Marketing Research*, *45*(6), 676–689.

Keren, G. (1991). Calibration and probability judgments: Conceptual and methodological issues. *Acta Psychologica*, *77*, 217–273.

  (2013). A tale of two systems: Scientific advance or a theoretical stone soup? Commentary on Evans & Stanovich. *Perspectives on Psychological Science*, *8*(3), 257–262.

Keren, G., & Schul, Y. (2009). Two is not always better than one: A critical evaluation of two-system theories. *Perspectives on Psychological Science*, *4*(6), 533–550.

Kerr, N. L., & Tindale, R. S. (2004). Group performance and decision making. *Annual Review of Psychology*, *55*, 623–655.

Kessler, J., & Vesterlund, L. (2015). The external validity of laboratory experiments: The misleading emphasis on quantitative effects. In G. R. Frechette & A. Schotter (Eds.), *Handbook of experimental economic methodology*, 391–404. Oxford, UK: Oxford University Press.

Kim, B. K., & Zauberman, G. (2009). Perception of anticipatory time in temporal discounting. *Journal of Neuroscience, Psychology, and Economics*, *2*(2), 91.

King, M. F., & Bruner, G. C. (2000). Social desirability bias: A neglected aspect of validity testing. *Psychology and Marketing*, *17*(2), 79–103.

Kirzner, I. M. (1973). *Competition and entrepreneurship*. Chicago, IL: University of Chicago Press.

Klass, G., & Zeiler, K. (2013). Against endowment theory: Experimental economics and legal scholarship. *UCLA Law Review*, *61*, 2–64.

Klayman, J., Soll, J. B., Gonzalez-Vallejo, C., & Barlas, S. (1999). Overconfidence: It depends on how, what, and whom you ask. *Organizational Behavior and Human Decision Processes*, *79*(3), 216–247.

Klayman, J., Soll, J., Juslin, P., & Winman, A. (2006). Subjective confidence and the sampling of knowledge. In K. Fiedler & P. Juslin (Eds.), *Information sampling and adaptive cognition*, 153–182. Cambridge, UK: Cambridge University Press.

Klein, D. B. (2004). Statist quo bias. *Econ Journal Watch, 1*(2), 260–271.

Klick, J., & Mitchell, G. (2006). Government regulation of irrationality: Moral and cognitive hazards. *Minnesota Law Review, 90,* 1620–1663.

Knight, F. H. (1921). *Risk, uncertainty and profit.* Boston, MA: Houghton Mifflin.

Koehler, J. J. (1996). The base rate fallacy reconsidered: Descriptive, normative, and methodological challenges. *Behavioral and Brain Sciences, 19*(1), 1–17.

Koop, G. J., & Johnson, J. G. (2012). The use of multiple reference points in risky decision making. *Journal of Behavioral Decision Making, 25*(1), 49–62.

Kopczuk, W., & Slemrod, J. (2005). Denial of death and economic behavior. *Advances in Theoretical Economics, 5*(1).

Koppl, R. (2018). *Expert failure.* Cambridge, UK: Cambridge University Press.

Korobkin, R. (1998). The status quo bias and contract default rules. *Cornell Law Review, 83*(3), 608–682.

Korzybski, A. (1958). *Science and sanity.* Lakeville, CT: International Non-Aristotelian Library.

Kraemer, H. (2013). Statistical power: Issues and proper applications. In J. S. Comer & P. C. Kendall (Eds.), *The Oxford handbook of research strategies for clinical psychology,* 213–226. Oxford, UK: Oxford University Press.

Kreps, D. M. (2013). *Microeconomic foundations I: Choice and competitive markets,* Vol. 1. Princeton, NJ: Princeton University Press.

Kroese, F. M., Evers, C., & De Ridder, D. T. (2011). Tricky treats: Paradoxical effects of temptation strength on self-regulation processes. *European Journal of Social Psychology, 41*(3), 281–288.

Krueger, J. I., & Funder, D. C. (2004). Towards a balanced social psychology: Causes, consequences and cures for the problem-seeking approach to social behavior and cognition. *Behavioral and Brain Sciences, 27*(3), 313–327.

Kruglanski, A. W., & Gigerenzer, G. (2011). Intuitive and deliberative judgments are based on common principles. *Psychological Review, 118*(1), 97–109.

Kuczmarski, R. J. (2007). What is obesity? Definitions matter. In S. Kumanyika & R. C. Brownson (Eds.), *Handbook of obesity prevention: A resource for health professionals,* 25–44. Boston, MA: Springer.

Kuczmarski, R. J., & Flegal, K. M. (2000). Criteria for definition of overweight in transition: Background and recommendations for the United States. *American Journal of Clinical Nutrition, 72*(5), 1074–1081.

Kudryavtsev, A., Cohen, G., & Hon-Snir, S. (2013). "Rational" or "intuitive": Are behavioral biases correlated across stock market investors? *Contemporary Economics, 7*(2), 31–53.

Kunda, Z. (1987). Motivated inference: Self-serving generation and evaluation of causal theories. *Journal of Personality and Social Psychology, 53*(4), 636–647.

Kuran, T., & Sunstein, C. R. (1998). Availability cascades and risk regulation. *Stanford Law Review, 51,* 683–768.

Kurzban, R., Duckworth, A., Kable, J. W., & Myers, J. (2013). An opportunity cost model of subjective effort and task performance. *Behavioral and Brain Sciences, 36*(6), 661–679.

Kwong, J. Y., Wong, K. F. E., & Tang, S. K. (2013). Comparing predicted and actual affective responses to process versus outcome: An emotion-as-feedback perspective. *Cognition, 129*(1), 42–50.

Laibson, D. I., Repetto, A., Tobacman, J., Hall, R. E., Gale, W. G., & Akerlof, G. A. (1998). Self-control and saving for retirement. *Brookings Papers on Economic Activity*, *1998*(1), 91–196.

Le Grand, J., & New, B. (2015). *Government paternalism: Nanny state or helpful friend?* Princeton, NJ: Princeton University Press.

Lee, J. (2007). Repetition and financial incentives in economics experiments. *Journal of Economic Surveys*, *21*(3), 628–681.

Leland, J. W. (2002). Similarity judgments and anomalies in intertemporal choice. *Economic Inquiry*, *40*(4), 574–581.

Lerner, J. S., Li, Y., Valdesolo, P., & Kassam, K. S. (2015). Emotion and decision making. *Annual Review of Psychology*, *66*, 799–823.

Leslie, I. (2016). The sugar conspiracy. *The Guardian*, April 7. Retrieved from www.theguardian.com/society/2016/apr/07/the-sugar-conspiracy-robert-lustig-john-yudkin

Leu, R. E., & Schaub, T. (1983). Does smoking increase medical care expenditure? *Social Science & Medicine*, *17*(23), 1907–1914. Retrieved from www.sciencedirect.com/science/article/pii/0277953683901685

Levi, I. (1983). Who commits the base rate fallacy? *Behavioral and Brain Sciences*, *6*(3), 502–506.

(1996). Fallacy and controversy about base rates. *Behavioral and Brain Sciences*, *19*(1), 31–32.

(2002). Money pumps and diachronic books. *Philosophy of Science*, *69*(S3), S235–S247.

Levine, L. J., Lench, H. C., Kaplan, R. L., & Safer, M. A. (2012). Accuracy and artifact: Reexamining the intensity bias in affective forecasting. *Journal of Personality and Social Psychology*, *103*(4), 584–605.

(2013). Like Schrödinger's cat, the impact bias is both dead and alive: Reply to Wilson and Gilbert (2013). *Journal of Personality and Social Psychology*, *105*(5), 749–756.

Levitt, S. D., & List, J. A. (2007). Viewpoint: On the generalizability of lab behaviour to the field. *Canadian Journal of Economics*, *40*, 347–370.

Lichtenstein, S., & Fischhoff, B. (1977). Do those who know more also know more about how much they know. *Organizational Behavior and Human Performance*, *20*(2), 159–183.

Lichtenstein, S., Slovic, P., Fischhoff, B., Layman, M., & Combs, B. (1978). Judged frequency of events. *Journal of Experimental Psychology: Human Learning and Memory*, *4*(6), 551–578.

Light, L. (2004). A fatally flawed food guide. *Conscious Choice*. Retrieved from http://web.archive.org/web/20090207074229/http://consciouschoice.com/2004/cc1711/wh_lead1711.html

Lipsey, R. G. (2001). Successes and failures in the transformation of economics. *Journal of Economic Methodology*, *8*(2), 169–201.

Lipton, E. (2016). A lobbyist wrote the bill. Will the tobacco industry win its e-cigarette fight? *The New York Times*, September 2. Retrieved from www.nytimes.com/2016/09/03/us/politics/e-cigarettes-vaping-cigars-fda-altria.html

List of Cognitive Biases. (n.d.). *Wikipedia*. Retrieved from https://en.wikipedia.org/wiki/List_of_cognitive_biases

List, J. A. (2003). Does market experience eliminate market anomalies? *Quarterly Journal of Economics, 118*(1), 41–71.

(2004). Neoclassical theory versus prospect theory: Evidence from the marketplace. *Econometrica, 72*(2), 615–625.

(2011). Does market experience eliminate market anomalies? The case of exogenous market experience. *American Economic Review, 101*(3), 313–317.

List, J. A., & Gallet, C. A. (2001). What experimental protocol influence disparities between actual and hypothetical stated values? *Environmental and Resource Economics, 20*(3), 241–254.

List, J. A., & Millimet, D. L. (2008). The market: Catalyst for rationality and filter of irrationality. *The BE Journal of Economic Analysis & Policy, 8*(1).

Little, I. M. D. (1957). *A critique of welfare economics.* Oxford, UK: Oxford University Press.

Lode, E. (1999). Slippery slope arguments and legal reasoning. *California Law Review, 87*(6), 1469–1543.

Lodge, M., & Hamill, R. (1986). A partisan schema for political information processing. *American Political Science Review, 80*(2), 505–519.

Loewenstein, G. (1996). Out of control: Visceral influences on behavior. *Organizational Behavior and Human Decision Processes, 65*(3), 272–292.

(1999). Experimental economics from the vantage-point of behavioural economics. *Economic Journal, 109*(453), F25–F34.

(2000). Emotions in economic theory and economic behavior. *American Economic Review, 90*(2), 426–432.

(2007). Affect regulation and affective forecasting. In J. J. Gross (Ed.), *Handbook of emotion regulation,* 180–203. New York: Guilford Press.

(2011). Confronting reality: Pitfalls of calorie posting. *American Journal of Clinical Nutrition, 93*(4), 679–680.

Loewenstein, G., & Ubel, P. (2010). Economics behaving badly. *New York Times,* July 15. Retrieved from https://nytimes.com/2010/07/15/opinion/15loewenstein.html?_r=2&hp

(2008). Hedonic adaptation and the role of decision and experience utility in public policy. *Journal of Public Economics, 92*(8), 1795–1810.

Loewenstein, G., John, L. K., & Volpp, K. (2012). Using decision errors to help people help themselves. In E. Shafir (Ed.), *The behavioral foundations of public policy,* 361–379. Princeton, NJ: Princeton University Press.

Löfgren, Å., Martinsson, P., Hennlock, M., & Sterner, T. (2012). Are experienced people affected by a pre-set default option: Results from a field experiment. *Journal of Environmental Economics and Management, 63*(1), 66–72.

Long, R. T. (2010). Wittgenstein on rule-following. In K. D. Jolley (Ed.), *Wittgenstein: Key concepts,* 81–91. Durham, UK: Acumen Press.

Loomis, J. (2011). What's to know about hypothetical bias in stated preference valuation studies? *Journal of Economic Surveys, 25*(2), 363–370.

Lopes, L. L., & Oden, G. C. (1991). The rationality of intelligence. *Poznan Studies in the Philosophy of the Sciences and the Humanities, 21,* 199–223.

Lord, C. G., Ross, L., & Lepper, M. R. (1979). Biased assimilation and attitude polarization: The effects of prior theories on subsequently considered evidence. *Journal of Personality and Social Psychology, 37*(11), 2098–2109.

Lovelace, B., Jr. (2017). FDA commissioner: Safer tobacco products can provide 'satisfying levels of nicotine' to people who want it. CNBC, August 24. Retrieved from www.cnbc.com/2017/08/24/fda-tobacco-product-innovations-can-provide-satisfying-levels-of-nicotine.html

Lucas, G. M., Jr. (2012). Paternalism and psychic taxes: The government's use of negative emotions to save us from ourselves. *Southern California Interdisciplinary Law Journal, 22*, 227–302.

(2015). Out of sight, out of mind: How opportunity cost neglect undermines democracy. *NYU Journal of Law & Liberty, 9*, 249–343.

Lucas, G. M., Jr., & Tasic, S. (2015). Behavioral public choice and the law. *West Virginia Law Review, 118*, 199–264.

Luce, R. D., & Raiffa, H. (1957). *Games and decisions: Introduction and critical surveys.* New York: Wiley.

Lundgren, S. R., & Prislin, R. (1998). Motivated cognitive processing and attitude change. *Personality and Social Psychology Bulletin, 24*(7), 715–726.

Lusardi, A., & Mitchell, O. S. (2014). The economic importance of financial literacy: Theory and evidence. *Journal of Economic Literature, 52*(1), 5–44.

Lusardi, A., Keller, P. A., & Keller, A. M. (2009). New ways to make people save: A social marketing approach. In A. Lusardi (Ed.), *Overcoming the saving slump: How to increase the effectiveness of financial education and saving programs,* 209–235. Chicago, IL: University of Chicago Press.

Macdonald, R. R., & Gilhooly, K. J. (1990). More about Linda: Or conjunctions in context. *European Journal of Cognitive Psychology, 2*(1), 57–70.

McGinley, L., & Dennis, B. (2016). The federal government is about to begin regulating the booming e-cigarette market.*Washington Post*, May 5. Retrieved from www.washingtonpost.com/national/health-science/the-federal-government-is-about-to-begin-regulating-the-booming-e-cigarette-market/2016/05/05/d22ddec0-130b-11e6-93ae-50921721165d_story.html

Machlup, F. (1974). Spiro Latsis on situational determinism. *British Journal for the Philosophy of Science, 25*(3), 271–284.

Maciejovsky, B., & Budescu, D. V. (2007). Collective induction without cooperation? Learning and knowledge transfer in cooperative groups and competitive auctions. *Journal of Personality and Social Psychology, 92*(5), 854–870.

McKenzie, C. R. (2003). Rational models as theories – not standards – of behavior. *Trends in Cognitive Sciences, 7*, 403–406.

McKenzie, C. R., & Nelson, J. D. (2003). What a speaker's choice of frame reveals: Reference points, frame selection, and framing effects. *Psychonomic Bulletin & Review, 10*(3), 596–602.

McKenzie, C. R., Liersch, M. J., & Finkelstein, S. R. (2006). Recommendations implicit in policy defaults. *Psychological Science, 17*(5), 414–420.

McKenzie, C. R., Liersch, M. J., & Yaniv, I. (2008). Overconfidence in interval estimates: What does expertise buy you? *Organizational Behavior and Human Decision Processes, 107*(2), 179–191.

McNamara, J. M., Trimmer, P. C., & Houston, A. I. (2014). Natural selection can favour "irrational" behaviour. *Biology Letters, 10*(1), 20130935.

McNeill, A., Brose, L. S., Calder, R., Hitchman, S. C., Hajek, P., & McRobbie, R. (2015). *E-cigarettes: An evidence update.* Public Health England. Retrieved from https://

assets.publishing.service.gov.uk/government/uploads/system/uploads/attachment_data/file/733022/Ecigarettes_an_evidence_update_A_report_commissioned_by_Public_Health_England_FINAL.pdf

Maler, K.-G., & Vincent, J. R. (2005). *Handbook of environmental economics*, Vol. 2. Burlington, MA: Elsevier.

Malmendier, U., & Taylor, T. (2015). On the verges of overconfidence. *Journal of Economic Perspectives, 29*(4), 3–7.

Manzini, P., & Mariotti, M. (2006). A vague theory of choice over time. *Advances in Theoretical Economics, 6*(1), 1–27.

(2009). Choice over time. In P. Anand, P. Pattanaik, & C. Puppe (Eds.), *The handbook of rational and social choice*, 240–270. Oxford, UK: Oxford University Press.

Maor, M. (2012). Policy overreaction. *Journal of Public Policy, 32*(3), 231–259.

Marewski, J. N., Gaissmaier, W., & Gigerenzer, G. (2010). Good judgments do not require complex cognition. *Cognitive Process, 11*, 103–121.

Markey, O., Le Jeune, J., & Lovegrove, J. A. (2016). Energy compensation following consumption of sugar-reduced products: A randomized controlled trial. *European Journal of Nutrition, 55*(6), 2137–2149.

Marzilli Ericson, K. M., & Fuster, A. (2014). The endowment effect. *Annual Review of Economics, 6*(1), 555–579.

Mas-Colell, A., Whinston, M. D., & Green, J. R. (1995). *Microeconomic theory*. New York: Oxford University Press.

Mast, B. D., Benson, B. L., & Rasmussen, D. W. (1999). Beer taxation and alcohol-related traffic fatalities. *Southern Economic Journal, 66*(2), 214–249.

Mattes, R. D., & Popkin, B. M. (2009). Nonnutritive sweetener consumption in humans: Effects on appetite and food intake and their putative mechanisms. *American Journal of Clinical Nutrition, 89*(1), 1–14.

Menger, C. (1981). *Principles of economics*. Translated by I. Dingwall & B. F. Hoselitz. New York: New York University Press.

Merton, R. C. (1973). An intertemporal capital asset pricing model. *Econometrica, 41*(5), 867–887.

Messer, W. S., & Griggs, R. A. (1993). Another look at Linda. *Bulletin of the Psychonomic Society, 31*(3), 193–196.

Mick, D. G. (1991). Giving gifts to ourselves: A Greimassian analysis leading to testable propositions. In H. H. Larsen, D. G. Mick, & C. Alsted (Eds.), *Marketing and semiotics: Selected papers from the Copenhagen symposium*, 142–159. Copenhagen, Denmark: Handelshojskolens Forlag.

(1996). Self-gifts. In C. Otnes & R. F. Beltramini (Eds.), *Gift giving: A research anthology*, 99–120. Bowling Green, OH: Bowling Green State University Popular Press.

Mick, D. M., & DeMoss, M. (1990). Self-gifts: Phenomenological insights from four contexts. *Journal of Consumer Research, 17*(3), 322–332.

Mill, J. S. (1989 [1859]). *On liberty and other writings*. Edited by S. Collini. Cambridge, UK: Cambridge University Press.

Miller, V., Mente, A., Dehghan, M., Rangarajan, S., Zhang, X., Swaminathan, S., ... & Bangdiwala, S. I. (2017). Fruit, vegetable, and legume intake, and cardiovascular disease and deaths in 18 countries (PURE): A prospective cohort study. *The Lancet, 390*(10107), 2037–2049.

Miloyan, B., & Suddendorf, T. (2015). Feelings of the future. *Trends in Cognitive Sciences, 19*(4), 196–200.

Minger, D. (2014). *Death by food pyramid: How shoddy science, sketchy politics and shady special interests have ruined our health* [Kindle version]. New York: Primal Nutrition.

Miron, J. A., & Zwiebel, J. (1995). The economic case against drug prohibition. *Journal of Economic Perspectives, 9*(4), 175–192.

Mirpuri, V. (2016). Non-discrimination testing: The basics of IRS 401(k) compliance [Blog post]. *Human Interest Blog*, May 27.

Mischel, W., Shoda, Y., & Rodriguez, M. I. (1989). Delay of gratification in children. *Science, 244*(4907), 933–938.

Mises, L. von. (1949). *Human action: A treatise on economics*. New Haven, CT: Yale University Press.

Mitchell, G. (2002). Why law and economics' perfect rationality should not be traded for behavioral law and economics' equal incompetence. *Georgetown Law Journal, 91*, 67–168.

(2005). Libertarian paternalism is an oxymoron. *Northwestern University Law Review, 99*(3), 1245–1277.

Moore, D. A., Tenney, E. R., & Haran, U. (2015). Overprecision in judgment. In G. Wu and G. Keren (Eds.), *The Wiley Blackwell handbook of judgment and decision making*, 182–209. Chichster, UK: Wiley-Blackwell.

Morewedge, C. K., & Buechel, E. C. (2013). Motivated underpinnings of the impact bias in affective forecasts. *Emotion, 13*(6), 1023–1029.

Morewedge, C. K., Shu, L. L., Gilbert, D. T., & Wilson, T. D. (2009). Bad riddance or good rubbish? Ownership and not loss aversion causes the endowment effect. *Journal of Experimental Social Psychology, 45*(4), 947–951.

Morris, J., & Khan, A. U. (2016). The vapour revolution: How bottom-up innovation is saving lives. Reason Foundation Working Paper. Retrieved from https://reason .org/wp-content/uploads/2016/08/vapour_revolution_working_paper.pdf

Mousavi, S., & Gigerenzer, G. (2014). Risk, uncertainty, and heuristics. *Journal of Business Research, 67*(8), 1671–1678.

Muraven, M., & Baumeister, R. F. (2000). Self-regulation and depletion of limited resources: Does self-control resemble a muscle? *Psychological Bulletin, 126*(2), 247–259.

Murphy, J. J., Allen, P. G., Stevens, T. H., & Weatherhead, D. (2005). A meta-analysis of hypothetical bias in stated preference valuation. *Environmental and Resource Economics, 30*(3), 313–325.

Myers, R. L. (2007). *The 100 most important chemical compounds: A reference guide*. Westport, CT: Greenwood Press.

Myrseth, K. O. R., Fishbach, A., & Trope, Y. (2009). Counteractive self-control: When making temptation available makes temptation less tempting. *Psychological Science, 20*(2), 159–163.

Nestle, M. (1993). Food lobbies, the food pyramid, and US nutrition policy. *International Journal of Health Services, 23*(3), 483–496.

Nickerson, R. S. (1998). Confirmation bias: A ubiquitous phenomenon in many guises. *Review of General Psychology, 2*(2), 175–220.

Nicolle, A., Fleming, S. M., Bach, D. R., Driver, J., & Dolan, R. J. (2011). A regret-induced status quo bias. *Journal of Neuroscience, 31*(9), 3320–3327.

Nilsson, H., Olsson, H., & Juslin, P. (2005). The cognitive substrate of subjective probability. *Journal of Experimental Psychology: Learning, Memory, and Cognition, 31*(4), 600–620.

Niskanen, W. A. (1971). *Bureaucracy and representative government.* Chicago, IL: Aldine, Atherton.

(1991). A reflection on bureaucracy and representative government. In A. Blais and S. Dion (Eds.), *The budget-maximizing bureaucrat,* 13–33. Pittsburgh, PA: University of Pittsburgh Press.

Nolen-Hoeksema, S., & Corte, C. (2004). Gender and self-regulation. In R. F. Baumeister & K. D. Vohs (Eds.), *Handbook of self-regulation: Research, theory, and applications* (2nd ed.), 411–421. New York: Guilford Publications.

Non-discrimination testing: The basics of IRS 401(k) compliance. (2016). *Human Interest,* May 27. Retrieved from https://humaninterest.com/blog/non-discrimination-testing-ndt-the-basics-of-401k-compliance

Nozick, R. (1993). *The nature of rationality.* Princeton, NJ: Princeton University Press.

Oaksford, M., & Chater, N. (1996). Rational explanation of the selection task. *Psychological Review, 103*(2), 381–391.

(2009). Précis of Bayesian rationality: The probabilistic approach to human reasoning. *Behavioral and Brain Sciences, 32*(1), 69–84.

O'Donoghue, T., & Rabin, M. (1998). Procrastination in preparing for retirement. University of California-Berkeley Working Paper. Retrieved from www.wiwi.uni-bonn.de/kraehmer/Lehre/Beh_Econ/Papiere/ODonoghue-Rabin-retire.pdf

(2003). Studying optimal paternalism, illustrated by a model of sin taxes. *American Economic Review, 93*(2), 186–191.

(2006). Optimal sin taxes. *Journal of Public Economics, 90*(10), 1825–1849.

(2015). Present bias: Lessons learned and to be learned. *American Economic Review, 105*(5), 273–279.

O'Donoghue, T., & Sprenger, C. (2018). Reference-dependent preferences. In B. D. Bernheim & S. Della Vigna, & D. Laibson (Eds.), *Handbook of behavioral economics: Foundations and applications,* Vol. 2. Amsterdam: North Holland.

Oliver, J. E. (2006). *Fat politics: The real story behind America's obesity epidemic.* Oxford, UK: Oxford University Press.

Olson, M. (1965). *Logic of collective action: Public goods and the theory of groups.* New York: Schocken Books.

Olsson, H. (2014). Measuring overconfidence: Methodological problems and statistical artifacts. *Journal of Business Research, 67*(8), 1766–1770.

Open Science Collaboration. (2015). Estimating the reproducibility of psychological science. *Science, 349*(6251). http://dx.doi.org/10.1126/science.aac4716

Oppenheimer, D. M. (2004). Spontaneous discounting of availability in frequency judgment tasks. *Psychological Science, 15*(2), 100–105.

Otsuka, R., Watanabe, H., Hirata, K., Tokai, K., Muro, T., Yoshiyama, M., ... & Yoshikawa, J. (2001). Acute effects of passive smoking on the coronary circulation in healthy young adults. *Journal of the American Medical Association, 286*(4), 436–441.

Patt, A., & Zeckhauser, R. (2000). Action bias and environmental decisions. *Journal of Risk and Uncertainty, 21*(1), 45–72.

Payne, J. W., Bettman, J. R., & Johnson, E. J. (1992). Behavioral decision research: A constructive processing perspective. *Annual Review of Psychology, 43,* 87–131.

Pechacek, T. F., & Babb, S. (2004). How acute and reversible are the cardiovascular risks of secondhand smoke? *British Medical Journal, 328*(7446), 980–983.

Peters, J. C., & Beck, J. (2016). Low calorie sweetener (LCS) use and energy balance. *Physiology & Behavior, 164,* 524–528.

Peters, J. W. (2007). In small packages, fewer calories and more profit. *New York Times,* July 7, C1.

Plan Sponsor Council of America. (2018). *60th annual survey of profit sharing and 401 (k) plans.* Chicago, IL: Plan Sponsor Council of America.

Plott, C. R., & Zeiler, K. (2005). The willingness to pay–willingness to accept gap, the "endowment effect," subject misconceptions, and experimental procedures for eliciting valuations. *American Economic Review, 95*(3), 530–545.

(2007). Exchange asymmetries incorrectly interpreted as evidence of endowment effect theory and prospect theory? *American Economic Review, 97*(4), 1449–1466.

Politzer, G., & Bonnefon, J. F. (2009). Let us not put the probabilistic card before the uncertainty bull. *Behavioral and Brain Sciences, 32*(1), 100–101.

Posner, R. A. (2007). Libertarian paternalism: Posner's comment [Blog post]. Retrieved from www.becker-posner-blog.com/2007/01/libertarian-paternalism–posners-comment.html

(1972). A theory of negligence. *Journal of Legal Studies, 1,* 29–96.

Prelec, D. (2004). Decreasing impatience: A criterion for non-stationary time preference and "hyperbolic" discounting. *Scandinavian Journal of Economics, 106*(3), 511–532.

Puri, M., & Robinson, D. T. (2007). Optimism and economic choice. *Journal of Financial Economics, 86,* 71–99.

Quinn, M. (2014). Turns out the 113th Congress wasn't the "least productive." *Daily Signal,* December 30. Retrieved from http://dailysignal.com/2014/12/30/turns-113th-congress-wasnt-least-productive

Rabin, M. (1998). Psychology and economics. *Journal of Economic Literature, 36,* 11–46.

(1999). Comment. In H. Aaron (Ed.), *Behavioral dimensions of retirement economics,* 247–252. Washington, DC: Brookings Institution Press.

Rabinowicz, W. (2000). Money pump with foresight. In M. Almeida (Ed.), *Imperceptible harms and benefits,* 123–154. Dordrecht, Netherlands: Kluwer.

Raloff, J. (2014). Health risks of e-cigarettes emerge. *Science News,* June 3. Retrieved from www.sciencenews.org/article/health-risks-e-cigarettes-emerge

Read, D. (2001). Is time-discounting hyperbolic or subadditive?. *Journal of Risk and Uncertainty, 23*(1), 5–32.

(2004). Intertemporal choice. In D. Koehler & N. Harvey (Eds.), *Blackwell handbook of judgment and decision making,* 424–443. John Wiley & Sons.

(2006). Which side are you on? The ethics of self-command. *Journal of Economic Psychology, 27*(5), 681–693.

Read, D., & Grushka-Cockayne, Y. (2011). The similarity heuristic. *Journal of Behavioral Decision Making, 24*(1), 23–46.

Read, D., Frederick, S., & Airoldi, M. (2012). Four days later in Cincinnati: Longitudinal tests of hyperbolic discounting. *Acta Psychologica, 140*(2), 177–185.

Read, S. (1995). *Thinking about logic: An introduction to the philosophy of logic.* Oxford, UK: Oxford University Press.

Redelmeier, D. A., & Kahneman, D. (1996). Patients' memories of painful medical treatments: Real-time and retrospective evaluations of two minimally invasive procedures. *Pain, 66*, 3–8.

Redelmeier, D. A., Rozin, P., & Kahneman, D. (1993). Understanding patients' decisions: Cognitive and emotional perspectives. *JAMA, 270*(1), 72–76.

Reinhard, M. A., Schindler, S., Raabe, V., Stahlberg, D., & Messner, M. (2014). Less is sometimes more: How repetition of an antismoking advertisement affects attitudes toward smoking and source credibility. *Social Influence, 9*(2), 116–132.

Rescher, N. (1987). How serious a fallacy is inconsistency? *Argumentation, 1*(3), 303–316.

(1988). *Rationality: A philosophical inquiry into the nature and rationale of reason.* Oxford, UK: Clarendon Press.

Rich, Nathaniel. (2011). Bad things happen to bad children. *Slate.com*, October 24.

Rizzo, M. J. (2005). The problem of moral dirigisme: A new argument against moralistic legislation. *NYU Journal of Law & Liberty, 1*, 789–843.

(2007). Trust us. *Forbes*, June 18, 30. Retrieved from www.forbes.com/columnists/forbes/2007/0618/030.html?partner=whiteglove_google

(2014). James M. Buchanan: Through an Austrian window. *Review of Austrian Economics, 27*(2), 135–145.

(2016). Behavioral economics and deficient willpower: Searching for akrasia. *Georgetown Journal of Law & Public Policy, 14*, 789–806.

Rizzo, M. J., & Whitman, D. G. (2003). The camel's nose is in the tent: Rules, theories, and slippery slopes. *UCLA Law Review, 51*(2), 539–592.

(2007). *Meet the new boss, same as the old boss: A critique of the new paternalism.* Unpublished manuscript, New York University, New York.

(2009a). Little brother is watching you: New paternalism on the slippery slopes. *Arizona Law Review, 51*, 685–739.

(2009b). The knowledge problem of new paternalism. *Brigham Young University Law Review, 2009*(4), 905–968.

Robbins, L. (1935). *An essay on the nature & significance of economic science* (2nd ed.). London: Macmillan.

Rockenbach, B., Sadrieh, A., & Mathauschek, B. (2007). Teams take the better risks. *Journal of Economic Behavior & Organization, 63*(3), 412–422.

Roelofsma, P. H., & Read, D. (2000). Intransitive intertemporal choice. *Journal of Behavioral Decision Making, 13*(2), 161–177.

Rosenthal, R. (1979). The file drawer problem and tolerance for null results. *Psychological Bulletin, 86*(3), 638–641.

Rothman, A. J., & Schwarz, N. (1998). Constructing perceptions of vulnerability: Personal relevance and the use of experiential information in health judgments. *Personality and Social Psychology Bulletin, 24*, 1053–1064.

Rouvray, D. H. (1992). Definition and role of similarity concepts in the chemical and physical sciences. *Journal of Chemical Information and Computer Sciences, 32*(6), 580–586.

Rozenblit, L., & Keil, F. (2002). The misunderstood limits of folk science: An illusion of explanatory depth. *Cognitive Science, 26*(5), 521–562.

Rubinstein, A. (2003). "Economics and psychology"? The case of hyperbolic discounting. *International Economic Review, 44*(4), 1207–1216.

Rubinstein, A., & Salant, Y. (2008). Some thoughts on the principle of revealed preference. In A. Caplin & A. Schotter (Eds.), *The foundations of positive and normative economics: A handbook*, 116–124. Oxford, UK: Oxford University Press.

Russo, J. E., & Leclerc, F. (1991). Characteristics of successful product information programs. *Journal of Social Issues, 47*(1), 73–92.

Safe Kids Worldwide. (2013). Poisoning safety fact sheet. Washington, DC.

Sambrook, T. D., Hardwick, B., Wills, A. J., & Goslin, J. (2018). Model-free and model-based reward prediction errors in EEG. *NeuroImage, 178*, 162–171.

Samson, A. (Ed.). (2014). *The behavioural economics guide.* Retrieved from www.behavioraleconomics.com/introduction-behavioral-economics/

Samuelson, P. A. (1938). A note on the pure theory of consumer's behaviour. *Economica, 5*(17), 61–71.

Samuelson, W., & Zeckhauser, R. (1988). Status quo bias in decision making. *Journal of Risk and Uncertainty*, 1, 7–59.

Sandroni, A., & Katz, L. (2014). Why law breeds cycles. Unpublished manuscript, Northwestern University, Evanston, IL.

Savage, L. J. (1954). *The foundations of statistics.* New York: John Wiley.

Sawyer, K. R., Beed, C., & Sankey, H. (1997). Underdetermination in economics: The Duhem-Quine thesis. *Economics and Philosophy, 13*(1), 1–23.

Sayman, S., & Öncüler, A. (2009). An investigation of time inconsistency. *Management Science, 55*(3), 470–482.

Scargle, J. (2000). Publication bias: The "file-drawer" problem in scientific inference. *Journal of Scientific Exploration, 14*(1), 91–106.

Schauer, F. (1985). Slippery slopes. *Harvard Law Review, 99*(2), 361–383.

Scheall, S., Butos, W. N., & McQuade, T. (2018). Social and scientific disorder as epistemic phenomena, or the consequences of government dietary guidelines. *Journal of Institutional Economics, 15*(3), 1–17.

Schelling, T. C. (1978). Egonomics, or the art of self-management. *American Economic Review, 68*(2), 290–294.

(1984). Self-command in practice, in policy, and in a theory of rational choice. *American Economic Review, 74*(2), 1–11.

Schimmack, U. (2012). The ironic effect of significant results on the credibility of multiple-study articles. *Psychological Methods, 17*(4), 551.

Schimmack, U., Heene, M., & Kesavan, K. (2017). Reconstruction of a train wreck: How priming research went off the rails [Blog post]. *Replicability Index.* Retrieved from https://replicationindex.wordpress.com/2017/02/02/reconstruction-of-a-train-wreck-how-priming-research-went-of-the-rails/

Schmidt, F. L., & Hunter, J. E. (2015). *Methods of meta-analysis: Correcting error and bias in research findings.* Thousand Oaks, CA: Sage Publications.

Schooler, L. J., & Hertwig, R. (2005). How forgetting aids heuristic influence. *Psychological Bulletin, 112,* 610–628.

Schultz, W. (2015). Neuronal reward and decision signals: From theories to data. *Physiological Reviews, 95*(3), 853–951.

(2016). Dopamine reward prediction error coding. *Dialogues in Clinical Neuroscience, 18*(1), 23–32.

Schultz, W., & Dickinson, A. (2000). Neuronal coding of prediction errors. *Annual Review of Neuroscience, 23*(1), 473–500.

Schulze, C., & Newell, B. R. (2016). More heads choose better than one: Group decision making can eliminate probability matching. *Psychonomic Bulletin & Review, 23*(3), 907–914.

Schumpeter, J. A. (2010 [1908]). *The nature and essence of economic theory.* Translated by B. A. McDaniel. New Brunswick, NJ: Transaction Publishers.

Schutz, A. (1962). Common–sense and the scientific interpretation of human action. In M. Natanson (Ed.), *Collected papers I: The problem of social reality,* 3–47. The Hague, Netherlands: Martinus Nijhoff.

Schwarz, N. (1998). Accessible content and accessibility experiences: The interplay of declarative and experiential information in judgment. *Personality and Social Psychology Review, 2*(2), 87–99.

Schwarz, N., Bless, H., Strack, F., Klumpp, G., Rittenauer-Schatka, H., & Simons, A. (1991). Ease of retrieval as information: Another look at the availability heuristic. *Journal of Personality and Social Psychology, 61*(2), 195–202.

Searle, J. (1969). *Speech acts: An essay in the philosophy of language.* Cambridge, UK: Cambridge University Press.

Sedlmeier, P., Hertwig, R., & Gigerenzer, G. (1998). Are judgments of the positional frequencies of letters systematically biased due to availability? *Journal of Experimental Psychology: Learning, Memory, and Cognition, 24*(3), 754–770.

Sen, A. (1993). Internal consistency of choice. *Econometrica, 61*(3), 495–521.

(1997). Maximization and the act of choice. *Econometrica, 65*(4), 745–779.

(2007). Unrestrained smoking is a libertarian half-way house. *Financial Times,* February 11. Retrieved from www.ft.com/cms/s/0/c8617786-ba13-11db-89c8-0000779e2340.html

Shackle, G. L. S. (1961). *Decision, order, and time in human affairs.* Cambridge, UK: Cambridge University Press.

Shafir, E. (Ed.). (2012). *The behavioral foundations of public policy.* Princeton, NJ: Princeton University Press.

Shah, A. K., Shafir, E., & Mullainathan, S. (2015). Scarcity frames value. *Psychological Science, 26*(4), 402–412.

Sharot, T. (2011). The optimism bias. *Current Biology, 21*(23), R941–R945.

Sharpe, M. J., Chang, C. Y., Liu, M. A., Batchelor, H. M., Mueller, L. E., Jones, J. L., . . . & Schoenbaum, G. (2017). Dopamine transients are sufficient and necessary for acquisition of model-based associations. *Nature Neuroscience, 20*(5), 735–742.

Sher, S., & McKenzie, C. R. (2006). Information leakage from logically equivalent frames. *Cognition, 101*(3), 467–494

Shimokawa, S. (2016). Why can calorie posting be apparently ineffective? The roles of two conflicting learning effects. *Food Policy, 64,* 107–120.

Shogren, J. (2005). Experimental methods and valuation. In K. G. Mäler & J. R. Vincent (Eds.), *Handbook of environmental economics*, Vol. 2, 970–1027. Burlington, MA: Elsevier.

Siegel, M. (2007). Is the tobacco control movement misrepresenting the acute cardiovascular health effects of secondhand smoke exposure? An analysis of the scientific evidence and commentary on the implications for tobacco control and public health practice. *Epidemiologic Perspectives & Innovations*, 4(1), 1–13. http://doi:10.1186/1742-5573-4-12

Siegmund, B., Leitner, E., & Pfannhauser, W. (1999). Determination of the nicotine content of various edible nightshades (Solanaceae) and their products and estimation of the associated dietary nicotine intake. *Journal of Agricultural and Food Chemistry*, 47(8), 3113–3120. Retrieved from www.ncbi.nlm.nih.gov/pubmed/10552617

Sifferlin, A. (2015). Health experts angry FDA still doesn't regulate e-cigarettes. *Time*, May 1. Retrieved from http://time.com/3843214/e-cigarettes-regulation-health-experts/

Simard, F. (2004). Self-interest in public administration: Niskanen and the budget-maximizing bureaucrat. *Canadian Public Administration*, 47(3), 406–411.

Simonson, I. (1989). Choice based on reasons: The case of attraction and compromise effects. *Journal of Consumer Research*, 16(2), 158–174.

Simonson, I., & Tversky, A. (1992). Choice in context: Tradeoff contrast and extremeness aversion. *Journal of Marketing Research*, 29(3), 281–295.

Sloan, F. A., Mathews, C. A., & Trogdon, J. G. (2004). Impacts of the Master Settlement Agreement on the tobacco industry. *Tobacco Control*, 13(4), 356–361.

Slonim, R., Wang, C., Garbarino, E., & Merrett, D. (2013). Opting-in: Participation bias in economic experiments. *Journal of Economic Behavior & Organization*, 90, 43–70.

Smith, A. (1976 [1776]). *An inquiry into the nature and causes of the wealth of nations*. Oxford, UK: Clarendon Press.

Smith, A. C., & Yandle, B. (2014). *Bootleggers & Baptists: How economic forces and moral persuasion interact to shape regulatory politics*. Washington, DC: Cato Institute.

Smith, C. A., & Ellsworth, P. C. (1985). Patterns of cognitive appraisal in emotion. *Journal of Personality and Social Psychology*, 48(4), 813–838.

Smith, V. L. (2005). Behavioral economics research and the foundations of economics. *Journal of Socio-Economics*, 34(2), 135–150.

Smith, V. L., & Walker, J. M. (1993). Rewards, experience and decision costs in first price auctions. *Economic Inquiry*, 31(2), 237–244.

Sniezek, J. A., & Henry, R. A. (1989). Accuracy and confidence in group judgment. *Organizational Behavior and Human Decision Processes*, 43(1), 1–28.

So, J., Kim, S., & Cohen, H. (2017). Message fatigue: Conceptual definition, operationalization, and correlates. *Communication Monographs*, 84(1), 5–29.

Soll, J. B., & Klayman, J. (2004). Overconfidence in interval estimates. *Journal of Experimental Psychology: Learning, Memory, and Cognition*, 30(2), 299–314.

Soman, D., Ainslie, G., Frederick, S., Li, X., Lynch, J., Moreau, P., . . . & Wertenbroch, K. (2005). The psychology of intertemporal discounting: Why are distant events valued differently from proximal ones? *Marketing Letters*, 16(3), 347–360.

Somin, I. (2016). *Democracy and political ignorance: Why smaller government is smarter* [E-reader version]. Stanford, CA: Stanford University Press.

Soto, D., Mäntylä, T., & Silvanto, J. (2011). Working memory without consciousness. *Current Biology, 21*(22), R912–R913.

Spencer, H. (1981 [1884]). The coming slavery. In E. Mack (Ed.), *The man versus the state*, 31–70. Indianapolis, IN: Liberty Classics.

Spiegler, R. (2015). On the equilibrium effects of nudging. *Journal of Legal Studies, 44*(2), 389–416.

Sprenger, C. (2015). Judging experimental evidence on dynamic inconsistency. *American Economic Review, 105*(5), 280–285.

Stanovich, K. E., & Toplak, M. E. (2012). Defining features versus incidental correlates of type 1 and type 2 processing. *Mind & Society, 11*, 3–13.

Stauffer, W. R., Lak, A., & Schultz, W. (2014). Dopamine reward prediction error responses reflect marginal utility. *Current Biology, 24*(21), 2491–2500.

Stevens, J. R. (2016). Intertemporal similarity: Discounting as a last resort. *Journal of Behavioral Decision Making, 29*(1), 12–24.

Stigler, G. J. (1971). The theory of economic regulation. *Bell Journal of Economics and Management Science, 2*(1), 3–21.

Stochastic Dominance. (n.d.). In *Wikipedia*. Retrieved from https://en.wikipedia.org/wiki/Stochastic_dominance

Strahilevitz, M. A., & Loewenstein, G. (1998). The effect of ownership history on the valuation of objects. *Journal of Consumer Research, 25*(3), 276–289.

Strotz, R. H. (1955–1956). Myopia and inconsistency in dynamic utility maximization. *Review of Economic Studies, 23*(3), 165–180.

Sugden, R. (2015). Looking for a psychology for the inner rational agent. *Social Theory and Practice, 41*(4), 579–598.

Sullivan, K., & Kida, T. (1995). The effect of multiple reference points and prior gains and losses on managers' risky decision making. *Organizational Behavior and Human Decision Processes, 64*(1), 76–83.

Sunstein, C. R. (2014). *Why nudge? The politics of libertarian paternalism*. New Haven, CT: Yale University Press.

(2015). Nudges, agency, and abstraction: A reply to critics. *Review of Philosophy and Psychology, 6*(3), 511–529.

Sunstein, C. R., & Thaler, R. H. (2003). Libertarian paternalism is not an oxymoron. *University of Chicago Law Review, 70*(4), 1159–1202.

Sweanor (2018). www.clivebates.com/tobacco-control-and-the-tobacco-industry-a-failure-of-understanding-and-imagination/

Taber, C. S., & Lodge, M. (2006). Motivated skepticism in the evaluation of political beliefs. *American Journal of Political Science, 50*(3), 755–769.

Tang, N., & Lachance, M. E. (2012). Financial advice: What about low income consumers?. *Journal of Personal Finance, 11*(2), 121–158.

Tannenbaum, D., & Ditto, P. H. (2011). Information asymmetries in default options. Working Paper. Retrieved from http://home.uchicago.edu/davetannenbaum/documents/default%20information

Tasic, S. (2009). The illusion of regulatory competence. *Critical Review, 21*(4), 423–436.

(2011). Are regulators rational? *Journal des conomistes et des tudes Humaines, 17*(1), 1–19.

Tavernise, S. (2015). Swedish company asks F.D.A. to remove warnings from smokeless tobacco product. *New York Times*, April 8.

Taylor, S. E., & Thompson, S. C. (1982). Stalking the elusive "vividness" effect. *Psychological Review, 89*(2), 155–181.

Tentori, K., Crupi, V., & Russo, S. (2013). On the determinants of the conjunction fallacy: Probability vs. inductive confirmation. *Journal of Experimental Psychology: General, 142*(1), 235–255.

Tergesen, A. (2011). 401(k) law suppresses savings for retirement. *Wall Street Journal*, July 7. Available at www.wsj.com/articles/SB10001424052702303365804576430153643522780

(2018). 401(k) or ATM? Automated retirement savings prove easy to pluck prematurely. *Wall Street Journal*, August 10, B8.

Thaler, R. H. (1981). Some empirical evidence on dynamic inconsistency. *Economics Letters, 8*(3), 201–207.

(1985). Mental accounting and consumer choice. *Marketing Science, 4*(3), 199–214.

(1991). *Quasi rational economics.* New York: Russell Sage.

(2015a). *Misbehaving: How economics became behavioural.* London, UK: Allen Lane.

(2015b). *Misbehaving: The making of behavioral economics.* New York: W. W. Norton.

Thaler, R. H., & Benartzi, S. (2004). Save more tomorrow: Using behavioral economics to increase employee saving. *Journal of Political Economy, 112*(1), S164–S187.

Thaler, R. H., & Rizzo, M. J. (2007). Should policies nudge people to make certain choices? *Wall Street Journal*, May 25. Retrieved from www.wsj.com/articles/SB117977357721809835

Thaler, R. H., & Sunstein, C. R. (2003). Libertarian paternalism. *American Economic Review, 93*(2), 175–179.

(2008). *Nudge: Improving decisions about health, wealth, and happiness.* New Haven, CT: Yale University Press.

(2009). *Nudge: The gentle power of choice architecture* [Kindle version].

Thaler, R. H., Tversky, A., Kahneman, D., & Schwartz, A. (1997). The effect of myopia and loss aversion on risk taking: An experimental test. *Quarterly Journal of Economics, 112*(2), 647–661.

Tiihonen, J., Ronkainen, K., Kangasharju, A., & Kauhanen, J. (2012). The net effect of smoking on healthcare and welfare costs: A cohort study. *BMJ Open, 2*(6), 1–6. Retrieved from http://doi:10.1136/bmjopen-2012-001678

Tobler, P. N., O'Doherty, J. P., Dolan, R. J., & Schultz, W. (2006). Human neural learning depends on reward prediction errors in the blocking paradigm. *Journal of Neurophysiology, 95*(1), 301–310.

Todd, P. M., & Goodie, A. S. (2002). Testing the ecological rationality of base rate neglect. In B. Hallam, D. Floreano, J. Hallam, G. Hayes, and J. A. Meyer (Eds.), *From animals to animals 7: Proceedings of the Seventh International Conference on Simulation of Adaptive Behavior.* Cambridge, MA: MIT Press. 215–223.

Todd, P. M., Gigerenzer, G., & ABC Research Group (Eds.). 2012 *Ecological rationality: Intelligence in the world.* Oxford, UK: Oxford University Press. Cambridge, MA: MIT Press/Bradford Books.

Tompson, T., Benz, J., Agiesta, J., Brewer, K. H., Bye, L., Reimer, R., & Junius, D. (2012) *Obesity in the United States: Public perceptions.* Chicago: The Associated Press-NORC Center for Public Affairs Research.

Trope, Y., & Fishbach, A. (2005). Going beyond the motivation given. In R. R. Hassin, J. S. Uleman, & J. A. Bargh (Eds.), *The new unconscious*, 537–565. Oxford, UK: Oxford University Press.

Tversky, A. (1975). A critique of expected utility theory: Descriptive and normative considerations. *Erkenntnis, 9*(2), 163–173.

Tversky, A., & Kahneman, D. (1973). Availability: A heuristic for judging frequency and probability. *Cognitive Psychology, 5*(2), 207–232.

(1974). Judgment under uncertainty: Heuristics and biases. *Science, 185*, 1124–1130.

(1980). Causal schemata in judgments under uncertainty. In M. Fishbein (Ed.), *Progress in social psychology*, Vol. 1, 49–72. Hillsdale, NJ: Erlbaum.

(1983). Extensional versus intuitive reasoning: The conjunction fallacy in probability judgment. *Psychological Review 90*(4), 293–315.

(1986). Rational choice and the framing of decisions. *Journal of Business, 59*(4), S251–S278.

(1992). Advances in prospect theory: Cumulative representation of uncertainty. *Journal of Risk and Uncertainty, 5*(4), 297–323.

US Department of Health, Education and Welfare. (1964). *Smoking and health: Report of the advisory committee to the Surgeon General of the public health service.* Report No. 1103. Washington, DC: US Government Printing Office.

Uzawa, H. (1956). Note on preference and axioms of choice. *Annals of the Institute of Statistical Mathematics, 8*(1), 35–40.

Van Baal, P. H., Polder, J. J., de Wit, G. A., Hoogenveen, R. T., Feenstra, T. L., Boshuizen, H. C., ... & Brouwer, W. B. (2008). Lifetime medical costs of obesity: Prevention no cure for increasing health expenditure. *PLoS Medicine, 5*(2), e29. Retrieved from http://journals.plos.org/plosmedicine/article?id= 10.1371/journal.pmed.0050029

Van Dillen, L. F., Papies, E. K., & Hofmann, W. (2013). Turning a blind eye to temptation: How cognitive load can facilitate self-regulation. *Journal of Personality and Social Psychology, 104*(3), 427–443.

VanEpps, E. M., Roberto, C. A., Park, S., Economos, C. D., & Bleich, S. N. (2016). Restaurant menu labeling policy: Review of evidence and controversies. *Current Obesity Reports, 5*(1), 72–80.

van Gaal, S., De Lange, F. P., & Cohen, M. X. (2012). The role of consciousness in cognitive control and decision making. *Frontiers in Human Neuroscience, 6*(121), 1–15.

Varian, H. R. (1992). *Microeconomic analysis* (3rd ed.). New York: W. W. Norton.

(2010). *Intermediate microeconomics: A modern approach*, Vol. 6. New York: W. W. Norton.

Varki, A. (2009). Human uniqueness and the denial of death. *Nature, 460*(7256), 684.

Veer, E., & Rank, T. (2012). Warning! The following packet contains shocking images: The impact of mortality salience on the effectiveness of graphic cigarette warning labels. *Journal of Consumer Behaviour, 11*(3), 225–233.

Velleman, J. D. (1988). Brandt's definition of "good." *Philosophical Review, 97*(3), 353–371.

Villareal, W. (2015). Vaping shops say FDA regulation could put them out of business. *Los Angeles Times*, August 10. Retrieved from www.latimes.com/business/la-fi-vaping-shops-20150810-story.html

Villejoubert, G., & Mandel, D. R. (2002). The inverse fallacy: An account of deviations from Bayes's theorem and the additivity principle. *Memory & Cognition, 30*(2), 171–178.

Vineberg, S. (2011). Dutch book arguments. In E. N. Zalta (Ed.), *The Stanford encyclopedia of philosophy* (Summer 2011 ed.). Retrieved from http://plato.stanford.edu/archives/sum2011/entries/dutch-book

Viscusi, W. K. (1990). Do smokers underestimate risks? *Journal of Political Economy, 98*(6), 1253–1269.

(1994). Cigarette taxation and the social consequences of smoking. NBER Working Paper No. w4891. National Bureau of Economic Research. Retrieved from www.heartland.org/_template-assets/documents/publications/w4891.pdf

Viscusi, W. K., & Gayer, T. (2015). Behavioral public choice: The behavioral paradox of government policy. *Harvard Journal of Law & Public Policy, 38*, 973–1007.

Viscusi, W. K., & Magat, W. A. (1987). *Learning about risk: Consumer and worker response to hazard information*. Cambridge, MA: Harvard University Press.

Vohs, K. D., Baumeister, R. F., & Loewenstein, G. (Eds.). (2007). *Do emotions help or hurt decision making? A hedgefoxian perspective*. New York: Russell Sage Foundation.

Volokh, E. (2003). The mechanisms of the slippery slope. *Harvard Law Review, 116*(4), 1026–1137.

von Neumann, J., & Morgenstern, O. (1953 [1944]). *Theory of games and economic behavior* (3rd ed.). Princeton, NJ: Princeton University Press.

von Wright, G. H. (1963). *The logic of preference*. Edinburgh, Scotland: Edinburgh University Press.

Walasek, L., & Stewart, N. (2015). How to make loss aversion disappear and reverse: Tests of the decision by sampling origin of loss aversion. *Journal of Experimental Psychology: General, 144*(1), 7–11.

Walton, D. (1992). *Slippery slope arguments*. Oxford, UK: Clarendon Press.

Wansink, B., & Hanks, A. S. (2013). Slim by design: Serving healthy foods first in buffet lines improves overall meal selection. *PloS One, 8*(10), e77055.

Ware, W. B. (2012). *Humor, hope, and vocational grief in a nursing sample*. Virginia Beach, VA: Regent University.

Wason, P. C. (1966). Reasoning. In B. M. Foss (Ed.), *New horizons in psychology*. Harmondsworth, UK: Penguin, 135–151.

Weintraub, E. R. (2002). *How economics became a mathematical science*. Durham, NC: Duke University Press.

Welsh, M. B., & Navarro, D. J. (2012). Seeing is believing: Priors, trust, and base rate neglect. *Organizational Behavior and Human Decision Processes, 119*(1), 1–14.

Wertenbroch, K. (1998). Consumption self-control by rationing purchase quantities of virtues and vice. *Marketing Science, 17*(4), 317–337.

Whitman, D. G. (2006). Against the new paternalism: Internalities and the economics of self-control. *Policy Analysis, 563*, 1–16.

Whitman, D. G., & Rizzo, M. J. (2006). Paternalist slopes. *NYU Journal of Law & Liberty, 2*, 411–443.

(2015). The problematic welfare standards of behavioral paternalism. *Review of Philosophy and Psychology, 6*(3), 409–425.

Wicksteed, P. H. (1967). *The common sense of political economy*, Vol. 1. New York: Augustus M. Kelly. (Original work published 1910)

Wilson, T. D., & Gilbert, D. T. (2013).The impact bias is alive and well. *Journal of Personality and Social Psychology, 105*(5), 740–748.

Winkielman, P., & Trujillo, J. L. (2007). Emotional influence on decision and behavior: Stimuli, states and subjectivity. In K. D. Vohs, R. F. Baumeister, & G. Loewenstein (Eds.), *Do emotions help or hurt decision making? A hedgefoxian perspective*, 69–92. New York: Russell Sage Foundation.

Winman, A., & Juslin, P. (2006). I am m/n confident that I am correct. In K. Fiedler & P. Juslin (Eds.), *Information sampling and adaptive cognition*, 409–439. Cambridge, UK: Cambridge University Press.

Winman, A., Hansson, P., & Juslin, P. (2004). Subjective probability intervals: How to reduce overconfidence by interval evaluation. *Journal of Experimental Psychology: Learning, Memory, and Cognition, 30*(6), 1167–1175.

Wiseman, A. E., & Ellig, J. (2007). The politics of wine: Trade barriers, interest groups, and the Commerce Clause. *Journal of Politics, 69*(3), 859–875.

Wolfe, E. (2004). Medicare redefines obesity as an illness. Associated Press, July 16. Retrieved from http://investorshub.advfn.com/Boards/read_msg.aspx?message_id=3575814

Wong, S. (2006). *Foundations of Paul Samuelson's revealed preference theory: A study by the method of rational reconstruction*. London: Routledge.

Wunderlich, K., Smittenaar, P., & Dolan, R. J. (2012). Dopamine enhances model-based over model-free choice behavior. *Neuron, 75*(3), 418–424.

Yandle, B. (1983). Bootleggers and Baptists: The education of a regulatory economist. *Regulation, 7*, 12.

(1999). Bootleggers and Baptists in retrospect. *Regulation, 22*, 5–7.

Yaniv, I., & Foster, D. P. (1995). Graininess of judgment under uncertainty: An accuracy-informativeness trade-off. *Journal of Experimental Psychology: General, 124*(4), 424–432.

(1997). Precision and accuracy of judgmental estimation. *Journal of Behavioral Decision Making, 10*(1), 21–32.

Zamir, E. (2014). *Law, psychology, and morality: The role of loss aversion*. Oxford, UK: Oxford University Press.

Zauberman, G., Kim, B. K., Malkoc, S. A., & Bettman, J. R. (2009). Discounting time and time discounting: Subjective time perception and intertemporal preferences. *Journal of Marketing Research, 46*(4), 543–556.

Zhang, Y., & Fishbach, A. (2010). Counteracting obstacles with optimistic predictions. *Journal of Experimental Psychology: General, 139*(1), 16–31.

Zhu, S. H., Zhuang, Y. L., Wong, S., Cummins, S. E., & Tedeschi, G. J. (2017). E-cigarette use and associated changes in population smoking cessation: Evidence from US current population surveys. *BMJ, 358*, j3262. www.bmj.com/content/358/bmj.j3262

Zuwerink, J. R., & Devine, P. G. (1996). Attitude importance and resistance to persuasion: It's not just the thought that counts. *Journal of Personality and Social Psychology, 70*(5), 931–944.

Zywicki, T. J. (2018). The behavioral economics of behavioral law and economics. *Review of Behavioral Economics, 5*(3–4), 439–471.

Index

Lightning Source UK Ltd.
Milton Keynes UK
UKHW010154190821
389094UK00004B/56

9 781107 016941